Handbook of Digital Public History

Handbook of Digital Public History

—

Edited by
Serge Noiret, Mark Tebeau, and Gerben Zaagsma

DE GRUYTER
OLDENBOURG

ISBN 978-3-11-135275-6
e-ISBN (PDF) 978-3-11-043029-5
e-ISBN (EPUB) 978-3-11-043037-0

Library of Congress Control Number: 2021950491

Bibliographic information published by the Deutsche Nationalbibliothek
The Deutsche Nationalbibliothek lists this publication in the Deutsche Nationalbibliografie;
detailed bibliographic data are available on the Internet at http://dnb.dnb.de.

© 2023 Walter de Gruyter GmbH, Berlin/Boston
This volume is text- and page-identical with the hardback published in 2022.
Cover image: THATCamp | The Humanities and Technology Camp 2013 at George Mason University in the RRCHNM, Fairfax, Virginia on the 13 Oct 2013. © Serge Noiret.
Typesetting: Integra Software Services Pvt. Ltd.
Printing and binding: CPI books GmbH, Leck

www.degruyter.com

Contents

Serge Noiret, Mark Tebeau, and Gerben Zaagsma
Introduction —— 1

Part 1: **Historiography**

Anaclet Pons
The Historiographical Foundations of Digital Public History —— 19

Serge Noiret
Crowdsourcing and User Generated Content: The Raison d'Être of Digital Public History —— 35

Serge Noiret
Sharing Authority in Online Collaborative Public History Practices —— 49

Mary Larson
Shifting the Balance of Power: Oral History and Public History in the Digital Era —— 61

Chiara Bonacchi
Digital Public Archaeology —— 77

Sophie Gebeil
Identities – a historical look at online memory and identity issues —— 87

Joshua MacFadyen
Digital Environmental Humanities —— 97

Emily Esten
Combining Values of Museums and Digital Culture in Digital Public History —— 107

Pierre Mounier
Open Access: an opportunity to redesign scholarly communication in history —— 121

Marcello Ravveduto
Past and Present in Digital Public History —— 131

Andreas Fickers
Digital Hermeneutics: The Reflexive Turn in Digital Public History? —— 139

Part 2: Contexts

Trevor Owens and Jesse A. Johnston
Archivists as Peers in Digital Public History —— 151

William S. Walker
History Museums: Enhancing Audience Engagement through Digital Technologies —— 165

Michelangela Di Giacomo, Livio Karrer
Interactive Museum & Exhibitions in Digital Public History Projects and Practices: An Overview and the Unusual Case of M9 Museum —— 175

Marii Väljataga
Digital Public History in Libraries —— 185

Rabea Rittgerodt
Publishing Public History in the Digital Age —— 199

Mills Kelly
"Learning Public History by doing Public History" —— 211

Kimberly Coulter, Wilko Graf von Hardenberg, and Finn Arne Jørgensen
Spaces: What's at Stake in Their Digital Public Histories? —— 223

Thomas Cauvin
Digital Public History in the United States —— 235

Priya Chhaya with contributions by Reina Murray
Technology and Historic Preservation: Documentation and Storytelling —— 243

Florentina Armaselu
Social Media: Snapshots in Public History —— 259

Part 3: **Best Practices**

Mark Tebeau
Curation: Toward a New Ethic of Digital Public History —— 279

Martin Grandjean
Data Visualization for History —— 291

Fred Gibbs
Mapping and Maps in Digital and Public History —— 301

Nico Nolden and Eugen Pfister
Gaming and Digital Public History —— 309

Tammy S. Gordon
Individuals in the Crowd: Privacy, Online Participatory Curation, and the Public Historian as Private Citizen —— 317

Rebecca S. Wingo and William G. Thomas III
Building Communities, Reconciling Histories: Can We Make a More Honest History? —— 327

Sandra Camarda
Cybermemorials: Remembrance and Places of Memory in the Digital Age —— 337

David Dean
Living History: Performing the Past —— 349

Lara Kelland
Activist Digital Public History —— 359

Jerome de Groot
Digital Public History: Family History and Genealogy —— 369

Valérie Schafer
Digital Personal Memories: The Archiving of the Self and Public History —— 377

Pierluigi Feliciati
Planning with the Public: How to Co-develop Digital Public History Projects? —— 385

Brett Oppegaard
As Seen through Smartphones: An Evolution of Historic Information Embedment —— 395

Part 4: Technology, Media, Data and Metadata

Matteo Di Legge, Francesco Mantovani, and Iara Meloni
What does it Meme? Public History in the Internet Memes Era —— 407

Paolo Mogorovich and Enrica Salvatori
Historical GIS —— 419

Gerben Zaagsma
Content Management —— 431

Carlo Meghini
Linked Open Data & Metadata —— 439

Frédéric Clavert and Lars Wieneke
Big Data and Public History —— 447

Gioele Barabucci, Francesca Tomasi, and Fabio Vitali
Modeling Data Complexity in Public History and Cultural Heritage —— 459

Yannick Rochat
History and Video Games —— 475

Dominique Santana
Historians as Digital Storytellers: The Digital Shift in Narrative Practices for Public Historians —— 485

Enrica Salvatori
The Audiovisual Dimension & the Digital Turn in Public History Practices —— 495

Raffaella Biscioni
Digital Public History and Photography —— 505

Seth van Hooland and Mathias Coeckelbergs
Exploring Large-Scale Digital Archives – Opportunities and Limits to Use Unsupervised Machine Learning for the Extraction of Semantics —— 517

Federica Signoriello
Infographics and Public History —— 531

List of Contributors —— 545

Serge Noiret, Mark Tebeau, and Gerben Zaagsma
Introduction

Abstract: This handbook provides a systematic overview of the present state of international research in digital public history (DPH). Detailed individual studies by internationally renowned public historians, digital humanists and digital historians elucidate central issues in the field and present a critical account of the major public history accomplishments, research activities, practices with the public and of their digital context. The handbook applies an international and comparative public history approach, looks at its historical development, focuses on technical background and on the use of specific digital media, software's and digital tools. It offers a bibliography adapted to each chapter. The Handbook analyses connections with local communities and different publics worldwide when engaging in digital activities with the past, and indicate directions for future research, practices and teaching activities. Its aim is to delimit the field as it is situated between digital humanities, digital history and public history.

Keywords: digital public history, digital history, digital humanities, public history, user-generated content, shared authority, publics, audience, citizen's history, curation

1 Origins of the Handbook

The emergence of the digital humanities coincided with the expansion of public history beyond North America and generated dialogue about the intersections of digital public history (DPH) that frame this volume. Two editors of the volume, Serge Noiret and Mark Tebeau, first discussed the possibility of this volume the 20–21 of March 2012 in Luxembourg City for the second symposium organized by the *Centre Virtuel pour la Connaissance de l'Europe* (CVCE) and the University of Luxembourg entitled "Digital Humanities Luxembourg" (#DHLU2012) as part of their joint research program *Digital Humanities Luxembourg: the future of research in humanities and social sciences.*[1] In subsequent meetings, at the National Council on Public History (NCPH) in Nashville, in Paris, and at the European University Institute in Florence the project took shape. The year 2015 saw the project's genesis through a series of digital meetings (well before the pandemic made them necessary) held by Noiret and Tebeau that outlined the structure of the Handbook, building on questions raised at the NCPH in February 2015.

---

[1] The CVCE was integrated in 2016 in the University of Luxembourg, with most of its staff joining the Centre for Contemporary and Digital History (C²DH: https://www.c2dh.uni.lu/) that was created in 2017. Its digital library was continued as CVCE.eu by uni.lu, https://www.cvce.eu/.

In agreement with Mark Tebeau, Serge Noiret proposed a session about defining DPH on 10 June, 2015 during the "unconference" THATCamp Paris with the intention to discuss a possible table of contents for the Handbook.[2] At that session, in Paris, the Handbook was born as we received feedback from an international community of digital and public historians. The possibilities of DPH or, in French, l'*Histoire Publique Numérique*[3] as a distinctive mode of inquiry became a central point of debate during the discussions. The meeting raised recurring questions about the differences between Digital History, public history, and DPH, as well as their points of intersection. Those tensions about the character of DPH, and about where and how public history overlaps with digital history, and digital humanities more generally, have decisively informed the development, organization and shape of this volume.

From those repeated discussions in Luxembourg, the United States, France, and later Italy, during the international conference "Public History and the Media" that was organized by the History Department at the EUI in March 2015,[4] this volume also acquired its distinctive international dimension, reflecting the expansion of the public history field, and challenging the often parochial ways that academic national communities (including, in particular, those in North America) imagine scholarship that crosses borders.

2 Defining the Tensions of the Handbook

This international sensibility challenges the field to think globally, even as many projects continue to be generated within local communities, defined by geography, politics, and fields of study. The emergence of an international dialogue about public history promises to transform the field in challenging ways, including reflecting on how much the existing literature has a relatively limited geographical scope defined by the historical practices of North America. The handbook has sought, wherever possible, to apply this international and comparative approach, drawing heavily on a broad international community of scholars. The editors asked authors to make this consideration in each of its chapters, something quite rare in the field of public history.

As the handbook developed, its authors grappled with the transformative ways that both the digital age and trends in public history accentuated and reinforced one another. User-centered digital practices have empowered individuals and communities, giving them the ability to control their own history. This, in turn, has challenged

---

[2] See *Définir le champ de l'Histoire Publique Numérique*, https://dph.hypotheses.org/785.
[3] See *ThatCamp Paris*, http://tcp.hypotheses.org/892.
[4] See *Public History and the Media*, workshop in Florence, February 11-12-13, 2015, https://ifph.hypotheses.org/352.

historians to embrace and make central the concept of shared authority that has migrated from oral history to public history, and now has moved to the center of both the digital humanities and the broader work of the professional historical community engaged in citizen's history practices.

Ultimately, we emerged with a working definition of DPH that recognized a new type of scholarly work, or curation, that melds digital tools and public engagement. DPH transcends the particulars of either the digital humanities or public history, working at the margins of both fields, and in particular it seeks not to build scholarship for one's scholarly peers but to find ways to collaborate directly with audiences beyond the academy. In this volume, we thus argue that digital public history entails the combination of academic knowledge of history with modern digital communication practices to engage the past while incorporating user-generated content and sharing authority with participating communities and publics.[5]

Building this volume proved to be an arduous and challenging journey for a variety of reasons. The ever-changing boundaries of the fields and their intersections, rapid advances and experimentation in technologies, the increasing technical and professional specialization of the fields covered in DPH, and the international dimensions of the work provided hurdles. Eventually, in 2019, Gerben Zaagsma joined the curatorial team in order to help complete the volume and its highly varied set of chapters. We (the curators) challenged individual authors to not just consider their area of expertise but to examine the intersections between digital humanities, digital history, and public history, as well as how each has been transformed by the digital. Unfortunately, certain topics proved elusive, and some questions we had initially hoped to take up could not be explored, including contributions that explored DPH's policy uses, its commercial landscape, and some of the more specialized technical aspects of archiving: the work of private contractors and commercial interests in DPH; and chapters dealing with specialized issues in archival settings.

As readers take up this volume, we want to challenge them to think about the ways that the global and local are converging and diverging in public history, as well as how the technical and theoretical intersect. We hope to spur dialogue that cross the usual geographic and field boundaries, creating greater transdisciplinary approaches. We want project directors to consider how to ground their DPH endeavors in their communities, while attending to broader international trends. This is a technically tricky effort – one that has grown even more challenging with the proliferation of specific technologies. And, yet, standards – for software, archiving, and project organizations – offer promise in providing the connective tissue that connects

---

[5] For more on how the work of curation has emerged at the heart of the DPH endeavor, see Mark Tebeau, "Curation: Toward a New Ethic of Digital Public History," and on user-generated content and sharing authority practices in DPH, see Serge Noiret's chapters in this hanbook.

our collective work. We challenge readers to see the intersections between the theories, practices, and technologies that frame both the digital humanities and public history. At the nexus of these conversations lies the world of DPH and the spirit of dialog at the heart of this volume.

3 Organization of the Handbook

This interplay between public history and the digital realm shapes the handbook, with many chapters inside the four main sections taking different angles on the intersections of public and digital. These discussions ranged widely, and the handbook is organized around four principal ideas that we call historiography, contexts, best practices, and technology. This organization reflects both the scholarly literature and theory, the diverse spaces in which DPH takes place, the nature of practice within the field (because DPH is fundamentally about doing and making things), and finally the nature of the digital itself, which continues to evolve.

Historiography

The first set of essays explores the historiography and traditions of both public history and the emergent world of digital humanities. Along the way, there was conceptual and theoretical work, of course, but ultimately the roots of this intersection come from a variety of historical subfields. Oral history, history preservation and cultural heritage. Other long-running conversations, about historical memory and the construction of identity have continued to resonate within the world of DPH, in no small part because of its activist bent (more on that later.) Other areas of practice within heritage and memory institutions, such as archives, museums, libraries and galleries – the foundation world of GLAMs – have long lineages in their own right, apart from their critical import in the world of DPH. In each essay, the writers take on key aspects of the topic, with attention to how the intersection of the digital and public has transformed these fields/themes.

In this section, Anaclet Pons explores the historiographical foundations of the discipline; Serge Noiret looks at the two mutually connected methods that are defining and supporting DPH practices, crowdsourcing and user-generated contents, and shared authority; Mary Larson describes a shifting balance of power between oral and public history in the digital era; Chiara Bonacchi explains how public archeology and the digital have revolutionized archeological practices; Sophie Gebeil considers the shift in identifying national identities; Josh MacFadyen writes about the emerging field of environmental humanities; Emily Esten writes about the emergence of DPH in museums, Pierre Mounier explores open access practices in DPH; and Marcello

Ravveduto deals with presentism in public history today. Finally, Andreas Fickers writes on digital hermeneutics and the reflexive turn in DPH.

Contexts

The second set of essays digs into some of the most interesting aspects of the practice of DPH – it happens not just in the ivory tower but within a variety of institutional and organization contexts, each with its own traditions, best practices, and specific goals. Thus, this section explores the spaces and specific places, in other words, the contexts, where DPH is practiced; it pays attention to scales of institution, locale (global, regional, national), and theoretical challenges faced in each domain. For example, a digital public historian working with museums has a different focus than one working with digital archives. The handbook sought to honor the specific ways in which each of these contexts generate a very particular flavor of DPH, one informed by the field broadly but nonetheless particular to its own goals.

How the digital transformed archival practices and how born-digital archives emerged is studied by Trevor Owens and Jesse A. Johnston in a chapter on archives and born digital archives and the new roles of archivists as peers in DPH projects. Chapters by Will Walker, and by Michelangela Di Giacomo and Livio Karrer look at history museums, virtual museums and exhibitions and how the digital transformed the interaction with the public in museum settings. Marii Väljataga explores DPH practices in libraries, considering the implications for large-scale digital library projects, such as dp.la and Europeana.

How we publish has changed and Rabea Rittgerodt considers the transformation of the publishing world because of new interactions with authors, technologies, and publics. Mills Kelly studies how digital and public history have altered university history classrooms. How the emergence of DPH has altered landscape history and environmental history in theory and practice is examined by Kimberly Coulter, Wilko Graf von Hardenberg, and Finn Arne Jørgensen. Thomas Cauvin describes the history of DPH in the United States; Priya Chayya, with Reina Murray, observe the kind of technology that is being used in historic preservation and has impacted documentation and storytelling. Finally, Florentina Armaselu looks at how social media has transformed the presence of the public in the history web.

Best Practices

This set of essays explores how public history practice has changed and new digital practices have emerged because of the intersection of public history with digital tools aimed at interacting with the public. This section takes the recurring tradition seriously in both public history and digital history that scholarship is not merely about theory but about making and doing – it is a dynamic social practice that engages public audiences. The handbook recognizes that these practices and approaches to knowledge each have different lineages, some developed well before DPH (such as the conceptual importance of shared authority) and others that emerged and were reinforced and facilitated precisely out of the digital age (such as crowdsourcing.) In each of these areas of practice, approaches have appeared for confronting the digital age. Not surprisingly, this section uses case studies and many examples.

Curation has become a central activity in the DPH landscape aimed at interacting with audiences and is looked at by Mark Tebeau. Martin Grandjean explores new forms of visualization of data that have appeared for showcasing networks and connections. Fred Gibbs writes about spatial DPH and GIS used for mapping. Nico Nolden and Eugen Pfister illustrate how gaming has become an important scene in which history encounters new publics. Tammy S. Gordon focuses on how concepts like privacy and online participatory curation, is transforming the ideas of the crowd. Rebecca S. Wingo and William G. Thomas III describe how communities can be built by reconciling histories through digital practices, making what they call "a more honest history." Sandra Camarda looks at "cyber memorials" as places of remembrance and memory in the digital age; David Dean examines how forms of Living History, revivals and reenactments have been changed through digital practices; Lara Kelland' explores DPH at the grassroots, considering the changing nature of activism. Jerome De Groote describes how genealogy is becoming a new public history discipline as more and more people engage with family history through the web. Valérie Schafer analyses how it is now possible to organize and preserve the self in the digital realm. Pierluigi Feliciati explains best practices for DPH project planning both for and with the public. Finally, Brett Oppegaard considers how the mobile revolution is remaking the interpretive work of DPH curators.

Technology, Media, Data and Metadata

The last part of the handbook stands at the core of DPH, which has become (at least in theory) a discipline that is both built upon and requires technical facility. The handbook remains agnostic about the import of technological tools, preferring instead to focus on the conceptual and practical application of technology. Technology and technical acumen take many forms in DPH, from an understanding of the basic technologies that are transforming the culture broadly and work in GLAMs particularly. Technological devices and software, such as mobile phones, geographic information systems, or content management systems are often the tools of the digital historian.

One of the challenges of commissioning essays on these topics is the speed with which they have continued to evolve. Likewise, key conceptual technologies for organizing knowledge – some of which emerged prior to both antecedent fields, public history and digital humanities – have become foundational to DPH. For example, at least some conceptual understanding of programming, data standards and metadata should be obtained by everyone in the field. More practical areas of work in the field, either on the web or with image and audio files, or even the techniques of big data and text mining have become key currencies of expertise within the field, with others, such as working with three-dimensional printing, emerging all the time. The challenge for authors within the handbook was to balance the very particular tools or techniques used in the field, with a conceptual understanding of how they have been used.

Matteo Di Legge, Francesco Mantovani and Iara Meloni investigate the presence of history in an era of Internet memes. Enrica Salvatori and Paolo Mogorovich study how the GIS is used in DPH practices; Gerben Zaagsma digs into the role of different content management systems used for publishing history. Carlo Meghini explains the importance of Linked Open Data and Metadata for DPH projects. Frédéric Clavert and Lars Wieneke look at big data and its impact in DPH projects. Gioele Barabucci, Francesca Tomasi and Fabio Vitali investigate ways of modeling data complexity in cultural heritage projects. Yannick Rochat considers the technologies used in historical video games; Dominique Santana enquires into the digital shift in narrative practices, considering when public historians become storytellers in digital media. Enrica Salvatori explores the considerations of working with different digital media. How photography has become a digital primary source for DPH projects is considered by Raffaella Biscioni. Seth Van Holland and Mathias Coeckelbergs write about text mining in history corpora. And, finally, Federica Signoriello thinks about the ways that a new visual medium such as the infographic presents history in new forms for different audiences.

4 Framing Digital Public History

Digital Turn

The emergence of digital public history is strongly related to what is sometimes called "the digital turn," which has deeply transformed the humanities, the practice of history as well as how the public engages in history. Not merely a change in focus or method, the digital turn represents a fundamental reworking of the tools used to study, construct, disseminate, and share history; it has broken down walls between historians working in the academy and those working in a variety of affiliated fields and settings, as well as invited publics into the process. Historians, archivists, librarians, preservationists, activists, communities, and publics have become curators of knowledge, constructing the historical record together and sharing responsibility and authority for interpreting the past. The advent of new tools may be the most conspicuous evidence of the shifting terrain, but make no mistake: it is not the tools that are driving change. It is the fundamental intersection of theory, techniques, and practices in the academy, in the oral history and especially public history movements that are configuring technology toward more democratic ends.[6]

At the intersection of public history and digital practice, we see the emergence of exciting new dimensions to the practice of history. If this handbook recognizes that the emergence of DPH is multivalent, it nonetheless draws attention to digital technologies, expanded roles for, and collaborations among historians, archivists, and publics, and the emergence of new theoretical and technical practices that one could argue have created a new ethos of curation that suffuses our endeavor. Additionally, the essays included in this handbook underscore the degree to which these developments eschew boundaries – of discipline, geography, and politics. And, yet, before turning toward those international developments and offering a definition of DPH for this volume, we should take a moment and think about the genealogy of the digital and the public in history.

Digital Public History

Developments in, and genealogies of, public and digital history form the broader context for the development of how we define DPH. The fields of public history and digital history both have decades long histories. They are also English-language descriptors for phenomena that, historically speaking, have been described with a wide variety of labels in different linguistic and spatial contexts. In both cases: different terminologies have been used for a broadly similar phenomenon. In a way, both were also the product of disciplinary developments that transcended national boundaries. The rise of "new" social (science) history in the 1960s, for instance, constituted a major impetus for both public oriented and "digital" approaches in history, be it in terms of subject matter or methodology. Social history helped to shift engagements with "the public," whether as a subject of historical research or audience, from top-down to more bottom-up approaches. At the same time, this reorientation engendered and called for quantitative approaches which could be greatly facilitated by early computing, whereas changing demands of museums prompted the first applications of computer technology there, with a view to better

---

[6] On the digital turn and its implication see, for example, Todd Pressner, Digital Humanities Manifesto 2.0 Launched, June 22, 2009; http://www.toddpresner.com/?p=7; accessed June 20, 2021 and Marin Dacos, "Manifesto for the Digital Humanities", 2010, THATCamp Paris, https://tcp.hypotheses.org/411, accessed June 30, 2021.

manage collection information for both scholars and the public and improve "research and educational services."[7]

The conceit of the emergence of the digital humanities in the 2000s has erased these antecedents and decades of experimentation in seeking to claim credit for the revolution. And as such, when discussing the digital revolution we should take a few moments (or more than a few moments) to also recognize the emergence of digital humanities and digital history, and consider the import of public history in fueling the transformation of historical practice.

Public history preceded digital history, and when the digital turn in history occurred at the turn of the century, public history had already matured and spread beyond its origins in the United States and the United Kingdom. But, truthfully, the origin story of the institutionalization of public history – that it is an American phenomenon – is largely derived from the formation of the National Council for Public History in the late 1970s.[8] Recently, a variety of scholars, including Paul Ashton, David Dean, Thomas Cauvin, and others, pointed out how public history's emergence happened separately in other contexts, including internationally.[9] For example, the British History Workshop movement which began in the late 1960s and propagated a history from below co-created by its protagonists was deeply influenced by new social approaches to history and spread internationally throughout the 1970s.[10]

Of course, public history also owes debts as a field to the emergence of oral history in the early twentieth century, not to mention recurring returns by historians to document the history of ordinary people. Decades of work by oral historians have also produced important methodological frames for public historians, and it was ultimately oral historians, not public historians, who first developed the concept of shared authority that suffuses so much of public history and digital humanities'

---

7 *Computers and their potential applications in museums: a conference sponsored by the Metropolitan Museum of Art, supported by a grant from the IBM Corporation, April 15,16,17 1968* (New York: Arno Press, 1968); Ellin, Everett, An Introductory Survey of Museum Computer Activity, *Computers and the Humanities* 3/2 (1968) 65–86; Rogalla von Bieberstein J., *Archiv, Bibliothek und Museum als Dokumentationsbereiche: Einheit u. gegenseitige Abgrenzung* (Verlag Dokumentation, Pullach 1975).
8 Even among public historians in the United States there is debate about the origins of public history, with scholars providing alternative genealogies of the field; see, for instance, the alternative history proposed by Denise D. Meringlo, Museums, Monuments, and National Parks: Toward a New Genealogy of Public History (Amherst: University of Massachusetts Press, 2012).
9 Cauvin, T. and Noiret, S. (2017) Internationalizing Public History. In Gardner, J. B. and Hamilton, P. (2017) *The Oxford handbook of public history*. Oxford University Press; Dean, D. and Etges, A. (2018) 'What Is (International) Public History?', *International Public History*, 1(1). DOI: 10.1515/iph-2018-0007; Ashton, P. and Trapeznik, A. (2019). *What Is Public History Globally? Working with the Past in the Present*. London, Bloomsbury; Cauvin, T. (2018). "The Rise of Public History: An International Perspective." In *Historia Crítica*, 68: 3–26.
10 Kynan Gentry, Ruskin, Radicalism and Raphael Samuel: Politics, Pedagogy and the Origins of the History Workshop, *History Workshop Journal* 76.1 (Autumn 2013): 187–211, https://doi.org/10.1093/hwj/dbs042.

rhetoric and methods.[11] Finally, public historians all too often ignore the importance of heritage and memory institutions, what we nowadays call the GLAM sector. Galleries, libraries, archives, and museums that have generated much interpretive excitement for many decades, long before and after "public history" and "digital history" began to be recognized as distinct fields. For example, the first truly mobile interpretive tool was developed at the Stedelijk Museum in the 1950s in which a centralized recording device was broadcast to museum visitors to engage publics.[12]

Genealogies of digital history usually start in the 1960s, when mainframe computing had taken of at universities, but if we broaden the scope to include the use of mechanical aids in both preservation/reproduction, as well as processing of information, we could trace its antecedents back to the early twentieth century. This is when German classicist Karl Krumbacher began to use photography for educational, reproduction, and research purposes.[13] Punched card systems made their entry into academic research in the 1930s and were soon used for historical data processing purposes. Indeed, the American historian, and digital history pioneer, William G. Thomas has argued for the recognition of at least two phases in the use of computing technologies by historians, those pioneers who were part of the "first phase of quantitative history" in the 1940s, and the "new" wave of social science historians from the 1960s.[14] As Daniel Greenstein has shown, the uptake of computers in the historical profession from the 1960s onwards hinged very much on the extent to which historiographical directions and research trends were conducive to computer-aided research.[15] In both Europe and the United States, "history and computing" as a methodologically oriented approach and scholarly community dates back to the late 1960s and early 1970s.[16] A key event was the methodological strand of the 13th International Congress of Historical Sciences in Moscow (1970), which

---

11 Woods, T.A (1989) "The Challenge of Public History." In *The Oral History Review* 17.2: 97–102; Frisch, M. H. (1990) *A shared authority: essays on the craft and meaning of oral and public history*. State University of New York Press, Hamilton, P. and Shopes, L. (2008) *Oral history and public memories*. Temple University Press.

12 Pavement, Peter, "The Museum as Media Producer: Innovation Before the Digital Age," in Kirsten Drotner, Vince Dziekan, Ross Parry, and Kim Christian Schroder, editors, *The Routledge Handbook of Museums, Media, and Communication* (Routledge, 2018), 67–70.

13 Krumbacher, Karl, *Die Photographie Im Dienste Der Geisteswissenschaften* (Leipzig: B.G. Teubner, 1906).

14 Thomas III, William, 'Computing and the Historical Imagination', In A Companion to Digital Humanities Edited by Susan Schreibman, Raymond George Siemens and John Unsworth. (Malden, MA: Blackwell Pub, 2004), 56–68, 59.

15 See, Zaagsma, G. (2013). On Digital History. *BMGN – Low Countries Historical Review*, 128(4), 3–29, here p.8, https://doi.org/10.18352/bmgn-lchr.9344.

16 Shorter, E. (1971) *The historian and the computer: a practical guide*. Englewood Cliffs, N.J: Prentice-Hall and Richard Jensen, "The microcomputer revolution for Historians," in *Journal of Interdisciplinary History* 14.1 (1983): 91–111. See also, *History and Computing*, a cura P. Denley, D. Hopkin, Manchester, Manchester University Press, 1987; *History and computing II*, edited by P. Denley,

brought together a varied international group of "computing" historians from East and West. Groundbreaking work, such as the Philadelphia Social History Project of the early 1970s, depended on mainframe computers running punch cards using Fortran and was instrumental in focusing on the histories of "ordinary" people that would inspire so much of the work that we now call public history. At the same time, the advent of the personal computer in the 1970s had begun to change how people engaged history, with the Oregon Trail Game being created in 1971 and propagating on PCs after 1974. Thus, we can observe parallel, albeit different trajectories in the USA and in various European countries of how computing technology was transforming historical practice and public outreach.[17]

Of course, the advent of personal computing in the 1980s, as well as the emergence of archival standards, such as Dublin Core in the 1990s, would become highly consequential for our topic of discussion. Of note, personal computing coupled with the development of the Internet and World Wide Web in the early 1990s would be the juncture at which the convergence of both fields can be located. Of course, these developments in historical research also had parallels in the heritage sector, where early mainframe and mini computing revolved in particular around collection cataloguing and management.[18] It was the combination of personal computing and the Internet/WWW that allowed these parallel tracks to become much more fundamentally entangled.

Even so, from a conceptual standpoint, these developments had precursors, most notably in the work and vision of the Belgian lawyer and information theorist *avant la lettre* Paul Otlet, who published his now well-known *Documentation Treatise* in 1934. Otlet's vision of the creation and circulation of scientific knowledge, in which publics throughout the world would participate, proved visionary: "[N]o book on the worktable; in its place a screen and a phone. All the books and information are over there, far away, in an immense building [. . .]. From there, the page to be

---

S. Fogelvik, C. Harvey, Manchester, Manchester University Press, 1989; *History and computing III: historians, computers, and data: applications in research and teaching*, edited by E. Mawdsley, Manchester, Manchester University Press 1990.

17 Daniel Greenstein, "Bringing Bacon Home: The Divergent Progress of Computer-Aided Historical Research in Europe and the United States," *Computers and the Humanities* 30.5 (1996): 351–364, 357. On the Philadelphia Social History Project, see Regan Kladstrup, "Philadelphia Social History Project," in The Encyclopedia of Greater Philadelphia (2015), https://philadelphiaencyclopedia.org/archive/philadelphia-social-history-project/, accessed 20 June, 2021; Hershberg, Theodore. "The Philadelphia Social History Project: A Methodological History." Ph.D. diss., Stanford University, 1973; on Oregon Trail, see Robert Whitaker, "'You Have Died of Dysentery,' – History According to Video Games," in *Not Even Past* (University of Texas, November 14, 2012), https://notevenpast.org/you-have-died-dysentery-history-according-video-games/ accessed June 29, 2021).

18 David Williams, 'A Brief History of Museum Computerization' in: Ros Parry, *Museums in a Digital Age* (London: Routledge, 2010) 15–22.

read will appear on the screen to find out the answer to the questions asked on the telephone, with or without wires."[19] The organizational structure of world knowledge desired by Otlet certainly anticipated the idea of a co-participated network of knowledge in the Mundaneum he co-founded with Henri la Fontaine, led to him now being regarded by some as one of the precursors of the Internet. However, as the contents of the network can neither be dominated nor indexed completely, Otlet's vision perhaps anticipated more the social and participatory encyclopedism introduced by Wikipedia in the new millennium.

Technology and the Changing Role of the Public

As we define DPH, we must recognize the importance that the emergence and dissemination of technology played in the production of the field, even if the practices and theories of DPH, as we mentioned earlier, are often agnostic about technologies. Technological innovation can occur through experimentation with existing tools, modifying technologies toward solving emerging problems, or building completely new types of technology. This practice of experiment has characterized how digital tools have made their way into historical research, teaching and publishing, including especially the emergence of the World Wide Web in the early 1990s. Historical sources now began to be put online in the form of databases and as text-based digital editions, accessible for all. Email and international exchanges through mailing lists changed the nature of scholarly communication and discussion. At the dawn of the twenty-first century, what was then called Web 2.0 introduced user generated content and saw the advent of social media. Based on collective collaboration, Web 2.0 engendered a new set of practices and processes of sharing history and memory.[20] Through new software and the use of digital media, a specific series of practices that we can now define as DPH was consolidated, in which historical processes and individual and social memory were translated into online projects involving a wide variety of audiences.

These developments moved "history" out of its traditional academic realm. Roy Rosenzweig and David Thelen were perhaps the first to understand how digital history helped to diffuse public history in redefining its engagement with the public in their seminal essay on the popular uses of history by Americans.[21] Rosenzweig and Dan Cohen subsequently further developed this understanding in their analysis of

---

19 Our English translation from French. See Paul Otlet, *Traité de documentation. Le livre sur le livre. Théorie et Pratique.* Bruxelles, Editiones Mundaneum, Palais Mondial, 1934, 342, in *Wikisource*, https://fr.wikisource.org/wiki/Trait%C3%A9_de_documentation.
20 Serge Noiret: *Digital History 2.0*, in Clavert, F. and Noiret, S. *L'histoire contemporaine à l'ère numérique = Contemporary history in the digital age.* Bruxelles, Peter Lang, 2013, 155–190.
21 Roy Rosenzeig and David Thelen, *The Presence of the Past. Popular uses of history in American life*, New York, Columbia University Press, 1998.

how new projects are facilitated by digital technologies[22] which deeply transformed public history practices and relations with "the public." What effectively happened here is a technologically induced shift that brought historians closer to audiences old and new, and audiences closer to historians.

Indeed, at the heart of the curatorial transformations of the twenty-first century has been an expanded conceptualization of the role of the public in the production of knowledge. Building on existing best practices, such as the concept of "a shared authority," new characteristics have emerged such as hitherto unavailable forms of online storytelling. Digital technologies have transformed the dissemination of historical knowledge and/or materials, and thereby enabled new ways of engaging with the public. Meanwhile, the "public" has radically changed from physical to vastly expanded online audiences, and its role in both the making of history and its consumption has been radically reshaped. No longer passive recipients of scholarly and museum expertise, broad publics have been invited into the work of knowledge production and exhibition development.

This development has to a large extent been enabled by new technologies which have created extraordinary new opportunities for historians working in a variety of environments. As Sharon Leon writes: "[T]he promise of digital technologies for public history is vast: new audiences, dynamic content, increased engagement, large-scale collaboration. But to achieve this promise, we must focus on the goals of public history and adapt our working practice to the new conditions created by the digital environment."[23] This scale and depth of available material is evident in a wealth of (born) digital primary sources, often available in open access, as well as new forms of publishing and digital storytelling, such as blogs, vlogs, social media, wikis, etc. and new transdisciplinary collaborations and network effects because of collective actions. Importantly, these tools have spread throughout the broad universe of GLAM institutions, with new tools and software helping us to build new knowledge, including knowledge that is more publicly accessible and co-created by and with the public.

User generated content practices, including crowdsourcing, in public history projects have grown enormously in the twenty-first century. Indeed, the impact of crowdsourcing projects on the work of heritage institutions, whose chronic lack of staff and funding have always presented challenges for engaging publics, has been profound. Digitally enabled public history is now integral in museum work, as virtual museums and exhibitions aim at broader audiences and more differentiated public communication and engagement. Not surprisingly, the social media revolution has

---

[22] Daniel J. Cohen and Roy Rosenzweig: Digital History: *A Guide to Gathering, Preserving, and Presenting the Past on the Web*, University of Pennsylvania Press, 2005, http://chnm.gmu.edu/digitalhistory/.

[23] *Sharon M. Leon*: "Complexity and Collaboration: Doing Public History in Digital Environments," in *The Oxford Handbook of Public History*, Edited by James B. Gardner and Paula Hamilton, 45.

accompanied and amplified the work of digital and public history toward developing and serving online and in-person communities. Taken collectively, these technological transformations have led to a reimagining of curation itself, giving new life to a traditional field. Bottom-up and top-down DPH practices have deeply transformed the way in which professional digital public historians engaged with individuals, communities and their sources as they offered and facilitated new forms of storytelling about the past. Critically, the co-creation of knowledge and citizen history have emerged as the new frontiers of DPH.

The revolution in both technology and public engagement continues to speed up, as it has since the emergence of Wikipedia in 2001. Indeed, the semantic web, through which data can be linked by encoding its meaning in a standardized format, has started to reshape the world through allowing the interoperability and linking of various data sources. Arguably, this vision (promoted by Tim Berners-Lee) remains in its infancy, but in the past decade these processes have accelerated noticeably due to the digitization boom in the heritage sector, rapid growth of available (historical) big data, the proliferation of new forms of online publications such as personal blogs, as well as online collaboration. Going forward, one imagines that linked data and the semantic web will continue to be transformative of the relation between curators and the public, demanding a deeper attention to the theory and practice of DPH.

Definitions

As this volume has developed, we've moved to develop a working definition for DPH – one that we hope will help the field confront the dizzying transformations ahead of us. We argue that DPH is characterized by the digitally enabled ways in which historians and their publics, in mutual interaction and co-dependency, gather, collect, consume, disseminate and engage with history and its sources. We seek to move beyond early definitions, such as that suggested by Fien Danniau in 2013 that "a definition for digital public history in relation to all digital history could be 'digital projects that primarily aim to communicate and interact with the public.'"[24] DPH is more though. Just as digital history overhauls and disrupts the field of history, revamping traditional ways of dealing with archives, analyzing sources and producing academic scholarship, DPH integrates the public into the virtual realm as co-participant. The digital turn has deeply transformed public history practices and the way historians work with archives, produce knowledge about the past and communicate such knowledge to and with the public, indeed the way in which public historians engage with their public.

---

[24] Fien Danniau, "Public History in a Digital Context: Back to the Future or Back to Basics?," *BMGN – Low Countries Historical Review* 128.4 (2013): 118–144.

Importantly, not all digital history is about public history: the online communication of digital history projects is not sufficient for it to become public history. Sheila A. Brennan indicated how the public was central for PH projects in the digital realm and digital tools fostered the possibility of a collaboration with the public.[25] And in an essay about the differences between digital humanities and digital history, Stephen Robertson also indicated the centrality of audiences as a key delineator. For Robertson, Valley of the Shadow or Digital Harlem "were designed to meet the needs and interests of the scholars who created them [. . .] placing them online made them publicly available but did not expand the scope of their audience. ('Be Online or Be Irrelevant'). They remained accessible, relevant, and useful primarily to those scholars and their colleagues [. . .]."[26]

Defining the tensions at the heart of this handbook, we argue that DPH is a combination of academic knowledge of history and modern digital communication practices that facilitate communities and publics to engage with the past through user-generated content and authority sharing. In other words, DPH is about more than producing digital work for one's scholarly peers; it is about finding ways to collaborate directly with audiences and engage in a process of co-creation through digital means, a form of citizen's digital history for the public and with the public.[27]

---

[25] Sheila A. Brennan, "Public, first," in *Debates in the digital humanities 2016*, eds. Matthew K. Gold and Lauren F. Klein (Minneapolis, MN: University of Minnesota Press, 2016), 384–389.
[26] Stephen Robertson: *The Differences between Digital History and Digital Humanities*, (23 May, 2014), http://drstephenrobertson.com/blog-post/the-differences-between-digital-history-and-digital-humanities/. See also S. Robertson: "The differences between digital humanities and digital history" in *Debates in the digital humanities 2016*, eds. Matthew K. Gold and Lauren F. Klein (Minneapolis, MN: University of Minnesota Press, 2016), 289–307.
[27] Salmi, Haanu, *What is digital history?* (Cambridge: Polity Press, 2021), 80–81.

Part 1: **Historiography**

Anaclet Pons
The Historiographical Foundations of Digital Public History

Abstract: Establishing the historiographical foundations in any field is a difficult or at least risky business. It entails granting a certain homogeneity and a good deal of coherence to practices, perspectives, and trends that do not necessarily have either of these properties and, to a great extent, to not aim to acquire them. This is more difficult in the case at hand because the adjectives "public" and "digital" refer in principle to two distinct branches or trends within the discipline of history, each of which has its own referents. Today, however, they tend on the whole to be confused with each other, or at least to overlap. If the aim of public history is to reach a wide audience that includes historians and citizens in the collective discussion of the past, then it must use the dominant ecosystem: the digital one. Obviously, public history encompasses very different practices, not only in terms of their origin but also because, for a few years now, and even more so with its internationalisation, it has been turning into a broad field where several realities that were previously separated now coexist. In turn, most digital history is public history, starting with the pioneering project "Valley of Shadow." In short, traditional history can continue to operate within the parameters of the printed world, but public history cannot and should not.

This text proposes looking at the backgrounds of digital history and public history separately. On the one hand (digital), it selects three precursors: Paul Otlet, Vannevar Bush, and Roberto Busa. On the other hand (public), it examines the original North American model, local history, and popular history, not to mention oral history. From there, it presents the moment in which the public and the digital overlap, presenting some of the problems and challenges public digital history faces.

Keywords: historiography, history, humanities, public, digital, archive

> If doctors meet patients in hospitals and lawyers join clients in the courtroom, where do we encounter our publics?[1]

---

1 Keith A. Erekson, "Putting History Teaching 'In Its Place'," *Journal of American History* 97, no. 4 (2011): 1070.

Notes: This article is part of a major research (HISMEDI: Historia, Memoria y Sociedad Digital. Nuevas formas de transmisión del pasado/History, Memory and Digital Society. New Ways of Transmitting the Past – with reference RTI2018-093599-B-I00 funded by MCIU/AE/FEDER. I especially appreciate the very helpful comments and suggestions from Serge Noiret.

https://doi.org/10.1515/9783110430295-002

Establishing the historiographical foundations in any field is a difficult or at least risky business. It entails granting certain homogeneity and a good deal of coherence to practices, perspectives, and trends that do not necessarily have it and, to a great measure, did not aim to have it. For this reason, the threads we choose to knit a specific historiographical warp with, in this case the digital one, can vary.

Jorge Luis Borges, a man of letters rather than a historian, was the person who better described this risk. In "Kafka and His Precursors", he wrote that he "once premeditated making a study of Kafka's precursors" and, in doing so, thought he recognized a first Kafkaesque voice in Zeno's paradox against movement, and then, by chance, his readings took him to a few more writers. There is no need to go that far in a retrospective quest; it is only necessary to notice that, as the Argentinian narrator said, each writer *creates* his or her own precursors: "If I am not mistaken, the heterogeneous pieces I have enumerated resemble Kafka; if I am not mistaken, not all of them resemble each other. This second fact is more significant". To the same extent and for similar reasons, the arrival of the digital world has created precursors and precedents. Paraphrasing Borges, we could say that in each of the precursors we find digital's idiosyncrasy to a greater or lesser degree, but if what is digital had not constituted itself as a differentiated field, we would not perceive this quality; in other words, it would not exist.[2]

When looking for precursors, without going too far back in time, we could choose three. Given that I have already mentioned Borges, the first precursor should be Paul Otlet, who anticipated some of the Argentinean writer's stories. Since the end of the nineteenth century he was concerned about the increase of information, the increasingly difficult management of the forever-growing number of publications. He introduced new and broader definitions about the terms document and documentation, proposing new methodologies for their use: "l'humanité est à un tournant de son histoire. La masse des données acquises est formidable. Il faut de nouveaux instruments pour les simplifier, les condenser ou jamais l'intelligence ne saura ni surmonter les difficultés qui l'accablent, ni réaliser les progrès qu'elle entrevoit et auxquels elle aspire".[3]

To solve this problem, he came up with a classification reform, an inventory according to topics and authors of all the publications from all countries, periods, and topics; and a place, the Mundaneum, where all that knowledge would be put in order. This kind of "World Museum" would also be a center of dissemination, a centralized mean of accessing the universal knowledge in all its formats (text, sound, images), previously electronically transformed thanks to microphotography. With this he came up with a kind of mechanic and collective brain, a memory where " a

---

[2] Jorge Luis Borges, "Kafka and His Precursors," in *Labyrinths*, ed. Donald A. Yates and James E. Irby (New York: New Directions, 1964), 201.
[3] Paul Otlet, *Traité de documentation: le livre sur le livre, théorie et pratique* (Bruxelles: Editiones Mundaneum, 1934), 430.

un degré moins ultime serait créée une instrumentation agissant à distance qui combinerait à la fois la radio, les rayons Rôntgen, le cinéma et la photographie microscopique. Toutes les choses de l'univers, et toutes celles de l'homme seraient enregistrées à distance à mesure qu'elles se produiraient" and thanks to which "chacun à distance pourrait lire le passage lequel, agrandi et limité au sujet désiré, viendrait se projeter sur l'écran individuel. Ainsi, chacun dans son fauteuil pourrait contempler la création, en son entier o u en certaines de ses parties".[4]

The second precursor was engineer Vannevar Bush, exactly a decade later, in particular his text "As We May Think",[5] where he reflects on the increase of information available and the mechanic ways to manage it in the future. Bush said that the ideas we generate are being stored alien to mechanic improvements, with totally artificially indexation systems. They are artificial because they are distant from human brain operation, which prioritizes association. Bush proposed another model, based on the web of trails carried by brain cells, which allow jumping from one place to another instantaneously. Let's learn from our brain, let's select by association and not by indexation, let's imagine a future device working as a private mechanized archive: the *memex*. Moreover, this would be advantageous for historian, who: "with his vast chronological account of a people, can parallel this with a skip-trail which stops only on the salient items; he can follow at any time contemporary trails which lead him all over civilization at a particular epoch. There will be a new profession of trailblazers, those who find delight in the task of establishing useful trails through the enormous mass of the common record.".[6]

The third precedent belongs to the humanistic field, conceived by Italian Jesuit Roberto Busa, whose machine endeavours started at the end of the forties.[7] It is important to point out this scholar not only for the work he did, but also because his particular dedication allows us to understand why philology and literature studies have dominated and shaped digital humanities. In 1946 Father Busa came up with a humongous project, creating an *index verborum* to gather all words contained in the works of Thomas Aquinas and other authors related to him, with over eleven million records. Given that he aimed to establish concordance of all the words recorded, something manually impossible, he spoke to IBM in order to do so mechanically. The results took time to come about, but the model was already in place and Busa wrote

---

4 Paul Otlet, *Monde: Essai d'universalisme connaissance du monde, sentiment du monde, action organisée et plan du monde* (Bruxelles: Editiones Mundaneum, 1935), 390–391.
5 Vannevar Bush, "As We May Think", *Atlantic Monthly* 176 (1945): 101–108, *accessed* September 13, 2018, https://www.theatlantic.com/magazine/archive/1945/07/as-we-may-think/303881/.
6 Vannevar Bush, "Memex revisited," in James M. Nyce and Paul Kahn, eds., *From Memex to Hypertext: Vannevar Bush and the Mind's Machine* (San Diego: Academic Press, 1991): 214.
7 Susan Hockey, "The History of Humanities Computing," in *A Companion to Digital Humanities*, ed. Susan Schreibman, Ray Siemens and John Unsworth (Oxford: Blackwell, 2004), 3–19, *accessed* September 13, 2018, http://www.digitalhumanities.org/companion/.

several papers during those years on the computing world and its hermeneutics. In his opinion, this mechanisation, "computerised speleology", marked the beginning of a new era.[8]

Based on Busa's work, the so-called *Humanities Computing* discipline started to thrive, especially in the sixties.[9] Those were also the years of the first centers, conferences, and associations, as well as the appearance of the first journal: *Computers and the Humanities* (1966). The consolidation did not come until the following decade, but reached its peak in the mid-eighties, especially with the gradual popularisation of PCs and e-mail. In turn, the nineties were the start of the current era, the Internet era, which began in 1993 with the first browser. After that, and with subsequent innovations, digital culture unfolded: the machine was no longer only interesting for computing and repetitive tasks, but was also used for elaborate texts: it was the new medium.

This brief journey could be summarized differently. First, we would have the heroic period, that of *Literary & Linguistic Computing*, initiated by Roberto Busa's project, characterized by the willingness to quantify the style of a text or author, measuring regularities. Secondly, the era prior to the Web, that of *Humanities Computing*, from the beginning of the eighties till the mid-nineties, the era of the creation of centers and networks around email. Finally, the arrival of the Web gave way to *Digital Humanities*. This would complete an evolution in which the term *Humanities* finally became the noun, and *Computing* the adjective, a term that ended up being replaced by a less technical, more humane word: *Digital*.

In the case of history, the acceptance of the new technologies came later, although the general features and impact were similar.[10] Thus, it is in the nineties when the new digital history appears. At that time, historians started using technology not (only) with the desire to compute data, but also to develop a new way of writing within the Internet. In this sense, at the beginning of the nineties there are two pieces of work we could consider pioneering in the new relationship with the digital context: *The Valley of the Shadow Project*, by Edward Ayers and William Thomas III, and *Who Built America?*, by Roy Rosenzweig, Steve Brier, and Joshua Brown.[11]

---

8 Roberto Busa, "Picture a Man . . . Busa Award Lecture", *Literary and Linguistic Computing* 14, no. 1 (1999): 5–10.

9 Dolores M. Burton published four papers about this on the *Computers and the Humanities Journal*. The first three appeared in volume 15 (1981) and the fourth in volume 16 (1982), all under the same title ("Automated concordances and word indexes . . .").

10 Serge Noiret, "Informatica, Storia e Storiografia: la Storia si fa digitale," *Memoria e Ricerca* 28 (2008): 189–201; Orville Vernon Burton, "Introduction: The Renaissance," in *Computing in the Social Sciences and Humanities*, ed. O.V. Burton (Champaign: University of Illinois Press, 2002), 1; Edward. L. Ayers, "Technological Revolutions I Have Known," in *ibidem*, 19–28.

11 A glance through what happened in the nineties with William G. Thomas III, "Blazing Trails Toward Digital History Scholarship," *Histoire Sociale/Social History* 34, no. 68 (2001): 415–426; as for the other project, please refer to Roy Rosenzweig and Steve Brier, "Historians and Hypertext: Is It

Besides those and other examples, digital history is understood in two ways. On the one hand, it is the result of a global process, whose effects are revolutionary: "Is the process by which historians are able to use computers to do history in ways impossible without the computer" and "is a revolution in the history profession that will change the way history is done at every level of scholarship and teaching".[12] On the other, it entails a new perspective and new methods: "Is an approach to examining and representing the past that works with the new communication technologies of the computer, the Internet network, and software systems", or is it a way "to create a framework, an ontology, through the technology for people to experience, read, and follow an argument about a historical problem".[13]

Broadly speaking, there have been three main types of digital practice in our discipline.[14] On the one hand, there is textual analysis (heavily linked to data mining), which comes from literary studies and is more common in digital humanities. On the other, there is the collection, preservation, and presentation of the past, more related to oral history and public history. Finally, there is the "visualisation" proposals generally linked to digital cartography, but also to other fields (iconography, photography, cartoons, 3d modelling, videogames). Obviously, these are not isolated fields, as they commonly overlap, some or all, at some time, but they represent the three more common formulae.

It is not necessary to present here the numerous examples of each of those practices,[15] or to deepen in all the issues deriving from them, but it is poignant to state that digital history has moved within the framework of digital humanities, reason why it has brought with it some of its discussions and features. This has led to some authors trying to point out the differences with the latter, always marked by the automatic processing of linguistic data. Thus, some of the historians who practice it consider that, if we have to accept the "digital" adjective, it would be more

---

More than Hype?", *Perspectives* 32, no. 3 (1994), *accessed* September 13, 2018, https://www.historians.org/publications-and-directories/perspectives-on-history/march-1994/historians-and-hypertext-is-it-more-than-hype.

12 Orville Vernon Burton, "American Digital History," *Social Science Computer Review* 23, no. 2 (2005): 207.

13 Daniel J. Cohen et al., "The Promise of Digital History," *The Journal of American History* 95, no. 2 (2008): 442–451.

14 Matthew K. Gold and Lauren F. Klein, eds., *Debates in the Digital Humanities 2016* (Minneapolis: University of Minnesota Press, 2016), *accessed* June 29, 2020, https://dhdebates.gc.cuny.edu/projects/debates-in-the-digital-humanities-2016. See also the volume edited by the same authors in 2019 and the volume that Matthew K. Gold compiled in 2012 (both with the same title and publisher), as well as Kristen Nawrotzki and Jack Dougherty, eds., *Writing History in the Digital Age* (Ann Arbor: University of Michigan Press, 2013), *accessed* September 13, 2018, https://doi.org/10.3998/dh.12230987.0001.001.

15 Examples of all of them: *Arguing with Digital History working group, Digital History and Argument*, white paper, Roy Rosenzweig Center for History and New Media (October 13, 2017), *accessed* September 13, 2018, https://rrchnm.org/argument-white-paper/.

appropriate to separate us from those digital humanities, displacing data mining.[16] As mentioned by Tom Scheinfeldt, calling our work "digital humanities" would have made it more difficult to make it understandable and respectable in the context of this discipline. He confesses that as a historian, the history of Father Busa is not his history. It is an important history, which he does not reject and that must be told, but as a digital historian who is not very involved in textual analysis, it is not a history he identified with, nor the only history that he believes can be told.[17] For instance, oral history would be an alternative precedent that would bring about fewer problems.[18]

But the latter does not solve the problem either, given that oral history, as close as it is in certain aspects to public history, is not exactly a precedent; they just share, as the others do, the effects of the digital shake-up.[19] That is, it has suffered a radical, democratising and transforming change, but is an effect of digitisation, and not a precedent.

For this reason, I would say that digital public history does not have exclusive precedents either in this specific field. We can assert that there is an academic use of data in digital humanities and history research, and another use in the construction of projects and narrative with and for the public thanks to the new technologies, projects that have given public history specific features,[20] just like they have potentially given these to all other areas with which they share those precedents. And that is only the case if we can talk today about a public history that is not digital. At the most, we could say that it can be consciously digital or unconsciously digital, given that the world around us is digital. The truth is that we all practice this profession under the conditions of the present, very different to the conditions of the last century, which was linked to printed technologies, with changes that are modifying the nature of the historic discipline itself.

---

16 Stephen Robertson, "The Differences between Digital Humanities and Digital History", in *Debates in the Digital Humanities*, ed. Matthew K. Gold and Lauren F. Klein, *accessed* September 13, 2018, http://dhdebates.gc.cuny.edu/debates/text/76.
17 Tom Scheinfeldt, April 7, 2014, "The Dividends of Difference: Recognizing Digital Humanities' Diverse Family Trees", *accessed* September 13, 2018, http://foundhistory.org/2014/04/the-dividends-of-difference-recognizing-digital-humanities-diverse-family-trees/.
18 Michael Frisch, *A Shared Authority: Essays on the Craft and Meaning of Oral and Public History* (Albany: State University of New York, 1990).
19 Clifford Kuhn, "The Digitization and Democratization of Oral History", *Perspectives on History* (November 2013), *accessed* September 13, 2018, https://www.historians.org/publications-and-directories/perspectives-on-history/november-2013/the-digitization-and-democratization-of-oral-history.
20 Sharon Leon, "Complexity and Collaboration: Doing Public History in Digital Environments," in *The Oxford Handbook of Public History*, ed. James B. Gardner and Paula Hamilton (New York: Oxford University Press, 2017), 44–68; Serge Noiret, "Digital Public History," in *A Companion to Public History*, ed. David Dean (Hoboken: Wiley-Blackwell, 2018), 111–124.

Tom Scheinfeldt's idea of finding other precedents to digital history helps us understand that public history has perhaps benefited the most from this change, partly in its origin; we could even assert that the digital element is inseparable from its practices. We must remember that, as established by Robert Kelley, public history refers "to the employment of historians and historical method outside of academia", with emphasis, as added by Thomas Cauvin, in communication "to non-academic audiences, a public participation, and the application of historical methodology to present-day issues."[21] That is, public history is forced to be digital, in particular because it impacts on the communication element, either reflecting on the way in which we preserve and create the past to introduce it socially as history, or is concerned about how people relate with the past, thinking always about how to interact with different audiences and how to attract different audiences to the projects. That is why it needs to be digitally aware, to reflect on the redefinition, reconfiguration, and reinvention of objects with which we work and the way in which we make history, a digital mode, therefore open and participatory.

In my opinion, digital history and public history overlap. In fact, I would dare say that most "digital history" is public digital history, starting with the pioneering project Valley of Shadow. Obviously, some parts are not, but there are others with a purely academic basis, research projects, that share this trait.[22] The reason for this convergence seems evident to this author, if one considers that what characterizes public historians is not their fundamental knowledge of the discipline but rather that they work outside of academia. All historians, wherever they work, must master the same skills and methods. Ultimately, the difference rests in the way of communicating and the nature of the medium employed to do it, a nature that sticks with and affects our work. The "academic" historian uses prominently printed text, whereas public historians must use digital media. Thus, whilst a printed text is devoted to an individual reader – although there are collective readings or collective texts – digital technology and the medium where it circulates are intrinsically social and, by employing one and using the other to disseminate our knowledge, our discourse is modified. This is why all digital history is forced to enter the public arena, something that cannot be said equally about "academic" history, based on print, to the extent that, as stated by Serge Noiret, we could ask ourselves: "Existerait-il alors une histoire

---

21 Robert Kelley, "Public History: Its Origins, Nature, and Prospects," *The Public Historian* 1 (1978): 16; Thomas Cauvin, "The Rise of Public History: An International Perspective," *Historia Crítica* 68 (2018): 4, *accessed* September 13, 2018, doi: 10.7440/histcrit68.2018.01. Cauvin's ideas are more and better developed in *Public History. A Textbook of Practice* (New York: Routledge, 2016).
22 For instance: Vincent Brown, "Slave Revolt in Jamaica, 1760–1761. A Cartographic Narrative" (2012), http://revolt.axismaps.com/; Gregory P. Downs and Scott Nesbit, "Mapping Occupation: Force, Freedom, and the Army in Reconstruction" (2015), http://mappingoccupation.org. *Accessed* December 10, 2021.

numérique 2.0 pour un plus vaste public, et une histoire faite en usant de médias traditionnels pour le seul public universitaire?".[23]

In fact, traditional history can continue to operate within the parameters of the printed world, but public history cannot and should not. In any case, this use also has degrees: it depends on how we do it. We could do it by considering historians as the only active party, the one that controls the process thanks to their knowledge and academic dexterity, with the public as the passive party, a mere spectator or consumer. With this approach, history would be something given, with a top-down operation, skilfully transformed by experts into an accessible product. In this case, it does not matter if some people write brainy books and others organize museum exhibitions, because they share the same basis. But we could do public history or approach it from a different perspective, focusing on the process according to which the past and present become history, a process where the public is an active player and not a mere recipient.

Obviously, public history includes very different practices, not only in terms of origin, but also because for a few years, increasingly more with its internationalisation, it has become a broad field where several realities that were previously separated now coexist. In my opinion, public history nowadays is an umbrella that includes the North American original model, local history and popular history, as well as their closeness and overlapping with other fields, such as the already mentioned oral history. In this sense, we could say that the proposal by Robert Kelley, with all its virtues, was mainly institutional, top-down, focused on the dissemination of history through institutions (museums, archives, associations, etc., whether present on the Web or not). Raphael Samuel did not have the same aim with the movement *History Workshop*.[24] In the first issue of the journal devoted to those workshops, its promoters mentioned several clearly rejuvenating aspects. One of them was British society's interest in history as part of a dual model: history consumption via mass media versus academic production reserved only to experts, distanced from its social function.

In Samuel's opinion, one of the solutions to this dilemma was to turn the corner and walk down the street, listen to the echoes of the past in the markets, read them on the walls, and follow their footprints in the fields.[25] That is, gauging the past in a different way, building even an archive, partly restoring the importance of those lives without written trace. Later, Samuel referred to this in terms of "popular history", an appropriate way of rethinking history bottom-up, approaching all those initiatives

---

[23] Serge Noiret, "La digital history: histoire et mémoire à la portée de tous," in *Read/Write Book 2: Une introduction aux humanités numériques*, dir. Pierre Mounier (Marseille: OpenEdition Press, 2012), 51, *accessed* September 13, 2018. DOI: 10.4000/books.oep.226.
[24] "Editorial," *History Workshop Journal* 1, no. 1 (1976): 3.
[25] Raphael Samuel, "Local History and Oral History," *History Workshop Journal* 1, no. 1 (1976): 191–208.

that showed willingness to democratize history production, enlarging the list of those who wrote it, with the will to bring closer the limits of history to those of people's lives.[26]

This duality (top-down versus bottom-up) does not have any type of connotations. There could be and there is excellent public history of the former and latter types, but bad history could also be present in both approaches. Something is not necessarily good just because it comes from the bottom; it is obviously a direct way to connect with the public, but also demands the historian's mediation and, thus, is in some way institutional. In fact, popular interest may go against academic interest, as it often happens when comparing memory and history. It is of worth recalling what David Loventhal said a few years back, albeit excessively, about differentiating between historians and heritage fashioners: "History cannot be wholly dispassionate, or it will not be felt worth learning or conveying; heritage cannot totally disregard history, or it will seem too incredible to command fealty. But the aims that animate these two enterprises, and their modes of persuasion, are contrary to each other".[27]

Thus, although there are many ways to do public history – and all of them have to combine this duality, those two ways of persuasion – I believe the digital change affects the aspect identified by Samuel in the eighties. This is so because new tools cannot just be seen simply as a mean, as a software that allows us to better expose or disseminate; they have to be seen in all their complexity, as a change of era that affects how people perceive the world and how they build it, a world where the public is an active player. If we go back to Samuel, this is the case because the list of those writing history has expanded thanks to new technologies and because the limits of history are already those of the lives of people.

In other words, the interest for history was there, but it now has boomed. Samuel stressed that interest, which is exactly the same pointed out by Roy Rosenzweig and David Thelen in 1998 when they questioned the presence of the past in US society. Moreover, they both stated a clear preference for a history without intermediaries, so that the public preferred a direct experience with the past, without professional historians and their conventional narrations in the role of intermediaries. That is, the American public "participated regularly in a wide range of past-related 'activities', from taking photos to preserve memories, to watching historical films and television programs, to taking part in groups involved in preserving or presenting the past"; this "particularly connected to the past in a range of different settings, from museums and historical sites to gatherings with their families". If the past was omnipresent, history "as it is usually defined in textbooks was not".[28]

---

26 Raphael Samuel, ed., *People's History and Socialist Theory* (London: Routledge, 1981).
27 David Lowenthal, *Possessed by the Past: The Heritage Crusade and the Spoils of History* (New York: Free Press, 1996), xi.
28 Roy Rosenzweig and David Thelen, *The Presence of the Past: Popular Uses of History in American Life* (New York: Columbia University Press, 1998), 9.

Therefore, we must understand that the digital world enhances all of this, because it has multiplied the ability to take photos, view or upload videos, create blogs, use social media, etc. Given that the past is a key element in the lives of people, it is logical that they use it and reclaim it in their own way. In other eras, that possibility was reduced, or even silenced by communication constrains. However, the surge of new technologies enables an unknown democratization, in the sense that it makes it possible to give voice to those who normally did not have it, a voice that is constantly expressed in many ways, either challenging the official version, modifying it, or creating a different history. For this reason, the "Participatory Historical Culture" mentioned by Thelen and Roy Rosenzweig is not a possibility, but a daily expressed reality.[29] That is why, in history just like in other places, old dualities (public/private, professional/amateur, academic/popular) are now obsolete and, without a direct dialogue with the audience on the uses and abuses of the past, history thus risks becoming a merchandise and a show, left in the hands of others.

All this change, offering users never-ending possibilities, is possible due to the new digital ecology, a modification with several aspects upon which every historian should reflect, of which I will highlight two in particular. The first refers to changes in traditional media, and their dematerialisation. As stated by Roger Chartier,[30] we have witnessed changes in the materiality with which information circulates or, better said, changes to the media, something that has changed the production and reproduction techniques, enabling, for instance, new types of writing and, therefore, new ways of reading. That is why, amongst other things, the physical continuity of the medium (for instance, the book, which is the object that has monopolized our textual culture) is replaced by digital mobility, changing the set of perceptions that we used to relate to texts (and sounds and images).

By changing the materiality, there is a revolution in the order of discourses, the one that for instance made it possible for a book to be a material and intellectual object clearly identifiable and immediately differentiated from a letter or a magazine. That is, the materiality in which discourses were set no longer differentiates them, given that the screen makes all presentations look similar. Finally, there is also another deep change, that of reasons, the rhetoric we can use in the way of arguing and representing. The printed text, with its linear, closed, and hierarchical logic gives way to a flexible, open, and uncontrolled and interactive hypertext, subject to all types of handling by the recipient, even that of algorithms.

I believe all those elements need to be taken into account by any public historian, even if the latter can continue combining conventional and new media, both

---

29 Some examples in: Meg Foster, "Online and Plugged In?: Public History and Historians in the Digital Age," *Public History Review* 21 (2014): 1–19. Also in Kristen Nawrotzki and Jack Dougherty, eds., *Writing History in the Digital Age*.
30 Roger Chartier, "Languages, Books, and Reading from the Printed Word to the Digital Text," *Critical Inquiry* 31, no. 1 (2004): 133–152.

regarding the ways of cultural production, at anyone's disposal currently, but also the reasoning and representation, which compete with those of everyday people and foster an exuberant presence of the past on the Web. Wikipedia could be an obvious example of that exuberance, but there are many other examples on the Web.

Secondly, if we have to deal with several media, we have to know their effects, just like we don't only deal with the past, but also with the way it is processed. In this sense, as highlighted by French philosopher Lous Déotte, we could say that eras are not necessarily defined by events, but by the way in which we seize them, which is down to "technical" issues.[31] For instance, it is not that events cease to be important, and not that they stop influencing an era; everything has to do with our way of perceiving them, meaning events quickly go by and are replaced by others, but the way of capturing them is maintained.

Obviously, Déotte's ideas have a "Benjamin" root. Benjamin, when analyzing the technical reproducibility, said, "the mode of human sense perception changes with humanity's entire mode of existence. The manner in which human sense perception is organized, the medium in which it is accomplished, is determined not only by nature but by historical circumstances as well."[32] Obviously, these ideas also remind us of Marshall McLuhan and Harold Innis. In any case, the important thing here is the awareness of change, a conscience that is nowadays mediatic. Because these media, these "apparatus", shape the way reality and the events that take place are captured.

This is what happens with our current recall of events, which depends on the new immaterial medium and also on the way we interact with it. As stated by José Van Dijck, memory is not only caused by objects, but happens through those objects. That is, materiality is inseparable from the cultural practices to which it is connected and depends upon, the specific rituals and circumstances within which objects are taken up.[33] In other words, by changing the material basis of our memories, the nature of our collections and the way of remembrance are reconfigured.

We could mention many examples of this phenomenon, but only need to remember how the public perceived each of the events that have shaken the world in recent times. The fall of the Berlin Wall and the Gulf War were televised phenomena, but the multiple terrorist attacks or the financial crisis of the twentieth-first century cannot be comprehended without social media or Wikileaks and Edward Snowden. If, in the mid nineties, David Thelen wondered how citizens in the TV era

---

31 Jean-Louis Déotte, *L'époque des appareils* (Paris: Lignes-Léo Scheer, 2004).
32 Walter Benjamin, "The Work of Art in the Age of Mechanical Reproduction," in *Illuminations*, ed. Hannah Arendt (New York: Schocken Books, 1969), 222.
33 José Van Dijck, *Mediated Memories in the Digital Age* (Stanford: Stanford University Press, 2007).

were,³⁴ today the means employed to challenge political initiatives or relate to the past have changed.

Lastly, I would like to focus on an issue of interest for all, particularly for public historians: the archive. Besides many other considerations, we can say that the concept of archive, the term itself, has become a universal metaphor for any type of memory and storage.³⁵ Thus, we challenge its traditional nature and its own physical monumental character because we do not live "in a society that uses digital archiving", but "in an information society that is a digital archive".³⁶ It used to be paper and stone; now it is electronic bits. Whilst in the past it was the power that documented, via administrative and control actions or certain civil society institutions, now there is the constant presence of the "I", the possibility for everyday citizens to express, archive themselves, and reorganize others' archives. Thus, it could be said that the archive changes from source to matter, from unquestionable storage house to a history that hopes to be found in controversial places for the creation of the identity and memory.³⁷

Because of this, because of the predominance of participatory culture, the Internet offers the public new opportunities to share experiences and interpretations, and to do this in a parallel manner with institutions and the work of professionals, whether they are historians or other experts. Thus, it is more than ever possible to do history bottom-up and to give voice to the voiceless, because the people of the present are not merely users and consumers of the Internet; they have and exercise their power to be active producers of their own history, managing the archive of their own lives.

Historian Ian Milligan gave a very illustrative example of the American case that can be applied in general.³⁸ He proposes thinking about the hosting service GeoCities, founded in 1994 and which closed down in 2009 when it had seven million users. Internet Archive and the Wayback Machine now keep those registries, with over one hundred and eighty million different URLs. Contrary to this example, Milligan mentions a traditional archive, the Old Bailey. Between 1674 and 1913 this Court

---

34 David Thelen, *Becoming Citizens in the Age of Television* (Chicago, IL: University of Chicago Press, 1996).
35 Wolfgang Ernst, *Stirrings in the Archives: Order from Disorder* (Lanham-Maryland: Rowman and Littlefield, 2015).
36 Arjen Mulder and Joke Brouwer, "Introduction," *Information is Alive: Art and Theory on Archiving and Retrieving Data*, ed. Joke Brouwer and Arjen Mulder (Rotterdam: NAi Publishers, 2003), 6.
37 Terry Cook, "The Archive(s) is a Foreign Country: Historians, Archivists and the Changing Archival Landscape," *American Archivist* 74, no. 2 (2011): 600–632.
38 Ian Milligan, "The Problem of History in the Age of Abundance," *The Chronicle of Higher Education* 63, no. 17 (December 16, 2016), *accessed* September 13, 2018, https://www.chronicle.com/article/The-Problem-of-History-in-the/238600. Milligan's ideas are more and better developed in *History in the Age of Abundance: How the Web is Transforming Historical Research* (Montreal, McGill-Queen's University Press, 2019).

collected the transcriptions of 197,745 court rulings, becoming the "largest body of texts detailing the lives of non-elite people ever published".[39] Comparing this with the seven million users and the one hundred and eighty-six million "documents" generated by GeoCities in fifteen years gives us quite a clear idea about the huge scale of the problem faced by historians.

There is a dual process here that Jacques Derrida warned us about. On the one hand there is a general impulse for preserving, for archiving, an mal d'archive, for which anyone has machines/tools similar to the psychic system, the memory, that represents it and therefore affects it. On the other, this "archiving earthquake" entails a bottom-up mutation, a transformation in the printing and preservation of what surrounds us, because now the archive (any digital memory) ends up determining what is archived. That is, "l'archivation produit autant qu'elle enregistre l'événement".[40]

Because of this and other reasons, one of the most significant consequences of this is the loss of that fetish status that archives had, in the dual sense mentioned by Derrida, as physical, historical, or ontological places that refer us back to the origin and, as for a specific place, to the residence of those who rule. Contrary to this, the archive now is everywhere. And this also relates to the other key element in order to understand the rise of public history: the correlation between technology changes and the rise of the so-called age of memory – with its subjective dimension – and age of commemoration, of statements and heritage, with the emergence of all kinds of initiatives that have reignited and modified the sense of archives, of heritage, of museums, of oral history, etc.

Thus, documenting, archiving, and disseminating are complex processes that are nowadays at everyone's disposal, due to the ease provided by new technologies. We no longer keep our memories in shoeboxes; we store everything in digital repositories and, sometimes, we share them. They are newly invented, fragmented archives, mediated by the digital technologies, totally disconnected from the traditional way of building archives in the past. There are people who show and archive their present or past lives, who tweet events, letters, diaries, who even build archives.[41]

This never-ending activity is also present in public history. In fact, just like I stated that all digital history ultimately has a feeling of public history, I would risk speculating that most digital public history is an archive, or at least the act of archiving. It is an archive of the one built with *Valley of the Shadow*, but also with

---

39 "GeoCities Special Collection 2009"; https://archive.org/web/geocities.php; "Old Bailey Proceedings Online," https://www.oldbaileyonline.org/index.jsp. *Accessed* September 13, 2018.
40 J. Derrida, *Mal d'archive* (Paris: Galilée, 1995), 34.
41 For instance, the archive ordered by Diarmid Mogg, a parliamentary reporter in the Scottish Parliament in Edinburgh: "Small Town Noir," *accessed* September 13, 2018, https://smalltownnoir.com.

many others.[42] And so are the multiple existing oral history archives over the world and so is, for instance, the proposal of public history *Histories of the National Mall*. This is so because, in fact, regardless of whether the documents contained can be found and consulted in a physical archive, those *Histories* and all the others become an act that digitally archives something that does not exist in another place and that, if it did, is now totally re-mediated.[43]

This archiving earthquake is an opportunity, because the past only exists and makes sense when a group of people give it meaning, give it a specific value, and integrate it in their culture. This idea of the digital archive is therefore not just a change of medium (from material to immaterial); it offers new opportunities to generate other relationships amongst individuals of a community and its symbolic dimension, building collective meanings in a collaborative manner. This presents a participation that is out there, in the dialogue on the Web, in the fora, in the social media reactions, and in crowdsourcing.[44]

Thus, it is understood that centers and projects that today state they do public history claim the use of "digital media and computer technology to democratize history: to incorporate multiple voices, reach diverse audiences, and encourage popular participation in presenting and preserving the past."[45] This combination of open access and emphasis on public commitment has made them think – and I share this view – about how digital technology can significantly help users to get involved with the abundance of materials that we currently have in digital format. Therefore, the final goal cannot be other than to enrich historic understanding to a broader audience.

And this supports the famous words by Ralph Samuel when he said, "history is not the prerogative of the historian, nor even, as postmodernism contends, a historian's invention. It is, rather, a social form of knowledge; the work, in any given instance, of a thousand different hands". That is, he refers back to the "ensemble of activities and practices in which ideas of history are embedded or a dialectic of past-present relations is rehearsed".[46]

---

42 For instance: "FBTEE: The French Book Trade in Enlightenment Europe" (http://fbtee.uws.edu.au/main/); "The Viral Texts Project" (http://viraltexts.org/); "Spatial History Project" (http://web.stanford.edu/group/spatialhistory/cgi-bin/site/index.php), etc., *accessed* September 13, 2018.
43 "Histories of the National Mall" (http://mallhistory.org/), *accessed* September 13, 2018.
44 Please refer for instance to what happened after the fire in the National Museum of Rio de Janeiro: "Wikipedia: Notice on the National Museum," *accessed* September 13, 2018, https://pt.wikipedia.org/wiki/Wikip%C3%A9dia:Comunicado_sobre_o_Museu_Nacional/en.
45 "Roy Rosenzweig Center for History and New Media," *accessed* September 13, 2018, http://chnm.gmu.edu/about/.
46 Raphael Samuel, *Theatres of Memory: Past and Present in Contemporary Culture* (London: Verso, 2012), 8.

Bibliography

Cauvin, T. *Public History. A Textbook of Practice*. New York: Routledge, (2016) 2022, 2nd edition.
Gold, M. K., and L. F. Klein, eds. *Debates in the Digital Humanities 2019*. Minneapolis: University of Minnesota Press, 2019.
Ernst, W. *Stirrings in the Archives: Order from Disorder*. Lanham-Maryland: Rowman and Littlefield, 2015.
Mounier, P., dir. *Read/Write Book 2: Une introduction aux humanités numériques*. Marseille: OpenEdition Press, 2012.
Nawrotzki, K., and J. Dougherty, eds. *Writing History in the Digital Age*. Ann Arbor: University of Michigan Press, 2013.

Serge Noiret
Crowdsourcing and User Generated Content: The Raison d'Être of Digital Public History

Abstract: Digital History is different from digital public history (DPH) and this essay describes the central role of crowdsourcing practices in defining the specificity of DPH. At the end of the 1970s, public history (PH) divided its field from a more traditional academic history, engaging with the public in different ways. In the new millennium, DPH developed new forms of interaction with the audience in cultural heritage settings and with communities, and made it possible, thanks to the web 2.0 facilities, to engage in new forms of collective interactions about the past, harvesting citizen's knowledge. This essay will first define the term of "crowdsourcing," then look at how the literature discusses the concept and finally describes different forms of crowdsourcing and user generated content (UGC) activities in DPH projects.

Keywords: user generated content, crowdsourcing, citizen's history, shared authority, public participation, audiences, digital data, participative history

Introduction

Through the 1990s and, even more, with the new millennium when the web economy became more about access to contents (the commons) and less about their property,[1] crowdsourcing became a fundamental practice that also redesigned the field of PH building on direct public engagement in co-creating these contents. This essay aims to illustrate how a digital dimension and a virtual interaction with individuals and community's citizen's knowledge, skills and sources entered the process of making history through crowdsourcing practices.

A series of studies published by Mark Hedges and Stuart Dunn from 2012 onwards, quote some of the endeavors that can be accomplished by the public in user generate contents digital projects: "[T]ranscribing, correcting and modifying content, collaborative tagging, categorizing, cataloging, linking, contextualizing, recording and creating content, commenting, critical responses and stating preference, mapping, georeferencing, translating."[2] They also identified different typologies of crowdsourcing methods because "processes act as connectors, linking assets [sources]

---

[1] Jeremy Rifkin: *The Age of Access: The New Culture of Hypercapitalism, Where All of Life is a Paid-for Experience* (New York: J.P. Tarcher/Putnam, 2000).
[2] Mark Hedges and Stuart Dunn: *Academic Crowdsourcing in the Humanities: Crowds, Communities, and Co-production* (Cambridge: Chandos Publishing, an imprint of Elsevier, 2018), 30.

https://doi.org/10.1515/9783110430295-003

with outputs [projects] via tasks [practices]."³ These many user generated contents methods, tasks and roles are performed by different publics connected to local history institutions but also to academic/public web-based projects.

In 2020, crowdsourcing the knowledge and workforce of the public is made of a vast area of practices involving many disciplines in transdisciplinary ways. It remains complicated to define the many forms of co-production of contents within the field of digital public history (from now on DPH). For this essay, we will focus on crowdsourcing activities being those about historians working on online projects with the public and co-producing contents with interested communities, and about communities directly creating their archives, memory, and stories publicly.

Defining Crowdsourcing in Digital Environments

Crowdsourcing is a neologism associated with Web 2.0 (2004) digital collaborative practices. It was introduced by Jeff Howe in *Wired* in 2006,⁴ as a business/oriented form of outsourcing work to less expensive publics or an audience of concerned volunteers facilitated by web open technologies.⁵ In the *Cambridge English Dictionary*, crowdsourcing is defined as "the activity of giving tasks to a large group of people or to the general public, for example, by asking for help on the internet."⁶ These practices even sometimes bring the danger of "crowdsploitation" of volunteer labor in cultural heritage crowdsourcing.⁷ In his book on *Crowdsourcing*, Daren C. Brabham defines the term as an "online, distributed problem-solving and production model that leverages the collective intelligence of online communities to serve specific organizational goals" through the work of engaged volunteers.⁸ The definition is so blurred that different meanings should be compared "in order to conceive one

---

3 Mark Hedges and Stuart Dunn: *Academic Crowdsourcing in the Humanities: Crowds, Communities, and Co-production* (Cambridge: Chandos Publishing, an imprint of Elsevier, 2018), 29–30. The different types of processes are described in a paper by the same authors: "Crowd-Sourcing Scoping Study: Engaging the Crowd with Humanities Research.", Centre for e-Research, Department of Digital Humanities King's College London, Humanities and Research Council, 2012, https://bit.ly/2EKFhy8.
4 Jeff Howe, "The Rise of Crowdsourcing," *Wired Magazine*, N.14, (1 June, 2006), http://www.wired.com/wired/archive/14.06/crowds_pr.html; "Crowdsourcing a definition," (2 June, 2006), https://crowdsourcing.typepad.com/cs/2006/06/crowdsourcing_a.html; and Jeff Howe *Crowdsourcing: Why the Power of the Crowd Is Driving the Future of Business* (New York, Crown Business, 2008).
5 Mark Hedges and Stuart Dunn, *Academic Crowdsourcing in the Humanities: Crowds, Communities, and Co-production* (Cambridge: Chandos Publishing, an imprint of Elsevier, 2018), 27.
6 "Crowdsourcing," https://dictionary.cambridge.org/dictionary/english/crowdsourcing.
7 Mia Ridge, ed. *Crowdsourcing Our Cultural Heritage* (London: Routledge, 2014), 8.
8 Daren C. Brabham: *Crowdsourcing* (Cambridge: MIT Press, 2013), XVIII.

which could be valid in all circumstances."[9] The word has increasingly been used after 2006,[10] and was left untranslated and in doing so *crowdsourcing* also became a neologism in many languages.[11]

Tim O'Reilly described crowdsourcing as being a form of "user-generated content,"[12] a concept that has been used in very different cultural contexts by heritage and memory institutions, (GLAM), often to rely on a supplementary workforce to achieving a project. It is a collaborative or cooperative form of generated content in which participants in the project were sharing their skills, knowledge, memories, documents, and everything related to the project itself. This happens of course thanks to the capacity of experts to verify the scientific value of generated (crowdsourced) contributions. Ignored, dispersed, or forgotten memories can be retrieved through crowdsourcing activities and past cultures can be historicized and consolidated online through Web 2.0 technologies. This can happen online directly with community's members and/or through the mediation of expert historians.

Within the DPH field, the aim of crowdsourcing practices is primarily to work together with an audience to supply original historical content in the form of data creation like comments/tagging, collections of documents, oral testimony, community/family memories, etc. Participative knowledge sharing creates public awareness about these pasts in our present.

With the web 2.0, a second phase of the history of the web started in which web users became direct protagonists of content creation.[13] Indeed, when people do have knowledge to share, they want to communicate with others and want their stories, artefacts, and memories to become part of the "big history" written by historians.[14] This not always mediated or collaborative creation of knowledge is nevertheless a new form of citizen's history in which, through different forms of dialogue, public historians may become mediators and/or interlocutors or even interpreters of crowdsourced public knowledge and memories, that have to be verified as original sources

---

9 E. Estelles Arolas, and F. González-Ladrón-De-Guevara, "Towards an Integrated Crowdsourcing Definition," *Journal of Information Science* 32.2 (2012): 189–200, DOI:10.1177/0165551512437638.
10 See *Google NGRAM viewer* usage of the word, https://books.google.com/ngrams.
11 In Italian, *crowdsourcing* in one word is a neologism introduced in 2008, as we can see from the Treccani Dictionary of the Italian Language: http://www.treccani.it/vocabolario/crowdsourcing_%28Neologismi%29/.
12 Tim O'Reilly, "What Is Web 2.0. Design Patterns and Business Models for the Next Generation of Software," September 2005, https://www.oreilly.com/pub/a/web2/archive/what-is-web-20.html.
13 *Serge Noiret, "Digital Public History,"* in *A Companion to Public History*, edited by David Dean (Hoboken: Wiley-Blackwell, 2018), 111–124.
14 Documented already at the end of the twentieth century by David Thelen and Roy Rosenzweig in their seminal study *The Presence of the Past. Popular Uses of History in American Life* (New York: Columbia University Press, 1998).

and contextualized within history.[15] Quality crowdsourcing, "uniquely, combines a bottom-up, open, creative process with top-down organizational goals."[16]

Often, who is collaborating makes the job because they accepted to be involved in it convinced by the cultural interest of a project. Crowdsourcers are often not generating qualitative knowledge contents but a quantitative addition of data into a project for which guidelines have been traced. It is always about people's time and dedication, the technical capacity to input data into databases, and to achieve the goals of a project which needs many hands but isn't theirs to lead and control.

Mia Ridge, first in her PhD thesis,[17] and then in a very successful series of essays she coordinated has been studying "the theory and practice of the emerging field of cultural heritage crowdsourcing."[18] Marii Väljataga, in her contribution to this handbook, looks at specific forms of crowdsourcing in libraries that can be extended to other cultural heritage institutions and that go beyond "the original 2006 definition of crowdsourcing by Jeff Howe [. . .] concerned with outsourcing activities previously performed by employees."[19] Johan Oomen and Lora Aroyo "categorize crowdsourcing activities in the GLAM sector according to the main activities and workflow of heritage institutions. [. . .] They maintain that crowdsourcing may play a role in each of the five stages [of a project]: creating, discovering, managing, describing, and using/reusing digital content."[20]

Mark Hedges and Stuart Dunn identify four elements in the life cycle of academic crowdsourcing: assets (primary materials and sources), tasks (what volunteers accomplish with assets), processes ("combination of tasks related to assets") and outputs (results of such an activity).[21] Milena Dobreva and Daniela Azzopardi suggested that "there are three types of projects: contributive, collaborative, and co-created. By their different nature they provide different opportunities for citizen

---

15 See Anita Lucchesi and Bruno Leal Pastor de Carvalho, "História digital: Reflexões, experiências e perspectivas," in *História pública no Brasil: Sentidos e itinerários*, edited by Ana Maria Mauad, Juniele Rabêlo de Almeida, and Ricardo Santhiago (São Paulo: Letra e Voz, 2016), 149–163, 158–159.
16 Daren C. Braham, *Crowdsourcing* (Cambridge: MIT Press, 2013), 19.
17 Mia Ridge, "Making Digital History: The Impact of Digitality on Public Participation and Scholarly Practices in Historical Research." PhD thesis. The Open University, 2016, http://oro.open.ac.uk/45519/.
18 Mia Ridge, ed. *Crowdsourcing Our Cultural Heritage* (London: Routledge, 2014), 1.
19 See Marii Väljataga, *Digital Public History in Libraries*, notes 11, 29 and 30. See also Laura Carletti, Derek McAuley et al., "Digital Humanities and Crowdsourcing: An Exploration," in *Museums and the Web 2013*, edited by Nancy Proctor and Rich Cherry (Silver Spring: Museums and the Web, 2013).
20 Johan Oomen and Lora Aroyo, "Crowdsourcing in the Cultural Heritage Domain: Opportunities and Challenges," in *Proceedings of the 5th International Conference on Communities and Technologies* (New York: Association for Computing Machinery, 2011).
21 Mark Hedges and Stuart Dunn, *Academic Crowdsourcing in the Humanities: Crowds, Communities, and Co-production* (Cambridge: Chandos Publishing, an imprint of Elsevier, 2018), 28.

scientists to participate in research, ranging from merely helping with trivial data collection tasks to formulating new research questions."[22]

Crowdsourcing in Literature and Historiography

Within a PH environment, outsourcing work to specific audiences is made of different processes and practices that engage citizens in the collective making of digital history contents, the output of the whole process. Nonetheless, even if practitioners agree that an ethical and professional interaction between historians and their public is the holy grail of any PH practice, especially within the digital realm, very few PH manuals engage directly with the definition of crowdsourcing practices.

In general, international PH historiography describes digital collaborative processes around UGC activities, as a path for a history from below that would aggregate the knowledge of the people through shared authority practices. Notwithstanding these well-established field activities, it is interesting to note that PH manuals that are mostly collective enterprises with different authors had no specific chapters dealing with crowdsourcing and shared authority before the digital revolution in the twenty-first century before a chapter dealing with the *9/11DigitalArchive* was added in 2006, in the revised "Essays from the Field" edition by James Gardner and Peter LaPaglia.[23]

Paul Martin in his *Public History Reader* coordinated with Hilda Kean (2013), a series of re-published essays by different authors, defined crowdsourcing (there in two words) as "a method by which objectives are achieved through popular outreach, not, in essence, a new phenomenon" which has been boosted to an extraordinary degree through digital and social media.[24] Kean shows how much community archives offer the possibility of common authority ownership between the public as users and archivists through the process of crowdsourcing documents.[25]

More recent manuals of PH written by single authors, engage with the importance of UGC within PH practices in the digital realm. In 2008, Jerome De Groote's *Consuming History* became the first PH manual written by a single author to deal

---

[22] See Milena Dobreva and Daniela Azzopardi, "Citizen Science in the Humanities. A Promise for Creativity," University of Cyprus, Nicosia, 2014, https://www.um.edu.mt/library/oar/handle/123456789/987.
[23] James T. Sparrow, "On the Web: The September 11 Digital Archive," in *Public history: Essays from the Field*, edited by James B. Gardner and Peter S. LaPaglia (Malabar Florida: Krieger Pub. Co., 2006), 397–415, 398. See the chapter on "Shared Authority" in this handbook.
[24] Paul Martin, "The Past in the Present. Who is Making History?" in *The Public History Reader*, edited by Hilda Kean and Paul Martin (Abingdon: Routledge, 2013), 1–10, 6–9.
[25] Hilda Kean: "Materials and Approaches to Making History," in *The Public History Reader*, edited by Hilda Kean and Paul Martin (Abingdon: Routledge, 2013), 147–156.

with these practices.²⁶ Some years later, Faye Sayer in 2015,²⁷ and Thomas Cauvin in 2016,²⁸ integrated reflections on crowdsourcing within DPH practices in their respective manuals. Sharon Leon writes that historians are "data creators" but within a crowdsourced activity that she prefers to call a community generated activity or "community sourcing."²⁹ It happens that the public itself becomes a producer of digital historical data and sources. Sometimes, people may play with their own stories in public without being filtered by professional historians.

Crowdsourcing in Heritage and Communities' Digital Public History Projects

Before the launch of social media and web 2.0 platforms and their disruptive impact on societies,³⁰ forms of co-creation of contents – mainly primary sources collections to be used in teaching activities – were orchestrated indirectly through the usage of emails, phone calls, oral interviews, and collecting of objects. In the case of the seminal Italian project MUVI (*Museo Virtuale della Memoria Collettiva della Lombardia*) (Figure 1), the indirect use of radio transmissions opened testimonies and storytelling to everyone.³¹ It has been a pioneer of socio-anthropological UGC already adapted in 1999 to a "virtual museum" and heritage website. Adding people's podcasts and videos to the site, MUVI promoted individual experiences in its virtual stances and narrated the traditions of Lombardy communities thanks to stories provided by the audience. Photographs were published online, and the public participated in the museum collections' captions, sending comments to the curators in a process of co-creation of senses that would be called "crowdsourcing" just a few years later.

Crowdsourcing in DPH projects is largely about the collective creation of digital archives. With the advent of the twenty-first century, we are witnessing a permanent "glocal" race to capture everyone's written, spoken, filmed, photographed, or

---

[26] Jerome De Groot, *Consuming History: Historians and Heritage in Contemporary Popular Culture* (New York, Routledge, [2008] 2016).
[27] Faye Sayer, *Public History: A Practical Guide* (London: Bloomsbury, (2015) 2nd edition 2019).
[28] Thomas Cauvin, *Public History: A Textbook of Practice* (New-York, Routledge, 2016), 179–181.
[29] Sharon Leon, "The Peril and Promise of Historians as Data Creators: Perspective, Structure, and the Problem of Representation," *[bracket], images, teaching, technology*, 24 November, 2019, http://www.6floors.org/bracket/2019/11/24/the-peril-and-promise-of-historians-as-data-creators-perspective-structure-and-the-problem-of-representation/.
[30] José van Dijck, Thomas Poell, and Martijn de Waal, *The Platform Society: Public Values in a Connective World* (New York: Oxford University Press, 2018).
[31] MUVI della Lombardia, http://www.muvilo.it. Information on its history is available in the *Internet Archive* here, https://web.archive.org/web/20060512165432/http://www.muvilo.it/index.htm.

Fig. 1: The MUVI website. https://web.archive.org/web/20190805112522/http://www.url.it:80/muvi/.

interviewed testimonies. Multimedia documents and sources are generated in digital formats by the public and shared in many crowdsourced projects that are built explicitly to think about the audience with which they engage at a very early stage of the projects.[32] This is why Sheila Brennan reminds us that a PH web project is created for and with a specific audience.[33]

Libraries, for example, were concerned about bad OCR performances in projects that transcribe textual primary sources. *Trove*, the newspaper project at the National Library of Australia, launched in 2008, was established to correct digitized texts and not to reflect on the power of UGCs and public endeavors.[34] One of the pioneering international projects is Flickr's *The Commons*, which involves the public to help to catalogue the world's public photo archives, adding tags and comments.[35] *The*

---

[32] Sharon Leon: "Complexity and Collaboration: Doing Public History in a Digital Environment," in *The Oxford Handbook of Public History*, edited by Paula Hamilton and James B. Gardner (Oxford: Oxford University Press, 2017), 44–66.

[33] Sheila A. Brennan, "Public, first" in *Debates in the Digital Humanities 2016*, edited by Matthew K. Gold and Lauren F. Klein (Minneapolis: University of Minnesota Press, 2016), 384–389.

[34] Rose Holley, "Crowdsourcing Based Curation and User Engagement in Digital Library Design," in *Rose Holley's Blog – Views and News on Digital Libraries and Archives* (2017). See Marii Väljataga's contribution to this handbook.

[35] On the contrary, Julia Thomas asserts, "that the meanings of illustration refuse to be fixed through collaborative procedures" (Julia Thomas, "Crowdsourcing" in *Nineteenth-Century Illustration and the Digital. Studies in Word and Image* [London: Palgrave Macmillan, 2017], 65–93, 65, DOI https://doi.org/10.1007/978-3-319-58148-4_4).

Commons was launched in January 2008 by the Library of Congress and was extended to numerous libraries and archives worldwide.[36]

On the other hand, a few years later, *Transcribe Bentham* at UC London, has been recognized by scholars in digital humanities as the first important collaborative project for which common people helped to transcribe online the papers of the English philosopher Jeremy Bentham. *Transcribe Bentham*, made people worldwide aware of the importance of a labor generated contribution to the digitization of texts.[37] Another extremely popular project has been "*What's on the menu*," a text that became a searchable database thanks to the work of volunteers digitizing New York City's restaurants' menus conserved at the New York Public Library.[38] *Shakespeare's World* marked the 400th anniversary of Shakespeare's death in 2016.[39] Volunteers numbering 3,926 participated through the *Zooniverse* platform of "people powered research" which favors citizen science and collaborative transcriptions projects.[40] Three genres of material were transcribed: letters, 'receipts' (recipes), books, and newsletters (early handwritten news sheets) written by Shakespeare's contemporaries. The idea behind the transcribing project was not only to foster the study of Shakespeare's works but to contextualize the sixteenth-century world in which he lived (1564–1616). The *Zooniverse* platform has been used for structured data collaborative transcription and contains many other historical user generated projects.

In 2013, in France a governmental project, the *Mission du Centenaire*, initiated the commemoration of the centenary of the First World War.[41] One of the specific tasks was, using a form which added data in an online public database,[42] to realize

---

[36] See Raffaella Biscioni, "The digital age is also the digitization age. La digitalizzazione del patrimonio fotografico fra digital cultural heritage e public history" in *Fotografia e Public History. Patrimonio storico e comunicazione digitale* (Pisa, Pacini, 2019), 45–120; see also her contribution to this handbook.

[37] Melissa Terras and Tim Causer, "Crowdsourcing Bentham: Beyond the Traditional Boundaries of Academic History," *International Journal of Humanities and Arts Computing* 8.1 (2014): 46–64.

[38] Michael Lascarides and Ben Vershbow: "What's on the Menu? Crowdsourcing at the New York Public Library" in *Crowdsourcing Our Cultural Heritage*, edited by Mia Ridge (London: Routledge, 2014), 113–138.

[39] *Shakespeare's World* is a collaboration between the Folger Shakespeare Library in Washington, DC, Zooniverse.org at Oxford University, and the *Oxford English Dictionary*, https://www.zooniverse.org/projects/zooniverse/shakespeares-world.

[40] See https://www.zooniverse.org/.

[41] @Mission1418, "Mission Centenaire, Actualités, publications et informations sur le centenaire de la Première Guerre mondiale," https://twitter.com/mission1418. The mission in Twitter used the official hashtag #Centenaire and supports the website project "14–18, Mission Centenaire," http://centenaire.org.

[42] "Rejoignez le programme d'indexation collaborative et participez à l'enrichissement de la base des Morts pour la France de la Première Guerre mondiale," http://www.memoiredeshommes.sga.defense.gouv.fr/fr/article.php?larub=52&titre=annotation-collaborative.

an ambitious crowdsourcing project called "Mémoire des Hommes";⁴³ a collaborative digital transcription of all soldiers' ("Poilus") handwritten records who sacrificed their lives for France and are conserved in the Defense Ministry Figure 2.⁴⁴

Fig. 2: France – Ministère de la défense – Mémoire des Hommes- Première guerre mondiale – https://bit.ly/3pLbr1F.

Today collective transcription and crowdsourced volunteers' workforce are mainstream methods used worldwide in important DPH projects and by outstanding heritage institutions for digitizing or computing vast amounts of data offering new sources for research and outreach. Community and citizen's history projects are launched everywhere in the world and in many different historical, political, social, and cultural contexts.

Collecting the documents, comments, reactions of communities affected by a catastrophic event, has been one of the most important "glocal" user generated kind of projects. The archetype of such a successful interaction with local and global communities has been *September 11*, the 2002 digital archive project launched by the RRCHNM and archived at the Library of Congress.⁴⁵ Hurricanes and their impact on cities and local communities were dealt with in another important crowdsourced archive in 2005, the *Hurricane Digital Memory Bank* which has become the most important public archive for the memory of the Katrina and Rita hurricanes.⁴⁶ JDA, the *Japan Disasters Digital Archive*

---

43 See http://www.memoiredeshommes.sga.defense.gouv.fr/.
44 "Base de données des Morts pour la France de la Première Guerre mondiale," http://www.memoiredeshommes.sga.defense.gouv.fr/article.php?larub=24&titre=morts-pour-la-france-de-la-premiere-guerre-mondiale.
45 See https://911digitalarchive.org/; consult the chapter dealing with "Shared Authority" in this handbook.
46 "Hurricane Digital Memory Bank," http://hurricanearchive.org/.

regroups more than 600 collections of multimedia data dealing with the impact of the March 2011 Tsunami and the nuclear catastrophe in Japan.[47] Similar semantic web applications to accessing data could become extraordinarily useful in 2020 to connect the many worldwide projects that were launched about the Covid-19 global pandemic.[48]

At the University of Canterbury, New Zealand, the *Earthquake Digital Archive* is a "comprehensive digital archive of video, audio, documents and images" related to the 2010 and 2011 earthquakes in that country. The project started as a global interface for different existing decentralized crowdsourced data repositories, capable of bringing together at the national level through a single access point, all the knowledge and memories of the earthquakes published in many sites.[49]

A pioneering US digital history project called *Historical Harvest, our history is all around us*, initiated by William G. Thomas and Patrick D. Jones in spring 2013 at the University of Nebraska-Lincoln inspired similar projects collecting artifacts and stories bottom-up, throughout the USA and launched a "harvest movement" to include "people's history" into US federal history.[50] "We believe that our collective history is more diverse and multi-faceted than most people give credit for and that most of this history is not found in archives, historical societies, museums or libraries, but rather in the stories that ordinary people have to tell from their own experience and in the things – the objects and artifacts – that people keep and collect to tell the story of their lives."[51] The movement spread,[52] with similarities everywhere.[53]

Another federal US project promoted by the Library of Congress in Washington is *History Hub*, a research support community for everyone, including genealogists, historians, and citizen archivists. This is a project in which the public participates[54] in community projects with archival materials and allows crowdsourcers to contribute to developing the "Hub."[55] The engagement with a memory institution like the library of Congress is twofold, members of concerned communities work with their archives to make the history of their communities but, in doing so, they also become citizen archivists transcribing and tagging sources; this is a positive collaboration for keeping these collections alive and improving the way they can be accessed.

---

47 "Japan disaster digital archive," http://jdarchive.org/.
48 See IFPH, "COVID-19 Story-Collecting Initiatives," https://bit.ly/3b63oUn.
49 See http://www.ceismic.org.nz/.
50 "An Introduction to The History Harvest," 8 April 2013, https://youtu.be/X_ltt7q4N78.
51 See https://historyharvest.unl.edu/.
52 Google mapped the projects around the USA, https://bit.ly/34GhVol.
53 See for example the Harvest in the Rondo neighborhood in St. Paul, Minnesota, Marvin Roger Anderson and Rebecca S. Wingo: "Harvesting History, Remembering Rondo", in Rebecca S. Wingo, Jason A. Heppler, Paul Schadewald (eds.), *Digital Community Engagement. Partnering Communities with the Academy*, Cincinnatti, University of Cincinnati Press, 2020, DOI: 10.34314/wingodigital.00004.
54 See https://historyhub.history.gov/welcome.
55 See https://historyhub.history.gov/community/citizen-archivists.

Crowdsourcing and User Generated Content: The Raison d'Être of Digital Public History — 45

Fig. 3: Europeana 1914–1918: untold stories & official histories of WW1 – http://www.europeana1914-1918.eu/en.

Crowdsourced activities have become so important in a global process aimed at building pieces of citizen science,[56] that, in 2015, the US federal government launched a project outlining best practices and examples for those who wants to start user generated projects.[57]

For the centenary of the First World War, in November 2013 *Europeana* launched *Transcribe*, a PH project crowdsourcing European wide documents on the model of the French *Grande Collecte*. *Transcribathon Europeana 1914–1918* Figure 3,[58] crowdsourced a public transcription of what had been collected through a very popular competition. Teams of volunteers in different EU cities[59] were tasked with transcribing and digitizing as many documents (each character counted) as possible in as little time as possible.[60] The last WW1 *Transcribathon* competition, *Versailles on the Run*, was held in 2019, with "1,381 documents and over a million characters" added to the *Europeana 1914–1918* database.[61]

Fig. 4: Unesco Heritage Helpers: Put a World of Pictures into Words https://heritagehelpers.org/projects/view/details/project/unesco_tagging_photos.

---

56 See Fien Danniau's definition of citizen science as "the practice of collecting and processing scientific data by volunteers," in "Public History in a Digital Context. Back to the Future of Back to Basics," in *BMGN – Low Countries Historical Review* 128.4 (2013): 118–144, 131, DOI: http://doi.org/10.18352/bmgn-lchr.9355.
57 "This central information includes success stories and some of the challenges that developers faced in designing and carrying out citizen science and crowdsourcing projects," "Federal crowdsourcing and citizen science toolkit," http://www.citizenscience.gov/toolkit/.
58 See https://europeana.transcribathon.eu/runs/europeana1914-1918/.
59 "Our Motto is Think History," http://www.factsandfiles.com/en/home.html.
60 "For the 100th anniversary of the First World War, Europeana 1914–1918," https://www.europeana.eu/portal/en/collections/world-war-I.
61 "Versailles Run. The end of WW1?," https://europeana.transcribathon.eu/runs/europeana1914-1918/versailles-1919/.

A heritage international organization like UNESCO, with *Put a World of Pictures into Words* opened in 2019 and ended in 2021 such a digitization project of 5,050 photographs derived from all heritage campaigns organized from its inception in 1945. Heritage Helpers is the interactive platform used in the UK to favor many crowdsourcing projects Figure 4.[62] Requests to the public were twofold: transcribe information and existing keywords into metadata. The difference between the pioneering French crowdsourcing initiative *Photos Normandie*, a photographic archive of the 6 June, 1944, D-Day and the battle of Normandy, uploaded to *Flickr*,[63] was the pre-existence of keywords that had to be digitized. Instead, in describing the more than 3,200 pictures of D-Day, volunteers were asked to identify the pictures and eventually correct the existing captions, adding their own keywords and even their own pictures.

All these national and international initiatives can only be carried out through the active presence of a skilled public that possesses expertise, knowledge, and sometimes documents, but, above all, the existence of easy-to-manage technologies that enable DPH projects to connect with their participants. It has been observed that whoever collaborates with a user generated project is directly interested or concerned by their community issues and/or by the heritage crowdsourcing project.[64]

Conclusions

Up to now we have mentioned projects based on a collective transcription of manuscripts and different kinds of community archives harvested in the US and the EU thanks to the direct contribution of the public. But these are only some of the possible crowdsourcing practices in DPH projects and citizen's history.

Trevor Owens considers crowdsourcing to be part of the "values and missions' of cultural heritage organizations, [. . .] the value of crowdsourcing lies not only in the productivity of the crowd but in 'providing meaningful ways for the public to enhance collections while more deeply engaging with and exploring them".[65] As Sharon Leon writes, the publics who engage with DPH are more than passive audience members absorbing content expertise from historians. The Web offers a range of ways that those publics can be active participants – co-creators – of public history. [. . .] Platforms

---

[62] "Anyone can help make online archives accessible," https://heritagehelpers.co.uk/.
[63] "PhotosNormandie," Patrick Peccatte and Michel Le Querrec, http://www.flickr.com/people/photosnormandie. See Patrick Peccatte, "PhotosNormandie five years – a balance shaped FAQ," *Déjà vu. Carnet de recherche visuel*, http://culturevisuelle.org/dejavu/1097.
[64] Chiara Bonacchi, et al., "Participation in Heritage Crowdsourcing," *Museum Management and Curatorship* 34.2 (2019):166–182, DOI: 10.1080/09647775.2018.1559080.
[65] Trevor Owens, "Making Crowdsourcing Compatible with the Missions and Values of Cultural Heritage Organisations," in *Crowdsourcing Our Cultural Heritage*, edited by Mia Ridge (London: Routledge, 2014), 279. See the Trevor Owens chapter in this handbook.

offer visitors a way to talk back to public historians and engage content experts in dialogue about the past. These participatory projects stand as a testament to how deeply interested nonprofessional historians are in history and how willing they are to contribute to and share that content."[66] Collecting public data can help create citizen's history and to write a history from below in which the authoritative voice is not always that of expert historians but of "expert crowdsourcers" like in the memorial project museum about the Lodz Ghetto in which accuracy of the contents is an essential feature for the credibility of the whole endeavor.[67]

Crowdsourcing practices have become, thanks to the digital, a core method in PH processes, an intimate raison d'être in the discipline, because the web always requires who is engaging with an audience to define the kind of shared authority that is part of any DPH project. PH in becoming digital unveiled the enormous impact of all kinds of crowdsourcing practices, collaborative, and co-created, on the craft of public historians.

Bibliography

Braham, Daren C. *Crowdsourcing*. Cambridge: MIT Press, 2013.
Howe, Jeff. *Crowdsourcing: Why the Power of the Crowd is Driving the Future of Business*. New York, Crown Business, 2008.
Hedges, Mark, and Stuart Dunn. *Academic Crowdsourcing in the Humanities: Crowds, Communities, and Co-production*. Cambridge: Chandos Publishing, an imprint of Elsevier, 2018.
Ridge, Mia, ed. *Crowdsourcing Our Cultural Heritage*. London: Routledge, 2014.
Noiret, Serge. "La *digital history*: histoire et mémoire à la portée de tous." In *Read/Write Book 2. Une introduction aux humanités numériques*. Ed. Pierre Mounier. Marseille: OpenEdition Press, 2012, 151–177, https://books.openedition.org/oep/258.
Noiret, Serge. "Digital Public History," in A Companion to Public History, ed. David Dean (Hoboken: Wiley-Blackwell, 2018), 111–124.
See the chapters about *Archives, Library, Photography* and *Shared Authority* in this handbook.

---

[66] Sharon Leon: "The Peril and Promise of Historians as Data Creators: Perspective, Structure, and the Problem of Representation", *[bracket], images, teaching, technology*, 24 November, 2019, http://www.6floors.org/bracket/2019/11/24/the-peril-and-promise-of-historians-as-data-creators-perspective-structure-and-the-problem-of-representation/.
[67] "Since inaccuracies are often used to fuel the fires of Holocaust denial, no information generated by the Citizen History project is made available to the public until it is quality checked [. . .]." Elizabeth Merritt, Founding director of the Center for the Future of Museums, American Alliance of Museums: *More Crowdsourced Scholarship: Citizen History. The Children's of the Lodz Ghetto, a memorial research project*, https://www.aam-us.org/2011/07/28/more-crowdsourced-scholarship-citizen-history/.

Serge Noiret
Sharing Authority in Online Collaborative Public History Practices

Abstract: Forms of shared authority has become User-generated projects in the digital realm public history practices and projects. New collaborative forms of history making through web technologies are ubiquitous worldwide. User-generated projects democratized the making of history with public historians now engaged in sharing their authority actively with targeted communities. This essay discusses the critical issues related to the concept as it dealt with public historians' activities, its acceptance as a fundamental method for doing public history in the digital world, and the way Web 2.0 social practices contributed enormously in developing the field of digital public history to intertwine crowdsourcing with shared authority practices.

Keywords: sharing authority, shared authority, web 2.0, citizen history, user generated content, crowdsourcing, digital realm

Introduction. Sharing Knowledge and Authority: An Old Transdisciplinary Activity

In his *Dialogue*, Plato describes how Socrates engaged with his interlocutors in a collaborative process of questioning. Through precise demands, those talking with Socrates slowly revealed knowledge that was hidden deeply. This process of delivering knowledge, memories, or experiences, has been called *maieutic*, the capacity of giving birth to what individuals did not even know they had in their minds, a method used by Socrates to offer more concrete definitions to theoretical concepts. Such a process is dual, and Socrates used his authority to drive interlocutors in a collaborative creation of applied knowledge.

Roberto Minervini, an Italian filmmaker living in the USA, documented a forsaken America telling the story of marginal communities through direct sensitive contacts and shared experiences. *What you gonna do when the world's on fire* (2018) Figure 1 tells the story of members of the surviving group of the Black Panthers. Only a year after living within the community and getting to know some of its members very closely through full personal immersion in real time was he able to start filming. He built a powerful out of the box storytelling of the Black Panthers' community. Individuals were the direct protagonists of their personal life stories through the mediation of the camera and a whole community's way of life was revealed this way. Minervini shared his authority as filmmaker very slowly, not imposing himself on his characters but practicing continuous dialogue and observing the community, even

https://doi.org/10.1515/9783110430295-004

Fig. 1: Roberto Minervini: What you gonna do when the world's on fire (2018) https://www.filmaffinity.com/us/movie image.php?imageId=409475529.

before starting to film his protagonists. "The film is not about [. . .] my beliefs or preconceptions, I won't mitigate reality." The movie becomes the result of the work that the author and the characters perform together: "[B]y listening to them, I help them and put them in a position to tell their stories."[1]

This chapter is divided into three sections. The first one tackles the process of democratizing the making of history by sharing authority practices within communities. The second starts with the seminal work written in 1990 by Michael Frisch and investigates the promises and dangers of sharing authority. The third section digs into shared authority practices in the *9/11DigitalArchive* project of publicly generated documents and memories.

---

1 See "The World on Fire. The cinema of Roberto Minervini," in *59 festival dei Popoli. Festival Internazionale del Film Documentario, 3–10 novembre 2018*, (Prato, Baroni & Gori, 2018), 66–86, 77.

Sharing a Public Historian's Authority within Communities

In the 1970s and 1980s, pioneering works by American and British historians focused on the making of public history in direct contact with individuals and communities willing to contribute to the making of their history through personal memories and documents. Raphael Samuel wanted to collect oral memories of the 1984 to 1985 miners' strikes during the Thatcher government era. Working with the direct protagonists and their families, the cultural meaning of the strike would remain in collective memories.[2] In creating a memory archive of the strike in 1985, he shared his authority with the miners who were invited to collaborate: "[W]e argued – in the words of the invitation – that the meaning of the strike would not be determined by the terms of the settlement [. . .] but by how it is assimilated in popular memory [. . .] in the country at large."

Roy Rosenzweig analyzed how the making of history was transformed through digital and web practices. He explicitly mentioned as part of this transformation, new bottom-up and grassroots ways of writing history within communities. "Many earlier neighborhood and community history projects also embodied this ethic of shared authority. Such ventures – oral history programs, photo exhibits, walking tours, documentary films, union history classes – often grew out of the social movements of the 1960s and 1970s. Professional historians who were caught up in those movements tried to infuse a more democratic ethos into their historical practice."[3]

A long time practitioner of these shared authority practices in community projects in the UK, Paul Ward, tells us that "community research [. . .], consistently seeks to sustain our community, revitalize and return our people back to their culture and language."[4] This kind of knowledge co-production follows Rosenzweig's arguments about fostering a more democratic ethos in history-making practices and

---

2 Quoted in Yate & District Labour History Group, *The Miners' Strike, 1984–85* (Thornbury: Colin Burges, 2014), 1–2. For the detailed method in which Samuel and his co-workers describe the whole process of collecting memories and documents, see Barbara Bloomfield, Guy Boanas, Raphael Samuel, *The Enemy Within: Pit Villages and the Miners' Strike of 1984–85* (London, Routledge and Kegan Paul, [1986] 2017).
3 See comments by people who answered the survey realized in parallel with the writing of their book, by Roy Rosenzweig and David Thelen, *The Presence of the Past. Popular uses of history in American life*, in a web site *supplementing* "the book published by Columbia University Press in November 1998, offering additional tables beyond those included in the book as well as the full text of the survey questionnaires." "Roy Rosenzweig Afterthoughts," *Roy Rosenzweig: Everyone a Historian*, http://chnm.gmu.edu/survey/afterroy.html.
4 Paul Ward: "Doing Research Differently: Imagining Better Communities in Local and Global Contexts," in *Imagine. Connecting Communities through Research*, 18 July, 2017, http://www.imaginecommunity.org.uk/blog-doing-research-differently-imagining-better-communities-in-local-and-global-contexts-by-paul-ward/. Ward co-directed a UK based project called *Imagine: Connecting Communities*

community knowledge creation, offering "a more ethical way of working with communities,"[5] different from traditional academic research. Giving voice to individual and community memories, looking at traditions and at the history of minorities the way communities themselves wanted to focus on writing their history, can be accomplished better through a shared process of history making. This process, Rosenzweig suggests, can become a very political issue because of the shared authority it entails. It can also come into conflict with traditional academic powers: "[G]iving a platform to people not usually heard can provoke counter-reactions from those who have traditionally had more power in shaping historical accounts."[6]

Nevertheless, sharing authority raises major issues in PH projects. James B. Gardner warn us of the blurred line between opinion and knowledge when "trusting radically" the role of the public and giving up authority.[7] User Generated Content (UGC) can become very dangerous when public historians abandon their scientific role, in favor of the public to which one would entrust both the content and direction of the projects. Sharing authority with the public supposes instead that public historians do not accept the concept of "radical trust" but engage critically with the knowledge, documents and memories shared by the public. Public historians should remain in control of their projects, especially in the new digital era when opening to UGC can easily become uncontrolled. Sharing an authority is not about accepting everything that is coming from the public. A public historian must be able to professionally process contents, share methods, contextualize sources, and demonstrate why critical thinking is necessary. In doing so, both the project and the communities engaged in generating

---

through Research (2012–2017) which involved a wide range of universities and community organizations. *Connected Communities Programme*, https://connected-communities.org/.

5 See Durham Community Research Team, Centre for Social Justice and Community Action, Durham University, *Community-based Participatory Research: Ethical Challenges*, https://www.dur.ac.uk/resources/beacon/CCDiscussionPapertemplateCBPRBanksetal7Nov2011.pdf.

6 "Roy Rosenzweig Afterthoughts," *Roy Rosenzweig: Everyone a Historian*, http://chnm.gmu.edu/survey/afterroy.html.

7 James B.Gardner: "Trust, Risk and Public History: A View from the United States," *Public History Review* 17 (2010): 52–61, DOI: https://doi.org/10.5130/phrj.v17i0.1852, and "Trust, risk and historical authority: negotiating public history in digital and analog worlds" in *Making Histories*, edited by Paul Ashton, Tanya Evans, and Paula Hamilton (Oldenbourg: De Gruyter, 2020), 59–67. Gardner was part of a discussion about "radical trust" in museums: "[W]hile I believe strongly that museums should *share* authority with the public, I don't support abdicating our role and privileging the public's voice or simply doing what the public votes for, no matter what that might be." See Jim Grove, "History Bytes: Grappling with the Concept of Radical Trust," *History News* (8 July, 2010), now in the web archive, https://web.archive.org/web/20160312022445/http://aaslhcommunity.org/historynews/radical-trust/.

contents and the public historians can benefit from a controlled process of shared authority.

Public historians' activities with targeted communities have been enormously facilitated by the digital revolution started in the 1990s, with the explosion of personal websites and of the widespread public diffusion of participative Web 2.0 social practices in twenty-first-century social media. Interactive digital technologies offered new possibilities to engage with local communities, their individual and family knowledge of the past, and to collect documents. Sharing one's own stories on the web has become a very popular common activity. The new "homo digitalis" feels alive only through a self-reflective presence in social media and not because of a responsible and self-conscious knowledge of what technologies are offering to enhance human knowledge. Therefore, citizens' online generated knowledge should be fostered and directed by public historians as mediators towards different kinds of crowdsourced activities based on everyone's new digital presence. Memory institutions (GLAM) only had to find the best way to stimulate and coordinate communities to jump into new collaborative practices. What must be figured out is the best way professionals can engage with these publics and capture their attention and knowledge while maintaining a critical rigor in harvesting public content, knowledge and expertise.

Public historians' understanding of this new normality and of the necessity to actively engage with the public in the digital realm facilitated the widespread diffusion of forms of shared authority that are common today in digital public history collaborative practices and projects. But what is not yet clearly stated in these new forms of digital relationships, is how public history projects can do more than collecting, organizing, and adding metadata to publicly generated contents. A public historian's role in sharing his authority with the public is also to critically validate opinions against recognized scientific knowledge. As we wrote in the "crowdsourcing" essay in this handbook, user-generated content collaborative practices systematically fostered the sharing of authority between targeted communities and public historians as organizers and mediators/moderators in digital projects. The leading role of historians is to showcase and share his hermeneutical approach to the writing of history and its critical method with whoever is engaged in a public project.

Michael Frisch first used "shared authority" with enormous success in the title of his 1990 book discussing "the interaction of scholarly authority and wider public involvement in presentations of history."[8] Frisch applied the concept to oral history projects and other collaborative practices in making history in active ways when the public was engaged directly in a co-creation process of history making with historians as mediators. It was not about the creation of historical content as such, but

---

8 Michael H. Frisch: "A Shared Authority: Scholarship Audience and Public Presentation," in *A Shared Authority: Essays on the Craft and Meaning of Oral and Public History* (Albany: State University of New York Press, 1990), 179–181.

much more about the interactive process, a collaborative dialogue between educators (public historians) and an audience. (Such an oral history and shared authority activity was practiced the same way and at the same time in Italy by Alessandro Portelli).[9]

Frisch came back often to his book and the concept of shared authority, drawing a line between shared and sharing authority:

> Somewhat curiously [. . .] in many usually laudatory references, there is a subtle change: the title [of my book] seems understood as a call for "Sharing Authority." The difference in emphasis conveyed by a single word – Sharing, rather than Shared –, turns out to be revealing, and consequential. "Sharing Authority" implies that this is something we do, or ought to do, that "we" have authority, and that we need or ought to share it with others. [. . .]. In contrast, "A Shared Authority," suggests something that "is," that is the nature of oral and public history, "we" are not the sole authority, the sole interpreters, the sole author historians. Rather, the interpretive process and the meaning-making process there are already shared, by definition [. . .].[10]

One of the case studies Frisch develops in his book is about a visit to Ellis Island, New York's emigration historical park, in which he analyzes another possible dimension of the sharing of his authority closer to the way James B. Gardner imagines historians should share their professional knowledge and methods with their public. In Frisch's mind, it is the "process by which audiences actually approach, engage, and digest historical interpretations."[11] The public knowledge acquired visiting the park is made of two layers: first a mixture between visitors' memories and how and why they connect with the park's interpretation of migrations (millions of Americans reconnected to the island because of their own opinion and memories about immigration), and second, based on public historians' professional knowledge, an attention to how public historians interpreted Ellis Island's history, in the broader context of American migration's history. Shared authority is not built here on how – and if – audiences had collaborated directly to the narrative, but on the pedagogical experience fostered by public historians based on their own authority in the matter, eventually positively modifying visitors' opinions. Co-creation of knowledge, in this case, the shared authority, would happen when the curators' conversations with the

---

9 Alessandro Portelli, *The Death of Luigi Trastulli and Other Stories: Form and Meaning in Oral History* (Albany: State University of New York Press, 1991).
10 Michael H. Frisch, "'Public History is not a one-way street,' or, from a shared authority to the city of mosaics and back," in "Ricerche Storiche," 48.3 (2017): 143–150, 147. Differences between sharing and shared were already developed in Michael Frisch. See his "From *A Shared Authority* to the Digital Kitchen, and Back" in *Letting Go? Sharing Historical Authority in a User-Generated World*, edited by Bill Adair, Benjamin Filene, and Laura Koloski (Philadelphia: Pew Center for Arts & Heritage; Walnut Creek: Distributed by Left Coast Press, c2011), 126–137.
11 Michael Frisch and Dwight Pitcaithley, "Audience Expectations as Resource and Challenge: Ellis Island as a Case Study" in Michael H. Frisch: "A Shared Authority: Scholarship Audience and Public Presentation," in *A Shared Authority: Essays on the Craft and Meaning of Oral and Public History* (Albany: State University of New York Press, 1990), 215–224, 215.

audience – like in Socrates' *maieutic* – would allow for a better understanding of the truest possible historical and public narrative displayed in the park.[12]

Some years later, Roy Rosenzweig came back to Michael Frisch's definition of shared authority, which he called "one fruitful metaphor for reimagining the relationship between history professionals and popular history makers. [. . .] Frisch urges us to break down hierarchies by redistributing and redefining the meaning of intellectual authority for crafting historical narratives [. . .]."[13] Rosenzweig correctly stated that such an active and engaged activity able to validate the authority and knowledge of the other is not easy to apply during a collaborative process of history making and is often challenged by traditional ways of doing history in which historians do not want to lose their individual academic power. "Sometimes historians are also unprepared to deal with the political issues raised by efforts to share authority."[14]

The process of sharing authority with an audience and implementing shared authority methods in public history projects, remains a delicate activity from a professional point of view. Of course, it allows a positive process of interaction to be developed at different levels between audiences and public historians, the role of which is dual in the process of making history. First, a public historian confronts and integrates one's own knowledge listening to public memories and incorporating community documents. At the same time, he/she shares his/her professional knowledge and analytical methods with the public. Such a bi-directional process facilitated by digital means deepen, in Rosenzweig's words, the public historians' capacity to build a more democratic and collaborative interpretation of the past and of the way history can be told.

The delicate and difficult process of sharing with and listening to an audience should not become an acritical and one-sided acceptance of public opinions. A public historian is not a notary who limits itself to making inventories of the opinions and documents of others. Therefore, shared authority in a co-created digital public history project, is implemented correctly when collecting, filtering, and organizing digital information is based on critical methods.

The concept and method of a co-created history making developed until now, becomes especially handy in multimedia DPH projects with and for communities.[15]

---

12 Ibid, 219.
13 See note 6.
14 "Roy Rosenzweig Afterthoughts," *Roy Rosenzweig: Everyone a Historian*, http://chnm.gmu.edu/survey/afteroy.html.
15 "The personal connections people draw to public historical events [. . .] would make excellent subjects for exhibits, class projects, public humanities programs, or documentary films." Michael O'Malley and Roy Rosenzweig, "Brave New World or Blind Alley? American History on the World Wide Web," *Journal of American History* 84 (June 1997): 132–55; now online as "Roy Rosenzweig Afterthoughts," *Roy Rosenzweig: Everyone a Historian*, http://chnm.gmu.edu/survey/afteroy.html.

Community sourcing and co-creation of knowledge have become a natural extension and development of shared authority practices within the field of digital public history. Especially museums rediscovered the centrality of their audience offering a voice to their visitors.[16] Open authority functions in museums and exhibitions' web projects and integrates the collaboration of communities,[17] which can of course contribute data/objects but could also collaborate in explaining the data/objects themselves. Co-creation of knowledge in museums happens through digital tools when the participants join all the phases of a project monitored by curators. "Web 2.0 invites ordinary people to become their archivists, curators, historians, and designers."[18] For example, the *House of European History* in Brussels narrates the history of Europe after World War Two. In the physical rooms of the museum, there has been no space for an active collaboration of the visitors in the storytelling. However, online, *My House of European History*, is a web platform created to add stories about how visitors perceive the construction of Europe. Personal narratives and memories are told, and metadata added for everyone to retrieve them on the map of Europe.[19] As Sharon Leon explains:, "[S]everal popular technologies have been devised specifically to promote exchange between content creators and their audiences" [. . .] and "requires public historians to think carefully about community management strategies."[20] In doing so it is possible to "meet the challenge organizations face in balancing institutional expertise with the potential of collaborative online communities."[21]

These theoretical premises came to life with 911DigitalArchive.org. (Figure 2). The large-scale event of September 11, the terrorist attacks on US soil, drastically accelerated collaborative collecting practices with ordinary people. Many memory institutions (GLAM) initiatives built digital archives like the Smithsonian's National Museum of American History.[22] Of course, born-digital archives existed before like the *Internet*

---

16 Benjamin Filene, "History Museums and Identity: Finding "them," "me," and "us" in the Gallery," in *The Oxford Handbook of Public History*, edited by Paula Hamilton and James B. Gardner (Oxford: Oxford University Press, 2017), 327–348.
17 Lori Byrd Phillip, "The Role of Open Authority in a Collaborative Web" in *Crowdsourcing Our Cultural Heritage*, edited by Mia Ridge (London: Routledge, 2014), 247–268.
18 Bill Adair, Benjamin Filene, and Laura Koloski, "Introduction" in *Letting Go? Sharing Historical Authority in a User-Generated World*, edited by Bill Adair, Benjamin Filene, and Laura Koloski (Philadelphia: Pew Center for Arts & Heritage; Walnut Creek: Distributed by Left Coast Press, c2011), 10–15, 11.
19 "My House of European History: Make your story part of History," https://my-european-history.ep.eu/myhouse/myheh_project, accessed 20 March, 2021.
20 Sharon M. Leon: "Complexity and Collaboration. Doing Public History in Digital Environments", in *The Oxford Handbook of Public History*, edited by Paula Hamilton and James B. Gardner (Oxford: Oxford University Press, 2017), 44–66, 60.
21 Mia Ridge, "Crowdsourcing Our Cultural Heritage: Introduction," in *Crowdsourcing Our Cultural Heritage*, edited by Mia Ridge (London: Routledge, 2014), 11.
22 "September 11, Bearing Witness to History," https://amhistory.si.edu/september11/.

Fig. 2: Shared authority practices and co-created knowledge in Digital Public History projects: The case of the *9/11 Digital Archive*. (The September 11 Digital Archive – https://911digitalarchive.org/).

Archive that started archiving websites worldwide in 1996.[23] However, the September 11 terrorist attack happened at the same time the web was becoming social and everyone worldwide, not only in the USA, had a chance to document an epochal event and make a history of the present time in the digital realm. Individuals and families shared their own memories related to the fall of the Twin Towers adding their documents and stories to the archive. Public historians, archivists and curators verified and contextualized crowdsourced original materials. As Daniel Cohen noted, "the record of 9/11 was to be found in new media such as websites, email, and other forms of electronic communication and expression, forms that have become an increasingly significant part of America's and the industrialized world's cultural output."[24] Public history was radically transformed engaging with new digital practices. Memory institutions, historians, archivists, and librarians realized the power of grassroots knowledge that could be harvested in building digital projects based on shared authority principles. Average people, grassroot communities, outside of cultural heritage professions,

---

23 Niels Brugger, *The Archived Web: Doing History in the Digital Age* (Cambridge: MIT Press, 2018) and Francesca Musiani, et al., *Qu'est-ce qu'une archive du web?* (Marseille: OpenEdition Press, 2019), http://books.openedition.org.eui.idm.oclc.org/oep/8713.

24 Daniel Cohen, "The Future of Preserving the Past," in *The Public History Reader*, edited by Hilda Kean and Paul Martin (Abingdon, Oxon: Routledge, 2013), 214–223, 215.

now had a chance to be heard and become the protagonist of their own time and history. On the other hand, public historians, and curators' role in acknowledging and encouraging these new practices became even more important and delicate because of the need to reinvent different levels of authority-sharing in a digital environment.

Cohen describes many projects that arose immediately after the fall of the Twin Towers. One of the most relevant one was *The September 11 Digital Archive* at the Center for History and New Media (CHNM) at Fairfax in Virginia, in collaboration with the Central University of New York (CUNY). It was launched in January 2002 and on the first anniversary of the attack attracted over a million visitors, "who were willing to share their small part of history with the public." The September 11 archive allowed "ordinary Americans to literally make their own history."[25] The CHNM servers collected and showed thousands of visitors, photographs, emails, home movies, voicemail, blog posts, etc, all kinds of digital documents that were created during the events or registered later. In the end, more than 150,000 digital documents and memories about the attack populated the database, thanks also to the systematic use of different media that connected the local communities which suffered the blow. The CHNM/GMU and CUNY archive project 911DigitalArchive.org targeted communities that participated extensively in this large-scale collaborative popular history-making. In September 2003, 911DigitalArchive.org became the first crowdsourced born-digital project based on everyone's participation and the filtering of historians' content validation that had been archived by the Library of Congress. The library had launched digital public history archives before in the 1990s as part of the *American Memory Project*.[26] Nevertheless, direct participation of local communities where the attacks took place, in creating a brand-new "invented" archive, had never happened before. This iconic project, a first digital "memory site," opened the way to dozens of new digital public history projects worldwide. It also made clear that professionals from different eras should now engage with the public through collaborative processes based on shared authority when using digital technologies.

James Sparrow who contributed to the development of the digital platform at CHNM, mentioned that quality control of the uploaded documents was time-consuming. However, it "helped to maintain some basic level of control over the content" because "the need to exercise this sort of control was especially important given the highly charged climate after 9/11 and the inescapably sensitive

---

25 James T. Sparrow: James T. Sparrow: "On the Web: The September 11 Digital Archive," in *Public history: Essays from the Field*, edited by James B. Gardner and Peter S. LaPaglia (Malabar Florida: Krieger Pub. Co., 2006), 397–415, 402.
26 *American Memory Remaining Collections*, https://memory.loc.gov/ammem/index.html.

nature of the contributions that would come in."[27] Sharing authority took place through an improvement of the quality control employed in such a citizen's history project. It was based mostly on verification of copyright issues, and the capacity to assert the genuineness of crowdsourced documents. Also, the age of the authors had to be controlled when no minors had been allowed to load materials. The difficulty of asserting the accuracy of the context of digital documentation could have frustrated the scientific basis of the collective crowdsourced project. It was important to avoid leaving authority solely in the hands of contributors when, instead, historians needed to validate the contents of the database: "[H]ow could we know that our contributors were who they claimed to be and that what they contributed was genuine and belonged to them?" noted Sparrow.[28] Organizing a critical approach to the sources that were generated by the users was extremely time consuming. An ethical and professional approach to the project reinforced its credibility by keeping future historical research in mind.

Conclusion. Amateurs and Professionals Contribute to Citizen's History Making

Forms of shared authority that have been described for 911DigitalArchive.org have now become the norm in digital public history practices. Similar procedures are displayed today when collecting the memory of the Covid-19 pandemic worldwide. New collaborative forms of history making through web technologies are "glocal" and ubiquitous. They have completely renovated the practice of crowdsourcing, with historians now engaged in sharing their authority actively in web projects.

A few years after 9/11, the terms "citizen science" and "citizen history" were introduced to define the making of history with the public contributing to data harvesting and analysis. It is seen as "science conducted by average citizens, e.g., people who are not full- or part-time professional scientists, but have a keen interest in the scientific inquiry,"[29] or, in 2013, in an EU commission green paper,[30] as a "general

---

[27] James T. Sparrow: "On the Web: The September 11 Digital Archive," in *Public history: Essays from the Field*, edited by James B. Gardner and Peter S. LaPaglia (Malabar Florida: Krieger Pub. Co., 2006), 407.
[28] James T. Sparrow: "On the Web: The September 11 Digital Archive," in *Public history: Essays from the Field*, edited by James B. Gardner and Peter S. LaPaglia (Malabar Florida: Krieger Pub. Co., 2006), 406.
[29] Chandra Clark in "Citizen Science Center," http://www.citizensciencecenter.com/about-citizen-science/. See also Chandra Clark, *Be the Change: Saving the World with Citizen Science*, CreateSpace Independent Publishing Platform, 2014.
[30] Still available in the Internet Archive, https://web.archive.org/web/20140630015921/http://www.socientize.eu:80/sites/default/files/Green%20Paper%20on%20Citizen%20Science%202013.

public engagement in scientific research activities when citizens actively contribute to science [. . .]."[31] Today, Citizen History incorporates forms of user-generated content in a public participatory web, and fosters the emergence of collective societal intelligence through forms of collaborative knowledge of the past and shared authority methods.[32]

How historians' expertise will engage in challenging everyone's access to authority and keep their own in social media in what Luciano Floridi calls the "digital infosphere,"[33] is an open question. Public historians face a true professional challenge today when doing digital public history through new forms of shared expertise, best practices, and hermeneutics in "citizen's history" projects based on a shared authority.

Bibliography

Adair, Bill, Benjamin Filene, and Laura Koloski, eds. *Letting Go? Sharing Historical Authority in a User-Generated World*. Philadelphia: Pew Center for Arts & Heritage; Walnut Creek: Distributed by Left Coast Press, c2011.

Gardner, James B. "Trust, Risk and Historical Authority: Negotiating Public History in Digital and Analog Worlds," in *Making Histories*, edited by Paul Ashton, Tanya Evans, and Paula Hamilton. Oldenbourg: De Gruyter, 2020, 59–67.

Kean, Hilda. "Public History as a Social Form of Knowledge," *The Oxford Handbook of Public History*, edited by James B. Gardner and Paula Hamilton. Oxford: Oxford University Press, 2017, 403–422.

Leon, Sharon M. "Complexity and Collaboration: Doing Public History in a Digital Environment," in *The Oxford Handbook of Public History*, edited by Paula Hamilton and James B. Gardner (Oxford: Oxford University Press, 2017), 44–66.

Sparrow, James T. "On the Web: The September 11 Digital Archive," in *Public history: Essays from the Field*, edited by James B. Gardner and Peter S. LaPaglia. Malabar Florida: Krieger Pub. Co., 2006, 397–415

Wojdon, Joanna and Wiśniewska, Dorota. (Eds). Public in public history. New York: Routledge, 2021.

---

pdf, 21. It was relaunched in 2017 as "EU green paper on Citizen Science," https://ec.europa.eu/digital-single-market/en/citizen-science.

31 Yuri Gordienko, "Green Paper on Citizen Science," November 2013, https://www.researchgate.net/publication/259230549_Green_Paper_on_Citizen_Science.

32 Imke Kaufmann and Monika Hagedorn-Saupe, "Citizen Science in Humanities. Unlocking the Knowledge of the Crowd," *ViMMPlus Virtual Multimodal Museum +*, https://www.vi-mm.eu/wp-content/uploads/2018/05/Citizen-Science-Paper_AP_IK_MHS_final.pdf.

33 Luciano Floridi, *The Fourth Revolution. How the Infosphere is Reshaping Human Reality* (Oxford: Oxford University Press, 2014).

Mary Larson
Shifting the Balance of Power: Oral History and Public History in the Digital Era

Abstract: Oral history and public history have been interconnected for many years, sharing multiple points of commonality, including a frequent interest in documenting under-documented communities. Both have brought different strengths to the table in their intersections, but it has been the digital turn in method and practice that has allowed these two areas of interest to complement each other most fully. Digital technologies have finally allowed oral history to be more fully public, and they have encouraged public history further toward the collaborative approach that oral history has often taken, fulfilling long-time aspirations on the part of both groups. The overall result of this evolution is a more holistic and contextualized treatment of the historical record along with a shift in power dynamics tantamount to the beginning of the "shared authority" moment.

This essay is organized around some perceived joint concerns as a way of providing structure for the discussion. For both groups, there is an interest in presenting a more complete view of history in terms of perspectives, recipients, and mediation, and this comes across in three primary areas. First, there is concern about what/who is being documented: is the focus on capturing the stories of the elite, or is there more of an emphasis on gathering the perspectives of everyday people and under-represented voices? Also, who is doing the documentation and driving the research agenda, and how do new digital tools shift what is feasible? Second, and less often considered, is the issue of who is involved in the interpretation of history – not just who gets to tell a story, but who controls how, when, or in what contexts the story is told? In the past, the work of curation and interpretation has been claimed largely by professionals, but new technologies have opened up that terrain to communities as well, so that there can be more public engagement in presenting the culture and history of everything from neighborhoods and organizations to traditionally under-documented groups. The third and final shared area of concern revolves around who gets to hear the resulting stories: will only academics have access, or will the histories be presented to, and made meaningful for, the general public? Evolving electronic platforms have certainly changed how documented history can be disseminated, and while class, gender, and other demographic issues still contribute to the existence of a not insignificant digital divide, obstacles of geography, mobility, and physical access are at least reduced through the use of online portals. The ability to make audio and video easily available through digital platforms has also changed the level of mediation inherent in that dissemination.

As digital technologies lower the barriers for communities to document, interpret, and present their own histories, we are at an exciting turning point in the development of oral history and public history. Outreach and engagement may now evolve in very different ways as local groups have the potential to take a more active role in the documentation and representation of their stories, and as their autonomy in creating and curating projects grows, we may get to see some very creative approaches. Our roles as oral historians and public historians will almost certainly change, but as we become more aware of power imbalances and can collaborate more meaningfully with communities on their own terms, the result will surely be a richer historical record.

Keywords: oral history, public history, digital curation, community collaboration

Oral history and public history have danced around each other and passed one another in the halls of cultural institutions for years. Sometimes they have been enthusiastic partners, other times slightly shy acquaintances, but they share multiple points of commonality, including an interest (generally) in documenting under-documented communities. Both have brought different strengths to the table in their intersections, but I would argue that it has been the digital turn in method and practice that has allowed these two areas of interest to complement each other most fully. Digital technologies have allowed oral history finally to be more fully public, and they have encouraged public history further towards the collaborative approach that oral history has often taken, fulfilling long-time aspirations on the part of both groups. This is even more clear on an international stage, where the sense of what constitutes public history is at times a bit broader than it is in North America.[1] I believe that the overall results will be a more holistic and contextualized treatment of the historical record along with a shift in power dynamics tantamount to the beginning of the "Shared Authority" moment.

Having viewed public history largely through the lens of oral history, I fully admit that the vision presented here may be skewed by an emphasis on shared

---

[1] In defining "public history," the National Council on Public History (NCPH) glosses the meaning as "applied history", or what others in the current era might refer to as "alt ac" – history outside of academia. From my experience of public history scholarship in North America, however, I have seen a definite trend toward thinking of community engagement as a key component of the practice. In fact, the NCPH website states as much, noting, "Unlike many historians in the academy, public historians routinely engage in collaborative work, with community members, stakeholders, and professional colleagues, and some contend that collaboration is a fundamental and defining characteristic of what public historians do." (https://ncph.org/what-is-public-history/about-the-field/) In at least some European circles, however, and perhaps particularly in the UK, "public history" seems to equally refer to "people's history" – not in terms of who is *viewing* historical products but in terms of who is the subject of the historical products, and this seems to differ from the North American model. *The Public History Reader* by Hilda Kean and Paul Martin (New York: Routledge, 2013) provides a series of relevant examples. Other European public history traditions are more specific about the necessary inclusion of community collaboration, though, as seen in *Il Manifesto della Public History italiana* (https://aiph.hypotheses.org/3193#eng, accessed 14 August, 2020).

methodological issues, but I think it is important to lay out some perceived joint concerns at the start as a way of giving some structure to this chapter. For both groups there is an interest in presenting a more complete view of history in terms of perspectives, recipients, and mediation, and this comes across in three primary areas. First, there is concern about what/who is being documented. While some early oral history efforts in the United States had an emphasis on capturing the stories of elites (and there is still work that maintains that focus), it is probably safe to say that the majority of oral history projects and programs both in North America and the UK now focus more on "history from the bottom up." In other areas there is broader variability, however. In Europe, similar to the UK/US model, you have scholars like Miroslav Vaněk and Pavel Mücke (Czech Republic) documenting their nation's recent history with almost 300 interviews and their book *Velvet Revolutions*, as well as Luisa Passerini (Italy), who has so famously highlighted the recollections and observations of everyday citizens in a wide range of publications, including *Autoritratto di Gruppo*. At the same time, however, there is also a very extensive set of oral histories at the Historical Archives of the European Union (HAEU), which explores more of a "top-down" approach to documenting the past by interviewing those making political decisions at the upper levels of power.[2]

As with oral history, there are also public historians who prioritize "people's history," and in order to present a more complete and well-rounded view of the past, both groups document stories from communities and individuals who have been largely overlooked in spite of their importance to the historical narrative. Second, and less often considered, is the issue of who is involved in the interpretation of history – not just who gets to tell a story, but who controls how, when, or in what contexts the story is told? Will the narrative be mediated only by academics, or will communities have a say? The third and final shared area of concern revolves around who gets to hear the resulting stories. Will only academics have access, or will the histories be presented to, and made meaningful for, the general public? The remainder of this essay will focus on how digital technology has provided avenues for oral historians and public historians to collaborate on addressing these shared concerns.

Documentation

I believe that the digital turn has had the most impact on shared methodological and theoretical concerns in three particular aspects: community engagement in the documentation of history, community involvement in the interpretation of history,

---

[2] See, for example, Vaněk and Mücke's *Velvet Revolution: An Oral History of Czech Society* (Oxford: Oxford University Press, 2016) and Passerini's *Autoritratto di gruppo* (Firenze: Giunti, 1988) as compared to the HAEU's project at https://archives.eui.eu/en/oral_history/ (accessed 14 August, 2020).

and then presentation of that history – both to involved stakeholders and to a more general public. The first area is probably where evolving technology has had some of its most obvious impacts. In the not-so-distant past, high-quality recording equipment (whether reel-to-reel, cassette, digital, audio, or video) was costly and could only be afforded by larger institutions.[3] Under-resourced community groups needed to work closely with museums, libraries, archives, or universities if they wanted their own histories documented, and while the collaborative efforts may have been generally positive and productive, they also inadvertently perpetuated an imbalance of power in terms of access to means of (audio) production. While none of this may have been intentional, it would be naive to overlook the implications. In order to conduct oral histories or record local recollections, communities often had to partner with cultural heritage institutions such as universities or museums who owned the necessary equipment, so the collaborations, while a step in the right direction, were lopsided in respect to power dynamics.

As costs for audio and video recording equipment have dropped and the knowledge barriers to using technology are considerably lower, communities are not as reliant on outside institutions for at least the basic documentation tools. The ubiquity of cell phones internationally, both in economically developed and developing countries, has certainly made recording much easier for a broad cross-section of communities. The caveat, in this case, is that while capturing recollections might be simpler and less expensive, infrastructures may not be in place everywhere for archiving or preserving the resulting materials. That is a burden that is not addressed in depth in this essay, but it is an important aspect of both oral history and public history work and is a challenge that will need to be met.

One approach to solving this problem is to incorporate community generated content into larger archival projects, which is something being done by both the Archives of Lesbian Oral Testimony (ALOT) and the Chilocco History Project (United States). Having interviews generated in a digital format has simplified sharing them, and ALOT (Canada) has taken advantage of this capability with its newest initiative, "Bridging the Gap." Part of the more expansive ALOT initiative founded by Elise Chenier, the Bridging the Gap web pages allow international community members to upload their own interviews of LGBTQTS chroniclers to the larger archives, further developing documentation of the communities it serves. The site also introduces the ability to tag other oral histories for topic and content and to

---

3 For discussions of the expenses attendant to oral history over time, see, for example, Michael Frisch, "Oral History and the Digital Revolution: Toward a Post-Documentary Sensibility," in *The Oral History Reader*, ed. Robert Perks and Alistair Thomson (New York: Routledge, 2006), 111; Dale Treleven, "Oral History, Audio Technology, and the TAPE System," *International Journal of Oral History* 2.1 (1981): 27–28.

rate them for interest, thus boosting their visibility to and discoverability by researchers and the general public (Fig. 1).[4]

Fig. 1: ALOT founder Dr. Elise Chenier in the opening scene of a video discussing the "Bridging the Gap" initiative (https://alotarchives.org/bridging-the-gap/ [accessed 14 August, 2020]).

The Chilocco History Project (Fig. 2) takes a slightly different approach. Its interviews were all conducted as part of a collaborative effort undertaken between the Chilocco National Alumni Association and the Oklahoma Oral History Research Program at Oklahoma State University, but its website expands documentation of the Chilocco community by allowing alumni and their descendants to add their own recollections and images to the website.[5] In both instances, the added content is community generated, with larger archival projects providing an infrastructure for disseminating materials.

Archiving and preservation will be another area where the expertise of cultural institutions can be helpful throughout the process, but cheaper technology and wider public expertise with recording equipment have significantly reduced dependence on cultural organizations for the basic tools of the trade. That gives community groups an option to document their own stories with or without the assistance or mediation of academics, and at the same time it provides the potential for any future collaborations to be more honest, more balanced, and less fraught, which would certainly move us closer to the methodological democratization that we aspire to.[6]

---

4 Bridging the Gap, https://alotarchives.org/bridging-the-gap/ (accessed 14 August, 2020).
5 Chilocco Oral History Project, https://chilocco.library.okstate.edu/ (accessed 14 August, 2020).
6 Frisch, "Oral History and the Digital Revolution," 113; Douglas Boyd and Mary Larson, "Introduction," in *Oral History and Digital Humanities: Voice, Access, and Engagement*, eds. Boyd and Larson (New York: Palgrave Macmillan, 2014), 10.

Fig. 2: The home page for the Chilocco History Project portal (designed in Omeka) (https://chilocco.library.okstate.edu/ [accessed 14 August, 2020]).

Interpretation

The second area where digital capabilities have had an impact is interpretation, and while in the past this task has been claimed largely by professionals, new technologies have opened up that terrain to communities, as well. It is also an aspect of public and oral history that lends itself particularly well to the collaboration mentioned above. While interviews and histories are curated in many different ways, much of that curation has always involved contextualization of materials – situating them within larger frameworks and providing enough background information so that people from outside a culture, neighborhood, or institution could make meaning of what was being presented. This aspect of curation is what has been simplified, at least somewhat, by evolving digital technologies, and it allows for a more complete representation of histories and their contexts.

It is important to understand how quickly the landscape has changed in this regard and where we were just prior to the advent of these possibilities. The World Wide Web originated in 1989, and the first graphical browser was only launched for widespread public use at the end of 1993, so the time depth for online cultural heritage materials is relatively shallow.[7] In that short period, however, oral and public historians have made use of a range of interactive platforms, from digital exhibits and standalone interpretive kiosks, to carefully curated cultural databases, to an array of social media formats. (It is also important to note that all of these formats have been used both to disseminate and to gather histories).

As practitioners have worked collaboratively with communities to document histories, they have also begun to bring community members into this process of interpretation and contextualization, cooperating to design meaningful interfaces and provide additional online materials that allow both stakeholders and the general public to access deeper layers of meaning. This can manifest itself in a variety of ways. For example, when William Schneider (University of Alaska Fairbanks, US) was developing the Chipp-Ikpikpuk Meade Rivers Project Jukebox in the early 1990s, he worked very closely with Iñupiat Elders to help design the layout for the interface. The initial plan for the project, which was a bilingual, audio-and-text presentation of oral histories originally collected in the 1980s, had been to make the interviews accessible by a standard keyword search, but Elders suggested that it would be more meaningful to them to be able to access the cultural information by using maps and photographs. The portal was then expanded to include multiple points of entry into the oral history collection.[8] (Fig. 3)

Similarly, the Brooklyn Historical Society's "Crossing Borders, Bridging Generations" project also aimed to further contextualize its oral histories by providing more information on its online platform. They worked with their constituent communities to include guides for difficult conversations, public programming, and lesson plans into a website they designated as a "public homeplace" (Fig. 4).[9]

What results from this process in both of these instances is a much more thorough, complete recording of the context of oral history projects, but also a more balanced narration of the respective histories more generally.

---

7 Bruce R. Schatz and Joseph B. Hardin, "NCSA Mosaic and the World Wide Web: Global Hypermedia Protocols for the Internet," *Science* 265. 5174 (12 Aug 1994): 895–901, DOI: 10.1126/science.265.5174.895.
8 The University of Alaska Fairbanks Project Jukebox is available at http://jukebox.uaf.edu/site7/. Community-influenced design arose in the project's earliest, pre-web iterations, e.g., http://jukebox.uaf.edu/northslope/Chipp/html2/chiphome.html (accessed 8/14/2020). For more on the development of this particular approach, see William Schneider, "Oral History in the Age of Digital Possibilities," *Oral History and Digital Humanities*, 19–33.
9 "Crossing Borders, Bridging Generations" and its multiple components can be found at http://goddaddy.brooklynhistory.org/cbbg/, and the project is discussed in more detail in Sady Sullivan's chapter, "Public Homeplaces: Collaboration and Care in Oral History Project Design," *Beyond Women's Words*, eds. Katrina Srigley, Stacey Zembrzycki, and Franca Iacovetta (New York: Routledge, 2018).

Fig. 3: The current landing page for the Chipp-Ikpikpuk and Meade Rivers Project Jukebox (http://jukebox.uaf.edu/northslope/Chipp/html2/chiphome.html [accessed 14 August, 2020]). The original home page, designed in Hypercard, showed an Elder's photo (representing "People"), a map (representing "Places"), and a sample of index terms (representing "Topics"), so it was much more visual. When the site was redesigned for the web in 2000, the format was changed to be more easily reproducible online.

Through evolving technologies, it is much easier to include a variety of features in an online interface, and it is also easier for participants not only to choose what aspects of their lives would help people understand their interviews, but to document that context themselves. While the above examples show collaborations between larger institutions and community groups, there are also notable instances where communities are doing all of the interpretive work on their own. A very interesting project from the UK is "Voices of the Past," created by the Barton Hill History Group (BHHG). Taking oral histories that had been conducted thirty years earlier by BHHG interviewers, this organization digitized their existing tapes and collaborated with local musicians to create productions that use a combination of interviews, song, soundscapes, and images to contextualize their stories. These have been introduced at public art events and presented online on YouTube, Facebook, and via live streamed events, and they were entirely community generated (Fig. 5).[10]

While some communities will have the skills and wherewithal to take charge of both the documentation and curation of their histories, what is happening in practice is that there is a collaborative continuum, with local groups working closely with cultural

---

10 Voices of the Past, https://soundcloud.com/jakeodb/barton-hill-voices-of-the-past-clip, https://www.facebook.com/bartonhillhistorygroup, https://www.facebook.com/events/barton-hill-bristol/voices-of-the-past-live-stream/325272522188923/, (all accessed 14 August, 2020).

Shifting the Balance of Power: Oral History and Public History in the Digital Era — 69

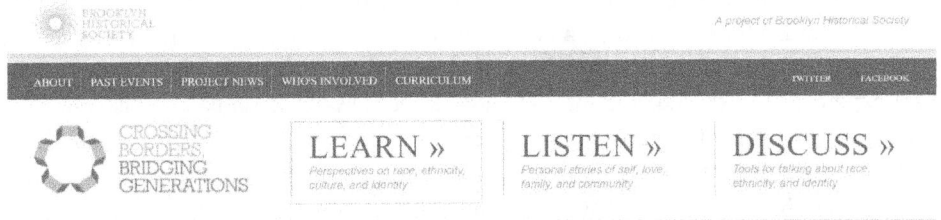

Fig. 4: The home page for Crossing Borders, Bridging Generations, with its three-tiered approach to contextualization ("Learn," "Listen," and "Discuss") (http://godaddy.brooklynhistory.org/cbbg/ [accessed 14 August, 2020]).

Fig. 5: Notice of the live stream for the Barton Hill History Group's "Voices of the Past" production (https://www.facebook.com/bartonhillhistorygroup [accessed 14 August, 2020]).

heritage organizations to help guide the interpretation of their histories for a broader public. What is important is that, as with recording technology, the barriers to entry for computer interface development have been lowered both in terms of financial outlay and expertise, and the hope is that this affects the power differential in this area as it might with documentation. Community groups can access basic recording tools and web-creation sites much more easily than they could have even a decade ago, with the result being that, no matter what part of the process they choose to take on, they have potentially more power over the presentation and contextualization of their own stories.

Presentation

The third area where digital technology has directly impacted the work of public and oral historians is the presentation of histories. How do people's stories get told so that they are available to stakeholders and the general public alike, beyond the bounds of scholarly journals or the walls of archives? Evolving electronic platforms have certainly changed how documented history can be disseminated, and they've also changed the level of mediation inherent in that dissemination.

As noted above, new technologies have definitely had an effect on how communities, oral historians, and public historians can contextualize histories for making meaning of interviews, and that has a bearing on outreach outside of scholarly or community circles. Ease of putting materials on the World Wide Web has given practitioners a more consistent public-facing platform. When trying to reach non-academic audiences in the past, public and oral historians made use of books, exhibits, roadside plaques, and audio or video documentaries, among other media. Until materials could be made available online or in easily navigable kiosks, however, efforts to disseminate this information far beyond the walls of cultural institutions were rather limited. As much as we might promote physical archives, museums, or historical sites and try to make them inviting to the public, they can still be difficult to access and, depending on context, can be intimidating to the general populace. The barriers for accessing online interviews or curated histories are significantly lower, with the development of open or inexpensive web platforms like Omeka and WordPress and growing access to the internet through cellular service internationally, public libraries (in North America, at least), and municipal wireless networks in urban areas around the globe, including in the economically developing world. While class, gender, and other demographic issues still contribute to the existence of a not insignificant digital divide, obstacles of geography, mobility, and physical access are at least reduced through the use of online portals.[11] In this respect, the digital

---

[11] As the outreach of online websites becomes increasingly international, translation of website materials and interfaces will be a growing challenge. Individual interviews or pages can, of course,

turn has allowed oral history to be more convincingly public history, which is something the methodology has largely aspired to for at least 50 years.

An example of a very publicly oriented site with multiple components is Passados Presentes: Memória da Escravidão no Brasil (Present Pasts: Memories of Slavery in Brazil) (Fig. 6). Developed by the Laboratory of Oral History and Images at the Universidade Federal Fluminense, the project generated an interactive website, films, and a mobile app with four different tour routes. Perhaps most notable in this context, beyond the multiple outward-facing products, is the fact that the presentation of all of these materials was very heavily influenced by the communities with which the researchers were collaborating, and they guided construction of the final products in significant ways. The project ended up being meaningful for multiple publics.[12]

Fig. 6: The project portal for Passados Presentes (http://passadospresentes.com.br/site/Site/index.php/principal/index?ling=br [accessed 14 August, 2020]).

Equally important to the publicly accessible presentation of information is the possibility, with these online platforms, for there to be less mediation of the histories being presented. While, as mentioned above, online access might reduce mediation of the historical experience in terms of access (whether cultural, spatial, demographic, etc.), it also allows for less mediation of actual voices. There has been a long-running conversation in oral history circles about the role and value of transcription, whether for access to content or for discoverability, but there has also been

---

be run through translation software, but on a larger scale, the impacts that language issues will have on overall accessibility cannot be overlooked. This will be particularly crucial when collaborating with bilingual communities, where equal representation of languages is critical to the success of a project.

12 Passados Presentes, http://passadospresentes.com.br/site/Site/index.php/principal/index?ling=br (accessed 14 August,/2020). For more discussion of the project, see Juniele Rabelo de Almeida and Larissa Moreira Viana, "Public History in Movement – Present Pasts: Memories of Slavery in Brazil," *International Public History* 1.1 (2018), DOI: https://doi.org/10.1515/iph-2018-0008.

an equal understanding that the original recordings need to be considered the documents of record and should be available to researchers and the general public.[13]

Transcripts by their very nature are a diminished representation of the oral history event. They flatten to one layer all the nuances of the interaction between interviewer and interviewee, including subtleties of body language and voice and all of the information that can be gleaned from those clues. As Gwendolyn Etter-Lewis noted of speech patterns, they can "reveal status, interpersonal relationships, and perceptions of language, self, and the world."[14] Standard written transcripts are unlikely to shed much light on these issues, but audio or video files can be more illuminating. Making this information available in these formats is even more critical when trying to situate the experiences of marginalized or under-represented communities, which historically have had their experiences devalued, appropriated, and otherwise mediated. Digital technology, even pre-web, introduced actual audio recordings into interactive computer programs, and evolving software platforms have made presenting audio or video online significantly more feasible.[15] The ability to hear someone else's voice enhances the possibility (but not the certainty) of building empathy and reinforcing the humanity of the people whose stories are being told.[16] As such, placing materials in interactive digital contexts not only has the potential to rebalance power dynamics, but it addresses two key concerns of oral historians, at least – issues with how transcription mediates a person's or a community's story, paired with a growing emphasis on the importance of the "oral" aspect of oral history – while interactive platforms address the shared public and oral history interest of making materials accessible to broader general audiences.

---

13 For more on issues surrounding transcription, see Teresa Bergen, *Transcribing Oral History* (Boca Raton: Taylor and Francis, 2019); Kathryn Anderson and Dana C. Jack, "Learning to Listen: Interview Techniques and Analyses," in *Women's Words*, 23; Frisch, "Oral History and the Digital Revolution", 102–103; Louis Shores, "Directions for Oral History," in *Oral History at Arrowhead: The Proceedings of the First National Colloquium on Oral History*, eds. Elizabeth Dixon and James Mink (Los Angeles: Oral History Association, 1966), 39; Elinor Mazé, "Deconstruction without Destruction: Creating Metadata for Oral History in a Digital World," in *Oral History and Digital Humanities*, 150.

14 Gwendolyn Etter-Lewis, "Black Women's Life Stories: Reclaiming Self in Narrative Texts," in *Women's Words: The Feminist Practice of Oral History*, eds. Sherna Berger Gluck and Daphne Patai (New York: Routledge, 1991), 44.

15 The ethics of putting oral histories online is a significantly more complex issue. While I have discussed this in detail elsewhere, I would argue that the difficulty of ethical issues increases in proportion to the decrease in the difficulty of technical issues. Care must be taken not to mistake simplicity on one side of the equation for simplicity on the other, and both oral and public historians should be conversant with the Oral History Association's Principles and Best Practices document (https://www.oralhistory.org/principles-and-best-practices-revised-2018/, accessed 14 August, 2020).

16 Steve Cohen, "Shifting Questions: New Paradigms for Oral History in a Digital World," *Oral History Review* 40.1 (2013):154–167.

A good example of research that emphasizes orality/aurality is the Australian Generations Oral History Project, developed through Monash University under the leadership of Alistair Thomson. While there are a number of other excellent products that came out of the effort, including a book, articles, a conference, a series of radio broadcasts, and a HistoryPin map, it is equally important that unmediated oral histories are also available to the public in their original audio through the National Library of Australia. In addition to providing a range of outcomes tailored to a wide range of audiences, the project team was also very intentional about the digital environment and its potential impact, taking into consideration both the capabilities made possible by digital developments and the related ethical concerns while also being cognizant of the methodological intersections between oral history and public history (Fig. 7).[17]

Fig. 7: The landing page for the Australian Generations Oral History Project (https://www.monash.edu/arts/philosophical-historical-international-studies/australian-generations [accessed 14 August, 2020].

---

17 Australian Generations Oral History Project, https://www.monash.edu/arts/philosophical-historical-international-studies/australian-generations and https://catalogue.nla.gov.au/Search/Home?lookfor=my_parent:%22(AuCNL)5973925%22&iknowwhatimean=1&filter%5B%5D=access_type:%22All%20online%22&page=1 (both accessed 14 August, 2020). Further information on the theoretical groundings of the research can be found on the project website and in the book by Anissa Puri and Alistair Thomson, *Australian Lives: An Intimate History* (Clayton, Victoria: Monash University Publishing, 2017).

Conclusion

In the end, all of these evolving digital capacities impact a very important, but often overlooked, component of community collaborations – accountability. As has been discussed already, while public and oral historians have often attempted to get their message out to larger audiences, that task has not always been easy. Written books, even when circulated through libraries, can only reach a certain number of people, and the same is true of circulating oral histories, regardless of whether they are in written or audio form (although the two formats might appeal to broadly different demographics and thus create slightly wider coverage). Physical exhibits reach only those who can visit them in person, which is also the case with archival reading rooms, and while most analog audio and video documentaries might fare a little better, their reach is still limited. The point is, up until recently most scholars could expect that very few of the community members they had worked with on a project would ever see the main products that derived from that effort. Even if researchers were diligent about sharing, the results were not often in formats that were meaningful for locals (although this is an area where oral historians have arguably been more proactive). Digital platforms and a heavier emphasis on community engagement have changed the equation, because if participants in a project have web access now, chances are very good that they will be following a project online. Practitioners who do not involve their communities in the development of their final web-based platforms do so at their own risk, because the balance of power has shifted in this regard, too. People will hold researchers accountable for how they are represented, and that is just part of the new calculus of collaboration.

As digital technologies lower the barriers for communities to document, interpret, and present their own histories, we are at an exciting turning point in the development of oral history and public history. Outreach and engagement may now evolve in very different ways as local groups have the potential to take a more active role in the documentation and representation of their stories, and as their autonomy in creating and curating projects grows, we may get to see some very creative approaches. In the last two and a half decades we have already seen close collaborations broaden and deepen the historical narrative, and as more community members gain technical expertise, we can expect that to continue. Our roles as oral historians and public historians will almost certainly change – maybe moving more toward training, curation, archiving, or preservation, maybe inching more toward advisory capacities – but that is not necessarily a bad thing. If it teaches us to be more aware of power imbalances, and if we learn to listen for what is contextually important to the communities with whom we work, then the end result will be a more holistic historical record.

Bibliography

Hamilton, Paula and Linda Shopes, eds. *Oral History and Public Memories*. Philadelphia: Temple University Press, 2008.
Perks, Robert and Alistair Thomson, eds. *The Oral History Reader*. London: Routledge, 2016.
Ritchie, Don. *Doing Oral History*. Oxford: Oxford University Press, 2015.
Ritchie, Don, ed. *Oxford Handbook of Oral History*. Oxford: Oxford University Press, 2012. (Of particular relevance to this topic is Graham Smith's chapter, "Toward a Public Oral History.")
Shopes, Linda. "The Evolving Relationship between Oral History and Public History," *Ricerche Storiche* 46.1 (2016): 105–118.

Chiara Bonacchi
Digital Public Archaeology

Abstract: This essay introduces Digital Public Archaeology and its relation with neighboring fields of research and practice. This is achieved by reviewing, exemplifying and critically reflecting upon a selection of relevant themes, including traditions, modes of digital engagement, crowdsourcing, 3D visualisation and simulation, and data science.

Keywords: public archaeology, digital engagement, data science, participation, representation, 3D, crowdsourcing, value

Traditions

Definitions of Public Archaeology are varied and variable. However, in recent years, there has been increasing agreement to frame this field as concerned with researching the relationship between archaeology and society, with the aim of improving such a relationship.[1] Within Public archaeology, the term Digital Public Archaeology (DPA) has often been utilized to refer to studies and practices that reflect on the impact and implications of the Internet, web platforms, digital technologies and devices to engage individuals and groups with archaeology-themed content, and to study these interactions, their dynamics and values.[2] Numerous publications have discussed the nature of the 'public' in public archaeology, stressing for example the three meanings of 'people,' 'state' and 'public opinion'[3] and, arguably, similar reflections could apply to DPA research and practice. Our conceptualization of the public is crucial in both defining and revealing the kinds of relationships that 'traditional experts' wish to establish with other citizens, as powerfully explained by Andrew Bevan's essay on "Value, Authority and the Open Society."[4] In this chapter, I will draw primarily from significant examples emerging from Anglophone practice and scholarship, partly because this has been proactive in undertaking pioneering research in the field and partly as a result of the personal and professional focus of my own work.

---

[1] A. Matsuda and K. Okamura, "Introduction: New Perspectives in Global Public Archaeology," in *New Perspectives in Global Public Archaeology*, ed. K. Okamura and A. Matsuda (London and New York: Routledge, 2011), 1–18.
[2] L. Richardson, "A Digital Public Archaeology?" *Papers from the Institute of Archaeology* 23.1 (2013), doi: http://doi.org/10.5334/pia.431; C. Bonacchi and G. Moshenska, "Critical Reflections on Digital Public Archaeology," *Internet Archaeology* 40 (2015), doi: 10.11141/ia.40.7.1.
[3] N. Merriman, "Introduction: Diversity and Dissonance in Public Archaeology," in *Public Archaeology*, ed. N. Merriman (London and New York: Routledge, 2004), 1–18.
[4] Bevan, "Value, Authority and the Open Society."

Because of the theoretical and methodological apparatus it draws upon, Digital Public Archaeology is in dialogue with a number of neighboring traditions, while retaining distinct features. For example, it often operates in synergy with computational archaeology, which has been exploring the potential of computer applications to answer questions about the human past.[5] Online citizen science, the practice of collaborating with citizen researchers to undertake scientific investigations,[6] is also a close ally of DPA to the point that the latter has sometimes been defined as online citizen archaeology, particularly in the context of crowdsourcing agendas and projects (see Crowdsourcing section below, for specific examples). Online citizen archaeology fully expresses the interlinking and interfacing between computational archaeology and public archaeology. The first is in fact leveraged in order to develop platforms and modular crowdsourcing templates useful to produce specific kinds of data of high research quality. Public archaeology feeds into this process, by reflecting on the dynamic tensions between public engagement and community development practices, on the one hand, and technical implementation and quality control on the other. Digital humanities are a further adjacent field, intent on experimenting with and testing methods for the digitization and analysis of data sources in the humanities.[7] Even stronger, perhaps, is the relationship between DPA and digital heritage, which is in the process of shifting from an original and more exclusive interest in digital heritage interpretation such as that expressed by Ross Parry's work[8] to a broader scope comprising the use of data generated by and through web infrastructures to examine how the past is being incorporated in present-day society.[9]

The difference between digital heritage and DPA deserves further attention and reflection. The former looks at the public experience and understanding of the past as mediated by and researched through digital means, while the latter concentrates on the appropriation of archaeological resources, methods, research and findings about the past by people who do not have professional training in archaeology. Digital heritage and DPA can intersect, especially when digital heritage examines the wider impact of expert practice in archaeology and how archaeological sites, museums and materials are 'lived' by contemporaries. Although they do not perfectly coincide, they can integrate and enhance each other substantially. Digital heritage can

---

[5] For example, see A. Bevan and M. Lake, eds, *Computational Approaches to Archaeological Spaces* (Walnut Creek, CA: Left Coast Press, 2013).

[6] M. Mordechai, S. Mazumdar. and J. Wardlaw, "Citizen Science for Observing and Understanding the Earth," in *Earth Observation Open Science and Innovation*, ed. P-P. Mathieu and C. Aubrecht (Cham: Springer International Publishing, 2018), 69–88.

[7] S. Schreibman, R. Siemens, and J. Unsworth, eds, *A New Companion to Digital Humanities* (Chichester: John Wiley & Sons Inc., 2016).

[8] R. Parry, R., *Recoding the Museum: Digital Heritage and the Technologies of Change* (London and New York: Routledge, 2007); R. Parry, ed., *Museums in a Digital Age* (London and New York: Routledge, 2010).

[9] Bonacchi, and Kryzanska, "Digital Heritage Research Re-theorised."

provide DPA with a broader context in which to inscribe its research, and DPA can help digital heritage to move beyond a stress on 'heritage discourse,' to more deeply consider the nuances of uses of the past by people who operate in different social, socio-cultural and physical contexts.[10] Laurajane Smith's notion of Authorised Heritage Discourse has been extremely useful to develop critical views of "officially sanctioned" heritage, but has been sometimes critiqued as being perhaps too monolithic and not recognising individual and networked agency to a sufficient extent.[11]

Practices

As I have I stressed elsewhere before, digital transformations should be carefully studied with an approach that remains sceptical towards both digital utopias and digital dystopias and acknowledges the substantive interdisciplinary literature that exist on this topic.[12] Understanding the impact of the Internet and digital technologies in public archaeology entails delving in matters of technicity, "technology considered in its efficacy or operating functioning."[13]

In my "Digital Media in Public Archaeology" piece, written for the *Key Concept in Public Archaeology* textbook edited by Gabriel Moshenska, I argued that digital media can activate two possible modes of communication, both viable and employed for DPA purposes in different combinations, a participatory mode and a broadcasting mode. The first welcomes and facilitates citizen's involvement in the creation of archaeological data, information and interpretations, whilst the second does not.[14] Whether one mode or another is preferred depends on the types of relationships that the initiators wish to establish as well as on the particular affordances of the platforms and tools that are chosen.[15] Research undertaken by Lorna Richardson for the UK in particular has proven that, at least up to 2013, the majority of archaeological organizations still prioritized hierarchical kinds of relationships and were less inclined to embrace participatory forms of engagement.[16] It should be

---

[10] See, for example, C. Bonacchi, "Understanding the Public Experience of Archaeology in the UK and Italy: A Call for a 'Sociological' Movement in Public Archaeology," *European Journal of Post-Classical Archaeologies* 4 (2014): 377–400.
[11] Laurajane Smith, *Uses of Heritage* (London: Routledge, 2006).
[12] Bonacchi, "Digital Media in Public Archaeology"; M. Shanks, and C. Witmore, "Archaeology 2.0? Review of *Archaeology 2.0: New Approaches to Communication and Collaboration* [Web Book]," *Internet archaeology* 32 (2012), doi: https://doi.org/10.11141/ia.32.7.
[13] A.S. Hoel, and I. Van der Tuin, "The Ontological Force of Technicity: Reading Cassirer and Simondon Diffractively," *Philosophy & Technology* 26 (2013): 187–202, doi: 10.1007/s13347-012-0092-5.
[14] Bonacchi, "Digital Media in Public Archaeology."
[15] Bevan, "Value, Authority and the Open Society."
[16] L. Richardson, "A Digital Public Archaeology?" *Papers from the Institute of Archaeology* 23.1 (2013), doi: http://doi.org/10.5334/pia.431.

noted that the latter also often require greater time, staff, skills and funds to be fully successful, and the limited availability of both can be a deciding factor for cultural institutions. Not withstanding this overall trend, efforts have been made by some professionals and organisations to develop more critically informed kinds of digital interpretations, often inviting or responding to inputs external to the 'academy.' Examples range widely from the work undertaken at the British Museum and the Fitzwilliam Museum, University of Cambridge, at the forefront of 3D modelling, 3D printing and open GLAM (Galleries, Libraries, Archives and Museums), or by the many cases where crowdsourcing was attempted as a way of enabling a new and different way of enjoying archaeological museum collections (e.g. Mary Rose Trust Museum, Egyptian Museum, Petrie Museum, etc.). Recent DPA literature and active projects express a concern with a rich array of themes. Here I highlight three areas that are *foci* of current research and practice in the UK, US and Europe.

Crowdsourcing

Crowdsourcing undertakings have been inviting citizens' input in the generation and – less frequently – in the analysis and interpretation of open archaeological and heritage data through bespoke websites, social media and forum technology. The first project to apply crowdsourcing in archaeology has been *Field Expedition: Mongolia*. Funded by the National Geographic, it asked for help with the identification of archaeological features online in search for Genghis Khan's Tomb.[17] Similarly, through the more recent GlobalXplorer,[18] anyone with interest and an Internet connection can inspect satellite imagery to identify threats to heritage sites around the world. Partly developing from ideas and collaborations linked to the Portable Antiquities Scheme, which has been implemented in the UK regions of England and Wales,[19] MicroPasts[20] has leveraged

---

[17] A. Lin, A. Huynh, G. Lanckriet, and L. Barrington, "Crowdsourcing the Unknown: The Satellite Search for Genghis Khan," *PLoS ONE* 9.12 (2014): e114046. DOI: 10.1371/journal.pone.0114046.
[18] https://www.globalxplorer.org.
[19] R. Bland, Lewis, M., Pett, D., Richardson et al., "The Treasure Act and Portable Antiquities Scheme in England and Wales," in *Key Concepts in Public Archaeology*, ed. G. Moshenska (London: UCL Press, 2017), 107–121.
[20] https://crowdsourced.micropasts.org. MicroPasts is a project originally developed as a collaboration between the UCL Institute of Archaeology and the British Museum, and now also involving the University of Stirling and the Fitzwilliam Museum, University of Cambridge. As part of this 'citizen archaeology' project, funded by the UK Arts and Humanities Research Council, the team developed an award-winning crowdsourcing platform and other web resources for the co-production and micro-financing of archaeological, historical and heritage research together with an unknown crowd of online participants.

crowd-based methods to co-produce archaeological, historical and heritage open data of research-quality, working with online contributors.[21] The project also briefly experimented with a crowd-funding component committed to micro-finance research into the human past that did not entail excavations and was designed jointly by 'traditional' researchers based in bespoke heritage institutions and communities.[22] Crowd-funded community archaeology centred on excavations has instead been pioneered, in the UK, by the social venture company DigVentures since 2012.[23]

Research linked to these and other projects of the same kind, together with more theoretical publications, has explored various intellectual and ethical issues. For example, Morgan and Pallascio have written about online remediations and the Trans-Atlantic slave trade, describing the potentially problematic nature of collaborative cultures revolving around difficult and contested heritage sites.[24] Others have underlined the danger that crowdsourcing might lead to homogenized narratives and undermine minority voices,[25] and fuel neoliberal agendas based on the exploitation of unpaid labor – offered to help with specific heritage conservation, management and interpretation tasks that could otherwise be completed by remunerated workers.[26] More generally, digital DIY (Do It Yourself) has been reviewed in opposite ways, both as a means of empowerment and "punk archaeology,"[27] and as an illusorily democratic tool that excludes many more than it 'frees.'[28]

3D Visualization and Simulation

Under the umbrella of 3D visualization and simulation we can include long-standing and sustained interest in 3D modelling for public communication purposes. Recent

---

[21] A. Bevan, D. Pett, C. Bonacchi et al., "Citizen Archaeologists. Online Collaborative Research about the Human Past," *Human Computation* 1.2 (2014): 185–199, doi: 10.15346/hc.v1i2.9.
[22] C. Bonacchi, D. Pett, A. Bevan, and A. Keinan-Schoonbaert, "Experiments in Crowd-funding Community Archaeology," *Journal of Community Archaeology & Heritage* 2.3 (2015): 184–198, doi: 10.1179/2051819615Z.00000000041.
[23] https://digventures.com.
[24] C. Morgan, and P.M. Pallascio, "Digital Media, Participatory Culture, and Difficult Heritage: Online Remediation and the Trans-Atlantic Slave Trade," *Journal of African Diaspora Archaeology and Heritage* 4.3 (2015): 260–278, doi: 10.1080/21619441.2015.1124594.
[25] R. Harrison, "Exorcising the 'plague of fantasies': Mass Media and Archaeology's Role in the Present; Or, Why We Need an Archaeology of 'now,'" *World Archaeology* 42.3 (2010): 328–340, doi: 10.1080/00438243.2010.497339.
[26] Perry and Beale, "The Social Web and Archaeology's Restructuring."
[27] C. Morgan, "Punk, DIY, and Anarchy in Archaeological Thought and Practice," *AP: Online Journal in Public Archaeology* 5 (2015): 123–146.
[28] L. Richardson, "I'll give you 'punk archaeology', sunshine," *World Archaeology* 49.3 (2017): 306–317, doi: 10.1080/00438243.2017.1333036.

projects in the UK have included, for example, ACCORD and HeritageTogether, with their focus on community co-creation of 3D scans of heritage sites and objects.[29] Both projects aimed to involve communities in different parts of the UK in the selection of heritage objects to 3D model and – in the case of ACCORD – also in conversations around the meanings they assigned to the scans and their perceived 'authenticity.' Amongst other things, these research ventures have generated novel insights and understanding of the social value of 3D visualization and of the public's perception of authenticity and 'realness' of digital records, compared to original artefacts and other physical counterparts such as 3D prints.[30] The place of 3D records in museum collecting has been increasingly researched, and so have their uses for purposes that span the design of digital interpretations on websites, in gallery spaces and on site, sometimes as part of Augmented and Virtual Reality Environments.[31] The latter are linked with the development of gaming, which remains an important strand of digital public archaeology today.[32] Attention has also been devoted to better understand the shifts in archaeological practice and narrative that all of these technological possibilities have been unlocking, also a result of more distributed and shared opportunities for

---

29 S. Griffiths, B. Edwards, K. Raimund et al, "Crowd-sourcing Archaeological Research: HeritageTogether Digital Public Archaeology in Practice," *Internet Archaeology* 40 (2015), doi: 10.11141/ia.40.7.3; M. Maxwell, "Power is in the Process: The ACCORD Project," *Internet Archaeology* 44 (2017): http://intarch.ac.uk/journal/issue44/10/index.html.

30 S. Jones, J. Stuart, M. Maxwell, A. Hale, and C. Jones, "3D Heritage Visualisation and the Negotiation of Authenticity: The ACCORD Project," *International Journal of Heritage Studies* 24.4 (2017): 333–353, doi: 10.1080/13527258.2017.1378905.

31 M. Jeater, "Smartphones and Site Interpretation: The Museum of London's Streetmuseum Applications," in *Archaeology and Digital Communication: Towards Strategies of Public Engagement*, ed., C. Bonacchi (London: Archetype Publications, 2012), 66–82; E. Watrall, "Public Heritage at Scale: Building Tools for Authoring Mobile Digital Heritage and Archaeology Experiences," *Journal of Community Archaeology & Heritage* 5.2 (2017): 1–14, doi: 10.1080/20518196.2017.1334619; H. Anderson, E. Galvin, and J. de Torres Rodriguez, "Museological Approaches to the Management of Digital Research and Engagement: The African Rock Art Image Project," *African Archaeological Review* 35 (2018): 321–337, doi: 10.1007/s10437-018-9280-8; S. Eve, "Losing our Senses, an Exploration of 3D Object Scanning," *Open Archaeology* 4.1 (2018): 114–122, doi: 10.1515/opar-2018-0007.

32 See, for example, A. Gardner, "Strategy Games and Engagement Strategies," in *Archaeology and Digital Communication: Towards Strategies of Public Engagement*, ed. C. Bonacchi (London: Archetype Publications, 2012), 38–49; Champion, E. *Critical Gaming: Interactive History and Virtual Heritage*. Farnham, Surrey: Ashgate, 2015; A. Reinhard, *Archaeogaming: An Introduction to Archaeology in and of Video Games* (New York: Berghahn Books, 2018); X. Rubio-Campillo, J.H. Caro Saiz, G. Pongiluppi et al, "Explaining Archaeological Research with Videogames: The Case of Evolving Planet," in *The Interactive Past: A Book on Video Games and Archaeology*, ed. A. Mol, C. Ariese-Vandemeulebroucke, K. Boom and A. Politopoulos (Sidestone Press, 2017), 153–165.

digital creativity.³³ These opportunities can be seized by those who have, not only interest, but also the time, skills, literacy and devices to participate.³⁴

Data Science

Data science in public archaeology is a newer and comparatively less established strand of DPA than digital cultural engagement. It results from an emerging realization that the web sites and methods facilitating public interaction can provide insights into participant profiles and behavior.³⁵ The 'deluge' of data points generated by web infrastructures at the time of a strongly interconnected and collaborative web is thus demanding substantial and widespread upskilling of DPA researchers in coding, quantitative methods and open science. Efforts of this kind are still in their infancy, with few but notable examples. For instance, Ben Marwick has developed and published Free and Open Source Software workflows for the extraction and analysis of tweets, using R to understand how Twitter supports conversations during anthropological conferences.³⁶ Shawn Graham has applied data science to the analysis of archaeological blogging and,³⁷ with Huffer, he has investigated textual data from Instagram posts to explore how human remains are valued and traded.³⁸ Chiara Zuanni has researched the archaeological 'audiences' of social media looking particularly at Twitter.³⁹ The author, with colleagues, has drawn on a 'big dataset' of Facebook

---

33 https://epoiesen.library.carleton.ca; C. Morgan, and J. Winters, eds, *Critical Blogging in Archaeology. Internet Archaeology* 39 (2015), doi: https://doi.org/10.11141/ia.39.11; G. Beale, and P. Reilly, eds, *Digital Creativity in Archaeology. Internet Archaeology* 44 (2017), http://intarch.ac.uk/journal/issue44/index.html; see also the newly established peer-reviewed journal *Epoiesen*.

34 See, for example, Bonacchi, "Digital Media in Public Archaeology" and Bonacchi et al. "Digital Heritage Research Re-theorised," for a discussion of the relationships between inequality in participation, socio-demographic characteristics and motivations of participants.

35 C. Bonacchi and G. Moshenska, "Critical Reflections on Digital Public Archaeology," *Internet Archaeology* 40 (2015), doi: 10.11141/ia.40.7.1; C. Bonacchi, "Digital Media in Public Archaeology."

36 B. Marwick, "Discovery of Emergent Issues and Controversies in Anthropology Using Text Mining, Topic Modeling, and Social Network Analysis of Microblog Content," in *Data Mining Applications with R*, ed. Y. Zhao and Y. Cen (Amsterdam: Academic Press, Elsevier, 2013), 63–93.

37 S. Graham, "Mapping the Structure of the Archaeological Web," *Internet Archaeology* 39 (2015), doi: 10.11141/ia.39.1.

38 D. Huffer, and S. Graham, "The Insta-Dead: The Rhetoric of the Human Remains Trade on Instagram," *Internet Archaeology* 45 (2017), doi: 10.11141/ia.45.5.

39 C. Zuanni, "Unintended Collaborations: Interpreting Archaeology on Social Media," *Internet Archaeology* 46 (2017), doi: 10.11141/ia.46.2.

posts, comments and replies to study the role of the ancient past in public discussions about Brexit.[40]

Towards the Future

This short essay has intended to provide a first and simple point of access to some of the key trends in Digital Public Archaeology research and practice today. Looking to the future, I suggest that there are four main directions that could be prioritized to further advance DPA. Firstly, the debates that have been occurring so far are still primarily concerned with the UK, Northern America and Australia; it would be helpful to ensure that this valuable work is integrated with discussions that extend beyond Anglophone countries and academic circles. Secondly, it could be useful to further strengthen existing synergies and collaborations between DPA, on the one hand, and both digital heritage and computational archaeology, on the other. Thirdly, it is precisely this empirical engagement with technicity that should be brought to the fore in combination with, and not as an alternative to, robust theoretical grounding.[41] Fourthly and finally, more extensive, larger-scale studies would be important to advance and detail our current understanding of the democratic and undemocratic, inclusive and exclusive, progressive and regressive stances of Digital Public Archaeology. Indeed, from this point of view, DPA has still to express much of its potential as an activist practice, undertaken in the public interest but also working in collaboration with people to determine what that public interest should be and the most appropriate and effective ways to actualize it. The public in Public Archaeology has been variously debated, and broken down into three core facets: the state, the people and the public opinion.[42] Digital methods allow us to establish new synergies and more participatory communications and programs of activities, within the limits of the social geographies of digital literacies and uptake and of the resources that are available to archaeologists and heritage institutions.

---

[40] C. Bonacchi, M. Altaweel and M. Kryzanska, "The Heritage of Brexit: Roles of the Past in the Construction of Political Identities on Social Media," *Journal of Social Archaeology* 8.2 (2018): 174–192, doi: 10.1177/1469605318759713.
[41] Bonacchi, and Kryzanska, "Digital Heritage Research Re-theorised."
[42] N. Merriman, "Introduction: Diversity and Dissonance in Public Archaeology," in *Public Archaeology*, ed. N. Merriman (London and New York: Routledge, 2004), 1–18; A. Matsuda, "The Concept of 'the Public' and the Aims of Public Archaeology," *Papers from the Institute of Archaeology* 15 (2004): 90–97. DOI: 10.5334/pia.224.

Bibliography

Bevan, A. "Value, Authority and the Open Society: Some Implications for Digital and Online Archaeology." In *Archaeology and Digital Communication: Towards Strategies of Public Engagement*, edited by C. Bonacchi, 1–14. London: Archetype Publications.

Bonacchi, C. "Digital Media in Public Archaeology." In *Key Concepts in Public Archaeology*, edited by G. Moshenska, 60–72. London: UCL Press, 2017.

Bonacchi, C. and M. Kryzanska. "Digital Heritage Research Re-theorised: Ontologies, Epistemologies and Ethics in a World of Big Data." *International Journal of Heritage Studies* (2019), doi: 10.1080/13527258.2019.1578989.

Perry, S. and N. Beale, "The Social Web and Archaeology's Restructuring: Impact, Exploitation, Disciplinary Change." *Open Archaeology* 1.1 (2015): 153–165, doi: 10.1515/opar-2015-0009.

Richardson, L. "A Digital Public Archaeology?" *Papers from the Institute of Archaeology* 23.1 (2013), doi: http://doi.org/10.5334/pia.431.

Sophie Gebeil
Identities – a historical look at online memory and identity issues

Abstract: Since the 1990s, profound changes linked to the globalization of both economic activities and information, as well as increased individual mobility have given rise to questions about national identities. This has occurred to such an extent that national "identity crises" have emerged, which collectively have become an important political issue. The Internet has become an active tool in these debates, contributing to increasing the circulation of knowledge, while at the same time disseminating new interpretations of past events on which the construction of collective and individual identities is based. Thus, since the 1990s, online content related to the past has become a newly documented subject matter for a cultural history of memory based on web sources with regard to identity creation. In this article, the web will be perceived as an object of study, used to analyze what relationship the past has to the construction of identities. By considering the web and its archives as a deposit for born-digital sources for the history of the 1990s to the present day, this chapter proposes to present some historiographical research fields concerning identity creation. We will thus examine to what extent the web and its archives constitute the sources that can open up avenues of research concerning the history of identity creation.

Keywords: web archives, memories studies, born-digital heritage, communities, witness

As a concept that combines multiple representations and uses, identity has developed into a bounteous historiographical field of study. Bringing together a set of diverse characteristics that merge into one, identity has become essential in historiography with regard to questioning the construction of collective identities and processes of identifying individuals within social groups over time.[1] As early as the 1960s, the field of oral history collected and studied individual and group testimonials – especially those of minorities and subalterns, which helped to affirm and legitimize the identity of those groups.[2] However, more recently, historiography has focused on the place of history and memory in the construction of collective identities.[3] Instilled by the reflections with regard to the regimes of historicity, the field questions the ways in which the

---

[1] Robinson Baudry and Jean-Philippe Juchs, "Définir l'identité," *Hypothèses* 10.1 (2007): 155, https://doi.org/10.3917/hyp.061.0155.
[2] Donald A. Ritchie, *The Oxford Handbook of Oral History*. Oxford: Oxford University Press, 2011.
[3] Maryline Crivello et al., *Concurrence des passés: usages politiques du passé dans la France contemporaine*, 1 vols, Le Temps de l'histoire (Aix-en-Provence, Publications de l'université de Provence, 2006).

identification process has projected the past and memories into the present.[4] The veracity of how the collective narratives have been constructed is not at stake, but rather the field questions how the representations that a society creates based on its history, its present and its future are analyzed at a given moment in time.[5]

Since the 1990s, profound changes linked to the globalization of both economic activities and information, as well as increased individual mobility have given rise to questions about national identities. This has occurred to such an extent that national "identity crises" have emerged, which collectively have become an important political issue.[6] The Internet has become an active tool in these debates, contributing to increasing the circulation of knowledge, while at the same time disseminating new interpretations of past events on which the construction of collective and individual identities is based. Thus, since the 1990s, online content related to the past has become a newly documented subject matter for a cultural history of memory based on web sources with regard to identity creation.[7] Subsequently, in this article, the web will be perceived as an object of study, used to analyze what relationship the past has to the construction of identities. Historicizing these sources has been derived from the history of representation, the uses of the past, public history as well as the history of the media, thereby attempting to decipher the evolution of mediation strategies. By considering the web and its archives as a deposit for born-digital sources for the history of the 1990s to the present day, this chapter proposes to present some historiographical research fields concerning identity creation. We will thus examine to what extent the web and its archives constitute the sources that can open up avenues of research concerning the history of identity creation.

The democratization of the web has opened up a new space to diffuse group identities. For minority groups, the Web is an additional tool that helps to affirm a collective identity that had previously not been fully realized. Thus many oral history initiatives developed in the 1960s and 1970s have now become more prominent on the web through the contents that bring the collected testimonials to the forefront,

---

4 François Hartog and Saskia Brown, *Regimes of Historicity: Presentism and Experiences of Time*, European Perspectives: A Series in Social Thought and Cultural Criticism (New York: Columbia University Press, 2015).
5 Moses I. Finley, *The Use and Abuse of History* (London: Hogarth, 1986); Henry Rousso, *Le Syndrome de Vichy: (1944–198 . . .)*, XXe Siècle (Paris: Éd. du Seuil, 1987); Pierre Nora, *Les Lieux de Mémoire*, Quarto ([Paris]: Gallimard, 1997).
6 Marie-Claire Lavabre, "Circulation, Internationalization, Globalization of the Question of Memory," *Journal of Historical Sociology* 25.2 (2012): 261–274.
7 During my doctoral research, I used the term "online memory content" to describe web content that offers a public narrative of a past event, regardless of who initiated it (memory creators). This hypermedia memory content is the result of the scenographic choices and the memory creators' interpretations of the past generated from social and economic contexts, hence the term "online memory mediation devices." See Sophie Gebeil, "The Digital Building of North African Immigration Memories on the French Web (1999–2014)," Aix-Marseille University, 2015.

thereby generating a feeling of belonging for a specific group. Whether the collective group is officially acknowledged or not, it will gain visibility and its memories can be shared thus obtaining the recognition of an affirmed specificity, associated or not with political demands (positive discrimination, subsidies, and compensation). Communities that have initiated cultural productions related to the past in the pre-web period build on this experience taking advantage of the simplification of online publishing during the 2000s. For example, the Outhistory.org site, created in 2008 by Jonathan Ned Katz, uses MediaWiki software to "compile community-created histories of LGBTQ life in the US and make the insights of LGBTQ broadly accessible."[8] The site was designed by a community of researchers, activists and enthusiasts to combine both public and digital history, subsequently providing access to an encyclopedia, archives and LGBT cultural news, as a continuation of previous works.[9]

For many minority groups such publishing tools, and specifically the emergence of the "participatory Web," have given them the opportunity to reclaim their own historical and memorial narrative, and so counter the dominant stigmatized representations. This work can be seen in the *Place of Memory* on the Amerindian web, thus promoting an "ethnic re-thinking" that opposes the colonial and reductive term "Indian."[10] For example, the contents of the *Indios online* blog give the groups' social memories visibility even though this heritage is not recognized as part of the official history. These practices contribute to strengthening a group's identity through the development and dissemination of a collective memory while defending the rights of the community. They also help forge a way of being in the world and relating to the world, as the blogger Yakuy Tupinambà explained: "The Internet makes our voices heard, which for such a long time were silent, smothered by the voices of those who considered themselves experts. Connecting to the world on the Internet is to have the right to a face, and to make our voice heard; it is also being aware of the events and interests that involve all humanity."[11]

With the continuity of the pre-existing media, the web is a place for discussion and sometimes confrontation about how past events are interpreted, as well as for the selection of references that make up identities, especially national identities. Through its participative dimension, the Web extends and broadens the range of

---

8 OutHistory.org, "About OutHistory," http://outhistory.org/about-outhistory, viewed March 7, 2018.
9 Lauren Jae Gutterman, "OutHistory.Org: An Experiment in LGBTQ Community History-Making," *The Public Historian* 32.4 (November 2010): 96–109, https://doi.org/10.1525/tph.2010.32.4.96.
10 Eliete da Silva Pereira, "O local digital das culturas: as interações entre culturas, mídias digitais e territórios" (text, Universidade de São Paulo, 2013), http://www.teses.usp.br/teses/disponiveis/27/27154/tde-06052014-110606/.
11 Yakuy Tupinambà, mentionned by José Ribamar Bessa Freire and Renata Daflon Leite, "Patrimoine en réseau: les cendres, la braise et les droits des Amérindiens au Brésil," in *Mémoire et nouveaux patrimoines*, ed. Cécile Tardy and Vera Dodebei (OpenEdition Press, 2015), https://doi.org/10.4000/books.oep.860.

spaces in which communities can discuss history and identity. These traces of conversations related to memory and identity generate new material for the historian, both online and in the Web archives in a perspective of the history of the present time.[12] I will illustrate my point by using a post-colonial interpretation on Maghreb immigration around 2005 in the French media space.[13]

In January 2006, the French press and television relayed the existence of a new militant group called the Movement of Indigenous People of the Republic (MIR). The group published an attack that drew attention for its radical nature within the online French anti-racist landscape. The text denounced the colonial character of the contemporary French Republic: "France is and remains a colonial state." Its authors seized upon the legal category used during a period of colonial history to designate themselves as 'Indigenous' and called to "decolonise the history of France." For the MIR, French society is divided into different categories founded on vague racial, religious, and colonial criteria: 'Black' and 'Arab' people fall into the 'Indigenous' category as opposed to the 'White' category. By combining colonial heritage and racial categorization, the MIR drew on ideas that have become an important component of French anti-racist activism over the last decade.

How then did this interpretation emerge at this date in a state based on secular republican unity?[14] Even though the emergence of colonial memories in 2005 was multi-factorial and was part of the continuity of debates boosted in the 1990s with regard to the "duty of memory," the web was instrumental in the expansion of the MIR. The French web archives, managed by the French National Library and the National Audiovisual Institute (INA), reveal the main dynamics at play in the origin of the MIR.[15] Beginning in 2003, the Web has shown the connections through the hyperlinks between numerous collective groups – Islamic, pro-Palestinian, feminist, far-left, and anti-racist groups – that opposed a proposed bill to ban the wearing of the Islamic veil in schools. From this point of view, the Muslim site Oumma.com

---

[12] For more about web archives and historiographical issues, see Niels Brügger, *Archiving Websites General: Considerations and Strategies* (Århus, Denmark: The Centre for Internet Research, n.d.), http://www2.scedu.unibo.it/roversi/SocioNet/bruegger_archiving.pdf; Valérie Schafer, Francesca Musiani, and Marguerite Borelli, "Negotiating the Web of the Past," *French Journal for Media Research*, La toile négociée/Negotiating the web, no. 6 (2016): http://frenchjournalformediaresearch.com/lodel/index.php?id=963; Sophie Gebeil, Website Story – Histoire, mémoires et archives du Web (INA, Bry-sur-Marne, France, 2021).

[13] Sophie Gebeil, "Temporalités Des Mémoires de l'immigration Maghrébine Sur Le Web Français (1999–2014): Une Histoire Entre Filiations et Recompositions," in *Temps et Temporalités Du Web*, ed. Valérie Schafer, Intelligences Numériques (Presses Universitaires de Paris Nanterre, 2018), 135–150.

[14] France does not recognize minority groups, and rejects any racial categorization (ethnic statistics are prohibited since World War Two).

[15] Sébastien Ledoux, *Le Devoir de Mémoire: Une Formule et Son Histoire* (Paris: CNRS éditions, 2016).

constituted an important space of debate in which the colonial argument was regularly raised.[16] Equally important was the scholar of Islam, Tariq Ramadan's open letter to the French President, which declared: "Muslims are no longer natives to colonise."[17]

The bill was finally passed in the National Assembly on March 15, 2004, but the controversies concerning the colonial past continued owing to another legislative project which sought to recognise the "positive role" of the French military presence overseas. Oumma.com published historian Pascal Blanchard's videos, a supporter of *Post-colonial French Studies*, whose work and political commitment emphasized the weight of the colonial past in the present.[18] The site showed an alternative vision of the news that was then punctuated by revolts in the poor neighborhoods at the end of 2005. Like many militant sites, Oumma.com denounced the racist and neo-colonialist treatment of the protestors by the mainstream media.[19] Consequently, for a minority of those opposed to the 2004 law, the colonial question emerged as the frame of reference at the origin of the MIR. Hence, the web archives helped to historicize the construction of this 'Iindigenous' identity, showing the online communication strategies and connections that resulted in a militant project in which the past played a fundamental role – highlighting the complex ways that French postcolonial ideas both intersected and were reshaped in online and off line contexts.

In the age of the Internet, blog posts, web pages, videos, tweets, etc, have shaped the visual representations that a society develops about past events. They add to the narratives conveyed by the mainstream media. Indeed, the identity of both our society as a whole as well as individuals and groups is embodied not only in disseminated memorial narrative, but also in the images produced and conveyed to the general public. Sometimes the icon, such as the national flag, a national symbol or a portrait is enough to embody group identity. The profusion of web content related to the past has become a source to study the public forms of identity construction from a scenographic and diachronic perspective combining cultural history, visual content, the role of the media and a public approach to history.

Through the web, digital memory content has been transformed into hypermedia that is potentially immersive and ubiquitously connected, which in turn has changed the modes of representing the past publicly online. The online content is structured

---

16 Concerning Muslim minorities online in Europe in the early 2000s, see Stefano Allievi and Jørgen S. Nielsen, *Muslim Networks and Transnational Communities in and across Europe*, Muslim Minorities v. 1 (Leiden Boston: Brill, 2003), http://www.sudoc.fr/071059741.
17 Tareq Ramadan, "Open letter to N. Sarkozy and J. Ferry"/"Lettre ouverte à M. Nicolas Sarkozy et à M. Jules Ferry," Oumma.com, February 7, 2003, http://www.oumma.com/article.php3?id_article=555, version du 15 février 2003, Internet Legal Deposit, BNF.
18 Pascal Blanchard, Nicolas Bancel, and Sandrine Lemaire, eds, *La fracture coloniale: la société française au prisme de l'héritage colonial* (Paris, France: la Découverte, 2005).
19 Alec G. Hargreaves, *Multi-Ethnic France: Immigration, Politics, Culture and Society* (Routledge, 2007), https://doi.org/10.4324/9780203962794.

by hypertextuality, and integrates sources that are often digitized and of a multifaceted nature (iconographic, sound, audiovisual, textual). The Internet user's place within this framework varies from experiencing them to participating in and leading the multiple narratives that are found in web documentaries.[20] Because connected, networked devices are involved, such narratives are subject to multiple processes of re-interpretation and re-routing, especially on social media. This process of engaging and then networking contributes to the construction of group identity as Dana Diminescu's e-Diasporas project shows. For example, the connections between Palestinian websites denote the manner in which individuals and groups struggle to form cultural and national identity, especially in the absence of a nation-state that is offline.[21] From another perspective, several recent studies have shown the re-deployment of Jewish identities and heritage on the web, connecting communities that no longer have a "physical" presence in countries like Morocco and Egypt.[22] To historicize this web material means to study both the interpretive evolution and the construction itself by applying them to different timescales and analyzing how and what is generated. Additionally, the visual expression of memory in digital spaces can thus be transformed according to the context, the opportunities, and the technical evolution of the web. Let's take the example of generiques.org created in 2000 by the eponymous association responsible for collecting and promoting the memoirs of immigration in France (figure1). The transformations experienced by the site from 2000 to the present day have resulted from many factors. The technical aspects are the most obvious: the first version of the homepage contained an animated GIF while the third and most recent version shows how there is a content management system backed up by a database. However, technical temporality is not enough to explain the evolution of the site's visual identity. Indeed, significant continuities can be seen, from the online publication of militant posters on the site as of 2004 through to composing a blog as of 2008. This element has been around for longer than the association, founded by the militants Saïd Bouziri (1947–2009), Driss El-Yazami (born in 1952), and Farid Aïouch, who dedicated their own collections to Génériques. Recent events, which fall within Braudel's "courte durée," have also shaped the visual identity of the site. For example, there was the Generations exhibition (2009–2011) that was organized by the Génériques Association and dedicated to the Maghreb migrants, as well as the

---

[20] Sophie Gebeil, "La Patrimonialisation Numérique Des Mémoires de l'immigration Maghrébine En France Dans Les Années 2000," *RESET – Social Science Research on the Internet*, no. 6 (4 November 2016), https://doi.org/10.4000/reset.853.

[21] A. Ben-David, "The Palestinian Diaspora on the Web: Between de-Territorialization and Re-Territorialization," *Social Science Information* 51, no. 4 (1 December 2012): 459–474, https://doi.org/10.1177/0539018412456769. Anat Ben-David, "Palestinian Corpus" I, e-Disaporas (dir. Dana Dimescu), http://www.e-diasporas.fr/wp/ben-david.html.

[22] Dario Miccoli, "Oltre l'archivio? Storie e Memorie Degli Ebrei Egiziani in Internet," *Memoria E Ricerca* 42 (May 2013): 189–201, https://doi.org/10.3280/MER2013-042012.

commemoration of the end of the Algerian War in 2012. Both events are visible and can be seen in the different versions on the website. Moreover, as certain material was neither available on the web nor in the web archives, it was essential to make use of both the written and oral sources in the association's written archives in order to understand the evolution of the website. With regard to Génériques, its website was created in 1999 by Réda Belkhodja (1939–2013), a volunteer and retired computer scientist who developed the first version of the site using File Maker Pro, a long-running database and web program. The association then received funding in 2007, which was used to develop the Odysséo database, dedicated to immigration archives, and hire a webmaster, Thomas Horner. This financial investment led to the site's third version being outsourced in 2014, entrusted to the webdesign company OneOfUs. Another critical element in the project's successful development was the presence of Naïma Yahi from 2005 to 2011 in the association, who was at that time a PhD student specializing in the history of music. She had skills in terms of digital mediation and data collection, referencing many Maghreb music archives that enriched the site. Génériques thus demonstrates how digital memory technologies, including their visual identity reflect the technical evolution of the web and its strategies as much as it does previous legacies. Given that the site's elements were not always accessible online, its development demanded that it adapted to the emergence of the web, as well as to broader shifts in the digital landscape.

Affirming collective identities on the web includes managing the digital presence of the users who can express multiple modes of identification through social media. For example, users may transmit an archived image via email or social media and/or click on "like" with regard to a specific a commemoration. Like their culinary tastes, Internet users' relationships to history are a facet of their cultural and digital identity.

From this perspective, born-digital sources have opened up avenues for analysis related to micro-history, focusing on the individual and the relationship between the group and the individual, and on the interactions between an individual's digital identity and his/her relationship to the group. For example, in "Reflet d'une mémoire (Reflection of a Memory)" put online in 2008, Karim and Djamel Achour revealed, through their parents' and relatives' testimonies, the story of a group of immigrants, who, for the most part were Algerians, and had lived in slums around the slaughterhouses before being relocated, near the current casino in the very touristic town of Aix-en-Provence. This reconstruction of a memory, of a group marginalized by the patrimonial and cultural narrative dominating the territory, mixes the individual memories and those of a group, while denying any assignment of identity. When asked about this, Djamel Achour refused to accept being labeled as an 'Arab,' 'Maghrebi,' or a 'Native.' On the contrary, he wanted to be considered a French citizen, living in Aix. Between the individual archives, the audiovisual archives, and the collective memories that break the institutional consensus, this example shows the complexity of the relationship to the past expressed online. It also testifies to the individual's ability to build a multi-faceted identity.

This type of highly conscious initiative co-exists with more fragmented and occasional practices in which history appears as a connected experience, in constant contact with the process of self-assertiveness on the web. The representation of history, in perpetual motion and accentuated within personal digital identity, is often iconic in the sense that it is both visual and symbolic. Thus the archives and testimonies, an incarnation of the proof of the past event, are adapted and distorted through individual practices and current events. Twitter is a good example of this, where commemorative controversies become the occasion of an "archive vs. archive" sparring, aimed at imposing one's own interpretation of the event. For example, during the debates generated by President Emmanuel Macron's proposal to commemorate the events that took place in May 1968, some tweets revealed that the *Office de radio diffusion télévision française*'s (ORTF) Gaullist propaganda de-contextualized their original records by glorifying the "hidden face" of May 1968. According to the INA archives, the images of demonstrations supporting General De Gaulle (figure 2) were in fact controlled images of propaganda. This process of documentary repurposing and re-authoring is now shaping the relationship between the past, the archive, the testimony, and the story, appearing as "a tiny whirlwind in a broader semiotic culture."[23]

The emergence of digital technologies has contributed to the emergence of a new sensitivity to the past since the 1970s, in the face of a future perceived as uncertain: the development of militant history aimed at giving a voice to the defeated and the forgotten was followed by an increase in the number of commemorations, a developed passion for heritage and an enthusiasm for historical reconstitutions, etc.[24] Hence, the user can draw on the historical references that build his/her own narrative identity and avoid those that are offensive.[25] The values of the present are thus projected onto past historical events, thus amplifying the presentification of history on a future horizon focused on the present, as can be seen by the many examples online.[26]

---

23 Luke Tredinnick, "The Making of History: Remediating Historicised Experience," in *History in the Digital Age*, ed. Toni Weller (London; New York: Routledge, 2013), 39–60; On repurposing, see Peter Stockinger, "The Repurposing (Re-Authoring) of Digital Audiovisual Resources in Cultural Heritage. A Concrete Example: The Huarpe Civilization and Culture," in *Unpublished* (2006), https://doi.org/10.13140/rg.2.1.1264.6800.
24 Maryline Crivello, "Let's Make a Spectacle of the Past! Genealogies and Historical Reconstitutions of Salon and Grans in Provence (19th–20th Centuries)," *Sociétés & Représentations* 12.2 (2001): 225, https://doi.org/10.3917/sr.012.0225; Frédéric Clavert and Serge Noiret, *L'histoire Contemporaine à l'ère Numérique* (Luxembourg (Luxembourg): Peter Lang, 2013).
25 Paul Ricœur, "Narrative Identity," *Philosophy Today* 35.1 (1991): 73–81, https://doi.org/10.5840/philtoday199135136.
26 François Hartog and Saskia Brown, *Regimes of Historicity: Presentism and Experiences of Time*, European Perspectives: A Series in Social Thought and Cultural Criticism (New York: Columbia University Press, 2015).

Conclusion: A Hstorian's Identity When Dealing with Deployments of Digital Narratives: A Crisis of Legitimacy or Opportunity?

In the 1990s, academic historians had already identified how the digital age was transforming the profession, including undermining historians' professional authority through questioning the fundamental concepts of the discipline: documentary abundance, volatility of content, technical constraints, specificities of web archives, and the increase in knowledge producers.[27] In these circumstances, several authors have concluded that there is a crisis of "relevance and legitimacy" for professional historians.[28]

At the same time, this new situation has opened up an opportunity for individuals and groups to contribute their own interpretive and documentary work; if this challenges the disciplinary authority of the historian, it nonetheless expands the field of history – especially through the production of born-digital sources. Ironically, through their work in creating digital memory technologies, ordinary people and groups validate the temporal approach of historians thus reinforcing the historian's ontology. Firstly, by placing contemporary usages online in the multiple temporalities of identity practices during the pre-web period, from the socio-technical evolution of the web from the late 1990s and the shorter memorialization period, the historian can help one better understand the daily Internet and identity practices that are often perceived as instantaneous. Secondly, historical survey methods rely on an in-depth study of the sources that underlie the technical choices made by the users, but which also take into account the individualities behind the screen. Finally, the contrast between the historian's digital presence and the non-specialist practices make it necessary to rethink the relationship between 'witnesses' who cannot just be considered as passive investigators but rather as actors who can participate in processes of co-construction of the past. This induces one to think of history as a set of specific skills that an amateur can also develop and recommends that professional historians collaborate with non-specialists in favor of building shared stories.

Bibliography

Baudrry, Robinson and Jean-Philippe Juchs. "Définir l'identité." *Hypothèses* 10.1 (2007): 155, https://doi.org/10.3917/hyp.061.0155.

Ben-David, A. "The Palestinian Diaspora on the Web: Between de-Territorialization and Re-Territorialization." *Social Science Information* 51.4 (1 December 2012): 459–474, https://doi.org/10.1177/0539018412456769.

---

[27] Roy Rosenzweig and David Paul Thelen, *The Presence of the Past: Popular Uses of History in American Life*, vol. 2 (Columbia University Press, 1998); Rolando Minuti, "Le incognite della 'pubblicazione' on-line," *Reti Medievali Rivista* 1.1 (15 June 2000): 1.

[28] Luke Tredinnick, "The Making of History: Remediating Historicised Experience," in *History in the Digital Age*, ed. Toni Weller (London ; New York: Routledge, 2013), 39–60.

Blanchard, Pascal, Nicolas Bancel, and Sandrine Lemaire, eds. *La fracture coloniale: la société française au prisme de l'héritage colonial*. Paris, France: la Découverte, 2005.

Clavert, Frédéric and Serge Noiret. *L'histoire Contemporaine à l'ère Numérique*. Luxembourg: Peter Lang, 2013.

Crivello, Maryline et al. *Concurrence des passés: usages politiques du passé dans la France contemporaine, 1 vols, Le Temps de l'histoire*. Aix-en-Provence, France: Publications de l'université de Provence, 2006.

Crivello, Maryline. "Let's Make a Spectacle of the Past! Genealogies and Historical Reconstitutions of Salon and Grans in Provence (19th–20th Centuries)." *Sociétés & Représentations* 12.2 (2001): 225, https://doi.org/10.3917/sr.012.0225.

Finley, Moses I. *The Use and Abuse of History*. London: Hogarth, 1986.

Freire, José Ribamar Bessa and Renata Daflon Leite. "Patrimoine en réseau : les cendres, la braise et les droits des Amérindiens au Brésil." In *Mémoire et nouveaux patrimoines*, edited by Cécile Tardy and Vera Dodebei. OpenEdition Press, 2015, https://doi.org/10.4000/books.oep.860.

Gebeil, Sophie. *Website Story – Histoire, mémoires et archives du Web*. INA, Bry-sur-Marne, France, 2021.

Gebeil, Sophie Gebeil. "Temporalités Des Mémoires de l'immigration Maghrébine Sur Le Web Français (1999–2014): Une Histoire Entre Filiations et Recompositions." In *Temps et Temporalités Du Web*, edited by Valérie Schafer, 135–150. Presses Universitaires de Paris Nanterre, 2018.

Gutterman, Lauren Jae. "OutHistory.Org: An Experiment in LGBTQ Community History-Making." *The Public Historian* 32.4 (November 2010): 96–109, https://doi.org/10.1525/tph.2010.32.4.96.

Hargreaves, Alec G. *Multi-Ethnic France: Immigration, Politics, Culture and Society*. Routledge, 2007.

Hartog, François and Saskia Brown, *Regimes of Historicity: Presentism and Experiences of Time, European Perspectives: A Series in Social Thought and Cultural Criticism*. New York: Columbia University Press, 2015.

Lavabre, Marie-Claire. "Circulation, Internationalization, Globalization of the Question of Memory." *Journal of Historical Sociology* 25.2 (2012): 261–274.

Ledoux, Sébastien. *Le Devoir de Mémoire: Une Formule et Son Histoire*. Paris: CNRS éditions, 2016.

Miccoli, Dario. "Oltre l'archivio? Storie e Memorie Degli Ebrei Egiziani in Internet." *Memoria E Ricerca*. 42 (May 2013): 189–201, https://doi.org/10.3280/MER2013-042012.

Minuti, Rolando. "Le incognite della 'pubblicazione' on-line." *Reti Medievali Rivista* 1.1 (15 June 2000): 1.

Pereira, Eliete da Silva. "O local digital das culturas: as interações entre culturas, mídias digitais e territórios." text, Universidade de São Paulo, 2013, http://www.teses.usp.br/teses/disponiveis/27/27154/tde-06052014-110606/.

Ramadan, Tareq. "Open letter to N. Sarkozy and J. Ferry"/"Lettre ouverte à M. Nicolas Sarkozy et à M. Jules Ferry." Oumma.com (7 Februrary 2003), http://www.oumma.com/article.php3?id_article=555.

Ricœur, Paul. "Narrative Identity." *Philosophy Today* 35.1 (1991): 73–81, https://doi.org/10.5840/philtoday199135136.

Ritchie, Donald A. *The Oxford Handbook of Oral History*. Oxford University Press, 2011.

Rosenzweig, Roy and David Paul Thelen. *The Presence of the Past: Popular Uses of History in American Life, vol. 2*. Columbia University Press, 1998.

Tredinnick, Luke. 'The Making of History: Remediating Historicised Experience." In *History in the Digital Age*, edited by Toni Weller, 39–60. London: New York: Routledge, 2013.

Joshua MacFadyen
Digital Environmental Humanities

Abstract: Over the last half century, the environmental humanities has become a new interdisciplinary and digitally engaged field with unique public impact and participation. Its fields include older disciplines such as history, literature, and geography and newer interdisciplinary subdisciplines such as public history, science and technology studies, environmental history, and ecocriticism. Many of these scholars were early adopters of digital research practices from Geographic Information Systems to digital photography, and as a small interdisciplinary field with global scope it benefitted from digital communications and networking. In the early age of environmental humanities research communication media changed relatively slowly, but now as they evolve more rapidly than the schools of thought they help disseminate, the digital media arguably influence and disrupt the fields themselves. Digital environmental humanities spaces shifted from being sites primarily of scholarly conversation into ones that were more publicly engaged, and over time non-academics have shaped the fields through digital participation as well. Through several waves of research and communication technologies, the turn toward public and digital humanities has transformed how we encounter the natural environment and how we define the field.

Keywords: digital humanities, environmental history, environmental humanities, historical geographic information systems, open access, anthropocene

The humanities have always been concerned with the relationships between the natural environment and human societies, but in the last half century the centrality of environmental and sustainability issues has helped create a new interdisciplinary and digitally engaged space for a field now generally recognized as environmental humanities. These approaches help account for the field's growth as well as its novel treatment of what might otherwise be tired tropes in subjects such as climate, agriculture, and energy. Climate variation was long a determinant and explanatory device for political theorists in the early modern past, but climate change has made humanity's agency, responsibility, and imagination core subjects of the humanities. Agriculture has long occupied the pages of books on peasant studies, but new approaches to interspecies relationships and concepts such as "care" are moving to the fore.[1] Energy-saving technologies fascinated the most metaphysical

---

[1] Multispecies Editing Collective, "Troubling Species: Care and Belonging in a Relational World," *RCC Perspectives: Transformations in Environment and Society* 1 (2017), DOI: org/10.5282/rcc/7768; see also Eben Kirksey, "Chemosociality in Multispecies Worlds: Endangered Frogs and Toxic Possibilities in Sydney," *Environmental Humanities* 12.1 (1 May, 2020): 23–50. DOI: https://doi.org/10.1215/22011919-8142198.

https://doi.org/10.1515/9783110430295-008

nineteenth-century historians, but to environmental historians, energy became a "regime" with all of its social implications.[2] As the cross pollination between arts and sciences introduces new concepts and draws attention to others – invasion ecology, island biogeography, or eco-pragmatism – the environmental humanities are well situated to debate their significance in cultural contexts.

Digital tools and communities are enhancing these collaborations and methodological innovations, giving rise to robust international networks, generative interdisciplinary scholarship, and born-digital publications like *Environmental Humanities*, the field's online-only open access journal. By virtue of studying natural environments, physical places, and scientific data, scholars in the environmental humanities were often early adopters of digital research practice from Geographic Information Systems to digital photos. And, as a small interdisciplinary field with a more global scope than some of the area studies, the environmental humanities benefitted from digital communications and networking. Whether enhancing public and interdisciplinary engagement, including citizen scientists in larger cultural research and analysis, or developing new methods for the humanities to observe and measure environmental phenomena, the environmental humanities has become a digital discipline.

Environmental humanities emerged as both a multi-disciplinary and publicly engaged field of scholarship in a manner that expresses well how both digital work and public work have propelled the academic toward new research models. The digital turn produced new modes of communication and public expression, collaborations that crossed the many disciplines at the heart of the environmental humanities. These fields include older disciplines such as history, literature, and geography and newer interdisciplinary subdisciplines such as public history, science and technology studies, environmental history, and ecocriticism. The interaction between environmental humanities and environmental sciences has been stronger because of common interests and a mutual, or at least parasitic, symbiosis between these groups. Many of the historical, literary, and geographic topics listed above were borrowed from discoveries or even emerging paradigms in the environmental sciences. But humanities scholars were there from the beginning of these developments, and they ought to continue shaping how discovery is applied across the academy as well as in the public and private sectors. For example, it was scientists who proposed the idea of "The Anthropocene" as a new geological epoch, but historians such as John McNeill were involved from early on.[3] Most of its proponents had been shaped by humanities scholars in ecofeminism, environmental history, and environmental philosophy, particularly the debates between anthropocentrism and deep ecology. Other scholars

---

[2] Brian C. Black, *Crude Reality: Petroleum in World History* (New York: Rowman & Littlefield, 2014), 9–10.
[3] Will Steffen, Paul J. Crutzen, and John R. McNeill, "The Anthropocene: Are Humans Now Overwhelming the Great Forces of Nature," *AMBIO: A Journal of the Human Environment* 36.8 (2007): 614–621.

responded by examining ecological catastrophe, resistance, and grief, culminating, perhaps in 2009 with the appearance of *Dark Green Religion*, by religious studies scholar Bron Taylor, the Dark Mountain Project, by writers Paul Kingsnorth and Dougald Hine, and essays on "dark ecology" by critical theorist Timothy Morton.[4] These and many other humanists responded to the Anthropocene debate with broad-minded accounts of environmental crises, responsibility, and human efforts to engage "wicked problems" and other system-wide stressors. One of the environmental historians who tackled the Anthropocene, Libby Robin has argued that the future is something we create, and the creative process requires all the tools from the sciences and the arts, including "history and the human imagination."[5]

Among the tools that can help leverage human imagination, environmental humanities scholars have made excellent use of digital research methods and digitally enhanced networks of professional and public engagement. The effects have been transformative for the humanities, as well as some of the sciences and the publics who engage with them. Digital humanities tools and communities are making research increasingly accessible, participatory, and decolonial. There have been multiple generations of digital engagement in the environmental humanities, and they differ somewhat depending on whether one examines their impact on research or communications and networking. There have been at least three generations in communications and networks, represented by the era of electronic mail and internet message boards, the Web 2.0, and the latest generation of social media communication. In digital humanities research, the same web-based generations apply, but there was also a previous era of centralized computer-assisted research and large-scale data initiatives. Digital humanities research is poised for another transformation through machine learning and big data, and, one hopes, through the renewed interest among granting agencies in coupled human-natural systems research, communicating sustainability, and funding for science with demonstrated commitment to knowledge mobilization. The pace of each new generation is quickening. In the early age of environmental humanities research – the aforementioned climate, agriculture, and early technology studies –, communication media changed relatively slowly, certainly slower than many larger schools of thought. Now as digital media evolve more rapidly than the schools of thought they help disseminate, they arguably influence and disrupt the fields themselves.

---

4 Bron Raymond Taylor, *Dark Green Religion: Nature Spirituality and the Planetary Future* (Berkeley: University of California Press, 2010); "The Origins of the Project," The Dark Mountain Project, https://dark-mountain.net/about/origins/, accessed 8 August 2020; Timothy Morton, "The Dark Ecology of Elegy," in *The Oxford Handbook of the Elegy*, edited by Karen Weisman (Oxford: Oxford University Press, 2010), 251–271.
5 Libby Robin, "Histories for Changing Times: Entering the Anthropocene?" *Australian Historical Studies* 44.3 (2013): 329–340, 339–40.

As the field's gravitational clusters began to form in the 1970s and 1980s, the environmental humanities took advantage of a limited number of digital tools and university-based computer infrastructure for enhancing their research. The best-known examples include the use of early Geographic Information Systems (GIS) for human geography, and a few environmental projects that formed the much larger cliometric era of quantitative history research. However, these were generally the exception. GIS fell out of favour among cultural geographers, and cliometrics were better suited for studying human rather than environmental topics over time.[6] Digital forms of research and engagement developed most rapidly in environmental humanities fields in the 1990s, and by the early twenty first century several scholarly groups were making extensive and transformative use of digital tools for research and public engagement. Environmental historians have been particularly active in the use of digital tools and platforms for expanding the reach of their scholarship. The American Society for Environmental History has used email listservs since the early 1990s, and in 2000 it adopted the name H-Environment to accommodate the growing interest from outside of the United States. H-Environment had 1200 members at that point, a quarter of its current membership, and new environmental history groups in Europe, Canada, Australia developed similar electronic networks in the early 2000s. Other disciplines were active as well. Groups such as the Canadian Association of Geographers boasted 730 subscribers to their listserv as early as 2004.[7]

As the second and third generation of digital communities emerged, these spaces shifted from being sites primarily of scholarly conversation into ones that were more publicly engaged, driven largely by the use of newly developing social media platforms. Popular listservs that for a time represented the backbone of scholarly communication, such as H-Net: Humanities & Social Sciences Online, have come to represent the mundane "busy work" of making announcements, rather than being part of the stimulating process of communicating with larger, more open networks over blogs and microblogs. H-Net and its 180 sub-networks is still very much alive with 300 volunteer editors and about 200,000 subscribers across its entire digital landscape at the time of writing (2019). Just under 5,000 of those subscribers follow H-Environment, although H-HistGeog (3007 subscribers at time of writing), H-Animal (1434), and H-Rural (1487)

---

[6] Anne Kelly Knowles, "Historical Geographic Information Systems and Social Science History," *Social Science History* 40.4 (2016): 741–750; Chad Gaffield,, "Clio and Computers in Canada and Beyond: Contested Past, Promising Present, Uncertain Future," *Canadian Historical Review* 101.4 (2020): 559–584.

[7] Dan Smith, "[Caglist] Subscription note," 23 April, 2004. https://lists.uvic.ca/mailman/private/caglist/2004-April.txt.

would have clear overlap.[8] The Canadian Association of Geographers maintains its listserv with over 3,000 members.[9]

Embracing this public turn of digital public history, environmental humanities groups began to create innovative platforms and portals for supporting research, teaching, and activism. Two notable examples were funded by national granting agencies, and then as a critical mass of volunteers and alternative funds materialized, they continued either unfunded or with reduced "soft" money. In 2004, several co-applicants from the fields of History, Geography, and Canadian Studies formed NiCHE: Network in Canadian History & Environment ~ Nouvelle initiative Canadienne en histoire de l'environnement. With Alan MacEachern as Director, the group secured federal funds dedicated to knowledge mobilization. Its members continued their research in environment and history, and its leaders focused primarily on website development so as to encourage member participation, publish news and articles on *The Otter ~ la loutre*, engage the public, and teach the value of digital communication technologies. Several other digital humanities projects, including the "Nature's Past" podcast, and the "Programming Historian" and "Geospatial Historian" open access tutorials started on the NiCHE website and continued as independent projects thereafter. Similarly, in 2009, Christof Mauch (LMU Munich) and Helmuth Trischler (The Deutsches Museum) established the Rachel Carson Centre with support from the German Federal Ministry of Education and Research. With a dual focus on bringing researchers to the centre in Munich and developing outreach through the museum, this group also focused heavily on digital environmental humanities and publics. It publishes the *RCC Perspectives* journal online, and its "Environment and Society" web portal makes digitized environmental humanities research and exhibits available to both academics and the public.[10]

In the United States, environmental humanities projects are often less interconnected due to independent funding agencies for the humanities and social sciences as well as the influence of private endowments and programs attached to individual or regional university systems. For example, the National Historical GIS is a product of IPUMS at the Institute for Social Research and Data Innovation based at the University of Minnesota, which receives funds from the National Institutes of Health,

---

8 Other groups such as H-Borderlands (1711) H-Urban (4597) and H-AmIndian (2347) certainly also feature scholars who do digital environmental humanities.

9 The American Association of Geographers manages its networks slight differently through subscription-based "Knowledge Communities." At the time of writing there were 67 communities, and membership ranged from 68 in the Bible Specialty Group and 76 in Senior Geographers to 1,600 in Urban Geographers.

10 Network in Canadian History & Environment | Nouvelle initiative Canadienne en histoire de l'environnement, https://niche-canada.org/; The Otter ~ la loutre, https://niche-canada.org/category/the-otter/; Rachel Carson Center for Environment and Society, https://www.carsoncenter.uni-muenchen.de/index.html; Environment and Society Portal, https://www.carsoncenter.uni-muenchen.de/digital_project/index.html, accessed 8 August, 2020.

the National Science Foundation, and the Food and Drug Administration. The Spatial History Project at Stanford is part of the Center for Spatial and Textual Analysis, which is funded by the university and private donors. Another group, HASTAC (Humanities, Arts, Science, and Technology Alliance and Collaboratory), was administered by individual universities, first Stanford and Duke and now City University of New York and Dartmouth College.[11] Although these groups have developed online communities with national and international membership, they are sometimes more insular than the models seen in Canada and Germany. The National Endowment for the Humanities maintains a Division of Public Programs, and its digital startup funds have helped launch spatial history projects from the Holocaust Geographies Collaborative, to the Curatescape and PlacePress mobile interpretive apps, to a gamified version of Walden.[12]

This digital turn has empowered the public itself to become vital contributors to the environmental humanities, broadening the field through citizen science networks and environmental activism. One of the most popular ways for the public to engage with environment data-gathering has been through climate history, and particularly the rescue and development of historical climate data. With the help of scholars who are equipped to explain climate and meteorological history and data creation, large numbers of citizen scientists have helped read and transcribe climate records in Germany, early Quebec, Oregon, the North Atlantic, and all of Canada. Most of these projects are described on HistoricalClimatology and NiCHE websites. The former also hosts the Climatological Database for the World's Oceans (CLIWOC), which was created from the weather observations contained in Dutch, English, French and Spanish sailing ship logs between 1750 and 1850. This sort of data rescue is highly popular among citizen scientists, and in the United States NOAA has designed "Old Weather," an entire web portal dedicated to crowdsourced data entry of ships logs worldwide. Old Weather uses the Zooniverse participatory interface to record weather, ocean, and sea-ice observations from over 1 million pages of ships' logs.[13]

Likewise, this public turn in imagining landscapes has been embodied in public history and Indigenous mapping of cultural values in the present, as well as planning and community mapping of values that will impact the future. Tools such as volunteered geographic information (VGI) and participatory GIS (PGIS) have

---

11 "About IPUMS NHGIS," https://www.nhgis.org/about; "About CESTA," https://cesta.stanford.edu/about/about-us; "About HASTAC," https://www.hastac.org/about-hastac, accessed 8 August, 2020.
12 "Holocaust Geographies Collaborative," https://holocaustgeographies.org/; "About Curatescape," https://curatescape.org/about/; "Walden, A Game," https://www.waldengame.com/, accessed 8 August, 2020.
13 "Climate History Databases," *HistoricalClimatology*, https://www.historicalclimatology.com/databases.html; DRAW: Data Rescue Archives & Weather, https://citsci.geog.mcgill.ca/en/; "Online Data Sets," *NiCHE*, https://niche-canada.org/research/canadian-climate-history/online-data-sets/; *Old Weather* https://www.oldweather.org/index.html, accessed 8 August, 2020.

opened geographic information and interpretation to millions of public cartographers and earth observers. VGI includes the OpenStreetMap and Wikimapia platforms for user contributed map features, the Panoramia (now defunct), Flickr, and Google Photo platforms for user-contributed geolocated photos, and the Google webmap and Google Earth platforms which enable a variety of geographic sharing and some public content creation. Historical map collections have come online through image rich scalable websites, and these interfaces have dramatically increased access to collections that previously were restricted to map and data libraries with limited hours and cumbersome storage cabinets.[14] The online collections often contained a web-based map viewer, and some repositories, such as the privately owned David Rumsey map collection, offered historical maps as fully georeferenced layers in Google Earth.[15] The Web 2.0 allowed increased interactions between map users and map servers, and high-speed internet connections enabled the transfer of increasingly large raster files, such as historical maps and aerial photographs. For public historians interested in environment and place, as so many are, these digital technologies expanded access to maps and spatial data at lower costs to researchers.

Digital platforms have created a new space for decolonization research and activism in ways that environmental humanities projects were unlikely to allow on their own. Some of the aforementioned geospatial tools are helping scholars map race and urban environments, for instance, from "Mapping Prejudice" in Minneapolis to mapping "Black ecologies" in New Orleans and "Black Eden" in Chicago. Many of these projects were imagined as public history. Other participatory research projects are helping decolonize the environmental humanities, from the "Decolonial Atlas" project to the Indigenous resistance to neocolonial wildlife management, food insecurity, and energy projects.[16] Indeed, by including Indigenous groups in the research exercise, some historians have even learned that terms such as "regime," so common across sciences and environmental humanities, are rooted in the language

---

[14] Don Lafreniere, et al, "Public participatory historical GIS," *Historical Methods: A Journal of Quantitative and Interdisciplinary History* 52.3 (2019): 132–149.

[15] David Rumsey and Meredith Williams, "Historical Maps in GIS," in *Past Time, Past Place: GIS for History*, edited by Anne Kelly Knowles (Redland: ESRI Press, 2002), 1–18; "David Rumsey Historical Map Collection," http://www.davidrumsey.com/, accessed 8 August, 2020.

[16] "Mapping Prejudice," https://www.mappingprejudice.org, accessed 8 August, 2020; "Mapping Inequality: Redlining in New Deal America," https://dsl.richmond.edu/panorama/redlining, accessed 8 August 2020; J.T. Roane and Justin Hosbey, "Mapping Black Ecologies," *Current Research in Digital History* 2 (2019), https://doi.org/10.31835/crdh.2019.05; Colin Fisher, "Multicultural Wilderness: Immigrants, African Americans, and Industrial Workers in the Forest Preserves and Dunes of Jazz-Age Chicago," *Environmental Humanities* 12.1 (2020): 51–87, https://doi.org/10.1215/22011919-8142209; "The Decolonial Atlas," https://decolonialatlas.wordpress.com, accessed 8 August 2020; Charlotte Coté, "'Indigenizing' food sovereignty: Revitalizing Indigenous food practices and ecological knowledges in Canada and the United States," *Humanities* 5.3 (2016): 57.

of colonialism.[17] Others invited Indigenous knowledge keepers to create artefacts such as a 35-foot-long sturgeon harpoon, and then immerse publics within a virtual river in order to understand Musqueam history and modern-day culture in the Lower Mainland of British Columbia, generations after their ancestors had ceased to fish sturgeon.[18]

Deeper modes of analysis of geographic landscapes have emerged that seek to build both scholarly conversation and engage publics. For example, using open-source Omeka-based platforms such as Curatescape, public historians and municipalities are also able to upload user generated content on place history to a shared community webmap. Using proprietary software such as ESRI's "Story Maps," it is also increasingly easy for users to let maps work in the background while scholars focus on the place-based stories and complex characters that make up the environmental humanities. In other place-based exercises, the historical imagery is brought to the foreground. For example, the "Dear Photograph" project invited people to "rephotograph" themselves in a scene of historical or personal significance by visiting that location and recording themselves holding a printed photograph. Other digital photography projects such as the USGS Northern Rocky Mountain Science Center's "Repeat Photography Project," the University of Victoria's "Mountain Legacy Project," and the Forest History Society's Repeat Photography for Sustainability and Working Forests were more systematic efforts to engage the public in measuring and communicating landscape change.[19]

Through several waves of research and communication technologies, the turn toward public and digital humanities has transformed how we encounter the natural environment. As digital humanities tools and communities continue to change, scholars and publics will encounter nature in new ways. Online publishing platforms focus on timely and accessible summaries of new scholarly research, but they also require feature images which orient the researcher toward visual research

---

[17] Brittany Luby, Andrea Bradford, and Samantha Mehltretter, with the Niisaachewan Anishinaabe Nation, "Building a Common Vocabulary: A Cornerstone of Community-Engaged Research," *Network in Canadian History & Environment / Nouvelle initiative Canadienne en histoire de l'environnement* (5 June, 2020), https://niche-canada.org/2020/06/05/building-a-common-vocabulary-a-cornerstone-on-community-engaged-research/.

[18] Dale Gintner, "Sturgeon Harpoon Knowledge Web wins Governor General's History Award," *Beaty Biodiversity Museum*, January 27, 2020, https://beatymuseum.ubc.ca/2020/01/27/sturgeon-harpoon-knowledge-web-wins-governor-generals-history-award/, accessed 8 August 2020.

[19] Curatescape, https://curatescape.org; ESRI Story Maps, https://storymaps.arcgis.com; Dear Photograph, https://dearphotograph.com; USGS Northern Rocky Mountain Science Center, "Repeat Photography Project," https://www.usgs.gov/centers/norock/science/repeat-photography-project/; The Mountain Legacy Project, http://mountainlegacy.ca/; The Forest History Society, "The Repeat Photography Project for Sustainability and Working Forests," http://www.repeatphotography.org/, accessed 8 August, 2020.

and views as well as publicly engaged scholarly practices.[20] Virtual reality and augmented reality have also shown great promise for communicating environmental history, and other advanced imaging may present ways to digitize and understand even more historical documents including handwriting or the very large collections of maps and aerial photographs that are currently still in analog form. As the tools change, engaging with digital methods and digital collaborators will introduce humanists to new time scales. Since humanities projects often take several years from conception to publication, and arguably live even longer public lives thereafter, the media landscape can shift several times over the life of a single humanities project.

Bibliography

Coulter, Kimberly, Hardenberg, Wilko Graf von, Jørgensen, Finn Arne, eds. *Ant Spider Bee. Chronicling digital transformations in environmental humanities.*

Gibson, Abraham, and Cindy Ermus. "The History of Science and the Science of History: Computational Methods, Algorithms, and the Future of the Field," *Isis* 110.3 (September 2019): 555–566, DOI: 10.1086/705543.

Jørgensen, Finn Arne. "The Armchair Traveler's Guide to Digital Environmental Humanities." *Environmental Humanities* 4 (2014): 95–1112

Kheraj, Sean, and K. Jan Oosthoek. "Online Digital Communication, Networking, and Environmental History." In *Methodological Challenges in Nature-Culture and Environmental History Research*. Eds. Jocelyn Thorpe, Stephanie Rutherford, and L. Anders Sandberg. London: Routledge, 2017, 233–247.

Knowles, Anne Kelly. *Placing History: How Maps, Spatial Data, and GIS are Changing Historical Scholarship*. Redland: ESRI Publishing, 2008.

---

20 Dolly Jørgensen, "Blogging as an environmental history research tool," in *Methodological Challenges in Nature-Culture and Environmental History Research*, edited by Jocelyn Thorpe, Stephanie Rutherford, and L. Anders Sandberg (London: Routledge, 2016).

Emily Esten
Combining Values of Museums and Digital Culture in Digital Public History

Abstract: Museum professionals have increasingly introduced technology into historical spaces, and history into technological spaces, to augment or transform the preservation of knowledge and artifacts; the sharing and creation of knowledge; and the visitor experience. This chapter reviews museum initiatives using technology and principles of digital public history to engage collections and audiences. It focuses on three aspects of museum work in digital public history: community building, collections enhancement, and experiential engagement. Considering the international, multifaceted, and multimodal work being done by the museum community, broadly conceived, the values of digital public history present themselves in the past and present of museum work.

Keywords: digital engagement, experience, museums, community, social media, crowdsourcing, collections

Introduction

Digital public history occurs broadly outside the academy, and effectively implemented within museums and cultural institutions.[1] As Tula Giannini and Jonathan Bowen wrote in "Museums and Digitalism," the strengths of digital culture – sharing, transparency, inclusiveness, and access – have influenced museums' incorporation of technology into historical spaces (and history into technological spaces).[2] Using technology, museums augment or transform the preservation of knowledge and artifacts; the sharing and creation of knowledge; and the visitor experience before, during, and after a visit have all created a space for engagement with history and culture.

In targeting a specific audience, good public history professionals think critically about their content and collections. Museums and cultural institutions provide unique opportunities in which to innovate with digital public history. As places of preservation, collection, display, and interpretation, museums actively engage with the role of narratives and objects. Public historians and museum professionals in the digital age are experts in creating new ways of displaying and preserving

---
[1] See Sheila A. Brennan, "DH Centered in Museums?" *Lot 49* (blog), (March 16, 2015), accessed September 2, 2018, https://web.archive.org/web/20181202182910/http://www.lotfortynine.org/2015/03/dh-centered-in-museums/.
[2] See Giannini and Bowen, "Museums and Digitalism."

objects, as well as new narrative forms, guided by principles of shared authority. In that sense, digital public history has much in common with the Museum 2.0 movement, which strives to make museums more open and accessible by enhancing their engagement with local communities. Coined by executive director Nina Simon, Museum 2.0 strives to transform the museum into a participatory space and make them more dynamic, relevant, and essential institutions within society.[3] Simon argued that museums, like the Internet, have had the opportunity over the last decade to become dynamic platforms of interaction, education, and sharing in centering users or visitors. Now that the tools and methodologies exist to craft new forms of digital narratives, a key question has become how new technologies can be harnessed to address old questions of engagement, participation, and relevance in the museum.

This chapter addresses how museums use technology for three primary purposes: community building, collections enhancement, and experiential engagement. In each example, technologies replace, augment, and transform aspects of museum projects and presentations.

Community Building

The presence of museums in the digital social sphere allows them to break barriers in engaging visitors. Digital users may not visit a museum regularly, if at all, but making use of online spaces "offers museums a chance to sidestep outdated perceptions and subvert expectations."[4] An important way to achieve this is crowdsourcing. Continuing the role of museums as centers of knowledge dispersion, the combination of participation and lifelong learning in crowdsourcing allows museums to build relations around cultural heritage that emphasize co-creation.[5] As Mia Ridge, digital curator for the British Library's Digital Scholarship team, has noted, such projects are not

---

[3] Simon, former executive director of the Santa Cruz Museum of Art and History, first uses the term in a blog post, but has expanded on it significantly through the blog and two books, *The Participatory Museum* (2010) and *The Art of Relevance* (2016). See Nina Simon, "What Is Museum 2.0?" *Museum 2.0* (blog), (December 1, 2006), accessed December 2, 2018, http://museumtwo.blogspot.com/2006/12/what-is-museum-20.html. See also Nina Simon, Shelley Bernstein in conversation with Cathy Brickwood, "Museum 2.0", in *Navigating E-culture*, ed. Cathy Brickwood and A. Dekker (Amsterdam: Virtueel Platform, 2009), 82–90.

[4] Russell Dornan, "Should Museums Have a Personality?" *Medium*(blog), (March 9, 2017), accessed September 4, 2018, https://web.archive.org/web/20181202183056/https://medium.com/@RussellDornan/museumpersonality-87ab2112ee9e.

[5] *Museum Education with Digital Technologies: Participation and Lifelong Learning*, report no. 6, RICHES Think Paper Collection, RICHES Project, (April 2016), accessed September 10, 2018, http://resources.riches-project.eu/riches-think-paper-06-museum-education-with-digital-technologies-participation-and-lifelong-learning/.

only an opportunity to generate content but can also represent a form of mutually beneficial engagement between audiences and institutions.[6]

Crowdsourced projects of any nature work to balance the productivity of volunteers (number of pages transcribed and added to the collection) with their public engagement (the conversations, investigation, and process.) The Smithsonian Transcription Center, launched in 2013, works with digital volunteers to transcribe historic documents and collection records and make collections publicly accessible.[7] One initiative, The Freedmen's Bureau Papers, includes nearly two million image files from this bureau, which was established by Congress in 1865 to assist in the reconstruction of the South and to aid formerly enslaved individuals' transition to freedom and citizenship. By contributing to this project, volunteers help to further historical and genealogical research.[8] In 2015, Canada launched its first archival crowdsourced transcription platform called Transcribe (Fig. 1). The site invited the public to transcribe historical records – letters, diaries, scrapbooks, journals, and government records – from the Royal British Columbia Museum (also referred to as the Royal BC Museum).[9] The Smithsonian Transcription Center promoted this process as a way to increase public engagement. The Royal BC Museum advertised Transcribe as an extension of the role volunteers already served at the museum; with the transcription platform, volunteers were no longer limited by their physical proximity to the museum in order to participate in its efforts to tell the stories of British Columbia.

Both platforms offer multiple entryways to take part in the project: volunteers can transcribe materials, review transcribed text, learn from primary source materials in context, or converse through forum and social media posts. The volunteer contributions in transcription and conversation not only help to make historical documents accessible, but they teach the process of being a historian as well – how does one read a primary source document? How do these fit in context with a time period? How can researchers use these materials to further research and work of the museum? Most importantly, these crowdsourcing projects recognize and credit the participation of volunteers in various ways, from providing opportunities to work with curators and content experts, to building on project work with new collections, to including the usernames of participants and transcribers in the final produced work.

---

[6] See Ridge 3–5.
[7] "About." Smithsonian Digital Volunteers: Transcription Center, accessed February 8, 2018, https://transcription.si.edu/about.
[8] "The Freedmen's Bureau Papers," Smithsonian Digital Volunteers: Transcription Center, accessed December 2, 2018, https://transcription.si.edu/instructions-freedmens-bureau.
[9] "Royal BC Museum: Transcribe." Royal BC Museum Transcribe, accessed June 28, 2020, http://transcribe.royalbcmuseum.bc.ca/about-the-project.

Fig. 1: Screenshot of the Transcribe platform. "Royal BC Museum: Transcribe," Royal BC Museum, accessed October 3, 2019. http://transcribe.royalbcmuseum.bc.ca/.

Crowd Curation

In addition to crowdsourcing for transcription and annotation of materials, crowd curation has been a successful model for museums to engage visitors. In 2013, the Chicago History Museum used its website to ask guests to provide ideas for the topic of an upcoming exhibition. Thousands of topics were submitted to the museum, which then selected 16 options that could be voted on by the public.[10] This innovative approach to exhibit development put the public in charge of the kind of content they would want to see in the museum.

Crowdsourcing can also take the form of collecting materials from outside the museum. Being able to contribute one's materials to an initiative or collection recognizes the value of visitor contributions. In preparation for the 150th anniversary of the proclamation of the Canadian confederation, science and technology museums as well as STEM Partners sought to create a "digital storybook" of the history of innovation within the country. To that end, a platform was built through which students, teachers, and amateur historians shared stories about their passion for science, technology, and innovation via video, story, social media, or comments

---

[10] Chicago History Museum, "Crowdsourcing Project to Design New Museum Exhibition," *Idea-CONNECTION* (December 29, 2015), accessed September 2, 2018, https://web.archive.org/web/20181202183636/https://www.ideaconnection.com/open-innovation-success/Crowdsourcing-Project-to-Design-New-Museum-Exhibition-00569.html.

about Canadian innovation history and their effects on the country's life today.[11] These submissions were then supported by the initiative's partner institutions, who curated news, articles, blogs, podcasts, and video content from which users could learn more about the technological innovations suggested. User-generated content also encouraged creativity and collaboration with regard to the initiative's theme, such as the Canadian "life hack" contest in which users submitted do-it-yourself tools and technologies used in day-to-day life. Putting these submissions alongside historical ones, and celebrating both in context with the initiative centered users within Canadian history of technology. Rather than state from the outset how technological or scientific history should be defined, the Canadian museum community encouraged the public to decide what was important and valuable to include within the storybook.

Crowdsourcing takes place in public. This prioritization of transparency in shared historical authority emphasizes co-creation and values the community as an equal partner in that process. For museums, crowdsourcing can help to facilitate public participation and strengthen the dialogue around history and culture with audiences. It expands a museum's audience to local, national, and international communities through the Internet. Most importantly, crowdsourcing provides a model for shared authority in that it broadens participation in the museum's knowledge creation and sharing process. It strengthens communal relationships to museums and the democratization of collections both physical and virtual.[12]

Collections Enhancement

As the driving force behind many museums, collections serve valuable purposes for research, teaching, and community-building. Digitized collections are nothing new – large museums have been building them for decades for both internal and public use, and many small museums have begun digitization projects too in recent years. Digitizing collections and releasing them online contributes to the core museum tasks of collecting, investigating, and mediating museum objects. Once available online,

---

[11] Sandra Corbeil, Fiona Smith Hale and Christopher Jaja, *Crowdsourcing A Nation*, working paper, Canada Science and Technology Corporation, (2017), accessed September 5, 2018, https://web.archive.org/web/20181202182802/https://mw17.mwconf.org/paper/crowdsourcing-a-nation/?s=crowdsourcing#. The site has been archived by Ingenium, the organization formerly known as the Canada Science and Technology Corporation. See https://ingeniumcanada.org/channel/innovation/.

[12] For more on the democratization and affordances of crowdsourcing platforms, see Joanna Iranowska, "Greater Good, Empowerment and Democratization? Affordances of the Crowdsourcing Transcription Projects," *Museum and Society* 17.2 (2019): 210–228, https://doi.org/10.29311/mas.v17i2.2758.

these virtual objects can be recontextualized on digital platforms with contextual and user enhancement for active reuse of collections.[13]

Opening Access to Collections

The Rijksmuseum, the Dutch national museum dedicated to art and history, launched its digital collections platform, Rijksstudio, in 2011 (Fig. 2). Giving online access to over 350,000 high-resolution digital images, the platform allows users to explore the collection, search for images, and download or save personal collections of objects and artwork. The collections platform aligns with the remixing culture of the Internet by encouraging the active use rather than passive viewing of the museum's collections. Its open data policy (free for commercial use) and attractive platform design provide deeper and personal engagement with the museum's collection for a wider audience of users, in an entirely new fashion.[14]

Fig. 2: Screenshot of the Rijksstudio platform. "RIJKSSTUDIO," The Rijksmuseum, accessed October 3, 2019. https://www.rijksmuseum.nl/en/rijksstudio.

---

13 See Bernadette Biedermann "'Virtual museums' as digital collection complexes. A museological perspective using the example of Hans-Gross-Kriminalmuseum," *Museum Management and Curatorship* 32.3 (2017): 281–297, DOI: 10.1080/09647775.2017.1322916.
14 Peter Gorgels, *Rijksmuseum Mobile First: Rijksstudio Redesign and the New Rijksmuseum App*, working paper, Rijksmuseum Amsterdam, (2018), accessed October 3, 2019, https://mw18.mwconf.org/paper/rijksmuseum-mobile-first-redesign-rijksstudio-the-new-rijksmuseum-app/.

Since Rijksstudio, other museum initiatives around the world, such as The National Portal and Digital Repository for Museums of India (launched in 2014) and Smithsonian Learning Lab (launched in 2016), have used digital collections platforms to continue expanding upon engagement opportunities with the images and metadata accessible. In particular, these two initiatives actively consider which audiences need and have an interest in accessing collections with additional content and features.[15] The National Portal brings together collections from 10 national museums, supplementing the digital objects with 3-D panorama experiences, scholarly essays, and timelines.[16] Designed for educators, Smithsonian Learning Lab provides tools for textual and visual annotation of museum objects by allowing users to upload, download, adapt, create, and share resources within the platform.[17]

If museums see themselves as archives of cultural assets, as Wiedemann, Schmitt, and Patzschke propose, then the process of documentation and open access of their materials continues the work of the museum for all.[18] Sharing digitized materials breaks free the objects (and museum's interpretation) from their physical domain. Furthermore, by providing users access to varied types of collections, supplementary content, and tools for annotating, it enhances the latter by adding dynamic multimodal experiences available in a digital environment.

Collections Existing Online

Digital objects and collections also allow museums to exist entirely without a physical presence. The Museu de Pessoa of Brazil represents an early example of a "virtual museum" and online digital archive. The museum (which translates as "Museum of the Person") has been active since 1997 as a public database of life stories of Brazilian

---

15 Dr. Dinesh S. Katre, *BOW Title: National Portal and Digital Repository for Museums of India*, working paper, Centre for Development of Advanced Computing, PUne, INDIA, (2015), accessed October 3, 2019, https://mw2015.museumsandtheweb.com/bow/national-portal-and-digital-repository-for-museums-of-india/.
16 See "National Portal of India," National Portal of India, accessed June 28, 2020, https://www.india.gov.in/spotlight/national-digital-repository-museums-india; "About," National Portal and Digital Repository: National Repository for Indian Museums: About, accessed June 28, 2020, http://museumsofindia.gov.in/repository/page/about.
17 The Smithsonian Learning Lab can be found at learninglab.si.edu. To read more about the extensive and ongoing research and evaluation of how educators and their students use the site, see Smithsonian Center for Learning and Digital Access with the School of Education at the University of California, Irvine (2018). Curation of Digital Museum Content: Teachers Discover, Create, and Share in the Smithsonian Learning Lab. Retrieved from http://s.si.edu/CurationofDigitalMuseumContent.
18 Julia Wiedemann, Eva Patzschke, and Susanne Schmitt, "Responding to Open Access: How German Museums Use Digital Content," *Museum and Society* 17.2 (2019): 193–209, https://doi.org/10.29311/mas.v17i2.2756.

citizens. The site includes timelines, oral histories, podcasts, blogs, and digital exhibitions of Brazilian communities (Fig. 3). Their methodology and collective focus began and continues to be directed at histories and experiences underrepresented or unrepresented in national memory, empowering communities to represent and find themselves within the state narrative. The site actively sought out and highlighted stories from immigrant communities, health workers, trade unions, football clubs. Not only were these citizens represented in the museum's digital space, but these communities were virtually brought together as part of a diverse alternate nationalistic identity.[19] Today, the Museu features 18,000 life stories, 6,000 photos and documents documenting the twentieth and twenty-first centuries of Brazilian history.[20] The Museu reflects upon the nation's past, present, and future realities by showcasing a multiplicity of personal and community experiences and perspectives, through the presentation and preservation of born-digital cultural objects.[21]

Fig. 3: Screenshot of the Museu de Pessoa collections platform. "Monté sua coleção," Museu de Pessoa, accessed October 3, 2019. https://acervo.museudapessoa.org/pt/buscar/conteudo/historia.

---

19 M.A. Clarke, "The Online Brazilian Museu da Pessoa," in *Save As . . . Digital Memories*, ed. J. Garde-Hansen, A. Hoskins and A.Reading (London: Palgrave Macmillan, 2009), 151–161.
20 "Linhas De Ação: Museu Da Pessoa," Linhas de Ação | Museu da Pessoa, accessed July 6, 2020, https://acervo.museudapessoa.org/pt/entenda/linhas-de-acao.
21 Maria José Vicentini Jorente and Karen Kahn, "Histórias De Vida Como Fato Museal Tratado Pelo Design Da Informação Na Curadoria Digital No Museu Da Pessoa," *Biblios: Journal of Librarianship and Information Science* 75 (2019): 16–24, https://doi.org/10.5195/biblios.2019.441.

Elsewhere in the world, the Virtual Museum of Soviet Repression in Belarus, a civic bottom-up initiative, contains audio and video recollections from prisoners and victims of repression.[22] The Museum with No Frontiers, which started from documenting Islamic art, architecture, and archaeology, prides itself on "virtual ensembles that could otherwise not exist."[23] The museum acts as a transnational resource, connecting objects, stories, and smaller institutions within its large platform. By existing entirely online and supporting independent spaces, these museums are able to tell stories that physical museums have long overlooked and thereby confront, and add to, the existing historiography of their respective topics.

Turning back to the values of digital culture noted by Giannini and Bowen – sharing, transparency, inclusiveness, and access – these platforms make museum collections accessible to the public for a variety of purposes. Both the development of digital collections platforms and the curation of collections in digital museums target particular user communities, and use the advantages of digital platforms to broaden collection use, visibility, and contents.

The Virtual Experience

In her visitor-centered research, professor of education Tiina Roppola notes that the modern museum exhibit is a platform for experience and the performance of making meaning.[24] As museums have become more visitor-centric, technology offers a way to enhance and transform visitor experiences.

Virtual Tours

The "standard" virtual tour experience, presented in 360-degree panoramic images or video, allows visitors to explore a museum from anywhere.[25] Replacing a visitor's

---

[22] "About the Project: Музей Савецкіх Рэпрэсій," About the project (English) (Belarusian Oral History Archive, The Open List, and Konrad Adenaeur Stiftung, 2007), http://represii.net/en/e_about.
[23] For more information see Nelly Bekus, "Historical Reckoning in Belarus." In *Transitional Justice and the Former Soviet Union: Reviewing the Past, Looking toward the Future*, ed. Cynthia M. Horne and Lavinia Stan (Cambridge: Cambridge University Press, 2018), 109–132; Eva Schubert, "Museum with No Frontiers," *Museum Museum*, accessed October 3, 2019, http://miriamposner.com/omeka/items/show/107.
[24] Donald Preziosi, "Foreword," in *Designing for the Museum Visitor Experience*, Tiina Roppola (New York: Routledge, 2012), xi.
[25] Standard is contained in quotation marks here by the author's choice. Virtual tours are becoming more and more popular each year, but are not very common in all countries due to cost, investment, and lack of interest. For more on the barriers and standard procedure for virtual tours, see

physical movement through a museum space, these tours attempt to give visitors a sense of presence as they click through exhibit halls, object labels, and closer looks at artifacts on display.

This kind of virtual tour has also proven itself valuable as a form of preservation. Following the September 2018 fire at the Museu Nacional Rio de Janeiro, just after the museum's 200th anniversary, an estimated 20 million objects were lost.[26] However, its digitization through Google Arts & Culture Street View imagery takes viewers through former gallery spaces, highlighting key artifacts of the collections through online exhibits. While certainly not a replacement for funding physical infrastructure and collections, the museum continues to share knowledge in its virtual form.

But virtual tours do more than just allow for the presentation of digitized collections and spaces. The digital environment offers an excellent opportunity for interacting with exhibits for an engaging learning experience. The National Palace Museum of Taiwan is home to the world's largest collection of Chinese art, as well as cultural artifacts of the Chinese-speaking world and East Asia. Even outside of the physical boundaries of the institution, technology supports experiential engagement for prospective and past visitors. Their virtual museum, accessible in both English and Chinese, offers an augmented reality game of the physical exhibitions, buildings, and halls (Fig. 4).[27] A treasure hunt game designed for children walks visitors through the galleries digitally, providing views of the exhibits alongside text while looking for specific objects to complete their mission.[28] The museum also provides extensive context for objects in the permanent collection through descriptions, metadata, and high-resolution images, helping visitors learn while completing the game.

This gamified virtual tour, as well as others provided by the museum, are primarily experience-based. Using the layout of the physical museum, visitors may feel as though they are actually walking through the halls of the palace. Audiences also have an opportunity to view the objects for themselves up-close, in a way that would never happen in a traditional setting. Rather than post an entire collections database online for visitors to browse, the virtual tours provided a targeted approach to engage materials and navigate through space even without a physical opportunity to visit.

Katerina Kabassi, Emmanuel Maravelakis and Antonios Konstantaras, "Heuristics and Fuzzy Multi-Criteria Decision Making for Evaluating Museum Virtual Tours," *The International Journal of the Inclusive Museum* 11.3 (2018): 1–21, https://doi.org/10.18848/1835-2014/cgp/v11i03/1-21.
26 "What's next for Museu Nacional? – Google Arts & Culture," Google (2018), https://artsandculture.google.com/theme/tAJiRqzzmenIIQ.
27 Alexa Huang, "Day 69: National Palace Museum Virtual Museum," Around DH in 80 Days, (August 29, 2014), accessed December 2, 2018, https://web.archive.org/web/20181202183150/http://www.arounddh.org/jekyll/update/2014/08/29/day69/index.html.
28 "Treasure Hunting," National Palace Museum, accessed December 2, 2018, http://www.npm.gov.tw/vrmuseum_en/game02/game02.html.

Fig. 4: Screenshot from the National Palace Museum tour. "Featured Routes," National Palace Museum, accessed October 3, 2019. https://tech2.npm.edu.tw/720vr/museumen/views.html.

Immersive Virtual Environments

Virtual reality (VR) creates an immersive experience through virtual content without making use of the user's physical environment. Augmented reality (AR), by contrast, imposes virtual content onto the physical environment through smartphones, tablets, or similar technologies. Successful virtual or augmented reality (VR/AR) interventions in the museum world include interactive content, emphasize visitor experience in their design and use, and allow public history audiences to learn about the past. Robert Costello, outreach program manager at the Smithsonian National Museum of Natural History noted that their use of augmented reality "playfully manipulat[ed] peoples' senses and experience preferences and us[ed] the information to deliver an experience rather than having the information be the experience."[29]

For history museums, the most powerful use of these platforms is in the digital re-creation of the past, illustrating the histories and issues at stake by placing the visitor directly within the experience. Archaeological excavations lend themselves nicely to virtual environments, traditionally communicated through excavated artifacts. The British Museum hosted a virtual reality experience event in 2015, in which visitors navigated a virtual reality Bronze Age roundhouse and 3D scans of objects from the Museum's collection. Showing these objects in context augmented the educational gap for British students studying the period by providing "physical"

---

29 Ding, "Augmented Reality in Museums."

evidence.[30] The Museu d'Arqueologia de Catalunya hosted a VR workshop as part of an exhibition of the La Draga neolithic settlement. There, families with children took part in 360-degree video walks and a gamified experience to view the exhibition's objects in virtual space.[31] In each of these archaeological VR opportunities, the interactive visualization allowed visitors to view the objects as they would have been viewed or used in the past. In each case, the technology helped to address visitors' gaps in knowledge of archaeological settlements by engaging specific histories or materials.

Whether educationally- or experientially-focused, immersive virtual environments inside and outside the museum create multimodal avenues to engaging collections. However, working with VR and AR is fraught with complex issues; immersive virtual environments can have physical and psychological impacts on users, for instance, including perceptions of disembodiment and loss of agency. For their part, museum professionals sometimes question what it means to remake these experiences and worry about VR/AR being an overhyped distraction from the content.[32]

Most importantly, the ethics of engaging a visitor in VR/AR experiences are complicated. For example, are virtual environments accessible given the visual, auditory, or physical limitations of visitors? Is immersion a responsible and effective methodology for all historical narratives, especially those with sensitive content? And are issues of privacy and agency communicated to the user before, during, and after engaging with such immersive technologies? In sum, an experiential focus may help institutions accomplish their educational missions and enhance engagement, but such experiences should be weighed alongside the intended educational and experiential innovations an institution achieves with their use.

---

30 "Virtual Reality Weekend at the British Museum," British Museum, 2015, accessed November 5, 2018, https://www.britishmuseum.org/about_us/news_and_press/press_releases/2015/virtual_reality_weekend.aspx. See also Juno Rae and Lizzie Edwards, *Virtual reality at the British Museum: What is the value of virtual reality environments for learning by children and young people, schools, and families?*, working paper, British Museum, 2016, accessed October 3, 2019, https://mw2016.museumsandtheweb.com/paper/virtual-reality-at-the-british-museum-what-is-the-value-of-virtual-reality-environments-for-learning-by-children-and-young-people-schools-and-families/.

31 Puig et al., "Lessons Learned from Supplementing Archaeological Museum Exhibitions with Virtual Reality."

32 Carrozzio and Bergamasco refer to this as the "Guggenheim effect." See Marcello Carrozzino and Massimo Bergamasco, "Beyond Virtual Museums: Experiencing Immersive Virtual Reality in Real Museums," *Journal of Cultural Heritage* 11.4 (2010): 452–458, https://doi.org/10.1016/j.culher.2010.04.001.

Moving Forward

A 2016 document issued by the Mu.SA (Museum Sector Alliance) project, highlights the emerging 'digital' job profiles that museums seek to fill: Digital Strategy Manager, Digital Collection Curator, Digital Interactive Experience Developer, and Online Community Manager.[33] At the same time, these titles highlight the continuation of the key concerns and ideas that have animated museums and cultural institutions for decades: engaging with publics, crafting narratives, and handling objects. In that sense, the uptake of the strengths and affordances of digital culture in the museum world, expand on institutional missions and recenter the public in museum practices. The technology may not always be the same, but the main concerns discussed in the projects above –building community, sharing content, and redefining experience – are still the driving force as the role of museums as community centers, creators of knowledge, and preservers of cultural heritage is reshaped.

Bibliography

Ding, Mandy. "Augmented Reality in Museums." Report. Arts Management & Technology Laboratory, Carnegie Mellon University. (May 2017), https://web.archive.org/web/20181202183955/https://static1.squarespace.com/static/51d98be2e4b05a25fc200cbc/t/5908d019f5e2314ab790c269/1493749785593/AugmentedRealityinMuseums.pdf.

Falchetti, Elisabetta. "The Cultural Value of Museums in Times of Transition." In *Melting Pro – Museum professionals in the digital era. Agents of change and innovation, Mu.SA Project*, edited by Antonia Salvaggi and Federica Pesce. Melting Pro, Museum Sector Alliance. (October 9, 2017), http://www.project-musa.eu/wp-content/uploads/2017/03/MuSA-Museum-professionals-in-the-digital-era-short-version.pdf.

Giannini, Tula and Bowen, Jonathan P. "Museums and Digitalism." In *Museums and Digital Culture*, edited by Giannini, Tula and Bowen, Jonathan P., 27–46. Cham: Springer, 2019.

Puig, Anna et al. "Lessons Learned from Supplementing Archaeological Museum Exhibitions with Virtual Reality." *Virtual Reality* (2019), https://doi.org/10.1007/s10055-019-00391-z.

Ridge, Mia, ed. *Crowdsourcing Our Cultural Heritage*. London: Routledge, 2017.

Simon, Nina. *The Participatory Museum*. Santa Cruz, CA: Museum 2.0, 2017.

---

33 Falchetti, "The Cultural Value of Museums in Times of Transition."

Pierre Mounier
Open Access: an opportunity to redesign scholarly communication in history

Abstract: While the adoption of open access to academic publications was slower and more difficult in the humanities and in particular in history than in the scientific and technical disciplines, it is today more and more widely accepted by the community of historians. The number of open access peer-reviewed journals is growing, thanks to the support of multidisciplinary platforms and tools, such as OpenEdition, Scielo and OJS. However, many journals still adopt an embargo period to protect the sales of their print edition. Research monographs in history are also more frequently available in open access. It is interesting to see that new academic presses, purely digital and adopting completely open access, such as UCL Press, Ubiquity Press and OBP were created in recent years to address the growing need of researchers in the humanities and social sciences. Finally, in the context of open science, which is larger than open access to publications, new forms of communication are experimented, that combine with open data (e.g. data journals) or with new ways of interacting with society (e.g academic blogs). These more recent explorations in open scholarly communications are promising perspectives for historians, in particular when they are involved in public history.

Keywords: open access, open science, academic blogging, publishing, scholarly communication, digital publishing

Introduction

The term "open access" traditionally refers to "open access to publications," which is different from "open data" – a term that covers open access to machine data, primary sources, and other materials used by the historians in their research work. Both open access and open data belong to the wider "open science" movement that aims at opening research to society at all levels; not only regarding the access to research output, but also the design and achievement of research itself – in that sense open science covers citizen science – and even evaluation: one of the latest offspring of this large movement towards openness being the development of open peer review practices.[1]

The development of open access started almost 30 years ago primarily in the STM (science, technology, medicine) disciplines, and notably in high energy physics

---
[1] T. Ross-Hellauer et al, "Survey on open peer review."

https://doi.org/10.1515/9783110430295-010

with the creation of the ArXiv server in 1991.[2] Two reasons explain why the physicists' community pioneered open access. Firstly, they were the first scientific community except computer scientists to have access to and use intensively computers to compute their data and to communicate their research. The other reason is more significant. Nuclear physicists have a longstanding tradition of immediately sharing their research results. This occurred initially through exchanges of letters, then through photocopied texts sent by postal mail. When their computers were interconnected, it seemed natural to them to use the new means of communication to share the drafts of their papers, named "preprints."[3]

Journals

The move towards open access through the Internet has not been so natural to researchers in the humanities and social sciences, particularly historians, because they have not been accustomed to sharing their preprints with peers. In those disciplines, the movement towards open access is mainly conveyed through digitization of traditional journals or the creation of new digital-born journals. In the former case, open access to full text articles is more difficult to obtain because online dissemination is usually added to print distribution and doesn't replace it. That's why in that case, to protect subscriptions to their print edition, journals open free access to the digital edition of their articles after an embargo period, which is typically quite long. Presently this period is three to five years on Jstor for English speaking journals and up to three years on Cairn for French language ones. The Italian service provider and publisher Casalini Libri opted for a no open access policy on most of their Torrossa platform that disseminate content mostly from Italy and Spain worldwide.

For that reason, a number of historians in different countries have ventured into the creation of full open access journals that are born digital, and often do not have a print edition. The advantages of this approach are counter-balanced by an important number of challenges, such as the technical skills needed, financial sustainability, and acquiring a journal reputation. For a long period, editors of such new journals have been left to achieve their goals without any support from the legacy publishers or from the most senior scholars and institutions. For equally long, open access journals in history have been considered as "bad quality," "non peer-reviewed," "vanity publishing" by a number of scholars in the selection and

---

[2] For full coverage of the open access movement in its different dimensions, see Suber, *Open Access*.
[3] Paul Ginsparg, "First Steps Towards Electronic Research Communication," *Computers in Physics* 8.4 (July 1994): 390–396, https://doi.org/10.1063/1.4823313.

evaluation committees.[4] Thanks to the generalization of open access in all academic disciplines and the momentum this model gained recently at policy level,[5] the situation has changed, even in history.

According to the practices and institutional structures specific to each country, new open access journals in the humanities, and in history in particular, can be supported by university libraries or national infrastructures. In some countries, technical hosting and dissemination services are offered through publicly funded infrastructures. This is the case in France where OpenEdition provides open access platforms for journals and books. As OpenEdition is funded by four higher education and research institutions as well as the Ministry of Research, access to the platforms for scholars editing the journals is free of charge. On OpenEdition, 150 journals in history and archeology are available open access. Croatia is another example of those countries structured around national infrastructures, with the Hrčak platform supported by Zagreb and Zadar universities that offers 80 open access journals.[6] In Latin America, the Scielo platform operates as a transnational infrastructure for journals in Spanish and Portuguese. But those examples are rather exceptions in the academic landscape worldwide. In most cases, technical resources and support for digital open access journals are provided locally through university libraries engaged in dissemination activities. In that case, they often rely on commonly used repositories management software, such as Dspace, or generic CMS, such as Drupal and Wordpress, or, more frequently, on CMS specially developed to manage online academic journals. In this latest case, Open Journal System (OJS), proposed by the Public Knowledge Project, a Canadian consortium based in Vancouver (Simon Fraser University) can be considered as a *de facto* standard.[7] Designed as an easy to install, configure and use software, OJS is widely implemented across the world. Around 8,000 open access journals from all disciplines use OJS,[8] though no figures are available concerning history journals more specifically. In Italy for example, the important public humanities and public history journal *Il Capitale Culturale. Studies on the value of cultural heritage* uses OJS.[9]

OJS and other similar publishing platforms should be considered as a major help for public history because they enable small and local institutions and scholarly as well as professional societies, closely connected to their community, to set up, develop

---

[4] David Nicholas et al, "Peer review: still king in the digital age," *Learned Publishing* 28.1 (January 2015): 15–21, https://doi.org/10.1087/20150104.
[5] Ministerie van Onderwijs, Cultuur en Wetenschap, "Amsterdam Call for Action on Open Science – Report – Government.nl," *Report*, April 4, 2016, https://www.government.nl/documents/reports/2016/04/04/amsterdam-call-for-action-on-open-science.
[6] Hrčak Platform, https://hrcak.srce.hr/.
[7] Brian Owen and Kevin Stranack, "The Public Knowledge Project and Open Journal Systems: Open Source Options for Small Publishers," *Learned Publishing* 25.2 (2012): 138–144, https://doi.org/10.1087/20120208.
[8] https://pkp.sfu.ca/ojs/ojs-usage/ojs-stats/.
[9] https://riviste.unimc.it/index.php/cap-cult.

and provide visibility for their journals at low cost. Remarkable examples exist: The Department of History, Faculty of Humanities, Diponegoro University, Central Java, publishes *Citra Lekha*,[10] an open access journal on Indonesian history with all the technical functionalities expected from an academic publication (Digital Object Identifiers, public statistics, formal peer review process management). The African Journals Online portal hosts three African journals in history, such as the *Lagos Historical Review*,[11] published by the Department of History of the University of Lagos. The library of York University in Toronto, Canada, hosts a portal dedicated to open access journals giving access to several highly specialized journals, such as *Historical papers: Canadian Society of Church History*.[12] OpenEdition hosts several community-based journals such as the *Revue d'Histoire des Chemins de Fer*,[13] published by the french Society for the history of railroads, or *Témoigner / Getuigen*,[14] by the Auschwitz Foundation. Other highly inspiring journals could be mentioned from different languages, countries, communities as well.

Books

If open access journals in history and public history are usually supported by university departments and scholarly societies, academic book publishing requires more resources and higher professional skills to be sustainable and to guarantee a minimal quality level. That's why the movement towards open access book publishing currently relies on university presses. In most cases, commercial publishers have yet to take this path, primarily because the business model is unsure for them. Recent surveys in Europe,[15] UK,[16] and North America,[17] have provided evidence that many university presses in those areas are currently experimenting with open access

---

[10] "Journal Sejarah Citra Lekha," accessed March 18, 2018, https://ejournal.undip.ac.id/index.php/jscl.
[11] "Lagos Historical Review," accessed March 18, 2018, https://www.ajol.info/index.php/lhr/index.
[12] "Historical Papers," *Canadian Society of Church History / Société Canadienne d'histoire de l'église*, October 22, 2010, https://csch-sche.ca/historical-papers/.
[13] "Revue d'histoire des chemins de fer," accessed March 18, 2018, http://journals.openedition.org/rhcf.
[14] "Témoigner. Entre histoire et mémoire – Revue pluridisciplinaire de la Fondation Auschwitz," accessed March 18, 2018, http://journals.openedition.org/temoigner.
[15] Ferwerda et al, "A Landscape Study on Open Access and Monographs," https://doi.org/10.5281/zenodo.815932.
[16] Geoffrey Crossick, "Monographs and Open Access, A Report to HEFCE." *HEFCE*, January 1, 2015, http://www.hefce.ac.uk/media/hefce/content/pubs/indirreports/2015/Monographs,and,open,access/2014_monographs.pdf.
[17] Michael A. Elliott, "The Future of The Monograph in the Digital Era: A Report to the Andrew W. Mellon Foundation," *Journal of Electronic Publishing* 18.4 (December 17, 2015), https://doi.org/10.3998/3336451.0018.407.

programs on at least one of their book series. As the monograph is a major format of publication in the humanities, it is not surprising that books in history are part of such programs. Oapen and OpenEdition Books platforms, two of the largest open access books platforms in the humanities and social sciences, give free access to 1,000 and 1,800 books in history, respectively. Contrary to journals, where new purely digital open access journals are far more numerous than traditional ones, most open access books also have a print edition. Several reasons explain this. First, technically, books offer fewer affordances than journals, particularly in the case of monographs. Whereas downloading and reading an article on a screen is pretty easy, the same cannot be said of a full book, particularly research monographs rather than edited books. Journals can be divided into small parts of texts, which is not the case with monographs. Therefore, for a continuous reading from the first to the last page of a book, most readers still need print editions. Nonetheless, digital editions have their own advantages, particularly for scholarly usage, such as searching, copy-pasting to cite, extracting data from the full content. As long as reading devices do not perform as well as print to support continuous reading, publishers will have to provide print editions alongside the digital open access ones.[18] That prevents publishers from reconfiguring their production workflow and explains why most digital editions are simply pdf files rather than other formats such as epub, which are adapted more to reading on screen but which are also both more complex to produce and require additional work from the publisher.

On the other hand, while open access business models are difficult to establish for journals because authors are not used to paying "article processing charges" in the humanities, the situation is quite different for monographs, as paying "book processing charges" (to cover editing costs) on research funding has been a common practice from the start of the print age. Therefore, the transition to open access seems paradoxically easier in some cases, as the BPC can now cover open access dissemination. Other business models are based on different funding schemes. For example, partnerships between libraries and/or research funding agencies are being developed: Knowledge Unlatched and OpenEdition Freemium programs are good examples. Surprisingly, the open access book sector, though less developed than that for journals, seems to be more creative under that perspective.

During the last few years, a number of new initiatives have emerged, particularly in the USA and the UK, two of the most innovative countries so far in that domain. Sometimes called "New University Presses" (NUP) and "Scholarly-led Presses" (SLP),[19]

---

[18] Terje Hillesund, "Digital Reading Spaces: How Expert Readers Handle Books, the Web and Electronic Paper," *First Monday* 15.4 (April 11, 2010), http://uncommonculture.org/ojs/index.php/fm/article/view/2762.
[19] Graham Stone and Janneke Adema, "Changing Publishing Ecologies. A Landscape Study of New University Presses and Academic-Led Publishing," *JISC*, July 1, 2017, http://repository.jisc.ac.uk/6666/1/Changing-publishing-ecologies-report.pdf.

new academic publishers started to publish open access research monographs and edited books relying on digital first workflows. In such cases, content is edited and structured primarily for digital formats, and print editions are usually provided but as secondary products by subcontracting to "print on demand" service providers. In the UK, Ubiquity Press, Open Book Publishers, and UCL Press are good illustrations of that situation. In the USA, the University of California Press is leading the sector with its dedicated imprint Luminos. Publishers in both countries have published several books in history amongst other social sciences and humanities disciplines. The other main advantage of these new initiatives is that they disseminate content in multiple formats, rather than pdf only. HTML and epub formats are the most common. In these cases, the book takes advantage of a better integration in the open web environment to increase visibility and usage. The content is more easily accessed, indexed and cited, particularly in social media. More generally, a recent report from Springer Nature showed that open access books are accessed, used and cited far more than traditional ones.[20]

The combination of open access dissemination with the integration of web formats and the reconfiguration of publishers' production workflows opens new and promising perspectives to the academic book in history and other disciplines in the humanities. Open annotation is one of them. This is a feature that – like open peer review – supports public history practices with book contents and has often been used for Digital Humanities books, for example. In that domain Hypothes.is, a company based in San Francisco, USA, took the lead with its Annotating All Knowledge initiative. This project gathers around 60 academic publishers and other digital publishing service providers to implement open annotation features on top of open access books and other types of academic content. Several experimental programs currently exist that explore how readers can be engaged with the content through annotation, public sharing of annotations and the building of open conversations through them. The perspective that annotation could open for public history is easy to understand, though it is probably too early to present many real examples so far.

Open Scholarly Communication

The development of the open web has also loosened the stronghold that traditional formats of publications – journals and books – have had on the way research results are communicated. Two different directions deserve mention: data publication and academic blogging. Regarding the former, the current development

---

[20] Christina Emery, Mithu Lucraft, Agata Morka, and Ros Pyne, "The OA Effect: How Does Open Access Affect the Usage of Scholarly Books?" *White paper. Springer Nature* (November 1, 2017), https://resource-cms.springernature.com/springer-cms/rest/v1/content/15176744/data/v3.

of open data, which is presented in another chapter, allows scholars to imagine new ways of calling up the primary sources on which the academic discourse is built and then embedding such materials inside the publication itself. This possibility, of giving direct access to the data used by the author of an article or a book, constitutes a major change for readers and an important improvement regarding the quality of academic publications in the humanities.[21] It gives to the reader the ability to better verify the soundness of an argument and to contest the way the primary sources were interpreted. In disciplines such as geography, anthropology, history, the possibility to include multimedia materials, such as high-resolution images, audio recordings, interactive maps, videos in an article or a book, to deliver what is sometimes named "enhanced editions," considerably enriches the argument and at the same time gives more latitude to the reader to develop his or her own perspective on the scholarship.

Sometimes, data are the main object of publications. The so-called "data journals" that appeared several years ago in science are not unheard of in the humanities. In archeology for example, Ubiquity Press hosts the *Open Archeological Data Journal*[22] that publishes data papers which do not contain research results, but rather a concise description of a dataset and where to find it. According to the journal,

> a data paper is a publication that is designed to make other researchers aware of data that is of potential use to them. As such it describes the methods used to create the dataset, its structure, its reuse potential, and a link to its location in a repository. It is important to note that a data paper does not replace a research article, but rather complements it. When mentioning the data behind a study, a research paper should reference the data paper for further details. The data paper similarly should contain references to any research papers associated with the dataset. Any kind of archaeological data is acceptable, including for example: geophysical data; quantitative or qualitative data; images; notebooks; excavation data, software, etc.

The important point here is that data papers are peer-reviewed exactly like standard articles.

Finally, it would be interesting to keep an eye in the future on how historians engage in new forms of open scholarly communication that are substantially different from the journal article or the book.[23] Academic blogging is probably one of the most interesting examples.[24] The flexibility of the blog as an editorial form makes it a convenient tool for researchers to communicate about their different research activities: fieldwork, but also seminars, research projects, bibliographical work and,

---

21 Stefan Buddenbohm et al, "State of the Art Report on Open Access Publishing of Research Data in the Humanities," *Report. DARIAH* (August 12, 2016), https://halshs.archives-ouvertes.fr/halshs-01357208/document.
22 https://openarchaeologydata.metajnl.com/.
23 Serge Noiret, "La digital history: histoire et mémoire à la portée de tous," in *Read/Write Book 2: Une introduction aux humanités numériques*, ed. Pierre Mounier (Read/Write Book. Marseille: OpenEdition Press, 2012), 151–177, http://books.openedition.org/oep/258.
24 Peter Haber and Eva Pfanzelter, *Historyblogosphere*.

of course, teaching. The main important difference between the blog and the traditional publication formats is that blogging allows for a continuous flow of communication during the research itself, and not only after it has been conducted, as with peer-reviewed articles and monographs. It allows for an on-going engagement with the readers through commenting. It allows for an informal presentation of archives, materials, readings, conversations, thoughts, hypotheses, drafts, all sort of news, and, of course, rants and potential mistakes that can be discussed, contested, and enhanced by readers through comments. The other important difference between blogs and articles is that blogs are not peer-reviewed. They allow researchers to communicate openly and directly with their readers who can be their colleagues and peers, but also a non-academic audience. Here again, provided the specificities of that means of communication are well understood by the different parties, blogs can be a powerful tool for the public historian to engage with a local or specialized community thanks to its conversational mode of communication. A famous example in France is how a team of prehistorians working on a cave in the south of France used their blog to engage with the local villages around the site for whom that cave was an important part of their cultural heritage.[25] The advantage of the blog here is not only that communication is continuous and simultaneous with the fieldwork itself, but also that an accessible discourse can be published without the academic jargon that usually prevents non-academic readers from benefitting from canonical publications.

Blogs can be collective as well as individual. In some cases, they can help emerging communities create a dynamic and structure themselves towards more institutional forms. Thus, they can support scholarly networks of researchers, academic and non-academic, by providing them with a lightweight and easy common place where they can exchange information, become visible and attract new members across institutional and cultural boundaries.

With more than 2,600 academic blogs in the humanities and social sciences, the Hypotheses.org platform is the most important community of academic bloggers. Around 1,000 history blogs are hosted on the platform which makes that discipline the most important one. Among them, several blogs deal more specifically with public history: Digital and Public History is the personal blog of Serge Noiret;[26] the Italian association of public history,[27] as well as the International Association of Public History,[28] have their own blogs on the Hypotheses platform.

---

[25] "Le blog de la grotte des Fraux | Site d'étude en écologie globale de l'INEE," accessed March 18, 2018, https://champslibres.hypotheses.org/.
[26] "Digital & Public History – @sergenoiret," accessed March 18, 2018, https://dph.hypotheses.org/.
[27] "AIPH – Associazione Italiana di Public History," accessed March 18, 2018, https://aiph.hypotheses.org/.
[28] "IFPH-FIHP – The International Federation for Public History Blog Promotes International Debates between Public Historians and Informs about the Activities of the IFPH-FIHP," accessed March 18, 2018, https://ifph.hypotheses.org/.

In a context where the public use of history remains intense alongside different ideological options, historians still need to engage outside their traditional academic audience to contribute to the public debate.[29] With the development of the web and social media, an important part of the public debate takes place in different online and open agora. Open access to history publications whatever the format, highly controlled and traditional as in articles and research monographs or more conversational and flexible as in blogs, is of the utmost importance and henceforth feasible in good conditions for all historians who want to take part in a larger movement towards open science.

Bibliography

Ferwerda, Eelco, Frances Pinter, and Niels Stern. "A Landscape Study on Open Access and Monographs: Policies, Funding and Publishing in Eight European Countries." Zenodo, August 1, 2017. https://doi.org/10.5281/zenodo.815932.

Haber, Peter, and Eva Pfanzelter. *Historyblogosphere, Bloggen in den Geschichtswissenschaften*. Berlin, Boston: De Gruyter, 2013. https://doi.org/10.1524/9783486755732.

Ross-Hellauer, T, A. Deppe, and B. Schmidt. "Survey on open peer review: Attitudes and experience amongst editors, authors and reviewers." *PLoS ONE* 12.12 (2017): e0189311. https://doi.org/10.1371/journal.pone.0189311

Suber, Peter. *Open Access*. Cambridge, Mass.: MIT Press, 2012.

---

[29] Serge Noiret, "Public History: A Necessity in Today's European Union?" *Public History Weekly* 5 (2017): 1–29, https://doi.org/10.1515/phw-2017-10113.

Marcello Ravveduto
Past and Present in Digital Public History

Abstract: The author examines the relationship between past and present to reflect on the perception of time in the era of the digital revolution. The time of digital presentism is not linear but circular. The arrival point coincides with the starting point: from present to present. A loop faster and faster which changed the perception of time for at least two generations of digital natives. The author uses Facebook as a case study to investigate the origin of the interreal (set of real and virtual) that restructured the relationship between past and present. In the social network, their link is no longer entrusted to the scientific rigor of history but to the disintermediated emotions of a ubiquitous memory which generates a wave of collective nostalgia.

Keywords: time, past, present, memory, interreality, metatechnology, facebook, public

Since ancient times, the relationship between the present and the past has been seen in terms of the *laudatio temporis acti*. Lucio Anneo Seneca idealizes the past, not without nostalgia, to exhort the Romans to react to the degradation of the present and move towards the future, recognizing, however, in the flow of time "the progressive maturation of a moral conscience."[1] Many centuries later Walter Benjamin in thesis IX, "On the Concept of History," emblematically depicts the past-present-future continuum through the interpretation of Paul Klee's *Angelus Novus*.[2] The angel turns his back on the future while directing his gaze to the past, the features of which are those of the catastrophe. An image suspended in a static present due to the juxtaposition of equal and opposite forces unleashed by the rubble of the past, and the inability to see the future. Billè argues:

> Making the past present means reactivating it to save it in memory; it is possible, therefore, to revive what has been, in the completely new moment of the present. [. . .] the angel portrays the horror of historical time through the expression of his face (an open mouth and eyes wide open in amazement and terror) and wings outstretched ready to take flight. He turns his back on the future and looks the past in the face: [. . .] instead of a chain of events that happen from the past to the present (and that are accumulated in cultural heritage), the angel sees the catastrophe, the ruins, the rubble of history.[3]

---

[1] François-Régis Chaumartin, "Sénèque lecteur de Posidonius," *REL* 66 (1988): 21–28; Enea Bertoli, "L"età dell"oro in Posidonio e Seneca", *QLLV* 7 (1982): 151–179.
[2] Walter Benjamin, *Angelus Novus. Saggi e frammenti* (Torino: Einaudi, 1962), 80.
[3] Giovanni Coppolino Billè, "L'immagine dialettica. Lettura delle tesi Sul concetto di storia di Walter Benjamin", *Dialegesthai* (2014): accessed November 3, 2018, https://bit.ly/2AlXnlb.

In our present, the "rebel" allegory of the German philosopher, the fruit of his anguished contemporary reality, seems to announce the prophecy of Günther Anders, and Francois Hartog's theory of the regimes of historicity.[4]

The West of the third millennium, having passed through the eras of pastism and modernism, today is living in the era of presentism: a dilated and one-dimensional present that chases after itself and sets in motion a series of mechanisms of sterile self-reproduction. Linear time has warped, giving rise to a circular time that is broken up into a sequence of repeated moments. Hartog writes: "Evoking an omnipresent present in no way exempts us from exploring ways out of it but quite the contrary: in a world in which presentism reigns supreme, the historian's place is more than ever 'vigilantly watch over the present [les guetteurs du présent],' in Charles Péguy's words."[5] Following the track marked by the French historian in the era of the digital revolution, we could compare presentism to a temporal loop in which the curvature of time constantly returns to the starting point: from present to present. Western man does not run towards the future, starting from the pedestal of the past, but runs after the present, anxious at not being able to grasp it while it is going around. We are reminded of the words of Seneca who in "The Shortness of Life" writes: "Present time is very short, so much so that to some it seems to be no time at all; for it is always in motion, and runs swiftly away [. . .]. Busy men, therefore, possess present time alone, that being so short that they cannot grasp it."[6]

The idea of circular time has even taken over the imaginary world. The film "Arrival" (2016) by Denis Villeneuve takes on board the theory of Edward Sapir and Benjamin Lee Whorf, according to which the language that we speak is determined by the organization of our mental processes and hence it conditions the way in which we perceive the world. The Indo-European languages have a form of writing that has a progressive, linear flow, moving from left to right. This means that thought takes on form by scanning a before and then an after. Everything we see, observe and experience is greatly influenced by the cognitive linguistic development that determines the prevailing interpretation.[7] The Chinese, for example, read

---

4 Günther Anders, *Die Antiquiertheit des Menschen*, Band II: *Über die Zerstörung des Lebens im Zeitalter der dritten industriellen Revolution* (Munich: Beck, 1980); "[. . .] [I]n the fear of change, the future flattens into the miserable repetition of the identical. Thus the present continues in its duty, with constant events that leave no space for the advent of the new and, bending back on itself, it closes in towards the past, completing the vicious circle"; accessed March 31, 2017, https://bit.ly/2VbdsTs; François Hartog, *Regimes of Historicity. Presentism and Experiences of Time* (New York: Columbia University Press, 2015).

5 Hartog, *Regimes of Historicity*, XVII.

6 Lucius Annaeus Seneca, *Minor dialogues. Together with the dialogue on Clemency* (London: George Bell and Sons, 1889) ed. Carlo Carena. Torino: Einaudi, 2013, p. 303. In Giuseppe De Rita and Antonio Galdo, *Prigionieri del presente. Come uscire dalla trappola della modernità*, (Torino: Einaudi, 2018), 4.

7 Edward Sapir *Selected Writings of Edward Sapir in Language, Culture, and Personality*, ed. David G. Mandelbaum (Oakland: University of California Press, 1985); Benjamin L. Whorf, *Language,*

from top to bottom and depict the succession of hours and days in the same way. This could mean that the linear nature of time, past-present-future, is conditioned by linguistic metaphysics. In the film, in fact, the protagonist verifies this theory by learning the language of the aliens, the Heptapods, who write in a circular manner without a progressive flow and without a specific reading order. Imagine writing a sentence with two hands, starting from both directions, already knowing what to write and the space to take up.

Such a language allows us to perceive time in a circular manner: past and future are the same as the present; everything exists contemporaneously in the mind of the linguist Louise Banks – played by Amy Adams. The protagonist experiences time no longer as linear, but as an entirety from where one can look either from right to left or vice versa: that which has been and that which is to come, co-exist. Louise sees the future as if it were a memory that she uses in the present. This paradox, together with the sequence in which the "memory of the future" appears with the semblance of a memory, is narrowed down until it comes together in a single point, which is the eternal present. Here once again, the loop of presentism reappears, in this case in the form of science fiction.

Let's pause a moment to consider the centrality of language. The spread of mobile phones and the immense use of text messages has transformed communication. First SMSs, then instant messaging Apps, have converted language into a type of "written spoken word," characterized by a lack of syntax and often a lack of grammar:[8] "[T]ext messages have specific linguistic forms that aim to compensate for the lack of communicative, gestural, mirroring and proxemic codes."[9] This new means of expression, which is fast and virtual, is an integral part of a specific "metatechnology,"[10] i.e. the practice that allows us to assimilate the individual and social use of a new technology. An original approach that signals a break with the past: technology transfer, in fact, is the sharing in the present of an innovation that becomes customary within a relational context; those who do not participate risk falling into the chasm of the "digital divide," a vacuum in which technology loses its meaning and becomes a problem rather than an opportunity.

A historian cannot fail to see, therefore, that the digital revolution is the result of a progression that began with the transition from the spoken word to writing, from writing to printing, from printing to industry, from industry to the means of mass communication. Changes in phases that have involved learning a new language through the absorption of technology. But whilst in the past this process could take a

---

Thought, and Reality: Selected Writings of Benjamin Lee Whorf, ed. John Carroll (Cambridge, MA: MIT Press, 2012).
8 Giuseppe Mininni, ed., *Virtuale.com. La parola spezzata*, (Napoli: Idelson-Gnocchi, 2002).
9 Giuseppe Riva, *Psicologia dei nuovi media. Azione, presenza, identità e relazioni nei media digitali e nei social media* (Bologna: Il Mulino, 2012).
10 Robert Wright, *Non-Zero: The Logic of Human Destiny* (New York: Pantheon, 2000).

long time, in today's digital world, time is compressed and accelerated. The domination of digital media in less than 20 years has imposed a new vision of the world. An example of this? In 2006 the five largest companies in the world were Exxon Mobil, General Electric, Microsoft, City Group and the Bank of America. Hence oil, manufacturing and finance, with the sole presence of one IT company. In 2017, the ranking of the Big Five based on stock market value, has changed its physiognomy: Apple, Google, Microsoft, Amazon and Facebook.[11] Digital has won the global industrial revolution. In fact, globalization itself is characterized by its evolutionary stages to such an extent that, since the beginning of the spread of the Internet, we can already identify four generations of digital natives: the text generation (using the text interface), that includes people born in the mid-1970s; the web generation (users of the Internet interface) referring to those born in the mid-1980s; the social media generation (web 2.0 interface users), that includes those born in the mid-1990s and the touch generation (touch interface users) – those born in the mid-2000s.[12]

These are the generations that, thanks to "metatechnology," on one hand have acquired the ability to use digital media intuitively, and on the other have learned to adapt to the virtual reality. After all, the relationship between man and the means is two-directional: man overcomes the constraints of his external environment through media but modifies his behavior through the use that he makes of it.[13] It is through the individual and social practice of the digital sphere, in terms of experience and meaning, that the fusion between the real world (offline) and the virtual world (online) is generated, giving rise to a spatial-temporal zone called "interreality":[14] an environment in which to live, an extension of the human mind, a mixture of algorithms and interfaces that intertwine with what is real, conditioning everyday life. One example of the influence of reality on digital world could be the link that exists between the icons of old and new media: the WhatsApp icon depicts the receiver of a telephone, and the Instagram logo is an analogue camera. Likewise, email services are identified through the symbol of an envelope, whilst the universal digital icon for "save" is the image of a floppy disc.[15] In this case, the relationship between the past and the present, in the exchange between material objects and immaterial symbols, appears in the self-referential circuit of mass media. On the other hand, one example of the influence of the digital on the real world is

---

[11] Galdo and De Rita, *Prigionieri del presente*, 20.
[12] Giuseppe Riva, *Nativi digitali. Crescere e apprendere nel mondo dei nuovi media* (Bologna: Il Mulino, 2014).
[13] Lev Semënovič Vygotskij, *Pensiero e linguaggio* (Firenze: Giunti, 2007).
[14] Jacob Van Kokswijk, *Hum@n, Telecoms, & Internet as Interface to Interreality* (Hoogwoud: Bergboek, 2003).
[15] Gabriele Balbi, "Ancora tu! L'emersione e la rilevanza della storia dei media nella vita quotidiana," *Mediascapes Journal* 8 (2017): 19.

tagging in social networks, that, linked to the sharing of compromising images, video or text, can alter the public image of the user in real life.

This reciprocal influence, however, not only affects symbolic aspects or the use we make of them. Transferring a part of one's own existence into the virtual world means accepting its rules of engagement. When we access a social network, we find ourselves in front of a wall that is being constantly updated. After an hour, a post is no longer visible, pushed out by the thousands of other posts that have turned it into a "past" event. But, if after one hour a piece of news is already considered as past and the future is still to come, we are faced with a time that is "always present." Digital time is an indefinite present, without breaks, in that it leaves a trace that is hard to erase from the Internet, so we seem to be always inside it, watching, intervening and participating in something. It is the paralysis of the present time: every "footprint" we leave seems to be put under glass, kept far away from the incessant flow of everyday life, between its progression and regression, and hence transformed into an instant that is static and forever there, in front of our eyes on computer screens.[16]

At the same time, beneath the surface of the fleeting present, the traces left by the information conceal a darkly static and stagnant past, that is always ready to resurface, preventing it from being filed away forever.[17] As Viktor Mayer-Schönberger observes, human beings "can no longer successfully run away from their past. That past follows them, ready to be tapped into by anyone with an Internet connection."[18] "Interreality" is causing the cognitive restructuring of the relationship between past and present: in a context which cultivates the moment of the click of a mouse, in which the need for information is satisfied in real time, following a subjective strategy of confirming one's own truth, there is no room for doubts or the unexpected, or even the time to research anything in more depth. Social networks reduce knowledge to a sum of disintermediate, emotional opinions that prevent critical thinking from arising. The result of this is that the link between the past and the present is no longer delegated to historical research, whose scientific rigor in the reconstruction of facts is too slow in comparison to the speed of the digital present. Its place has been taken by memory, the immediate use of which lends itself to the emotional experience of the interconnected public.[19] But what is the memory circulated by social networks?

If we analyze the posts published in Facebook groups, we will find a collective narrative based on the imagination of memory as the lowest common denominator. Users / witnesses share personal or family memories through the publication of photos,

---

16 Davide Sisto, "Digital Death. Una morte postumana?," *Lo Sguardo* 24 (2017): 160.
17 Davide Sisto, "Digital Death. Le trasformazioni digitali della morte e del lutto," *Lessico di etica pubblica* 1 (2018).
18 Viktor Mayer-Schönberger, *Delete. Il diritto all'oblio nell'era digitale* (Milano: Egea, 2010), 90.
19 Danah Boyd, "Taken Out of Context. American Teen Sociality in Networked Publics" (PhD diss., University of California-Berkeley, 2008), accessed November 23, 2018, https://bit.ly/2Q8SlO4.

videos or digitized objects to consolidate their identity and reread their experiences. An editing of the past, without distinction of sources or historical contextualization, which is presented as an opportunity to integrate, and often contrast, the small stories of the local communities with the official narratives of professional historians.[20]

A private and individualistic memory, that, becoming public, generates a wave of collective nostalgia. A nostalgia stimulated by the automatism of algorithms, such as that of the "Memories" function in Facebook (previously called "It happened today") that republishes photos from a recent past, the digital archiving of which was determined by the choices of the user in the moment in which they decided to share the images of their daily life on the social network. Hence, as a form of an external support to the human memory, Facebook revives memories virtually: a precise moment (day, time, place) that is (if we want) shared with and visible to a public who were unaware of it, but who now can participate (if they want) in the commemoration of an individual past event, that has become, in the moment in which it is shared, a fleeting social present.

Digital presentism crushes the temporal depth of history under the weight of the sharing of personal memories, opening up the path to pastism – in other words an unjustified attachment to the ideas, customs and traditions of the past; a conservative behaviour that always interprets the "after" as inferior to the "before."[21] The union of presentism and pastism provokes a true escape from time that seems to confirm the last hypothesis of Bauman: that we live in the era of "retrotopia," an inverted utopia, that manifests itself through the approach of placing our image of a better reality than that which we have now in the past rather than in the future.[22] This temporal misperception of the "interreality" dimension, characterizes the past through the lens of the imagination, building a perfect world that is now lost.

Hence in the memorial groups on social networks, it is not the memory of the event that is safeguarded, but an individual narrative that is shared and that fuels the imagination of the memory, on the one hand transferring an idealized past into the present, and on the other hand eluding the linear progression of time. It is no coincidence, therefore, that in the last 30 years the theme of time travel has won a significant place in the collective imagination of science fiction in the cinema and on television. Dozens of films and TV series have a time traveller as their main character who returns from the future to the present – which is our present – to adjust the things that are not working and give a new direction to the future, twisting the flow of time.

The archiving nature of the Internet, alongside the obsessive search for the fleeting moment, is changing the perception of the past and the present so profoundly that it is calling into question the social and cultural repression of death. The web is

---

[20] Stefania Gallini and Serge Noiret, "La historia digital en la era del Web 2.0. Introducción al dossier Historia digital," *Historia Crítica* 43 (2011): 31–32.
[21] Livia Romano, "La ricerca storica in educazione tra passato e futuro," *SPES* 7 (2018): 166.
[22] Zygmunt Bauman, *Retrotopia* (Cambridge: Polity Press, 2017).

constantly populated by the shadows of the dead, who replicate themselves through words and images. The digital media have built an environment in which it is possible to establish a reciprocal communication between those who are alive and those who are dead, to such an extent that an interface has been designed – the griefbot – that allows the dead to reply automatically to those who are alive. This means we can continue to talk to our loved ones, thanks to a software that automatically elaborates the response to the questions of those who are alive by reproducing the communicative style adopted on the social media, "imagining" the likely responses that the person would have given had they still been alive. The digital survival of the person who has died, within the virtual correlation between the instantaneous nature of the present moment and the insuperability of the past, demonstrates how digital technology is interfering with the traditional dichotomy of life and death. Every time that a unique, and unrepeatable biological life finishes, their parallel digital life continues to be operative in numerous forms and for an incalculable length of time. Suffice to think that on Facebook, there are approximately 50 million users who are dead, and recent studies predict that by the end of this century – obviously if this popular social network is still running – there will be a higher number of users who are dead than those who are alive (as happens in the real world). In other words, Facebook is, already today, the biggest cemetery in the world, accessible from anywhere that has Wi-Fi or a data connection and indifferently to the different beliefs of its users. It is an awareness of this fact that pushed the giant of Menlo Park to invent the "heir contract," in order to decide on the management of one's own profile post mortem.[23]

The cancellation of death supports the theory of the escape from time that is ultimately fuelled by the culture of narcissism, exalted by the individualistic use of social networks. The digital narcissist, closed in their nostalgic present, is no longer able to perceive the sense of history or imagine the future. Their life is a constant flow of isolated moments, dominated by fleeting and instinctive moods, in which the passion for new things and the obsession to relate all existing things back to their own ego, prevails. A cognitive loop that mutes their relationship with history: living for oneself means breaking the sense of historical continuity, the sense of belonging to a succession of generations that has its roots in the past and is projected into the future. This loss of historical time dissolves any sense of posterity, inducing them not to safeguard the inheritance of their ancestors, nor to conserve any legacy for their descendants.[24]

One answer to the temporal misperception of "interreality" is, in my view, Digital Public History – understood as the "metatechnology" of history in the virtual

---

23 Sisto, "Digital Death," 52–58.
24 Christopher Lasch, *The Culture of Narcissism. American Life in an Age of Diminishing Expectations* (New York: W. W. Norton & Company, 1979); Vincenzo Cesareo, Italo Vaccarini, *L'era del narcisismo* (Milano: Franco Angeli, 2012); Giovanni Orsina, *La democrazia del narcisismo. Breve storia dell'antipolitica* (Venezia: Marsilio, 2018).

context. An activity involving the re-intermediation of historical knowledge that can restore depth to the relationship between the past and the present. A bridge between the real and digital worlds founded on the active role of a new professional figure: the historical influencer, whose task will be, through debunking, to create narratives and content that is appropriate for the "interconnected public." In short, the historical influencer is a public historian who intermediates in first person with the presence of the past on the Internet, reacting to the emotional dominion of the memory with the critical thinking of scientific method.[25] This, in all likelihood, will be the social mission of the historian in the twenty-first century.

Bibliography

De Rita, Giuseppe, and Antonio Galdo, *Prigionieri del presente. Come uscire dalla trappola della modernità*. Torino: Einaudi, 2018.

Floridi, Luciano, *The Fourth Revolution. How the Infosphere is Reshaping Human Reality*. Northamptonshire: Oxford University Press, 2014.

Goldsmith, Kenneth, *Wasting Time on the Internet*. New York: Harper Perennial, 2016.

Gumbrecht, Hans Ulrich, *Unsere Breite Gegenwart*. Berlin: Suhrkamp Verlag, 2010.

Hartog, François, *Regimes of Historicity. Presentism and Experiences of Time*. New York: Columbia University Press, 2015.

---

[25] Serge Noiret, "Digital Public History," in *A Companion to Public History*, ed. David Dean (Malden: John Wiley & Sons Ltd, 2018), 111–124.

Andreas Fickers
Digital Hermeneutics: The Reflexive Turn in Digital Public History?

Abstract: The digital – be it in forms of data, infrastructures, or tools – interferes at all levels in the practice of doing public history. This chapter argues that digital public historians have to reflect more deeply on the epistemological consequences of their digital practices. It proposes the concept of "digital hermeneutics" as a conceptual framework for this reflection. As a "hermeneutics of in-betweenness," digital hermeneutics investigates the trading zone of digital public history where new digital methods and approaches meet disciplinary traditions and epistemic cultures of history.

Keywords: digital hermeneutics, historical data criticism, participatory design, ethics of algorithms

Introduction

In 1931, the outgoing President of the American Historical Association (AHA), Carl L. Becker, delivered his Presidential address at Minneapolis entitled "Everyman His Own Historian." In his provocative speech, Becker challenged the community of professional historians by arguing that history – when reduced to its basic terms – is the memory of things said and done, and that everyone, both the professional historian and "Mr Everyman," fuse personal memories and facts of the past in an act of imaginative creation. "The appropriate trick for any age is not a malicious invention designed to take anyone in, but an unconscious and necessary effort on the part of 'society' to understand what it is doing in the light of what it has done and what it hopes to do."[1]

More than eight decades later, another outgoing President, this time of the Organization of American Historians (OAH), revisited Becker's theses in the light of the digital condition. In "Everyone Their Own Historian," Ed Ayers – undoubtedly one of the pioneers of digital public history – stresses that the digital turn has morphed our private histories and the "artificial memories that constitute history" even more completely and to such a degree that boundaries between them blur and disappear as everyone has become their own historian, their own curator and archivist and

---

[1] The lecture, which was published in the *American Historical Review* 37.2 (1932): 221–236, can be accessed at the homepage of the American Historical Association: https://www.historians.org/about-aha-and-membership/aha-history-and-archives/presidential-addresses/carl-l-becker.

narrator.² Ayers celebrates "multiplicity in the forms of history because of our common bias of accountability to the historical record" and, just like Becker, concludes his address with a strong plea for civic engagement of historians: "Our profession will flourish by collaborating with everyone respectful of that evidence, with every teacher, every writer, every blogger, every podcaster, every filmmaker, every archivist, every interpreter of public history, by being an ally for everyone who explores American history for the greater good."³

Despite the considerable temporal distance between the two events, both speeches share a strong pathos and basically fight for the same cause: they emphatically call on the responsibility of historians as public actors based on their personal experiences and critical witnesses of their own times. Doing history, whether as professional, public or private historian, means critical engagement with both the past and the present – and whatever means used for reaching that goal are fine. Seen in that light, it would be tempting to identify the Internet and digital technologies as exactly the "malicious invention" mentioned by Becker and to interpret the digital condition of today's historical practice as "trick of our age."

Yet the aim of this chapter is to reflect on both the possibilities and limitations, the great potential and the risks that the digital offers to public historians in a time characterized by pragmatic hybridity. Instead of sketching the present state of hybridity as a bipolar discourse of hopes and fears, preachers of technological solutionism on the one side and digital luddites on the other – so typical of moments of disruptive innovation⁴ – this chapter tries to reflect on the heuristic potential, epistemological consequences, and ethical implications of digital approaches in public history in the light of digital hermeneutics.

Digital Hermeneutics: Hybrid Practices and Heuristics of In-Betweenness

Digital hermeneutics can be defined as a set of skills and competences that allow historians to critically reflect on the various interventions of digital research infrastructures, tools, databases and dissemination platforms in the process of thinking, doing

---

2 Edward L. Ayers, "Everyone Their Own Historian." *Journal of American History* 105.3 (2018): 505–513.
3 Edward L. Ayers, "Everyone Their Own Historian." *Journal of American History* 105.3 (2018): 511 and 513.
4 Sturken, Marita, Douglas Thomas, and Sandra Ball-Rokeach, eds. *Technological Visions. The Hopes and Fears that Shape New Technologies* (Philadelphia: Temple University Press, 2004).

and narrating history.⁵ Nowadays, all stages of realizing a public history project are to a lesser or stronger degree shaped by the use of digital infrastructures and tools. Be it browsing on the Internet, taking notes on an interview on a laptop, capturing digital photographs in archives or museum collections, the recording of an oral testimony on the mobile phone, or the organization of crowdsourcing activities on the Web – the workflow of historical research is characterized by digital interventions.⁶

While one can argue that most public historians have become digital by now, one has to emphasize the fact that many remain strongly embedded in analogue practices and traditions. This current duality or parallelism of analogue and digital practices forces public historians to experiment with the new while keeping established norms of valid historical practices alive. If we accept that "hybridity is the new normal,"⁷ I argue that we need an update of historical hermeneutics that problematizes the "in-betweenness" of our current public history practices.⁸ Instead of falling into the trap of asymmetric conceptions ("analogue" versus "digital"), the concept of digital hermeneutics proposes a critical framework for making the methodological and epistemological tensions involved in our public history practices explicit.

As Anita Lucchesi has demonstrated based on the example of building a digital memory platform on migration memories in Luxembourg, the hands-on approach of doing a collaborative and participatory digital public history asks for critical reflection on the "interferences" of digital tools, infrastructures and data in the co-creation of public history narratives.⁹ The co-design of an Internet platform such as *Memorecord* – taking place in the trading zones of digital public history practices – is characterized by many epistemological uncertainties and experimental heuristics of "grasping":¹⁰ turning a prototype of a website aiming

---

5 On the idea of digital hermeneutics, see Manfred Thaller, "The Need for a Theory of Historical Computing." *Historical Social Research* 29 (1991): 193–202; Joris Van Zundert, "Screwmeneutics and Hermenumericals: The Computationality of Hermeneutics," in *A New Companion to Digital Humanities*, edited by S. Schreibman, R. Siemens, and J. Unsworth (London: Wiley-Blackwell, 2016), 331–347; Stephen Ramsey, "The Hermeneutics of Screwing Around; or What You Do with a Million Books," in *Pastplay. Teaching and Learning History with Technology*, edited by Kevin Kee (Ann Arbor: University of Michigan Press, 2014), 111–120; Andreas Fickers, "Update für die Hermeneutik. Geschichtswissenschaft auf dem Weg zur digitalen Forensik?" *Studies in Contemporary History* 17.1 (2020): 157–168; Andreas Fickers, and Tim van der Heijden, "Inside the Trading Zone: Thinkering in a Digital History Lab," *Digital Humanities Quarterly* 14.3 (2020), see: www.digitalhumanities.org/dhq/vol/14/3/000472/000472.html.
6 On the notion of "digital intervention" in doing public history see Anita Lucchesi, "For a New Hermeneutics of Practice in Digital Public History. Thinkering with memorecord.uni.lu." Unpublished PhD thesis, University of Luxembourg, 2020.
7 Gerben Zaagsma, "On Digital History," *BMGN – Low Countries Historical Review* 128.4 (2013): 3–29.
8 Tara McPherson, "U.S. Operating Systems at Mid-Century: The Interwinning of Race and UNIX," in *Race after the Internet*, edited by L. Nakamura and P. Chow-White (New York: Routledge, 2012), 35.
9 See www.memorecord.uni.lu.
10 On the concept of trading zone and digital history see Max Kemman, "Trading Zones of Digital History." Unpublished PhD dissertation Université du Luxembourg, 2019.

at collecting "mediated memories" posted on social media platforms such as Facebook and Instagram into a public history platform was a non-linear, iterative process, characterized by many detours, serendipities, and even failures or mistakes. In fact, planning and realizing *Memorecord* turned the digital public historian into a "thinkerer":[11] an experimenter, playing with the possibilities of the digital while remaining self-critical towards its inherent possibilities and limitations.

Translated into the practice of doing public history in the digital age, it is the "digital kitchen" that we need to investigate as the place where the "raw" is transformed into the "cooked"![12] Building on the kitchen-metaphor, Anita Lucchesi describes the mediated memories (Facebook or Instragram posts) as "tira-gostos" (appetizers), the historical context as "menu," and the *Memorecord*-platform as the "digital kitchen" she used for producing the digital public history product.[13] To summarize, digital hermeneutics as hermeneutics of in-betweenness problematize the many tensions between the analogue and the digital, browsing and searching, scanning and reading, sharing and engaging, accessibility and interpretation inscribed into current practices of digital public history.[14] Such "hermeneutics of screwing around" not only ask for a self-reflexive approach of those doing digital public history projects, but are a real challenge when it comes to the documentation and ethical implications of such a work with and within the digital.[15]

---

11 The term "thinkering" has been introduced by media historian Erkki Huhtamo to describe the combination of "tinkering" and "thinking." See Erkki Huhtamo, "Thinkering with Media: On the Art of Paul DeMarinis," in *Buried in Noise*, edited by Paul DeMarinis (Heidelberg: Kehrer, 2011), 33–39. The concept of thinkering is close to similar conceptions of "heuristic groping" figuring under the term of "bricolage." See Andreas Fickers, "How to Grasp Historical Media *Dispositifs* in Practice?" in *Materializing Memories. Dispositifs, Generations, Amateurs*, edited by Susan Aasman, Andreas Fickers, and Joseph Wachelder (New York: Bloomsbury, 2018), 85–102.
12 Michael Frisch, "From 'A Shared Authority' to the Digital Kitchen, and Back," in *Letting Go? Sharing Historical Authority in a User Generated World*, edited by Bill Adair, Benjamin Filene, and Laura Koloski (London: Routledge 2011), 126–137.
13 Anita Lucchesi, "For a New Hermeneutics of Practice in Digital Public History. Thinkering with memorecord.uni.lu." Unpublished PhD thesis, University of Luxembourg, 2020, 282–287.
14 On the notion of inscription and the role of the digital infrastructures, objects, and tools as "actants" see Bruno Latour, *Reassembling the Social* (Oxford: Oxford University Press, 2005). On the impact of digital technologies as "actants" in a museum/pedagogical context, see Jonathan Westin, "The Interactive Museum and its Non-human Actants," *Nordisk Museologi* 1 (2011): 45–59.
15 Ramsey, op. cit.

Rethinking Shared Authority: Towards Fair Principles in Digital Public History

While the practices of public history are undoubtedly affected by digital technologies, most public history projects entertain a rather instrumental relationship with the digital as a mode of diffusion or representation of the past.[16] As public historians most decisively aim at co-producing and sharing historical knowledge with their audiences, we need to more systematically reflect on how this vision of "shared authority" is affected by the nature of the digital as the new ecosystem of historical practice.[17] If we acknowledge that the gap between the "raw" and the "cooked" in digital public history practice remains substantial as suggested by Michael Frisch,[18] we need to investigate how the digital interferes in the collaborative endeavor of making sense of the past all together. As the example of many public history projects in the making during the Covid-19 pandemic shows, the synchronic temporality and global connectivity of the Internet is impacting on how crowdsourcing activities are designed, managed and performed.[19] As Thomas Cauvin and Serge Noiret have argued, doing public history by using digital tools, infrastructures and platforms fosters new forms of collaboration, communication and production of "user generated content," but a systematic reflection on how the digital changes the thinking, doing, and telling of history in the age of abundance and accessibility is still lacking.[20]

Considering the plurality of publics that digital public history has to deal with, sharing authority between professional historians and those publics asks for a more systematic reflection on when, how and where those publics are involved in the co-production of historical knowledge.

Involving people in a mediated process of crowdsourcing or organizing history harvests with local communities not necessarily involves a real sharing of authority when it comes to the managing, curating or long-term accessibility and preservation of this data; the "crowd" rarely participates in the design or architecture of

---

16 Fine Danniau, "Public History in a Digital Context. Back to the Future or Back to Basics?" *BMGN – Low Countries Historical Review* 128.4 (2013): 118–144.
17 Sharon Leon, "Complexity and Collaboration. Doing Public History in Digital Environments," in *The Oxford Handbook of Public History*, edited by Paula Hamilton and James B. Garnder (Oxford: Oxford University Press 2017), 44–67.
18 Michael Frisch, "'Public History is Not A One-Way Street', or, From A Shared Authority to the City of Mosaics, and Back," *Ricerche Storiche*, XLVII.3 (2017): 143–150.
19 See Thomas Cauvin, "Making History Together: Public History and Digital Memories During COVID-19," online lecture hosted by the Institute for Holocaust, Genocide and Memory Studies of the University of Massachusetts Amhurst, 17 June, 2020. https://www.youtube.com/watch?v=DhtyIxRVzIw.
20 Serge Noiret, "Digital Public History," in *A Companion to Public History*, edited by D. Dean (London: Wiley, 2018), 111–124; Thomas Cauvin, *Public History. A Textbook of Practice* (London: Routledge, (2016) 2022).

databases or the definition of meta-data standards that ultimately define the limits and possibilities of the findability of information in a structured database. Digital public history projects with a real equality of ownership and responsibility of interpretation are rather rare, as acts of participation are often solicited, controlled and institutionally framed. But as the example of the *Pararchive*-projects shows,[21] systematic co-design can enable real community-based participatory research (CBPR) in the field of digital public history[22] – an approach which has successfully been tested and implemented in the field of public health.[23] But if the codes of web-based public history applications are not made available or shared on open source platforms such as Github, digital public history projects are susceptible of reinforcing knowledge asymmetries between historians, engaged participants and technical collaborators (such as coders, programmers, web-designers or data-stewards) instead of enabling truly democratic encounters.[24] Translating the concept of "shared authority" to the digital thus requires sharing research data and outputs based on the FAIR principles: co-produced data should be findable, accessible, interoperable and reusable.[25]

Shared authority also means shared responsibility. To thrive on open science, digital public historians have to be explicit about their responsibilities in co-producing historical data and sharing expertise and knowledge with their publics.[26] Many public history projects rely on a colloquial understanding of openness, participation, and interactivity, often concealing hidden power structures or "actants" outside the trading zone of digital public history projects (such as software, cloud infrastructures, or data protection and copyright laws). In a recent volume on "the participatory condition",

---

[21] See www.pararchive.com. The Pararchive Project "Open Access Community Storytelling and the Digital Archive" was a collaboration between a range of communities and two large institutional partners, the BBC and the Science Museum Group in the UK. It aimed at co-producing a new 'open' digital resource allowing anyone to search and collect on-line resources and to combine them with their own media (film, photographs and other ephemera) in order to tell their own stories and make new archives.

[22] Simon Popple and Daniel Mutibwa, "Tools you can trust? Co-design in community heritage work," in *Cultural Heritage in a Changing World*, edited by Karol Jan Borowiecki, Neil Forbes, and Antonella Fresa (Springer Open Access, 2016), DOI 10.1007/978-3-319-29544-2.

[23] Meredith Minkler and Nina Wallerstein, eds. *Community-based Participatory Research for Health: From Process to Outcomes* (San Francisco: Jossey-Bass, 2008).

[24] Julia Janes, "Democratic Encounters? Epistemic Privilege, Power, and Community-based Participatory Action Research," in *Action Research* 14.1 (2016): 72–87.

[25] Mark Wilkinson, et al. "The FAIR Guiding Principles for Scientific Data Management and Stewardship," *Scientific Data* 3.3 (2016):160018, DOI: 10.1038/sdata.2016.18.

[26] As a best practice, see "Building Histories of the National Mall. A Guide to Creating a Digital Public History Project", co-authored by Sheila Brennan and Sharon Leon, together with Megan Brett, Jannelle Legg, Michael O'Malley, Spencer Roberts, and Jim Safley (October 2015). http://mallhistory.org/Guide/index.html.

the editors warn that participation – styled as interactivity – has become a preferred engine of commerce, consent, and control.[27]

With regard to digital public history projects, we can see that interactive designs not only enable users to explore non-linear narratives; the democratic potential of such "database histories"[28] has to be read against the disciplining power of interactive and participatory designs.[29] Despite the "freedom" that users may experience in browsing through online exhibitions or crowdsourced collections, the explorative possibilities remain framed by indexical regimes and design principles of the content management system. This is what Barney et al. call the deep ambiguity of the participatory condition: on one side, participation has evolved into a leading mode of subjective interpellation, on the other, it increasingly informs business models in the cultural sphere. Participation, however, is not engagement, and interactivity is not shared authority.

Conclusion: The Ethics of Doing Digital Public History

This brings us to a last point of reflection: the ethics of doing digital public history. As our own experiential reality can no longer be thought of as separate from digital media,[30] the transformation of historical information – such as oral testimonies of Holocaust survivors – into data raises significant ethical issues too. Using the example of the database of the Shoah Visual History Archive (containing more than 50,000 survivor testimonies in 39 languages from 61 countries – amounting to more than 100,000 hours of testimony), Todd Presner has convincingly demonstrated the need to locate the ethical in digital and computational modalities of representation. His plea for "the ethics of the algorithm" is based on the assumption that computation as a "genre of historical representation that includes data, databases, algorithmic processing, and information visualization" is not a value-free process but instead requires ethical reflections on how information architectures, indexes, and

---

27 Darin Barney et al., eds., "The Participatory Condition. An Introduction," in *The Participatory Condition in the Digital Age* (Minneapolis: The University of Minnesota Press, 2016), p. XXXI.
28 On the concept of "database histories," see Steve F. Anderson, *Technologies of History: Visual Media and the Eccentricity of the Past* (Hanover, New Hampshire: Dartmouth College Press, 2011).
29 On the role of design as mediating interface and "actant" in the Latourian sense, see Anthony Masure, *Design et humanités numériques* (Paris: Éditions B42, 2017).
30 See Nick Couldry, "Deep Mediatization: Social Order in the Age of Datafication", online lecture, 18 October, 2017, https://cyber.harvard.edu/events/2017/10/CouldryHepp.

visual interfaces turn historical narratives into data.[31] As there are no transcripts of the video testimonies of the archive, a keyword indexing system consisting of a thesaurus linked to particular segments of a video is the only way to search the content of the testimonies. This process, also described as "defiguration" (as it evacuates all traces of the figurative in its literalism), is a fundamentally interpretative process characterized by the creation of a data ontology "that has expelled the latent, the performative, the figural, the subjunctive, the tone of questioning and doubt, the expressiveness of the face, and the very acts of telling (and failing to tell) that mark the contingency of all communication."[32] Without the critical repertoire of digital hermeneutics, I argue, the visitors of this "virtual in-between space"[33] can hardly engage in a critical dialogue with the past.

As Alina Bothe has shown, the USC Shoah Foundation has recently shifted towards less aestheticized virtual exhibition designs and organized workshops on "ethical editing" in which questions of digital source criticism and responsible practices of editing authentic historical testimonies were discussed with teachers and researchers.[34] These forms of training are a concrete example of applying digital hermeneutics in digital public history education. As future generations of digital public historians are likely to be confronted with the ethics of data integrity and algorithms, we need to sensitize the community to a careful reflection on how computational processes do intervene in the production of digital representations of past events and facts. We need to scrutinize the visual evidence and look of certainty of the increasingly complex visualizations of historical data in digital public history projects.[35] A better understanding of the complex interplay between what David Berry has called the "commodity layer" and the "mechanism layer" of continuous interfaces will become a key competence for digital public historians who ground their work ethics in the digital hermeneutics of in-betweenness.[36]

---

31 Todd Presner, "The Ethics of the Algorithm. Close and Distant Listening to the Shoah Foundation Visual History Archive," in *Probing the Ethics of Holocaust Culture*, edited by Claudio Fogu, Wulf Kantsteiner, and Todd Presner (Cambridge: Harvard University Press, 2016), 175–202, 182.
32 Ibidem, p. 192.
33 Alina Bothe, *Die Geschichte der Shoah im virtuellen Raum. Eine Quellenkritik* (Oldenbourg: De Gruyter 2019).
34 Ibidem, p. 365.
35 Drucker, Johanna, *Graphesis. Visual Forms of Knowledge Production* (Cambridge: Harvard University Press, 2014).
36 Berry, David, "The Commodity-Mechanism Form of Software/Code." Lecture at the "Unlike Us" conference in Amsterdam (2012). https://vimeo.com/39256099, accessed 20 March, 2021.

Bibliography

Day, Donald D. *Indexing it All. The Subject in the Age of Documentation, Information, and Data*. Cambridge: MIT Press, 2014.

Galloway, Alexander R. *The Interface Effect*. Cambridge: Polity Press, 2012.

Michel, Johann, *Homo Interpretans. Towards a Transformation of Hermeneutics*. London: Rowman & Littlefield, 2019.

Milligan, Ian, *History in the Age of Abundance. How the Web is Transforming Historical Research*. Montreal: McGill-Queens University Press, 2019.

Romele, Alberto, *Digital Hermeneutics. Philosophical Investigations in New Media and Technologies*. London: Routledge, 2020.

Part 2: **Contexts**

Trevor Owens and Jesse A. Johnston
Archivists as Peers in Digital Public History

Abstract: In the last three decades the web has enabled new digital means for historians to reach broader publics and audiences. Over that same period of time, archives and archivists have engaged in a parallel digital transformation. Archives are more engaged in community work through digital means and have developed methods to care for and make available digital material. This chapter explores the major convergence between the needs and practices of public historians and archivists. Historians' new forms of scholarship increasingly function as forms of knowledge infrastructure. Archivists work on systems for enabling access to collections are themselves anchored in longstanding commitments to infrastructure for enabling the use of records. In this context, we argue for the need for historians to engage more with archivists as peers in advancing both theory and method in digital public history.

Keywords: digital humanities, archival theory, community archives, digital collections, allyship, electronic records, collaboration

Bio: Dr. Trevor Owens is a librarian, researcher, policy maker, and educator working on digital infrastructure for libraries. Owens serves as the first Head of Digital Content Management at the U.S. Library of Congress. He is also a Public Historian in Residence at American University, and a lecturer for the University of Maryland's College of Information, where he is also a Research Affiliate with the Digital Curation Innovation Center. Owens previously worked as a Senior Program Officer and as Associate Deputy Director for Libraries at the United States Institute of Museum and Library Services (IMLS). Prior to that, he worked on digital preservation strategy and as a historian of science at the Library of Congress. Before joining the Library of Congress, he led outreach and communications efforts for the Zotero project at the Center for History and New Media at George Mason University. Owens is the author of three books, the most recent of which, The Theory and Craft of Digital Preservation, was published by Johns Hopkins University Press in 2018 and has won outstanding publication awards from both the American Library Association and the Society of American Archivists.

Dr. Jesse Johnston is an archivist and scholar based in Ann Arbor, Michigan. He has served as a Senior Librarian for Digital Content at the Library of Congress, Senior Program Officer for preservation and access programs at the National Endowment for the Humanities, and as an archivist at the Smithsonian Center for Folklife and Cultural Heritage. He holds a PhD in musicology and a Masters in archives and records management. He has taught archives and digital curation courses at George Mason University and the University of Maryland iSchool.

In the last 25 years we have seen the web enable new digital means for historians to reach broader publics and audiences. Over that same period of time, archives and archivists have been exploring and engaging with related strands of digital transformation. In one strand, both historians and archivists have focused their digital work toward community engagement. While historians have been developing a community of practice around public history, archivists and archives have similarly been reframing their work as more user centered and more closely engaged with communities and their records. A body of archival work and scholarship has emerged around the function of community archives that presents significant possibilities for further connections with the practices of history and historians. In a second strand, archivists and historians have developed new strategies for understanding and preserving digital cultural heritage. While historians have begun exploring using tools to produce new forms of digital scholarship, archivists and archives have been working to both develop methods to care for and make available digital material. Archivists have established tools, workflows, vocabulary and infrastructure for digital archives, and they have also managed the digitization of collections to expand access.

At the intersection of these two developments, we see a significant convergence between the needs and practices of public historians and archivists. Historians' new forms of scholarship increasingly function as a knowledge infrastructure that shapes both fields and disciplinary practice. Archivists work on systems for enabling access to collections are themselves anchored in longstanding commitments to infrastructure for enabling the use of records. At this convergence, there is a significant opportunity for historians to connect more with archivists as peers, as experts in questions of the structure and order of sources and records.[1]

In this chapter we explore the ways that archives, archivists, and archival practice are evolving around both analog and digital activities in ways that are highly relevant for those interested in working in digital public history.[2]

---

[1] For a longer view of the tensions between historians and archivists generally, see Francis X. Blouin, Jr. and William G. Rosenberg, *Processing the Past: Changing Authorities in History and the Archives* (Oxford: Oxford University Press, 2011); Terry Cook, "What Is Past Is Prologue: A History of Archival Ideas Since 1898, and the Future Paradigm Shift" *Archivaria* 43 (1997): 17–63, https://archivaria.ca/index.php/archivaria/article/view/12175/13184; Richard Cox, "Archivists and Historians: A View from the United States," *Archivaria* 19 (1984–85): 185–190, https://archivaria.ca/index.php/archivaria/article/view/11143/12080; Tom Nesmith, "What's History Got to Do with It? Reconsidering the Place of Historical Knowledge in Archival Work," *Archivaria* 57 (2004): 1–27, https://archivaria.ca/index.php/archivaria/article/view/12450/13553, accessed 21 March, 2021; Terry Cook, "The Archive(s) Is a Foreign Country: Historians, Archivists, and the Changing Landscape," *American Archivist* 74 (2011): 600–632, https://doi.org/10.17723/aarc.74.2.xm04573740262424, accessed 21 March, 2021.

[2] This essay synthesizes and extends aspects of work previously published in Trevor Owens, "Archives as a Service: From Archivist as Producer and Provider to Archivist as Facilitator and Enabler," in *Archival Values: Essays in Honor of Mark Greene. Society of American Archivists*, edited by Christine Weideman and Mary A. Caldera (Chicago: Society of American Archivists, 2019), and as

Archives: Digital and Analog Hybrids

When archivists and historians use the term "digital archive" they often mean different and overlapping things, which can be a source of tension and confusion. Much of this comes from the very flexible nature of the concept of an "archive." The popular email application Gmail has a button next to each message called "archive" that moves a message from your inbox to a folder for storage. In such popular vernacular, the concept of an archive can be any kind of set of content that has been moved from active use. Noting this casual usage, particularly in the realm of digital work, Margaret Hedstrom observed that "archivists have literally lost control over the definition of *archive*."[3] It is important to define specific uses and understandings around the work of archives in order to improve and deepen collaborative work between archivists and historians.

In this context, it makes sense that when public historians made their way to the web it made sense to talk about publishing and sharing digitized primary sources as "digital archives." Indeed, when historians at the Roy Rosenzweig Center for History and New Media launched the Omeka platform for publishing sources the default name the collection of all the digitized items in a given site was "My Archive."

This cavalier notion of an archive can often rankle archivists who might read this use of the term as a dismissal of their professional knowledge and a lack of understanding of the nature of their institutions. Archives are institutions, not websites.[4] More specifically, an institution that manages archives is generally referred to as an archives, and an archival collection is called an archive.[5] Of note, archival practice is itself the integration of multiple interrelated traditions: the manuscript tradition, often focused on organizing and managing personal papers; a public records tradition, anchored in the development of the bureaucracy of the modern nation state; and the development of documentation strategies, like oral history collecting.[6] In this context archives are institutions that take shape in myriad ways wherein archivists work with the communities they serve to acquire, arrange, describe, manage, and make available

---

the chapter on multimodal access, in Trevor Owens, *The Theory and Craft of Digital Preservation: An Introduction* (Baltimore: Johns Hopkins University Press, 2018).

3 Margaret Hedstrom, "Understanding Electronic Incunabula: A Framework for Research on Electronic Records," *American Archivist* 54 (1991): 334–354, https://doi.org/10.17723/aarc.54.3.125253r60389r011, accessed 21 March, 2021.

4 For an extensive exploration of issues with usage of "digital archive" see Kate Theimer, "Archives in Context and Archives as Context," *Journal of Digital Humanities* 1 (2012), http://journalofdigitalhumanities.org/1-2/archives-in-context-and-as-context-by-kate-theimer/, accessed 21 March, 2021.

5 See https://www2.archivists.org/glossary/terms/a/archive.

6 See, for example, Terry Cook, "What Is Past Is Prologue: A History of Archival Ideas Since 1898, and the Future Paradigm Shift" *Archivaria* 43 (1997): 17–63; Randall C. Jimerson, *Archives Power: Memory, Accountability, and Social Justice* (Chicago: Society of American Archivists, 2009); and Helen Samuels, "Who Controls the Past," *American Archivist* 49 (1986): 109–124.

records to users now and in the future. The essential focus here is to ensure that conversations about archives are always conversations about more than "the stuff." Archives cannot be understood without an understanding of their history and creation, organizational structure, and the expertise and labor of archivists and their record creators.[7]

Beyond the notion of archives as institutions, there is also something particularly significant about the structure and relationships that exist between items in an archival collection. Specifically, archival collections are generally understood to be the results of the accrual of records through the process of an individual or an organization's management and use of documents in support of its ongoing work. As a result, when archivists work to process and make available records they do that work in accordance with the idea that the characteristics of the items being preserved, their structure and interrelationship, and the history and contexts of their creation, accrual, and ownership are critical aspects of a collection's meaning and intellectual significance.[8] In archival collections, the context of the items and their relationships to each other tell as much if not more than any of the individual items. The whole is greater than the parts and the whole is only evident as a result of the accrual of records and their management as whole archives.

Archivists often contrast archival collections with "artificial collections." In this case, when highly curated collections of digitized resources are presented online in thematic interpretive presentations and referred to as archives they cut against many traditional concepts that animate archival thinking. Nonetheless, the "collecting tradition" has had a long history in the United States, with notable activity amongst community organizations (often state historical societies) and scholars to pull together or reconstruct bodies of records that support local narratives.[9] For example, the nineteenth-century *American Archives* series by Peter Force gathered and reprinted documents that demonstrated the history of the American Revolution, which have recently

---

[7] Michelle Caswell, "'The Archive' Is Not an Archives: On Acknowledging the Intellectual Contributions of Archival Studies," *Reconstruction* 16 (2016), https://escholarship.org/uc/item/7bn4v1fk, accessed 21 March, 2021; and Michelle Caswell, Ricardo Punzalan, and T-Kay Sangwand, "Critical Archival Studies: An Introduction," *Journal of Critical Library and Information Studies* 1 (2017), https://doi.org/10.24242/jclis.v1i2.50, accessed 21 March, 2021.
[8] A concise overview of these principles is offered in Luciana Duranti, "The Concept of Appraisal and Archival Theory," *American Archivist* 57 (1994): 328–344, https://doi.org/10.17723/aarc.57.2.pu548273j5j1p816, accessed 21 March, 2021.
[9] Overviews of this strand of American archival history are offered in Luke Gilliland-Swetland, "The Provenance of a Profession: The Permanence of the Public Archives and Historical Manuscripts Traditions in American Archival History," *American Archivist* 54 (1991): 160–175, https://doi.org/10.17723/aarc.54.2.w42580v137053675, accessed 21 March, 2021; and Randall C. Jimerson, *Archives Power: Memory, Accountability, and Social Justice* (Chicago: Society of American Archivists, 2009).

been transformed into a digital edition.[10] One constant in these two traditions of archival practice is the attention to primary sources, as well as an emphasis on provenance, the practice of recording the source and chain of custody of records, another key principle of archival work.[11] To this end, historians would do well to work toward somewhat more nuanced notions of what to call collections of digital resources and consider the multiple genealogies of this work.

While historians were developing notions of digital archives, archivists were simultaneously embracing digital technology as a means to expand access to archival records. For one, as archives become more and more focused on public engagement with records, many are moving to bulk digitization of archival collections. In this instance, archivists work to present the content online in ways that enable the presentation of whole sets of historical records to be read against each other in their original context and structure.

Beyond digitization as a method to expand access, archivists have also been dealing with significant amounts of born-digital records in collections. If the "paperless office" appears unlikely in the near term, the volume of digital materials continues to increase. This creates complex and increasingly diverse collections with both significant analog materials and increasingly large sets of digital records. Collections of personal papers now often come with floppy disks and hard drives and archivists have established practices and workflows for making copies of that content that can then be made available to researchers alongside the analog content of personal papers collections. Ongoing initiatives like the BitCurator software platform, which adapts digital forensics tools for use by archivists in an effort to demonstrate provenance and chain of custody for electronic materials, are advancing significant progress in supporting workflows for accessioning born digital content into archives.[12]

For public historians, this shift toward complex and born digital collections presents an opportunity for collaboration. To further their connections to archives, public historians must remember that the archive concept has different, often highly specific, meanings in different contexts. Understanding these differences in language, areas of domain expertise, and professional identity on all sides, will be critical for building partnerships between historians and archivists going forward.

---

10 Peter Force, compiler, *American Archives: Documents of the American Revolutionary Period, 1774–1776*, edited by Allan Kulikoff et al., http://amarch.lib.niu.edu/about, accessed 21 March, 2021.
11 A recent review of the provenance concept and its applications by archivists is offered by Jennifer Douglas, "Origins: Evolving Ideas about the Principle of Provenance," in *Currents of Archival Thinking*, edited by Terry Eastwood and Heather MacNeil (Oxford: ABC-Clio, 2010): 23–44. See also David A. Bearman and Richard H. Lytle, "The Power of the Principle of Provenance," *Archivaria* 21 (1985–1986): 14–27, https://archivaria.ca/index.php/archivaria/article/view/11231/12170, accessed 21 March, 2021.
12 See bitcurator.net.

Likewise, recognizing that archives are also working to enable access and use of archival collections, as well as developing innovative ways to connect with users, should help enable significant potential partnerships between historians looking for such rich partnerships.

Archives Are Becoming More Publicly Engaged and Participatory

Archives have been increasingly working to remake their connections with users. Archivists have reframed perceptions of their practices, as passive or "dusty" institutions, toward being actively engaged in enabling use. Most critically, however, archivists increasingly prioritize creating participatory relationships around records.[13]

One key area of engagement is to increase public access to archives and to encourage broader involvement in the processing of archival records. Following on notable work by Katie Shilton and Isto Huvila, Kate Theimer has defined a participatory archive one in which "people other than archives professionals contribute knowledge or resources, resulting in increased understanding about archival materials, usually in an online environment."[14] An example of such work is the "citizen archivist" campaign by the U.S. National Archives and Records Administration (NARA), a project to make available scanned records for public tagging and transcription.[15] This initiative is in support of NARA's strategic goal in its 2018 to 2022 strategic plan to "make access happen."[16] Likewise, the Australian Trove project provides a public access portal for digitized records as well as a platform for community input to correct auto-generated transcriptions, create lists, and tag items.[17] The result of this increasing turn toward public engagement is that archivists' work

---

[13] See, for example, Terry Cook, "Evidence, memory, identity, and community: four shifting archival paradigms," *Archival Science* 13 (2013): 95–120, https://doi.org/10.1007/s10502-012-9180-7, accessed 21 March, 2021.

[14] Kate Theimer, "Exploring the Participatory Archives," *Archives Next*, http://archivesnext.com/?p=2319, accessed 21 March, 2021. See Isto Huvila, "Participatory Archive: Towards Decentralised Curation, Radical User Orientation, and Broader Contextualisation of Records Management," *Archival Science* 8 (2008), https://doi.org/10.1007/s10502-008-9071-0, accessed 21 March, 2021; and Katie Shilton and Ramesh Srinivasan, "Participatory Appraisal and Arrangement for Multicultural Archival Collections," *Archivaria* 63 (2007): 87–10, https://archivaria.ca/index.php/archivaria/article/view/13129, accessed 21 March, 2021.

[15] As of July 2018, the Citizen Archivist portal is available at https://www.archives.gov/citizen-archivist.

[16] National Archives and Records Administration, *Strategic Plan*, https://www.archives.gov/about/plans-reports/strategic-plan/strategic-plan-2018-2022, accessed 21 March, 2021.

[17] National Library of Australia, *Trove*, https://trove.nla.gov.au/, accessed 21 March, 2021.

increasingly looks like work that public historians are engaging in. The possibilities for partnerships here are indeed significant. As archivists increasingly work to make archival collections available online there are significant opportunities for historians to develop new dynamic interpretive layers that help a wide range of user communities engage with and understand these materials.

The move to engage with users and communities and leverage digital platforms is not limited to large institutions. In fact, one of the key insights of the growing body of work in "community archives" is the validation and empowerment of communities to be the appropriate arbiters and stewards of their own records, rather than external organizations.[18] Some of the most exciting opportunities in these areas have been occurring at the intersection of local community based archiving efforts and digital tools. In founding the South Asian American Digital Archive (SAADA), Samip Mallick and Michelle Caswell were motivated by their finding that "only a few museums ever had organized exhibitions on South Asian Americans and no archival repository was systematically collecting materials related to South Asian American history." SAADA works closely with South Asian American community members to identify, gather, appraise, and digitize materials for online presentation. It follows a "post-custodial" model in which the archives as an organization do not hold physical custody of the archive, rather SAADA "borrows" records from their owners for digitization, returns the originals, then will "digitize them, archivally describe them in a culturally appropriate manner, link them to related materials in the archives, and make them freely accessible online to anyone in the world with an internet connection." Although collected, the project follows archival principles and gains value as new items that conform to its mission enter the collection; the principle of provenance, moreover, is also followed, though the source of the materials may in this case be considered to stem from the idea of the group, who shares an ethnicity and particular social experiences, as the source.[19] Caswell and Mallick, who bring subject matter knowledge as well as archival and digital preservation expertise to the project, describe the project as a "digital participatory microhistory project," which follows archival principles to collect and preserve access to culturally significant materials according to their collecting policy.[20]

---

18 See, for example, Andrew Flinn, Mary Stevens, and Elizabeth Shepherd, "Whose memories, whose archives? Independent community archives, autonomy and the mainstream," *Archival Science* 9 (2009): 71–86, https://doi.org/10.1007/s10502-009-9105-2, accessed 21 March, 2021; and Jeannette A. Bastian, "Play Mas: Carnival in the Archives and the Archives in Carnival: Records and Community Identity in the US Virgin Islands," *Archival Science* 9 (2009): 113–125, http://doi.org/10.1007/s10502-009-9101-6, accessed 21 March, 2021.
19 On the idea of "ethnicity as provenance," see Joel Wurl, "Ethnicity as Provenance: In Search of Values and Principles for Documenting the Immigrant Experience," *Archival Issues* 29 (2005): 65–76.
20 Michelle Caswell, "Seeing Yourself in History Community Archives and the Fight Against Symbolic Annihilation," *The Public Historian* 36.4 (2014): 26–37, http://doi.org/10.1525/tph.2014.36.4.26, accessed 21 March, 2021.

The *People's Archive of Police Violence in Cleveland* illustrates another significant potential that exists for this intersection between community-based archiving efforts and ideally the advancement of a more critical and directly publicly engaged form of digital public history. Created in 2015, the *People's Archive of Police Violence in Cleveland* is a local community created and managed online archive built using the Omeka platform. It's designed to be participatory in that it provides a means for community members to submit and tell their stories. The site is explicitly anchored in notions of participation, perspective and power and work on anti-oppression and the function that the creation and curation of community archives can have around belonging and community development.

Jarrett Drake, one of the key archivist facilitators in the development of the Cleveland archive, has described one of the key aspects of this work as a move toward a new kind of trust between archivists and communities. This trust is particularly critical with communities facing oppression, largely at the hands of the very powers that sustain the institutions that establish and maintain most archives. In Drake's words, archives must "build trust with the people, communities, and organizations around whose lives the movement is centered, a trust they should pursue not under the guise of collection development but under the practice of allyship."[21] While the example of *A People's Archive of Police Violence* is recent, it builds on work to liberate archives from their emphasis on and benefit to recording the memory of society's rich and powerful. Further, any appeal to the work of the archivist as technical or neutral in that work obfuscates the extent to which our institutions are aligned and complicit with wealth, power and privilege.[22]

In working on participatory and liberatory archives, archivists not only better serve those communities, but they also gain the opportunity to understand and represent records as the community understands them. Michelle Caswell and others suggest that by opening up the process of producing the archive, by making the production of an archive participatory, archives can serve communities by helping to create a sense of belonging.[23] Notions of participatory and liberatory archives are major challenges to the institutional status quo of archival institutions and practices. At this point, it is still not clear the extent to which this strand of thought will require the development of new kinds of archival

---

21 J.M. Drake, (27 June, 2016), "Expanding #ArchivesForBlackLives to Traditional Archival Repositories," https://medium.com/on-archivy/expanding-archivesforblacklives-to-traditional-archival-repositories-b88641e2daf6#.h1hobqzq3, accessed 4 December, 2016.
22 H. Zinn, "Secrecy, archives, and the public interest," *The Midwestern Archivist* 2.2 (1977): 14–26.
23 Michelle Caswell, Marika Cifor, and Mario H. Ramirez, "'To Suddenly Discover Yourself Existing': Uncovering the Impact of Community Archives," *The American Archivist* 79 (2016): 56–81, https://doi.org/10.17723/0360-9081.79.1.56, accessed 21 March 2021; and M. Caswell, "Assessing the Use of Community Archives US IMLS RE-31-16-0117-16," Institute of Museum and Library Services, 2016, https://www.imls.gov/grants/awarded/re-31-16-0117-16, accessed 4 December, 2016.

institutions or the extent to which existing institutional archival power structures can support this work without coopting community agency.

As archives and archival practice continues to increase engaging with communities of users as participants and co-producers of archival work and practices, the potential alignment between the work of digital public history and archives becomes stronger. At the same time, the lines between the work of historians as interpreters and archivists as enablers of access blurs further. The future of collaborations between these two professional communities can be found at the intersections where the lines between interpretation and documentation blur. By further understanding how archivists and historians can support and complement each other's work, such innovative digital projects will continue to remake the nature of public history as a field, both broadening it and creating a more participatory and welcoming space in which intellectual and project authority is shared and distributed.

Blurring Lines between Scholarship and Knowledge Infrastructure

The traditional connection between scholars and archivists has been punctuated by a line that clearly delineates their roles. Scholars produce books and articles and archivists and librarians facilitate access to primary and secondary sources for the production of that scholarship the concept of archivist and librarian as providing this commodity service to the scholar works relatively well. Archives and libraries are and continue to function as society's "epistemic infrastructure."[24] Of course, providing that kind of service, acting as a platform for scholarship, remains a vital role for librarians and archivists. However, digital history projects have emerged as hybrid forms, straddling the boundary between interpretating primary sources and providing direct access to those materials. At the same time, archivists increasingly produce resources for a wide range of audiences that include significant interpretive components. That is, archivists are increasingly not relying on historians as their primary users to provide value and use everyone from K-12 teachers and students, to community members, to genealogists.

Our contention is that the best way forward in these spaces is for archivists and historians to build establishing deeper and more significant kinds of partnerships. As new forms of digital scholarship take on larger and varied roles in knowledge

---

24 Margaret Hedstrom and John King, "Epistemic Infrastructure in the Rise of the Knowledge Economy," in *Advancing Knowledge in the Knowledge Economy*, edited by B. Kahin and A. Wycoff (Cambridge: MIT Press, 2005).

infrastructure than monographs or journal articles, it is increasingly necessary for historians to start treating archivists as peers and not service workers.[25] This builds on the observations of others working with large digital projects, who have noted that various types of expertise require acknowledgment, collaboration must be inclusive, and the concept of research should be capacious.[26] Archivists and librarians have developed both significant bodies of practice and scholarship on issues of organizing and structuring information resources and historians will do well to start directly engaging with that body of work. The expertise of the archivist and the librarian in the organization of knowledge and records is of core relevance to the design of digital scholarship. Digital librarians and archivists, for example, have been at the center of efforts to provide data management plans and input on digital preservation infrastructure, which have been made mandatory elements of planning by many funders; the *Chronicling America* resource of digitized American newspapers, likewise, has developed through the expertise of collection specialists who deeply understand the metadata and distribution of newspapers in collections across the country (in microfilm and paper holdings), as well as historians who have consulted on selecting the most significant newspapers for the resource.[27] If we are going to have sustainable and interoperable forms of digital scholarship that is increasingly a hybrid form of knowledge infrastructure, it becomes critical to view the librarians and archivists less as service providers and more as partners and co-creators.

There also exists significant potential for public historians to begin to take the digital and digitized collections that archives are making available for use as the basis to produce expressive interfaces and novel forms of scholarly interpretation. One of the most powerful examples of the potential for this kind of collaboration is evident in *The Real Face of White Australia Project*. In the early twentieth century, Australia established a series of immigration restrictions, called the White Australia Policy, that limited immigration of non-Europeans to the country. These racist policies weren't repealed until the middle of the twentieth century. The National Archives of Australia has extensive documentation of how and when these immigrant groups were controlled and oppressed. These materials were well described and

---

25 Roxanne Shirazi (July 2014). "Reproducing the Academy: Librarians and the Question of Service in the Digital Humanities." Presented at the American Library Association Annual Conference, Las Vegas. http://roxanneshirazi.com/2014/07/15/reproducing-the-academy-librarians-and-the-question-of-service-in-the-digital-humanities/, accessed April 16, 2016.
26 These conclusions come from an analysis of projects funded under the "Digging Into Data" initiative by Christa Williford and Charles Henry, *One Culture: Computationally Intensive Research in the Humanities and Social Sciences* (Council on Library and Information Resources, 2012), https://www.clir.org/pubs/reports/pub151/.
27 See the DMPTool (Data Management Plan Tool), including a library of humanities-focused project plans, at https://dmptool.org/ the *Chronicling America* resource can be found at https://chroniclingamerica.loc.gov/ (funding comes from the National Endowment for the Humanitie).

digitized in bulk, which enabled the possibility for the creation of this project. Through the *Invisible Australians Project*, historians Kate Bagnall and Tim Sherratt have set out to turn these documents of control into a means of surfacing the stories and narratives of the oppressed people they were created to control.[28] The primary output of this work is an interface that presents a wall of faces under the title *The Real Face of White Australia*.[29] Users can click on any of the faces to see the document each face was extracted from, the bulk of which come from the National Archives of Australia's digitized online collections. Where looking at the documents themselves reinforces the narrative of dominance and control, extracting just the faces of those who were oppressed functions to draw attention to the humanity and of each individual recorded in these documents. This work offers considerable potential for modeling how cultural heritage institutions might further develop and cultivate relationships with their users to develop modes of access and use for their collections.

Sherratt and Bagnall's work has resulted in substantive engagement with these records and with an underappreciated aspect of the history of Australia. The work was possible because of the depth of subject-matter expertise that Bagnall brought to understanding the collection and the technical chops and ingenuity of Sherratt. It is worth underscoring that by making digital collections available online, cultural heritage institutions create the possibility for this kind of use and reuse. Given the significance of these possibilities, archives would be wise to more explicitly seek out and support uses and reuses of collections instead of simply waiting for potential users to do so on their own.

The Path Forward: Archivists and Public Historians as Digital Peers

In hindsight, the seemingly tidy separate spheres of the work of archivists and historians at the end of the twentieth century will likely appear as an anomaly. The permeable membrane between the training and practices of archivists and historians in earlier periods can and should begin to remerge. Before substantive professionalization of both historians and archivists in the later part of the last century, historians and archivists were often trained together and moved back and forth between roles associated with collecting, organizing, describing, and

---

28 See Kate Bagnall, "Invisible Australians"; and Tim Sherratt, "Real Face of White Australia," http://invisibleaustralians.org/faces/, accessed on 21 March, 2021.
29 Tim Sherratt, "The Real Face of White Australia," http://invisibleaustralians.org/faces/, accessed on 21 March, 2021.

interpreting historical sources. We believe returning to cross train historians and archivists in each other's practices in the digital age can pay substantial dividends to both fields and to the communities they support.

Our contention is that work like archival crowdsourcing, the *South Asian American Digital Archive*, the *People's Archive of Police Violence in Cleveland*, and *The Real Face of White Australia* exemplify bright possibilities and future directions for both archives and for digital public history. In these cases, archivists can work with public historians in seeking ways to make their practices more relevant and directly engaged in critical issues for society, while drawing on expertise in organizing, selecting, and making available sources. These examples blur lines between organizing and structuring information and enabling forms of interpretation and story telling. As David Bearman noted in an early essay responding to the digital challenges (and opportunities) facing archives, new modes of digital, multimodal access increase the potential for connections with archives, and the "challenge is to make sense of the documentation – not to keep it. To deliver it where it is needed – not to store it."[30] Our discussion here shows a path forward for potential partnerships around common goals and objectives for archival and historical work.

With that noted, to make these kinds of partnerships more and more of the norm and not individual exceptions, both historians and archivists need to explicitly focus on how to further engage in collaborations. For archives, this likely means making more and more of their content available in ways that it can be used and identifying ways to create fellowships and support things like hackathons that open the doors wide and invite in historians in as co-producers of digital resources. For historians this increasingly means attending archives and digital library conferences as well including archival approaches to metadata and data curation in courses or course offerings. This also means turning to appreciate, respect, and read the literature and scholarship produced by archivists and librarians on the curation, management, design and organization of information. The future is bright for collaborations between archivists and public historians, but it's going to take explicit and focused work to build partnerships and collaborations to make that future a reality.

---

[30] David Bearman, *Archival Methods* (Pittsburgh: Archives & Museum Informatics, 1989), available at www.archimuse.com/publishing/archival_methods/.

Bibliography

Caswell, Michelle. (2014). Seeing Yourself in History: Community Archives and the Fight Against Symbolic Annihilation. *The Public Historian*, *36*(4), 26–37. https://doi.org/10.1525/tph.2014.36.4.26

Caswell, Michelle, Cifor, M., & Ramirez, M. H. (2016). "To Suddenly Discover Yourself Existing": Uncovering the Impact of Community Archives1. *The American Archivist*, *79*(1), 56–81. https://doi.org/10.17723/0360-9081.79.1.56

Cook, T. (1997). What is Past is Prologue: A History of Archival Ideas Since 1898, and the Future Paradigm Shift. *Archivaria*. https://archivaria.ca/index.php/archivaria/article/view/12175

Cox, R. J. (1984). Archivists and Historians: A View from the United States. *Archivaria*, 185–190.

Drake, J. M. (2016). RadTech Meets RadArch: Towards A New Principle for Archives and Archival Description. *On Archivy*. https://medium.com/on-archivy/radtech-meets-radarch-towards-a-new-principle-for-archives-and-archival-description-568f133e4325#.gk8s8781p

Duranti, L. (1994). The Concept of Appraisal and Archival Theory. *The American Archivist*, *57*(2), 328–344. https://doi.org/10.17723/aarc.57.2.pu548273j5j1p816

Flinn, A., Stevens, M., & Shepherd, E. (2009). Whose memories, whose archives? Independent community archives, autonomy and the mainstream. *Archival Science*, *9*(1), 71. https://doi.org/10.1007/s10502-009-9105-2

Hedstrom, M. (1991). Understanding Electronic Incunabula: A Framework for Research on Electronic Records. *The American Archivist*, *54*(3), 334–354.

Huvila, I. (2008). Participatory archive: Towards decentralised curation, radical user orientation, and broader contextualisation of records management. *Archival Science*, *8*(1), 15–36. https://doi.org/10.1007/s10502-008-9071-0

Nesmith, T. (2004). What's History Got to Do With It?: Reconsidering the Place of Historical Knowledge in Archival Work. *Archivaria*, 1–27.

Owens, T. (2018). *The theory and craft of digital preservation*. Johns Hopkins University Press.

Owens, T., & Johnston, J. (2019). Archives as a Service: From Archivist as Producer and Provider to Archivist as Facilitator and Enabler. In C. Weideman & M. Caldera (Eds.), *Archival Values: Essays in Honor of Mark Greene. Society of American Archivists*. Society of American Archivists.

Shilton, K., and Srinivasan, T., (2007). Participatory Appraisal and Arrangement for Multicultural Archival Collections *Archivaria* 63:87–101.

Theimer, K. (2012). Archives in Context and as Context. *Journal of Digital Humanities*, *1*(2). http://journalofdigitalhumanities.org/1-2/archives-in-context-and-as-context-by-kate-theimer/

William S. Walker
History Museums: Enhancing Audience Engagement through Digital Technologies

Abstracts: This essay argues that simply putting a museum's collection online, or creating a digital kiosk that includes a collections database, does not constitute audience engagement. History museums utilize the tools and methods of digital history to increase the visibility of their collections and engage with visitors. Consequently, museums' digital strategies must explicitly contend with the question of audience. The most successful projects combine key principles of museum education, interpretation, and outreach with the capabilities of digital tools. Approaching digital history with audience engagement in mind enables history museums to achieve more effectively critical goals related to relevance, collaborative practice, and community service.

Keywords: history museums, audience engagement, collections, exhibitions, podcasts, websites, interactives

History museums approach digital history in two main ways: 1) as a route to increasing the visibility and accessibility of their *collections* through digital collections databases, and 2) as a means of engaging with *audiences* through websites, online exhibitions, podcasts, and other digital initiatives. Sometimes these efforts overlap – for example, through popular crowdsourcing projects or social media campaigns that highlight collection items – but, more often, they are discrete endeavors, and critics and practitioners should not conflate them with one another. Both approaches to digital history work are valid pursuits for history museums, and both have tangible benefits for the public. Nevertheless, a strategy that is overly focused on digitizing collections without considering the importance of audience engagement is increasingly untenable as history museums strive to be more relevant and welcoming to multiple constituencies.

Simply putting a collection online does not mean that a museum is reaching its audience in meaningful ways. Audience engagement through digital history takes multiple forms in museums, including through interactive displays, websites, podcasts, crowdsourcing initiatives, apps, virtual reality and augmented reality, gaming, and social media campaigns. The most effective of these combine fundamental principles of museum education and interpretation with the capabilities of digital tools. Public historians and museum professionals who practice digital history in this way encourage audiences to make connections between history and their contemporary lives; explore historical ideas and narratives in deeply contextual and nuanced ways; understand better the processes of history making; participate in constructive dialogue on critical social issues; see communities, identities, and cultures through new lenses; and take action to address key societal challenges. Overall, approaching digital history with audience engagement in mind enables history museums to achieve more effectively critical goals related to relevance, collaborative practice, and community service.

In the United States, one of the earliest examples of the successful use of digital history in a history museum came as part of the Smithsonian National Museum of American History's landmark 1987 exhibition, "A More Perfect Union: Japanese Americans and the United States Constitution." To narrate individual Japanese Americans' experiences of incarceration during World War II, the exhibition's curators employed computers and the then-new digital technology of laserdiscs to share video oral histories through interactive displays. At the time, the use of oral histories in exhibitions was not unprecedented. A decade and a half earlier, the Anacostia Neighborhood Museum's "The Evolution of a Community," for example, had incorporated oral histories from over fifty residents of Washington, D.C. In "A More Perfect Union," however, visitors were able to interact with oral histories in a new way. Instead of simply including written quotations from transcripts, playing recordings on a loop, or having visitors trigger analog recordings with a push button, the exhibition's curators used touchscreens to allow visitors to select video oral history segments. To access interviews with Japanese Americans discussing their experiences in internment camps, visitors chose from a list of pre-determined questions, thereby evoking the conversational dynamic of oral history. This section of the exhibition, which was called "Conversations," often held visitors' attention for "many minutes" and encouraged careful listening to "multiple stories," according to Selma Thomas, who was the member of the exhibition team who conducted the interviews and produced the videos.[1] In this pioneering model, digital technology served as a critical tool for enabling deeper and more intimate visitor engagement with the intellectual and emotional content of the exhibition.

Due to the exhibition's popularity, it remained on display at the National Museum of American History (NMAH) for over a decade and a half. In addition, in 2001, museum staff created a companion website (http://amhistory.si.edu/perfect union/), which included the text from the traveling version of the exhibition as well as a collections database of over eight hundred items. It also contained lesson plans for elementary and secondary level students with the objective of helping "students become aware of, and sensitive to, the Japanese internment camp experience." A "Reflections" section encouraged users to share their responses to this history; categories in the section included: "Internment Stories," "Never Again?" "Citizenship," "Security vs. Liberty," and "Then and Now." Many of the contributions clearly came

---

[1] Selma Thomas, "Private Memory in a Public Space: Oral History and Museums," in *Oral History and Public Memories*, ed. Paula Hamilton and Linda Shopes (Philadelphia: Temple University Press, 2008), 95.

from junior and senior high school students completing classroom assignments. Nevertheless, quite a few offered thoughtful responses to the subject matter and reflected national discussions around civil liberties in the wake of September 11, 2001. The website debuted less than two months after the attacks, and its developers noted the resonance of the history of Japanese American incarceration with current events. Curator Jennifer Jones, who worked on both the original exhibition and the companion website, stated, "With the United States engaged in a war against terrorism – a war with no borders – we have to look to history to help us understand that individual rights and civil liberties will once again be tested."[2] In the immediate post-9/11 period, the relevance of this history was clear to many who were worried about how the federal government would balance security concerns with respect for constitutional rights, especially those of Arab Americans and Muslims. According to Franklin Odo, a curator for the online exhibition and director of the Smithsonian Asian Pacific American Program, "This exhibition looks at a time in our history when racial prejudice and fear tipped the delicate balance between citizen rights and the power of the state."[3] Such comments, as well as several of the user responses on the website, demonstrated that history could inform contemporary debates concerning national security, constitutional rights, and race.

The creators of "A More Perfect Union" used digital history – in the form of video oral histories, interactive displays, and, later, a website – to challenge broad and diverse audiences to critically examine the United States government's history of racism and constitutional violations. The combination of a relevant and timely historical topic with digital tools that enabled curators to bring it to audiences in compelling ways made for an enduring contribution to the field of public history.

In 1987, at the same time that "A More Perfect Union" was making its debut at the Smithsonian in Washington, D.C., the Union Française des Arts du Costume (UFAC) in Paris was also harnessing laserdisc technology, but for a different purpose – to digitize images and descriptions of their large collection of costumes, accessories, and designs. Since it occurred prior to the advent of the first web browsers and the emergence of the World Wide Web, the UFAC's effort led to the creation not of a website but a local computer network where curators and other researchers could access multiple items in the collection digitally without the need to disturb the originals. Although this set-up was quite innovative for its time, within a few years museum staff recognized that it had become dated and they started to envision ways

---

[2] "Smithsonian Launches Online Exhibition 'A More Perfect Union: Japanese Americans and the U.S. Constitution'," Smithsonian National Museum of American History, November 7, 2001, http://americanhistory.si.edu/press/releases/smithsonian-launches-online-exhibition-more-perfect-union-japanese-americans-and-us; see also, "A More Perfect Union: Japanese Americans and the U.S. Constitution (exhibition)," *Densho Encyclopedia*, https://encyclopedia.densho.org/A_More_Perfect_Union:_Japanese_Americans_and_the_U.S._Constitution_(exhibition)/.
[3] Ibid.

of providing much wider access through "an exhaustive catalogue of our collections which can be consulted by the whole profession and by schools and museums, in France and abroad."[4] The idea of making museum collections accessible via computer beyond the narrow confines of the museum's physical walls was coming into focus.

More than a decade earlier, international museum leaders had glimpsed the potential of computing technology to transform their practices – although they most certainly could not have foreseen the emergence of the internet and how it would radically alter the world. In October 1976, UNESCO, in collaboration with the International Council of Museums (ICOM), organized a conference in Barcelona to explore the "use of computers in museums." The report of the meeting stated that "experiences in several countries have now demonstrated that computer methodology makes it possible to communicate information cheaply and quickly anywhere in the world." Moreover, it went on to note that computers "make it possible to store, organize, and communicate . . . information [about cultural objects] dependably and rapidly."[5] Yet, even the most forward-thinking museum professionals could never have anticipated the breadth and depth of the changes to come, nor the challenges they would face as museums encountered the digital revolution.

In the late 1980s and early 1990s, as personal computing took off and more people began accessing the World Wide Web, individuals and institutions in the field came to understand how digital technology might fundamentally change museum practice. In 1994, British computer scientist Jonathan Bowen founded the "Virtual Library museums pages," an important directory of museum websites which tracked the international growth of museums in the digital realm in their formative years.[6] Bowen understood how the "advent of the Internet" enabled museums to reach audiences in "their homes, workplaces, schools, libraries, etc." and "to provide real content that is appealing to . . . users." Encouraging museums to think about what their "virtual visitors . . . might wish to gain from using the museum Web site, rather than just considering what the museum has to offer," Bowen recommended that museums avoid attempting to "re-create the 'traditional' museum experience." Instead, they should create appealing and easy-to-navigate homepages, virtual exhibitions, and image-rich spaces. At the same time, in this age before broadband when many people were still using dial-up modems to access the internet, Bowen warned that "large, slow-loading multimedia resources" could frustrate users who expected pages to

---

[4] Marie Hélène Poix, "A Computerized Interactive Catalogue," *Museum International* 179, Vol. XLV, no. 3 (1993): 33–35, quotation on p. 35. See also, "Fashion and Textiles," Musée de la Mode et du Textile, http://madparis.fr/en/about-us/collections-1307/nouvelle-traduction-20-mode-et.

[5] Robert G. Chenhall, "Museums and Computers: A Progress Report," *Museum International* XXX, no. 1 (1978): 52–54, quotations from p. 52.

[6] *Virtual Library museums pages*, http://www.historisches-centrum.de/vlmp/; "Virtual Library museums pages," *Wikipedia*, https://en.wikipedia.org/wiki/Virtual_Library_museums_pages.

"load quickly."[7] As communications infrastructure improved along with digital technologies, such concerns disappeared. Nevertheless, Bowen's recommendations that museums' digital efforts should take into account their users' interests and desires and prioritize ease of use remained at the core of best practices in the field. Increasingly, museum leaders envisioned digital technologies as being critical to efforts to attract new audiences. This perception led more and more museums to embrace interactive digital technologies in both physical and virtual spaces. Museums' rush to add digital "bells and whistles," however, often brought mixed success in large part because they only partially understood how users would engage with these elements.

One prominent example of an interactive-rich museum that offered an impressive array of video and computer-based displays and modules was the National Constitution Center in Philadelphia, which opened in 2003.[8] Two popular digital interactives at the Center engaged visitors directly in explorations of constitutional questions and voting rights in the United States. At one of them, visitors donned a robe and assumed the role of a U.S. Supreme Court justice deciding critical cases in U.S. history. At the other, visitors participated in a voting activity with a twist – character profiles illuminated for visitors who could and could not vote at different points in U.S. history and why particular individuals and groups were denied the franchise. In this way, visitors experienced both the empowering feeling of exercising one's constitutional right to suffrage and the marginalization that has resulted from restrictions on voting. Some critics have argued that the non-partisan Center favors an overly celebratory view of U.S. democracy and constitutional history, but this interactive made the important point that full participation in U.S. democracy has been limited in significant ways for particular groups.

Although the Center has avoided taking a position on contemporary voter restrictions that its patrons might construe as partisan, staff members have not ignored the topic and have utilized digital media to engage with it. The subject of voter restriction is increasingly relevant as U.S. Republican politicians and government officials have sought to put in place heightened requirements for individuals to exercise their voting rights, ostensibly in an effort to counteract voter fraud, a problem that is quite rare in the contemporary United States. Critics argue that these efforts are intended to limit black and Latino participation in voting, two constituencies that tend to vote in large numbers for the Democratic party. In 2016, as part of its podcast series, "We the People," the Center featured a debate about "Voting Rights in the Courts," which included both a liberal expert and a conservative expert who offered detailed explanations of current voting rights cases and provided competing interpretations of voter

---

[7] Jonathan Bowen, "The Virtual Museum," *Museum International* 52, no. 1 (2000): 4–7, quotations from pp. 4–5.
[8] "About the Constitution Center," *National Constitution Center*, https://constitutioncenter.org/about.

ID laws.[9] The podcast, which was hosted by the Center's president and CEO, studiously avoided advancing an institutional position on controversial questions, providing instead equal time for the airing of sharply different perspectives on the discriminatory (or non-discriminatory) intent and impact of these laws. In this way, the Center was able to maintain its posture of non-partisanship while engaging with a challenging topic. More recently, the podcast has featured a similar approach to gun rights, gerrymandering, and free speech. In each of these instances, the digital medium of the podcast offered an expansive and flexible platform for exploration of the issues. It also extended the museum's reach beyond its walls to audiences on the internet and allowed the museum to showcase the relevance of constitutional history to contemporary events.

Of course no museum's podcast may ever match the immense popularity and reach of the "History of the World in 100 Objects," hosted by British Museum director Neil MacGregor and originally broadcast on BBC Radio 4 in 2010. In the year of its debut alone, downloads totaled over 10.4 million and a companion book became a bestseller.[10] With his engaging style and uncanny ability to make the British Museum's vast collections relevant, MacGregor enthralled listeners and inspired them to visit the museum to see the objects in person. Visitors who did so were able to utilize an online guide to locate objects in the galleries and to discover more information about them.[11] The museum also gathered contributions of additional objects from museums across the United Kingdom and aggregated them on its website. Although one can quibble with the sheer audacity of such an effort, many museums clearly envied the British Museum's success, as evidenced by the numerous copycat efforts that followed.

Over the past two decades, digital interactives have become a popular way of connecting with museum audiences. Many so-called interactives are essentially collections databases, offering visitors access to a large body of items (objects, images, and documents) that curators were unable to include physically in exhibitions due to space considerations. Some digital interactive displays, however, aim for deeper levels of audience engagement beyond browsing collections.

Opened in 2009, el Museo del Caribe in Barranquilla, Colombia utilizes a wide array of digital installations to draw visitors into the rich history and culture of

---

9 "Voting Rights in the Courts," *We the People* (podcast), August 11, 2016, *National Constitution Center*, https://constitutioncenter.org/experience/programs-initiatives/podcasts/P90.

10 Maev Kennedy, "Radio 4's A History of the World in 100 Objects draws to a close," *The Guardian*, October 14, 2010, https://www.theguardian.com/media/2010/oct/14/radio-4-history-world-objects.

11 "A History of the World in 100 Objects," *The British Museum*, https://www.britishmuseum.org/explore/a_history_of_the_world.aspx.; Neil MacGregor, *A History of the World in 100 Objects* (New York: Viking, 2010).

Colombia's Atlantic coastal region.[12] Displaying few traditional museum objects, the museum instead relies on immersive video and interactive installations to dramatize the region's social, cultural, and environmental characteristics. Visitors first encounter beautifully rendered animations of Gabriel Garcia Marquez's stories and novels in an immersive space. Perhaps the most well known and widely admired Colombian of the past century, Marquez immortalized the region in his fiction, most famously in his novel *One Hundred Years of Solitude*. Moving beyond Marquez's works, interactive stations contain video oral histories with members of indigenous and Afro-Colombian communities and a particularly effective room-sized installation features musicians showcasing the diverse musical cultures of Colombia.

In 2011, when the New York Historical Society re-opened after a large-scale renovation, the centerpiece of the re-imagined space was an inviting entryway and introductory exhibition on "New York and the Nation" featuring a salon-style gallery of painting and sculpture. In the gallery, visitors encountered a row of large touchscreens on swivels that they could manipulate to discover more information about the collection items on display. These digital interactives were essentially high-tech exhibition labels, but the artful design and user interface encouraged a deeper level of engagement than traditional label texts typically inspire. Similarly, when it reopened to the public in 2014 after an extensive renovation, the Cooper Hewitt, Smithsonian Design Museum in New York City showcased flashy digital interactives that facilitated creative visitor engagement with the museum's collections. In the museum's newly conceived spaces, digital collections became central to the visitor experience rather than an ancillary feature. Large and enthusiastic crowds who flocked to the museum were eager not only to see physical collections but to play with innovative technology. Through large table-top touchscreens, visitors were able to access a digital repository of the museum's collections. Simply by drawing a shape, such as a circle or triangle, they were able to call up and manipulate collections items that shared a particular geometric design feature. The simple nature of the interactive made it accessible and appealing to visitors of all ages and abilities. Another playful digital interactive – the "Immersion Room" – allowed visitors to select and manipulate wallcoverings and see them projected on the walls of a room. The idea behind these and other digital interactives was to give visitors the experience of being designers by encouraging them to make choices and recognize patterns. The museum also provides visitors with a digital "pen," which allows them to "collect" objects during their visit and then access these objects later through the museum's website.[13] In this way, the physical experience of visiting the museum can be

---

12 Author's observations from visit to El Museo del Caribe, Barranquilla, Colombia, May 2016.
13 "Using the Pen," *Cooper Hewitt, Smithsonian Design Museum*, https://www.cooperhewitt.org/events/current-exhibitions/using-the-pen/.

linked directly to what museum staff hope will be a sustained connection with the museum's digital collections.

This combination of physical (in-real-life) and digital elements in interactive museum settings is the hallmark of a digital history practice that is attentive to audiences and the overall visitor experience. Although not every experiment has been successful, the evidence suggests that history museum leaders are increasingly finding productive ways to integrate digital history with the traditional educational, interpretative, and exhibitionary functions of their institutions. The staff of the Lower East Side Tenement Museum in New York City has been particularly creative in melding digital elements with in-person interpretation. In the "Shop Life" tour, which debuted in 2012, museum staff worked with exhibition designers to craft a digital installation that became an integral part of a new educator-led tour through the lower level of the museum's historic building at 97 Orchard Street. This space once housed a variety of commercial businesses from a saloon to a garment wholesaler. To narrate the history of these "shops" from the mid-nineteenth century to the late twentieth century, the museum's staff developed a mixture of immersive historic spaces, third-person interpretation, and digital installations. The final section of the tour brings all three elements together seamlessly. The guide invites visitors to sit at a long counter, which is also a projection screen and touchscreen, and instructs them to select a reproduction object from a shelf adjacent to the counter and place it in a designated spot on the counter/screen. Each individual object then triggers an array of texts, images, and videos that visitors can navigate independently to discover more about the history of commerce at 97 Orchard St.

More recently, the Tenement Museum has expanded its digital presence through a crowdsourcing website called "Your Story, Our Story" (http://yourstory.tenement.org/), which invites users to contribute objects and stories related to their families' migration histories. The website is part of a broader effort at the museum to collect and share contemporary immigration stories, building on the nineteenth- and early-twentieth-century narratives they have highlighted since the museum's founding in the 1980s. In addition to "Your Story, Our Story," museum staff have developed an exhibition and tour ("Under One Roof") at another historic building, 103 Orchard St., which tells the stories of Holocaust survivors as well as Puerto Rican migrants and Chinese immigrants of the mid to late twentieth century. As with "Shop Life," staff have integrated digital history with the physical, on-site experience, allowing visitors to see and hear from past occupants of 103 Orchard St.[14] A digital exhibition contextualizes the migration histories of Puerto Ricans, Chinese, and displaced persons and features former residents sharing their family stories, cultural narratives, material culture, and memories of the neighborhood. Conceptually, the "Under One Roof"

---

14 "Under One Roof," *Lower East Side Tenement Museum*, https://www.tenement.org/tour/under-one-roof/.

project has retained the museum's core approach of using the life stories of actual residents of a historic building to illuminate diverse histories of immigration, while adding new layers of digital storytelling in order to enrich and deepen visitors' experiences. By creating new on-site experiences and digital content – both crowdsourced and museum-curated – and expanding the chronology and scope of the history it presents, the Tenement Museum has sought to appeal to broader audiences, which previously may not have been attracted to the nineteenth- and early-twentieth-century histories of immigration the museum primarily showcased.

Over the past decade, the Smithsonian National Museum of American History – in partnership with the Roy Rosenzweig Center for History and New Media at George Mason University, the Institute of Oral History at the University of Texas El Paso, and the Center for the Study of Race and Ethnicity in America at Brown University, among other institutions – has undertaken a similar effort to document and share immigration history through the "Bracero History Project." As with the Tenement Museum's "Your Story, Our Story" website, this project combines crowdsourced materials with content produced by museum staff and affiliated public historians. The bulk of the digital "Bracero History Archive" (http://braceroarchive.org/) is a collection of oral histories conducted primarily in Spanish with former Braceros, or contract laborers who came from Mexico to the United States during and after World War II as part of a government-sanctioned guest worker program. In addition to the oral histories, the Omeka-based archive contains documents, such as identification cards and images, some of which have been contributed by site users who have personal connections to Bracero history. In addition to the digital archive, NMAH, along with the Smithsonian Institution Traveling Exhibition Service, has created a traveling exhibition and a companion online exhibition entitled "Bittersweet Harvest: The Bracero Program, 1942–1964." As with the Tenement Museum's recent initiatives, combining digital and physical elements to create a collaborative public history project that addresses a topic of continued relevance to contemporary society has been a recipe for success. Public historian Mireya Loza has written that the Bracero History Project has "contributed to the national dialogue about labor and immigration."[15] It has pushed audiences to confront the past and present of "guest workers" in the United States as well as broader questions concerning immigration reform.

The integration of digital history as part of multi-pronged efforts to engage audiences is essential as museums strive to build connections with old and new constituencies, demonstrate their continued relevance, and develop collaborative relationships with various communities. A growing number of digital projects emanating from history museums take this approach. The Detroit Historical Society's

---

15 Mireya Loza, "From Ephemeral to Enduring: The Politics of Recording and Exhibiting Bracero Memory," *The Public Historian* 38, no. 2 (May 2016): 25.

"Detroit 67: Looking Back to Move Forward" project (https://detroit1967.org/), for example, began with a digital archive (https://detroit1967.detroithistorical.org/) of both museum-collected and crowdsourced oral histories, followed by a physical exhibition at the Detroit Historical Museum as well as related public programs and community projects. The overall goal of the project is to use the history of the 1967 uprising in Detroit "as a catalyst to engage, reflect and provide opportunities to take the collective action that can help move our community forward."[16] In this way, project staff have intentionally linked digital history and public history to concrete actions related to community building in the present and future. Although challenging for museum professionals and public historians to execute, this type of multi-pronged approach which seeks to build community and address societal challenges through collaborative projects encourages the further development of a digital history practice that is relevant to, and of service to, our society.

This analysis has not attempted to offer a comprehensive accounting of the full range of digital history projects undertaken by history museums over the past three decades. Rather, it has provided detailed examples of how digital history practice can be fully integrated with the traditional educational, interpretative, and exhibitionary functions of museums and, more importantly, how digital history can enable museums to expand and deepen the ways in which they engage audiences. At its best, the skills and methods of digital history are essential components in all museum professionals' toolkits. More than just a way to provide access to collections, digital history is helping museums to become more relevant, engaging, and connected to their communities.

Bibliography

Bowen, J. "The Virtual Museum." *Museum International* 52, no. 1 (2000): 4–7.
Chenhall, R. G. "Museums and Computers: A Progress Report." *Museum International* XXX, no. 1 (1978): 52–54.
Cohen, D. J., and Rosenzweig, R. *Digital History: A Guide to Gathering, Preserving, and Presenting the Past*. Philadelphia: University of Pennsylvania Press, 2005. http://chnm.gmu.edu/digitalhistory/.
MuseWeb. https://www.museweb.net/.
Thomas, S. "Private Memory in a Public Space: Oral History and Museums." In *Oral History and Public Memories*, edited by P. Hamilton and L. Shopes. Philadelphia: Temple University Press, 2008.

---

[16] "Introducing Detroit 67: Looking Back to Move Forward," *Detroit Historical Society*, https://detroit1967.org/about/>.

Michelangela Di Giacomo, Livio Karrer

Interactive Museum & Exhibitions in Digital Public History Projects and Practices: An Overview and the Unusual Case of M9 Museum

Abstract: How are museums evolving in their mission of being institutions not any more dedicated only to collect and preserve heritage? What are some of the challenges museums face today? How is the impact of new technologies affecting the new mission and the renovated essence of museums? In this essay, the authors will briefly explain how museums have evolved from being places of collection to become places of storytelling; they will introduce some international examples of museums that make use of technological tools in their own visitor experiences; and finally they will analyze the experience of M9 – Museum of the 20th Century, an institution, opened in Venice in late 2018, that has made multimedia and interactive technology its distinguishing mark. In the conclusion, the authors will evaluate some of the most relevant critical issues that lay in the interaction among technologies and museum collections as presented in this essay.

Keywords: new technologies, exhibition design, visitor experience, new generation museums, museology and museography

Premise

Since 1995, more than 650 museums around the world have been opened or completely renewed. Even if those institutions are all different – for subjects, for funding, for structures, etc. – a green line connects many of them: a common interest in new technologies as drivers for more effective learning in the museum environment.[1] Technology has entirely affected our experience as human beings, deeply changing our skills, habits and cognitive ability. In a society in which visual, audio-visual, tactile, experiential have become bread and butter for billions of people – the same people that have gained a cheaper and easier access to culture and information, as protagonists of the so-called "knowledge society" – museums have to face these socio-anthropological revolutions.

---

[1] Guido Guerzoni, ed., *Museums on the Map 1995–2012* (Torino: Fondazione di Venezia/Umberto Allemandi & C., 2014).

Since a while, museums are places not anymore exclusively dedicated to heritage conservation, and among their tasks they can count communication, exhibition and transmission of memory, "for purposes of study, education and pleasure" (as defined by ICOM[2]). Adapting museology to contemporary forms of entertainment and communication – forms that are inherent to the society in which the museum as an institution lives and is part of – is, therefore, an essential prerequisite to carry out that mission. Beyond that: along with "critical museology," there come museums which are participated, widespread, inclusive – places of collective creation of knowledge through the interaction and involvement of both their territory and visitors.[3]

In this essay, we will briefly explain how museums have evolved from being places of collection to become places of storytelling; we will introduce some international examples of museums that make use of technological tools in their own visitor experiences; and in greater details we will analyse the experience of M9 – Museum of Twentieth-Century Italian History, an institution that has made multimedia and interactive technology its distinguishing mark. A museum whose planning we have followed and overseen, and which therefore allows us to give a detailed evaluation.

The starting premises for our next arguments are as follows:[4]

1) Museums are places of Public History: they are institutions founded on cultural projects connected to the construction of collective identities, whether they are local, national or supranational, with no regard to any underlying political motivation;

2) The use of "new" technologies is not in itself sufficient in order to assign a positive heuristic value to those experiences which employ these same technologies, whether they are exhibition-, museum- or entertainment-related;

---

[2] ICOM, General Conference, 9th, *The museum in the service of man: today and tomorrow. The museum's educational and cultural role: the papers from the Ninth General Conference of ICOM* (Paris: ICOM, 1972). New definition was born in 1974: "A museum is a non-profit making, permanent institution in the service of the society and its development, and open to the public, which acquires, conserves, researches, communicates, and exhibits, for purposes of study, education and enjoyment, material evidence of man and his environment," in "Development of the Museum Definition according to ICOM Statutes (2007–1946)": http://archives.icom.museum/hist_def_eng.html, last accessed April 13, 2020.

[3] Josep Ballart Hernández, *Manual de museos* (Madrid: Editorial Sintesis 2007); Tony Bennet, *The Birth of the Museum: History, Theory, Politics* (London; Routledge, 1995); Oscar Navarro Rojas, "Éticas, museo e inclusión: un enfoque crítico," *Museo y territorio* 4 (2011): 49–59.

[4] Ilaria Porciani, "La nazione in mostra. Musei storici europei," *Passato e presente* 79 (2010): 114; Joan Santacana i Mestre, and Francesc Xavier Hernàndez Cardona, *Museos de Historia. Entre la taxidermia y el nomadismo* (Gijòn: Trea, 2011); Berard Schiele, "Society Museums and their Identities in the Era of Globalization," in *Museums of Today. The New Museums of Society*, ed. Gabriel Alcalde i Gurt, Jusep Boya i Busquet, Xavier Roigé (Barcelona: Publicacions de l'ICRPC, 2012): 9–26; Kevin Walsh, *The Representation of the Past. Museuems and Heritage in the Post-Modern World* (London-New York: Routledge, 1992).

3) In our society there is a great demand for the 'past' and 'history' – it is enough to think about the huge development of the fictional entertainment industry (film industry, tv series, videogames, escapist literature, and so on) and the outburst of blogs, pages and groups in social media that feed on individual memories and nostalgia;
4) The distinctive difference between museums and all the media lies in the strict adherence, for what concerns the first ones, to scientific criteria of accuracy and source verification, together with a relocation into a wider historical and geographical perspective of individual memories and events.

This simple principle marks the distance between museums and entertainment industry in the use of technological instruments and storytelling techniques – that is, *de facto*, one of the fundamental principles of historical science: museums are certainly places of reconstruction and knowledge but, most of all, they are places of interpretation of the past.

From Collections to Experiences

Yet immediately after the Second World War, museums played a central function in the awkward process of reconstruction of national identities severely wounded during the conflict. The birth of institutions such as the International Council of Museums (1946) was a signal of public acknowledgment of the importance of history and heritage for looking forward to the future of the world. But it was in the 1960s, when museums changed into a more dynamic organization, that a "new museology" was born.[5] While in France the museologist George-Henry Rivière, father of the "new museology" applied to history museums, invented the "ecomuseum," in the United States "neighborhood museums" began to spread and also "visitor centers," based on the theories of Freeman Tilden.[6]

In museographical terms, "new museology" was realized through a blossoming of dioramas, widely diffused in every kind of museum – naturalistic, ethnographic, historical, etc. Inspired by the work of Artur Hazelius, yet at the beginning of the nineteenth century, the *mise en scène* of entire settings (as result of mixed original finds or completely replaced by crafted artefacts) has been the main "wow factor" at the disposal of museums in order to let the visitors truly enter the natural or social context treated. The settings of Smithsonian's Museum of Natural History and of the National Museum of American History were well-known, and they recreated anything, from the landing of Christopher Columbus in the "New World" to Julia

---
5 Luís Alonso Fernández, *Nueva Museología* (Madrid: Alianza Editorial, 2012).
6 Tilden Freeman, *Interpreting our Heritage* (Chapel Hill: University of North Carolina Press, 1957).

Child's Kitchen from her legendary tv show. Also, the Imperial War Museum in London displays famous reconstructions dedicated to the combat experience of the First World War, which are a pilgrimage destination for millions of tourists and have not been replaced until 2014.

But, somehow, the charm of dioramas seems to survive the digital revolution: still in the mid-1990s there were museums opening which considered diorama as the main tool for public engagement, although they included in their own constitutional statute the experimentation of new technologies for museology. That is the case, for example, of the Museu de Historia de Catalunya, inaugurated in 1996, which still today exposes fictitious reconstructions of battlefields, notable orators' balconies, sports bars, schools, war shelters, kitchens of the economic miracle period, factory interiors, etc., along with the case of Central Tejo converted in a heritage site as Electricity Museum (now incorporated in MAAT) in Lisbon; the entrenched routes of First World War in Dolomites Ecomuseum (Italy); the Wellington Museum in Waterloo.

The second main aspect is "All the power to the audience," a paradigm shift that has set the focus on the voice and vision of the visitors rather than putting the institution-museum at the center.[7] While the living rooms were being stuffed with televisions and VHS players; while the earlier personal computers began to render the mouse the natural extension of our hands; while the cable networks broadcasted better and better documentaries; while we were amazed by the early multimedia hypertexts, the imperative of museums became meeting the public taste for technologies. Museums started to provide rooms with displays where short documentaries and experiments made of hypertexts and interactive games were projected. And still, these first technological grafts were not always followed by any upgrade: there are museums which employ interfaces that were once innovative and that today have, indeed, disappeared from the common market – i.e. trackballs.

When does a multimedia content or a technological device become too old to succeed in its task to move, engage, entertain, intrigue the visitors, in order to raise their critical sense and desire for deepening and learning? Perhaps the point on which to reflect is not the technology employed, but rather the sense of its use. In a world that immerge us in a permanent process of "creating memory" through the 2.0 web instruments, museums are the space through which public historians can transform an oversized exposure of personal pasts in a common, shared past. To become such tools for educating citizenship education, they are now challenged to convert their contents into meaningful experience.[8]

---

[7] John D. Harrison, "Ideas of Museums in the 1990s," *The International Journal of Museum Management and Curatorship* 2 (1994): 166.
[8] Fiorenzo Alfieri et al., *Europa e musei. Identità e rappresentazioni* (Torino: Celid, 2003), E Monsterrat Iniesta, "Àgores 'Glocals': Museus per a la mediació: història, identitats i perplexitats," *Mnemòsine* 3 (2016): 35–50.

The Tour of the World through Interactive Displays

Technology is a fascinating language that gave to museum the opportunity to reconstruct, recreate and revive the past.[9] The old formula of learning through play and acquiring knowledge whilst having fun has not lost any of its strongpoints facing the challenge of technology. The challenge, indeed, is to ensure a balance between meaning and media, to use the first for enhancing the second. All the great museums of the world have thought about or are working on virtual areas that are self-sufficient in terms of narration and the increased experience of their exhibits, with some of them going as far as creating entirely multimedia itineraries: from the ones designed to zoom-in on the masterpieces of Art History (i.e. Van Gogh Immersive Experience,[10] or even the Google Art Project Bosch-capsules in museums such as the Royal Museum of Fine Arts in Brussels or the Ateliers des Lumières in Paris), to contemporary art installations in Virtual Reality (i.e. the Venice Biennale VR Experiences or the Alejandro Iñárritu's "Carne y arena" experiences hosted by Fondazione Prada in Milan[11]); from Augmented Reality Heritage and touristic apps (i.e. Augmented Expeditions or Izi Travel), to gamification in Museums (i.e. British Museum or Tate Gallery).[12]

The first distinction is between museums that are entering the multimedia world to bring back to life their collections and those new museums that have been designed totally as areas of multimedia narration, without collections or fundamentally important architectural elements. Apparently, there is a large diversity in terms of the philosophy of exhibiting and the nature of the experience.[13]

To the first kind belongs the Egyptian Museum in Turin, that has been completely set up afresh, removing a large part of the items of its enormous collection from exposition, and that now invites the visitor to interact with the same collection through a multimedia audio guide that extends the various contents and explores them through video-explanations by the Director of the Museum himself.[14]

---

9 Francesca Lanz and Elena Montanari, "Introduction. A Reflection on Innovative Experiences in 21st Century European Museums," in *Advancing Museums Practices*, ed. Francesca Lanz, Elena Montanari (Torino: Allemandi & C., 2014), 10–22.
10 The project is a perfect example about the new trend in blockbuster travelling exhibition. At this link a good video from the show in Paris: https://www.youtube.com/watch?v=gIc_533Uf54, last accessed April 13, 2020.
11 For 2019 Biennale VR public program, see https://www.labiennale.org/it/cinema/2019/venice-virtual-reality, and Inaritu's project: http://www.fondazioneprada.org/project/carne-y-arena/?lang=en, last accessed January 3, 2022.
12 Maria Luisa Bellido Gant, *Arte, museos y nuevas tecnologías* (Gijón: Trea 2001).
13 Kirsten Drotner, ed., *The Routledge Handbook of Museums, Media and Communication* (New York: Taylor and Francis, 2018).
14 For further information about the history of the renovation in the collection: https://museoegizio.it/en/discover/story/, last accessed January 3, 2022.

A middle way between these two kinds of approach is offered by the House of European History in Brussels which, although it has been projected and built *ex novo*, founds its visit on a mix of tangible objects and virtual supports. During the visit the narratives are provided by a tablet: without this device, that recognizes the visitors' position during the visit and allow to match the physical collection with the digital narratives, the visitor experience would be largely unsatisfying.[15]

Similarly, the DDR Museum in Berlin merges artefacts and technologies in which the visitor is involved with all his senses in a travel in the East Germany's everyday life: getting into a Trabant car and "driving" it through the streets of the DDR's public housing thanks to a VR video integrated in the windshield; entering a kitchen and exploring the food habits displayed on tablets; watching television lying on the sofa of a mutual living room.[16]

Also, in Brussels, to the second kind belongs the Parlamentarium. The visitor centre of the European Parliament, opened in 2011, is more advanced referring to the techno-museographic aspect. Without displaying any artefacts, big immersive exhibits (mixing architecture and projection) plunge visitors into a day of a parliamentarian and into the changing life of European people after the intervention of EU programs in their lives. It makes a massive use of technology and of interactive devices in order to let the visitor explores the history of the EU institutions and how they work.[17]

The world of media museums, with their focus on the history of communication, has produced many examples of excellent and completely interactive exhibition spaces: for example, the Netherlands Institute For Sound And Vision offers the visitors the chance to get on stage and challenge fellow visitors to a music competition, or even to join a TV broadcast set and create their own news – both of the situations are realized through a mix of scenographic elements and multimedia technology, such as cameras and motion sensors.

From a technological point of view, "new technologies" implemented in museums are not actually so "new."[18] Many reasons including: the stability of technology in itself; its availability on the market; its maintenance and, in the end, the visitors' habits in its use, lead museologists and designers to prefer "steady" technologies and with a long-time presence in the market. In a world in which interactive museum's

---

[15] The institution is entirely founded by the European Parliament; the whole process of content development is narrated in Andrea Mork, Perikles Christodoulou, *Creating the House of European History* (Luxembourg: Publication Office of the European Union, 2018).

[16] Sören Marotz, Elke Sieber and Stefan Wolle, eds, *DDR Museum Guide* (Berlin: DDR Museum Verlag GmbH, 2018).

[17] At this link is explained an educational project – good example of 'best practice' in public history – for schools and young visitors: https://www.europarl.europa.eu/visiting/en/education-learning/brussels/role-play-game, last accessed January 3, 2022.

[18] Alonzo Addison, ed., *Digital Heritage International Congress* (IEEE, 2018); Elisa Mandelli, *The Museum as a Cinematic Space: The Display of Moving Images in Exhibitions* (Edinburgh: Edinburgh University Press, 2019).

displays are basically based on projectors (the most famous kind is the "experience"/ touring exhibition dedicated to great artists, such as Van Gogh or Giotto; the Museum of Confluences in Lyon); on videowall (in this sense, the Cleveland Museum of Art is pioneering); touchscreens; AR devices (i.e. Google Glass and its followers, often employed in archaeological museums, such as Palazzo Baldini in Florence or the Histo-Pad Project for the Châteaux of the Loire Valley, and even the 3D reconstruction of Calafell citadel in Spain); also VR devices (such as Oculus and HTC Vive, along with the Louvre's project "Mona Lisa: Beyond the Glass," and also the experiment by National Museum of Finland, with whom the visitors can "dive" in 1863 and have a talk with the Emperor Alexander II); motion sensors (Bluetooth Beacon as in the Lavazza Museum in Turin, where everything interacts with a coffee cup provided with a motion sensor; and Kinect sensors, like the one used in sport museums); digital environments recreated with Unity; light design's scenographic effects (Memory and Tolerance Museum, Mexico City, or the opening soon Planet World in Washington DC) in or even olfactory experiments and gamification systems (narrative video games or trivia, as it shown at the International Spy Museum in Washington, in which the visitors have to take part in an undercover interactive spy adventure); or even web-based and social media apps (i.e. the Museum of Selfies in Glendale, California, that explores "40thousand years of selfies" and asks visitors to have fun taking photo of themselves in a broad series of scenarios); simulated sport action (i.e. FC Barcelona Stadium, Barcelona; Olympic Museum in Lausanne) – in a world like this, the contents do make the difference, as usual: in other words, both the work of the researcher and the quality of the research itself that are behind a museum's storytelling.

Why is M9 Unusual?

Regarding what has been seen so far, Italy can boast an uncommon case of avant-garde and experimentation: the newborn M9 – Museum of Twentieth-Century Italian History. Opened for a little more than a year, it is an experiment of construction of a semi-permanent exhibition space that could challenge the common understanding of "museum". In order to do that, it utilizes a massive amount of technologies sustaining a certain storytelling on a quite wide dimensional scale, focused on a poorly investigated topic in the Italian museums' system, and dedicated to an audience – composed of young and very young people – that, within the museological choices all around our Peninsula, has often been regarded as ancillary.

Italy has few other cultural institutions like it. Even if there are some other examples of all-digital and interactive museum in the country – i.e with no exhibits on display –, such as Joe Petrosino Museum in Padula (Salerno) or Museo del Tartufo di Acqualagna (Pesaro Urbino) or Stupor Mundi – Museo Federico II (Jesi, Ancona), M9 is the bigger experiment, counting on almost 3k square feet of permanent exhibition.

M9 aims to be a collective journey into the rich heritage of modern Italian history, a bridge between past and present, as the youngest citizens are not familiar with their past. M9 curators wanted to create a different kind of place where visitors were free to find their path and not being forced by chronology. Moreover, in every section the storytelling tries to match the didactic elements related with the exhibit main theme with the entertainment aspects which allow visitors to amuse themselves while learning. They will have the thrill of being in a crowded square listening to great orators; they will feel crushed by the experience of two massive wars. They will also grasp the harshness of factory work, being subjected to the pace of the assembly line. They can immerse themselves in the clothing, houses and kitchens of their great-grandparents, grandparents and parents, reliving their everyday lives. They will play with all the Italian dialects, and so much more.

Come into being without a readymade collection of exhibits, the museum's exhibitions are being developed by first writing a narrative framework and then linking up a network of the partner archives providing the specific items to be shown. M9 illustrates the last century using its own cultural heritage: the twentieth century brought photography, films, television, radio and mass media. Huge quantities of cartographical, printed, audio, video and photographic material have been digitalized and edited into interactive, sound and tactile installations.[19]

An unusual crowd-designing system, that has involved 5 multimedia and interaction design studios, an architect and a graphics coordinator – as well as more than 42 specialists of diverse historical, humanistic, social, statistical and ICT disciplines – has led to stage over 60 different interactive installations that call out the visitors to have always new approaches to knowledge. On the one hand, the attempt is to adapt the visual language to the scientific content to be transmitted in every section; on the other hand, to keep the visitors' attention throughout a long exhibition route.

M9 is a multisensorial and multimedia space, a museum with few objects but plenty of constantly renewed contents. It is built around seven core technologies: 3D graphic development using 2D sources; virtual reality scenarios; immersive scenarios; motion detection and tracking; digital displays; oleographic 3D interactive installations; audio-oriented distribution; Arduino motherboard; laser tracking; and digital signage.

Just one year after the opening, it is possible to obtain some evaluations of the success of this operation. On the one side, the visiting route appears to be quite tiring for more than a reason, including the darkness of the place; the excessive amount of contents to read and to look at; the need to interact with the installations in constantly new ways. On the other side, almost all the audiences (in different

---

[19] About M9 project there is no literature yet, but more information is available on the museum guide: Cesare De Michelis, ed., *M9 – The Museum of the 20*th *Century* (Venezia: Marsilio, 2018).

age groups) claim to be enthusiastic about the lived experience in the museum-environment – especially professors and school groups confirm they deeply benefit from this kind of approach to historical contents[20] – and they are likely to consider that this site may dispel many common place conceptions of the alleged tiresomeness of history as a discipline and of the "museum" idea itself, too.

The intergenerational relationship among different age groups, that is being established in the museum, is also meaningful: if the elderly appear to be scared of the digital technologies' approach, they are likely to prove important when it comes to decoding the historical contents for the younger ones, who, in return, serve as "tech-mediator" for the adult members of their family. Within a period of five years, the estimated time for the renovation of the permanent exhibition, these initial evaluations will perhaps look outdated, but they already provide some guidelines for reflection.

Conclusions

We still live in an era of digital enthusiasm and we are hardly capable of being objective about multimedia and interactive technologies' diffusion as tools at the service of museums' missions. We can observe, in embryonic form, that quite often technologies do not actually contribute to the spread of knowledge, and also, they do not always integrate with the museological collections.

Even when they are considered not just as tools designed to provoke the so-called "wow effect," sometimes they remain simple additions to a previous traditional museography. Whereas, on the contrary, technological instruments are harmoniously implemented in the visitors' ways in, they can be useful to touch the interest of different target audiences, who are generally disinterested in history's insights, but are likewise immersed in digital communication. But in this case, the point is not the "newness" of technology, but rather the logic lying behind its employment. Since now the trend consists in "digitalizing" the museums, the interest, or rather the challenge, will be whether this model of museum will endure over time or whether it will be made obsolete by new forms of representation and thus buried under the rubble of the model of 2.0 communication used in today's society. If museums have often used newer technologies whenever they have been available, soon – the outlines are uncertain – will it be mandatory to change everything in order to change nothing? Namely, will it be necessary to search for new tools in order to realize the museums' original mission, that is to contribute to the education of future citizens?

---

20 We pointed out more educational issues related to the collection in Livio Karrer and Michelangela Di Giacomo, "M9 – Un Ponte tra Presente, Passato e Futuro," *Bollettino di Clio* 11–12 (2019): 172–178.

Bibliography

Studio Azzurro, *Musei di narrazione. Percorsi interattivi e affreschi multimediali*, Cinisello Balsamo: Silvana Editoriale, 2011.
De Michelis, Cesare, ed. *M9 Museo del '900*, Venezia: Marsilio, 2018.
Moore, Kevin, *Museum and Popular Culture*, London and Washington: Cassel, 2000[2].
Santacana i Mestre, Joan, Hernàndez Cardona, Francesc Xavier, *Museos de Historia. Entre la taxidermia y el nomadismo*, Gijòn: Trea,2011.
Mandelli, Elisa, The museum as a cinematic space: the display of moving images in exhibitions, Edinburgh: Edinburgh University Press, 2019.

Marii Väljataga
Digital Public History in Libraries

Abstract: This chapter explores digital public history practices in libraries and points to the opportunities, imperatives, successes, and challenges therein. It discusses contemporary library operations and the novel ways in which libraries are engaging the public: crowdsourcing transcriptions, content, and image data; inviting users to contribute their expertise and experience, to interact with collections, and to co-curate. Examples of crowdsourcing and digital engagement reveal libraries to be an interesting arena for historically informed interactions and highlight the shift toward Library 2.0, a new library model that incorporates online collaboration and user-centered change.

Keywords: libraries, digital libraries, crowdsourcing, co-curation, patron engagement, transcription, library 2.0

Introduction

Advances in digital and networking technologies have vastly transformed the way people use libraries, and the way libraries, in turn, reach out to their users. The physical catalogue, the former heart of the library operation, is now displayed, space permitting, as something of a nostalgia piece from the institutional past, while increasingly intelligent and interconnected search sites run on patrons' personal laptops. Relevant hits link to immediately available e-versions of the desired content, copyright permitting. The radically remodelled logistics of consulting material empowers the user and alters the roles in information communication. If two decades ago people came into the library's ecosystem, and engaged with a pre-configured, passive repository of knowledge, it is now the library that seeks to position itself, alongside Google, in the life of the user, reaching out through various Internet tools and social media.[1] The communicative space that arises in this shift

---

[1] Diana L. H. Chan and Edward F. Spodick, "Transforming Libraries from Physical to Virtual," in *Digital Information Strategies: from Applications and Content to Libraries and People*, ed. David Baker and Wendy Evans (Oxford: Chandos, 2016); Lynn Silipigni Connaway, *The Library in the Life of the User: Engaging with People Where They Live and Learn* (Dublin, Ohio: OCLC Research, 2015). The shift in service design thinking from 'patron in the life of the library' to 'library in the life of the user' is, of course, not unique to said settings. With considerations of visitor engagement dating to the late 1980s, museums have similarly moved the 'user' to the centre of their design, replacing conservation and the educational agenda as their main focus. Jerome De Groot, *Consuming History: Historians and Heritage in Contemporary Popular Culture* (New York: Routledge, 2009), 244–245.

https://doi.org/10.1515/9783110430295-016

from collections to *connections*[2] is a promising arena for digital public history experiments, spanning grand global crowdsourcing projects and less conspicuous everyday practises of tagging and key wording that accomplish the use-based crowd-managing of the library's online offer.

The ideals of digital history – such as 'gathering, preserving and presenting the past' on the Internet[3] – suggest a promising resonance with humanities libraries and their mission as memory institutions. Libraries hold and care for the community's – or the nation's, or humanity's – written heritage, and strive to make it accessible, as per the technological culture and user expectations of the time. Commonly the repositories of publications (doubtless a problematic term in the era of multiform online production), libraries' primary mission has been to grant public access to information, to the shared body of recorded knowledge and intellectual output.[4] Library materials are systematized and maintained for *use*.[5] The aim is providing better access, enabling more effective reading practices, and supporting the creation of new research.[6] Early digitization projects of historic newspapers, manuscripts, maps and images were essential for establishing public interest in digital libraries, as well as enhancing the work of researchers.[7] However, digital *public* history implies presenting and digitally narrating history for and *with* the public.[8] Web accessibility alone does not guarantee such interaction to any collection or history

---

[2] Henrik Jochumsen, Dorte Skot-Hansen, and Casper Hvenegaard Rasmussen, "The Four Spaces of the Public Library," in *The End of Wisdom? The Future of Libraries in a Digital Age*, ed. David Baker and Wendy Evans (Cambridge, Massachusetts: Chandos, 2017).
[3] Daniel J. Cohen and Roy Rosenzweig, *Digital History. A Guide to Gathering, Preserving, and Presenting the Past on the Web* (Philadelphia: University of Pennsylvania Press, 2006).
[4] 'Publication' is necessarily dissynonymous with 'printed', its formerly prevalent meaning in library context. Regardless of media, it refers to material made available to members of the public. Terminological confusion arises as libraries (mostly national libraries) create and manage *Web archives*, which in most cases contain *public* content from the Web, rather than non-public material traditionally entrusted to the domain of archives. The term *Webrary* has been suggested to more accurately capture the essence of such a collection of Web publications. Niels Brügger, "Webraries and Web Archives – The Web Between Public and Private," in *The End of Wisdom? The Future of Libraries in a Digital Age*, ed. David Baker and Wendy Evans (Cambridge, Massachusetts: Chandos, 2017).
[5] https://libguides.ala.org/library-definition.
[6] Jeffrey A. Rydberg-Cox, *Digital Libraries and the Challenges of Digital Humanities* (Oxford: Chandos, 2006). Since subject access has traditionally been the focus of libraries, the digital access turn brings about a lesser rupture here than, for example, in archival practice. Oliver Gillian, "The Digital Archive," in *Evaluating and Measuring the Value, Use and Impact of Digital Collections*, ed. Lorna M. Hughes (London: Facet Publishing, 2012). Libraries have affirmed their commitment to the access ideal in the IFLA (International Federation of Library Associations) address to the United Nations, which included information access as one of its sustainable development goals in 2015.
[7] E.g. Gallica, Picture Australia, Papers Past. Karen Calhoun, *Exploring Digital Libraries* (London: Facet Publishing, 2014).
[8] Serge Noiret, "Digital Public History," in *A Companion to Public History*, ed. David Dean (Hoboken, NJ: Wiley, 2018).

project, and quantitative metrics of an item's Web page activity fail to capture the whole story of its public impact.[9] In various examples, libraries have engaged the public beyond the consultation of sources, and established themselves as an important setting for user–specialist interaction over historical themes and materials.

Transformed from their pre-digital tradition of social engagement, libraries' functions now include providing support and navigation in the changed information realm, and serving as an active gateway to skills, including media and digital literacy. The speedy information service is increasingly complemented by makerspaces as well as online interactions that define and serve collaborative group goals, such as crowdsourced transcription projects.[10] With the growing repertoire of Web engagements, libraries' public-historical activities often times blend into those of museums and archives. This chapter discusses some of the prevalent forms of online user engagement in libraries today – crowdsourcing for transcriptions, content, and image information.[11] Crowdsourcing in its various designs speaks to libraries' potential for historically informed interactions, and exemplifies the shift towards Library 2.0, a new library model that incorporates online collaboration and user-centred change to deliver effective services.

What is a Digital Library?

Among the varied tools and digital environments evolving from humanities computing, digital libraries are defined through their *organized* quality, their imposition of order on content. Digital libraries are 'focused collection[s] of digital objects [. . .], along with methods for access and retrieval, and for selection, organisation and maintenance of the collection'.[12]

---

9 Thomas Cauvin, *Public History. A Textbook of Practice* (New York: Routledge, (2016) 2022); Paula Bray et al., "Rethinking Evaluation Metrics in Light of Flickr Commons," in *Museums and the Web 2011: Proceedings*, ed. Jennifer Trant and David Bearman (Toronto: Archives & Museum Informatics, 2011).
10 See: Rose Holley, "Crowdsourcing: How and why should libraries do it?," *DLib Magazine*, no. March/April (2010).
11 The original 2006 definition of crowdsourcing by Jeff Howe was concerned with outsourcing activities previously performed by employees. Since then, more comprehensive definitions have emerged (see: Laura Carletti, Derek McAuley et al., "Digital Humanities and Crowdsourcing: An Exploration," in *Museums and the Web 2013*, ed. Nancy Proctor and Rich Cherry, Silver Spring, MD: Museums and the Web, 2013). It is, however, important to note that not all instances of online user participation constitute crowdsourcing. Interactions that do not have a specific goal towards library-held digital content, such as sharing and discussing discoveries, would tend to fall outside its scope.
12 Ian H. Witten and David I. Bainbridge, *How to Build a Digital Library* (San Francisco: Morgan Kaufmann, 2003), 6. For an overview of relevant definitions at the close of digital libraries' first decade, and for tensions between content-focussed research perspectives and institutionally oriented librarian perspectives, see Christine L. Borgman, *From Gutenberg to the Global Information*

Project Gutenberg, the first and oldest digital library dating from 1971, provides electronic access to older works of world literature (public domain texts) shortly after their copyright term expires.[13] Gallica, the digital library of the Bibliothèque Nationale de France launched in 1997, brought to the remote user a range of materials from manuscripts to audio recordings.[14] Digital repositories hosted by 'traditional' libraries typically form part of hybrid environments, where electronic and paper-based sources co-exist. In such settings, emphasis shifts from transactions to *flows* between different repositories of information, and between the repositories and their users.[15] Europeana, an aggregate pan-European online library providing a single access point to the continent's cultural heritage was launched in 2010.[16] The ultimate access and searchability ideal with minimal selection or preservation agenda is introduced in the broadest, most ambitious digital repositories: Google Books and Open Content Alliance, announced in 2004 and 2005 respectively.[17] They strive to 'extend online convenience to offline wisdom'.[18] While falling outside the stricter definitions of digital libraries that require institutional guidance and curation in minimal form, these projects nevertheless stretch our imagination of what a library is, and condition the future of the institution by habituating user preferences, introducing lower-cost access digitization, and driving use-value based decisions in service development.

The path and nature of digital libraries appear compatible with the idea of increasing web interactions and collaboration with the user. However, in her discussion of Dan Cohen's 2010 advocacy of digital libraries as active, open, 'chatty' social platforms, Karen Calhoun points to libraries' long-established traditions and practices that could potentially obstruct a painless march forward: the values of engagement

---

Infrastructure, ed. William Y. Arms, Digital Libraries and Electronic Publishing (Cambridge, Massachusetts: The MIT Press, 2000), 35–52.
13 www.gutenberg.org; Calhoun, *Exploring Digital Libraries* (London: Facet Publishing, 2014), 17, 55.
14 https://gallica.bnf.fr.
15 Lorcan Dempsey, *The Network Reshapes the Library* (Chicago: American Library Association, 2014); Lorcan Dempsey, "Library Places and Digital Information Spaces: Reflections on Emerging Network Services," *Alexandria* 11, no. 1 (1999), 54.
16 https://www.europeana.eu.
17 Mass digitization projects such as Google Books and Open Content Alliance engage in access *digitization*, which is technologically less demanding than producing preservation-grade digital items that strive for quality and faithfulness. See, for example: Kalev Leetaru, "Mass book digitization: The deeper story of Google Books and the Open Content Alliance," *First Monday* 13, no. 10 (2008).
18 Scott Rosenberg, "How Google Book Search Got Lost," *Wired*(2017), https://www.wired.com/2017/04/how-google-book-search-got-lost/ Unlike the Open Content Alliance, the Google Books project is still continued today, even though the scanning process has drastically slowed down since its peak in 2010–2011 – a decade-long legal battle arising from copyright infringement allegations caused the project to lose both momentum and ambition. See: ibid.

and user-created content are not necessarily easily integrated with the librarians' values of authority and authenticity.[19]

When considering the digital space where the library interacts with its public, another recent shift is apparent. Traditionally, the library has endeavoured to bring in the broadest attainable range of material, the world of knowledge, and facilitate its local use. While this continues to be a salient ambition, the very opposite process has gained momentum. The post-digital turn library increasingly concerns itself with curating local material and making it available for the public outside, on the Internet.[20] This occurs through national libraries digitizing postcards, public libraries digitizing their city's menus, university libraries enabling access to doctoral theses through institutional repositories and potentially changing the landscape of monograph publishing. Libraries participate in the glocal knowledge promotion characteristic of international public history, and through their online presence, enable local pasts to resonate as universally relevant and cross-culturally relatable.

New Ways of Engaging the Public: Texts and Beyond

Libraries' move online is more complex than digitizing and uploading content. In order to achieve the usefulness and usability expected of an information source today, additional work needs to be done to convert older, non-standard material into searchable documents. Such steps for the libraries include text segmentation, optical character recognition (OCR), annotating, keywording and archiving the content. Libraries perform the technology-reliant formatting and the standardized exercises of metadata creation and treatment. However, crowdsourcing the subsequent high-volume operations that allow for content exploration, such as transcribing or correcting the digital image, makes the transition from analogue to digital feasible and cost-effective, and, quite invaluably, invites the user to engage with the library, and with the historical material in new, interactive ways.

The first public crowdsourcing effort to correct texts that do not easily lend themselves to satisfactory machine-readings was the *Trove* newspapers project at the National Library of Australia, launched in 2008 and internationally celebrated for its wide-scale success (Fig. 1). At a time when little was known about crowdsourcing behaviour, this innovative project was motivated by a desire to offer high

---

19 Calhoun, *Exploring Digital Libraries* (London: Facet Publishing, 2014), 213.
20 Andrew Prescott, "The Digital Library," in *Evaluating and Measuring the Value, Use and Impact of Digital Collections*, ed. Lorna M. Hughes (London: Facet Publishing, 2012), 20.

quality search, rather than ideals of user engagement.²¹ Libraries worldwide followed suit, enlisting the help of their patrons, and now such volunteering often simply blends into the library's digital operation as one of the activity options offered when viewing an item. The National Library of Estonia hosts a freely accessible newspaper archive *Digar* with titles dating back to 1821 (Fig. 2). Estonian newspapers, published in blackletter typeface up until the 1940s, are in need of correction, as the OCR-assisted transcripts are often erroneous to the point of non-comprehension. Upon coming across articles of interest, users can easily settle into the process of correcting the texts. As the video campaign for Europeana's *Transcribathon* suggests, this activity can be rather addictive,²² and the *Digar* staff rejoice over instances where users log on in search of an article and remain online to correct an entire year's worth of editions for their newspaper of interest.

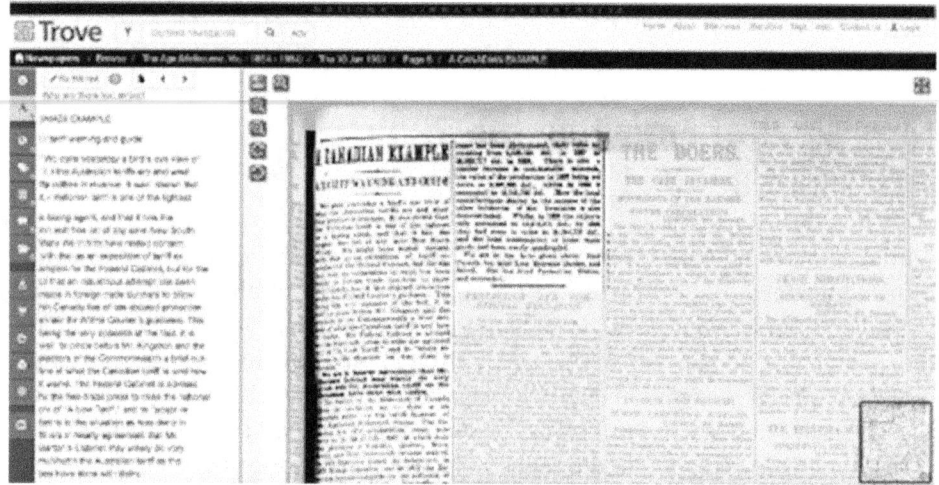

Fig. 1: The Trove online service was launched at the National Library of Australia in 2008 as the first public crowdsourcing effort to correct digitized texts: https://trove.nla.gov.au/ (accessed 19.11.2019).

In 2010, University College London, together with the UCL Library and the UCL Centre for Digital Humanities, launched *Transcribe Bentham*, a collaborative initiative to transform previously unpublished manuscripts by British philosopher Jeremy Bentham into searchable documents, for accessibility and long-term preservation.²³ The material is fascinating to browse, and the volunteer may feel like a history detective,

---

21 Rose Holley, "Crowdsourcing Based Curation and User Engagement in Digital Library Design," in *Rose Holley's Blog – Views and News on Digital Libraries and Archives* (2017).
22 https://transcribathon.com/en/.
23 http://blogs.ucl.ac.uk/transcribe-bentham/.

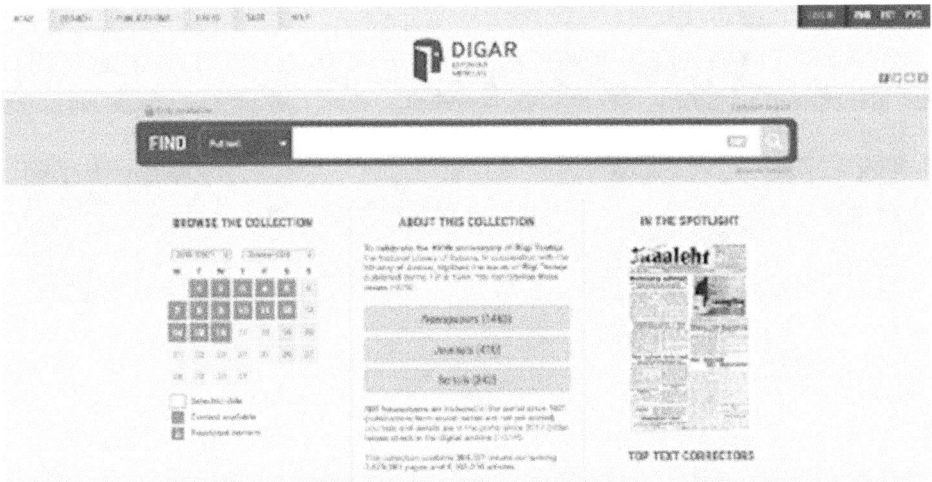

Fig. 2: The digital newspaper archive Digar at the National Library of Estonia features the top text correctors on its main page: https://dea.digar.ee/ (accessed 19.11.2019).

deciphering handwriting with all its corrections and strikethroughs, delving into the thought process, mannerisms and humour of the author. The project website features a *Benthamometer* to visually convey the progress of the transcription works, and volunteers have been credited in the published volumes of the *Collected Works*, which can be consulted freely online. Transcripts have proven to be of a high standard. Transcribers have thus played an instrumental part, co-creating this body of knowledge with the researchers who edit the transcripts for publishing. They have contributed to uncovering a more nuanced, humane Bentham, who had long been portrayed as a 'cold calculator of pleasures and pains'.[24]

Europeana, the platform that unites libraries, archives and museums across Europe, launched their first international *Transcribathon* in 2016, inviting volunteers to competitively decipher and transcribe handwritten stories from World War I. Europeana 1914–1918 is a digital archive that organises collection days and exhibits digitized personal records, such as diaries, sketchbooks, letters, postcards, certificates, but also objects like helmets, uniforms and embroidered badges. In order to improve the usability of handwritten documents, the designated tool *Transcribathon.eu* was created, where volunteer transcribers can 'bring history to life' and explore the intimate accounts from 100 years ago (Fig. 3). While one may engage in the activity anytime,

---

24 Tim Causer et al., "'Making Such Bargain': Transcribe Bentham and the Quality and Cost-Effectiveness of Crowdsourced Transcription," *Digital Scholarship in the Humanities* 33, no. 3 (2018), 483. See also: Tim Causer and Melissa Terras, "Crowdsourcing Bentham: Beyond the Traditional Boundaries of Academic History," *International Journal of Humanities and Arts Computing* 8, no. 1 (2014).

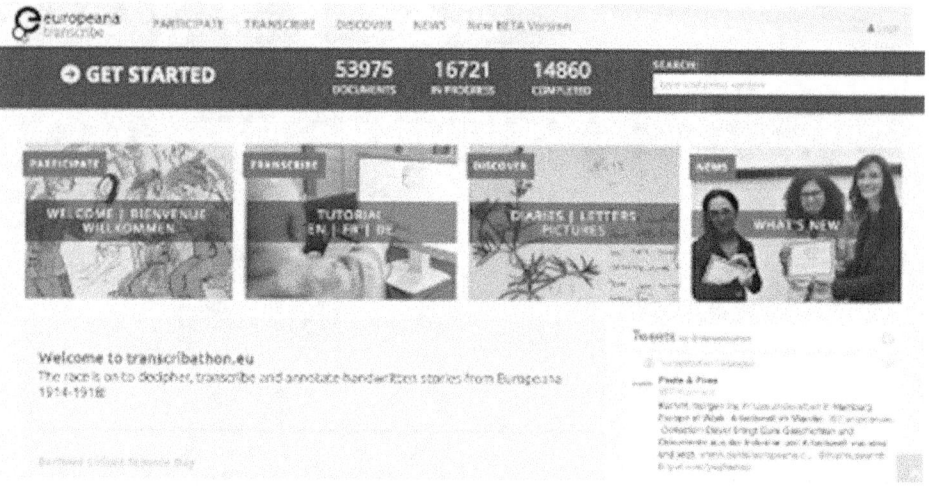

Fig. 3: Europeana's Transcribathon.eu (accessed 19.11.2019).

anywhere, special *Transcribathon* runs are also organised, such as the Transcribathon Campus in June 2017 at the Berlin State Library, or the Centenary Tour Finale Transcribathon, hosted at the House of European History in Brussels in November 2018, marking the end of Europeana's campaign commemorating the centenary of the First World War. Such runs see historians, students and history enthusiasts compete in transcribing and annotating unique, digitalised, hand-written testimonies. The exercise is managed within institutional frames – providing access to documents involves curation, and transcription outcomes are assessed by a jury of historians, thus upholding the professional standards for the sources created while expanding the sense of public ownership of heritage and resources. The participatory endeavour brings the transcriber into thorough, intimate contact with wartime experiences and lives, and renders the distant historical conflict an experience that continually invokes emotions as part of a shared, living legacy.[25] Transcribing may just turn the volunteer into an 'evangelist for the importance of history to contemporary life'.[26]

Traditional libraries have also successfully incorporated user transcription into their online offer, making collections more interactive and ultimately more accessible. In 2011, the New York Public Library launched their award-winning website *What's on the Menu?*, crowdsourcing the transformation of their digitised restaurant menus (9,000 images) into a searchable resource for culinary history. The project's

---

[25] Ross Wilson, "Volunteering for Service: Digital Co-Curation and the First World War," *International Journal of Heritage in the Digital Era* 1, no. 4 (2013).
[26] Curt Hopkins on the U.S. War Papers crowdsourcing project, quoted in Hilda Kean and Paul Martin, eds., *The Public History Reader* (New York: Routledge, 2013), 8.

popularity exceeded expectations and the staff had to re-prioritize digitisation queues to meet user demand for new menus to transcribe.[27]

Working with texts is an active yet leisurely way of acquiring cultural-historical information, and habituating users to this practice has the potential to improve the reach and impact of library collections. It provides users with an experience of direct, seemingly unmediated exploration of historical sources (which may be, for better presentation, selected and contextualized by specialists), and empowers them to create useful, usable documents for future visitors and researchers on the site. Through the shared task of creating and improving access, the user assumes part of the library's mission. Nowadays, artificial intelligence software such as OverProof, trained on the manual corrections in the Australian newspaper archive, can be used to improve OCR-detected texts, so user participation could, in the future, be particularly relevant for more difficult sources, and resemble archival detective work.[28]

The digital library user also engages with resources beyond text improvement, as crowdsourcing initiatives cover the entire life cycle of digital content.[29] Depending on the library, users may have the opportunity to organise content into thematic categories, contribute keywords, assess, grade, and comment on sources, compile public 'shelves' and reading lists, correct annotations, 'georectify' historical maps, and participate in hackathons aimed at improving the use of library datasets.[30] Libraries increasingly encourage users to structure and contextualise library-held knowledge, relying on their own expertise.[31] This follows the ideal of a user-driven environment and user-to-user sharing that the library helps facilitate – reading lists, thematic content groups and keywords can be adopted and added to by other users, and, as libraries endeavour to become interactive platforms, users are given tools for sharing and discussing the sources. Libraries adopt the concept of curation, as it expands beyond the field of museums and comes to signify something of a mapmaking endeavour

---

[27] Michael Lascarides and Ben Vershbow, "What's on the Menu?: Crowdsourcing at the New York Public Library," in *Crowdsourcing our Cultural Heritage*, ed. Mia Ridge, *Digital Research in the Arts and Humanities* (London: Routledge, 2014).

[28] Rose Holley, "National Digital Library of India," in *Rose Holley's Blog – Views and News on Digital Libraries and Archives* (2017).

[29] Johan Oomen and Lora Aroyo categorize crowdsourcing activities in the GLAM sector according to the main activities and workflow of heritage institutions. Using the Digital Content Life Cycle model from the National Library of New Zealand, they maintain that crowdsourcing may play a role in each of the five stages: creating, discovering, managing, describing and using/reusing digital content. Johan Oomen and Lora Aroyo, "Crowdsourcing in the Cultural Heritage Domain: Opportunities and Challenges," in *Proceedings of the 5th International Conference on Communities and Technologies* (New York: Association for Computing Machinery, 2011).

[30] See: Robin Camille Davis, "Hackathons for Libraries and Librarians," *Behavioral & Social Sciences Librarian* 35, no. 2 (2016).

[31] For example, browsing the digital archive of the National Library of Estonia, the user is invited to contribute keywords to the content that he or she is familiar with, thus creating content groups with items that belong together, according to the user's thematic expertise.

that opens new routes through a subject or a people.³² An interesting example of digital curation is British Library Labs and their open-source, participatory, social platform Curatorial, born at the Library's 2-day hackathon event in 2013. Its aim was to provide a dynamic, user-led encounter with digital cultural heritage collections, allowing users to discover, annotate and directly share findings on social media.³³

A library built together with its users has become the ideal across different library types, meaningfully involving users has become part of their essence. Crowdsourcing reveals important information about the library's role and status as an active arena for public-historical interactions. The NYPL had prepared to considerably enhance their interface for the Menus project after the initial beta, employing principles of game design to keep the user intrigued, but instead found themselves having to supply more generous amounts of digitised images for the eager public to transcribe. The Bentham project similarly concluded that engaging content is what brings and hooks people to a participatory transcription project. Libraries have the power to harness people's inborn curiosity in novel ways, and enter the general economy of engagement for the good of historically charged explorations and community building. The interesting sources and the public mission inspire participants to give their time. Trevor Owens at the Library of Congress observes the broader cultural commitment and appeal of library crowdsourcing: "It is about offering your users the opportunity to participate in public memory."³⁴

Following the ideals of user engagement, the activities of museums, archives and libraries occasionally overlap. Libraries not only crowdsource for text correction and improved metadata, but also for actual content to be included in their diverse collections. The National Library of Singapore collects moments and memories related to the city-state from people, companies, organisations and groups in the framework of the Singapore Memory Project (Fig. 4). Submissions of texts, images, video and audio files are invited with the aim to expand and enrich the city's historical record, as published sources and the oral history tradition complement each other in the library's holdings.³⁵ The library's mission to collect and structure knowledge no longer necessarily refers to published material alone. Not only users' expertise but also users' *experience* matters, and the library proposes itself as a platform for the collection, preservation and sharing of this experience, thus opening itself up as a more nuanced, co-created carrier of memory.

---

32 Hans Ulrich Obrist, *Ways of Curating* (New York: Farrar, Straus and Giroux, 2014).
33 http://labs.bl.uk/Curatorial+2.
34 Quoted in Lascarides and Vershbow, "What's on the Menu?: Crowdsourcing at the New York Public Library," in *Crowdsourcing our Cultural Heritage*, ed. Ridge, *Digital Research in the Arts and Humanities* (London: Routledge, 2014), 115.
35 www.singaporememory.sg.

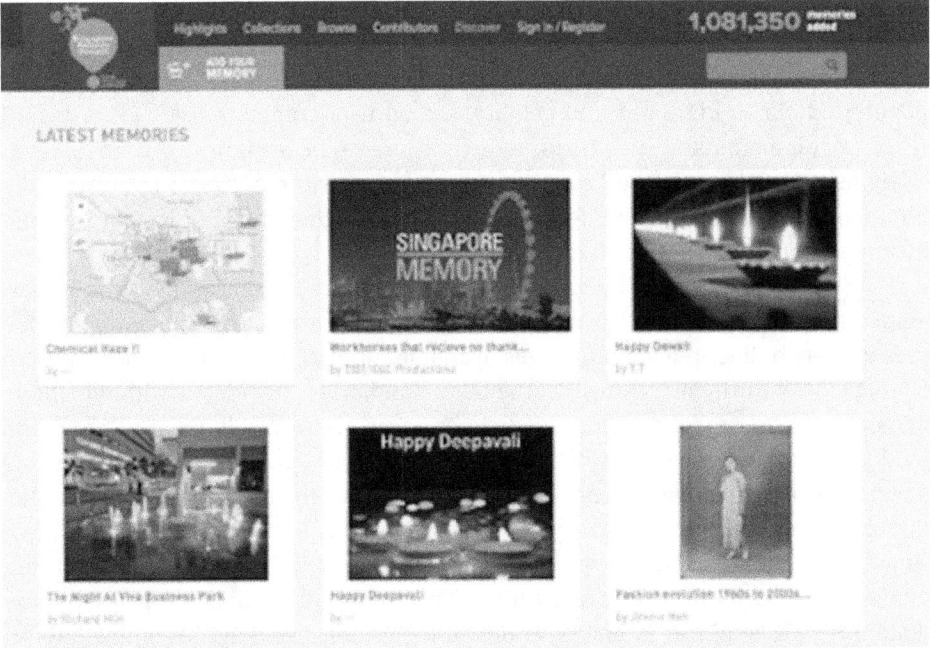

Fig. 4: The Singapore Memory Project – the National Library of Singapore collects texts, images, video and audio files linked to the city-state to enrich the nation's shared memory and foster community engagement (accessed 19.11.2019).

Image and Place

Images are a particularly potent medium to capture the imagination of users. Visual collections appeal to diverse audiences, and the digitization of photographs documenting people, events, and life at large has been an important driver for popular interest in digital libraries. Imagery invites interaction on social media, and serves as an important tool for exchanging historical information in libraries. 2008 saw the launch of Flickr Commons, a partnership of memory institutions on a social media platform to allow for greater visibility of image collections, and provide opportunities to interact with the material, tagging, discussing, annotating, reusing it. Libraries, alongside archives and museums – 114 institutions in 2022 – expose their collections through the platform, encourage people to help identify the events, persons and locations depicted, and facilitate conversation towards deduction and discovery. The information uncovered is then used to improve image metadata, and links to the relevant user comments may find their way into the library catalogue.

The reach and impact of the libraries' Flickr presence is assessed through quantitative metrics such as 'likes' and qualitative measures such as the content of the discussion occurring between users, and the interventions of library staff.[36] Amid expressions of general delight, commentators contribute historical context to the photos, and reference the sources used. The Library of Congress even ran a special page on Flickr to highlight and celebrate good user commentary.[37] Library staff react to comments and questions, and link photos in response to user interest. Users ask about the pictured event or the extent of war damage to the city in the photo, and libraries provide information. The photos thus inspire two-way communication of historical knowledge.

On the one hand, digital photo collections alter our relationship to space. For example, a monument researcher may be able to conduct visual and iconographic analyses entirely online, relying on images available through digital collections, without having to visit the memory sites. On the other hand, user interactions with the library demonstrate that the place and lived experiences are precisely what activate and lend relevance to image collections. The postcards and old place photographs are among the most frequently consulted sources in *Digar*, the digital archive at the National Library of Estonia. Corrections to item descriptions are actively submitted, sometimes for images featuring as little as a simple stone wall, which a local tour guide recognises to be a castle in her town. The incorporation of user-suggested information regarding places in images is one of the established ways for online interactions to yield new knowledge for libraries, and for users to experience a more active, personal relationship to the institution.

Conclusion

The transforming library in the digital era presents a number of contrasts. The physical and the digital collections coexist, but their full integration into a seamless information experience is, in most cases, still sought after. The institutional image and professional identity of staff continue to be linked to an educational repository of 'confirmed' knowledge, while crowd participation and user engagement are accepted as the new ideals going forward. Crowd-contributed material and corrections mostly appear with special markings in library catalogues, and whether this distinction could ultimately be abandoned remains to be seen. A balance is sought between fears of losing reliability, and the model of fruitful co-curation between library professionals and their publics. Libraries experiment with new ways of retaining relevance and continuing the mission to present their collections. The new,

---

[36] Bray et al., "Rethinking Evaluation Metrics in Light of Flickr Commons," in *Museums and the Web 2011: Proceedings*, ed. Trant and Bearman (Toronto: Archives & Museum Informatics, 2011).
[37] https://www.flickr.com/photos/library_of_congress/sets/72157623212811048/.

crowdsourced content is monitored by librarians, as the institution seeks to uphold its standards of knowledge mediation.

The library's position between the narrating museum and the documenting archive is increasingly challenged. Unlike archives, libraries assume an educational mission, but unlike museums, they are not very good at providing context for the collections. Increased searchability means fragmented narratives, decontextualization, eroding source-criticism, and use-value based selection of texts and formats by users to work with. Digital libraries could do more to consider the implications of digital reading, and respond to information needs not only in terms of ever-greater accessibility, but by providing context and navigation in the digital information realm.

The state of digital public history has been criticized as presenting 'many collections, little history'.[38] Co-curation is oftentimes little more than collective shelving. Digital databases and image banks lack historical narratives and solid ideas for users on how to work with the source material offered. Contemplation over *why* material is released online, and how exactly co-produced discussions are to be used, often remains in the background as digital collections grow and interaction tools multiply. The collaboration between Europeana and the Digital Public Library of America (DPLA) on Europeans migrating to the United States in the 19th and 20th centuries is a splendid example of meaningful online availability with expert commentary and contextualisation.[39] Collaboration with other memory institutions and external specialists on community engagement projects is a fruitful way to add substance to digital public history activities in libraries.

As libraries search for novel ways to matter, to share their collections and invite user interaction with held material, crowdsourcing and other participatory endeavours are in increasing limelight. User interest in transcription projects has suggested that libraries as public institutions of knowledge continue to have the power to capture people's curiosity and invite participation in public memory making. As Library 2.0 emerges to be an interactive platform, it has the chance to expand the library's role in curation and, through meaningful feedback and conversation, encourage users to contribute information backed by evidence, thus advancing source-critical co-creation of historical knowledge.

---

38 Fien Danniau, "Public History in a Digital Context," *Low Countries Historical Review* 128, no. 4 (2013), 135.
39 https://pro.europeana.eu/post/new-virtual-exhibition-leaving-europe-a-new-life-in-america.

Bibliography

Lascarides, Michael, and Ben Vershbow. "What's on the Menu?: Crowdsourcing at the New York Public Library." In *Crowdsourcing our Cultural Heritage*, edited by Mia Ridge. London: Routledge, 2014.

Calhoun, Karen. *Exploring Digital Libraries*. London: Facet Publishing, 2014.

Evans, Wendy, and David Baker, eds. *The End of Wisdom? The Future of Libraries in a Digital Age*. Cambridge, Massachusetts: Chandos, 2017.

Evans, Wendy, and David Baker, eds. *Digital Information Strategies: from Applications and Content to Libraries and People*. Oxford: Chandos, 2016.

Causer, Tim, Kris Grint, Anna-Maria Sichani, and Melissa Terras. "'Making Such Bargain': Transcribe Bentham and the Quality and Cost-Effectiveness of Crowdsourced Transcription." *Digital Scholarship in the Humanities*, no. 3 (2018).

Rabea Rittgerodt
Publishing Public History in the Digital Age

Abstract: Publishers have to adapt their work, service and support through all kinds of changes being brought on by the digital age. Historians, especially public historians, have long been very active and innovative when publishing findings and sharing their research online. What does digital publishing mean in 2020? And what does publishing public history entail, specifically?

Keywords: hardcopy, e-book, database, open access, subsidy, print-on-demand, journal

Introduction

The publishing world is going through a revolution – once again. With over four billion people being online, the printed book can no longer be the only way to provide academics with scholarly content anymore. New and not so new digital developments like e-books, databases, and open access publications are setting new standards, and publishing houses need to adapt to these, or be in danger of becoming expendable and useless. This article describes what publishing models are used in academic publishing houses, and what they do to serve the needs of their customers and the fast-growing online community.

Every bit of information on the internet is optimized to fit our need for instant and easy access. This change has made a vast impact on how (public) historians do research, and also on how publishers publish and grant access to it afterwards. If we agree on the very broad definition of public history as something that "create[s] and shape[s] historical knowledge in the public sphere for and with a non-academic audience,"[1] any kind of scholarly publication on history is, by definition, public history. Scholarly publishing, and also (some) non-fiction publishing, is one means to push historical research into the public sphere, and make the public interact with it. Book presentations (digital or analog) are one example of non-academics interacting and engaging with historians and their research. This direct form of "sharing authority"[2] is, in essence, what public history is all about. And its in the interest of publishers and public historians to kindle and nurture the public's interest.

---

[1] See Ljubinka Petrovic-Ziemer, "Public History – a short introduction." https://www.frient.de/en/blogdata/tj-blog/public-history-a-short-introduction, accessed 23 March, 2021.
[2] Michael Frisch, *A Shared Authority. Essays on the Craft and Meaning of Oral and Public History* (Albany: State University of New York Press, 1990).

https://doi.org/10.1515/9783110430295-017

The "digital" transformed (and still is transforming) the traditional publishing world. This is specifically true for history publishing. Public historians, it seems, are using more digital tools and digital data to tell their stories, and thus are more successful in including and attracting a non-academic audience than other academics, because their main focus is interacting with the public. Open peer review for example is one form especially used by public historians, in order to get their research and their agenda spread and make it openly accessible. People don't have to be academics to criticize or comment on articles/chapters, so this opens up a whole different world.

With the advent of the Internet and information technologies, the ways in which we (and the public generally) both produce and consume knowledge has changed significantly, as has its transfer and spread; everyone can write/publish and read about everything everywhere. This gives a whole new meaning to the word "public," and public historians might have been among the first ones to acknowledge this, because it changed how they worked.

Publishers are aware of this shift as well, in no small part because it has shaped the industry so dramatically and has widened their target group. The historian and the publisher share a lot of common ground, the most important one being the role of the communicator.[3] Both professions want to share the product of research and reflection with a larger audience,[4] if for diverging reasons. Traditionally, historians have sought a large academic audience to share their findings with, be it for academic reputation, for sparking new discussions, for career purposes. Commercial publishers, on the other hand, want to share acdemics works with an academic and non-academic audience mostly for financial reasons,[5] as they want to sell. University presses are somewhat different, because they don't rely as heavily on profit, but still have to cover their own costs and do everything they can to sustain scholarship (which is something non-university presses do as well of course). At present, university presses in the US/UK are going through an especially harsh period with governments cutting down their financial institutional support, especially in the humanities. Since most of the UPs depend upon their institutions' endowments, this is not good news.

In this chapter I will look at different kinds of publications, from the conventional (but far from boring!) hardcover, to more innovative models like e-books and

---

[3] James P. Roscow, "Crossing Over Between History and Publishing," *The Public Historian* 4.2 (1982): 29–34.

[4] Of course, there is a difference between the historian being the creator of said research while the publisher is only engaging on a more technical level (editing, typesetting, printing, distributing etc.) with the research. Still, both parties want a big audience, a big public, to interact and engage with the published research.

[5] Some of the history departments in publishing houses also really do believe in their "duty" to publish well researched and profound content, even if that sometimes doesn't equal making lots of money.

e-databases and also new ways in which publications can be means of open interaction between academics.

Models of Publication

Publishing remains a key mode of bringing knowledge into the world. Especially within the field of public history publishing means more than just printing a book, uploading an article, or writing a blog post. Quite often it also specifically calls for interaction with the public, for example on social media platforms such as Twitter,[6] Facebook[7] or Instagram.[8] So how exactly does one publish historical findings, how does one share research with the public? How does one make sure of reaching the widest possible audience, and make sure people interact? This is important for historians, but absolutely essential for the work of public historians. Sharing research with an audience outside the academic sector is vital to the field.

a) Print

The first and most obvious thing that comes to mind is the printed book. Hardback or softcover, linen bound or paperback, sewn or glued, printed in offset or digitally. Those are the most common ways for (humanitites) academics to publish their findings, and already within this one product there are endless possibilities. Digital print is actually what most bigger publishing houses are using today,[9] since the quality of the print has improved enormously during the last decade. Its faster, less expensive, and equally good as offset print. The manuscript is typeset and printed, and afterwards ready to be shipped and distributed worldwide.

The vast majority of academic books is not sold in bookstores, but to almost every library and university institute across the globe. Because that is where they are needed most.[10] The negative side effect is quite obvious: The "public" is not involved

---

6 See https://twitter.com/Herstory_Club/status/1304857396913807361.
7 See https://www.facebook.com/thomas.cauvin.5/posts/10215180854234506.
8 See https://www.instagram.com/p/CEbs0-0Hpcc/.
9 Offset printing technology uses plates, usually made from aluminum, which are used to transfer an image onto a rubber "blanket," and then rolling that image onto a sheet of paper. It's called offset because the ink is not transferred directly onto the paper. Digital printing doesn't use plates the way offset does, but instead uses options such as toner (like in laser printers) or larger printers that do use liquid ink. When each piece needs a unique code, name or address, digital is the only way to go.
10 Academics writing for other academics is still common practice, so publishing houses will feed into that behaviour as long as they can make good money out of it.

in academic discourse, knowledge is not shared. Publishers see the need for open access publications in books that are dealing with certain topics, but when they decide on distributing books to the trade market, its because they hope they will sell well – no noble motive involved. Public historians write books specifically for the public, which means they aim to write in a more accessible and direct way, to encourage engagement, to 'bridge the gap.' Plus, they write books about where history scholars and the public work together (in politics for instance),[11] to make a case for interacting on different levels. And, of course, they also write textbooks for colleagues and students, talking about what exactly it is their field tries to do, and how to get involved.[12]

b) E-Books

When e-books came into the picture (I am talking about mass usage of e-books in trade publishing starting in the late 1990s, not the development of the first book on floppy disk) – first the simple PDF, afterwards the more evolved EPUB (the first one being available in 2007) – publishers were diffident on investing in them. After all, printed books had existed for 1800 years, so there was some hesitance towards the "new" technology. Publishers are quite conservative and it takes them a while to get used to new ideas. But little by little, academic publishers started to adapt to the changing market situation. It is still common to publish e-books only as a side-product of the printed version, but its usually done in one go. The data is there, so why not use it for two different formats. Converting word files into XML is rather easy, and not expensive either. This opens up the product to different and more diverse user groups. Books published by (academic) publishing houses have a huge reach, and almost all big libraries worldwide receive a copy.

Once libraries buy the e-book, everyone affiliated with said library can access the content at any given time (access to the network provided). The big fear among publishers (that readers would print out the e-book version and copy it many times for all their fellow colleagues or students) has not (completely) come true.

During the last five to seven years, more authors/societies asked to publish their manuscripts e-only, which means they did not want a printed book at all. But the majority of (humanities) authors still wants a hardcopy of their book on their shelf, so publishers still offer a printed version, too. Also, no one knows how people will read in 10 to 15 years from now, and although it has been predicted many times that the e-book will

---

10 Academics writing for other academics is still common practice, so publishing houses will feed into that behaviour as long as they can make good money out of it.
11 See Alix R. Green, *History, Policy and Public Purpose: Historians and Historical Thinking in Government*, (London: Palgrave Macmillan, 2016).
12 See Thomas Cauvin, *Public History: A Textbook of Practice* (London: Routledge, (2016) 2022).

take over the print book, figures show that while the usage of e-books has risen from 3 to 7% within the last five years, the print book sales have not dropped accordingly.

Libraries prefer e-books though. They want digitized material on their servers to serve the needs of students and scholars, and make it possible for them to read at all times and places. It is also much more elegant to embed digital content like podcasts, video and audio material, websites in general, animations and images in an e-book. A printed book can only provide a URL which you have to copy manually into an electronic device. Since it is highly probable that we will use even more digital content in the future (no matter what subject), e-books seem like the obvious choice.

c) E-Journals

One rather new development is the hypbrid (print plus digital) and online only, the e-journal, which, contrary to traditional journals, is not available in print unless someone absolutely insists on the print version. This does not necessarily mean open access, but it still helps to enhance access to academic content for a broader audience. A perfect example of this new journal format is the e-journal of the International Federation for Public History (IFPH): *International Public History*. The very first issue is open access,[13] to show as many people as possible what current debates in the field are, and what doing public history means. Another example is the *History Workshop Journal*, which is "committed to innovative scholarship, accessible writing and lively engagement with the politics of historical knowledge continue to attract readers within and beyond the academic community."[14] And while they predominantely publish in print, they also offer e-only versions for institutional or corporate customers.

If you are an academic publishing house with a strong focus on the humanities it is only natural to see yourself as an agent of public history. At least that holds true for myself and my colleagues in the history department. And while we are certainly not without an agenda, we do care about the field, its authors, and the readers. To make academic findings, discussions and observations public is what makes publishing houses so valuable.

E-journals are not only journals published as e-books. They allow a new way of publishing articles: as they come in, and not necessarily in a fixed number of issues per year. "Storytelling" via digital means is something new e-journals are focusing on, giving scholars the chance to tell their "story" online and let other people in on the (digital) method they used to find the evidence to prove or disprove their findings. One example is the open access blog journal Public History Weekly.[15] The editors state that

---

13 See https://www.degruyter.com/view/j/iph.2018.1.issue-1/issue-files/iph.2018.1.issue-1.xml.
14 See https://academic.oup.com/hwj/pages/About.
15 See https://public-history-weekly.degruyter.com/.

it "thrives on the diversity of its authors' voices and opinions" and also encourage active participation: "Comments on published contributions are most welcome – true to our endeavour to encourage active and spontaneous debate and to dissolve the strict separation between authors and "consumers." At the same time, we strive to maintain high standards for all contributions appearing in Public History Weekly. Submissions are hence subject to careful review. Comments form an integral part of the body of texts published and are archived with the original contribution. This is an essential form of public history publishing: It is academic publishing (peer reviewed by scholars and published in a Scopus listed academic journal), with outreach into the public (open access), and a concrete invitation to comment on articles.

Digital Resources

Most publishing houses also host databases. Some "only" host a collection of open access books, for instance the Brill Open e-Book Collection, focusing on Asian studies,[16] or Gutenberg-e, where emerging scholars are presented with new possibilities for online publications.[17] Other databases show content processed in a specific way, like the World Biographical Information System Online (WBIS)[18] which provides biographical information on over six million people from the eight-century BC to the present. And, of course, there are major databases like JSTOR, "a not-for-profit organization helping the academic community use digital technologies to preserve the scholarly record and to advance research and teaching in sustainable ways."[19]

In particular, open access databases, like the Digital Public Library of America,[20] or the Library of Congress Digital Collection,[21] help scholars and people interested in (digital) history to effortlessly access content they are interested in. Databases have the big bonus of including material you can also find in printed or electronic books, but mostly either combined with additional material or presented in a different way, and hence create a greater value to the reader. Some publishing houses are extremely open to new digital developments, so new forms of digital products are emerging as well: Manifold, an "innovative platform to publish and read open-access books online,"[22] or Cambridge Open Engage, an "early and open content and collaboration platform",[23] which includes preprints, presentations, working papers, etc.

---

16 See http://booksandjournals.brillonline.com/content/brill_open_e-book_collection.
17 See http://www.gutenberg-e.org/.
18 See https://wbis.degruyter.com/?lang=en_US.
19 See https://www.jstor.org/open/.
20 See https://dp.la/.
21 See https://www.loc.gov/collections.
22 See https://manifold.umn.edu/.
23 See https://www.cambridge.org/engage/coe/public-dashboard.

Self-Publishing

Internet retailers like Amazon, Lulu, Books-on-Demand etc. help authors publish e-books and also print copies. Here, every decision remains with the author, every right stays with the author, royalties are supposedly okay, but also: all risks and work (marketing!) stays with the author, too.

Self-publishing may sound attractive to some, but it asks for a lot of commitment. It works for authors of fictional works who have a huge fan base, but not so much for academic publications. If its not done to earn money though, it does help accessibility. If a public historian self-publishes an article and uploads it on academia.net or a blog, for example hypotheses.org, it is instantly accessible and open to everyone. People can read and quote, sometimes also download it. This helps scholarly reputation (if it's referenced correctly) and starts public engagement on a broader lever. Self-publishing authors are in (more) control over the entire publication process, and they possibly earn more money from their publications.[24]

But the services publishers provide, quality checks (peer review, plagiarism checks etc.), professional copy editing, marketing and distribution, dealing with all kinds of specific problems academics have never thought existed before; all of this is left to the author to deal with alone.

Open Access

Open access means putting electronic content into free access, contemporaneous with the publication of the print copy (if there is one). Everyone is able to access the published work at once, which helps democratizing scholarly content, which also increases the visibility of texts that would otherwise not be read as often or frequently. But open access also means the publishing house is not able to sell the book, so someone needs to make up for this loss. Costs for all services (typesetting/production/marketing/A&I,[25] and sometimes printing) stay almost the same. In some countries, where political pressure to publish in open access is high, institutes provide funds for authors (Scandinavian countries are a good example for this policy). In other places, funding institutions like the Swiss National Fonds (SNF), the Austrian Science Fund (FWF), and the European Research Council

---

24 At a panel discussion at the London Book Fair 2017, Glasstree's Daniel Berze quoting from a recent survey of 25,000 academics undertaken by Glasstree, suggested that more than three-quarters of academic writers responding to the survey said they wanted more control over the entire publication process, with nearly two-thirds saying they are keen to earn more from publication. See https://publishingperspectives.com/2017/03/self-publishing-scholarly-writing-debate-lbf-2017/.
25 Abstracting and Indexing.

(ERC) offer to pay lump sums to the publisher in order to help authors publish in immediate open access.

Open access comes in different forms: There is "gold" open access, which means the immediate open access of content. And there is "green" open access, which means free access after a certain embargo period. The former is at the same time more attractive and more problematic, because publishing houses have to compensate for what they cannot sell, and authors – naturally – cannot afford to come up with sums reaching from 6,000 euros to 10,000 euros, which is the average fee asked by most European publishing houses.

Publishing the "green way" is a lot easier, because authors don't have to come up with as much or any fee at all, depending on the length of the embargo period. However, the downside is that the publication is 12+ months old when it is put in open access, meaning it might lose some of its relevance.

There are different types of licenses. The most commonly used is the Creative Commons Attribution-NonCommercial-NoDerivatives 4.0 International (CC BY-NC-ND 4.0) license, which does not allow commercial re-usage of the content.[26] Another one is CC-BY only, which basically allows anything after publication of the content, as long as the content is referred to correctly.

Open access publication also means primarily publishing the e-book, not necessarily a printed version. Although complimentary copies for contributors, authors, and editors will be printed, if a customer wishes for a printed version of an open access publication, she/he will have to live with a print-on demand copy. Nowadays this doesn't mean they also have to live with lower quality, since most printers can produce high-quality print-on-demand copies without problems.

As stated above, e-books allow authors to embed digital content easier and make its usage much more elegant. Since printed books "only" provide URLs, having a digital-only version of a book is not as unattractive as it once was. Open access e-publications therefore are something both publishing houses and authors should focus on and think more about. But the payment model is in need of further development. The most famous one is the Elsevier pay and publish model, which caused (and still causes) a lot of outrage in the scholarly world, due to Elsevier's powerful standing as a commercial publisher. They hold almost 37% of the world's scholarly content and are able to set high prices for paywalls and/or hefty subscription fees. Numerous consortia/universities have taken a stand since 2017 and are no longer willing to have terms 'dictated' by Elsevier.[27] In most recent developments, Elsevier has now reacted to the fact that academics, who can't access some journals anymore because their university library dropped out of the deal with Elsevier, are

---

[26] See https://creativecommons.org/licenses/by-nc-nd/4.0/.
[27] See https://www.theatlantic.com/science/archive/2019/03/uc-elsevier-publisher/583909/.

sharing in so-called "shadow libraries." They announced they will invest heavily in "protecting the scholarly infrastructure" – with spyware.[28]

In 2019, another contract was signed between the German consortium DEAL and Wiley,[29] which aims to "draw out of expensive subscription contracts and flip to publish and read agreements."[30]

Open Peer Review

A special form of open access (pre-)publication is "open peer review." Here authors publish their manuscript on a platform online and invite colleagues to publicly comment on the manuscript for a certain period of time. This process is usually edited by either the author or a second party involved, to make sure comments stay within editorial guidelines. It is a way to make sure academic content is openly accessible before it is published, plus scholars are able to talk about it, to discuss ideas, to argue, and to do all of this publicly. It helps engage the community, and, provided people are not too hesitant to comment openly and under their real name, can spark a real academic discussion. It also helps the author with revisions. Public historians are predestined to use this publishing model, because it unites their intentions of a) public interaction, and b) academic publishing/gaining credit points. Examples of open peer review can be found on the DG opr platform.[31] Its success is extremely dependent on how well experts (from either inside or outside academia) interact with it and also how well it is publicized. Quite a pure form of open access publication, but, obviously, not the best business model for publishing houses if there is no additional funding or subsidy making up not being able to sell the final product (because everyone has access to the pre-publication). This might be an opportunity for new agents of public history to join the world of publishing, ones who don't have to make money out of content, because they are funded otherwise or have different business models.

Digital Developments

New publishing possibilities led publishers to new ways of thinking, and to opening up to new digital formats in publishing. New digital ressources are being set up (as mentioned earlier) with functions developed to suit the needs of public historians (only

---

[28] See https://www.snsi.info/news-and-events/cybersecurity-landscape/.
[29] See https://www.lepublikateur.de/2019/01/16/pay-to-publish-open-access-deal-wiley-agreement/.
[30] 'Publish and read' refers to the fact that the publishers' job is to publish and, thus, they should be paid on the basis of the publishing – not the reading – volume.
[31] See https://opr.degruyter.com/.

think of the new C²DH's digital exhibition about the Great War in Luxembourg launched in 2018.[32] The database is open and growing, which means new material can be added all the time, and it is also created to serve the needs of people with "with varying interests and degrees of expertise." New book series are being developed to use digital material (see enhanced e-books), so they offer a much smoother reading and accessing of the material. New journals with a focus on digital developments, especially within the field of public history, are being born. Electronic only versions thus add more value to the reader: Automatically embedded links and all sorts of media (audio/video etc.), immediate accessability, searchability that helps find topics/keywords/theses easier and quicker (quicker being the most important feature here, because if there's one thing public historians/academics don't have enough of its time[33]). They also make the reading experience more "interactive" in the sense that GIFs/videos etc. are starting to play instantly, as if you were scrolling down a Facebook/Twitter/TikTok feed. Writing about digital exhibitions, public involvement, online source material and academic findings makes a lot more sense when published electronically.

Publishers are aware of new possibilities, but also of problems arising at the same time. Problems, because traditional institutions (like universities and also politics) sometimes are a little bit less encouraging when it comes to digital developments, and they can be a reason for publishers (and academics) to hold back. What is the best journal for academics in order to gain tenure track credit points (keyword impact factor/REF) might not always be what is the most digital evolved, publicly cited, and modern journal. Governments don't see the need to work with commercial publishers to develop new business models for open access publications, because they don't see the added value (yet). Since they fund academia almost exclusively in most countries, and commercial publishers are making money by selling what academics produce, it should be on the agenda though. And some countries have started the discussion already: in Switzerland (SNF), Austria (FWF), the Netherlands (NOW) and in some parts/cities of Germany its fairly easy to apply for state-funded open access. But those obstacles have to be overcome before launching a new online platform. Luckily, public historians are a great help when it comes to finding clever and modern solutions.

---

32 See https://www.c2dh.uni.lu/news/official-launch-eischte-weltkrich-remembering-great-war-luxembourg.
33 See, for instance, the new e-journal of the International Federation for Public History: International Public History, https://www.degruyter.com/view/j/iph.

Conclusion

One could argue that public historians don't nesseccarily need publishers anymore. The tools to publish research online (open access or not) are freely accessible on the Internet, everyone can learn how to use them. Even printing a couple of books is easily done. Repositories and libraries can take over being a "publisher's platform,"[34] at least in theory.[35] And authors can also do self-marketing of course; ask colleagues to rate their books on Amazon, present it at conferences, do book talks, etc. Another important point is if they sell their book themselves, they get to keep all the incoming money, which has, even if it's never that much, some psychological value of its own. Publishers usually only pay little royalties or up-front lump sums. Most of the time, authors will not recognize a difference in their bank account, even if their book sold reasonably well. Publishing without a press also means keeping all the rights. Authors can re-publish, translate, re-use whatever, whenever and wherever they want. Having this freedom is not nothing.

But, on the other hand, publishers are still of value. They offer professional services like quality control (which includes plagiarism checks and peer review), copy editing, typesetting, printing, distributing. In combination with their insights into the market, publishers are experts when it comes to the production and distribution of books/content/knowledge. Existing networks and established relationshsips between publishers and book sellers and libraries/institutions often are very strong and make it realtively easy for publishers to introduce new book formats or even digital/virtual projects/products to the market. It helps public historians share their knowledge more widely and publicly. Its this expertise (interdisciplinary and world-wide marketing/distribution plus the 'old-fashioned' services listed above) that make them an important partner for public historians/academics.

But all of this is worth next to nothing if publishers don't start looking for new and innovative ways to publish similarly innovative and often digital content. Only if they manage to adapt to this new situation, if they try and find new ways of collaborating, will they remain the first choice for a public historian when it comes to publishing research.

Publishers (no matter whether commerical or non-commercial) need to make sure they are on eye-level with their academic partners, their authors. They need to create new forms of publishing, use automated processes and artifical intelligence (for example tagging content automatically). They need to be prepared for a time when textbooks are read out by Alexa or Siri, when computer learning takes over,

---

34 See Cadmus, for example: http://www.cadmuspublishing.com/. Also, online repositories of universities, etc.
35 In theory, because they will never reach the same audience a publisher's platform will. More often than not, if they do not rank well enough on Google they are simply not found. It's an alogrithm world, the internet.

when books are merely vessels to populate bigger (digital) content. They have to consider using personalizations (like algorithms used by Google or Facebook). The future is digital, and if publishers want to stay a responsible and valued partner for public historians, they have to stay on top. Developing new historical digital products and making them freely accessible to a wide public, while taking care of quality control and maintaining academic standards must become the main objective.

Bibliography

Thomas Cauvin, *Public History: A Textbook of Practice* (London: Routledge, (2016) 2022).
Michael Frisch, *A Shared Authority. Essays on the Craft and Meaning of Oral and Public History* (Albany: State University of New York Press, 1990).
Alix R. Green, *History, Policy and Public Purpose: Historians and Historical Thinking in Government*, (London: Palgrave Macmillan, 2016).
Ken Hyland, *Academic Publishing: Issues and Challenges in the Construction of Knowledge*, (Oxford: Oxford University Press, 2015).
James P. Roscow, "Crossing Over Between History and Publishing," *The Public Historian* 4.2 (1982): 29–34.

Mills Kelly
"Learning Public History by doing Public History"

Abstract: How should we teach public history undergraduate students the digital literacy and skills they will need in their future careers as public historians? This essay examines the current state of teaching digital public history at American universities and considers our obligations as public history educators when it comes to preparing our students for future careers in public history work. Using a case study from one digital public history course, the essay also discusses some of the many challenges faced by public history educators as we teach our students to be more digitally proficient.

Keywords: digital, public, history, humanities, digital humanities, teaching, students, digital public history, public history

Several years ago, I was leading a team of conservation volunteers doing backcountry trail maintenance in one of our national parks. My team was made up of eight men and women, all US Marines, who were taking the day off from their military service to do some volunteer work in the woods. They were glad to be out of uniform, glad to be away from their commanding officer, and glad to be out in nature getting dirty. About an hour into our work, one of the men in the group came up to me and said, "Sir, you have to understand. I just wanna move some shit." I pointed to the large stump of a tree that had recently fallen across the trail. I had cut away the trunk of the tree on an earlier work day, but the stump remained, half out of the ground and blocking the trail. A big smile broke out on his face and he and one of his colleagues spent the next 90 minutes digging, chopping, and eventually rolling that stump out of the trail, to the sound of a lot of cheering from their friends. I had assumed that I needed a backhoe or some dynamite to move that stump. What I really needed was two US Marines.

On my way home that evening, it occurred to me that "moving some shit" is exactly what our undergraduate students want to do. To be sure, they are very interested in the content of history, but they also want to *make*, to create history. In short, they want to be able to look back from the vantage point of being done with a project and see something tangible that they have accomplished – something more than a well-crafted essay or a successfully completed examination.[1] In the

---

[1] On how students' use of digital media differs from those in older generations, see Mizuko Ito, Becky Herr-Stephenson, Dan Perkel, and Christo Sims. *Hanging Out, Messing Around, and Geeking Out* (Cambridge, Mass: MIT Press, 2009), http://mitpress.mit.edu/catalog/item/default.asp?ttype=2&tid=11889.

United States, and I assume globally, our students studying the humanities are increasingly concerned about their job prospects after graduation and want tangible products that they can show to potential employers and say, "I did that."[2] Public history, especially digital public history, gives our students the opportunity to create those kinds of work products.[3]

It might feel a bit obvious to emphasize the "doing" of public history in an essay such as this, because it seems such a reasonable assumption that *every* public history course gives students the opportunity to make history, even if in very small ways. Unfortunately, that is not the case, at least in the United States. For this essay, I selected at random 20 undergraduate public history syllabi from American universities for the years 2015–2017, and examined the assignments given to students in those courses. The institutions in my sample ranged across institutional categories – large/small, public/private, selective/non-selective, national/regional. Only one more than half of the courses I examined included the creation by students of actual public history, in the sense that the students' work would be made available to a public audience. The other half of the syllabi I looked at limited students to writing essays about public history, writing grant applications, surveying the various employment categories for public historians, or to producing mock ups of, or concept proposals for public history projects, and of those that did include public assignments, two-thirds of those included digital public history work. That digital work was primarily, but not exclusively the creation of a very basic website (usually with a low bar of entry platform such as WordPress) or a digital exhibit within a larger digital public history project. I was not in a position to evaluate the work that the students did in these various courses, only the instructions they received from their professors. That said, in every case where the students were expected to do digital work, the syllabi reflected the professors' understanding that digital public history required different modes of presentation, or offered different opportunities for interactivity, and that it presented its own complications (beyond the tech skills) for students to deal with separate from what they might confront in a non-digital assignment.

A sample of only 20 syllabi, even one properly randomized, cannot allow us to draw definitive conclusions about the ways in which undergraduate public history courses are taught in the United States. However, the data I collected are instructive, given that so many historians in the United States are still in whole or in part in thrall to the coverage model of teaching history, i.e., to making sure they "cover"

---

[2] Cristina Sin, Orlanda Tavares and Alberto Amara, "Who is responsible for employability? Student perceptions and practices." *Tertiary Education and Management* 22.1 (2016), doi:10.1080/13583883.2015.1134634.
[3] Mills Kelly, "Helping Students Make History: Community Engaged Learning," *Public History Weekly*, May 25, 2017: doi: dx.doi.org/10.1515/phw-2017-9357; and Leon et al., "Imaging the Digital Future of The Public Historian," 8–27.

all the relevant content for their particular course. As Lendol Calder argues, the desire to ensure "coverage" is a significant problem in history education, because in attempting to cover all aspects of a particular historical topic, too often we end up obscuring some of the most important parts of what our students need to learn.[4] My random survey of American syllabi also reminds us just how wedded historians are to writing about the past, because every one of the 20 courses I examined included writing assignments as a substantial portion of the work assigned. While writing skills are not to be minimized, writing about public history is a bit like writing about ice hockey . . . it lacks a certain level of authenticity.[5] After graduation, if our students are called upon to do something they have only written about, those first few days on the job will surely awkward, whether they are working as a public historian or as a member of an ice hockey team.[6] For example, try to imagine the plight of a recently-graduated public historian in his or her first job who is asked to create a visualization from a dataset acquired by the museum or archive where they end up working. Has our newly hired historian ever played with data visualizations? Or has she/he only written about them? Has our newly hired historian ever considered the ethical dilemmas that the dataset poses in the first place?[7] Has she/he adjusted her/his practice as a historian based on a sophisticated knowledge of these dilemmas?

In addition to the 20 undergraduate public history syllabi I examined, I also selected an additional randomized group of 10 undergraduate digital public history syllabi. All but one of these courses included assignments that made students' work public, an unsurprising result given the very public nature of digital work. Because doing digital public history, almost by definition, gives our students the opportunity to "move some shit," to create digital things from the raw material they find in their research, students will emerge from digital public history courses with valuable and translatable skills, but also with a sense that they were able to create history on their own terms. To use the previous example about visualizations, students who have learned both how to play with data to create compelling visualizations and to think critically about the ethical issues the collection, organizing, and presentation of those data raise, will be better prepared to take on new roles as digital public historians. For example, one of my public history students this year has

---

4 Lendol Calder, "Uncoverage: Toward a Signature Pedagogy for the History Survey," http://www.journalofamericanhistory.org/textbooks/2006/calder/, and Kelly, *Teaching History in the Digital Age*, 8–9.
5 On the importance of authentic learning in public history, see Janis Wilton, "Oral History in Universities: From Margins to Mainstream," Donald A. Ritchie, ed., *The Oxford Handbook of Oral History*, (Oxford: Oxford University Press, 2011): 478–479.
6 Stéphane Lévesque. *Thinking Historically: Educating Students for the Twenty-First Century*. (Toronto: University of Toronto Press, 2008): 16–17.
7 Katherine Hepworth and Christopher Church, "Racism in the Machine: Visualization Ethics in Digital Humanities Projects," *Digital Humanities Quarterly* 12.4 (2018): http://www.digitalhumanities.org/dhq/vol/12/4/000408/000408.html.

created a database of historical pandemics in the American state of Virginia between 1912–1945 and is comparing health outcomes in the black and white communities in that state. One of her challenges is deciding how best to represent these differences in outcomes both graphically and geospatially. The data tell her that influenza killed whites at a much higher rate during the 1918 pandemic, but that tuberculosis killed blacks at much higher rates, but only in certain years. But her research also shows that various diseases (measles, diphtheria, typhoid) killed Virginians, whether black or white, at higher rates in certain parts of the state and not others. As a digital public historian, her task is to determine how to show the complexity of these findings in ways that are accessible to a public audience, while retaining the sophistication of her analysis. When she is done with this project, she will have a final product that she can show not only to her professor, but also to potential employers. Given the fact that the vast majority (70%) of employers in the United States who hire entry level public historians in the US believe that digital media development and production skills will be essential in the future, it seems more than a little obvious that these skills should be part of any curriculum in public history.[8] Although this survey is limited to an American audience for public historians, I suspect a survey almost anywhere else in the world would find similar results.

However, several problems confront the historian who wants to teach digital public history. These include having a perceived or real lack of digital skills as compared to what we believe to be the high level of skills our students have, or a lack of familiarity with the various digital platforms our students might use to create a digital public history project using platforms such as Omeka, a lack of knowledge about essential underlying standards such as the Dublin Core Metadata Initiative, just to name a few.[9] Of course, faculty members cannot possibly master every digital platform or skill, just as we cannot master the historiography of every subject. However, just as we are capable of mastering one or two historiographies, we are also more than capable of mastering a set of digital skills and at least one platform, such as Omeka, that will allow us to teach the critical digital public history skills our students need.[10] While it is the case that many faculty members may not have the same level of digital skill as their students, it is also the case that just because our students are adept *users* of technology, it does not follow that they are adept *learners* with technology. Moreover, almost none of them have ever had the opportunity to use any of their digital skills in the creation of public history, which is a problem given the previously cited data about employer expectations of digital

---

8 *Report from the task force on public history education and employment*, National Council on Public History, April 14, 2015: http://ncph.org/history-at-work/report-public-history-education-and-employment/.
9 "DCMI: Home," accessed January 16, 2018, http://dublincore.org/.
10 For more on the Omeka platform, see http://omeka.org.

proficiency. This gap between what our students are being asked to learn and what employers (at least in the United States) are expecting them to be able to do means that we as public history educators have to take seriously our obligation to teach *digital* public history skills, not just public history skills, as part of the public history curriculum in our universities. At the same time, digital public history done right also requires faculty members to turn our students loose – to let them create history in the ways they want rather than in the ways we insist on, even as we seek to maintain the disciplinary standards we care about.[11] If we can bring ourselves to give them room to maneuver, to provide space for their creative impulses, to use the technology in ways we hadn't anticipated, there is no telling how they will surprise us. If, however, we restrict what they do, defining topics, setting boundaries around what they can and cannot do, then we will continue to receive competent, if often uninspiring work from our students.

What might it look like to give students in a digital public history course this sort of freedom? In 2016, I did just that in a digital public history course on the history of the Appalachian Trail, America's oldest and most iconic long distance (2,192 miles/3,528 kilometers long) hiking trail. The course was designed to provide students with an introduction to the methods of the public historian, to digital public history as a sub-category, to the history of the Appalachian Trail, and to give them the opportunity to create public history in both the analog and digital worlds. I taught this class twice over two consecutive semesters to a total of 28 students. None of the students had any prior experience with either public or digital history, only a few had ever created any online historical content, and only one had ever hiked on the Appalachian Trail, so both the larger topic (digital public history) and the more finite topic (the Appalachian Trail) were wholly unfamiliar to my students. At the beginning of the semester, we read together in the theory and practice of public and digital public history, then turned to readings about the history of the Appalachian Trail itself. During that first half of the semester, the students discussed the readings, wrote about what they learned, and began to think about potential research topics. Three of the issues I spent extra time on were considerations of audience (something undergraduate students rarely think much about), a careful look at the architecture of digital information (something undergraduate students almost never think about), and how writing for digital presentation (and for a public history audience) was significantly different than writing a well-crafted essay to be turned in to one's professor.

For example, we placed the text from a typical history essay into a digital exhibit and then analyzed it as a means of presentation in the online environment. The students instantly noticed how poorly suited the essay form of writing was to digital presentation. Seeing was believing. We then played with the content of the

---

11 Kelly, *Teaching History*, 129–130.

essay and boiled it down to a very brief, compelling, and engagingly written text that fit easily on a laptop screen with no scrolling. This kind of radical editing and rewriting of historical scholarship to make those ideas and conclusions engaging for a public history audience is something that public historians know how to do already. Going one step further and making that text work on a screen was challenging but instructive for the students. With each iteration, the students' rewritten texts became shorter, more audience-centric, and less formal. Some of them took to this new style of writing right away, while others found it almost impossible to let go of a writing form they have mastered through more than a dozen years of schooling. Each week we also spent some time on the platform they would be using for their work (Omeka) and on technical topics such as metadata, copyright and fair use, and image sizing.[12]

For their public history project, the students had to work as a group to create a large analog display of the history of the Appalachian Trail, and they had to create their own digital public history exhibit on a topic of interest to them within the larger history of the Trail. For the analog project, I secured permission from my university to use an 80 foot (24 meter) long wall in the building where my department is housed on which the students could paint the Appalachian Trail. Beyond securing them permission to use this wall and purchasing all the materials they needed to create their display, I offered no advice or assistance, other than regularly reminding them to keep their audience(s) in mind. I left it to them to make all the creative decisions. They had little trouble deciding on color schemes, or on what geographic features (national parks and forests, landmarks such as mountain summits, cities and towns along the route of the Trail) to include. The issue that engendered the most discussion and even argument among the students in the first iteration of the course was the orientation of the map they were creating. Should the northern terminus of the Trail – Mount Katahdin in Maine – be on the left, or should it be on the right as the audience (people walking down the hall) viewed it? Opinions on this subject were strong, debate was heated, but in the end, the group decided that North would be left and South would be right. Once this most basic of decisions had been made, they managed to create the entire map of the Trail in just four 90-minute class periods.

The digital work took much longer, because it was so much more open-ended, and required original research on their part. For the wall map, all they had to do was replicate an existing map in ways they felt were suited to the goals of their project. But for their individual exhibits, they had to select a topic, research that topic,

---

[12] On using Omeka in the classroom, see Jeffrey W. McClurken, "Teaching With Omeka," ProfHacker Blog, *The Chronicle of Higher Education*, August 9, 2010: https://www.chronicle.com/blogs/profhacker/teaching-with-omeka/26078, accessed January 7, 2018; and "Omeka in the Classroom" University of Pennsylvania Libraries: https://guides.library.upenn.edu/omeka/teachwithomeka, accessed January 7, 2018.

convert analog or digital sources (images, texts, maps, etc.) into items in our Omeka database, and then use Omeka's Exhibit Builder to create their own exhibits.[13] Those exhibits required creativity, careful attention to writing for their perceived audience, and the mastery of a relatively simple software tool. Once completed, the students' exhibits were then highlighted on the wall map they had created with a museum-style card giving the title of the exhibit, the student creator's name, and the year it was created. Each card also contained a QR code that passersby can use to gain quick access to individual exhibits and the website URL was posted in several different locations along the wall. As one would expect from a mixed group of undergraduate students, the quality of those exhibits reflected their academic abilities, their motivations, and the time they had to commit to the work. Some were excellent, some were good, and some were just acceptable. What was striking, however, was how their selection of research topics was so wildly different from the traditional historical scholarship on the Appalachian Trail that they had read in the first half of the semester.

Scholars who write about the history of the Appalachian Trail have largely concerned themselves with a fairly limited number of topics. These include critical investigations of the building of the Trail in the 1920s and 1930s, of the later federalization of the Trail in the 1960s as it was incorporated into the National Park system, of the "builders" of the Trail – those men and women who came up with the idea and then made it a reality – and of those who have hiked the trail, especially the "thru hikers" who have traversed the entire 2,192 miles from Georgia to Maine in a single year.[14] By contrast, not one of my students created an exhibit that fit under the general headings of these topics favored by professional historians. Instead, because I set them free to choose their own topics, they chose topics that interested them and would, they hoped, resonate with their primary audience–students, faculty, and staff members walking down the hall where the analog exhibit lives, and/or people who found their way to the website we were building via a search engine result.

Perhaps because only one of my students had any prior experience with backcountry hiking (I did take them on the Trail during the semester), a significant number were particularly interested in matters of risk along the Trail. Their interests in this topic ranged from the potential for interactions with wildlife (especially bears),

---

[13] The students' exhibits can be found at: http://appalachiantrailhistory.org/exhibits/browse?tags=Student+Exhibit.
[14] Recent examples of this scholarship include: Sarah Mittlefehldt, *Tangled Roots. The Appalachian Trail and American Environmental Politics* (Seattle: University of Washington Press, 2013); Jeffrey H. Ryan, *Blazing Ahead. Benton MacKaye, Myron Avery, and the Rivalry That Built the Appalachian Trail* (Boston: Appalachian Mountain Club Books, 2017); Larry Anderson, *Benton MacKaye. Conservationist, Planner, and Creator of the Appalachian Trail* (Baltimore: Johns Hopkins University Press, 2002); and Adam Berg, "'To Conquer Myself': The New Strenuosity and the Emergence of 'Thru-hiking' on the Appalachian Trail in the 1970s," *Journal of Sport History* 42.1 (Spring 2015): 1–19.

to the possibility of being a victim of a violent crime, to what happens if a hiker gets lost. As the last three cells in the table below indicate, they were also quite interested in the question of who gets to hike on the Appalachian Trail? Is it a place where people with disabilities can succeed? Do people of color, or those in the LGBTQ community, take on greater risk than those in our society's dominant groups? Many students were also very interested in issues around rural development, rural poverty, and rural cultures that have been impacted positively or negatively by the appearance of hikers coming from "away" or "down the mountain," as some residents of Appalachia put it. Given the pressing concerns generated by climate change, it is not surprising that a significant number also wanted to examine environmental change in the Appalachians in their research. Most importantly, we see in the table below what happens when we turn our students loose to purse their own interests rather than asking them to focus on what the historiography privileges. In my analysis of what happened in this course, the digital nature of the project assignment was not what led to the wide variety of topics explored by my students. Rather, it was the conscious choice I made to encourage them to explore whatever topic they chose. Once given this kind of freedom, they ran with it. However, the fact that they were presenting the results of their research in a public (digital) form did influence the *way* that they presented the research. For instance, one of my students created a project in the "danger" category in this table that was focused on the still-unsolved murder of a lesbian couple on the Appalachian Trail in the 1990s. Understanding that her exhibit had the potential to be widely viewed by anyone searching for information about danger on the Trail made her think very carefully about how she presented each aspect of the tragedy. The fact that her project was immediately public and was not a classroom-only assignment forced her into a series of decisions that a classroom-only assignment would not have required and led to a number of in-depth conversations about ethics and ways we write about and present human tragedy.

As pleased as I was with the wide-ranging nature of my students' research, and as pleased as I was with the quality of their exhibits (given that none of them had ever done this sort of work before), not everything about the course was a success. Despite my spending what seemed to me like a lot of time on information architecture, especially metadata, most of my students either did not learn what I was teaching or did not internalize the lessons of that learning sufficiently enough to put them into practice. Far too many of the items they created for the database lacked complete or accurate metadata; in some cases, the possessed hardly any metadata at all beyond a basic caption and date. Before enrolling in my course, they knew how to do their research online or in the library. With only a little bit of instruction they were capable of writing strong descriptive text about their database entries, but almost all of them proved unable or unwilling to complete the most basic tasks of correctly filling out metadata fields, such as item type, format, or creator in the project database. Given the increasingly rich and networked databases of humanities content such as Europeana that are being created around the

Tab. 1: Student Exhibit Topics (N=38).[15]

Topic	Percent of total
Danger/Crime	26%
Hiking culture	18%
Impact on rural communities	13%
Environmental	11%
Rural poverty	8%
Trail management	8%
LGBTQ	5%
Disability	5%
Race	5%

world, inattention to metadata standards by public historians (even if they are students in a public history course who are making their work public) means that digital content being created will not be as visible or discoverable in a world of linked open data.

My students understood this problem intellectually, but I found it all but impossible to convince them to care enough about metadata to be attentive to it and so their approach to this essential aspect of their work was haphazard at best. It's up to me to find a new way to teach about information architecture that resonates with novice digital public historians.[16] Further, because close attention to the standards or the Dublin Core is a very important skill for the digital public historian, I had to rethink how I teach these skills for the next iteration of this course which I taught in the Fall 2018 semester. To address my failings as an instructor when it came to teaching about metadata, I created a new series of assignments designed to help them start taking ownership the metadata they were creating. Of the various interventions I tried, the one that worked the best was to have them create a first (and private) item in the database that described a loved one (parent, sibling, romantic partner) as though that item would become a public record. Suddenly, they wanted the metadata to be done right because it described someone who they cared about.

---

15 There are currently 27 student exhibits on the project website, one of which is not public. Some were coded to more than one topic.
16 On this issue, see, for instance, Jake Carlson and Marianne Stowell Bracke, "Planting the Seeds for Data Literacy: Lessons Learned from a Student-Centered Education Program," *International Journal of Digital Curation* 10.1 (2015), doi:10.2218/ijdc.v10i1.348.

I did see some improvement in their attentiveness to the importance of proper metadata, but still not enough to satisfy me as a public historian.

A second issue, that is more a function of the university where I teach, is that only a small number of my students were able to bring a mobile device (laptop or tablet) to class and so we were not able to do much production work during our class sessions. This would likely be less of a problem at an institution where all, or almost all, students have portable devices, but even on those campuses instructors face the problem of students having different devices with different operating systems and interfaces. Using a resource like Omeka, which is not platform specific, helps to mitigate this issue, but teaching digital public history will always require at least some tech support from the instructor, if only to help the students navigate to the resources they need.

Conclusion

Far too few of the public history course syllabi I examined included opportunities for students to make their work public beyond the classroom. Moreover, it remains the case that public digital history is still less commonly taught in history departments in the United States, than is what we might call "traditional" public history. Given that almost three-fourths of American employers of public history graduates feel that having digital skills will be essential for our students in the future, it is incumbent on us to create more opportunities for our students to learn these skills. Faculty fear of mastering digital skills is not a good excuse. The skills we teach in all public history courses are the same skills we teach in a digital public history course, and I would argue that in the current global political environment that includes an all-out assault on facts, truth, and accuracy in the presentation of history, these skills are essential to the functioning of free societies. The only real difference is the platform we use for that teaching. But adding digital history to the public history curriculum is not enough.

Given what we know about how students use, manipulate, experiment with, and play with digital media, we also need to give them the space they need to use the technology in ways that make sense to them. It is up to us to help them connect their creative impulses to what we know are the essential skills of the public historian. They can be as creative as they want, but if they forget that public history thrives on audiences, that creativity will not result in a successful final project. They can be very entrepreneurial in their choices of topics, but if they don't do the hard work of getting their metadata correct, whatever they create will be incomplete. In this era of transition in public history to an increasingly digital world, we have a vital role to play when it comes to the standards of our profession, but we also have to be willing to get out of our students' way as they make history for themselves.

Bibliography

Calder, Lendol. "Uncoverage: Toward a Signature Pedagogy for the History Survey." *The Journal of American History* 92.4 (March 2006).
Faulkenbury, Evan. "Teaching Public History to Sophomores." *History @ Work*, February 9, 2018.
Kelly, T. Mills. *Teaching History in the Digital Age*. Ann Arbor: University of Michigan Press, 2016.
Leon, Sharon M. et al. "Imaging the Digital Future of The Public Historian." *The Public Historian* 35.1 (February 2013): 8–27.
Posner, Miriam. "How Did They Make That?" *Miram Posner's Blog*, August 29, 2013.

Kimberly Coulter, Wilko Graf von Hardenberg, and Finn Arne Jørgensen
Spaces: What's at Stake in Their Digital Public Histories?

Abstract: Public histories of spaces are often at the heart of territorial claims: they can cultivate emotional identification, or even build legitimizing facts on the ground. Digital technologies have increased public awareness of, and ability to mobilize, the power of public histories of spaces. This means more influence for both official and grassroots channels to spread, augment, or contest spatial narratives. We argue that those who take care of spaces and their archival records, and interpret them for the public, have the opportunity to play an important public role. Through diverse examples, this chapter shows how control of iconography, access, and ownership is at stake.

Keywords: space, place, environment, iconography, access, ownership, narratives

Compared to other public histories, public histories of spaces may be distinguished by their direct relationship to territorialization. Spaces are the heart of territorial claims: they are not only symbols cultivating emotional identification, but also the bricks that build legitimizing facts on the ground. Perhaps to inoculate against blindness to malignant nationalism, late twentieth century humanities scholars emphasized that communities like "the nation" are not natural, but narrated; they called for a shift in focus from territory as a given fact to territorialization, the ongoing social processes and discourses by which humans claim and control space. Geographers have asserted the importance of place in studies of nationalism, called for more boundary-crossing analyses, emphasized the social relations behind landscapes, and urged attention to appeals made to territorial interests and identities in their production and distribution of historical narratives and artifacts.[1]

The digital age has increased public awareness of, and ability to mobilize, the power of public histories of spaces. This means more influence for both official and grass-roots channels to spread, augment, or contest spatial narratives. As an example,

---

[1] Benedict Anderson, *Imagined Communities: Reflections on the Origin and Spread of Nationalism*, Revised edition (London; New York: Verso, 2006); Homi K. Bhabha, *Nation and Narration* (London: Routledge, 1990); Anssi Paasi, "Boundaries as Social Practice and Discourse: The Finnish-Russian Border," *Regional Studies* 33.7 (1999): 669–680; Cosgrove and Daniels, *The Iconography of Landscape*; Tim Edensor, "National Identity and the Politics of Memory: Remembering Bruce and Wallace in Symbolic Space," *Environment and Planning D: Society and Space* 29 (1997): 175–194; Rose Gillian, "The Cultural Politics of Place: Local Representation and Oppositional Discourse in Two Films," *Transactions of the Institute of British Geographers* 19.1 (1994): 46–60; Kimberly Coulter, "Territorial Appeals in Post-Wall German Filmmaking: The Case of *Good Bye, Lenin!*," *Antipode: A Radical Journal of Geography* 45.4 (2013): 760–778.

https://doi.org/10.1515/9783110430295-019

take the US National Mall. Envisioned as a public space for the American capital, it became a symbol of national identity and a site for recreation and protest. A digital project funded by the National Endowment for the Humanities and awarded the Outstanding Public History Project for 2015 by the US National Council on Public History, the Roy Rosenzweig Center for History and New Media's *The Histories of the National Mall* (http://mallhistory.org/) augments the experience of visitors with mobile devices while also bringing history to those far from the capital (Fig. 1). It presents diverse document-based histories of the space: as home of some 80 Nacotchtank people before their decimation by disease or conflict with Europeans; a residence for presidents, their families, paid staff, and enslaved people; a dynamic working-class neighborhood; an evolving setting for presidential inaugurations.[2]

This carefully researched and presented public history stands in sharp contrast to the disregard for nuance, science, and facts already apparent at the very beginning of the Trump administration. When the US National Park Service's twitter account shared an unflattering comparison of aerial photos of the 2017 (Trump) and 2009 (Obama) inauguration crowds, the juxtaposition went viral (Fig. 2). In response, Trump ordered the agency to temporary shutdown its Twitter activities and demanded a more flattering image of the crowd at the Mall.[3]

At the same time, the new administration began to cleanse government sites of other inconvenient facts, such as references to climate change.[4] This prompted an immediate backlash from some US National Parks Service workers and others charged with conservation and interpretation of public spaces, perhaps most familiar to the public in the role of the trusty park ranger. In the *New York Times*, Timothy Egan lauds their resistance:

> From Badlands National Park came a tweet about more carbon dioxide in the atmosphere than any time in the last 650,000 years. From the Redwood park, a note about the saving grace of ancient trees. From Death Valley, a reminder that Japanese-Americans had once been interned there.
>
> Heroes in uniform? No, not by normal standards in normal times. Informing people is what park rangers do.[5]

---

[2] This chapter was written in early 2017; all mentioned projects but one were accessible online as of July 1, 2020. In the one instance where the site was already defunct we decided to provide the link to the relevant page on the Internet Archive Wayback Machine (https://archive.org/web/), where most other sites are also archived. The one exception is a user page within Flickr (http://flickr.com), as the site does not allow archiving.

[3] Eli Rosenberg, "After Silent Period, Park Service Says It Regrets 2 Trump-Related Retweets," The New York Times, January 21, 2017, sec. U.S., https://www.nytimes.com/2017/01/21/us/national-park-service-trump-tweet.html.

[4] Coral Davenport, "How Much Has 'Climate Change' Been Scrubbed From Federal Websites? A Lot," *The New York Times*, October 3, 2018, https://www.nytimes.com/2018/01/10/climate/climate-change-trump.html.

[5] Timothy Egan, "Park Rangers to the Rescue," *The New York Times*, January 20, 2018, https://www.nytimes.com/2017/01/27/opinion/park-rangers-to-the-rescue.html.

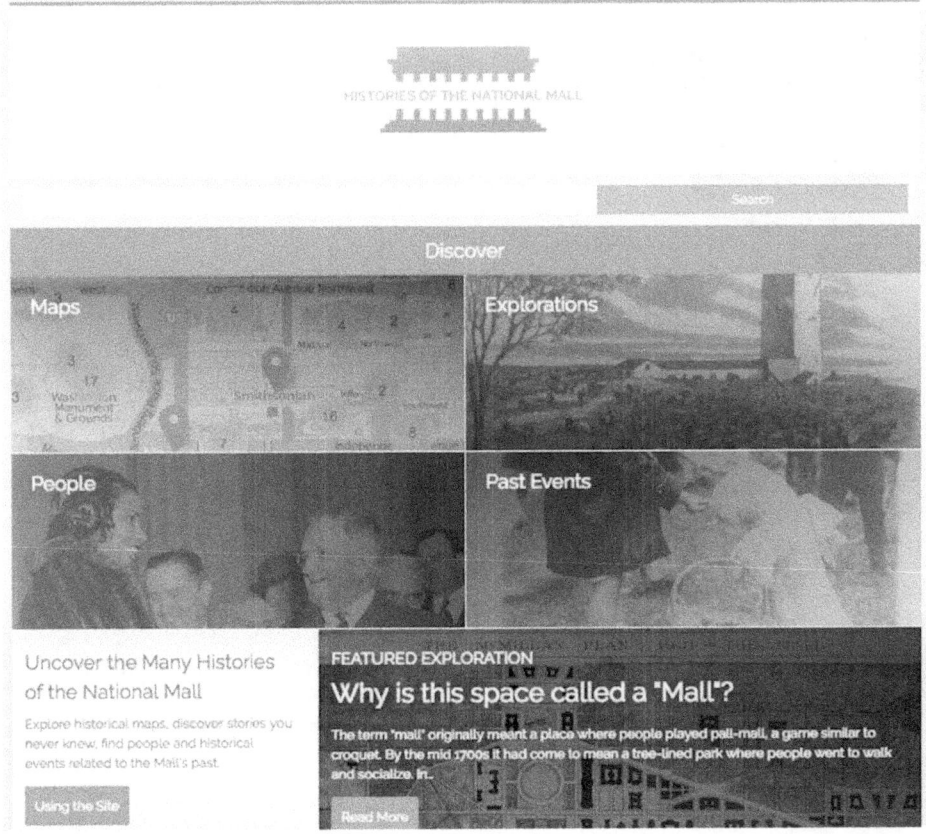

Fig. 1: Screenshot of *Histories of the National Mall* (http://mallhistory.org). Accessed 10 February 2017.

As soon as the Trump administration censored these employees' tweets, "alt" national park accounts appeared that claimed to be from US National Park Service staff gone rogue. Anonymity, while understandable, deprived the tweeters of the trust they would have garnered as verifiable rangers or scientists. And it is trust – feelings of integrity, dependability, and confidence – in such figures that plays a critical role in shaping public opinion in politicized debates.[6] Those who take care of spaces and their archival records, and interpret them for the public, have the opportunity to play an important public role. At stake in these public histories is control of iconography, access, and ownership.

---

[6] National Academies of Sciences, Engineering, and Medicine, *Trust and Confidence at the Interfaces of the Life Sciences and Society: Does the Public Trust Science? A Workshop Summary* (Washington, DC: The National Academies Press, 2015), https://doi.org/10.17226/21798.

Fig. 2: Screenshot of since-deleted retweet from the US National Park Service as reported in William Turton, "National Park Service Banned From Tweeting After Anti-Trump Retweets [Updated]," *Gizmodo*, January 20, 2017, https://gizmodo.com/national-park-service-banned-from-tweeting-after-anti-t-1791449526.

Iconography

First, the iconography of public spaces – their visual appearance and symbolic interpretation – cultivates public identification with these spaces. Wherever national narratives are constructed – whether around the National Mall in Washington DC, Soviet monuments as "petrified utopias" in Poland, or Roman archeological sites in Fascist Italy – political claims tied to the representation of landscapes and public spaces have been crucial in the institutionalization of *lieux de mémoire*, or realms of memory for the public use of history.[7] Such use of iconography to cultivate

---

[7] See Pierre Nora, *Realms of Memory: Rethinking the French Past* (Chicago: University of Chicago Press, 1998); Joshua Arthurs, *Excavating Modernity: The Roman Past in Fascist Italy* (Ithaca, NY: Cornell University Press, 2013); Katarzyna Trzeciak, "The Petrified Utopia: Monumental Propaganda, Architecture Parlante, and the Question about (De)Materialisation of Monuments," *Philosophy Study* 5.1 (January 28, 2015), https://doi.org/10.17265/2159-5313/2015.01.004; Ian Tyrrell, "America's National Parks: The Transnational Creation of National Space in the Progressive Era," *Journal of American Studies* 46.1 (February 2012): 1–21, https://doi.org/10.1017/S0021875811001320.

identification with space has long been employed by territorially invested actors. Since the late nineteenth century, the organization of public memory grew increasingly centralized. Preservation and public history efforts cultivated national identity by promoting identification with landscapes' beauty, recreation opportunities, development potential, or historical value for their connection to memorabilia. New national narratives have often been superimposed on local places and diverse cultural landscapes to form symbols of the nation, as has been particularly visible in the German nation-building process.[8]

Following the broad 1960s engagement that paved the way for public histories to reach more diverse communities, the digital age presents an opportunity to invite new participants to add interpretive layers to the iconography and representation of landscape and public space. Both commercial and non-profit mobile and web tools can enhance and inform enjoyment of protected areas and heritage sites through various degrees of augmented reality.[9] One particularly relevant example is the "Digital Wonderland" prototype app, an attempt to offer tourists a state-of-the-art interactive environmental and cultural history of the Yellowstone National Park that blends narratives, maps, photographs, games, and social media.[10] Many more examples of how place interpretation may be improved through the addition of interpretive layers often developed by or in conjunction with a diverse array of local communities can be found on the many place-based mobile projects that use the Curatescape platform (https://curatescape.org/projects/), whether in Spokane, Washington; Adelaide, South Australia; or Kisumu, Kenya.

Such application of interpretive layers has found popular resonance in histories of iconic national landscapes that stir patriotic feeling, such as battlefields. Commemorative tours of Civil War battlefields are a traditional undertaking for many American families and battlefield tourism became also a crucial element of memorialization in post-World War One Europe.[11] New mobile technologies, combined with the centenary of World War One, have renewed interest in such practices. The Somme 14–18 app (http://www.zevisit.com/application/somme1418/), for instance, funded by

---

[8] Thomas Lekan and Thomas Zeller, eds., *Germany's Nature: Cultural Landscapes and Environmental History* (New Brunswick, NJ: Rutgers University Press, 2005).
[9] Brennan, "Public First"; Christen and Mighetto, "Introduction: Environmental History as Public History," 12.
[10] Yolonda Youngs, "Creating a Digital Wonderland: Environmental and Cultural History in the Digital Age," *Ant Spider Bee* (blog), July 21, 2015, http://www.antspiderbee.net/?p=11386.
[11] Bill Bryson, *The Lost Continent: Travels in Small-Town America* (New York: Harper & Row, 1989), 131–132; Marco Armiero, "Nationalizing the Mountains: Natural and Political Landscapes in the First World War," in *Nature and History in Modern Italy*, Marco Armiero and Marcus Hall, eds., (Athens, Ohio: Ohio University Press, 2010), 300; Wilko Graf von Hardenberg, "Beyond Human Limits. The Culture of Nature Conservation in Interwar Italy," *Aether – The Journal of Media Geography* 11 (February 2013): 55–56.

the Somme regional tourism development agency, promotes a region normally off the beaten track, offering tourists a new perception of the battlefield. But tourism is not the only interpretive motor behind initiatives of this kind: the memory of fallen soldiers is central in many similar initiatives. The Nga Tapuwae website and app (https://ngatapuwae.govt.nz), which follows the trail of New Zealand's military in Gallipoli and the Western Front is funded by the government as a way to allow New Zealanders to retrace the paths of their ancestors. Another project that layers historical information in an effort to provide users with an immersive understanding of a landscape is an app, called "Kioku no Kaito" (Rebooting Memories), that shows how Hiroshima appeared prior to its destruction by nuclear weapons.[12] Thanks to the ability to add layers and additional information with each visit, the iconography of past landscapes can thus be experienced, understood, and interpreted on the fly via smartphone.

Access

Digital public histories of spaces work not only as iconographic symbols; this information actually affects access to the spaces themselves (and their archives). Access to, and common ownership of, public spaces and their data are central to democratic values. Those concerned with these values should pay close attention to the digital transformation of public histories of parks, landscapes and monuments; the management, conservation, and communication of public spaces can enable or stifle opportunities for their recreational enjoyment, scientific study, public protection, and the promotion of environmental justice. Digital public history projects may encounter a variety of obstacles, not least due to the vagaries of national copyright legislation.[13]

Beyond this, limitations may be due to the explicit desire of a government to restrict access to certain information like climate data. Open data are a crucial part of the possibility to do environmental science and their preservation should be of fundamental concern. Of course, the digital divide is characterized not only by divergent access to data, but also to the Internet itself and hardware. According to the World Bank, as of 2016 less than half the world's population used the Internet.[14]

---

[12] "Hiroshima App Shows Tourists Pre-Bomb Sights," *BBC News*, February 6, 2017, http://www.bbc.com/news/blogs-news-from-elsewhere-38882394; Kanoko Tsuchiya, "AR-Based App Brings Prewar Hiroshima to the Modern World," *The Asahi Shimbun*, February 18, 2019, http://www.asahi.com/ajw/articles/AJ201902180001.html.
[13] Serge Noiret, "Storia pubblica digitale," *Zapruder. Storie in movimento*, 36 (January–April 2015). 8–23; Coulter and Hardenberg, "Cultivating the Spirit of the Commons in Environmental History".
[14] The World Bank, "Individuals Using the Internet (% of Population)," 2019, https://data.worldbank.org/indicator/IT.NET.USER.ZS.

Even as digital tools enable the collection of large data sets and empower alternative narratives, the ability to contribute, use, or just access data certainly does not overlap with being affected by it.

For this reason, it is important not to lose sight of the many ways digital tools and platforms can influence access to public spaces and their data. Most immediately, the digitization of archival materials for the public and for the scientific community is pivotal to an informed public history of the environment. Some examples are the efforts of many botanical gardens, libraries, and museums around the world in such joint ventures such as Global Plants on JSTOR (http://plants.jstor.org) and the Biodiversity Heritage Library (www.biodiversitylibrary.org). By making data accessible, digital public history projects empower people to make spaces and environments accessible. The "spirit of the commons," with its emphasis on open access, is the tie that connects landscapes and the new digital environments.[15] In the digital age, public histories of spaces not only define places, they also connect them, enabling interaction between top-down and grassroots processes, between official and subversive efforts. For instance, Linked Open Data allows "siloed" digital projects in different parts of the world to speak to each other and information about place and space to be reused in creative ways. The digital even allows for a "long tail" approach to audiences, meaning that local initiatives can find niche audiences anywhere in the world.[16]

Of course, just because history is digital does not mean that it is public-facing or even accessible. For instance, many documents digitized as part of the US-based Hathi Trust partnership (https://www.hathitrust.org) end up being inaccessible to those countries in which the documents were originally produced because of often misplaced worries about copyright restrictions. Regrettably, it is not even sufficient for researchers seeking access to have an academic affiliation: it needs to be an American one. This forces researchers and institutions outside the US who are interested in accessing or preserving specific documents to invest money, time, and work to redo work that has already been done. This should not be the case, considering the ease and facility with which digital copies could be transferred and shared.[17]

In the case of public history initiatives, it becomes even clearer how digitization alone is wholly insufficient; materials need to be made accessible and discoverable, for example by creating multiple pathways to data or targeting specific audiences. The Open Parks Network (https://openparksnetwork.org), a collaboration of Clemson

---

15 Coulter and Hardenberg, "Cultivating the Spirit of the Commons in Environmental History."
16 Chris Anderson, *The Long Tail: Why the Future of Business Is Selling Less of More* (New York: Hyperion, 2006).
17 A recent example of the need for one such re-digitization project is provided by Measuring the Earth: A Digital Repository for the History of Modern Geodesy at the Max Planck Institute for the History of Science in Berlin and the GeoForschungsZentrum in Potsdam: https://www.mpiwg-berlin.mpg.de/research/projects/measuring-earth-digital-repository-history-modern-geodesy.

University and the US National Park Service, set up in 2010 with funding from the Institute of Museum and Library Services, shows how digital tools can help national parks and other protected areas to make their collections of historical imagery available to both a broader public and the specific audiences that visit the parks. This venture is supported by the US federal government to promote the historical relevance of the treasures hidden in the libraries, archives and museums of more than 20 US national parks and protected sites. To broaden its reach, it also collaborates with the Internet Archive (https://archive.org/) to foster the digitization of grey literature produced by the US nature conservation complex. Still, setting up a digitization project need not require large-scale infrastructure and massive resources: on a shoestring budget, the Perito Francisco P. Moreno Central Library and Documentation Center of the Argentinian National Parks Administration has been using Flickr (https://www.flickr.com/photos/22495431@N00/) to upload selected pictures from its archives. Enabling discovery of such data requires not only digitization, but thoughtful interpretive curation and application of metadata in the backend, as well as a user-friendly interface that offers users pathways to connection and interpretation. In Germany, the Environment & Society Portal (http://www.environmentandsociety.org) of the Rachel Carson Center for Environment and Society offers map, timeline, and keyword discovery tools to create exploration pathways through open-access archival resources and interpretive multimedia content.

The potential for open access to data to pave paths on the ground makes digital projects attractive to activists. Environmental historian and activist Jenny Price and software developers Ben and John Adair developed the "Our Malibu Beaches" smartphone app (https://ourmalibubeaches.com) as an "owner's manual" to public beaches in Malibu. The accessways to these public beaches are often hard to find due to private development and intimidation. The app aims to enable the public to reclaim access to public space by providing legal and geographic information. The app and related performative and digital work of the public art collective Los Angeles Urban Rangers (http://laurbanrangers.org) to which Price belongs, challenges more traditional historical and scholarly community to higher standards of interpretation and engagement in their work.

The increasing ease with which such digital tools can be financed, produced, and distributed suggests great potential for increasing grass-roots engagement with public spaces and data. The Our Malibu Beaches app was partially funded by a successful Kickstarter crowdfunding initiative which made it possible to keep the app free to download.[18] Volunteer-led practices are experiencing a renaissance. The now-defunct Haiti Memory Project (https://web.archive.org/web/20191209064125/http://haitimemoryproject.org/) was, for instance, developed as a fast and low-

---

[18] Kimberly Coulter, "Open Access to the Beach," *Ant Spider Bee* (blog), February 18, 2014, http://www.antspiderbee.net/2014/02/18/open-access-to-the-beach/.

budget alternative undertaken by a single PhD student to large and high-profile digital public history projects with considerable institutional support and funding.[19]

Ownership

Due in part to their ability to build identification with places and influence access to places and their data, public histories of space can also work to materialize facts on the ground. Digital histories can advance public protection and advocate for environmental justice transnationally by destabilizing national narratives and reframing these across boundaries. By supporting or discrediting claims of ownership they may contribute to disenfranchisement or empowerment.

Funded by the US National Institutes of Health through its Science Education Partnership Award, a collaboration between the Chemical Heritage Foundation and the University of Pennsylvania Perelman School of Medicine, *Resources for Education and Action for Community Health in Ambler* (http://reachambler.sciencehistory.org/) provides a local community with documentation on its history of asbestos production and remediation at the BoRit Superfund site. A multi-platform public history concerning environmental, health, demographic, and economic consequences of this resource exploitation, it presents diverse views of local residents and institutions and aims to help the community shape its future.

Digital public histories of spaces can also contribute to the rebuilding of communities following periods of war and conflict. For example, *A Liberian Journey: History, Memory, and the Making of a Nation* (http://liberianhistory.org), a multi-platform (film and website), collaborative, transnational project centered around the restoration of historical documentation and its restitution to local communities in Liberia, demonstrates such a reframing. The website digitizes and repurposes the photographic and early film documentation collected on a 1926 Harvard scientific expedition to Liberia in part sponsored by the Firestone Tire and Rubber Company, and returns this documentation to Liberians seeking to reclaim a forgotten past and support a new future. It also records oral interviews with elders (under the "stories" tab). The projects advocates for the local re-appropriation of what Ann Stoler has termed "ruins of empire" within present politics and the writing of a more inclusive history; this is an issue of particular importance in a country whose recent past is marked by a brutal civil war.[20] Another core issue this project has effectively addressed is the need to actively consider the limits and disparities caused by the

---

19 Claire Payton, "'Hacking' Public History," *Dissertation Reviews* (blog), January 5, 2015, http://dissertationreviews.org/archives/10472.
20 Ann Laura Stoler, *Imperial Debris: On Ruins and Ruination* (Durham, NC: Duke University Press, 2013).

digital divide when developing projects that aim to bring public history through digital means to peripheral and infrastructurally underserved communities, by making the website accessible to those with smartphones but low bandwidth. Everyone should be empowered to access the results of academic work that affects their lives and lands. Drawing on the same documentation, a corresponding film, *The Land Beneath our Feet* (http://thelandbeneathourfeet.com/) addresses the current debates about radical land reform in Liberia, advocating for the empowerment of communities and displaced people via a historically sensitive understanding of communal land ownership.

Claims of ownership depend on memory and legal standing, which in turn depend on claimants' access to data. The ongoing sustainability and long-term preservation of digital projects is also important with projects that develop an active user base for whom the digital content becomes a critical part of the public understanding of, experience of, or claims to a place. Finn Arne Jørgensen demonstrates how the disappearance of geosocial networks like Gowalla led to the loss of entire communities engaging with public places.[21] On a much larger scale, recent data rescue efforts such as Data Refuge (https://ppeh.sas.upenn.edu/experiments/data-refuge), motivated by silencings and erasures ordered by the Trump administration, are intended as pivotal elements of a future strategy towards an open and accessible public history of environmental issues.

In conclusion, while public histories of spaces are still often authored under the auspices of territorially invested institutions (such as state agencies, local chambers of commerce, or tourism councils), the popularization of digital media and methods potentially removes barriers and amplifies impact. Digital tools can expand the scope of data drawn upon; they enable access to broad audiences, and often seek to engage those audiences in novel ways; they invite public input; they facilitate connections. They are democratic in the sense that they may be used by everyone (whether or not they are community-sourced); yet they are only instruments of public transformation – blind to political and social ends. The same tools that challenge populist agendas and nationalist propaganda may also empower such efforts, twisting them in unforeseen ways. As the use of digital tools increases, if combined with a growing indifference to facts and interests, battles over control of these spaces and their meanings will intensify.

Effective digital public histories of spaces need to be built with possible risks in mind. Efforts to create sustainable archives for environmentally relevant data that transcend the local dimension of public spaces need to be favored and fostered. At a time of accelerated and amplified messages, we urgently need critical attention to territorial appeals and effects in digital public histories; encouragement of more transnational histories; and a renewed understanding of the role (whether dominant

---

21 Jørgensen, "Walking with GPS".

or not) of trained experts and scientists. We have an opportunity to get out of our ivory towers and make digital histories that truly serve democratic values, the environment, and the public good.

Bibliography

Brennan, Sheila. "Public First." In *Debates in the Digital Humanities: 2016*, edited by Matthew K. Gold and Lauren F. Klein, 384–389. Minneapolis, MN: University of Minnesota Press, 2016.

Christen, Catherine, and Lisa Mighetto. 2004. "Introduction: Environmental History as Public History." *The Public Historian* 26.1 (2004): 9–20.

Cosgrove, Denis and Stephen Daniels, eds. *The Iconography of Landscape: Essays on the Symbolic Representation, Design, and Use of Past Environments*. Cambridge: Cambridge University Press 1988.

Coulter, Kimberly and Wilko Graf von Hardenberg. "Cultivating the Spirit of the Commons in Environmental History." In *Methodological Challenges in Nature-Culture and Environmental History Research*, edited by Jocelyn Thorpe, Stephanie Rutherford, and L. Anders Sandberg, 260–271. Abingdon: Routledge, 2017.

Jørgensen, Finn Arne. "Walking with GPS: An Object Lesson." In *Methodological Challenges in Nature-Culture and Environmental History Research*, edited by Jocelyn Thorpe, Stephanie Rutherford, and L. Anders Sandberg, 284–297. Abingdon: Routledge, 2017.

Thomas Cauvin
Digital Public History in the United States

Abstract: Digital history goes, by definition, beyond national frontiers, but can one decipher national specificities in its practices and projects? This chapter explores the birth, development, and institutionalization of digital public history in the United States. Issued from a strong network of digital history practitioners, the success of digital public history in the United States stemmed from its connection with pre-existing public history academic centers and projects. Through projects like the *Valley of the Shadow* or, later, the 9/11 Digital Archives, digital historians re-imagined the concept of authority and relations with the public. The Center for History and New Media was created by Roy Rosenzweig in 1994 and rapidly became one of the main actors in the move from digital to digital public history. Finally, the chapter explores the future of digital public history in the United States, its institutionalization as a discipline, and its increased focus on user-generated projects.

Keywords: United States of America, institutionalization, user-generated, Rosenzweig, public history, shared-authority, crowdsourcing

The recently published Oxford Handbook of Public History proposes a first part on "The Changing Public History Landscape". One of the two main changes put forward by the Handbook – in addition to "International Public History" – is about "Doing Public History in Digital Environments".[1] This essay, written by American historian Sharon Leon, is symbolic of the rise of digital public history in the United States. Likewise, Andrew Hurley points out that "Students entering the field [public history] are encouraged, if not required, to acquire fluency in database management, digitization techniques, and collaborative writing software."[2] The rise of digital public history in the United States should not be surprising since this is where the institutionalization and academic teaching of public history has been taking place since the 1970s. This chapter explores the birth of a specific field of digital public history in the United States, its vectors, and institutionalization – through university programs, projects, and funding opportunities – as well as its impact on a broader international context.

---

[1] Sharon Leon, "Complexity and Collaboration: Doing Public History in Digital Environments," in *Oxford Handbook of Public History*, ed. James Gardner and Paul Hamilton (Oxford: Oxford University Press, 2017), 44–68.
[2] Andrew Hurley, "Chasing the Frontiers of Digital Technology. Public History Meets the Digital Divide," *The Public Historian* 38, no. 1 (February 2016): 69–88.

https://doi.org/10.1515/9783110430295-020

Digital History and Public History: Recent Encounter

The uses of computers in history and humanities have a long and international history that dates back at least to the 1950s. Serge Noiret reckons that "Digital history has transformed the kinds of sources used by historians, and the tools for accessing, storing, and managing them, without having thoroughly discussed their critical use".[3] Symbolized by the creation of the Association for History and Computing in 1986, digital history was, at first, mostly limited to quantitative research, with little direct public engagement. However, the last twenty years witnessed the proliferation of debates on the "promises of digital history", especially in the United States. In a 2008 discussion in the *Journal of American History* led by Dan Cohen, historians defined digital history as "based on the use of new media and computers in order to analyze and understand historical information and/or to communicate its results."[4] The development of digital technologies have allowed historians to not only process data but also to share and communicate them with the public. This move opened the door for a major reflection on historical practices as a whole. Thus, the first part of *History in the Digital Age*, edited by Toni Weller in 2012, is entitled "Re-conceptualizing history in the digital age."[5]

Digital communication tools fostered new interest among historians. The World Wide Web was born in 1991, and already in the Nineties, historians such as Edward Ayers and Roy Rosenzweig proposed a reflection on the use of digital tools to communicate history. Based on hypertexts, the Internet affected how historical narratives were constructed and communicated. Website navigation and hyperlinks changed the overall structure of digital history.[6] Based on a book written by Edward Ayers and Anne Sarah Rubin, the *Valley of the Shadow* was one of the most famous examples of new digital history.[7] Developed at the University of Virginia, the project presented the experiences of two local communities during and after the Civil War. Used at first to communicate historical research to a larger public, the project became

---

[3] Serge Noiret, "Digital Public History," in *Companion to Public History*, ed. David Dean (Wiley-Blackwell, forthcoming 2018), 111.
[4] Daniel J. Cohen, Michael Frisch, Patrick Gallagher, Steven Mintz, Kirsten Sword, Amy Murrell Taylor, William G. Thomas, III and William J. Turkel, "Interchange: The Promise of Digital History," in *The Journal of American History* 95, no. 2 (Sep., 2008): 452–491.
[5] Toni Weller, *History in the Digital Age* (London/New York: Routledge, 2012).
[6] Sherman Dorn, "Is (Digital) History More Than an Argument about the Past?" in *Writing History in the Digital Age*, ed. Jack Dougherty and Kristen Nawrotzki (Ann Arbor: University of Michigan Press, 2013), https://writinghistory.trincoll.edu (accessed January 8, 2019).
[7] Edward Ayers, *The Valley of the Shadow*, http://valley.lib.virginia.edu/ (accessed December 11, 2017).

a laboratory to reflect on the links between historians and audiences.[8] Historians had begun to think about communicating history in new multi-media ways, presenting also primary sources through the web hypertext and ways of considering how these tools could engage publics with the results of a new historiography about the war. In their 2005 ground-breaking book *Digital History: A Guide to Gathering, Preserving, and Presenting the Past*, Roy Rosenzweig and Dan Cohen proposed a practical approach to digital history instead of echoed public history.[9] For instance, Rosenzweig and Cohen explored how historians should consider and participate not only in the interpretation but also in the preservation of digital archives.[10] Digital technologies provided new opportunities for historians to deal with archival materials. Historian Sharon Leon rightly explains "The promise of digital technologies for public history is vast: new audiences, dynamic content, increased engagement, large-scale collaboration." But Leon also warns that "to achieve this promise, we must focus on the goals of public history and adapt our working practice to the new conditions created by the digital environment."[11] The promise and use of digital technologies for historians was accompanied by a reconsideration of the relations between the different actors of the process, especially between historians and the public.

From Digital History to Digital Public History

The birth of the World Wide Web in the 1990s transformed digital practices. The Internet became a mode of communication for digital historians and cultural institutions. For instance, the U.S Library of Congress launched the *Selected Civil War Photographs* collection in 1994 for people to browse materials from the Civil War.[12] Due to the limited format of the first years, digital history on the Web initially appeared to be a collection of materials with little historical interpretation. Additionally, the emergence of the Internet began a process of democratizing public access to information. As Roy Rosenzweig noticed, anyone could become a historian

---

8 Serge Noiret, "Y a t-il une Histoire Numérique 2.0?" in *Les historiens et l'informatique. Un métier à réinventer*, ed. Jean-Philippe Genet and Andrea Zorzi (Rome: Ecole Française de Rome, 2011), 265–267.
9 Roy Rosenzweig and Dan Cohen, *Digital History. A Guide to Gathering, Preserving, and Presenting the Past on the Web* (Philadelphia: University of Pennsylvania Press, 2005), http://chnm.gmu.edu/digitalhistory/ (accessed December 2, 2017.); Serge Noiret, "La "nuova storiografia digitale" negli Stati Uniti (1999–2004)," in *Memoria e Ricerca* 18 (January-April 2005): 177–178.
10 Roy Rosenzweig, "Scarcity or Abundance? Preserving the Past in a Digital Era," *American Historical Review* 108, no. 3 (June 2003): 735–762; Daniel J. Cohen, "The Future of Preserving the Past," in *CRM: The Journal of Heritage Stewardship* 2, no. 2 (Summer, 2005): 6–19.
11 Leon, "Complexity and Collaboration," 45.
12 Leon, "Complexity and Collaboration," 45.

thanks to the Web.[13] It became easier to create and manage personal websites and share stories, interpretations, and historical narratives. The web contributed to the publication of a variety – in format and quality – of views on the past. Beyond the discourse of how to best communicate historical narratives through hypertexts, the web forced digital historians to reconsider authority and public participation once new interactive Web 2.0 technologies appeared between 2001 and 2004.

The advent of the so-called "participatory web", or Web 2.0, augured even more transformative changes, with the advent of blogging and content management software. As the web grew more dynamic, users become active participants in crafting stories and narratives. Leon explains that "users developed ways to talk back and interact with the content being served on the Web."[14] For instance, the book *Writing History in the Digital Age* – published in 2013 by the University of Michigan Press – was a born-digital, open-review project. In addition to questioning whether the digital revolution transformed how we write about the past, the collective project received twenty-eight essays and more than one thousand comments – used for the final draft – from visitors.[15] Likewise, De Gruyter publishing now proposes open peer review projects in which authors can engage publicly with reviewers and readers.[16] Participation transformed digital history into digital public history. This move was encouraged by key actors in the United States, among which the Center for History and New Media has had a particular importance.

In his recent essay on digital public history, Serge Noiret reckons that "Roy Rosenzweig, who (. . .) was already dealing with the Web at the end of the 1990s, invented the field of digital public history in this way."[17] Rosenzweig, a historian who specialized in urban and social history and historic preservation, created the Center for History and New Media (CHNM) in 1994 at George Mason University in Fairfax, Virginia. The CHNM's mission has been to "use digital media and computer technology to democratize history: to incorporate multiple voices, reach diverse audiences, and encourage popular participation in presenting and preserving the past."[18] The CHNM promoted, developed, and theorized the use of digital tools in historical practices. It also framed digital public history as a field of study and practice. In 2014 during the twentieth anniversary celebrations of the center, Stephen Robertson (Director of the Center) highlighted the importance of digital media in

---

[13] Noiret, "Digital Public History," 118.
[14] Leon, "Complexity and Collaboration," 45.
[15] "Writing History in the Digital Age," https://writinghistory.trincoll.edu (accessed December 12, 2017).
[16] De Gruyter "Open Peer Review," *De Gruyter website*, https://opr.degruyter.com (accessed December 29, 2018).
[17] Noiret, "Digital Public History," 118.
[18] "About," CHNM, http://chnm.gmu.edu/about/ (accessed December 11, 2017).

forging a new history profession.[19] Different CHNM tools and projects have offered new perspectives to move from digital history to digital public history.

Of particular note, the CHNM promoted the development of multiple perspectives, voices, and interpretations in digital works. *Gulag: Many Days, Many Lives* was the first online exhibition designed by the CHNM in 2006. It "immerses visitors in the varied experiences of the vast and brutal Soviet prison camp system."[20] While proposing "a strong narrative voice," the project also allowed "users to trace the lives of more than two dozen different prisoners who had vastly different experiences with the Soviet forced-labor concentration camp system."[21] Presenting the complexity of the past through multiple voices also answered digital public history's effort to expand and develop a variety of audiences for history. For example, Sheila Brennan, a former student and staff member at CHNM, considers "understanding audiences" as key in digital projects and tested it through her recent project *Histories of the National Mall*.[22] Brennan and the project team "tested the site architecture, content, functionality, and terminology with different users using paper mock-ups" and "identified tourists and individuals new to the D.C. area (e.g., summer interns) as the primary audiences for its mobile public history project."[23] This project showcases the emerging user-centered approach to digital history. In 2015 Sharon Leon, also a former student and member of the CHNM staff, conceived "User-Centered Digital History: Doing Public History on the Web" as a project to "offer a clear introduction for practicing public historians, those who teach public history, and their students, who want to embark on digital work."[24] The focus on user-centered history is a key difference between academic digital history and digital public history.

Digital public history has also given audiences a role in the process of creating history – both in terms of user contributions but also in the development of digital tools. For instance, the CHNM has developed tools to collect digital-born materials from the public. The *September 11 Digital Archive* was user centered. It collected "more than 150,000 digital items, a tally that includes more than 40,000 emails

---

19 Noiret, "Digital Public History," 113.
20 "Gulag: Many Days, Many Lives," CHNM website, http://chnm.gmu.edu/gulag-many-days-many-lives/ (accessed December 11, 2017).
21 Leon, "Complexity and Collaboration," 49.
22 Sheila Brennan, "Public First," in *Debates in the Digital Humanities 2016*, edited by Matthew K. Gold (Minneapolis: University of Minnesota Press, 2016), http://dhdebates.gc.cuny.edu/debates/text/83 (accessed December 12, 2017); *Histories of the National Mall* takes users "on a tour of the National Mall's rich past by offering historical maps, a chronology of past events, short bios of significant individuals, and episodes in the Mall's history." "About" Histories of the National Mall website, https://mallhistories.tumblr.com/about (accessed December 11, 2017).
23 Brennan, "Public First."
24 Sharon Leon, "User-Centered Digital History: Doing Public History on the Web," *[bracket], images, teaching, technology*, https://www.6floors.org/bracket/2015/03/03/user-centered-digital-history-doing-public-history-on-the-web/ (accessed December 12, 2017).

and other electronic communications, more than 40,000 first-hand stories, and more than 15,000 digital images" related to the attacks on the World Trade Center.[25] These invented-archives are based on the concept of crowdsourcing first used by Jeff Howe in 2006 and defined as "the act of taking work once performed within an organization and outsourcing it to the general public through an open call for participants."[26] User-generated projects, through crowdsourcing, have redefined the concept of authority in digital public history.

Of equal note, the September 11th Digital Archive was built around a digital content management system created by CHNM specifically for the project. That tool would eventually become the widely-used Omeka content management system. Today Omeka.net hosts more than 36000 sites to create digital archives. Arguably Omeka has emerged as one of the most influential tools developed during the digital turn of the historian. Tools, such as Omeka, are a vital part of how historians are engaging publics – not just in giving them a voice through traditional historical projects but also giving publics digital platforms through which they can document and tell their own stories.

The Future of Digital Public History

More than in any other historical fields, changing technologies greatly affect digital public history practices. The democratization of Internet access and mobile phones has allowed historians to better connect contents and users. Although not limited to the United States, mobile computing has recently emerged as a major role in digital public history. One of the first examples of using mobile technologies for digital curation was the *Cleveland Historical* project developed by Cleveland State University's Center for Public History and Digital Humanities.[27] As a Web app, *Cleveland Historical* functions through Curatescape that geolocalises stories and user-generated materials about urban heritage (Cleveland, but also Spokane, Baltimore, New Orleans, and many others).[28]

CHNM participated in the development of mobile technology for digital public history. In 2008, the CHNM created a project team – led by Sharon Leon and Sheila Brennan – to develop mobile technology for museums.[29] Likewise, Curatescape uses Omeka as its content management system to upload, manage, and provide

---

25 "About," *September 11 Digital Archive*, http://911digitalarchive.org (accessed December 11, 2017).
26 Mia Ridge, *Crowdsourcing our Cultural Heritage* (London/New York: Routledge, 2014), 1.
27 "Home," *Center for Public History and Digital Humanities*, https://csudigitalhumanities.org (accessed December 12, 2017).
28 "Home," Curatescape, http://curatescape.org (accessed December 8, 2017).
29 "Mobile for Museums," CHNM, http://chnm.gmu.edu/labs/mobile-for-museums/ (accessed December 7, 2017).

contents in the different versions of *Cleveland Historical*. As Noiret asserts, Curatescape is "a trailblazer in the new element of individual access to the virtual content of digital public history."[30] Through new projects in Kenya, England, and Australia, Curatescape contributes to a mobile-app oriented digital public history.

User-centered and user-generated digital public history also led to more discussion about activism and how the historian could be part of current debates. Historian Denise Meringolo has worked on *Preserve the Baltimore Uprising,* a digital crowdsourced repository project that documents the death of Freddie Gray in 2015 and the resulting protest in Baltimore.[31] Many other digital public history projects aim to strengthen the voices of under-represented communities. In a 2016 article entitled "What LGBT Digital Public History Requires," Claire Potter explained how digital tools could empower communities through preservation of archives as well as user-generated contents.[32]

Finally, digital public history has benefited from, and will continue to develop as part of, academic institutionalization in the United States. The CHNM has offered *Doing Digital History* summer institutes that have helped to nurture digital public history projects and expertise.[33] Additionally, from August to December 2017, four out of the seven tenure-track Assistant Professor positions in public history offered in the United States listed digital public history among the skills required.[34] Even more impressive is the number of public history programs that now include digital public history components. Rather than coming from digital humanities strongholds, digital public history has taken advantage of the long-established network of public history university programs. The success of digital public history in the United States suggests that the field represents the evolution of public history towards digital practices, rather than a development from digital humanities towards public practices.

---

30 Noiret, "Digital Public History," 124.
31 "About," Preserving the Baltimore Uprising 2015 Archive Project, http://baltimoreuprising2015.org/about (accessed December 12, 2017).
32 Claire Potter, "What LGBT Digital Public History Requires," *outhistory*, http://outhistory.org/blog/what-digital-public-history-requires/ (accessed December 11, 2017).
33 Sheila Brennan, "White Paper Summary," Doing Digital History: 2016, http://history2016.doingdh.org (accessed December 12, 2017).
34 Colorado State University, University of Cincinnati, George Mason University, and Virginia Tech.

Bibliography

Brennan, S. "Public First." In *Debates in the Digital Humanities 2016*, edited by Matthew K. Gold (Minneapolis: University of Minnesota Press, 2016), accessed December 12, 2017, http://dhdebates.gc.cuny.edu/debates/text/83.

Leon, S. "Complexity and Collaboration: Doing Public History in Digital Environments." In *Oxford Handbook of Public History*, edited by James Gardner and Paul Hamilton, 44–68. Oxford: Oxford University Press, 2017.

Noiret, S. "Digital Public History." In *Companion to Public History*, edited by David Dean (Wiley-Blackwell, forthcoming 2018).

Ridge, M. *Crowdsourcing our Cultural Heritage*. London/New York: Routledge, 2014.

Making digital history: The impact of digitality on public participation and scholarly practices in historical research. PhD thesis Open University, 2016. http://oro.open.ac.uk/45519/, accessed January 2, 2019.

Priya Chhaya with contributions by Reina Murray
Technology and Historic Preservation: Documentation and Storytelling

Abstract: Over the last few decades transformation within the field of historic preservation has involved the nearly parallel tracks of expanding the histories being preserved and a constantly shifting technological landscape. This digital transformation has reshaped historic preservation practice and community engagement by making new tools and methods available for documentation and place-based storytelling. This chapter examines how technological advancements such as geographic information systems, Lidar, photogrammetry, drones, mobile applications, and social media translate data and information into a more useable and accessible format for both professional and public use.

Keywords: historic preservation, digital documentation, heritage conservation, interpretation, GIS, social media, virtual reality, augmented reality

In its June 2017 report on the implications of connectivity, the Pew Research Center for Internet & Technology found, "49 percent of the world's population is connected online and an estimated 8.4 billion connected things are in use worldwide."[1] For the field of historic preservation, the effects of this digital transformation are reflected at nearly every level of work, creating complex tools and resources that are also leading to growing opportunities for public engagement with cultural and historical fabric.

In the United States, this digital transformation goes hand-in-hand with a broader shift in historical methodologies to uncover the many facets of the American story. Ongoing efforts acknowledge individuals and communities whose stories were subsumed by the traditional narrative of the rich, the white, and the powerful. For historic preservation, this includes a critical shift in expanding definitions of significance to include buildings and neighborhoods based on their historical and cultural meaning, not only for their architectural style.[2] Instead of focusing on grand, emblematic buildings, such as George Washington's Mount Vernon, preservationists began to

---

[1] Lee Rainie and Anderson, Janna, "The Internet of Things Connectivity Binge: What Are the Implications?" (Pew Research Center: Internet and Technology, 6 June, 2017), http://www.pewinternet.org/2017/06/06/the-internet-of-things-connectivity-binge-what-are-the-implications/.
[2] National Park Service, "Secretary of the Interior's Standards and Guidelines," https://www.nps.gov/history/local-law/arch_stnds_5.htm, accessed 7 August, 2019. Today, in the United States, preservationists follow a series of guidelines that are developed by the Secretary of the Interior. They play an essential role in what information should be including in all documentation.

protect smaller, more vernacular structures, such as barns, enslaved quarters, tenements, and factories.[3]

Internationally, there are movements to document sites in a wide variety of ways. Since 1992, United Nations Educational, Scientific and Cultural Organization (UNESCO) has sought to document sites of universal value to include the natural and the built environment through the development of a list of Intangible Cultural Heritage, or the Creative Cities Network.[4] The field of heritage conservation values the preservation of culture – beyond buildings and structures – to include intangible heritage such as language and indigenous cultural practice.[5]

Running on nearly parallel tracks, these conversations about preserving history and the constantly shifting technological explosion have opened doorways for historic preservationists to adapt old methodologies and create new tools to document, protect, and interpret historic places. The digital transformation has reshaped historic preservation practice both within the field and through community engagement by making new tools and methods available for documentation and storytelling.

Documentation

A central aspect of historic preservation work is the practice of documentation. Without knowledge of what resources exist, preservationists cannot know what places to save, protect, and interpret for the future.[6] Formal preservation efforts date

---

[3] "The Period of Significance Is Now," *Forum Journal* 28. 4 (Summer 2014): 43–51. One of the shifts in the field is related to determining or revaluating a site's period of significance. This includes connecting the different layers to present day issues.

[4] For more on global practices and philosophies visit www.unesco.org and www.icomos.org. For the purposes of this essay, historic preservation will be used to refer to American practice, and heritage conservation for global practice. While there is a movement to change the language in the United States, preservation is still in common use. That being said, my definition of cultural heritage and historic preservation refers to the practice of preserving places and practices of the past. Traditionally, this is limited to buildings only but in recent years (in the United States) this includes landscapes, intangible heritage, and traditional cultural practice as well. UNESCO, "Creative Cities Network," https://en.unesco.org/creative-cities/content/why-creativity-why-cities, accessed 4 August, 2019. Other international organizations doing this work are ICOMOS, the International National Trusts Organisation (INTO) and World Monument Fund.

[5] While this essay will primarily be focused on preservation and technology in the United States (my primary expertise), I have tried to include a few global examples to show connections across practice.

[6] Jeff Joeckel and Shannon Bell, "Guidelines for Local Surveys: A Basis for Preservation Planning, National Register of Historic Places (Nrb 24)," 29 December, 2001, https://www.nps.gov/nr/publications/bulletins/nrb24/iNDEX.htm, accessed 20 March, 2021.

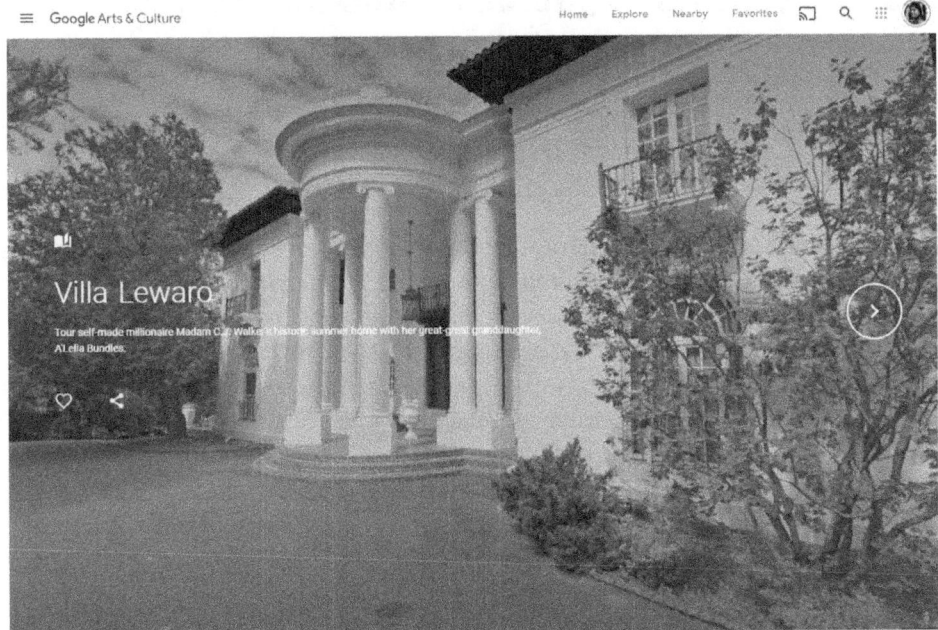

Fig. 1: Screen capture of a 3D Visualization of Madame C.J. Walker's home in Irvington, NY. Madame Walker was a cosmetics and business pioneer and a self-made millionaire.
Credit: Google Arts & Culture "Villa Lewaro," accessed August 24, 2021, https://artsandculture.google.com/exhibit/villa-lewaro-national-trust-for-historic-preservation

to the nineteenth century and earlier, but systematically identifying sites of preservation is a more recent phenomenon. In the United States, the Historic American Buildings Survey (HABS) began in 1933 with the backing of the American Institute of Architects, the Library of Congress, and the US federal government.[7] Recent technological advances introduced aerial photography, precise mapping, and three-dimensional modeling have had significant impact on how preservationists documented and surveyed different kinds of historic resources at varying levels of detail Figure 1.

---

[7] As these shifts occurred in the field, HABS was joined by the Historic American Engineering Record (HAER) and the Historic American Landscapes Survey (HALS). These three programs, managed by the National Park Service, continue to provide the most extensive documentation of America's historic resources today. National Park Service, "Historic American Building Survey," accessed February 18, 2018, https://www.nps.gov/hdp/habs/index.htm.

Mapping with Geographic Information Systems

Historic preservation is intrinsically place-based, making mapping frameworks like Geographic Information Systems[8] important for the documentation of cultural resources. By capturing and managing precise spatial information, GIS connects data with geography, allowing for the linkage of what things are with where things are.

Traditional historic and cultural resource surveys, required on-site surveyors who measured and mapped locations and manually completed forms in the field. Increasingly, mobile applications are replacing pen and paper, allowing for data capture to integrate with GIS databases.[9] In 2016, the Los Angeles Office of Historic Resources completed an ambitious 10-year comprehensive survey of the city's resources. One of the first comprehensive surveys of its kind, SurveyLA Figure 2 recorded over 30,000 individual historic resources and historic districts over 500 square miles, Designed with the goal of informing better overall citywide planning, the results of the survey were shared with other city agencies allowing the survey data to be layered and analyzed in relation to other crucial city data, such as zoning codes, transportation routes and/or brownfield locations.[10]

GIS has also provided preservationists with a compelling way to communicate about historic places, especially using web GIS to communicate with publics about the historic landscape. For example, in 2017 the Washington DC Historic Preservation office launched HistoryQuest DC, a mapping project that provided historical data on the city's 127,000 buildings. The project also "links to documentation about properties listed on the National Register of Historic Places, information on historical residential subdivisions, and identification of the city's historic districts and their boundaries. HistoryQuest will help the Historic Preservation Office achieve its

---

8 Much of this portion of the essay is based on conversations and content formulated in partnership with Reina Murray, former GIS Analyst for the National Trust for Historic Preservation's 2017 PastForward Conference. In most ways my understanding of the role present technologies influence and manifest in preservation's documentation and process is informed by her on the ground experience.

9 Emilie Evans, "Smartphone Survey Contributes to Detroit's Rightsizing Conversation," Forum Blog (blog), 11 March, 2014, http://forum.savingplaces.org/blogs/special-contributor/2014/03/11/smartphone-survey-contributes-to-detroits-rightsizing-conversation, accessed 20 March, 2021.

10 Janet Hansen Cruz, and Sara Delgadillo, "Top Tips from SurveyLA, Los Angeles' Citywide Historic Resources Survey," *Forum Blog* (blog), 28 July, 2017, https://forum.savingplaces.org/blogs/special-contributor/2017/07/28/top-tips-from-surveyla-los-angeles-citywide-historic-resources-survey, accessed 20 March, 2021. Enriquez, Annabel Lee, Myers, David, and Dalgity, Alison, "The Arches Heritage Inventory and Management System for the Protection of Cultural Resources," *Forum Journal* (Technology Transforming Preservation) 32.1 (June 2018): 30–38. At the time of this article, the SurveyLA demo site used Archesv4. The Arches-hosted inventory is also available online to the public at historicplacesla.org, where users can search for resources through filters such as theme, architect, or period of significance.

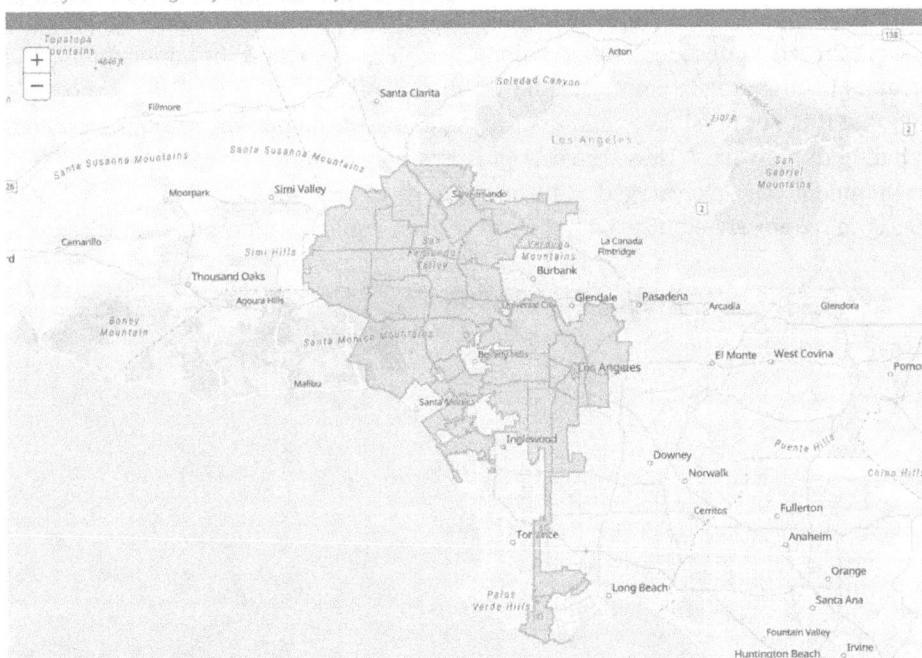

Fig. 2: A screen capture of the Survey LA portal with the districts that were a part of the survey shaded in orange. Further down the website (not pictured) are various filter options for the survey. Credit: "Historic Resources Surveys," accessed August 24, 2021, https://planning.lacity.org/preservation-design/historic-resources-survey.

ongoing goal of identifying and evaluating historic properties and planning for their preservation."[11] In a similar vein, as a way to make accessing GIS information more public facing, ESRI created a tool called Story Maps which allows the addition of extra contextual information and images within the mapping interface.[12]

In 2016 the University of Richmond's Digital Scholarship Lab launched Mapping Inequality Figure 3 an interactive GIS application that documented the role of redlining in the 1930s. Digitizing the maps of the Home Owners' Loan Corporation, helps users to see at a neighborhood level and national scale systematic discrimination

---

[11] "HistoryQuest DC: Tracking the City's Historical Fabric, Building by Building," *Forum Blog* (blog), http://forum.savingplaces.org/blogs/special-contributor/2017/03/28/historyquest-dc-tracking-the-citys-historical-fabric-building-by-building, accessed 18 February, 2018.

[12] ESRI, "Story Maps and the Digital Humanities," https://collections.storymaps.esri.com/humanities/, accessed 4 August, 2019. To dig deeper into these examples look for "Hokusai: The Many Views of Mount Fuji," and "Re-Envisioning Greater Cahokia." Both of these Story Maps leverage location specific data to provide their publics with an understanding between history, art and place.

against African Americans through federal housing programs.[13] Mapping Inequality inspired Mapping Prejudice, which analyzes restrictive racial covenants on property deeds that led to decades of discriminatory housing practices in Minneapolis. The creators of this project emphasize how "this history has been willfully forgotten," and that it is not possible to address the inequities of the present without an understanding of the past.[14] These projects illustrate how the imaging of the historic built environment can be leveraged to inspire change in existing local and national policies, arming preservationists with tools to support equitable planning strategies.

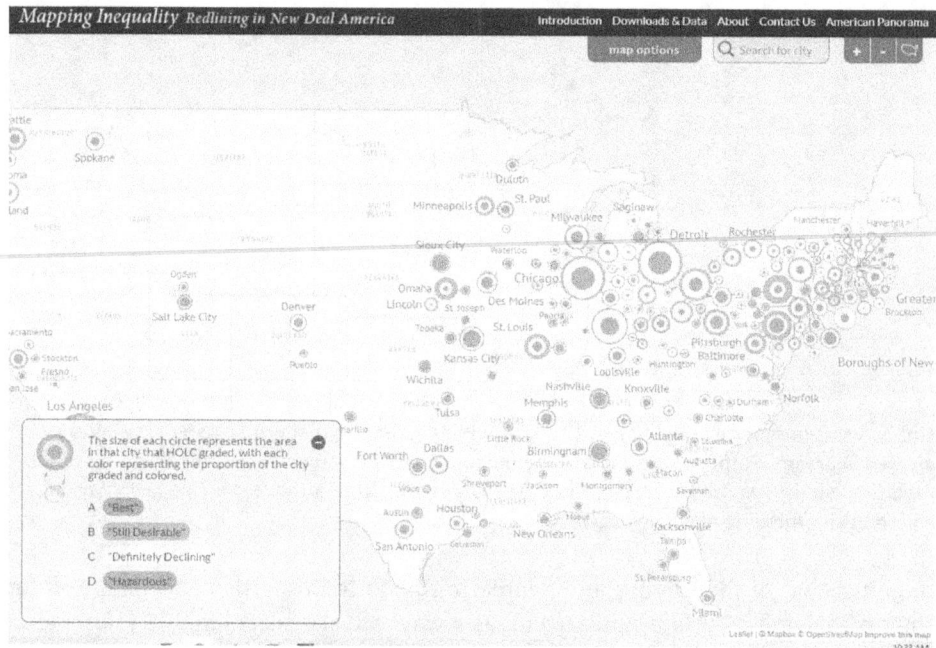

Fig. 3: Mapping Inequality uses GIS mapping technology to illustrate the role Redlining played during a specific period of American history. Technology like this inspires other projects like Mapping Prejudice which connects historical documents with practices in present day.
Credit: University of Richmond, Digital Scholarship Lab, "Mapping Inequality," n.d., https://dsl.richmond.edu/panorama/redlining/#loc=5/39.1/-94.58.

---

13 University of Richmond, Digital Scholarship Lab, "Mapping Inequality," n.d., https://dsl.richmond.edu/panorama/redlining/#loc=5/39.1/-94.58, accessed 20 March, 2021.
14 "Mapping Prejudice," https://www.mappingprejudice.org, accessed 7 August, 2019.

Lidar, Photogrammetry, and Drones

Advancements in laser scanning technology (such as LiDAR), as well as photogrammetry, have enabled preservationists to collect detailed measurements of entire buildings or landscapes too large to measure by hand. These images are used to develop sophisticated 3D models that capture the state of a structure in time, establishing a baseline for its continued monitoring and evaluation. Such new tools have become vital at both visualizing a broader range of historical landscapes but doing so more thoroughly and less expensively than was previously possible. This has fostered an era of new archeological discovery. In 2018, using LiDAR technology, researchers identified the ruins of 60,000 human-made features in the jungles of Guatemala. This new evidence has provided essential information for archaeologists to understand and document Mayan civilization.[15]

Such tools have also helped preservationists and urban planners in their work in documenting heritage landscapes under threat. For example, after a flash flood caused significant damage to the buildings along Ellicott City's Main Street in Maryland in late July 2016, companies specializing in aerial imaging and 3D modeling documented the extensive damage to historic structures in order to facilitate preservation work by creating a record.[16] The ability to combine a birds-eye view from the drones, with the accurate measurements collected by the laser scans, provided recovery teams with a comprehensive picture of the work and resources needed to bring Ellicott City back.[17]

The importance of these methods of documentation also became evident in April 2019 when the historic Notre Dame Cathedral was ravaged by fire. The late Andrew Tallon led a team at Vassar College to document Notre Dame by combining laser scanning and panoramic photography to generate a three-dimensional model of this structure Figure 4. This documentation is aiding preservationists to repair and rebuild the cathedral.[18]

---

[15] Tom Clynes, "Exclusive: Laser Scans Reveal Maya 'Megalopolis' Below Guatemalan Jungle," 1 February, 2018, https://www.nationalgeographic.com/news/2018/02/maya-laser-lidar-guatemala-pacunam/, accessed 20 March, 2021.
[16] Terry Kilby, and Belinda Kilby, "A Different View: Using Drones to Document Historic Places," Forum Journal (Technology Transforming Preservation) 32.1 (June 2018): 13–21.
[17] The work Elevated Element did was following the 2016 flood. In 2018 another 1000-year historic flood hit the town, making this work all the more valuable.
[18] Rachel Hartigan Shea, "Historian Uses Lasers to Unlock Mysteries of Gothic Cathedrals," 16 April, 2019, https://www.nationalgeographic.com/news/2015/06/150622-andrew-tallon-notre-dame-cathedral-laser-scan-art-history-medieval-gothic/, accessed 20 March, 2021. In the aftermath of the fire, Tallon's work was seen as a saving grace, potentially providing critical documentation for how to rebuild the vaunted cathedral.

Fig. 4: Screen capture of a Andrew Tallon capturing data as he documents Notre Dame Cathedral. (Taken August 8, 2019).
Credit: Shea, Rachel Hartigan, "Historian Uses Lasers to Unlock Mysteries of Gothic Cathedrals," April 16, 2019, https://www.nationalgeographic.com/news/2015/06/150622-andrew-tallon-notre-dame-cathedral-laser-scan-art-histo

Interpretation and Storytelling

Where technologies such as GIS and laser scanning provide historic preservationists and heritage conservationists with the ability to gather data for documentation process, these same tools, can power place-based storytelling.

Technology in Place

One of the greatest assets of new technologies (such as mobile devices) is its ability to convey information despite the user's physical location. Mobile apps and websites provide opportunity to not only broaden the historical record but also provide visitors with additional information that is easily adaptable.

The Tenement Museum uses digital storytelling techniques within its historic structures and online to help visitors better understand the histories of different generations of immigrants and American who occupied their buildings on the Lower East Side of Manhattan. Touch tables in the "Shop Life" exhibit invite visitors to

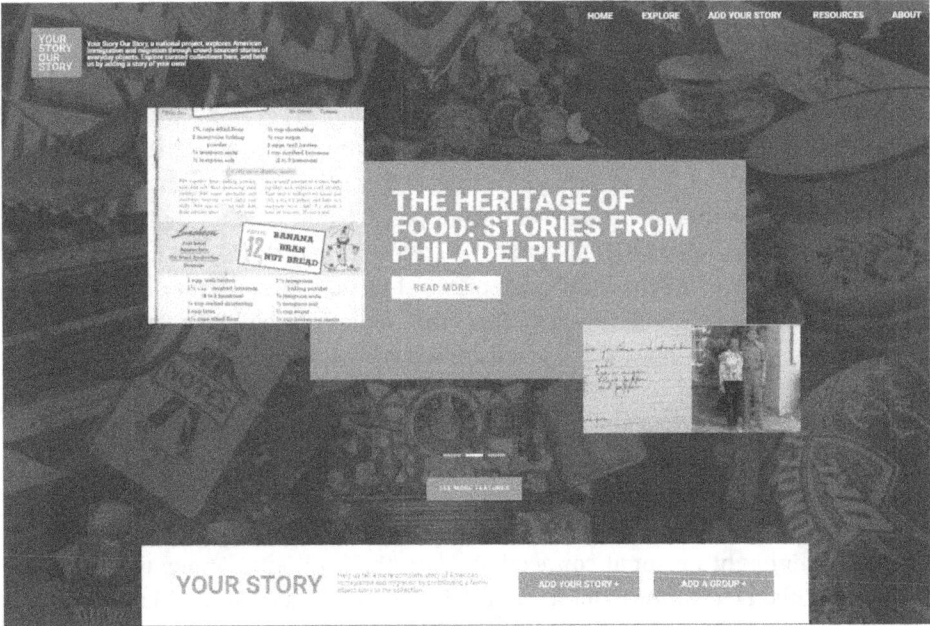

Fig. 5: Homepage of the "Your Story, Our Story" portal on the Lower Eastside Tenement Museum's shows how users can add to the database with images and stories of their own.
Credit: "Your Story, Our Story," accessed February 18, 2018, https://yourstory.tenement.org/.

interact with digital objects and sources that reconstruct stories of people living on Orchard Street in the early twentieth century. Their web project "Your Story Our Story" invites online visitors to share the photo of meaningful personal objects and pin it on a map to connect stories of immigration and migration across the US Figure 5. An individual using the platform can make connections that are both deeply personal, but also revealing the commonalities of human experience.[19]

Similarly, mobile and web apps use geolocation to connect narrative text, images, and audio (oral histories) for the everyday user. These applications provide visitors with an interactive experience to explore place around them and are often used to develop field trips, or tours related to the more underrepresented stories of a community. The Curatescape application platform, for example, is used to tell the history of Ottawa's LGBT community (Ottawa Village Legacy Project), or HistoryPin which has a collection focused on Greenbook Sites across the United States.[20]

---

[19] "Your Story, Our Story," https://yourstory.tenement.org/, accessed 18 February, 2018.
[20] Curatescape, "Curatescape: Public Projects," accessed August 4, 2019, https://curatescape.org/projects/. One additional example is HistoryPin, which uses Google Maps to "pin" objects and additional historical information about various places in one place. Visit www.historypin.org for more information. Additional innovative platforms and approaches from around the United States, both

Social Media as Storytelling

Social media options have expanded considerably since the advent of MySpace (2003) and Facebook (2004). While Facebook remains a mainstay – along with Twitter and Instagram – the ways in which audiences engage with these and other social media platforms have shifted. For preservationists, social media seeks to engage users in the moment and create narratives for them about place. Sarah Heffern, former director of social media at the National Trust for Historic Preservation, notes that ephemeral and live events have become the focal point of social media engagement. As a result, she writes, "[o]ur strategy combines storytelling and community building. Saving places is full of stories, whether they tell the history of a place; of the people who lived, worked, and played there; or of the preservationists who have worked to save it. We use our social media channels to share those stories and to allow people doing such work to talk to us and to each other."[21]

Perhaps one of the best examples of this work is the National Trust for Historic Preservation's This Place Matters campaign. Started in 2008, the program was intended to highlight personal connections with the built environment.[22] Using the hashtag #ThisPlaceMatters, photo competitions on Instagram, and conversations over Twitter invited audiences to interact with the broader message of the National Trust and to share with the world that important historic sites are not merely the grand structures designed by famous architects Figure 6. Using social media networks, people told their own stories emphasizing the power of place in their lives.

Engagement over social media can be a strategy for building more inclusive preservation efforts as organizations build, expand, and respond to their communities. Historic Charleston Foundation uses their Instagram channel to both encourage visitation and also discuss their city's complex and painful history with slavery and the slave trade.[23] An inclusive preservation movement must address and acknowledge

---

championed by scholars and place-based interpreters, including Next Exit History, Detour Guided Walking Tours, the Whole Story, and Jane's Walk. "Detour – Guided Walking Tours, 'The World's Coolest Audio Guides,'" https://www.detour.com, accessed 18 February, 2018. I had the opportunity to use Detour during a 2017 visit to London. "The Whole Story," accessed 18 February, 2018, https://thewholestoryproject.com/, accessed 18 February, 2018.
21 Sarah Heffern, "An Evolving Approach to Social Media," *Forum Blog* (blog), 27 July, 2017, http://forum.savingplaces.org/blogs/sarah-heffern/2017/06/27/an-evolving-approach-to-social-media, accessed 20 March, 2021.
22 National Trust for Historic Preservation, "'This Place Matters' Campaign Brings Historic Preservation to Twitter, Instagram," https://savingplaces.org/stories/this-place-matters-campaign-brings-historic-preservation-to-twitter-instagram/, accessed 18 February, 2018.
23 Lauren Northup, "Historic Charleston Foundation Launches Preservation App, Part I," *Forum Blog* (blog), 6 December, 2017, https://forum.savingplaces.org/blogs/special-contributor/2017/12/06/historic-charleston-foundation-launches-preservation-app-part-i, accessed 20 March, 2021.

Fig. 6: A screen capture of the hashtag #ThisPlaceMatters on Instagram shows the array of places tagged by users. While the hashtag has been officially retired, the tag persists as a way for individuals to highlight places where people have a meaningful connection.
Credit: "#ThisPlaceMatters," accessed August 24, 2021, https://www.instagram.com/explore/tags/thisplacematters/

systemic barriers to fully engaging communities in the protection of their neighborhoods and historic resources.

This was evident in 2020, when in response to social unrest due to COVID-19 and the movement for Black lives, preservationists began to confront the role the movement plays in issues around equity. While these discussions are ongoing, the role social media plays in public engagement on historic preservation issues can be illustrated by the intensity of discussions following statements by major historical organizations calling for the removal of Confederate memorials in the United States in June 2020. Amidst the deluge of comments, and misguided calls for the protection of property over people, the National Trust decided to retire the popular #ThisPlaceMatters campaign, "out of respect for Black Lives Matter and the important message behind it."[24]

---

24 Megan White, "A Look Back as We Look Forward to Our 100,000th #ThisPlaceMatters Post," 4 December, 2018, https://savingplaces.org/stories/a-look-back-as-we-look-forward-to-our-100000th-thisplacematters-post. The full text of the note is: "Note: This Place Matters is a campaign that the National Trust started in 2009, before Black Lives Matter had come into being as a movement. Out of respect for Black Lives Matter and the important message behind it, we retired the campaign in June 2020. We encourage National Trust supporters to instead celebrate places that are important to them using the hashtags #SavingPlaces or #TellTheFullStory." National Trust for

Social media is complex and can invite hostility and harmful false counternarratives to basic historical facts.[25] Despite this challenge, Jessica Marie Johnson reminds us that the accessibility of social media platforms are "creating some of the most innovative, daring, and radical space" for individuals to write and share their own stories.[26]

The Future of Technology and Preservation

Technology's impact on the saving, interpreting, and telling the full history of old places will continue to evolve as long as the technology itself is evolving. In 2013, Andy McAfee, the associate director of the Center for Digital Business at MIT Sloane School of Management, explained that we are only at the beginning of the potential exponential growth for computing power and access.[27] At this moment the vanguard of using technology to tell stories at historic sites is centered around virtual and augmented reality.

Virtual Reality can also be used to transport visitors to locations they cannot physically visit, either because they are closed to the public, or are no longer in existence. One example is the Virtual Reality tour of Nina Simone's childhood home presented by the National Trust for Historic Preservation. This 360-degree view of the home allows visitors to see not only the space where Nina Simone began her life as a musician, but also to see the deterioration of the site. This tool was used as part of a crowdfunding campaign to protect and preserve this important historic site. Both projects were funded by Google Arts and Culture but provide users with a more interactive experience than through simple photographs.[28]

Historic Preservation "Statement on Confederate Monuments." https://www.facebook.com/NationalTrustforHistoricPreservation/photos/a.433757211101/10159909208141102/, accessed 16 September, 2020. The post resulted in 1.7k comments, most of which contained racist vitriol and imagery.

25 Hunt Allcott, Matthew Gentzkow, and Chaun Yu, "Trends in the Diffusion of Misinformation on Social Media," n.d., https://web.stanford.edu/~gentzkow/research/fake-news-trends.pdf. This is just one source of many that are tracking this phenomena in terms of fake news. For history twitter the best example are the twitter conversations between Princeton Historian Kevin M. Kruse and various individuals. His threads providing evidence against counternarratives is one example of how the push back against misinformation is occurring: https://twitter.com/KevinMKruse/status/1146131616785489921.

26 Jessica Marie Johnson, "Social Stories: Digital Storytelling and Social Media," *Forum Journal* (Technology Transforming Preservation) 32.1 (June 2018): 39–46.

27 Capgemini Group, *Digital Transformation – We Haven't Seen Anything Yet*, https://www.youtube.com/watch?v=AZ5ePL36BbU, accessed 18 February, 2018.

28 National Trust for Historic Preservation, "Take a Virtual Tour of Nina Simone's Childhood Home," *SavingPlaces* (blog), 16 July, 2019, https://savingplaces.org/stories/take-a-virtual-tour-of-nina-simones-childhood-home; National Trust for Historic Preservation, "Take a Virtual Tour of Villa Lewaro," *SavingPlaces* (blog), 18 July, 2018, https://savingplaces.org/places/villa-lewaro-

Where virtual reality places an individual in a new environment, augmented reality takes the existing tour apps one step further, allowing users to see information overlaid on the physical place they are visiting. The potential of this technology lies in its ability to show, in person, the transformation of a historic site as it changes through time. The future of interpretation and storytelling at historic sites is likely to further push the boundaries of personal interaction with the past.[29] The Jinsha Site Museum (a site where an ancient Chinese civilization used to gather to pray) leverages augmented reality to provide visitors with a closer look at the over 5,000 relics unearthed by archaeologists. The application provides a 3D view of objects along with additional contextual information.[30]

Perhaps the most promising future is one in which the work of preservationists comes together – in which advanced digital documentation techniques intersect with the more subjective work of memory, identity, and story. That is when the work of protecting and preserving a site through detailed physical documentation goes hand in hand with telling the stories of the historic sites for posterity.

One example is Project Anqa, which focused on at risk sites, primarily in Iraq and Syria. The project planned to deploy on-the-ground teams to produce 3D documentation of sites endangered by warfare. The intent was not only to protect and preserve historic places under constant threat of destruction but also to build capacity for this kind of work in the Middle East. The accompanying web platform focused on three views: 3D, conservation, and storytelling. In a research paper, the project authors reveal the importance of balancing technology with storytelling.[31] Specifically, they state how they "also emphasize the importance of documentation using what we call the 'subjective eye,' which is based on a list of intangible categories. [. . .] Photographs, videos, and interviews of building caretakers/users, on-site observations of rituals and processes, and the recording of peculiarities of a build-

---

madam-c-j-walker-estate/updates/take-a-virtual-tour-of-villa-lewaro. The importance of emerging tools related to site interpretation and engagement was clear in the Spring of 2020 when historic sites around the world had to pivot to digital programming to tell their story. At the National Trust for Historic Preservation this building a month-long campaign around "Virtual Preservation Month." https://savingplaces.org/preservationmonth, accessed 17 September, 2019.

29 "ARtGlass – Augmented Reality for Cultural & Historic Sites,", http://artglassus.com/, accessed 18 February, 2018.

30 "Jinsha Site Museum," http://english.jinshasitemuseum.com/, accessed 4 August, 2019; Jennifer Billock, "Five Augmented Reality Experiences That Bring Museum Exhibits to Life," *Smithsonian.Com* (blog), 27 June, 2017, https://www.smithsonianmag.com/travel/expanding-exhibits-augmented-reality-180963810/, accessed 20 March, 2021.

31 ICOMOS, "Project Anqa: Final Report," April 2019, https://www.icomos.org/images/DOCUMENTS/Secretariat/2019/Project_Anqa_Final_Report_20190419.pdf; Carleton University, "Project Anqa," https://cims.carleton.ca/anqa/#1, accessed 4 August, 2019.

ing all help in the storytelling process and conveying the importance of cultural heritage preservation for the purposes of posterity."[32]

Conclusion

Throughout this chapter we've seen how public historians, preservationists, and heritage conservationist have deployed technology to protect, preserve, and interpret the places which make up the world's cultural heritage. The value of these tools – from GIS to Social Media – lies in their inherent ability to take data and information and translate it into a useable format, for professional or public use. Sometimes it is to protect a place in danger of destruction, such as those projects illustrated by Project Anqa's work. Other times they provide an interpretive framework connecting people with places far removed from their physical location, as we can see in the virtual reality project to show Nina Simone's childhood home.

As the other examples cited here suggest, we are not at the limits of how technology can and will shape the world of heritage protection. But in its very shifting nature there are some broader issues still to face. Despite the expanding potential of technology, it is important to note the challenges that many historical organizations face when it comes to technology – namely, capacity and funding. In a piece for *Forum Journal*, Tom Scheinfeldt, emphasizes the need to go into technical projects with clear, organizationally relevant goals. He explains the importance of paying attention to building capacity, noting that, while tools will change over time, it is critical to ensure that organizations have the right people in place to manage their technological innovations.[33] Funding challenges can be met, at least in part, by embracing open source tools. Annabel Lee Enriquez, David Myers, and Alison Dalgity state (in reference to the open source Arches system) that

> its software code can be downloaded and modified by anyone. Arches' code is free, although preservation organizations must host the software themselves, on either a local or cloud server. Users are not subject to annual license fees and there are no limits on how many users can access any Arches implementation. And improvements to the software code must be made available to all, so they can be implemented by any institutions that find them useful [. . .]. The Arches software platform is strengthened by its community of users interacting and helping each other through direct support and the development of features that benefit the entire preservation field.[34]

---

[32] S. Akhtar et al., "Project Anqa: Digitizing and Documenting Cultural Heritage in the Middle East," 2017.
[33] Tom Scheinfeldt, "Making Sustainable Technology Choices," *Forum Journal*, (Technology Transforming Preservation) 32.1 (June 2018): 5–10.
[34] Annabel Lee Enriquez, David Myers, and Alison Dalgity, "The Arches Heritage Inventory and Management System for the Protection of Cultural Resources," *Forum Journal* (Technology Transforming Preservation) 32.1 (June 2018): 30–38.

While in some ways, technology has opened up the conversation to a wide variety of voices, it does not guarantee a balanced distribution of whose voices are included. In a lot of ways there are two sides to how technology can support society and it is only with a clear-eyed understanding that we can innovate, and question how technology can support historical work in the future. The first is an acknowledgement of technology's limitations. Or as Jasper Visser, author of the Museums of the Future blog, states, in some ways technology has failed to live up to its promise of democratized engagement and shared authority: "Overall, technology has not liberated us. There are still gatekeepers; there is still censorship. I do not believe technology or digital media are broken, perse, but like our societies, we need a new approach to fix what is wrong with them [. . .]."[35]

But with that in mind, the potential and opportunity for documenting and telling more stories remains. In a presentation for the PastForward conference in late 2017, artist and futurist Zenka emphasized this, stating "if we can bring [technological experts and preservationists] to the table, we can really make magic happen and give this technology a purpose and a path forward." The role technology and digital tools play in the future of historical and cultural preservation depends largely on those who develop and use these tools. With collaboration and the right partnerships, the future is limitless.[36]

Bibliography

Priya Chhaya, and Reina Murray, eds. *Forum Journal* (Technology Transforming Preservation) 32.1 (National Trust for Historic Preservation, June 2018).
National Trust for Historic Preservation, "Preservation for People: A Vision for the Future" (National Trust for Historic Preservation, May 2018). https://forum.savingplaces.org/viewdocument/preservation-for-the-people-a-visi
University of Richmond, Digital Scholarship Lab, "Mapping Inequality," n.d., https://dsl.richmond.edu/panorama/redlining/#loc=5/39.1/-94.58, accessed 20 March, 2021.
ICOMOS, "Project Anqa: Final Report," April 2019, https://www.icomos.org/images/DOCUMENTS/Secretariat/2019/Project_Anqa_Final_Report_20190419.pdf, accessed 20 March, 2021.

---

35 Jasper Visser, "Futureproofing the Digital Museum," *The Museum of the Future* (blog), http://themuseumofthefuture.com/2018/01/25/futureproofing-the-digital-museum/, accessed 25 January, 2018.
36 National Trust for Historic Preservation, *TrustLive: Tech Keynote – Zenka*, https://www.youtube.com/watch?v=qHeEsvSBXQ0, accessed 18 February, 2018.

Florentina Armaselu
Social Media: Snapshots in Public History

Abstract: This chapter provides an overview of how social media foster the application of public history and communication with the public, and what types of institutions, projects, and communities are involved in the process. Without claiming to be exhaustive or referring to a representative selection, the study is based on an exploration of seventy-three public history websites and the methods they use to engage audiences via social media.

Keywords: public history, social media, digital humanities

Introduction

Although the definition of the term "public" in public history has varied in time and place, there seems to be a general consensus that the public historian is acting as a "mediator" or "communicator" when dealing with large audiences, by both sharing authority and defending historical analysis of the past.[1] As Sayer observes, social media platforms, such as Facebook, Twitter, Instagram and Pinterest, have influenced public history practices and modes of communication, and over the past decade, the creation of social media profiles has become essential for a large majority of public history organizations and projects.[2]

The aim of this chapter is to provide an overview of how social media foster the application of public history and communication with the public, and what types of institutions, projects, and communities are involved in the process. Without claiming to be exhaustive or referring to a representative selection, the study is based on an exploration of seventy-three public history websites[3] and the methods they use to engage audiences. The second section presents the categories of projects and organizations examined in the study. Starting from the assumption that the reader is

---

[1] Thomas Cauvin, *Public History: A Textbook of Practice* (New York and London: Routledge, Taylor & Francis Group, (2016) 2022), 10, 15.
[2] Faye Sayer, *Public History: A Practical Guide*, 2nd edition (London, Oxford, New York, New Delhi, Sydney: Bloomsbury Academic, 2019), 126.
[3] The data collection and first analysis of these websites were performed at the end of 2017. The figures were updated in February and March 2019.

Acknowledgement: The author would like to thank Sarah Cooper, from the Language Centre of the University of Luxembourg, for English proofreading.

https://doi.org/10.1515/9783110430295-022

already familiar with social media practices, the third section proposes a discussion on the use of this technology as observed for the selected websites, including social media analytics. The fourth section concludes the chapter and suggests avenues for further research.

Types of Projects and Institutions

The projects and institutions considered for analysis were either mentioned in digital and public history publications[4] or identified using Google searches and public history-related queries. The criteria for selection were intended to provide variety and were thus based on relevance in illustrating a certain project category, institutional scale, location, or social media language, and on the availability of at least one social media profile for the project or its coordinating organization (if there was no profile for the project itself). However, given the three main sources considered and the Google search results, a certain dominance of US/UK and English-oriented examples can be observed.

Figure 1 illustrates the typology of these projects, the language of communication via social media platforms, and the location and scale of the corresponding establishments (see also Appendix – Tables). Seven categories of projects were identified. The largest includes projects (18) that vary from heritage sites or houses to heritage visitor centers, community archaeology, and heritage museum campaigns. The second category covers shared community memories and oral, family, and people's history (13). The third type includes journals and blogs (13) and the fourth groups together projects dedicated to education and media production (8), such as exhibitions, museum programs, and teaching resources, as well as radio or TV series, films, and books.

The remaining categories include museum sites, exhibitions, and collections (8), digital libraries, archives, and crowdsourcing projects (5), and commemoration, anniversary, and chronicling (8). Regarding the scale, the most numerous are projects and institutions at national level (39), followed by those at international (14), local (13) and regional (7) level. As far as the location and language are concerned, the first three most represented locations are the US (25), the UK (11) and France (7), with a majority of the seventy-three social media profiles expressed in English (52) or multi-language, i.e. more than three languages (9).

Examples of projects by category and their approach in involving the public are briefly discussed below. *Heritage* includes *The excavations of the Roman Theatre in*

---

[4] Cauvin, *Public History*; Sayer, *Public History*; Daniel J. Cohen and Roy Rosenzweig, *Digital History. A Guide to Gathering, Preserving, and Presenting the Past to the Web* (Philadelphia: University of Pennsylvania Press, 2006).

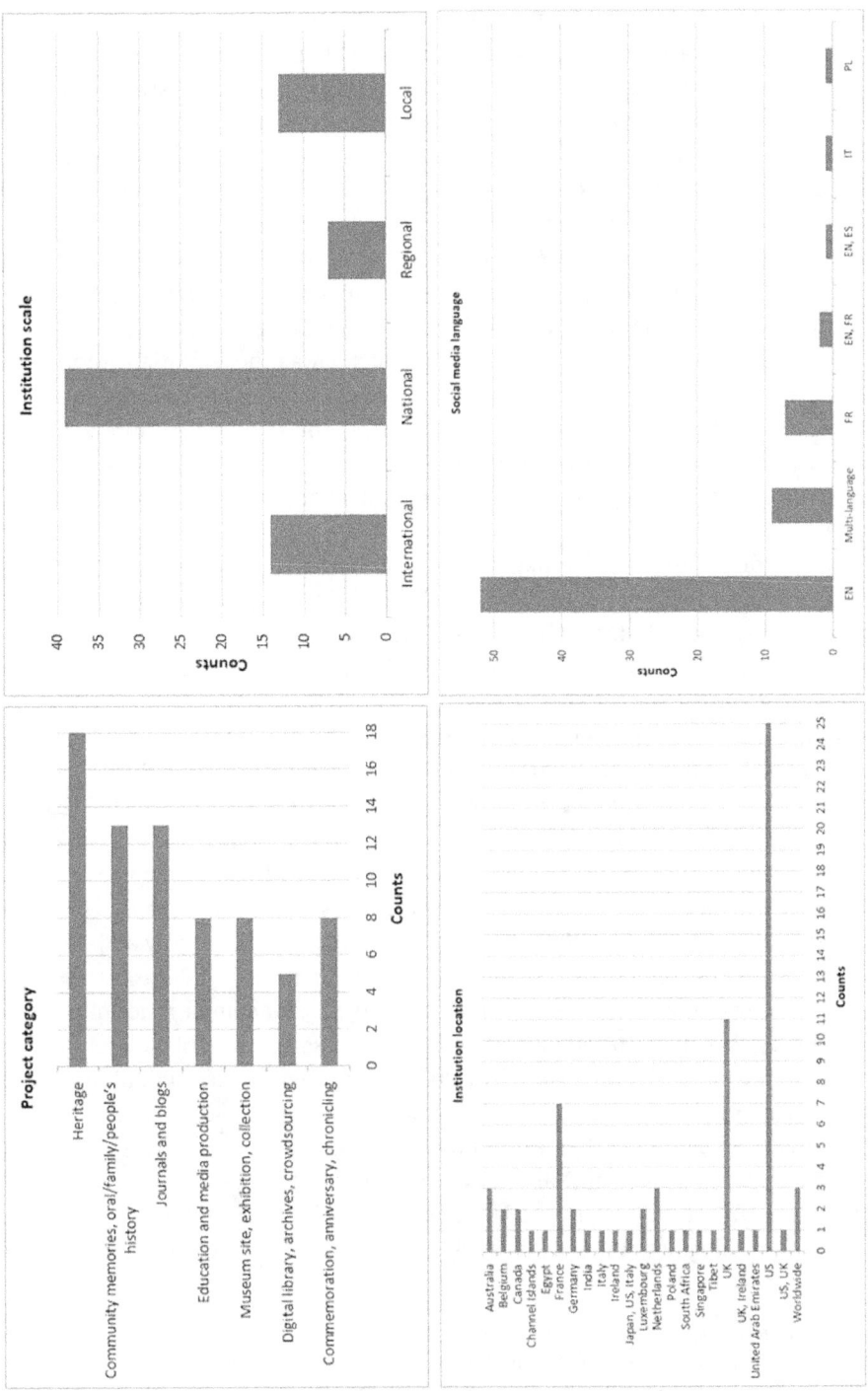

Fig. 1: Project types, institution scale and location, social media language (computed March 4, 2019, data snapshot February 23 – March 2, 2019).

Florence,[5] which proposes audio tour apps to be downloaded on a smartphone or tablet for the exploration of an archaeological area beneath the Palazzo Vecchio, from the Roman Florentia to the mediaeval Fiorenza. While the excavations and audio guide content are managed by the Archaeological Heritage of Tuscany and the Florentine Civic Museums, the storytelling platform is provided by an international team specializing in free applications for audio guides in museums and city tours around the world. Other types of institution, acting at national level, such as English Heritage in the UK, the US Forest Service, and the Musée du Louvre in France, invite the public to visit prehistoric monuments (*Stonehenge*) or participate in the preservation of natural, archaeological and cultural heritage (*Passport in Time*, *Tous mécènes!*). Regional and local actors, such as the Victorian Aboriginal Heritage Council in Australia, Colonial Williamsburg and the Oak Alley Foundation in the US, the Château Ramezay Museum in Canada, and the Centre d'innovation et de design (CID) au Grand-Hornu in Belgium, offer a variety of on-site activities, from community-related events to historical re-enactments, guided tours, and traditional seasonal parties.

In the second category, international, national and regional organizations engage the public in preserving and sharing *Community or personal collections* in a variety of forms, from photographs and texts to audio and video. Examples of this type of project are *Memoro, The Bank of Memories*, led by an international association with branches in Africa, North and Latin America, Asia, and Europe; *Memory Book*, initiated by the Smithsonian National Museum of African American History & Culture; *The September 11 Digital Archive*, conducted by the American Social History Project/Center for Media and Learning and the Roy Rosenzweig Center for History and New Media; and *First Days Project*, sharing stories of immigrants' first days in the United States, presented by the South Asian American Digital Archive (SAADA). Other websites included in this category cover the areas of community-based oral history (*Tibet Oral History Project, Bangalore Storyscapes*), as well as family and people's history (*Family History Library*, TV series *Who Do You Think You Are?*, *History Pin*).

Unlike the two first categories, *Journals and blogs* foster communities of readers and writers by theorizing public history. Among the selected publications are the Germany-based *Public History Weekly*, published by De Gruyter Oldenbourg, the *Cultures of History Forum*, focusing on how Central, Eastern and Southeastern Europe address the meaning of the past in public, led by Imre Kertész Kolleg, *The Public Historian*, published by the National Council on Public History (NCPH) and the University of California Press in the US, and *South African History Online (SAHO)*. The selection of blogs contains items such as *Europeana blog*, *Les billets d'humeur*

---

5 Laura Longo, *New Technologies to Preserve and Promote Cultural Heritage: The Italian Experience* (workshop on: Immersive exhibits & Storytelling: engaging the public, bringing the past to new life, Tbilisi, Georgia, September 26, 2018), accessed February 22, 2019, https://ambtbilisi.esteri.it/ambasciata_tbilisi/resource/doc/2018/09/programma-eng.pdf.

du CVUH, proposed by the Comité de Vigilance face aux Usages publics de l'Histoire (CVUH) in France, and *History Matters*, by the History Department at the University of Sheffield in the UK. In 2018, the International Federation for Public History (IFPH) website opened *Bridging*, a blog informing the public about the IFPH's activities and promoting debates among public historians.

Although the educational aspect is, to a certain degree, implicit in the cases presented so far, the *Education and media production* category includes projects that explicitly target the public for this purpose. Examples from this category are *A History of the World in 100 Objects*, a radio series developed by the BBC and the British Museum, *Chicago Architecture*, from the Educators section of the Chicago History Museum, and *Forging a Modern Society*, a book and exhibition open to the public featuring a collection from the industrial archives, conducted by the Luxembourg Centre for Contemporary and Digital History (C^2DH) and the Centre national de l'audiovisuel (CNA). The selection also contains *Primary Source Workshop*, an educational program proposed by the Mystic Seaport Museum in the US, the *Historiquement show* series, broadcasted by the Histoire TV channel, and *Historiana*, an online educational portal led by the European Association of History Educators (EUROCLIO).

Museums create other opportunities to involve the public with historical topics, such as through on-site games including *Escape Tunnel*, proposed by the Jersey War Tunnels Museum in the Channel Islands, and exhibitions such as *The Great Inka Road* from the Smithsonian National Museum of the American Indian, the *Exposition permanente du Musée bruxellois des industries et du travail* in Belgium, and *Magiques Licornes* by the Musée de Cluny in France. Collections are also proposed, e.g. the *Chinese-Australian Historical Images in Australia* from the Chinese Museum in Melbourne's Chinatown and the *Hundred Years' War* from the Royal Armouries Museum in the UK.

The next category contains *Digital library* resources, such as *Primary Source Set* (Digital Public Library of America) and the *Memory of the Suez Canal* (Bibliotheca Alexandrina in Egypt), as well as digital archives involving crowdsourcing projects, such as *Transcribe Bentham* (University College London) and Europeana's *Transcribathon*.

Other forms of public involvement included in the study are exhibitions and events occasioned by historical *Commemorations and anniversaries*, e.g. the *Centenaire de la Grande Guerre* (Archives nationales de France), *Warsaw Rising 1944* (Warsaw Rising Museum in Poland), and the *154th Anniversary of the Battles for Chattanooga* (Chickamauga & Chattanooga National Military Park in the US). This category also includes pedagogically-oriented projects such as *La Grande Guerra più 100* (Università di Trento, Italy) and *World War I goes Twitter* (University of Luxembourg), as well as *Documenting the Now* (University of Maryland, University of Virginia, US), a project chronicling historically significant events through the public's use of social media.

Analysis of Social Media Usage

All these projects and their organizations make use of a variety of methods to engage audiences, supported by Web technology. Social media profiles, accessible from the project or institutional home pages, create additional incentives for interaction.

Fuchs characterizes social media as enabling three "modes of sociality" (or "integrated sociality") manifested by the creation of content (cognitive level), its publication, allowing others to comment upon it (communicative level), and the manipulation and remixing of content eventually determining "multiple authorship" (cooperation level).[6] In the context of public history, social media have been considered from a variety of perspectives, for instance as a way to support "user-centered digital history" by enabling public historians to increasingly encounter their audiences through digital means instead of more traditional "face-to-face encounters" and at "physical sites."[7]

Other studies point out the tensions with user-created content and the notion of "radical trust," suggesting "greater equality between museum and the user" as a potential "threat" to the history organization's "voice of authority," and the need for these institutions to "expand their dialogue with the public" in the social media realm.[8] Further inquiries focus on the typologies of "engagement," "content," and "approach" related to sharing historical content on social media,[9] the ways of creating a community in connection with archives/archivists,[10] or the more general use of social media by researchers in digital humanities.[11]

---

6 Christian Fuchs, *Social Media, a Critical Introduction*, second edition (Los Angeles, London, New Delhi, Singapore, Washington DC, Melbourne: Sage, 2017), 50.
7 Sharon M. Leon, "User-Centered Digital History: Doing Public History on the Web," *[bracket] images, teaching, technology*, March 3, 2015, accessed March 10, 2019, https://www.6floors.org/bracket/2015/03/03/user-centered-digital-history-doing-public-history-on-the-web/.
8 Tim Grove, "New Media and the Challenges for Public History," *Perspectives on History*, American Historical Association, May 2009, accessed March 10, 2019, https://www.historians.org/publications-and-directories/perspectives-on-history/may-2009/intersections-history-and-new-media/new-media-and-the-challenges-for-public-history.
9 Martin Grandjean, "[Twitter Studies] Rewriting History in 140 characters," *Humanités*, November 10, 2014, accessed March 10, 2019, http://www.martingrandjean.ch/rewriting-history-140-characters/.
10 Russell D. James, "Using Facebook to Create Community: The SAA Group Experience," *The Interactive Archivist, Case Studies in Utilizing Web 2.0 to Improve the Archival Experience*, SAA, Society of American Archivists, May 18, 2009, accessed March 10, 2019, http://interactivearchivist.archivists.org/case-studies/facebook-saa-group/.
11 Emmanuel Mourlon-Druol, "L'usage des réseaux sociaux pour chercheurs," in *Expérimenter les humanités numériques. Des outils individuels aux projets collectifs*, edited by Cavalié Étienne, Clavert Frédéric, Legendre Olivier and Martin Dana, "Parcours numériques" collection (Montréal: Les Presses de l'Université de Montréal, 2017), accessed March 10, 2019, http://www.parcoursnumeriques-pum.ca/l-usage-des-reseaux-sociaux-pour-chercheurs.

Within this context, an overview of the types of social media profiles and interactions for the studied cases is provided. In general, an average of 3.4 social media profiles per case were observed[12] for the seventy-three websites considered.

Figure 2 presents more details. The average number of profiles by project category varies from 2.76 (*Journals and blogs*) and 2.87 (*Commemoration and chronicling*) to 3.8 (*Digital library*) and 4.3 (*Education*). For the selected sample, the values indicate that institutions (e.g. NCPH, IFPH, UTS Press Australia, JSTOR) and projects (*World War I goes Twitter*, *Documenting the now*) in the former categories tend to use fewer and more specialized social media profiles, perhaps because of the design and goals of the institutional websites themselves or the particularity of the projects. On the other hand, the latter categories exploit a wider diversity of social media profiles to reach the public (e.g. the University of Virginia, Europeana, Bibliotheca Alexandrina, the Chicago History Museum, and the British Museum).

The institution scale shows higher figures for national and local entities (3.48, 3.46). Examples in these categories with more than four profiles are museums, public authorities such as the US Census Bureau and the Archives nationales de France, and heritage establishments such as the Oak Alley Foundation and the Château Royal de Blois. Lower values are observed for international and regional entities (3.07, 2.57). Examples of this type of projects or coordinating institutions with fewer than three profiles are *Historiana* and La Fonderie. As far as the top three institutional locations are concerned, France has a higher average number of social media profiles (4), possibly given the selection of museums, archives, and heritage sites in the sample, followed by the US (3.72) and the UK (3.45).

Regarding social media usage,[13] a high percentage of the total of seventy-three projects/institutions have a profile on Facebook (94.52%), followed by Twitter (93.15%), Instagram (46.58%), YouTube (36.99%), and Pinterest (19.18%). Values from 4% to 7% are observed for LinkedIn, Google+, Tumblr, project blog, and Snapchat, and less than 3% for other platforms (Flickr, DailyMotion, Vimeo, Scoop.it, SoundCloud, and Sketchfab). While Facebook is also ranked first in general statistics (Statista January 2019[14]) by number of active users in millions (2,271), the other social media networks exhibit a slightly different ranking within the top 20: YouTube – 2nd place (1,900), Instagram – 6th place (1,000), Twitter – 12th place (326), LinkedIn – 14th place (303), Snapchat – 17th place (287), and Pinterest – 19th place (250).

The high number of public history Facebook profiles recorded in the present study may be related to the variety of features and means of engagement offered by

---

[12] An increase as compared with the average of 3.07 profiles computed at the end of 2017.
[13] Instagram and YouTube show noteworthy increases (by 10.97% and 4.13% respectively), as compared with the values computed at the end of 2017.
[14] "Statista," accessed March 6, 2019, https://www.statista.com/statistics/272014/global-social-networks-ranked-by-number-of-users/.

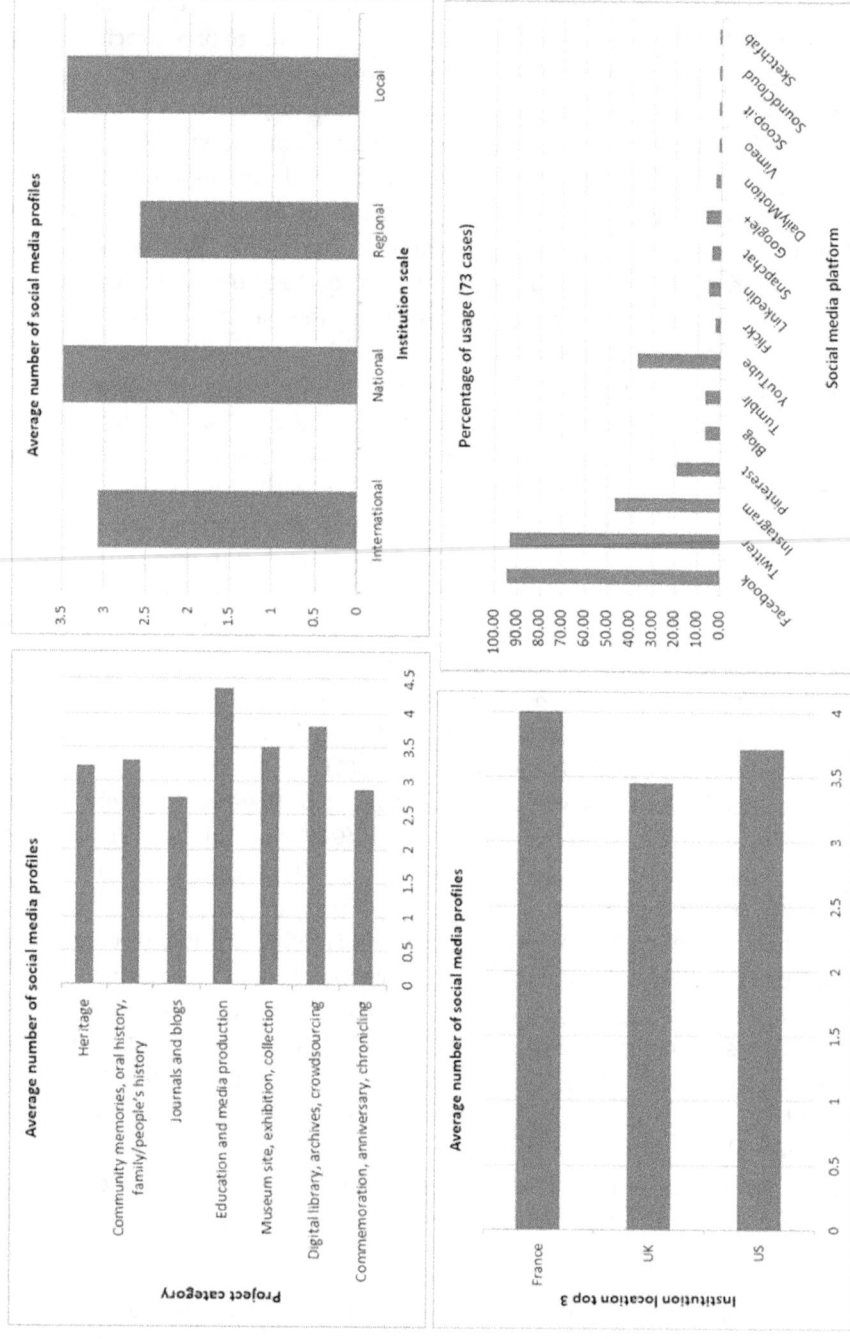

Fig. 2: Average number of social media profiles by project category, institution scale and location. Percentage of social media platform usage by projects/institutions (computed March 4, 2019, data snapshot February 23 – March 2, 2019).

the platform, e.g. photos, videos, posts, events, reviews, liking, sharing, and following, as well as links with other social media. In this respect, Sayer notes that "Facebook has enabled public history sectors to develop narrative and visual commentary and dialogs with audiences."[15] Despite having fewer features, limits on text length and a lower ranking in general statistics, Twitter comes in second place among the analyzed public history cases. A possible explanation may reside in the fact that it facilitates approaches to specific themes, historical sources or "real time" experiences[16] and supports the work of historians exploring "collective memory" and "current time events."[17]

Instagram, especially popular with the younger generation, seems to be increasingly used by public history institutions and projects to promote their activities and collections and engage with viewers owing to its visual and storytelling appeal. Likewise showing increasing usage, YouTube aims to involve the public by featuring history-related events, conferences, interviews, performances, collections, and heritage site presentations through audio/video means, sometimes combining speech, music, enactment or spectacle-like *mise en scene*. Pinterest, mainly featured by museums and heritage sites in the sample, possibly owes its fifth position, as Sayer observes, to its "ability to create themes and narratives through image boards,"[18] including both archival and current images taken by the institution and the public.

Although outstripping Pinterest in the general statistics, Snapchat shows lower figures for the selected cases, perhaps given the specific age range involved, primarily millennials, and the conversational nature of the platform, not yet assimilated at a larger scale by the public history arena. Less used in the current selection are SoundCloud and Sketchfab, two specialized social media-like platforms based on online audio distribution and 3D models. Institutions such as the British Museum and the Musée de Cluny have found ways to promote their educational programs and exhibitions through this type of resource, which is potentially interesting in the future for further public history scenarios.

More details on audience engagement are presented in Figure 3, via average values for the four most used types of social media profiles of projects/institutions (rendered on a logarithmic scale to cover wide ranges), and the project categories considered so far.[19]

---

15 Sayer, *Public History*, 127.
16 Grandjean, "[Twitter Studies]."
17 Sofia Papastamkou and Frédéric Clavert, "Twitter Data as Primary Sources for Historians: A Critical Approach. Lessons from two Projects: The 2015 Greek Referendum and the Centenary of the Great War on Twitter" (paper presented at the *Digital Hermeneutics in History: Theory and Practice* Conference, Luxembourg Centre for Contemporary and Digital History, University of Luxembourg, October 25–26, 2018), accessed March 10, 2019, https://www.c2dh.uni.lu/thinkering/digital-hermeneutics-history-theory-and-practice.
18 Sayer, *Public History*, 130.
19 The data were collected from the profile pages for each type of social media platform.

Facebook profiles with the highest average numbers of people liking and following are related to the category *Education*, and those with the highest average numbers of people reviewing to *Heritage*, while the lowest values are observed for *Journals*. Generalizations about the meaning of these figures are, of course, to be pondered with care, given the construction of the sample. However, they can hint at a certain awareness or intent characterizing the institutions or projects within a given category. For instance, Papacharissi draws attention to Facebook emerging as the "architectural equivalent of a glass house," providing tools that "may be used to project more carefully crafted presentations of the self and to posit performances of taste that lead to sociocultural allegiances or differentiations."[20] Similarly, in their discussion on building "communities of practice," understood as "groups of people" sharing "a set of problems, or a passion about a topic," Gunawardena et al. recommend the use of Facebook to generate "a sense of social presence and community."[21] Therefore, although they are not to be considered as absolute indicators, the numbers may suggest that these entities are more or less aware of or interested in promoting the sociocultural and community-shaping facet fostered by this type of social media profile.

For Twitter, the category with the most tweets on average is *Museum*, while *Education* has the highest values for following and followers. *Commemoration* has the highest average figure for liking (tweets by others), while *Journals* and *Community* make most use of lists and moments, respectively.[22] The lowest average number of tweets belongs to *Heritage* (although this category nevertheless has a high average of followers, ranked third after *Education* and *Museum*). The lowest figures for following and lists were observed for *Commemoration* and the lowest number of followers for *Journals*. Liking (tweets by others) is least represented for *Digital library*, while moments are completely absent from *Digital library*, *Museum* and *Education*. Although "Twitter can lack the scope and space for public active interaction that Facebook provides,"[23] figures for tweets, following, followers, and likes displayed by categories such as *Museum, Education, Heritage,* and *Commemoration* might be interpreted in Grove's terms, i.e. as "exhibition developers" and "educators" making use of technology as a "vehicle to teach or communicate."[24] To this can be

---

20 Zizi Papacharissi, "The Virtual Geographies of Social Networks: A Comparative Analysis of Facebook, LinkedIn and ASmallWorld," *New Media & Society* 11, no. 1–2 (2009), 215, accessed March 8, 2019, https://journals.sagepub.com/doi/10.1177/1461444808099577.
21 Charlotte N. Gunawardena, Mary Beth Hermans, Damien Sanchez, Carol Richmond, Maribeth Bohley and Rebekah Tuttle, "A Theoretical Framework for Building Online Communities of Practice with Social Networking Tools," *Educational Media International* 46, no. 1 (2009), accessed March 8, 2019, https://doi.org/10.1080/09523980802588626.
22 However, lists and moments seem less used, the average number for the former ranging from 0.5 to 3.9, and for the latter from 0 to 1.08 (not represented on the logarithmic scale).
23 Sayer, *Public History*, 129.
24 Grove, "New Media."

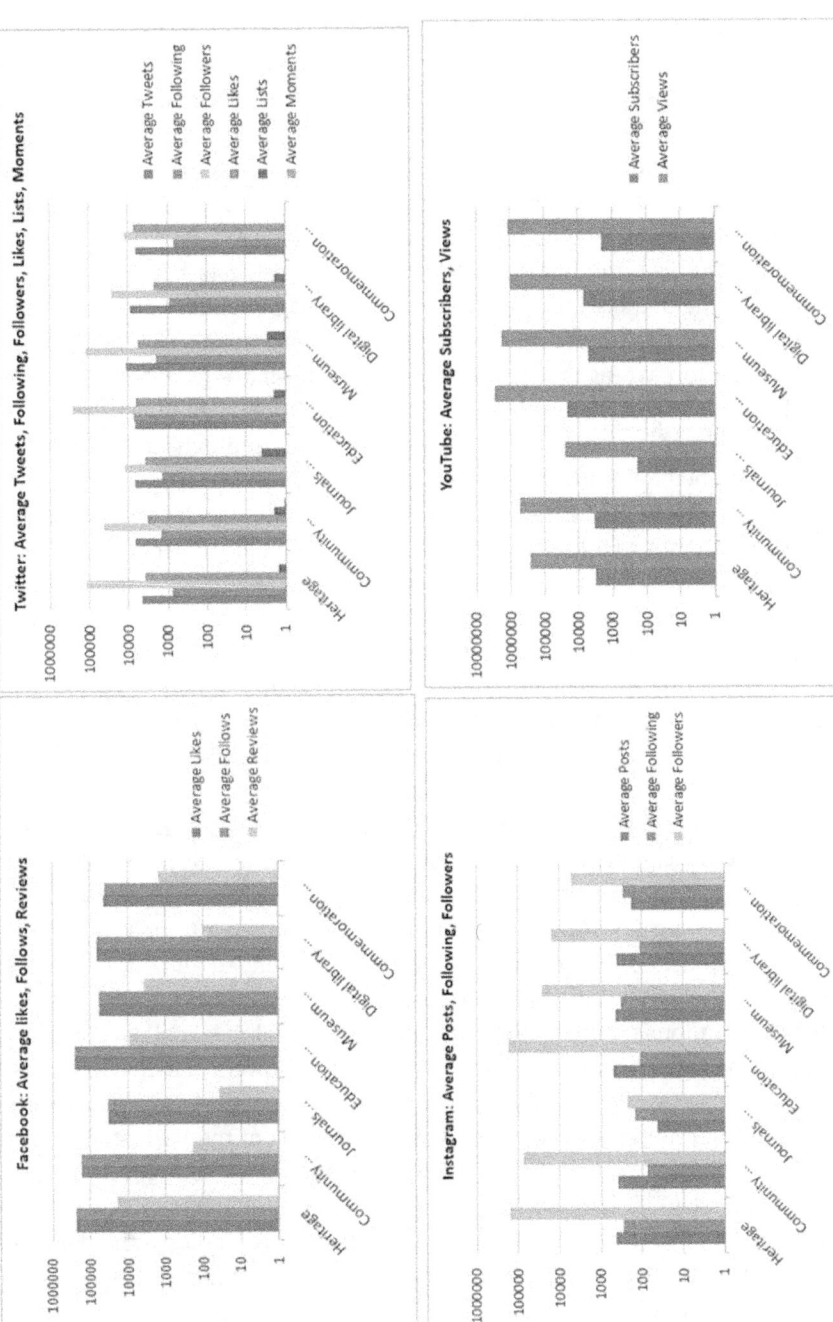

Fig. 3: Average values for social media profiles of projects/institutions by project category (logarithmic scale, base 10) (computed March 4, 2019, data snapshot February 23 – March 2, 2019).

added the notion of connecting with others, since following and liking others' content also represents a way of engaging with the public. More favored by *Journals* according to the data, lists focus on curated groups of Twitter users, so as to better target particular audiences. This may be an indicator that institutions and projects in this category are possibly aiming more at depth, i.e. reaching specialized audiences, than at a wider reach. This hypothesis appears to be supported by figures also observed for the other social media platforms under study.

In Instagram profiles, the highest average numbers of posts and followers are for *Education* and the highest following figures for *Museum*, while *Journals* exhibits the lowest average figures for posts and followers and *Community* the lowest for following. YouTube's top averages for subscribers and views are recorded by *Education*, while the lowest values for both are for the category *Journals*. Given the nature of these two social media platforms, featuring visual and audiovisual content, the value they are ascribed for education and entertainment purposes is not surprising.

Irrespective of the project categories, the most engaging social media profiles belong to museums and, to a lesser degree, heritage sites. For instance, the Musée du Louvre outperforms other institution/project profiles with top values for likes, follows and reviews on Facebook, liking on Twitter, and followers on Instagram. Top posts and following on Instagram are recorded by Colonial Williamsburg and the Oak Alley Plantation, respectively. The Science Museum, London, presents the highest values for tweets, while the British Museum has the largest following and number of followers on Twitter and the highest number of subscribers and views on YouTube.

This seems to confirm the status of museums as "bastions of expertise and scholarship," a "most trusted source of information," and a means of "learning about the past," along with historical sites,[25] which are also often supported by the Web and social media technologies. However, as mentioned before, when interpreting the data it is important to reflect on the depth versus breadth of intended audiences together with the nature of the institution or project itself.

Another observation is related to the way in which social media allow communities to develop over large distances. Figure 4 illustrates followers' locations analyzed via *Followerwonk*,[26] a Twitter analytics software. Four types of project categories and institutional scales are represented for the Twitter accounts of the IFPH, the Chickamauga & Chattanooga National Military Park, the Victorian Aboriginal Heritage Council, and the Jersey War Tunnels Museum.

Although red and magenta (the larger spots in the figure) indicate the points of highest concentration related to the real location of the coordinating institution or the most affected community, the maps suggest that wider community areas can be

---

25 Grove, "New Media."
26 https://moz.com/followerwonk/.

reached through social media platforms. From this perspective, the strict distinctions by institutional scale or project category seem to be blurred.

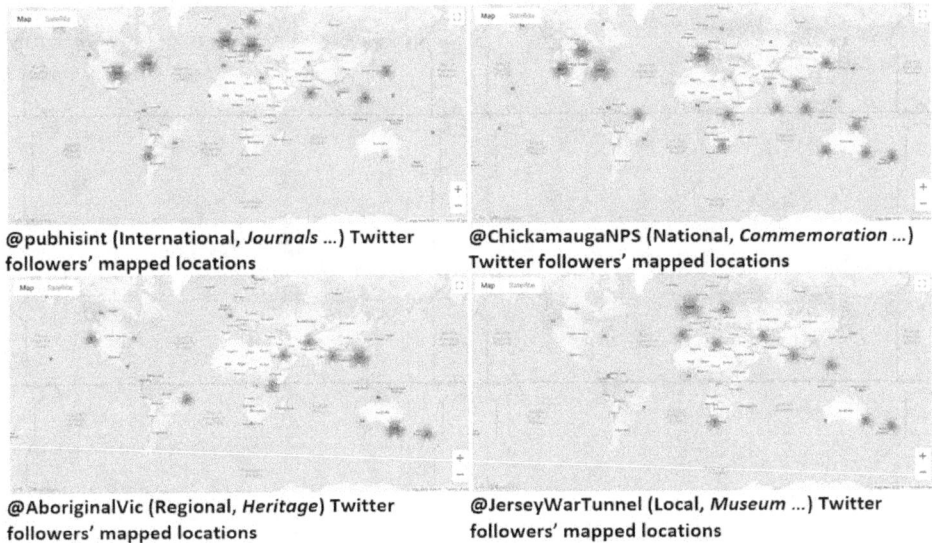

@pubhisint (International, *Journals* ...) Twitter followers' mapped locations

@ChickamaugaNPS (National, *Commemoration* ...) Twitter followers' mapped locations

@AboriginalVic (Regional, *Heritage*) Twitter followers' mapped locations

@JerseyWarTunnel (Local, *Museum* ...) Twitter followers' mapped locations

Fig. 4: Twitter followers' mapped locations – examples by institution scale and project category (Followerwonk free version) (computed March 10, 2019).

On the other hand, the use of different social media platforms may shape public engagement depending on the variety of content proposed via each type of profile. Figure 5 presents top posts/videos by engagement for the Musée du Louvre and its Facebook, Twitter and YouTube accounts, through a Keyhole[27] snapshot from November 2018 to February 2019.

For instance, this Facebook post from January 2019 features architectural objects, the cour Napoléon, the roof of the Islamic Arts department, and the arc du Carrousel, under a white coat of snow. The tweet also exploits a momentary reference to connect Valentine's Day with one of the masterpieces from the museum's collections, *Psyché et l'Amour*.

The YouTube entry points to a special event, the twelfth edition of the Journées Internationales du Film sur l'Art 2019, exploring the creative process and role of art in society, with the museum as one of its leading promoters. The posts or the accounts themselves also provide links to the other social media profiles of the institution: Facebook to Twitter, Instagram, Pinterest, and YouTube; Twitter to Pinterest; and YouTube to Facebook, Twitter, and Instagram.

---

27 http://keyhole.co/.

These examples show not only fine communication skills but also awareness and appropriation of the possibilities offered by the technology and each type of social media platform.

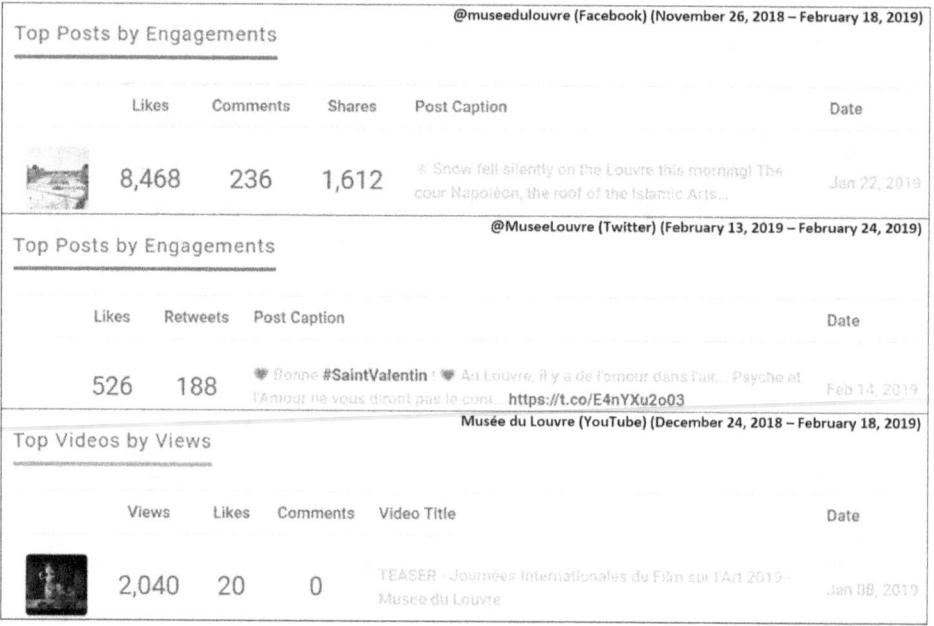

Fig. 5: Top posts/videos by engagement, Musée du Louvre (Facebook, Twitter, YouTube) (Keyhole free version) (computed February 24, 2019).

Conclusion and Future Research

The chapter provides an overview of how the use of social media by public history projects and institutions fosters new ways of engaging audiences that seem to blur more traditional distinctions between local and global, voice of authority and dialog, and institutional and community-driven approaches.

Although the figures presented in the study vary and should not be considered in an absolute sense given the nature and limitations of the data sample, it may be assumed that public history institutions and projects have generally succeeded in exploiting social media technology to reach their target audience. This usage apparently enables different "modes of sociality," as suggested by Fuchs,[28] at a cognitive, communicative, and cooperative (or connective) level, but it should also be viewed

---

[28] Fuchs, *Social Media*.

in conjunction with the type of entity, since the intended coverage and depth of engagement may vary from larger communities to more specialized audiences. However, for further and more robust insights into the topic, and especially the effectiveness of using this technology for public history purposes, a more comprehensive selection and analysis is necessary, including, for instance, a larger variety of projects and social media analysis tools, as well as languages and areas less represented in the study (e.g. Eastern and Southern Europe, Asia, Africa), combined with a close reading of relevant cases.

Appendix

Types of public history projects and institutions included in the study (computed March 5, 2019, data snapshot February 23 – March 2, 2019).

Project type	Scale of coordinating institution	Location of coordinating institution	Language (social media)	Total/ Subtotal
Heritage (site/house, visitor center, community archaeology, museum campaign)				18
	International	United Arab Emirates (1)	Multi-language (1)	1
	National	France (1); Ireland (1); UK (2); US (3)	EN (6); EN, FR (1)	7
	Regional	Australia (1); UK (1); UK + Ireland (1)	EN (3)	3
	Local	Belgium (1); Canada (1); France (1); US (4)	EN (4); EN, FR (1); FR (2)	7
Community memories, oral history, family/people's history				13
	International	Worldwide (2); Japan + Italy+ US (1); UK + US (1)	Multi-language (3); EN (1)	4
	National	US (6)	EN (6)	6
	Regional	Tibet (1); US (1)	EN (2)	2
	Local	India (1)	EN (1)	1
Journals and blogs				13
	International	Germany (2); Netherlands (1); UK (2); US (1); Worldwide (1)	Multi-language (1); EN (6)	7
	National	Australia (1); France (1); South Africa (1); UK (1); US (2)	EN (5); FR (1)	6

(continued)

Project type	Scale of coordinating institution	Location of coordinating institution	Language (social media)	Total/ Subtotal
Education and media production (exhibition, museum program/teaching resources, radio, TV, film, book)				8
	International	Netherlands (1)	EN (1)	1
	National	France (2); Luxembourg (1); UK (2); US (1)	EN (3); FR (2); Multi-language (1)	6
	Local	US (1)	EN (1)	1
Museum (site, exhibition, collection)				8
	National	Canada (1); France (1); UK (2); US (1)	EN (3); EN, ES (1); FR (1)	5
	Regional	Belgium (1)	Multi-language (1)	1
	Local	Australia (1); Channel Islands (1)	EN (2)	2
Digital library, archives, crowdsourcing				5
	International	Netherlands (1)	Multi-language (1)	1
	National	UK (1); US (2)	EN (3)	3
	Regional	Egypt (1)	Multi-language (1)	1
Commemoration, anniversary, chronicling				8
	National	US (3); France (1); Italy (1); Luxembourg (1)	EN (4); FR (1); IT (1)	6
	Local	Poland (1); Singapore (1)	EN (1); PL (1)	2

Further Readings

Cauvin, T. *Public History: A Textbook of Practice*. New York and London: Routledge, Taylor & Francis Group, (2016), Second edition 2022.

Fuchs, C. *Social Media, a Critical Introduction*. Second edition. Los Angeles, London, New Delhi, Singapore, Washington DC, Melbourne: Sage, 2017.

Grove, T. "New Media and the Challenges for Public History." *Perspectives on History*, American Historical Association, May, 2009. Accessed March 10, 2019. https://www.historians.org/publications-and-directories/perspectives-on-history/may-2009/intersections-history-and-new-media/new-media-and-the-challenges-for-public-history.

Papacharissi, Z. "The Virtual Geographies of Social Networks: A Comparative Analysis of Facebook, LinkedIn and ASmallWorld." *New Media & Society* 11, no. 1–2 (2009): 199–220. Accessed March 8, 2019. https://journals.sagepub.com/doi/10.1177/1461444808099577.

Sayer, F. *Public History: A Practical Guide*. Second edition. London, Oxford, New York, New Delhi, Sydney: Bloomsbury Academic, 2019.

Bibliography

"154th Anniversary of the Battles for Chattanooga." Accessed March 4, 2019. https://www.nps.gov/chch/planyourvisit/154thchattanooga.htm.

"Aboriginal Victoria." Accessed December 22, 2021. WayBack Machine archive (March 12, 2019): https://web.archive.org/web/20190312023820/https://w.www.vic.gov.au/aboriginalvictoria/about-aboriginal-victoria.html.

"A History of the World in 100 Objects." Accessed March 4, 2019. http://www.bbc.co.uk/programmes/b00nrtd2/episodes/downloads.

"Bangalore Storyscapes." Accessed December 22, 2021. WayBack Machine archive (November 10, 2019): https://web.archive.org/web/20191110182237/http://srishti.ac.in/disciplines/public-history.

"Bridging: The International Federation for Public History blog." Accessed March 4, 2019. https://ifph.hypotheses.org/category/bridging.

"Centenaire de la Grande Guerre." Accessed March 4, 2019. http://www.archives-nationales.culture.gouv.fr/centenaire-de-la-grande-guerre.

"Château Ramezay." Accessed March 4, 2019. http://www.chateauramezay.qc.ca/fr/.

"Chicago Architecture." Accessed March 4, 2019. https://www.chicagohistory.org/chicago-architecture/.

"Colonial Williamsburg." Accessed March 4, 2019. https://www.colonialwilliamsburg.com/.

"Cultures of History Forum." Accessed March 4, 2019. http://www.cultures-of-history.uni-jena.de/home/.

"Documenting the Now." Accessed March 4, 2019. https://www.docnow.io/.

"Escape Tunnel." Accessed December 22, 2021. WayBack Machine archive (February 12, 2018): https://web.archive.org/web/20180212095736/http://jerseyescapetunnel.com/.

"Europeana blog." Accessed March 4, 2019. http://blog.europeana.eu/.

"Exposition permanente du Musée bruxellois des industries et du travail." Accessed March 4, 2019. https://www.lafonderie.be/expositions.

"Family History Library." Accessed March 4, 2019. https://www.familysearch.org/wiki/en/Family_History_Library.

"First Days Project." Accessed March 4, 2019. http://www.firstdaysproject.org/.

"Forging a Modern Society." Accessed March 4, 2019. https://www.c2dh.uni.lu/fr/thinkering/forging-modern-society-photography-and-corporate-communication-industrial-age-arbed–1911.

"Historiana." Accessed March 4, 2019. https://historiana.eu.

"Historiquement show." Accessed December 22, 2021. https://histoire.fr/actualités/historiquement-show.

"History Matters." Accessed March 4, 2019. http://www.historymatters.group.shef.ac.uk/.

"History Pin." Accessed March 4, 2019. https://www.historypin.org.

"Hundred Years' War (1337–1453)." Accessed March 4, 2019. https://collections.royalarmouries.org/hundred-years-war.html.

"La Grande Guerra più 100." Accessed March 4, 2019. http://www.lagrandeguerrapiu100.it/.

"Les billets d'humeur du CVUH." Accessed March 4, 2019. http://cvuh.blogspot.lu/p/les-billets-dhumeur-du-cvuh.html.

"Magiques Licornes." Accessed March 4, 2019. https://www.musee-moyenage.fr/activites/expositions/expositions-passees/exposition-magiques-licornes.html.

"Memoro. The Bank of Memories." Accessed March 4, 2019. http://www.memoro.org/index.php.

"Memory Book." Accessed March 4, 2019. https://nmaahc.si.edu/explore/initiatives/memory-book.

"Memory of the Suez Canal." Accessed December 22, 2021. https://www.bibalex.org/en/project/details?documentid=238&keywords=memory%20of%20the%20suez%20canal.

"Oak Alley Plantation." Accessed March 4, 2019. https://www.oakalleyplantation.org/.

"Passport in Time." Accessed March 4, 2019. http://www.passportintime.com/index.html.

"Primary Source Set." Accessed December 22, 2021. https://web.archive.org/web/20170710135638/https://www.mysticseaport.org/learn/k-12-programs/primary-source-workshops/.

"Primary Source Workshop." Accessed March 4, 2019. Wayback Machine archive (July 10, 2017): https://www.mysticseaport.org/learn/k-12-programs/primary-source-workshops/.

"Public History Weekly." Accessed March 4, 2019. https://public-history-weekly.degruyter.com/.

"South African History Online (SAHO)." Accessed March 4, 2019. http://www.sahistory.org.za/.

"Stonehenge. English Heritage." Accessed March 4, 2019. http://www.english-heritage.org.uk/visit/places/stonehenge.

"The Chinese-Australian Historical Images in Australia (CHIA)." Accessed March 4, 2019. http://www.chia.chinesemuseum.com.au/.

"The excavations of the Roman Theatre in Florence." Accessed December 22, 2021. https://izi.travel/en/9fe0-the-excavations-of-the-roman-theatre-in-florence/en.

"The Grand Hornu." Accessed March 4, 2019. http://www.grand-hornu.eu/.

"The Great Inka Road." Accessed December 22, 2021. WayBack Machine archive (May 6, 2021): https://web.archive.org/web/20210506202540/https://americanindian.si.edu/explore/exhibitions/item?id=945.

"The Public Historian." Accessed March 4, 2019. http://tph.ucpress.edu/.

"The September 11 Digital Archive." Accessed March 4, 2019. http://911digitalarchive.org/.

"Tibet Oral History Project." Accessed March 4, 2019. https://www.tibetoralhistory.org/.

"Tous mécènes!" Accessed March 4, 2019. http://www.tousmecenes.fr/fr.

"Transcribathon." Accessed March 4, 2019. https://transcribathon.com/en/.

"Transcribe Bentham." Accessed March 4, 2019. http://blogs.ucl.ac.uk/transcribe-bentham/.

"Warsaw Rising 1944." Accessed March 4, 2019. http://www.warsawrising.eu.

"Who Do You Think You Are?" Accessed March 4, 2019. https://www.imdb.com/title/tt1365047/.

"World War I goes Twitter." Accessed March 4, 2019. http://h-europe.uni.lu/?page_id=621.

Part 3: **Best Practices**

Mark Tebeau
Curation: Toward a New Ethic of Digital Public History

Abstract: This essay argues that a new curatorial ethic has emerged at the heart of digital public history, reflecting a flourishing of curatorial work in the broad culture. Everyone has become a curator: the disc jockey who spins records at a club or selects playlists for Internet radio as well as the creator of a born digital archive who collects and shares cultural records. This curatorial turn has shattered the thick walls that once existed between various public history professional specializations – such as libraries, archives, and scholars. As digital public historians redefine the fields from which their practice is drawn, they create new possibilities for engaging and building wide public communities; and yet building this new curatorial ethic remains challenging because its inclusive promise depends heavily on mastering and navigating increasingly specialized technical and administrative conversations about the management and organization of digital materials.

Keywords: curation, crowdsourcing, rapid-response archives, galleries, libraries, archives, museums, mapping, storytelling, games

A new curatorial ethic has emerged at the heart of digital public history. The digital and public turns have expanded the purview of curators and seen a flourishing of curatorial work, which has happened simultaneously with the emergence of curation as a metaphor that pervades the digital age. In some ways, it is this ubiquity of the curator in everyday culture of the twenty-first century that is revealing of the shift in the world of digital public history. Everyone has become a curator: the disc jockey who spins records at a club or selects playlists for Internet radio; the shoe salesperson who selects products for sale at their boutique, as well as their online store, and (of course) the creator of a born digital archive who collects and shares cultural records. Early in the twenty-first century, this shift made its way into the popular press. For example, in 2009, the *New York Times* noted this trend in reporting that curation "has become a fashionable code word among the aesthetically minded, who seem to paste it onto any activity that involves culling and selecting." By 2020, the *New York Times* would follow up on the ubiquity of curation, quoting a marketer for luxury brands noting, "I hate the word. It's everywhere." As the word and concept has entered the mainstream, "content curation" has become a professional activity that adds "value," without any

https://doi.org/10.1515/9783110430295-023

real sense of what such value might be – and surely devoid of its origins in the arts and in museums where curators had specialized field or topical expertise.[1]

Digital public history has transformed how professionals work in the context of galleries, libraries, archives, and museums (GLAMS) and the field of history work. The new curatorial turn that has emerged has shattered the thick walls that once existed between various historic fields – such as libraries, archives, and historians. Also, the space between publics and historical professionals has become decidedly more porous. Digital and public historians have modeled new approaches to making knowledge, to building arguments, and to disseminating their work. In many ways, the curatorial turn has embodied the manner in which public history and the digital humanities have transformed one another.

This transformation in the world of digital and public history has too many roots to be documented easily, but it was clearly articulated in the Humanities Manifesto 2.0 in 2009, which stated that curating in the twenty-first century has moved beyond its staid roots in gentlemen collectors of the nineteenth century: the digital humanities, it argued, "recasts the scholar as curator and the curator as scholar."[2] It also argued that this would reinvigorate historical scholarship and renew the scholarly mission of GLAMS. In many respects, the manifesto has proven to be prescient, though it all but ignored how this conversation has been transformed by both public historians and publics.

Curation – whether of physical or digital materials – has expanded beyond the specialized worlds of galleries, libraries, archives, and museums, each with its own training and traditions. It includes a variety of components, such as the following: a) the process of collecting and classifying materials, as well as conserving them; b) the practices of sharing those digital and physical items beyond the institution and connecting them to other collections both inside and outside the host GLAM; c) the work of interpreting (or contextualizing) and creating meaning within the broader scholarship and culture. Dividing the work of curation into several elements highlights the ways that the work of digital and public historians have transformed the field, exposing the paradoxes at the heart of twenty-first-century curation. Among the more notable transformations has been the broadening of the field, as well as the emergence of specialized conversations related to digital materials. This essay will focus less on all the specialties within digital public history, more emphasizing the ways that public and digital historians have transformed their fields with a new

---

1 Lou Stoppard, "Everyone's a Curator Now: When Everything is Curated What Does the Word Even Mean," *New York Times* (3 March, 2020); https://www.nytimes.com/2020/03/03/style/curate-buzzword.html (accessed October 10, 2020); Alex Williams, "On the Tip of Creative Tongues," *New York Times* (2 October, 2009), https://www.nytimes.com/2009/10/04/fashion/04curate.html, (accessed 10 October, 2020).
2 Todd Pressner, Digital Humanities Manifesto 2.0 Launched, (22 June, 2009), http://www.toddpressner.com/?p=7 (accessed 10 October, 2020).

curatorial turn that emphasizes technical innovation and public engagement. This essay takes a historians' view of the emergence of the field of digital history and its points of intersection with public history, emphasizing especially digital archival work, technologies and tools, as well as the dynamism of Web 2.0 as spaces where the digital & public history intersected to build a new curatorial ethic.[3]

The possibilities of digital curation exploded in the 1990s with the emergence of personal computing, portable data, and eventually the Internet. In particular, the creation of digital archives emerged as a first form of digital curatorial activity and a foundational activity among historians working digitally with public audiences. Among the earliest was the *Valley of the Shadow* whose origin on CD-ROM reflected early challenges of sharing digital archival materials, though by the late 1990s it had moved to the Internet. *Valley of the Shadow* reflected analog sensibilities with its organization as a library with shelves of data but quickly emerged as a model archive – organized around the experiences of two communities before, during, and after the Civil War. The project took a sophisticated approach to curating the materials from Virginia and Maryland, gesturing toward the collaborative team-oriented approach that included students as archive curators and also imagining a project that crossed media formats – what communications scholars now call transmedia – when project leader Ed Ayers published an award-winning book *In the Presence of Mine Enemies*, whose footnotes connect back to the archive.[4] Ever more sophisticated digital archival projects, notable for the quality of their metadata, design, and features, emerged in the twenty-first century with award-winning efforts such as *Digital Harlem* and the *Proceedings of the Old Bailey*, a series of London court records, being especially impressive. Both projects forged new models for digital public history as curatorial teams collaborated and worked in the space between the traditional scholarly researcher and the archivist or museum professional.[5] The development of Proceedings of the Old Bailey, in particular, reveals how effective use of metadata – in this case xml mark-up – allowed these court records to be richly searchable, and extended for use with other datasets with similarly robust metadata,

---

[3] As we delve into these fields, it is worth posing a simple definition about what curators do. Curators make choices and build context. They choose what to collect, preserve, and display. They assign metadata, conduct research, and develop interpretive arguments. Curators help design, represent, and organize knowledge in domains that include museums, the Internet, and urban landscapes. Each aspect of this work requires the curator to make distinctions and selections based on professional best practice, institutional missions, and academic knowledge. Effective curation is equal measures of science, craft, and art.
[4] Edward L. Ayers, The Valley of the Shadow, https://valley.lib.virginia.edu/, (accessed 10 October, 2020).
[5] Digital Harlem, Everday Life, 1915–1930, http://digitalharlem.org/, (accessed October 10, 2020).

which is evident in its inclusion in efforts such as *Digital Panopticon, LondonLives,* and *connectedhistories* among others.⁶

Perhaps nowhere is the emergence of this new sense of curation as a fundamental work of a range of history professionals more evident than in the work of digital collecting in response to crises. The digital turn in public history emerged forcefully in the days following 9/11, as the Center for History and New Media at George Mason forged what is arguably the first crowdsourced digital archive. In building the *September 11 Digital Archive* the team collected more than 150,000 artifacts working within the context of the basic database software that existed at the time. The effort occurred as the internet was shifting toward becoming a "commons," or a public space in which individuals shared knowledge, accessed data, and engaged one another, and even before the coining of the phrase Web 2.0, which signaled the dynamic web of social media. The work included collecting materials from a variety of sources, as well as assigning basic metadata. Such early efforts included little descriptive metadata and did not emphasize that work nearly as much as later work, reflecting the degree to which public historians and GLAM professionals were just beginning to develop a new curatorial ethic.⁷

More broadly, the development of rapid response archiving as a formal response to crises illustrated how scholars and a variety of historical professionals reimagined the work of curation. Rapid-response archiving crystalized around the destruction and ravaging of New Orleans by Hurricane Katrina. *The Digital Memory Bank* emphasized how collaborative teams of researchers and communities could collect digital objects, reflecting the increasing importance of broad publics in the historical endeavor, something that would grow more important with the digital turn. In addition, the worlds of programming, design, and technical acumen began to make its way into curatorial work, as the project became the first instantiation of *Omeka*, an open-source content management software whose use has become a standard (or model) for digital public history practice. Over two decades, *Omeka* has become a go-to tool for a new generation of curators, as scholars, librarians, students, and communities. *Omeka* itself has continued to respond to changing *Omeka* as a tool for collecting, classifying, and historical knowledge. Omeka – and tools like it – have shaped professional digital curatorial practices – moving the conversation from how to collect historical narratives toward how to use metadata to describe those stories and make them interoperable with other tools.

More recent efforts, such as *Documenting Ferguson* and *Our Marathon*, have spurred intensive discussions of the logistics and ethics of contemporaneous digital collection and have modeled community partnerships as the basis for ethical and

---

6 Tim Hitchcock, Robert Shoemaker and Jamie McLaughlin, et al., The Old Bailey Proceedings Online, 1674–1913, version 8.0, (March 2012), www.oldbaileyonline.org, (accessed 10 October, 2020).
7 Dan Cohen and Rosy Rosenzweig, Digital History: A Guide to Gathering, Preserving, and Presenting the Past on the Web (2005), see especially Chapter 7, http://chnm.gmu.edu/digitalhistory/collecting/7.php, (accessed 10 October, 2020).

diverse collecting. In 2020, academic institutions, libraries, archives, and community organizations around the world have drawn on the best practices developed in these contexts to develop their approach to documenting the coronavirus pandemic.[8] In an effort to create conversations about the pandemic, *Made by US* and the *International Federation for Public History* have compiled a list of global digital collecting projects, based on project director reports solicited through Facebook; it includes nearly 100 projects.[9] Archive-It has compiled 173 collections, presumably initiated by those institutions' arrangements with the Internet Archive.[10] Additionally, a quick perusal of the landscape of collecting institutions reveals that countless state, regional, and local city/town historical agencies across the globe are collecting at least some materials in response to the pandemic. The overwhelming response suggests just how ubiquitous the curatorial turn has become across the institutional spectrum, revealing the depth and breadth of the field of digital public history. What began as a guerilla movement in the 1970s among historians (public history) and in the 2000s among humanists (digital humanities) has emerged as a powerful force within the broader academic and GLAM sectors.

The development of rapid response archives depended on the emergence of the dynamic Internet, or Web 2.0, that created an interactive relation between publics and scholars and GLAM curators – once housed in their ivory towers or inaccessible halon-protected archival repositories. The origins of this collaborative endeavor that connects publics and history professionals also had its origins in citizen involvement in science, often astronomy. This work led to the creation, in 2007, of Zooniverse a resource for "people powered" research. With a community of nearly two million participants, Zooniverse dozens of citizen science projects, many pertaining to the environment, such as Climate Australia or Sounds of New York City.[11] In the humanities, early aggregation

---

8 See, the Roy Rosenzweig Center for History and New Media, which developed the September 11 Digital Archive, Hurricane Digital Memory Bank, and was involved in Our Marathon – A community project hosted at Northeastern University. On the evolution of crises archives, compare Sheila Brennan and T. Mills Kelly, Why Collecting History Online is Web 1.5 – Roy Rosenzweig Center for History and New Media, *RRCHNM Blog* (March 2009); Sheila Brennan, "What's Next for Digital Memory Banks?," *Lot 49*, (6 May, 2013). On social activism, ethics, and collecting, see The Occupy Archive and Documenting Ferguson. On rapid-response archives, see Pam Schwartz, Whitney Broadaway, Emilie S. Arnold, Adam M. Ware, and Jessica Domingo, "Rapid-Response Collecting After the Pulse Nightclub Massacre," *The Public Historian* 40.1 (2018): 105–114.
9 Made By US and International Federation for Public History, "You are the primary source: COVID-19 Story-Collecting Initiatives"; a search of "covid-19 archive" yielded more than 250 items.
10 On early collecting that included Archive-It, see also Oya Y. Rieger, Documenting the COVID-19 Pandemic: Archiving the Present for Future Research, Ithaka S+R Blog, (6 April, 2020). As of 20 June, 2020, Archive-It reported 173 collections (https://archive-it.org/explore?q=covid-19&show=Collections).
11 Alison Klesman, "Zooniverse: A Citizen Science Success Story," *Astronomy*, (26 September, 2018), https://astronomy.com/magazine/2018/09/a-citizen-science-success-story, (accessed 10 October, 2020).

projects, such as NINES, largely have promoted scholarly discussion and data aggregation in an effort to connect the material archive of the nineteenth century with twenty-first-century digital methods. By contrast, the shift toward involving publics in research has been embodied most impressively in The New York Public Library's *What's on a Menu* project. In 2011, the NPYL asked the community to transcribe historic menu's in its collection, which has resulted in more than 17,000 menus being translated to date. Later efforts, such as *Building Inspector*, moved the bar further, by asking communities to document what's on fire insurance atlases and then maps as a way to train computer algorithms to do a better job at evaluating the digital maps.[12] Europeana also used similar methods to help it crowdsource the history of World War I, accepting digital objects from a broad range of communities from across the continent. Such efforts spawned the development of *CrowdHeritage*, an open platform for collecting better, more granular metadata and to connect the collections to broad public audiences.[13] Even more lightweight digital tools, such as *Scripto*, have become useful at allowing annotation of historical documents or even oral histories, making more and deeper metadata available.[14] Even so, many archives and libraries remain slow at letting "crowds" supplement their archival metadata, although this surely will become an ever more powerful practice in their future.

Perhaps an even more striking way that Web 2.0 has generated a new curatorial ethic has been through the social media revolution that has transformed digital and public history. This change in thinking about the work of curation has transformed museums' relation to their audiences in striking ways. In 2010, in *The Participatory Museum*, Nina Simon urged curators to use social media to transform their interactions with both publics and historical materials. She argued that social media had more uses than merely informing publics about upcoming events. Rather, she argued that social could be used to encourage the development of communities around their

---

[12] New York Public Library, What's On A Menu, 2011–2020, http://menus.nypl.org/, (accessed 10 October, 2020); New York Public Library, Building Inspector. Make Time. Make History, 2013–2020, http://buildinginspector.nypl.org/, (accessed 10 October, 2020).

[13] Stephen Bull, "Europeana 1914–1918: Showcasing Crowdsourcing and User Generate Content as the 'New' History," *Europeana Pro* (2 March, 2016); "Europeana launches crowd source campaign to decipher unique First World War testimonies," *Digital Meets Heritage*, (9 November, 2016), https://www.digitalmeetsculture.net/article/europeana-launches-crowd-source-campaign-to-decipher-unique-first-world-war-testimonies/, (accessed 10 October, 2020); Caroline Boswell, "Crowdsourcing World War I: 'The Lives of the First World War,'" *North American Conference of British Studies*, (20 August, 2014), https://www.nacbs.org/blog/crowdsourcing-world-war-i-the-lives-of-the-first-world-war/, (accessed 10 October, 2020); Marine Baron and Marco Rendina, "CrowdHeritage: A Crowdsourcing Platform for Enriching Europeana Metadata," *Europeana Pro*, (2 December, 2019), https://pro.europeana.eu/post/crowdheritage-a-crowdsourcing-platform-for-enriching-europeana-metadata, (accessed 10 October, 2020).

[14] Roy Rosenzweig Center for History and New Media, Scripto, 2019, https://scripto.org/, (accessed 10 October, 2020).

institutions, and especially to build conversations around artifacts themselves. Simon's formulation of "social objects" shifted the work of curation from one in which scholarly curators held forth on history, art, or culture to one in which the stuff of history – material culture itself – became part of a conversation. Engaging and interpreting objects came alive through dialogue – including dialogues with public audiences. Just as archives and libraries had begun to turn to publics for help in understanding their collections, so to did museums seek to build conversations about historical artifacts.[15]

At the same time, digital curators began to experiment with implementing this new participatory ideal. In London, University College, London's Centre for Digital Humanities, UCL Centre for Advanced Spatial Analysis, and UCL Museums and Collections at the Grant Museum of Zoology developed *QRator*, which experimented with a new form of digital interpretation that involved publics and curators in a two-way conversation about museum objects. The citation of the *UK Museums and Heritage Award for Excellence 2012 in the Innovation* described the work as "impressive in the way it encourages participation within museums but also, importantly, in maintaining that participation beyond the walls of the museum when visitors have returned home."[16] Judging from the involvement of broad publics in historical documentation and in interpretive conversations, the curatorial turn of digital public history has moved the center of the conversation toward broad public audiences in decisive ways that are driving the development of scholarly collecting and analysis.

And, yet, the curator's role as expert – or at least as a framer of debate remains, perhaps more powerfully than ever before. The curatorial turn in digital public history has underscored the creativity and expertise required to build interpretive contexts for digital arguments and objects. These vary from the work of building archives with inventive strategies for search, to building mobile tools for interpreting landscapes as one might curate an exhibit in a museum, to building creative projects that imagine new ways of presenting materials the break the linear nature of historical argument. The ecosystem of tools, data, and resources available to curators – underscored by the implementation of data standards – surely has made digital curation more collaborative and increased its impact and audiences. But it

---

15 Nina Simon, The Participatory Museum, 2010, http://www.participatorymuseum.org/, (accessed 10 October, 2020); more broadly, the critical role of museums as centers of community conversations has become a central theme within the GLAM field, and one that extends worldwide. See, for instance, the International Council for Museums, International Museum Day: Museums as Cultural Hubs, (2019), https://icom.museum/en/news/imd2019-museums-as-cultural-hubs-the-future-of-tradition/, (accessed 26 January, 2021).
16 QRator: A Digital Dialogue on Museum Collections, Grant Museum of Zoology, 2011 to 2015, Exhibition, University College London, https://www.ucl.ac.uk/culture/projects/qrator, (accessed 10 October, 2020).

has also come to depend on complex new scholarly and institutional perspectives and collaborations.

The growth of GIS mapping tools has, for example, provided a complex set of visualization tools that are widely available, and increasingly used by curators developing historical archives to document the past. One approach to this work has been to create new map layers, often built on historic maps. The David Rumsey collection, the New York Public Library's *Map Rectifier*, and *Hypercities* all reflected work to make the work of "thick mapping" deeper and more historically oriented. Equally compelling have been projects that use maps (and data layers) to take deep dives into cities. Such projects have sprouted up across the globe, usually oriented around urban history; they have connected archives to neighborhoods (*Digital Harlem*) or connected multiple historical databases to a city's history (*LondonLives*), or simply doc. Many digital curators now use mapping tools to provide alternative ways of visualizating archival materials, whether they are government documents from the (*Photogrammar*) or disaster in Japanese History (*Japanese Disasters Digital Archive*.)[17]

As mapping tools have become ubiquitous as an approach to visualizing archival data, scholar curators have used maps as a frame for presenting historical arguments. Such projects are less about presenting archival materials than they are about using interpretive approaches that emphasize digital storytelling. This work ranges from crowdsourced efforts, such as *HistoryPin*, that seek to present local history within map contexts, suitable for use in walking tours through the landscape navigated by local phones.[18] Other efforts, such as *Curatescape* have adapted open-source software, such as Omeka, for use by local preservation organizations and scholars to create locally curated mobile & web apps.[19] Increasingly, curators in GLAMS and the academy, are also moving toward completely virtual tours, reconstructing historical experiences that have been lost, such as *Gulag Online* seeks to represent "the basic form and dimensions of Soviet repression through a virtual reconstruction of a Gulag camp, specific life stories, selected objects, documents and

---

[17] Photogrammar, http://photogrammar.yale.edu/map/, (accessed 10 October, 2020); Japanese Disasters Digital Archive, https://jdarchive.org/en, (accessed 10 October, 2020); Digital Harlem, Everday Life, 1915–1930, http://digitalharlem.org/, (accessed 10 October, 2020); Locating London's Past, Version 1.0, (December 2011), https://www.locatinglondon.org/, (accessed 10 October, 2020); Gulag*CZ, Gulag Online, 2013–2020, http://www.gulag.online/?locale=en, (accessed 10 October, 2020); imagineRio, https://imaginerio.org/#en, (accessed 10 October, 2020); Todd Presner, David Shepard, and Yoh Kawano, HyperCities: Thick Mapping in the Digital Humanities, Harvard University Press, https://www.hypercities.com/, (accessed 10 October, 2020).
[18] Shift Design, Inc., HistoryPin, 2010–2020, https://www.historypin.org/en/, (accessed 10 October, 2020).
[19] Center for Public History + Digital Humanities, Curatescape; 2010–2020, https://curatescape.org/, (accessed 10 October, 2020); Roy Rosenzweig Center for History and New Media, Omeka, https://omeka.org/, (accessed 10 October, 2020).

texts." All of these projects, and so many more across the globe, seek to use the historic map as a layer of interpretation but also to place interpretive data (not just archival data) on maps as a way to enhance the depth of scholarship as well as its public accessibility.

Finally, the work of outreach in GLAMS has been thoroughly transformed by the blurring of lines between archivist and specialist interpreters as everyone becomes a storyteller. Indeed, this process of creating stories has emerged as a characteristic of the new curatorial ethos. This shift has emphasized that curation is not merely the storage and display of data, but the act of forming it into narratives. Increasingly, scholars and practitioners have moved toward sharing historical narratives in more and more innovative ways. Some of these modes have represented entirely novel forms of digital scholarship. The NYPL's *Biblion: World's Fair*, for example, presented a dizzying array of interpretive and archival materials around the 1939 New York's World's Fair presented through a user interface that provided a range of subject, document, and interpretive framing connections.[20] Other work emphasizes gaming as an approach to teaching and learning history, dating to the fondly-remembered Oregon Trail video game that originated in the early days of computing and was an innovative education program available on personal computers of the 1980s and 1990s.[21] Gaming, or more aptly, gamification – the process of turning learning into a game has emerged as an important choice made by curators to entertain public audiences in the digital age. Platforms, such as ARIS, have emerged as a way to encourage the expansion of this approach to curating a historical experience. And, finally, so-called augmented reality (with its emphasis on 3D virtual tours) has emerged as yet another way to engage publics – either those visiting historical landscapes or sitting in their easy chairs.) The goal of such technologies is to augment reality in ways that bring the past into the present, transporting publics into the past.[22]

---

[20] "NYPL Biblion: Frankenstein," *Kirkus Review* (4 June, 2012), https://www.kirkusreviews.com/book-reviews/new-york-public-library/nypl-biblion-frankenstein/, (accessed 10 October, 2020); Steve Sande, "NYPL Biblion: World's Fair iPad App a Compelling Look at Yesterday's Future," *Endgadget* (18 June, 2011), https://www.engadget.com/2011-06-18-nypl-biblion-worlds-fair-ipad-app-a-compelling-look-at-yesterd.html, (accessed 10 October, 2020); Elissa Turner, "Biblion Roars to Life on the IPad," *The New Yorker* (16 May, 2011), https://www.newyorker.com/books/page-turner/biblion-roars-to-life-on-the-ipad, (accessed October 10, 2020).
[21] The Oregon Trail (series), Wikipedia; https://en.wikipedia.org/wiki/The_Oregon_Trail_(series), (accessed 10 October, 2020); see, for instance, Play the Past, https://www.playthepast.org/, (accessed 10 October, 2020); Jeremy Antley, "Games and Historical Narratives," *Journal of Digital Humanities* 1.2 (Spring 2012), http://journalofdigitalhumanities.org/1-2/games-and-historical-narratives-by-jeremy-antley/, (accessed 10 October, 2020); Field Day Learning Games, ARIS: Create Location-Based Games and Stories, https://fielddaylab.org/make/aris/, (accessed 10 October, 2020).
[22] Karen Schrier, Revolutionizing History Education: Using Augmented Reality Games to Teach Histories, MIT Graduate Program in Comparative Studies, (1 August, 2005), https://cms.mit.edu/rev

As the curatorial turn has transformed the way digital public history represents knowledge it has also created a space that demands ever broader and complex skill sets – both for individuals and research teams. The growing complexity of the field has generated new ways to engage broader publics, but also demands higher levels of collaboration. Innovative projects, such as the *Venice Time Machine*, offer cautionary tales about what is possible but also what might stand in the way of innovation. Promising to bring a thousand years of the city's history together into an open research archive that could be used by researchers and also that presented the city's rich history, the *Venice Time Machine* was suspended in 2019 over disputes about the data standards being used.[23] More recently, the project as re-emerged as a broader European Union effort connecting archives and universities in a wider effort to invigorate European history with "big data from the past." As digital public historians work through standards and interoperability, it is imperative to note that such increasingly specialized techniques and practices emerging at the center of the field makes the curatorial turn especially challenging, even as it promises more democratic access to the past. The digital age has blurred the lines between historians and archivists and traditional curators. Everyone is a curator in a world where the digital shapes public and historical dialogues. As this shift has broken barriers both among professional historians and between those historians and various publics, it demands broad technological competence and relies on increasingly specialized technical expertise, often only available through collaboration. Ironically, this collaborative culture both opens up new possibilities and closes them off – representing a central paradox at the heart of the digital public humanities.

Bibliography

Adair, Bill, Benjamin Filene, and Laura Koloski, eds. *Letting Go? Shared Historical Authority in a User-Generated World*. New York: Routledge, 2011.

Ayers, Ed, *In the Presence of Mine Enemies: The Civil War in the Heart of America, 1859–1864: War in the Heart of America 1859–1863*. New York: W. W. Norton, 2004.

---

olutionizing-history-education-using-augmented-reality-games-to-teach-histories/, (accessed 10 October, 2020).

23 EPFL, Venice Time Machine, https://www.epfl.ch/research/domains/venice-time-machine/, (accessed 10 October, 2020);; Davide Castelvecchi, Venice Time Machine Project Suspended Amid Data Row, *Nature* (October 25, 2019), https://www.nature.com/articles/d41586-019-03240-w, (accessed October 10, 2020); EPFL Booted from Venice Time Machine Project, *Swissinfo.ch*, (September 24, 2019), https://www.swissinfo.ch/eng/surprise-move-_epfl-booted-from-venice-time-machine-project-/45252134, (accessed 10 October, 2020); Time Machine, https://www.timemachine.eu/about-us/, (accessed 10 October, 2020). To learn more, see Barabucci, Tomasi, and Vitali, "Modeling Data Complexity in Public History and Cultural Heritage" in this handbook.

Boyd, Douglas and Mary Larson. *Oral History and Digital Humanities: Voice Access, and Engagement*. New York: Palgrave, 2014.
Burdick, Ann, Johanna Drucker, Peter Lunenfeld, Todd Presner, and Jeffrey Schnapp, *Digital Humanities*. Cambridge, MA: MIT Press, 2012.
Finn, Ed. *What Algorithms Want: Imagination in the Age of Computing*. Cambridge, MA: MIT Press, 2017.
Salmi, Hannu. *What is Digital History?*. London: Polity, 2021.

Martin Grandjean
Data Visualization for History

Abstract: It is logical that the generalization of digital approaches in history is leading to a democratization of the graphic representation of the data produced by these processes. Rather than presenting long series of examples, this very cursory chapter seeks to fuel reflection on our uses: why do we visualize historical data? Is it for illustrative purposes, to "show" our historical object and make it understandable to a large audience? Or is it, on the contrary, because the raw data is unintelligible to us, and visualization is therefore a heuristic tool intended for their exploration? The central point of my argument is based on a typology of sources and uses, a double entry table which is intended as a kind of decision-making aid for those seeking to make their data speak in the right way to the right audience.

Keywords: data visualization, digital history, digital humanities, infographics, visual analytics

Introduction

The widespread use of visual representations in historical science reflects the public's passion for historical questions in general: as this subject arouses a strong and lasting interest from society and as such a rich iconographic tradition has made history intelligible to so many people for so long, the integration of graphics into historical narratives is now common.[1] Presently, this practice is mainly descriptive, taking advantage of relatively universal visual codes to summarize an object or a historical phenomenon, "simplifying" it to make it more understandable. Of course, visualization is not a prerogative of history. Far from it. It is primarily a cross-curricular skill inspired by the hard sciences and statistical methods, spreading into all areas of research. It is this hybridization that drives a large community of historians, researchers in social sciences, economics, literary, or artistic studies, journalists, and graphic designers to produce visual representations that go far beyond the mere presentation of results toward more analytic and exploratory approaches. In this essay, we will focus on issues related to visualization in history practice, without disregarding the works of some references in neighboring areas,

---

[1] Johanna Drucker, 2015. "Graphical Approaches to the Digital Humanities," in *A New Companion to Digital Humanities*, ed. Susan Schreibman, Ray Siemens and John Unsworth (John Wiley & Sons, Ltd., 2008), 238–50; Martyn Jesson, "Digital Visualization as a Scholarly Activity," *Literary and Linguistic Computing* 23 (3): 281–293.

such as those of Tukey, Tufte, and others.² Process automation, corpus massification,³ "distant reading,"⁴ interactivity, and data sharing have emerged as methods for sharing research and involving audiences. Nonetheless, the evolution from an illustrative visualization to visualization that integrates the research process, or allows readers or exhibition visitors to navigate the data for themselves, raises many questions.

Rather than provide an inventory of projects and methods, this paper offers a more conceptual reflection around the production of these graphic representations, from the author's ideas to the reader's comprehension. While data visualization is a prevalent practice in historical science and its ancillary disciplines, at least in its simplest forms, the recourse to these sometimes fascinating visual objects demands a critical discussion and typology of uses.

A History of Visualizing Data

It is important to remember that visualization is only one step among others when processing a dataset. Visualizations simplify and, thus, are not always able to express the richness of the object they describe. If this visual product naturally makes it possible to "see" the historical data, or at least one of its facets, a graphic representation may not be the perfect end point of a demonstration or an exhibition.

But this visual simplification, which is a very ancient practice, is of course beneficial to information dissemination. For example, representing territory in the form of a map augmented with markers indicating elements of physical (such as mountain ranges in rock paintings) or human geography is a form of visualization that preceded formal writing. Next came symbolic and political cartography,⁵ the objectification of the "frontier", which made territory maps and cadastral plans performative visualizations. Celestial cartography, which is suspected to be even older than its earthly counterpart, is also a perfect example of simplifying information for

---

2 See John W. Tukey, *Exploratory Data Analysis* (Reading: Pearson, 1977); Edward R. Tufte, *The Visual Display of Quantitative Information* (Cheshire: Graphics Press, 1983); Amy Maxmen, "Three Minutes with Hans Rosling Will Change Your Mind about the World," *Nature* no. 540 (2016): 330–33; Michael Bostock, Vadim Ogievetsky, and Jeffrey Heer, "D3: Data-Driven Documents," *IEEE Trans. Visualization & Comp. Graphics* (2011).
3 Shawn Graham, Ian Milligan and Scott Weingart, *Exploring Big Historical Data, The Historian's Macroscope* (London: Imperial College Press, 2015); Andreas Fickers, "Towards a New Digital Historicism? Doing History in the Age of Abundance," *VIEW Journal of European Television History and Culture* (2012): 19–26.
4 Franco Moretti, *Distant Reading* (Verso Books, 2013).
5 Christian Jacob, *L'empire des cartes. Approche théorique de la cartographie à travers l'histoire*. (Paris: Albin Michel, 1992).

practical purposes: even if, since the Antiquity, certain astronomical atlases sought to be as complete as possible, most were simplified maps of the brightest stars and major constellations for sailors and travelers. In the register of highly codified visual representations, we also find medieval family trees. On one or more sides of the cenotaph of a recumbent, for example, the representation in bas-relief of the coats of arms were organized according to marriages and relatives. This allowed the viewers to glance over the genealogy of the monarch, understand the alliances formed, and reconstruct the recent history of power without needing to know how to read. This is an early example of a "public" history – a history that was available for all to see.

More recently, during the enlightenment, engineer William Playfair is often credited with the first graphical representations of statistical data.[6] Inspired by the timelines of Priestley who, in 1765, visualized the lifespan of two thousand personalities along an axis of time spanning almost three millennia,[7] Playfair offered many time series documenting the British foreign trade balance and can be therefore considered as the inventor of the histogram (the bar graph). In 1869, Charles Joseph Minard made the "first" emblematic historical visualization that grew from a statistical framework. That graphic, *Carte figurative des pertes successives en hommes de l'armée française dans la campagne de Russie* (1812–1813), was described by Robinson[8] and notably popularized by Tufte (Fig. 1).[9] This map simplified the constantly decreasing number of soldiers in the Napoleonic army into a graphic that very effectively demonstrated Napoleon's ill-fated march; it still inspires many graphic designers today. At the beginning of the twentieth century the use of graphs that combined statistical data, conceptual plans, and geographical maps grew dramatically,[10] although the practice is far from being generalized in the humanities. From the rise of statistical atlases and their fascinating thematic maps developed in the second half of the nineteenth

---

6 William Playfair, *Commercial and Political Atlas: Representing, by Copper-Plate Charts, the Progress of the Commerce, Revenues, Expenditure, and Debts of England, during the Whole of the Eighteenth Century* (London (1786), recently reissued by Howard Wainer and Ian Spence, eds. 2005); *The Commercial and Political Atlas and Statistical Breviary* (New York: Cambridge University Press, cited by Michael Friendly, 2007); "A Brief History of Data Visualization," in *Handbook of Computational Statistics: Data Visualization*, edited by C. Chen, W. Härdle and A. Unwin (Heidelberg: Springer), 1–34.
7 Joseph Priestley, *A Chart of Biography* (London: British Library, 1765), 611.I.19.
8 Arthur H. Robinson, "The Thematic Maps of Charles Joseph Minard," *Imago Mundi* 21, no. 1 (1967): 95–108.
9 Tufte (1983).
10 Charles van den Heuvel, "Building Society, Constructing Knowledge, Weaving the Web: Otlet's Visualizations of a Global Information Society and His Concept of Universal Civilization," in *European Modernism and the Information Society*, edited by W. Boyd Rayward (London: Ashgate, 2008), 127–153.

Fig. 1: Visitors in front of a giant reproduction of Minard's 1869 map at the Mundaneum, in Mons (Belgium). CC-BY-SA Martin Grandjean 2021.

century to "graphic semiology",[11] the modes of representation have evolved and stabilized. In this field, their use remains nevertheless relatively descriptive and heuristic data visualizations are still rare.

Typologies of Visualization: Sources and Uses

Having data that can be visualized does not mean that it needs to be visualized, or at least not in any way for any audience. Thus, we propose a typology for visualization adapted to (public) history. It unfolds along to two main axes (see Fig. 2): a typology of historical sources that distinguishes representations that are drawings based on information aggregation from those that are based on quantitative datasets; and a typology of use that differentiates the representations intended to illustrate or describe a situation in a simple way to make it immediately understandable, those produced to make data accessible through an interactive interface, and those likely to be the analyst's tool to generate new knowledge in a research process.

Axis 1: Which Sources? Infographics and Data Visualizations

The relationship between a researcher and his sources is a fundamental distinguishing characteristic of historical science. Thus, we expect a high degree of

---

[11] Jacques Bertin, *Sémiologie Graphique. Les Diagrammes. Les Réseaux. Les Cartes* (Paris: Mouton et Gauthier-Villars, 1967).

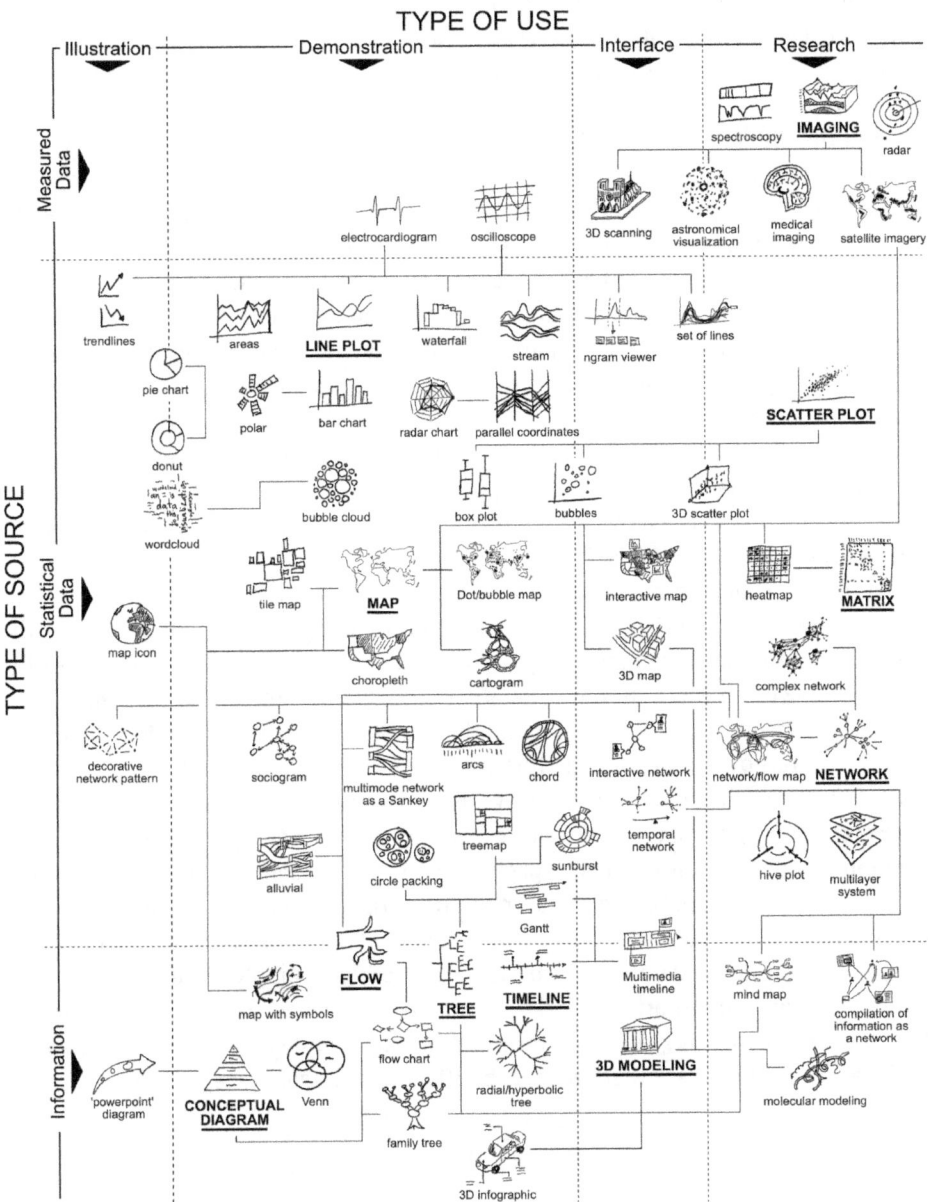

Fig. 2: Typology of data visualization along two axes: the type of data sources (vertical) and the type of use (horizontal). This table is intended to fuel reflection, to support the realization of a visualization. It cannot contain all the scenarios but offers 70 examples of frequent graphic forms, organized in families, to serve as reference points. CC-BY-SA Martin Grandjean 2021.

precision from historical visualization as regards the type of data that lies beneath the graphical representation. The nuance between an "infographic" and "data visualization" can be difficult to see, as the terms are often used interchangeably, especially now that the use of such visual aids has increased, especially in digital public history practices.

But the difference is important: making a representation based on a compilation of information (and on short historical narratives) is an act that involves a graphic and manual layout, whereas the visualization of a dataset is an operation that can be automatically done by software. And so, it is according to the type of sources used, and their serial processing, that one distinguishes "infographics" from "data visualizations", even though they sometimes may be visually similar. For example, the historical literature is very fond of maps – which may be created from quite different sources. A map of global movements of populations, battlefields, or railway networks may be an object that is "drawn" by its author on the basis of the information it graphs (Fig. 2 "map with symbols"). By contrast, a map with markers of industrial production, population density, or the position of monuments may not be a drawing at all, but the product of a formalized procedure based on a list of geographical coordinates and values (Fig. 2 "dot/bubble map").

In the field of information graphics, we therefore find all representations that are not based on numerical data. Thus, a diagram that clarifies the hierarchy or the succession of several elements (Fig. 2 "flow chart") and a dendrogram describing the structure of an institution or a family (Fig. 2 "family tree") are "drawings" because they do not imply a formal data table. Conversely, a curve tracing the evolution of a value over time (Fig. 2 "line plot"), a set of points in a two-dimensional space (Fig. 2 "scatter plot"), or a histogram of a value that evolves over time (Fig. 2 "bar chart") are pure statistical representations. This is a category in which we also find much more complex forms, especially when it represents relational data (Fig. 2 "matrix" and "network"), like social relations or the circulation of goods, people, or documents.[12] This typological axis might suggest that information design is a less noble art than data visualization because it produces simpler images or those in which technical connotation is less pronounced. However, it must be remembered that these two types of graphic representations are complementary rather than hierarchical. They simply show sources with different characteristics.

---

12 A more precise classification of historical networks is proposed in Martin Grandjean, "Analisi e visualizzazioni delle reti in storia. L'esempio della cooperazione intellettuale della Societa delle Nazioni," *Memoria e Ricerca* 55, no. 2 (2017): 371–393.

Axis 2: What Uses and Which Audiences? Demonstration, Interface, and Research

Is a graphic created for the purpose of synthesizing a historical object intended for an audience? Or is it made in order to understand a massive research object and to crunch data for new knowledge – in which case it will probably only be useful to the historian? This typology of uses between "demonstration" and "research" can be traced back to Tukey[13] and applied to history.[14] They also can be refined, using an intermediate stage that relates particularly to public history. Indeed, visualizations can now serve as an "interface" to explore data and access more information or for the audience to add some data by themselves, in a collaborative process. These three uses are implicitly classified from the simplest to the most complex. First, the "demonstration" visualization is usually straightforward so that the reader can immediately understand, such as a diagram that classifies elements into sets (Fig. 2 "Venn") or a flow diagram for simple relational data (Fig. 2 "alluvial"). For its part, the "interface" visualization can be more complex since the public can interact with it and it is not limited to a unique view, like a timeline, which allows the public to choose the temporality and to display additional information (Fig. 2 "multimedia timeline"), or frequency curves of words, which makes it possible to return to the indexed text (Fig. 2 "ngram viewer"). More and more frequently, these visualizations are turned into dashboards that accumulate indicators, allowing the public to navigate between the screens. Finally, the "research" visualization is sometimes illegible for someone other than its author – as the scholar (often alone) has gone through the whole development of processing and analysis, such as in very dense graph analyses (Fig. 2 "complex network"). Heuristic drawings are quite similar as they represent the organization of concepts or research ideas (Fig. 2 "mind map"), where only the author can understand the intrinsic logic. It should be noted that these three different uses depend on the evolution of technology. For example, the data visualization remained very descriptive or demonstrative until the development of the computation power of the personal computer, making the visualizations more affordable as research tools. And it has been the emergence of web technology, mobile applications, and touch screens that today favor the exploitation of visualization interfaces in online publications, databases, or museums.

---

[13] Tukey (1977).
[14] Martin Grandjean, "Introduction à la visualisation de données: L'analyse de réseau en histoire," *Histoire et Informatique* no. 18 (2015): 107–126.

Maintaining a Critical Discussion on Visual Representations

Visualization provides a unique and increasingly important avenue through which to convey historical knowledge. However, sometimes the intended effect is completely spoiled by misinformed or faulty practices. Thus, it remains critical that the graphic representation is not dissociated from the data; we also must provide critical and demanding discourse to support the data modeling process.[15]

The aesthetic and heuristic aspects of visualization often unintentionally reinforce the impression that these graphical representations are self-sufficient and that they can become a substitute for traditional scholarly methods. To visualize is to objectify, to "totalize" a historical object, sometimes giving the impression that complex subjects can be grasped at once. Although this may serve the general public, it is an open door for the positivist temptation to reduce this object to its empirically measurable part. Yet, visualization should not replace the fundamental material of the historian: the figures, the organization charts, and the timelines are hiding the people who make history. This reminder is all the more important because the innovative and extremely specific aspect of certain technologies forces those who use them to isolate themselves in scientific communities that sometimes cut them off from the public. This leads those historians, designers, or cultural institutions to make visualizations that deprive their audience of important critical information and necessary context. Moreover, and this is also a point that needs to be discussed in any research project or public history work, the tools themselves are rarely designed for historical analyses and narratives. Using them in other ways is a rich and fascinating task but exploiting them without discerning that they need to be adapted to the contexts of arguments and audience can lead to irrelevant conclusions.

The recent developments of "digital history",[16] which have been accompanied by a democratization of access to visualization tools, only accentuates such issues. While it is obviously valuable that software resources are not monopolized by a caste of specialists, audiences sometimes lack the analytic or technical skills to use such resources and understand their added value. Network analysis is a classic case of complex and extremely powerful tools that sometimes are used naïvely for projects that wish to benefit from the impressive and complicated expression of deep entanglements evident in such representations. But, for unsophisticated audiences, these graphs may be inexplicable. Adding complexity in this manner may

---

15 Frederick W. Gibbs, 2016. "New Forms of History: Critiquing Data and Its Representations," *The American Historian*, http://tah.oah.org/february-2016/new-forms-of-history-critiquing-data-and-its-representations/.

16 Serge Noiret and Frédéric Clavert, eds., *L'histoire contemporaine à l'ère numérique – Contemporary History in the Digital Age* (Bern: Peter Lang, 2013).

ultimately obscure more than it reveals and create an artificial distance with the public. Likewise, it is also common for museums and the media to use visual objects that have the characteristics of a visualization but that do not explain or illustrate the subjects they are meant to elucidate. Instead, they fill empty spaces to impress the audience with a debauchery of aestheticism.

Conclusion: Historians' Responsibilities to Audiences

The main pitfall facing the producers of historical data visualization is probably that they are not always able to predict the reception of their audience and design a product that matches their needs. Although it is now common to encounter graphic representations of statistical data in mass media publications, the use of such objects is still relatively underdeveloped in scientific publications in history or in their popularization to the general public. It is often limited to very simple and intuitive forms: histograms, curves, or geographical maps. Consequently, using a visualization resulting from complex data processing, such as a multiple correspondence analysis or a network graph, whose codes are unfamiliar to the majority of people, often produces mixed reactions. Some do not understand or refuse these visualizations as a means of proof. Others may be so fascinated by the object, its attractive aesthetic, and the impression of completeness, that they accept the interpretation without questioning the modeling choices. Problems also arise when interactive data visualizations are proposed to the public. In practice, many museum visitors confronted with an interactive audiovisual interface or Internet users who browse a heritage database on a website are lost after the first click because the interface was not designed with the user in mind. In some cases, such visualizations may offer so much browsing freedom that the visitor is immediately disoriented or overwhelmed.

In the end, all these reactions are the product of the same cause, a form of "visual illiteracy", an inability to read these graphs and understand the visualization issues that underlie them. However, it is not a question of ridding ourselves of our responsibility by blaming audiences. On the contrary, it is crucial to take into account the fact that they are not always educated to read such objects. Audiences, therefore, must be accompanied – often metaphorically through text or user design – with the historians' guidance when decrypting these graphic representations. For public historians, whose work is so much a part of historical dialogues with diverse audiences, this is especially true. And as with great powers come great responsibilities, we have the mission to produce visualizations that are up to the rigor of historical sciences, respecting their data on the one hand and the public of readers on the other.

Bibliography

Cairo, A. *The Functional Art: An Introduction to Information Graphics and Visualization*. Indianapolis: New Riders, 2012.

Drucker, J. *Visualization and Interpretation. Humanistic Approaches to Display*, Cambridge: MIT Press, 2020.

Graham, S., I. Milligan, and S. Weingart. *Exploring Big Historical Data, The Historian's Macroscope*. London: Imperial College Press, 2015.

Kee, K., and T. Compeau, eds. *Seeing the Past with Computers: Experiments with Augmented Reality and Computer Vision for History*. Ann Arbor: University of Michigan Press, 2019.

Rosenberg, D., and A. Grafton. *Cartographies of Time: A History of the Timeline*. New York: Princeton Architectural Press, 2010.

Fred Gibbs
Mapping and Maps in Digital and Public History

Abstract: As maps have become ubiquitous digital interfaces, we have become increasingly numb to how they shape our perception of reality. Digital maps in the context of public history are exciting opportunities to engage a wider public in critical cartography. They give us a chance to pull back the curtain of how digital maps, perhaps even more than their analog counterparts, do not simply objectively depict some external reality, but in fact create and sustain the world around us and our perceptions of it.

Keywords: digital mapping, cartography, public history, community engagement

Introduction

As maps have become ubiquitous digital interfaces, we have become increasingly numb to how they shape our perception of reality. Especially in a world presumptively fueled by "Big Data," it is all too easy to assume that the sheer bigness of the data behind digital maps smooths out anomalies and omissions, and therefore mitigates against human fallacies and biases. The assumed completeness of data-driven digital maps makes it easy to forget that the process of their creation is no less selective, interpretive, and argumentative than even the most polemic analog map.

As remarkably seductive interfaces, it is unsurprising that maps have featured centrally in many outstanding digital public history projects. Considering these, their success, and the general trend of technological sophistication, the trajectory of digital mapping and public history seems to be clearly established in terms of producing more technically sophisticated digital maps that foreground the complexity in which humanists revel. Certainly, we should continue to explore the potential of digital maps along these lines. Yet there are also many good reasons to move beyond maps as historic data visualization tools or interfaces to historical interpretations.

Digital maps in the context of public history are exciting opportunities to engage a wider public in critical cartography. They give us a chance to pull back the curtain of how digital maps, perhaps even more than their analog counterparts, do not simply objectively depict some external reality, but in fact create and sustain the world around us and our perceptions of it. They can help us represent and reflect upon the rhetorical and political power that maps both create and suppress. They can help us rethink how digital maps continually shape and reshape our relationship to space, community identity, and cultural heritage. Digital history and public history scholars are perfectly primed to take a leadership role in rethinking the cartographic potentials and fostering critical interrogation of digital maps.

A Brief History of History on the Map

Over the last decade, digital mapping has blossomed for myriad reasons, many fueled by the increasing accessibility of digital tools.[1] From a technology standpoint, it has never been easier to make and share maps. Google Maps and later alternatives like OpenStreetMap and MapBox have provided relatively easy tools and platforms to create engaging web-based maps. The continued development and improvement of QGIS, the free and open-source desktop GIS (Geographic Information System) software that rivals its expensive but predominant competitor ArcGIS, has brought powerful desktop mapping tools to most scholars. The continued growth of the geospatial web, which makes available and visible all kinds of contemporary and historical data for use with digital maps, has provided what were even a short time ago almost unimaginable possibilities for geospatial visualizations.

The implications for both public and scholarly history were immediate. With the increasing accessibility of digital mapping tools and data, early humanist proselytizers extolled the virtues of GIS technologies to their colleagues, often labeled as historical GIS or hGIS. Unsurprisingly, many historians were skeptical about the positivist implications baked into GIS and the requisite technical skills. Early adopters emphasized in particular the value of cartographic data visualization during the research process.[2] To be sure, imagining changes over large geographic or chronological distances is far easier with a map (or set of maps) than with raw data alone. Perhaps most importantly, the ability to juxtapose different kinds of data – whether demographic, economic, geographic, or cultural – within space and to visualize how these changed over time continues to hold great potential to broaden historical inquiry and analysis.

---

[1] For an excellent overview of the history of GIS and its movement into the humanities, see Todd Presener and David Shepard, "Mapping the Geospatial Turn," in *A New Companion to Digital Humanities*, ed. Susan Schreibman, Ray Siemens, and John Unsworth (Malden, MA and Oxford: Wiley-Blackwell, 2016), 201–212.

[2] Foundational literature includes David J. Bodenhamer, "Creating a Landscape of Memory: The Potential of Humanities GIS," *International Journal of Humanities and Arts Computing* 1.2 (2007): 97–110; Ian N. Gregory and Paul S. Ell, *Historical GIS: Technologies, Methodologies, and Scholarship* (Cambridge: Cambridge University Press, 2007). For early examples of using GIS in historical research, see Amy Hillier and Anne Kelly Knowles, ed. *Placing History: How Maps, Spatial Data, and GIS Are Changing Historical Scholarship*. Redlands (CA: ESRI Press, 2008). For an overview and examples of how historical GIS and spatial history have converged, see Ian N. Gregory and A. Geddes, *Toward Spatial Humanities: Historical GIS and Spatial History* (Bloomington, IN: Indiana University Press, 2014).

As digital mapping technologies matured, a growing number of Digital Humanities and Digital History initiatives (and research centers) aggregated the necessary humanist and technical skills to design and develop innovative digital maps to make historical archives and scholarship more accessible to a broader public. A steady stream of digital projects continually encouraged (and still does) the blending of map interfaces and historical interpretations, ranging across a wide spectrum of projects.[3] To be sure, projects that have developed complex maps (whether as interfaces or data visualizations) have provocatively expanded historiographical imaginations. However, perhaps the siren's song of technological sophistication now distracts from more important opportunities.

Resurfacing from the Deep

As digital maps in public history projects have grown more sophisticated and impressive, a parallel theoretical development that continues to shape project agendas (and grant applications) is the idea of "deep mapping," a way of reinvigorating the humanist potential of GIS and mitigating some of its positivist and reductivist tendencies.[4] As leading proponents have described it, "[d]eep maps augment the infrastructural physical, and environmental themes of conventional mapping to include the cultural, emotional, and perceptual experiences of human behavior."[5] It shares a natural affinity to hGIS, which facilitates "unique postmodern scholarship, an alternate construction of the past that embraces multiplicity, simultaneity, complexity, and subjectivity."[6]

Speculative futures of any field, not least of something as nascent and dynamic as spatial humanities, usually land somewhere between wishful thinking and idyllic fantasy. Without doubt, deep or thick maps are theoretically and rhetorically seductive. But their execution is another matter entirely, and their design and implementation are almost always glossed over altogether. We have to ask: are deep maps really possible without resorting to (more or less) standard web maps as background eye-candy for

---

[3] Recent projects, such as *Placing Segregation* and *Visualizing Emancipation*, have rightfully received accolades as impressive examples of using maps as compelling interfaces to historical interpretations.
[4] David J. Bodenhamer, John Corrigan, and Trevor M. Harris, "Deep Mapping and the Spatial Humanities," *International Journal of Humanities and Arts Computing* 7.1–2 (2013): 170–175.
[5] Trevor M. Harris, John Corrigan, and David J. Bodenhamer, "Conclusion," in *Deep Maps and Spatial Narratives*, ed. David J. Bodenhamer, John Corrigan, and Trevor M. Harris (Bloomington: Indiana University Press, 2015), 232.
[6] David J. Bodenhamer, "Creating a Landscape of Memory: The Potential of Humanities GIS," *International Journal of Humanities and Arts Computing* 1.2 (2007): 97–110, 107.

narratives that appear in pop-up windows or awkwardly scrolling text blocks?[7] Is the interpretive revelation worth the technical investment? Some scholars have suggested that such depth could be conveyed on the production side through more robust data practices, such as deeper metadata or better mapping ontologies;[8] others have focused on the consumption side, such as building narrative into maps.[9] Arguably, some of the most successful implementations of deep maps have been primarily artistic endeavors.[10]

Although scholarship promoting deep mapping has not much mentioned digital or web-based maps as a potential solution to their tangible creation, there seems to be much promise at first glance. After all, many of the early calls for deep mapping came when many digital mapping tools and platforms were relatively new, and nascent technologies are often a tough sell to humanists accustomed to the impressive stability of print and the hegemony of the narrative. Given the continued innovation with mapping technologies and web interfaces, it is tempting to think that we now stand on (or have just crossed) the precipice of a revolution in the digital humanities, at least at the intersection of cartographic technology and humanistic inquiry.

I contend that such a precipice remains a mirage because of the still largely impossible trade-off between depth and usability. Deep maps can become even less engaging than their "shallow" counterparts because the complexity detracts from the fundamental purpose of a map: to improve legibility. Although humanists frequently cringe at the reductive nature of data visualizations, such simplification remains the primary function of any map. Calls for thicker or deeper maps, even in the abstract, quickly summon Borges' (very) short story, "Del rigor en la ciencia," which describes how the Map of the Empire achieved cartographical perfection only after the map and the empire completely coincided (i.e adopting a 1:1 scale). Furthermore, just as usability usually decreases with depth, so does sustainability in the face of the rapid evolution of digital mapping technologies. Exactly what is the historical payoff for tremendous investment in necessarily fragile cartographic interfaces?

---

7 For an interesting critique of deep mapping as related to spatial and digital humanities, see Les Roberts, "Deep Mapping and Spatial Anthropology," *Humanities* 5.5 (2016): 1–7.
8 Nadine Schuurman, "Metadata as a site for imbuing GIS with qualitative information" in *Qualitative GIS: A Mixed Methods Approach*, ed. Meghan Cope and Sarah Elwood (Los Angeles: SAGE, 2009), 41–56. John Corrigan, "Qualitative GIS and Emergent Semantics" in *The Spatial Humanities: GIS and the Future of Humanities Scholarship*, David J Bodenhamer, John Corrigan, and Trevor M Harris (Bloomington: Indiana University Press, 2010), 76–88.
9 P.J. Ethington and N. Toyosawa, "Inscribing the Past: Depth as Narrative in Historical Spacetime," in *Deep Maps and Spatial Narratives*, ed. D. J. Bodenhamer (Bloomington, IN: Indiana University Press, 2014), 72–101.
10 For a fascinating array of deep maps in practice, all of which seem more like art than cartography, see the special issue "Deep Mapping" of *Humanities* 5.1 (2016). See also Iain Biggs, "'Deep mapping': A Brief Introduction," in *Mapping Spectral Traces*, ed. Karen E. Till (Blacksburg: Virginia Tech College of Architecture and Urban Studies, 2010), 5–8.

Cartographic Transparency and Epistemology

Rather than deeper and more complex (and less usable) maps, future work at the intersection of public history and digital maps might endeavor to promote cartographic transparency and data literacy. Whether considering premodern territorial claims or twenty-first-century gerrymandering, the idea that maps reify power and social hierarchies is hardly new.[11] Yet recent digital mapping and web technologies now afford historians distinctly new ways to show, rather than simply describe, the true power of maps. Potentially useful guiding questions: how can digital public history maps serve as objects of critique as much as epistemological statements or arguments? How can we engage with the many ways that cartographic representation directly shapes the kind of knowledge being represented?[12]

While raising vital questions, critical cartography has been directed primarily at geographers and cartographers in almost exclusively theoretical terms.[13] Take for instance the important suggestion that map theory should shift its focus from the nature of maps to their production process – from ontology to ontogenesis.[14] Although now over a decade old, it has been difficult to imagine how this idea could move from theory to practice without simply writing about it in academic journals (as has been the case). Yet the recent intersection of digital mapping and public history has appropriated new digital mapping tools, platforms, and digital publishing techniques that now allows precisely this kind of critical cartography to be implemented more effectively and accessibly. Digital maps with relatively simply interfaces can illustrate and engage (rather than merely explain) map various kinds of map limitations, such as why we should be skeptical of ubiquitous choropleths and clines.[15]

---

11 For two early and now classic formulations, see J.B. Harley, "Deconstructing the Map," *Cartographica* 26.2 (1989): 1–20; Denis Wood, *The Power of Maps* (New York: Guilford Press, 1992).
12 For an example, see Margaret Wickens Pearce and Renee Pualani Louis, "Mapping Indigenous Depth of Place," *American Indian Culture and Research Journal* 32.3 (2008): 107–126.
13 For an interesting history of philosophical engagement of cartographers, with a very useful bibliography for critical cartography, see Jeremy W. Crampton and John Krygier, "An Introduction to Critical Cartography," *ACME: An International E-Journal for Critical Geographies* 4.1 (2006): 11–33; Rob Kitchin, Chris Perkins, and Martin Dodge, "Thinking about Maps," in *Rethinking Maps: New Frontiers in Cartographic Theory*, ed. Martin Dodge, Rob Kitchin, and Chris Perkins (London and New York: Routledge, 2009), 1–25.
14 Rob Kitchin and Martin Dodge, "Rethinking Maps," *Progress in Human Geography* 31.3 (2007): 331–44.
15 Jeremy Crampton, "Rethinking Maps and Identity. Choropleths, Clines, and Biopolitics," in *Rethinking Maps: New Frontiers in Cartographic Theory*, ed. Martin Dodge, Rob Kitchin, and Chris Perkins (London and New York: Routledge, 2009), 26–49. Ian N. Gregory, "'A Map Is Just A Bad Graph': Why Spatial Statistics Are Important In Historical GIS," in *Placing History: How Maps, Spatial Data, and GIS Are Changing Historical Scholarship*, ed. Anne Kelly Knowles and Amy Hillier (Redlands: ESRI Press, 2008), 123–149.

Of course there's a lot more to this than simply choosing the right kind of geographical representation or cartographic conventions. We must also innovate technically simple cartographic ways to show the ambiguity and uncertainty of data. Digital maps and the digital platforms on which they are published allow us highlight, for instance, the (usually invisible) nitty gritty methodological work that goes into creating any map. While we have access to a fantastic bibliography of justifications for hGIS and deep mapping, the difficult work required to move from raw data to legible maps often remains a dangerous mystery. Digital maps in public history provide limitless opportunities to foreground the slippery nature of data, particularly the frequently serpentine process of moving from across spectrum of analog archive, data creation, normalization, and visualization. Although far from easy, this is a significantly more approachable design challenge than the daunting technical coding challenge presented by deep digital maps.

It should be clear that maps alone cannot reframe cartographic thinking. Successful practitioners at the intersection of digital and public history might experiment with new approaches to cartographical essays on digital publishing platforms that interweave various kinds of maps within a cohesive historical narrative. Although historians do not normally foreground epistemological uncertainties inherent in their field, digital maps should engage as much with the particular data behind and the interface around the map as with the map itself.[16] While not necessarily ends in themselves, cartographic transparency and critique should be treated at least as equal to what the map is supposed to communicate on its own.

Cartographic Engagements

Ultimately, it is my hope to bring together a new synergy between critical cartography, spatial humanities, digital mapping, and public history. It may be especially useful to consider maps beyond mere products, but rather as cartographic experiences. By way of conclusion, I want to encourage more post-representational mapping that foregrounds map/data literacy through unconventional cartography and deepens our engagement with maps and how they shape our sense of place.

Precisely because of prevailing assumptions of accuracy and completeness of digital maps, future digital mapping should challenge conventional assumptions about spatial data and the significance of space. We should embrace the

---

[16] For provocative questions that we should apply to maps as well as interfaces, see Stan Ruecker, "Interface As Mediating Actor for Collection Access, Text Analysis, and Experimentation," in *A New Companion to Digital Humanities*, ed. Susan Schreibman, Ray Siemens, and John Unsworth (Malden, MA and Oxford: Wiley-Blackwell, 2016), 397–407.

role for experimental cartography that shakes up expectations and provokes critical reflection on spatial awareness.[17] Some maps may find considerable overlap with the ways in which artists have long used maps to both inspire and ground their social and political commentary.[18] Although unconventional maps have a long history, digital versions uniquely encourage readers to rethink the objectivity of data behind the digital maps they see and use every day. Counterfactual or hypothetical datasets can challenge the authority of the digital over the analog and the myth of objective data representation.

Experimental and counter-mapping projects can reach far beyond individual map users. Community mapping initiatives and projects can nourish collective memories and identities, fostering a sense of shared governance and ownership in the community.[19] Participatory mapping within a public history context can provide a medium through which planners, developers, archivists, scholars, and citizens can better understand the intersection of space and place on local, regional, and national levels. By embracing principles of minimal computing, we can engage with more people through a wider range of mobile devices that help people think more critically about the space they pass through and occupy daily.

Especially within public history, maps have an unusual power to resonate with their broad audiences. We must not settle for the typical map as data representation, but rather design and create objects that encourage critical reflection on how maps are made, what they are, and how they can be used. Multivalent maps in self-reflexive contexts not only provide richer historical interpretations (with an emphasis on plurality), but also cultivate much stronger map literacy and challenge our uncritical assumptions about maps that rise from their ubiquity and presumed data-driven objectivity.

---

17 Stuart C. Aitken and James Craine, "Into the Image and Beyond: Affective Visual Geographies and GIScience," in *Qualitative GIS*, ed. Meghan Cope and Sarah Elwood (Los Angeles: SAGE, 2009), 139–55. For a fun set of examples, see https://www.pinterest.com/claudioenrico/maps-alternate-history/.
18 C. D'Ignazio, "Art and Cartography," in *International Encyclopedia of Human Geography*, ed. Rob Kitchen and Nigel Thrift (Oxford: Elsevier, 2009), 190–206.
19 For more on these points, see Clayton Aldern, "Cartographers without Borders," *Logic* 3. Accessible at https://logicmag.io/03-cartographers-without-borders/; L. C. Manzo, "Finding Common Ground: The Importance of Place Attachment to Community Participation and Planning," *Journal of Planning Literature* 20.4 (2006): 335–350.

Bibliography

Mitchell, Katharyne, and Sarah Elwood. "Engaging Students through Mapping Local History," *The Journal of Geography*, vol. 111,4 (2012): 148–157. Accessible at: https://www.ncbi.nlm.nih.gov/pmc/articles/PMC4306806/

Pacheco, Denise and Velez, Veronica Nelly, "Maps, Mapmaking, and Critical Pedagogy: Exploring GIS and Maps as a Teaching Tool for Social Change," *Seattle Journal for Social Justice*, vol. 8.1, Article 11 (2009): 273–302. Accessible at: https://digitalcommons.law.seattleu.edu/sjsj/vol8/iss1/11

Wieck, Lindsey Passenger, "Blending Local and Spatial History," *Perspectives on History*, September 25, 2017. Accessible at: https://www.historians.org/publications-and-directories/perspectives-on-history/september-2017/blending-local-and-spatial-history-using-carto-to-create-maps-in-the-history-classroom

Wilmott, C. "'Mapping-with': The Politics of (Counter-)classification in OpenStreetMap". *Cartographic Perspectives*, no. 92 (2019): 43–57. Accessible at: https://cartographicperspectives.org/index.php/journal/article/view/1451/1749

Young, Christopher J. and Joseph Ferrandino, "The Old Is New Again: Digital Mapping as an Avenue for Student Learning," *Educause Review*, October 8, 2018. Accessible at: https://er.educause.edu/articles/2018/10/the-old-is-new-again-digital-mapping-as-an-avenue-for-student-learning

Nico Nolden and Eugen Pfister
Gaming and Digital Public History

Abstract: Over the past 50 years the part of digital games in our everyday's media use has consistently grown. They are thus an extremely revealing source for public history. This chapter argues that digital games are among other things a 'historical form.' They are not merely products of entertainment, but as cultural artifacts communicate perceptions of history. Digital games are also 'historical sources.' Because they are developed from the inside of societies, they are shaped by cultures and politics. Furthermore, digital games are 'historical research tools'. Historical simulations can help to understand historical structures and processes. There are however practical, methodical and technical challenges for public historians. Historians must have a comprehensive knowledge of a vast field of academic disciplines from game and media studies, political sciences, sociology to anthropology and philosophy. A historical analysis of games must search for historical game influences but also for other historical conditions and influences.

Keywords: digital history, digital games, video games, popular culture, history of ideas, media history, cultural studies, public history

Locating the Work Field for Public Historians

1. Digital games are a 'historical form.' They are not merely products of entertainment but as cultural artifacts also communicate perceptions of history. Their interactive character distinguishes them however from other mass media, as only they simulate historical agency of players,thus, enabling a new form of constructivistic historical understanding. Historical settings in games have conquered a remarkable share of the global market.[1] They enrich historical culture, and influence historical consciousness, uniting players in communities of commemorative cultures. Public historians should therefore attempt to better understand this new

---

[1] Angela Schwarz, "Computerspiele: Ein Thema für die Geschichtswissenschaft?," in *"Wollten Sie auch immer schon einmal pestverseuchte Kühe auf Ihre Gegner werfen?": Eine fachwissenschaftliche Annährung an Geschichte im Computerspiel*, edited by Angela Schwarz (Münster: Lit, 2012), 10–14; Carl Heinze, *Mittelalter Computer Spiele: Zur Darstellung und Modellierung von Geschichte im populären Computerspiel* (Bielefeld: Transcript, 2012), 109–113; "Deutscher Games-Markt 2018," GAME Bundesverband, https://www.game.de/marktdaten/deutscher-games-markt-2018/, accessed 30 August, 2018; "Gaming in Austria 2019," ovus Österreichischer Verband Unterhaltungssoftware, accessed 27 January, 2020, https://www.ovus.at/news/ueber-fuenf-millionen-oesterreicher-spielen-videospiele/.

historical form (as a source). This would open up classical historical narratology to user interaction, for example,[2] as games allow a nexus of textual traditions and history performances. As a research interest of 'newer cultural history,' digital games require also increased socio-cultural reflection on their technological history.[3] From a perspective of global history on the other hand their players gather globally on a common technological basis. They exchange individual historical perceptions in communities, and form a commemorative culture interwoven worldwide.[4]

2. Digital games are 'historical sources.' Because they are developed from the inside of societies, they are shaped by cultures and politics. Whether intentionally or unintentionally they bear witness to political, social and cultural discourses. As historical sources they allow insights into the inner logic of collective identities and processes of collective memory construction.[5] A history of digital games can only be written meaningfully if they are embedded as artifacts in social, cultural and economic histories. The most urgent challenges right now are the preservation, accessibility and archiving of digital games as sources, because of magnetic, chemical, and technological decay. Museums, exhibitors, and (web) archives struggle to preserve their history in a representative and scientifically satisfying form.[6]

3. Digital games are 'historical research tools.' Historical simulations can help to understand historical structures and processes. Their use for didactic purpose has already been theorized and put into practice.[7] Most historians however still lack the toolkit to implement games as experimental environments. In collaboration with game developers, scientists might better understand how digital games evoke history perceptions in players, how they mediate historical knowledge in communities, and how to utilize both in class.[8]

---

2 Jakob Krameritsch, *Geschichte(n) im Netzwerk. Hypertext und dessen Potenziale für die Produktion, Repräsentation und Rezeption der historischen Erzählung* (Münster: Waxmann, 2009).
3 Martina Heßler, *Kulturgeschichte der Technik* (Frankfurt a. M.: Campus, 2012).
4 Nico Nolden, "Keimzellen verborgener Welten. Globalisierungsprozesse beim MMORPG The Secret World als globalhistorische Zugriffswege," in *Weltmaschine Computerspiel. Digitale Spiele als globalgeschichtliches Phänomen*, edited by Josef Köstlbauer, et al (Vienna: mandelbaum, 2018), 181–201.
5 Eugen Pfister, "'Man spielt nicht mit Hakenkreuzen!' Imaginations of the Holocaust and Crimes Against Humanity During World War II in Digital Games," in *Historia Ludens: The Playing Historian*, edited by Alexander von Lünen et al. (London: Routledge, 2019), 267–284.
6 Raiford Guins, *Game After. A Cultural Study of Video Game Afterlife* (Cambridge: MIT Press, 2014).
7 See Jeremiah McCall, *Gaming the Past* (Routledge: London, 2011).
8 Dawn Spring, "Gaming History: Computer and Video Games as Historical Scholarship," *Rethinking History* 19 (2015): 207–221.

Properties and Methods

Most of the previous historiographic analyses of historical computer games have used a mixture of quantitative and qualitative methods. These have yielded some promising insights.[9] But the lack of a well established common methodological ground made it necessary for each researcher to develop a method on his or her own.

Five attempts to find the core historical properties of digital games showed promise. Carl Heinze for one proposed a model based on the technical system between hardware and software. He only considers as historically relevant what is functionally integrated into game mechanics.[10] By contrast, Martin Zusag's systems analysis model concentrates on the act of digital gaming as an interacting productive-receptive space.[11] The "ecological approach" adapted by Adam Chapman focuses on the trias between players, technological artefacts, and gaming experience, phenomenologically describing digital games as a space where simulation, epistemology, time, space, and affordances form the historical gaming experience.[12] The *History-Game Relations (HGR) framework* of Vincenzo Casso and Mattia Thibault combines structured investigations of game elements and their interplay with research perspectives of historical theory (Historicism, *Annales*, and narratology).[13] Finally, Nico Nolden investigated how interdependent components constitute digital game worlds as a system of historical knowledge supply, that dynamically changes by player's agency, paying special attention to their exchange in a commemorative culture around multiplayer games.[14] Each of these approaches reminds

---

[9] Andrew B.R. Elliott and Matthew Kapell, "To Build a Past that will 'stand the test of time' – Discovering historical Facts, Assembling Historical Narratives," in *Playing with the Past. Digital Games and the Simulation of History* (New York: Bloomsbury, 2013); Alexis Blanchet, *Des Pixels à Hollywood. Cinéma et jeu vidéo, une histoire économique et culturelle* (Paris: Pix'n love, 2010). Also see Eugen Pfister, "Das Beste, was wir von der Geschichte der Computerspiele haben, ist der Enthusiasmus, den sie erregt' – Eine kurze Bestandsaufnahme aktueller Publikationen zur Computerspielhistoriografie," *Neue Politische Literatur* 63.3 (2018): 385–394.
[10] Carl Heinze, *Mittelalter Computer Spiele: Zur Darstellung und Modellierung von Geschichte im populären Computerspiel* (Bielefeld: Transcript, 2012), 23–131, in particular 107.
[11] Martin Zusag, "Digitale Spiele in der Geschichtswissenschaft: Betrachtungen zum Quellenwert und zu den methodischen Grundlagen ihrer wissenschaftlichen Analyse," diploma thesis, University of Vienna (2013), 93.
[12] Adam Chapman, "Affording History: Civilization and the Ecological Approach," in *Playing With the Past: Digital Games and the Simulation of History*, edited by Matthew. W. Kapell and Andrew B. R. Elliott, (London: Bloomsbury, 2013), 62–63; Adam Chapman, *Digital Games as History: How Videogames Represent the Past and Offer Access to Historical Practice* (New York: Routledge, 2016), 20.
[13] Vincenzo I. Casso and Matthia Thibault, "The HGR Framework: A Semiotic Approach to the Representation of History in Digital Games," *gamevironments* 5 (2016): 156–204, http://nbn-resolving.de/urn:nbn:de:gbv:46-00015661-11, accessed 25 September, 2018.
[14] Nico Nolden, *Geschichte und Erinnerung in Computerspielen. Erinnerungskulturelle Wissenssysteme* (Berlin: De Gruyter, 2019), 534–544.

us however of the importance to overcome the tendency of historians, to focus on and the narrative of games while neglecting their aesthetics and ludic elements.

Keeping in mind, that the imagination of history in popular culture is effectively interlinked with our understanding of history, it is remarkable that game developers have so far never been investigated for their conceptions of history.[15] In our own experience, we have encountered four re-occurring types:[16] (1) Some developers focus on objects and material culture, pursuing the idea to reconstruct buildings and artefacts for an authentic representation of history.[17] (2) Others understand history as the individual arrangement of historical perceptions by players from networks of narratives by their own action.[18] (3) The next group favors macro-historical models that simulate military, economics, societal processes, and even concepts like medieval piety on larger scales.[19] (4) A more recent concept emerges as micro-historical world designs. Here developers try to stage everyday historical processes like the late medieval life of various villagers.[20]

Based on this, four aspects can be seen of particular interest for public historians:[21] (1) Digital games show conceptions of any historical period, reaching from prehistoric to contemporary history. (2) They serve as historical sources for the cultural, political and social discourses of their production time. (3) Digital games deal with the history of their industry, the evolution of game design principles or certain game forms as games themselves. (4) Digital games should be seen as epistemological or 'knowledge systems' where the structural elements of their historical form, as stated above, and the forms of depiction, mentioned here, interfere and influence each other. These systems dynamically evolve through player's actions and developer's updates. If a great number of players converge and communicate about their historical perceptions in games, they create a form of commemorative culture.

Because of the constant evolution, the heterogeneity and complexity of digital games, public historians here face some practical, methodical and technical challenges. On the one hand we still lack a common, reliable vocabulary to describe these historical aspects in games. Furthermore, we tend to neglect the historicity of

---

[15] For the partial aspect of "accuracy", examined in more than 150 interviews: Tara Copplestone, "Videogames between Creators, Consumers and Critics", Rethinking History, 21 (2017); S. 415–38. Outlining how to overcome obstacles in order to conduct more comprehensive studies: Yannick Rochat, "A Quantitative Study of Historical Video Games (1981–2015)," in *Historia ludens. The Playing Historian*, edited by Alexander von Lünen et al. (New York: Routledge, 2020), 5–19.
[16] Nico Nolden, *Geschichte und Erinnerung in Computerspielen. Erinnerungskulturelle Wissenssysteme* (Berlin: De Gruyter, 2019), 42–56.
[17] *Anno 1800* (Blue Byte Mainz / Ubisoft, 2019).
[18] *Battlefield 1* (Digital Illusions Creative Entertainment [DICE] / Electronic Arts, 2016).
[19] *Crusader Kings II* (Paradox Development Studio / Paradox Interactive, 2012).
[20] *Kingdom Come: Deliverance* (Warhorse Studios, Warhorse Studios, 2018).
[21] Nico Nolden, *Geschichte und Erinnerung in Computerspielen. Erinnerungskulturelle Wissenssysteme* (Berlin: De Gruyter, 2019), 169–219.

hardware platforms, that is their historical specificity during different time periods. Another deficit is the continuing disregard for the performativity of digital games, i.e. the agency of the players. Digital games essentially form a stage where players themselves produce their individual historical perception.[22] Hence we are dealing with a new variant of historical practices comparable to reenactment or improvisational theatre, already discussed as "doing history."[23] Therefore researchers themselves must reflect on this performative peculiarity in their research, when exploring game worlds and referencing findings. Furthermore, the impact of digital games on commemorative culture has to be considered. Following Aleida Assmann, the 'historical knowledge system' of digital games can thus be regarded as a technical form of our collective historical memory that has been adapted to the needs and circumstances of societies in the digital network age.[24]

In order to do justice to the new medium, we must therefore develop methods and instruments to better analyze the digital game as a historical source. For this we need a comprehensive knowledge of a vast field of academic disciplines from game and media studies, political sciences, sociology to anthropology and philosophy. A historical approach that combines rigid source criticism and historical contextualization will thus eliminate current historiographic misconceptions, such as the persistent master narrative that imagines the history of digital games as pioneer work and economic success of a handful of males, mostly European, American and Asian. Instead, we should consider them as artefacts of specific geographic and functional cultures and economies. Furthermore, most of the accounts on the history of digital games were written by games practitioners. These lean almost exclusively on personal interviews, lack scientific standards and often become uncritical hagiographies. Former employees, and journalists communicate their personal beliefs on history, looking back on games, individuals, enterprises, technologies, platforms, as well as production and creative processes. While such texts are vital for Historians as sources, they must be handled with maximum scientific caution.

A historical analysis of games must search for historical game influences but also for other historical conditions and influences: economic paradigms (neoliberalism e.g.), or influence of international relations on game trends (the cold war or the war on terror for example). We should also regard surrounding sources like marketing material, reviews, forums, manuals, solving aids and cover art. Keeping the performative character in mind, and with it the player, the audio-videographic documentation of the researcher's perspective is vital. It may be accompanied by

---

22 Daniel Giere, *Computerspiele – Medienbildung – historisches Lernen. Zu Repräsentation und Rezeption von Geschichte in digitalen Spielen* (Frankfurt a. M.: Wochenschau, 2019).
23 Sarah Willner, Georg Koch, and Stefanie Samida, eds., *Doing History. Performative Praktiken in der Geschichtskultur* (Münster: Waxmann, 2016).
24 Aleida Assmann, *Erinnerungsräume. Formen und Wandlungen des kulturellen Gedächtnisses* (5th rev. ed., Munich: C. H. Beck, 2010), 19–20.

screenshots and textual descriptions. In digital games, players use various technologies to communicate, like voice communication (VoIP), text chat and so-called "emotes" (in-game gestures of the avatars). A solution to document this fluid, volatile exchange has yet to be found. Until then historical discussion threads among players in game forums are offering initial insights.

Developing Historical Game Studies

Since the 2010s, there has been substantial progress in historical approaches to digital games with the work of historians such as Angela Schwarz, Adam Chapman, Alexis Blanchet, to name only a few.[25] Gaming has also become a topic in academic teaching, but it is still not a regular part of the curricula, despite a continuous demand by students. Social media and digital publishing made historical game studies visible and cross-linked. Blogs inform colleagues, teachers, journalists and developers about specific research.[26] Through Twitter and Facebook young professionals developed research networks, national and cultural borders notwithstanding, experimented with video channels,[27] and audio podcasts.[28] In order to bundle interests, to enable greater interdisciplinary research, and provide advice for societal partners, a German-speaking workgroup for "historical science and digital games" was established in 2015 (AKGWDS). Collaboratively the workgroup negotiated, how to deal appropriately with digital games in historical perspectives, compiling the results into the comprehensive guidelines of a "Manifesto."[29] Since then, many joint publications have originated from members, like an anthology on global history, and an extensive overview of the field at Docupedia.[30]

In the past few years, the history department of the University of Hamburg also gained experience in dealing with digital games.[31] The working group Public History

---

[25] Adam Chapman, Anna Foka, and Jonathan Westin, "Introduction: What is Historical Game Studies?," *Rethinking History* 21.3 (2017): 358–371, https://doi.org/10.1080/13642529.2016.1256638, accessed 2 February, 2020.
[26] Nico Nolden, "Keimling. Innovationen in digitalen Spielen und im Digital Game-Based Learning," https://keimling.niconolden.de, accessed 26 September, 2018; Eugen Pfister, "Spiel Kultur Wissenschaften," https://spielkult.hypotheses.org/, accessed 26 September, 2018.
[27] For example, Romain Vincent, "Jeu vidéo et histoire," http://jeuvideohistoire.com/ and Jan Heinemann, "Let's play history!," https://lepetitcapo.wordpress.com/.
[28] For example, "History Respawned," https://www.historyrespawned.com/.
[29] "gespielt. Blog," Arbeitskreis Geschichtswissenschaft und Digitale Spiele, https://gespielt.hypotheses.org/, accessed 26 September, 2018.
[30] Eugen Pfister and Tobias Winnerling, "Digitale Spiele," *Docupedia-Zeitgeschichte*, https://docupedia.de/zg/Pfister_Winnerling_digitale_spiele_v1_de_2020, accessed 7 February, 2020.
[31] "GameLab und Ludothek," Public History Hamburg, https://www.geschichte.uni-hamburg.de/arbeitsbereiche/public-history/forschung/gamelab.html, accessed 7 February, 2020.

implemented digital games as a historical subject for academic education by analysis, production, presentation and review. A proper *GameLab* has been established to use as a media laboratory and for project seminars. The central apparatus, a live recording box, allows researchers and students to produce audio-visual material as references for research texts. A digital game collection – the *Ludothek* – contains more than 400 items. Both were used by students in project seminars to analyze digital games, to apply historical theories and methods, while allowing them to develop innovative methods and discover new topics. Thus, they were able to translate game content into other media forms like exhibitions or videos. The students presented their work publicly, for example on streaming platforms or in public exhibitions. As public historians they could for example counsel game developers in the future on the appropriate use of history and of the media properties.

Conceptions of History and Commemorative Culture

In the recent past there have been several cases, that have clearly proven the connection between computer games, history and politics: in 2014, for example, French politician Jean-Luc Mélenchon started a dispute concerning the French interpretative sovereignty of the French Revolution on the occasion of *Assassin's Creed: Unity*.[32] In 2018 German journals (and television) debated if digital games should be allowed to use the swastika and other Nazi symbols.[33] In 2019, the German rating institution USK (Unterhaltungssoftware Selbstkontrolle) decided to allow the use of Nazi symbols, if they serve an artistic or educational motive ("Sozialadäquanzklausel").[34] The commemoration of the *Shoah* belongs as an integral part to European Identity and never has been restricted to schoolbooks, documentaries and memorial sites, but had always had a central place in our popular culture. This memory should be kept alive in digital games on a regular basis, as societies negotiate their values and norms through popular culture too. These examples show particularly clearly the importance of a historical reappraisal of digital games not only for science but for society in general.

Future research must also take into account the communities of multiple players, because they establish commemorative cultures. Online-Communities often seem

---

32 *Assassin's Creed: Unity* (Ubisoft Montréal/Ubisoft, 2014). Eugen Pfister,"'Des patriotes, ces abrutis!' Imaginationen der französischen Revolution im digitalen Spiel *Assassin's Creed: Unity*," *Frühneuzeit-Info* 27 (2016): 198–201.
33 Eugen Pfister, "'Man spielt nicht mit Hakenkreuzen!' Imaginations of the Holocaust and Crimes Against Humanity During World War II in Digital Games," in *Historia Ludens: The Playing Historian*, edited by Alexander von Lünen et al. (London: Routledge, 2019), 267–284.
34 Eugen Pfister, "'Man spielt nicht mit Hakenkreuzen!' Imaginations of the Holocaust and Crimes Against Humanity During World War II in Digital Games," in *Historia Ludens: The Playing Historian*, edited by Alexander von Lünen et al. (London: Routledge, 2019), 267.

disreputable, but it has been proven for the contemporary Multiplayer-Shooter *Battlefield 4* and the World War Two scenario of *War Thunder*, that players often discuss historical topics in a civilized manner and on a regular basis.[35] Therefore it is crucial to investigate player communities in and around multiplayer games in a collaborative way, as was carried out by members of the AKGWDS as a pilot project focused on the late medieval-based title *Life is Feudal* in 2016.[36] A detailed case study on the online role-playing game *The Secret World* showed that its players exchanged views over a period of ten years, moreover the historical discourse addressed most of the aspects, that were described above in section 2 on properties and methods.[37] By researching such genuine game forms and their communities, historians may add more detail to show how historical perceptions are negotiated.[38]

Such examples clearly demonstrate that a public history approach to digital games must focus on identities and collective memory, on commemorative culture and a history of ideas in digital games, i.e. the construction and negotiation of a popular understanding of history, as it is shown in games. This is of paramount importance to better understand not only popular perceptions of history, but also a historian's motivations for his or her research, because they too have been socialized by the same imaginations of history in popular culture.

Bibliography

Chapman, Adam. *Digital Games as History: How Videogames Represent the Past and Offer Access to Historical Practice*. New York: Routledge, 2016.

Elliott, Andrew, and Kapell, Matthew, eds. *Playing with the Past. Digital Games and the Simulation of History* New York: Bloomsbury, 2013.

Guins, Raiford. *Game After. A Cultural Study of Video Game Afterlife*. Cambridge: MIT Press, 2014.

Nolden, Nico. *Geschichte und Erinnerung in Computerspielen. Erinnerungskulturelle Wissenssysteme*. Berlin: De Gruyter, 2019.

Pfister, Eugen and Tobias Winnerling. "Digitale Spiele" in *Docupedia-Zeitgeschichte*, https://docupedia.de/zg/Pfister_Winnerling_digitale_spiele_v1_de_2020.

---

[35] Nico Nolden, *Geschichte und Erinnerung in Computerspielen. Erinnerungskulturelle Wissenssysteme* (Berlin: De Gruyter, 2019), 212–214. *Battlefield 4* (Digital Illusions Creative Entertainment (DICE) / Electronic Arts) 2013. *War Thunder* (Gaijin Entertainment / Gaijin Entertainment) 2012.

[36] Nico Nolden, "Life is Futile? Studie des Arbeitskreises am MMO 'Life is Feudal.'" 13 May, 2016, https://gespielt.hypotheses.org/502, accessed March 28, 2019; *Life is Feudal: Your Own* (Bitbox / Bitbox 2015), http://lifeisfeudal.com/.

[37] Nico Nolden, *Geschichte und Erinnerung in Computerspielen. Erinnerungskulturelle Wissenssysteme* (Berlin: De Gruyter, 2019), 531–532.

[38] See Nico Nolden, *Geschichte und Erinnerung in Computerspielen. Erinnerungskulturelle Wissenssysteme* (Berlin: De Gruyter, 2019), 543, for several suggestions.

Tammy S. Gordon
Individuals in the Crowd: Privacy, Online Participatory Curation, and the Public Historian as Private Citizen

Abstract: This essay examines *NC HB2: A Citizens' History*, a digital project that gathers materials related to North Carolina House Bill 2, also known as "the bathroom bill," legislation that promoted discrimination against transgender people and drew protest in the form of direct action and boycott. Drawing on the author's experience as the site's creator, the essay argues that digital crowdsourcing increases the tension between public historians' professional roles and their roles as private citizens and amplifies the power dynamics that shape co-creation.

Keywords: transgender people, privacy, crowdsourcing, digital curation, public historians

On March 23, 2016, the North Carolina (US) Legislature passed House Bill 2, a bill that limited municipal governments' powers to pass nondiscrimination acts, eliminated the right of workers to file discrimination suits in state courts (a feature later amended), and required transgender citizens when in state facilities (including schools) to use the bathrooms that corresponded to the sex listed on their birth certificates.[1] The bill, signed by Governor Pat McCrory shortly before midnight on that same day, became an international symbol of discrimination against transgender people in particular and against LGBTQ citizens more broadly. It ignited vehement protest and economic boycotts both within and outside the state. After a close and contested gubernatorial election in which Democrat Roy Cooper narrowly won over incumbent Republican Pat McCrory, the legislature and the new governor agreed on a repeal. House Bill 142, which repealed HB2 but left the regulation of bathrooms in state facilities under the jurisdiction of the General Assembly and put a moratorium on local non-discrimination ordinances until 2020, became state law on March 30, 2017. While LGBTQ activists and others argued that HB142 undermined transgender individuals' access to civil rights protections, sporting organizations and other entertainment industries were satisfied enough to call off their boycotts. House Bill 2 came and went from North Carolina quite quickly, but it fits into a larger history of public spaces – especially intimate spaces that involve the need for privacy but also close contact between bodies such as

---

[1] The author would like to thank the editors, Mark Tebeau and Serge Noiret, for their suggestions for this essay and digital public historians Sheila Brennan and Sharon Leon for the experience of Doing Digital 2016. For an introduction to transgender history, see Stryker, *Transgender History*.

https://doi.org/10.1515/9783110430295-027

swimming pools, skating rinks, restaurants, clothing stores, and bathrooms – used to enforce racial and gender segregation and dominant white, cisgender norms.[2]

I created *NC HB2: A Citizens' History* in early April of 2016 as an Omeka-powered forum to collect materials related to individuals' experiences of HB2. As of May of 2019, the collection included 173 contributions that range from videos and photos of protests (especially those related to arts and music), letters and photos related to universities, documentation of business reactions, and even bathroom selfies. The site privileges materials related to individual experiences. If you've come to this essay to find an example of best practices in crowdsourcing, digital archives, or community curation, you may be disappointed in this case study. I developed the tool and the policies at the same time, working them out as I processed donations. Relying instead on personal conversations with transgender people I knew, I conducted no formal listening sessions and developed no collaborative vision or strategy. The project included no formal needs assessment study, no summary of research on discrimination against transgender men and women and no analysis of how historical resources may be applied to solutions to the problem. I asked no one for funding. When university lawyers wanted to put a large disclaimer on a black bar directly across every single page of the site, I got irritable and maybe a bit unprofessional. Quite honestly, I deeply feared HB2 and the violence it encouraged, and I created the site rapidly, motivated by the desire to quickly let others know how such a law affected individuals' lives. When afraid and angry, I looked at my training in methodical, careful, data-driven collaborative public history as slow, unresponsive, and unsuitable for the task at hand.

The site and the experiences I have had working on it demonstrate the promises and problems of digital community curation as they relate to privacy, personal safety, and the role of public historians in contemporary political culture. Work on the site has reinforced the importance of public history designed not for, with, or by a mass "public" but by individuals, people who are always more complex, more nuanced, and more powerful than any community to which they or others – including public historians – assign them. In crowdsourcing projects, it is imperative for public historians to work with individuals in all their complexities. This essay centers my experience as a public historian and private citizen in the hope of helping others creating digital history projects who also may find unresolvable tension between some of the field's expectations for public disclosure and the need for privacy.

---

[2] For more on the history of intimacy and public spaces, see Victoria W. Wolcott, *Race, Riots, and Roller Coasters: The Struggle over Segregated Recreation in America* (Philadelphia, Pennsylvania: University of Pennsylvania Press, 2012), and Andrew Kahrl, *The Land Was Ours: African American Beaches from Jim Crow to the Sunbelt South* (Cambridge, Massachusetts: Harvard University Press, 2012). See also Ara Wilson, "The Infrastructure of Intimacy," *Signs: Journal of Women in Culture and Society* 41.2 (2016): 247–280.

Social media users adamantly defend their rights to privacy and control of their content as political dialogue can escalate to abuse rather quickly online. Donations to *NCHB2: A Citizens' History* demonstrate the kinds of materials people feel comfortable sharing in a politically aggressive culture. Of the 173 items donated to the site, most have related to anti-HB2 activism. Protest against the bill emerged from diverse organizational sources: LGBTQ organizations, churches, synagogues, mosques, artists and musicians, and longstanding, experienced civil rights organizations like the North Carolina National Association for the Advancement of Colored People (NAACP). National organizations like the Human Rights Campaign (HRC), the American Civil Liberties Union (ACLU) as well as regional groups like the Campaign for Southern Equality mobilized against the law and in support of LGBTQ civil rights. New associations formed around protest against HB2, such as TurnOUT NC, a local group focused on voters and supported by the ACLU, the HRC, EqualityNC, and the Campaign for Southern Equality. The Air Horn Orchestra, a grassroots weekly protest outside the governor's mansion, gathered anti-HB2 activists to make as much noise as possible for a short time – usually with air horns but also with any noisemaker, demonstrations conducted as "performances" – to insist that pro-HB2 Governor Pat McCrory was not listening to North Carolinians (their motto was "Can You Hear Us Now Pat?"). *NCHB2: A Citizen's History* provided a forum through which activists could amplify their messages: photos of signs and crowd size and videos of protests or individual speakers at protests became a common part of the site.

The site facilitated links among diverse cultural expressions such as music, visual arts, and other media. Music emerged as a mechanism for protesting HB2, and *NCHB2: A Citizen's History* reflected this. When states, and even a country in the case of the United Kingdom, warned against visiting North Carolina or boycotted travel there,[3] event organizer Mike Allen came up with a non-boycott solution that involved support for those affected by the law: the Stand Against HB2 concert series. The series gave musicians in six venues throughout North Carolina the opportunity to express their dissatisfaction with the bill and gather support for repeal. Donors associated with the series placed forty items in the site, including poster artwork for each venue and professional photographs of performers.[4] One of the earliest donations came from members of two bands, Mel Melton and the Wicked Mojos and the Beauty Operators, a photo of all of them squeezed into the bathroom of Deep South The Bar in Raleigh, North Carolina in protest of the bill.[5] One contributor even

---

[3] "UK.gov Notice to British Travellers to North Carolina," screenshot, gordontammy5, "UK.gov notice to British travelers to NC," *NC HB2: A Citizens' History*, accessed April 30, 2019, https://nchb2history.omeka.chass.ncsu.edu/items/show/15.
[4] https://nchb2history.omeka.chass.ncsu.edu/collections/show/5.
[5] Mary Melton, "Mel Melton & The Wicked Mojos and Beauty Operators," *NC HB2: A Citizens' History*, accessed July 30, 2018, https://nchb2history.omeka.chass.ncsu.edu/items/show/68.

donated a home bathroom guitar performance called "This Stall is Your Stall" set to the tune of the Woody Guthrie's "This Land is Your Land."[6]

Donors also chose to share visual culture, such as memes and photos of signs. North Carolina digital artist Eagle White shared 13 memes that protested HB2, often ridiculing particular politicians. White explained the work as a way to use specialized skills:

> I've always been creative, and taught myself a bit of photo-manipulation technique using an online site. I had always used it to put my head/face into absurd situations/pictures, for the amusement of readers of my FB friends. Then HB2 happened. As soon as I could find a copy of the bill (in its entirety) online, I read it, and realized the enormity of its scope, and the spiteful intention of those who passed it. In the days that followed, I became angry that it was being dealt with entirely as a "bathroom bill," when the other portions of the law were equally, if not more damaging. I began making up graphics to post online (using my warped sense of humor, I called them "Art Projects.") It just took off from there.[7]

Photos of signs – mostly expressing anti-HB2 stances – also spoke to a lively visual culture of the debate. Signs made of toilet seats decrying "potty politics," made of poster board declaring "NC Voters and Businesses Did Not Ask for This," and signs of different materials outside businesses declaring the owner's position on the issue (one outside a bookstore declaring the retail space was "now featuring (un) common sense bathrooms") made up about 15 percent of the total number of donations.

As Michel-Rolph Troulliot and the public historians following his lead have shown, silences shape historical memory.[8] While protests, music, and visual culture became well represented, gaps became noticeable. Donors shared written information about visual materials, but only one donor, a professor from the University of North Carolina Wilmington, shared a written piece, a moving account of the challenges facing LGBTQ people, particularly in universities in North Carolina.[9] Donations from people supporting HB2 represented a glaring silence. Items, such as the road sign that declared "We support our govenor [sic] on HB2" outside a business on Highway 49 and photos from a pro-HB2 rally were items I donated. Some HB2 proponents cited university professors (and the media) as individuals seeking to impose liberal values on the Christian Right, and so a site created by a professor hosted on a university server in the political context of HB2 was unlikely to inspire trust. By summer of 2016, the pro-HB2 group the North Carolina Values Commission launched its

---

6 brianmoyerb1, "This Stall is Your Stall," *NC HB2: A Citizens' History*, accessed July 30, 2018, https://nchb2history.omeka.chass.ncsu.edu/items/show/149.
7 Eagle White quoted in "Eagle White Art Project Collection," https://nchb2history.omeka.chass.ncsu.edu/collections/show/6.
8 Troulliot, *Silencing the Past*.
9 peelk, "Postcard from North Carolina," *NC HB2: A Citizens' History*, accessed July 30, 2018, https://nchb2history.omeka.chass.ncsu.edu/items/show/43.

own "share your story" site, with options for family members, business owners, and educators to make contributions, but did not make donations public.[10]

Donations from transgender individuals were few, and those came from activists. This silence is not surprising given that HB2 forced transgender individuals using public spaces to declare their identities as transgender when they may or may not have declared this identity to friends, coworkers, and sometimes even families. Such outing made transgender people even more vulnerable to potential harassment. Hate crimes researcher Rebecca L. Stotzer, in her synthesis of research on violence against transgender people, found multiple studies showing shockingly high rates of violent crimes committed against transgender people, with first victimizations starting commonly in the early teens.[11] Donations from transgender activist like Janice Covington Alison, a long-time democratic activist, and Angela Bridgman, who marched with her birth certificate outside Governor McCrory's house during an Air Horn Orchestra demonstration, represented perspectives of activists used to putting their transgender identities at the forefront. Some individuals helping with *NCHB2: A Citizen's History* did so behind the scenes, assisting with promotion and other tasks, but chose not to donate materials, even anonymously, or be recognized as site creators. Such silences speak to the importance of considering both privacy and safety when designing online, public-facing collections projects. Donations that represented perspectives of transgender activists instead of a broader sample of transgender people was also due to the field's tradition of middle-class white scholars capitalizing on the stories of marginalized communities, "processes [that] ensure and enshrine the co-option of grassroots projects by the nonprofit-industrial complex," as noted by public historian GVGK Tang in the important essay "We need to talk about public history's columbusing problem."[12]

Unquestioned assumptions about the value of making all information public can pair with the rapid response feature of digital collection to undermine individuals' privacy. Traditionally, the needs of local, state, and federally funded museums and historic sites drove our field to embrace a commitment to showing all sides of a topic. Our funders, boards, and visitors often accuse us of lacking objectivity when we highlight history that confronts contemporary power relations. What they are really asking us to do is to function as tools for justifying the status quo. Having worked for 20

---

10 The NC Values Commission provided three versions for contributing stories, one each for family members (https://www.ncvalues.org/share_your_story_family?utm_campaign=2016721_survey&utm_medium=email&utm_source=ncvalues), business owners (https://www.ncvalues.org/share_your_story_business_owners?utm_campaign=2016721_survey&utm_medium=email&utm_source=ncvalues), and educators (https://www.ncvalues.org/share_your_story_educators?utm_campaign=2016721_survey&utm_medium=email&utm_source=ncvalues).
11 Rebecca L. Stotzer, "Violence Against Transgender People," 170–179.
12 GVGK Tang, "We Need to Talk About Public History's Columbusing Problem," History@Work, June 25, 2020, https://ncph.org/history-at-work/we-need-to-talk-about-public-historys-columbusing-problem/#14.

years in public institutions as a historian, curator, and educator, I knew the best practices of engagement: work closely with those living with the effects of historical phenomena through such tools as community forums, listening sessions, shared research, and other ways of communicating and listening that public historians have employed for the last 40 years. But in my haste to get the site live, I cut corners roundly. Very roundly, in big arcing curves. To be honest, the site was a knee-jerk response on my part to the rapidity of the law's passage and the dangers to which it subjected people in my life about whom I care deeply (I am not transgender but instead am pansexual and identify as female, which is what I was assigned at birth). In the moment, when the law passed over night and many of us working in public institutions funded by the state of North Carolina scrambled to come to grips with its implications, I chose to create the site as a way that people outside of North Carolina could hear directly from the people dealing with the law and the political environment that created it. From initial idea to going live took about a week, and I developed policies, language, and site structure based on my experiences curating exhibitions. My decision to use a university server, a decision based on sustainability, slowed the process, for revising the language that university lawyers required to appear and negotiating the disclaimer's appearance on the site took some time. For the most part, I processed donations by myself, staying up late at night moving items through Omeka and conducting conversations with donors via e-mail, Facebook messaging, and Twitter. While others contributed to the promotion and maintenance of the site, they chose not to be named for reasons of privacy, so I became the public face of the project, discretely and carefully channeling inquiries to a small group of individuals who could then choose what to do with them. I sometimes struggled with the absolute necessity of privacy, made many mistakes, and worked to fix them. My best work on this project centered not on getting materials to a cisgender audience who may (or may not!) empathize with transgender people, but in amplifying the activism that led to the law's repeal. Too often our field defaults to what might be termed an "all stories matter" approach to collaboration that has facilitated public access. When peoples' lives are in danger, though, our field's commitment to representing the cacophony of voices borders on malpractice.

Amidst my struggles with maintaining privacy and developing the site quickly, I made two choices that relied on crowdsourced projects' potential for bringing people together for face-to-face conversation. First, as the public face of the project, I attended public events to have conversations, share the site's business card, and encourage donations. In public talks, private conversations, and twitter accounts, I asked people to share what they felt comfortable sharing. Sometimes they wanted to donate, but did not want to use the site's donation tools, so they sent things through email, Facebook, and Twitter, and I gathered the information on the items and uploaded them on their behalf. Sometimes they did not want to donate anything, only to share their experiences with another person. While the site served as an easy way to share materials, many donations came as a result of bodily attendance at an event, from talking with strangers face to face. As a public historian, I knew I would face criticism if I failed to record an event through multiple perspectives, that I would hear it was important to collect items from "all sides," but the law was mean, disingenuous, and potentially dangerous not only to my fellow citizens whom I didn't know well, but also to people very close to me. As a private citizen, I took the project very personally, which confronted my professional commitments to understanding broader public dialogue. Writing in *American Archivist* in 2015, Mario H. Ramirez argued that an archivist's positionality affects the composition of archives and hence the eventual historical narrative. Elucidating the dangers of white privilege on archival efforts, Ramirez notes that "continued assertions of neutrality and objectivity, and a rejection of the 'political,' take for granted an archival subject that is not only homogenous (free of racial stereotypes, societal influence, prejudice, and political opinions), but that also supports whiteness and white privilege in the profession."[13] Like whiteness, heteronormativity in the guise of professional objectivity ultimately damages public historians' abilities to document the present for future historical study. Second, I drew on a community of experts. I was lucky enough to be able to attend Doing Digital 2016, a training camp for public historians new to digital history. Learning from Sharon Leon, Sheila Brennan, and Eric Gonzaba (creator of the award-winning Omeka site *Wearing Gay History*[14]) of the Roy Rosenzweig Center for History and New Media and the other participants in that workshop in the summer of 2016 provided invaluable guidance as the site developed. My technical and theoretical proficiency increased exponentially with such support.

The project revealed to me the power of digital curation to confront our assumptions about and methods for all curation. In traditional exhibit development, much of the collaboration with communities happens during the feasibility assessment and development stages, and ideally the collaboration continues during and after the run of the exhibit. Digital community curation projects can be put together and changed with rapidity, a feature with high potential for responsiveness, but it also moves the bulk of the collaboration out of the fairly neat development timeline traditionally followed for exhibits. This does not mean that crowdsourced, digital curation projects require less engagement or that the public historian's identity and positionality cease to affect the outcome of the project. The potential rapidity of digital projects forces public historians to better confront their own positionality, to negotiate their own citizenship with their professionalism, and to practice managing public service with private life. As Ramirez notes, public historians whose identities come with racial, gender, or class privilege are not used to having their identities constantly assessed in terms of their professionalism and so must make an effort to be conscious of positionality. Our field has a nasty old habit of framing work in terms of "giving people a voice." Such an idea privileges the public historian and condescends

---

13 Mario H. Ramirez, "Being Assumed Not to Be," 340.
14 Eric Gonzaba, *Wearing Gay History*, https://wearinggayhistory.com/.

to the broad range of participants in any public history project. Instead of bestowing the gift of speech, we should be listening carefully and deeply, all the time, so that when the need arises, we are ready to implement projects that meet needs effectively. At the same time, we should not be afraid to use our own voices, loudly if necessary.

Scholars of oral history provide helpful guidance for decision making when framing digital historical projects intended to serve contemporary needs. Margo Shea, writing about her oral history project with women of Northern Ireland, advocates that feminist oral historians move away from the oversimplified idea of "giving a voice" and instead to theorize the functions and methods of contemporary, digital storytelling. Such advice is germane to all public history practice:

> By utilizing an array of digital spaces and embracing the democratic possibilities of social media while maintaining focus on *how* we tell stories and construct meaning together, feminist oral historians stand poised to amplify their own work while inserting an important counterpoint to the shape and tenor of the curated narrative self-representations that proliferate in social media and other digital platforms.[15]

My goal for *NCHB2: A Citizen's History* now is to develop a long-range plan, collaborate more broadly when determining its future, and revisit policies and funding. It should also continue to provide access to individuals' perspectives, for the discrimination at the base of the law continues in our state. My position as a tenured academic both limits and expands possibilities for long-term sustainability for this project. My university provides resources for hosting and for research support, both of which can be utilized to offer more historical perspective on the issue and build a richer archive on the long-term effects of the bill. The university, however, is a state facility, a type of place that transgender people in North Carolina will remember for a long time as unsafe space.

NCHB2: A Citizens' History drew on digital media's major strength of responsiveness; it also drew on digital media's major weakness of responsiveness. At the center of the project was a lesson about the fragility of the core concept of our field: the public. As public historians' innovate in organizing, gathering, and presenting historical information or generating resources for the historians of the future, we must remember that the "crowd" is ultimately a construct, a label that flows and bends with meaning as contexts change and as individuals – including public historians – express and assert their own complexities.

---

15 Margo Shea, "Feminist Oral History Practice in an Era of Digital Self-representation," 295. See also Mary Larson, "'We All Begin with a Story,'" 157–171.

Bibliography

Larson, Mary. "'We All Begin with a Story': Discovery and Discourse in the Digital Realm." In Douglas A. Boyd and Mary A. Larson, *Oral History and Digital Humanities: Voice, Access, and Engagement*. New York: Palgrave Macmillan, 2014: 157–171.
Ramirez, Mario H. "Being Assumed Not to Be: A Critique of Whiteness as an Archival Imperative," *The American Archivist* 7.2 (Fall/Winter 2015): 339–356. DOI: 10.17723/0360-9081.78.2.339.
Shea, Margo. "Feminist Oral History Practice in an Era of Digital Self-representation." In Katrina Srigley, Stacet Zembrzycki and Franca Iacovetta, *Beyond Women's Words: Feminisms and the Practices of Oral History in the Twenty-First Century*. London and New York: Routledge, 2018.
Stotzer, Rebecca L. "Violence Against Transgender People: A Review of United States Data." *Aggression and Violent Behavior* 14.3 (May-June 2009): 170–179.
Stryker, Susan. *Transgender History*. Berkeley, California: Seal Press, 2008.
Troulliot, Michel-Rolph. *Silencing the Past: Power and the Production of History*. Boston, Massachusetts: Beacon Press, 2015.

Rebecca S. Wingo and William G. Thomas III
Building Communities, Reconciling Histories: Can We Make a More Honest History?

Abstract: Using case studies, Rebecca S. Wingo and William G. Thomas III seek to define how historians define and engage with "community" in digital spaces. They identify three types of digital communities (user groups, hybrid projects, and digital group formation) and further posit a checklist of questions designed to ensure equitable academic-community partnerships.

Keywords: community engagement, community formation, ethics, history harvest

Since the social and cultural turn of the 1960s, public historians have created more inclusive and participatory historical spaces through community engagement and a deliberate incorporation of a shared authority.[1] One need look no further than the National Museum of African American History and Culture (NMAAHC) in Washington, DC, to see the power of these twin methods. The museum invited contributions from the public to tell the history of African Americans in the United States and hundreds of people and organizations responded. One of the objects donated to the museum came from Hagerstown, Maryland. It was a slave auction block, but for decades a local organization displayed it to commemorate and celebrate election speeches delivered from it by Andrew Jackson and Henry Clay in 1830. Yet, as President Barack Obama noted during his speech at the museum opening, the slave block told multiple histories: "[D]ay after day, for years, men and women were torn from their spouse or their child, shackled, and bound, and bought, and sold, and bid like cattle, on a stone worn down by the tragedy of over 1,000 bare feet."[2] Exhibited for decades as a monument to two of America's leading political figures, both slaveholders, the auction block held other stories and latent meanings. Voices

---

[1] For more, see Rebecca S. Wingo, Jason A. Heppler, and Paul Schadewald, "Introduction," in *Digital Community Engagement: Partnering Communities with the Academy*, ed. Rebecca S. Wingo, Jason S. Heppler, and Paul Schadewald (University of Cincinnati Press, 2020), especially fn 5. In 1990, Michael Frisch popularized the term "a shared authority" to describe the mechanism by which academics could treat the public as an equal partner in knowledge creation. Frisch, *A Shared Authority: Essays on the Craft and Meaning of Oral and Public History* (Albany: SUNY Press, 1990). See also, Frisch, "From A Shared Authority to the Digital Kitchen, and Back," in *Letting Go?: Sharing Historical Authority in a User-Generated World*, ed. Bill Adair, Benjamin Filene, and Laura Koloski (Philadelphia: The Pew Center for Arts and Heritage, 2011): 126–137.

[2] Katie Reilly, "Read President Obama's speech at the Museum of African American History and Culture," *Time* (September 24, 2016), accessed August 7, 2018, http://time.com/4506800/barack-obama-african-american-history-museum-transcript/.

long silenced included those who also stood on its rough surface, other men, women, and children who played just as much of a role in shaping the nation as the slaveholders who gave stump speeches from its height.

Obama's reinterpretation of the block in a museum dedicated to the history of the people enslaved on it exemplifies a more critically aware conversation about the representation and re-presentation of history in American public spaces. From this same ethos stems discussions of Confederate monuments. After debates over public history turned deadly in Charlottesville, it became increasingly clear to many Americans that objects, whether monuments or named buildings, offered a particular version of historical memory, that a series of historical interpretations came with the stone and marble, and that these could be, and should be, critiqued and reconsidered.[3]

Meanwhile the medium for public discussion around history has expanded to include digital spaces and platforms.[4] As the web moved from "read-only" to "read-write," and as social media communities exploded, non-academic critics suddenly had a means to communicate their interpretations of historical objects and sites.[5] Digital tools like geomapping offered opportunities online to re-present historical objects and work with communities to reach a more honest, more complete account of our shared past. We believe digital public historians are poised to make advances in community engagement by pushing the traditional definitions of community, and even the ways in which they form. In so doing, historians can buttress the tenants of a shared authority and continue to challenge the traditional role of scholars as the primary, even privileged, keepers and producers of history.

---

3 Joe Heim, "Recounting a Day of Rage, Hate, Violence and Death," *Washington Post* (August 14, 2017), accessed November 6, 2018, https://www.washingtonpost.com/graphics/2017/local/charlottesville-timeline/; and Farah Stockman, "Who were the Counterprotesters in Charlottesville?" *New York Times* (August 14, 2017), accessed November 6, 2018, https://www.nytimes.com/2017/08/14/us/who-were-the-counterprotesters-in-charlottesville.html.

4 Contributors to Dorothy Kim and Jesse Stommel's *Disrupting the Digital Humanities* comprise a self-described "motley crew" that seek to critically engage issues around digital humanities' own "embedded practices in relation to issues around multilingualism, race, gender, disability, and global praxis." Of any recent volume, it does the most work at picking at loose threads and critiquing digital humanities' narrative of egalitarianism. See Dorothy Kim and Jesse Stommel, *Disrupting the Digital Humanities* (New York: Punctum Books, 2018).

5 Sharon Leon, "Complexity and Collaboration: Doing Public History in Digital Environments," in *The Oxford Handbook of Public History*, ed. Paula Hamilton and James B. Gardner (New York: Oxford University Press, 2017), 58–63.

Types of Digital Community Engagement

Communities have traditionally formed by three intersecting spaces: geography, demography, or shared interest.[6] Through spaces like these, Benedict Anderson argues, communities are bound by a "deep, horizontal comradeship."[7] Digital platforms have added new, exciting spaces for community formation, especially around history. Dynamic online communities are imagined by their constituencies and the past is the unifying force that brings them together. They are bonded by both common interest and shared motivation even though they may have never gathered in person. In fact, members of these communities increasingly become acquainted in virtual spaces first and in person only later, if they ever do meet. Such communities have grown up alongside HTML protocols, chatrooms, and digital history projects. They are the public – online.

Digital community formation in historical projects typically falls into one of three categories. The first is through user communities that form around a historical question or mission. Many of these are digitization projects. For example, the New York Public Library's award-winning project *What's on the Menu?* asked the public to transcribe the corpus of menus in their archives. As of 2019, a community of volunteers transcribed more than 1.3 million dishes from over 17,500 historic New York City menus.[8] The *Mapping Prejudice* project investigating housing covenants and restrictions in Minneapolis, Minnesota, also tapped into a vibrant transcription community through a crowdsourcing tool called Zooniverse.[9] Similarly, the Civil War Photo Sleuth project out of Virginia Tech uses BetaFace facial recognition software and a community of users to identify unknown Civil War soldiers in their archival photographs (Fig. 1).[10]

As demonstrated in these projects, the public is eager to contribute to and become part of historical dialogue in digital spaces.[11] The communities that formed around each project play a powerful role in the projects they help produce. Their

---

[6] Wingo et al., "Introduction."
[7] Benedict Anderson, *Imagined Communities: Reflections on the Origin and Spread of Nationalism* (New York: Verso, 2016), 7.
[8] *What's on the Menu?*, New York Public Library, accessed July 28, 2019, http://menus.nypl.org/.
[9] Kirsten Delegard and Ryan Mattke, *Mapping Prejudice*, accessed September 12, 2018, http://mappingprejudice.org/.
[10] Kurt Luther, Ron Coddington, and Paul Quigley, *Civil War Photo Sleuth*, accessed July 11, 2019, https://www.civilwarphotosleuth.com/. See also Kurt Luther, "Photo Sleuth: New Digital Tool Redefines Photo Sleuthing," *Military Images Magazine* 35.3 (Summer 2017), https://militaryimages.atavist.com/photo-sleuth-summer-2017.
[11] For a candid conversation about developing trust and empowering citizen scholars to assert their own dialogic place in the presentation and re-presentation of history, see John Kou Wei Tchen and Liz Ševčenko, "The 'Dialogic Museum' Revisited: A Collaborative Reflection" in *Letting Go? Sharing Historical Authority in a User-Generated World*, ed. Bill Adair, Benjamin Filene, and Laura Koloski (Philadelphia: The Pew Center for the Arts & Heritage, 2011), 80–95.

expertise may even shape the ways in which scholars ask their questions as the users often spend more time investigating the minutia of historical sources than the academic partners. Their expertise comes in many forms – noting the make and model of a Civil War locomotive and ascertaining its exact specifications and year of production, for instance – and contributes to the richness of new knowledge. Their work often advances the project's overall mission in clearly discernable ways. But despite these contributions, user communities do not often share authority with the project scholars.

Fig. 1: Artwork by Ron Coddington, Civil War Photo Sleuth Project, 2017.

The second type of digital community engagement uses digital outcomes for more traditional engagement. A good example of this hybrid community project is the History Harvest, a community-based, student-driven digital archive.[12] Students

---

[12] The History Harvest was developed at the University of Nebraska-Lincoln by William G. Thomas III and Patrick D. Jones. For more information, visit http://historyharvest.unl.edu. See also Thomas, Jones, and Andrew Witmer, "History Harvests: What Happens When Students Collect and Digitize the People's History?" *Perspectives* (January 1, 2013), https://www.historians.org/publications-and-directories/perspectives-on-history/january-2013/history-harvests and Rebecca S. Wingo and Amy C. Sullivan, "Remembering Rondo: An Inside View of the History Harvest," *Perspectives* (March 1, 2017), https://www.historians.org/publications-and-directories/perspectives-on-history/march-2017/remembering-rondo-an-inside-view-of-a-history-harvest.

organize a one-day event in which community members bring their items of significance, students digitize them and record a story about the items, and then contributors take their items back home. The format might be compared to Antiques Roadshow, except that understanding the historical rather than monetary value is the goal.

The objects people bring to a History Harvest are often stunning. At the North Omaha History Harvest in 2011, Warren Taylor contributed an 1840 penny and a collapsible drinking cup that belonged to his great-great-grandmother. She carried the "Liberty" penny with her until the day she died, he told the students, because when she was enslaved she was not allowed to have any money. On a small, folded piece of paper with the outline of the penny still visible, Taylor's great-aunt wrote: "This was my grandmother's penny." (Fig. 2) At the 2016 Remembering Rondo History Harvest in Minnesota, an anonymous contributor brought a unique scrapbook of ephemera relating to the Inner City Players, a short-lived Black theatre company founded by Abdul Salaam el Razzac in the 1970s. The collection is truly one-of-a-kind.[13]

The History Harvest, and projects like it, rely heavily on building trust with communities. This is difficult, however, without face-to-face engagement. There is no substitute for making announcements at church services, asking local businesses to hang flyers, or attending community functions as a representative of the academic partnership. The Harvest emphasizes the value of the community partners as citizen scholars, as experts of their own histories. This is much closer to a shared authority than developing a user community, but also requires a deeper investment from the community involved.

Fig. 2: The penny from Warren Taylor's great-great-grandmother and the note from his great-aunt. Warren Taylor Collection, North Omaha History Harvest, 2011, University of Nebraska-Lincoln, https://historyharvest.unl.edu/items/show/105 accessed August 1, 2020.

---

13 "Scrapbook of the Inner City Players," *Rondo History Harvest*, accessed July 12, 2019, http://omeka.macalester.edu/rondo/items/show/40.

The third type of digital community engagement occurs when historians create or curate communities that did not know they shared a common past. Scholars have done this on both local and national stages. For example, Amy Sullivan (Macalester College) organized a History Harvest to collect stories from Minneapolis' harm reduction community active in the 80s and 90s. Before harm reduction became synonymous with needle exchange programs in the current opioid crisis, grassroots activists worked with homeless youth, passed out condoms to prevent the spread of AIDS/HIV, and provided outreach to women and LGBTQIA populations. While these communities worked in the same city at the same time, their efforts were rarely coordinated if they were aware of each other at all. Sullivan used Facebook to unite a community of these organizers and generate excitement over the History Harvest. Until they assembled for the event in May 2017, these important activists did not realize they were part of a collective history.[14] With a minimal budget, Sullivan leveraged a digital platform to create a community that met in person to contribute to a digital project about an untold history.

At Georgetown University a similar process unfolded, one not directed or controled by the university. In 2016 the *New York Times* published a leading story on the university's 1838 sale of 272 enslaved men, women, and children to sugar planters in Louisiana. Two descendant community organizations subsequently emerged. The Louisiana-based GU272 Descendants Association brought together modern descendants of the families the university sold. Separately, a Georgetown alumnus began the Georgetown Memory Project and used DNA testing to identify all living descendants of the families. Both groups formed quickly and outside of the university, and both communicated and grew through digital spaces, such as Ancestry.com and 23andme. Again, digital platforms united people who did not otherwise know they comprised a community.

Despite these communities, there was no clearly defined role for the descendants in shaping the memory and interpretation of the history of the sale. And the history at stake in the Georgetown case concerns the actions of the university, the Society of Jesus, and the Catholic Church, because each participated both in the sale itself and in the subsequent historical omission. When the university formed a working group to study the matter, the administration turned exclusively to professional historians, lawyers, and academics. The university's working group did not include a single descendant. Nevertheless, the group met with descendant stakeholders and drafted a final report recommending several ways Georgetown should repair the historical

---

[14] Amy Sullivan, "Seen and Heard: Using DiCE to Reconnect Communities and Enrich Pedagogy," in *Digital Community Engagement*, eds. Rebecca S. Wingo, Jason A. Heppler, and Paul Schadewald (Cincinnati: University of Cincinnati Press, 2020), https://ucincinnatipress.manifoldapp.org/read/digital-community-engagement/section/ca505396-0d0b-4bad-ba6e-8dbb79679265. See also Sullivan, *When 'Rock Bottom' Means Death* (Minneapolis: University of Minnesota Press, 2020) and http://amycsullivan.net/mnopioidproject/archive/.

trauma of the sale. Georgetown University and the Society of Jesus apologized for the sin of enslavement. The university renamed buildings and began digitizing its archival materials related to slavery. Descendants were accorded preferential status in admission decisions at the university. But the omission of descendants from the working group proved difficult for Georgetown to overcome. Initially, the university decided on its own to rename a building "Isaac Hall" for the first person listed in the 1838 sale. But descendants quickly pointed out that his full name should be used – Isaac Hawkins – and that it was presumptive and an insult to his memory not to do so. Georgetown's administration renamed the building "Isaac Hawkins Hall." The university and the descendant community organizations continue to navigate and negotiate what a more honest, more complete history means for one other.[15]

Community Engagement in Practice

Georgetown's missteps in developing a working group dis not model the best practices for building trust between communities and their academic partners. But the project does align with nascent efforts in digital public history to repair, reconstruct, and make visible what has been otherwise rendered invisible in the artifacts and records. By opening digital opportunities for communities to engage in ways they have not before, historians are being pulled deeper into a phase of public work where we are called on to help repair the past.[16] What could historians accomplish if we worked with communities through digital media to create, interpret, and represent history? If we invest in a shared authority with the public, could we reach a more honest history?

We have assembled a list of questions that, when considered in advance, can augment the equity of the community partnership – with or without a digital component:[17]

---

[15] Report of the Working Group on Slavery, Memory, and Reconciliation to the President of Georgetown University, Summer 2016, accessed November 8, 2018, http://slavery.georgetown.edu/. See also, William G. Thomas III, *A Question of Freedom: The Families Who Challenged Slavery from the Nation's Founding to the Civil War* (New Haven: Yale University Press, 2020) and http://earlywashingtondc.org/.

[16] While there are many solitary and unique examples of this type of work, foremost in the field is the International Coalition of Sites of Conscience, founded in 1999, that brings together places "united by their common commitment to connect past to present, memory to action." "About Us," International Coalition of Sites of Conscience, accessed November 1, 2018, https://www.sitesofconscience.org/en/who-we-are/about-us/. See also Arguing with Digital History working group, "Digital History and Argument," white paper, Roy Rosenzweig Center for History and New Media (November 13, 2017): 10, https://rrchnm.org/argument-white-paper/.

[17] Inspiration for these questions come from Sheila Brennan, "Public, First," in *Debates in the Digital Humanities*, ed. Matthew K. Gold and Lauren Klein (Minneapolis: University of Minnesota Press,

1. Is the partnership mutually beneficial and reciprocal?
2. Are all stakeholders represented among the leadership and on the editorial boards or committees?
3. Are the goals, objectives, and governance of the partnership co-created and clearly defined?
4. Are meetings/gatherings and project updates accessible to all stakeholders?
5. Is there a clear understanding of how the project will be assessed?

Digital tools can change the dynamics, longevity, and sustainability of a project. We have identified three questions that pertain directly to the lifespan of a digital community engagement project:

6. Who controls / will control the digital content?.
7. Are any of the tools used proprietary and how will on-going costs be covered?
8. Is there a clear data management plan with explicit agreements about project sustainability?

Not all of these questions will remain relevant as technologies change, but one thing remains constant: the need for scholars and community stakeholders alike to generate ethical partnerships that draw upon the core tenants of a shared authority and thoughtful engagement. The questions we present here are offered as starting points, as guiding ideas, and as a means to reframe and reorient how we work with and in communities. It is up to scholars and the communities with whom they collaborate to make sure the partnerships in the present and future rectify rather than replicate old power structures of intellectual elitism and mask historical injustices.[18]

The role of the digital public historian is changing alongside the technologies they use – shifting as history is performed, reconstituted, and repaired in digital form – and recognition for that work is inconsistent. Community-engaged digital public history projects present new challenges to versioning that traditional scholars have taken for granted. We know what a book looks like; we also know what a book will look like in 50 years. Digital projects have a different life-cycle. They are flexible and dynamic, both as a result of technology and their expansion (or contraction). The first release is rarely the final version, which means that we have an ephemerality of scholarship relative to our peers. With community-based projects

---

2016) and Nina Simon, *The Participatory Museum* (Santa Cruz: Museum 2.0, 2010), 270–271, as well as our own experiences working with communities through the History Harvest.

18 Nina Simon cites the community engagement work of the Wing Luke Asian Museum as one of the leaders in the field of community engaged practices that embrace a shared authority over their history and presentation. Simon, *The Participatory Museum*, 264–271. The Wing Luke Asian Museum has also published extensively about their model: Cassie Chinn, *Wing Luke Asian Museum Community-based Exhibition Model* (Seattle: Wing Luke Asian Museum, 2006). See also, Arguing with Digital History working group, "Digital History and Argument," 10.

in particular, control may transition back to the community, or the project may never reach formal "completion." Our national organizations have collectively issued guidelines for valuing community engaged work, but it has yet to filter downstream.[19]

Digital public historians create projects for many reasons. Community engagement remains a principal design strategy as ways to build and support audience for digital projects. Often, digital public historians enter into community partnerships which offer both obstacles and opportunities. Harnessing the power of digital projects to engage with communities, or even redefine community formation, holds new promise and new challenges for historians. Perhaps the bigger challenge is training historians to see that the public is always around us, online and otherwise.

"Come here and see the power of your own agency," Obama beckoned in his remarks at the NMAAHC, a museum that accentuated the actions people took to change history. Historical contributions like those made to the NMAAHC offer a different paradigm for public history, a re-presentation of historical objects whose full histories have yet to be told. Can we ensure that digital (and hybrid) spaces hold the same promise?

Bibliography

Gold, Matthew K. and Klein, Lauren F., eds. *Debates in the Digital Humanities*. Minneapolis: University of Minnesota Press, 2016.
Adair, Bill, Benjamin Filene, and Laura Koloski, eds. *Letting Go? Sharing Historical Authority in a User-Generated World*. Philadelphia: The Pew Center for the Arts & Heritage, 2011.
Kim, Dorothy and Jesse Stommel, eds. *Disrupting the Digital Humanities*. New York: Punctum Books, 2018.
Simon, Nina. *The Participatory Museum*. Santa Cruz: Museum 2.0, 2010.
Wingo, Rebecca S., Jason A. Heppler, and Paul Schadewald, eds. *Digital Community Engagement: Partnering Communities with the Academy*. Cincinnati: University of Cincinnati Press, 2020.

---

19 Kristin Ahlberg et al, "Tenure, Promotion, and the Publicly Engaged Academic Historian: A White Paper by the Working Group on Evaluating Public History Scholarship," 6–7, https://www.oah.org/site/assets/files/1041/engaged_historian_white_paper_-final.pdf; and Modupe Labode, "Does it count? Promotion, tenure, and evaluation of public history scholarship," National Council of Public History, (December 6, 2017), accessed August 5, 2018, http://ncph.org/history-at-work/does-it-count/.

Sandra Camarda
Cybermemorials: Remembrance and Places of Memory in the Digital Age

Abstract: The rise of user-generated media culture and the diffusion of digital technologies have contributed to the production of new forms of mnemonic practices that coexist with, enhance, or altogether replace traditional memorial sites.

Cybermemorials range from virtual spaces on the Internet, such as webpages and social media platforms, to physical memorials enhanced by means of digital artefacts and mixed-reality technologies. While the design and scope of these new forms of collective memorialization can vary significantly, they display formal analogies and reflect a general trend towards a de-institutionalization of commemoration through spontaneous participation, emotion, and feeling.

The prosumer culture generated by digital media offers new possibilities to build narratives around historical events and collaboratively construct public memory. Through interactive communication platforms, digital memorials are able to simultaneously address a global audience, enticing new forms of democratic participation and understanding.

Keywords: digital memorials, participation, public memorialisation, user-generated media culture, digital technologies, virtual environments

Introduction

Throughout history, monuments and memorials have embodied societal values, functioning as sites for the collective mourning and remembrance of the dead, the celebration of national heroes and the profession of ideological statements. As familiar elements of the urban landscape, they provide a focal point for the communities to mourn, sustain the recollection of historical events, and come to terms with death and loss.[1] From conventional bronze statues, plaques, headstones and plinths, to memorial parks and landmarks, their presence – or absence[2] – entices different rituals

---

[1] Michael Rowlands, "Trauma, Memory and Memorials," *British Journal of Psychotherapy* 15.1 (1998): 54–64.
[2] Several scholars have pointed out how the destruction and absence of memorials are equally relevant in constructing cultural meanings and identities. Far from being a linear process, the relation between remembering and forgetting always displays a tension deriving from what is there and what is not. The absence of the monument – the empty space left behind – evokes its presence, pointing to what is amiss and reminding the community of specific historical events. See Mary Douglas and Baron Isherwood's seminal work *The World of Goods: Towards an Anthropology of*

and social practices, while their meaning and reception shifts and overlaps with time revealing clues about the processes of identity construction and historical re-orientation. For their ability to promote active remembering and continually refashion, reinforce or challenge social traditions and identities, memorials have been at the center of heated public debates and controversies and a topic of interest for a vast array of disciplines ranging from art history to anthropology, sociology, architecture, cultural geography, and memory studies.

During the late nineteenth and early twentieth centuries, the sites of public memorialization tended to be highly institutionalized spaces controlled predominantly by religious or governmental authorities.[3] Since the end of the Second World War, however, the modes and practices of commemoration have begun to change and broaden.[4] Over the past decades, there has been an extraordinary proliferation of public memorials dedicated to a wide variety of causes, from grandiose, carefully planned and state-sanctioned architectural endeavours, to impromptu forms of vernacular memorialization – such as temporary shrines for leaving flowers or tokens set up spontaneously by local communities in the wake of public tragedies.[5]

Contemporary commemorative culture has experienced a major shift from 'traditional' monuments, increasingly perceived as aesthetically, politically, and ethically obsolete, to memorials focused on the sentiment and the experiential, rejecting monolithic master narratives in favour of more diverse, conflicting and subjective perspectives.[6] As argued by Erika Doss, memorials embody a cultural turn toward public feeling, where the understanding of history, memory and identity occur through the experience of affect and emotion.[7] The leaning of contemporary memorials towards the representation of individual memories and traumas is evident in the architectural choices, symbolism, and in the social practices surrounding the sites.[8] Additionally, after the end of the Cold War, the impact of globalization and the emergence of a

---

Consumption (London: Allen Lane, 1979). Also, see Victor Buchli, Gavin Lucas, and Cox, Margaret. *Archaeologies of the Contemporary Past* (New York: Routledge, 2001), 80; Arjun Appadurai's *Fear of Small Numbers: An Essay on the Geography of Anger* (London: Duke University Press, 2006), and Thomas M. Hawley's *The Remains of War: Bodies Politics, and the Search for American Soldiers Unaccounted for in Southeast Asia* (Durham: Duke University Press, 2005).

3 John R Gillis, *Commemorations: The Politics of National Identity* (Princeton: Princeton University Press, 1994), 12–13.

4 Andrew M. Shanken, "Planning Memory: Living Memorials in the United States during World War II," *The Art Bulletin* 84:1 (2002): 130–147.

5 Erika Doss, *The Emotional Life of Contemporary Public Memorials: Towards a Theory of Temporary Memorials* (Amsterdam: Amsterdam University Press, 2008).

6 Erika Doss, *Memorial Mania: Public Feeling in America* (Chicago: University of Chicago Press, 2010), 5. On the topic of anti-monumentalism, see Andreas Huyssen, "Monumental Seduction," *New German Critique* 69 (1996): 181–200.

7 Erika Doss, *Memorial Mania: Public Feeling in America* (Chicago: University of Chicago Press, 2010).

8 Sabina Tanović, *Designing Memory: The Architecture of Commemoration in Europe, 1914 to the Present* (Cambridge: Cambridge University Press, 2019), 66–78.

global public sphere have dramatically reconfigured the spaces of memory.[9] Tragedies such as the Holocaust have been used as universal tropes for historical trauma,[10] and memorials have started to be erected not only to commemorate the victims of wars and catastrophes but also as a form of reparation for historical injustices such as slavery, dispossessions, and persecutions.[11]

In relation to this experiential turn, Alison Landsberg argues that a new form of public cultural memory, a "prosthetic memory," emerges when a person is confronted with a historical fact presented at an experiential site.[12] Modern technologies of mass culture have the ability to function as technologies of memory, transporting individuals through space and time and allowing them to learn about historical events through feeling and experience. Moreover, they contribute to further blur the distinction between individual and collective memories, introducing the experiential as a key mode of knowledge acquisition.[13]

The rise of user-generated media culture and the diffusion of digital technologies have contributed to the production of new forms of mnemonic practices that coexist with, enhance, or altogether replace traditional memorial sites. Andrew Hoskins describes how the very use of these systems contributes to the creation of an "emergent digital network memory," forged and driven by the interactions and connectivities enabled by digital social networks.[14] Under the impact of the digital, memories have evolved along unpredictable trajectories, undergoing constant transformations and becoming more dynamic, ephemeral and fluid.

'Digital memorials' or 'cybermemorials' are wide umbrella terms that emerged in the late-1990s to describe a variety of commemorative sites ranging from virtual spaces on the Internet, such as webpages and social media platforms, to physical memorials enhanced by means of digital artefacts and mixed-reality technologies. While the design and scope of these new forms of collective memorialization can vary significantly, they display formal analogies and reflect a general trend towards a de-institutionalization of commemoration through spontaneous participation and feeling. Furthermore, through interactive communication platforms, digital memorials

---

[9] A. Assmann and S. Conrad, eds., *Memory in a Global Age: Discourses, Practices and Trajectories*, Palgrave Macmillan Memory Studies (London: Palgrave Macmillan, 2010), 1–2.
[10] Andreas Huyssen, *Present Pasts: Urban Palimpsests and the Politics of Memory* (Stanford: Stanford University Press, 2003), 13.
[11] See Jie-Hyun Lim, "Victimhood Nationalism in Contested Memories: National Mourning and Global Accountability" in *Memory in a Global Age*, edited by A. Assmann and S. Conrad, 138–162.
[12] Alison Landsberg, *Prosthetic Memory: The Transformation of American Remembrance in the Age of Mass Culture* (New York: Columbia University Press, 2004), 2.
[13] Alison Landsberg, Prosthetic Memory: The Transformation of American Remembrance in the Age of Mass Culture (New York: Columbia University Press, 2004), 1.
[14] Andrew Hoskins, "Digital Network Memory" in *Mediation, Remediation, and the Dynamics of Cultural Memory*, edited by Astrid Erll and Ann Rigney, in Collaboration with Laura Basu and Paulus Bijl (Berlin: De Gruyter, 2009), 92.

are able to simultaneously address a global audience, enticing new forms of democratic participation and understanding of historical events.[15]

Starting from the above considerations, this contribution will provide an overview of these emerging patterns of collective remembrance, identifying their inherent characteristics, their modes of production and fruition, and the struggles over public memory emerging from official and vernacular narratives within digital commemorative environments.

Web Memorials

The earliest examples of digital memorials began to appear in the late-1990s when the extensive adoption of the Internet allowed for new modes of communication and interaction.[16] The proliferation of virtual communities and the progressive integration of a digital dimension into people's daily lives affected also the manifestations of grief and commemoration. Networks providing social support for mourning families and individuals, bereavement online resources and sites with virtual graves and obituaries have become increasingly common.[17]

Aside from these forms of individual commemorative practices, physical memorial sites started to have a presence online, with webpages serving as promotional and fundraising instruments or providing general information on the accessibility to the locations, the history of those particular memorials and the events they commemorate.[18]

From the early 2000s, the advent of blogs, social media platforms and easy-to-use content management systems, has greatly facilitated the creation and publishing of content online. Gradually, users have become "prosumers" – simultaneous producers and consumers – and the number of online memorials has grown exponentially.[19]

---

15 A. Assmann and S. Conrad, eds., *Memory in a Global Age: Discourses, Practices and Trajectories*, Palgrave Macmillan Memory Studies (London: Palgrave Macmillan, 2010), 4–5.
16 Manuel Castells, *The Rise of the Network Society*. 2nd ed., 1942- Information Age; v. 1 (Oxford: Wiley-Blackwell, 2010), 355–406.
17 Early examples include the American database "Find a Grave" (https://www.findagrave.com); commemorative sites such as the World Wide Cemetery (https://cemetery.org) and the Pet Loss Grief Support (https://www.petloss.com). See: Carla J. Sofka, "Social Support 'Internetworks,' Caskets for Sale, and More: Thanatology and the Information Superhighway," *Death Studies* 21.6 (1 November, 1997): 553–574; Pamela Roberts, "Here Today and Cyberspace Tomorrow: Memorials and Bereavement Support on the Web," *Generations* 28.2 (2004): 41–46; Scott H. Church, "Digital Gravescapes: Digital Memorializing on Facebook," *Information Society* 29.3 (5 June, 2013): 184–189; "Hans Geser: Death Memorials in the http://socio.ch/intcom/t_hgeser07.htm, accessed 6 May, 2020.
18 Johanna Hartelius, "'Leave a Message of Hope or Tribute': Digital Memorializing as Public Deliberation," *Argumentation and Advocacy* 47.2 (1 September, 2010): 68.
19 Timothy Recuber, "The Prosumption of Commemoration: Disasters, Digital Memory Banks, and Online Collective Memory," *American Behavioral Scientist* 56.4 (2012): 531.

One of the distinctive traits of web memorials is their interactive and participatory nature. Whether through a forum, guestbook or by means of a digital alias, visitors are prompted to share their stories online. The result is a prosumer-oriented accumulation of personal narratives in the form of digital archives and memory banks.[20] Other than functioning as therapeutic channels for grief and commemoration, these platforms collect users' interpretations of historical events and absorb them into the memorial's overall message prompting an ongoing public dialogue.[21]

Pierre Nora argues that modern memory is, above all, archival, predicated on the urge to record, collect and classify historical material traces, a task traditionally carried out by institutions of memory – such as museums and archives – associated with the rise of capitalism and the modern nation-state.[22] Digital memory, however, as contended by Ekaterina Haskins, "collapses the assumed distinction between modern 'archival' memory and traditional 'lived' one" by combining the function of the archive with the transmission of shared experiences through participatory performance and interactivity.[23]

In concurrence with a chain of tragic events such as devastating terrorist attacks, hurricanes, tsunamis and other catastrophes, the Internet has provided countless opportunities for the construction of web memorials as outlets for mourning and commemoration.[24] In order to underpin the inherent characteristics of these diverse forms of digital memorialisation with their various degrees of social interaction, participation, and design possibilities, several scholars have proposed conceptual interpretative models.

Kylie Veale has developed a "Memorial Attribute Model" based on the motivations for creating web-based memorials, revolving around expressions of grief, bereavement and loss, unfinished business, social presence, and/or historical significance.[25] Kirsten Foot, Barbara Warnick and Steven Schneider focus on the characteristics of Internet memorials, both institutional and individual websites, and formulate a series of questions to identify seven dimensions of the memorialising process: 1) the object or focus of the commemoration; 2) the evidence of a co-productive process between actors

---

20 Timothy Recuber, "The Prosumption of Commemoration: Disasters, Digital Memory Banks, and Online Collective Memory," *American Behavioral Scientist* 56.4 (2012), 537.
21 Johanna Hartelius, "'Leave a Message of Hope or Tribute': Digital Memorializing as Public Deliberation," *Argumentation and Advocacy* 47.2 (1 September, 2010): 68.
22 Pierre Nora, "Between Memory and History: Les Lieux de Mémoire," *Representations* 26 (1989): 13.
23 Ekaterina Haskins, "Between Archive and Participation: Public Memory in a Digital Age," *Rhetoric Society Quarterly* 37.4 (2007): 402.
24 Timothy Recuber, "The Prosumption of Commemoration: Disasters, Digital Memory Banks, and Online Collective Memory," *American Behavioral Scientist* 56.4 (2012), 531.
25 Kylie Veale, "Online Memorialisation: The Web as a Collective Memorial Landscape for Remembering the Dead," *The Fibreculture Journal* 3 (2004). http://three.fibreculturejournal.org/fcj-014-online-memorialisation-the-web-as-a-collective-memorial-landscape-for-remembering-the-dead/, accessed May 12, 2020.

involved; 3) the voice, single (individual or collective) or multiple; 4) the temporal distance of the memorial from the event it commemorates; 5) the dynamic or static nature of its form and content; 6) the intended audience; and 7) the relational positioning of the victims.[26]

More recently, Wendy Moncur and David Kirk have outlined a framework based on notions of actors, inputs, form, and message, including also non-web-based forms of cybermemorials. Digital memorials are mapped according to the individuals or institutions involved in their creation, management, and consumption; the reasons and circumstances under which they are designed and what type of content they display; their form and structure – completely digital or hybrid, static or evolving – which often determine the users' level of engagement and participation; and, finally, according to the message they convey, whether cultural or personal, sacred or secular.[27]

The edges of these categorizations, however, are never neat, particularly the differences between websites sponsored by authorized institutions and those produced by private individuals. The earlier mentioned progressive shift from a nationalist and militarist framework to globalism and humanitarianism with a focus on suffering and trauma[28] has promoted digital responses that oscillate between the public and the private sphere, the official and the vernacular.

Memorials dedicated to the victims of terrorism are today among the most heated sites of public culture: sacred sites of bereavement, morbid dark tourism destinations, as well as ideological rallying grounds that can be used to further political agendas.[29] In the wake of the 9/11 terrorist attacks, Aaron Hess counted nearly 40 web memorials,[30] displaying a variety of personal responses and ranging from complex state-endorsed websites[31] to smaller individual initiatives.[32]

The urgency with which communities tend to demand the erection of memorials, whether physical or digital has been put in relation to the need for a material

---

[26] Kirsten Foot, Barbara Warnick and Steven M. Schneider, "Web-Based Memorializing after September 11: toward a Conceptual Framework," *Journal of Computer-Mediated Communication* 11.1 (1 November 2005): 72–96.
[27] Wendy Moncur and David Kirk, "An Emergent Framework for Digital Memorials," in *Proceedings of the 2014 Conference on Designing Interactive Systems*, DIS '14, Vancouver, BC, Canada: Association for Computing Machinery (2014): 965–974.
[28] See Christina Simko, "Marking Time in Memorials and Museums of Terror: Temporality and Cultural Trauma," *Sociological Theory* 38.1 (March 2020): 51–77.
[29] Erika Doss, *Memorial Mania: Public Feeling in America* (Chicago: University of Chicago Press, 2010), 119.
[30] Aaron Hess, "In Digital Remembrance: Vernacular Memory and the Rhetorical Construction of Web Memorials," *Media, Culture & Society* 29.5 (2007): 816.
[31] "9/11 Memorial and Museum." *The 9/11 Memorial & Museum*. https://www.911memorial.org, accessed 14 May, 2020.
[32] "Mike's 9/11 Memorial Page." http://www.mshepp.com/20010911.htm, accessed 14 May, 2020.

substitute for the absent bodies: commemorating that absence ultimately requires a representation of presence, a sacralized space of pilgrimage where families and visitors can focus on specific historical events, perform their rituals, and heal.[33] While divorced from the material world and lacking the phenomenological experience deriving from walking past real memorial sites, the web is able to provide readily available memorial spaces, accommodating both official and unorthodox readings of events.[34] As seen in the aforementioned tragedies such as 9/11 or the 2004 Boxing Day Tsunami, where the places of the disasters were no longer freely accessible, hypertextuality could effectively compensate for the absence of embodied experiences.[35] Affect and emotion – as heuristic modes of apprehending historical events – can be triggered by the employment of transmedia storytelling strategies such as audio-visual recordings, multimedia features and interactivity. The result is a multi-layered digital space where the relationship between individual and public memory is deeply intertwined.[36]

#EnMémoire, a web memorial created by the French newspaper *Le Monde* to commemorate the victims of the 13 November, 2015 attacks in Paris, offers a good example of how digital media translate the interplay between vernacular accounts, curated stories, and official national narratives. The website displays an interactive grid gallery with the crowdsourced photos and biographies of the deceased. These are linked to the five locations of the attacks, on one level digitally recreating a spontaneous memorial shrine but also reading those sites as multicultural hubs inhabited by a global community that embody the traditional Parisian cultural values of tolerance and liberty.[37] The interactive features of the site allow the dynamic overlapping of biographies and geographies, ultimately shaping how those narratives of the event will be stored and retrieved.

---

[33] Allyson Booth, *Postcards from the Trenches: Negotiating the Space between Modernism and the First World War* (Oxford, New York: Oxford University Press, 1997), 41.

[34] Lee Jarvis, "Remember, remember, 11 September: memorializing 9/11 on the Internet," *Journal of War & Culture Studies* 3.1 (2010): 74.

[35] Aaron Hess, "In Digital Remembrance: Vernacular Memory and the Rhetorical Construction of Web Memorials," *Media, Culture & Society* 29.5 (2007): 820. In his study on cybermemorials, Edwin Martini has highlighted the potential of hypertext in facilitating expression. See Edwin Martini, "Virtual Walls, Virtual Memories? Cybermemorials and the Performance of Memory Online" (unpublished presentation discussed during the conference of the International Association of Internet Researchers 2.0, Minneapolis, October 2001); see Kirsten Foot, Barbara Warnick and Steven M. Schneider, "Web-Based Memorializing after September 11: toward a Conceptual Framework," *Journal of Computer-Mediated Communication* 11.1 (1 November 2005): 78.

[36] Johanna Hartelius, "'Leave a Message of Hope or Tribute': Digital Memorializing as Public Deliberation," *Argumentation and Advocacy* 47.2 (1 September, 2010): 70.

[37] "Un Mémorial pour les morts du 13 novembre". *Le Monde*. 26 November, 2015. https://www.lemonde.fr/attaques-a-paris/article/2015/11/26/un-memorial-pour-les-morts-du-13-novembre_4818363_4809495.html, accessed 10 April, 2020.

Memorials in Virtual Worlds and Online Video Games

An especially immersive form of digital memorials is represented by memorials created in virtual worlds and online video games. In Massively Multiplayer Online Games (MMOGs), players can explore fantasy environments and socially interact with fellow gamers through individual avatars (in-game alter-egos representing the users). While generally maintaining a ludic dimension, areas of these virtual worlds have been appropriated by both players and game developers to commemorate deceased members of the gaming community, with pilgrimages to virtual shrines and collective rituals analogous to those practised around real memorial sites.[38]

Other online worlds such as *Second Life* allow users to modify the virtual environment creating objects and building structures that can be visited by other players. Among these digital destinations, browsable through a directory,[39] several virtual memorials have been erected. These range from replicas of existing sites, like the Vietnam Veterans Memorial Wall, to completely original constructions such as a mausoleum for the victims of 9/11, a site dedicated to the fallen aviators from the great conflicts of the twentieth century, a monument to the transgender victims of hate crimes, and an educational virtual exhibit "Witnessing History: Kristallnacht, the 1938 Pogroms" set up by the US Holocaust Memorial Museum.

Similarly, the popular sandbox video game *Minecraft*, with a player base of over 120 million monthly users, revolves around the construction of a variety of 3D structures, including digital memorials. The significant time and effort required to single-handedly or collaboratively harvest resources and build such digital structures translates into an expression of grief through labour and dedication.[40]

More recently, Nintendo's *Animal Crossing: New Horizon* (a customizable virtual world where players can create, inhabit and explore villages populated by anthropomorphic animals), launched in 2020 amidst the ongoing COVID-19 global pandemic, reached extraordinary popularity offering, in times of social distancing, the possibility to virtually socialise but also launch political protests,[41] celebrate funerals and erect shrines to mourn the victims of the virus.[42] By the creative exploitation

---

38 M. Carter, M, Gibbs, and J. Mori, "Vile Rat: Spontaneous Shrines in EVE Online," (Proceedings of the First International Workshop on Eve Online, Foundation of Digital Games, 2013).
39 "Destination Guide." *Second Life*. https://secondlife.com/destination/, accessed 10 April, 2020.
40 Michael Arnold et al., *Death and Digital Media* (Abingdon: Routledge, 2017), 3.
41 "Nintendo game pulled from Chinese platforms after Hong Kong protest." Reuters. 10 April, 2020. https://www.reuters.com/article/us-nintendo-china-animalcrossing/nintendo-game-pulled-from-chinese-platforms-after-hong-kong-protest-idUKKCN21S11F, accessed 21 March, 2020.
42 "How Animal Crossing helped one gamer mourn their dead mom". *Inverse*. 17 April, 2020. https://www.inverse.com/gaming/animal-crossing-new-horizons-memorial, accessed 14 May, 2020.

of game mechanics, players transform the customary tropes for grieving and memorializing generating innovative hybrid forms of private and public remembrance.[43]

In HCI (Human-Computer Interaction), the term digital memorials is employed to describe the design and application of new digital technologies to commemorative settings, in particular the use of augmented-reality applications to integrate multimedia elements in physical environments.[44] Mobile technologies and location-based interactive devices, beacons or QR-codes, placed in historically salient places or at existing memorial locations, can enrich the experience of the site allowing the audience to listen to survivors' testimonies,[45] view digital renditions of artefacts or holographic stories,[46] or actively intervene in the environment by adding virtual objects to the landscape. These mixed-reality interventions can prove effective for both sustaining and subverting existing commemorative narratives. For example, the *Black Monument Project*, launched by the *Mic*'s editorial team in response to the controversial debate over the Confederate monuments in the US, employs augmented-reality monuments dedicated to prominent African-American figures to help people visualize alternative scenarios where they can be duly represented. Through their mobile devices, users can erect 3D-digital monuments of black heroes in the real world as a means to challenge the underrepresentation of marginalized communities and contribute to the conversation.[47]

Conclusions

Cybermemorials represent an emerging and evolving set of commemorative spaces mediated by computer networks, digital objects and environments. While displaying features comparable to both official physical memorials and vernacular shrines, they exhibit unique elements of hybridity, dynamism and participation. In line with a general tendency towards the emotional and the sentimental, they effectively

---

[43] Michael Arnold et al., *Death and Digital Media* (Abingdon: Routledge, 2017), 3.
[44] Moncur and Kirk, "An Emergent Framework", 966.
[45] See, for instance, the project *Sonic Memorial* discussed by E. L. Cohen and C. Willis, "One nation under radio: digital and public memory after September 11," *New Media & Society* 6.5 (2004): 591–610.
[46] "When monuments come to life thanks to augmented reality". *Hoverlay*. 14 October, 2019. https://www.hoverlay.com/when-monuments-come-to-life-thanks-to-augmented-reality, accessed 14 May, 2020.
[47] "The Black Monuments Project." *Mic*. 2018. https://black-monuments.mic.com, accessed 14 May, 2020. See also: "Augmenting reality in the Black Monuments Project." *Medium*. February 23, 2018. https://medium.com/readme-mic/augmenting-reality-in-the-black-monuments-project-4448a2262210, accessed 14 May, 2020.

exploit the possibilities of the digital medium to build narratives around historical events and collaboratively construct public memory.

To varying degrees digital memorials provide opportunities for the public to have a voice;[48] the question remains open whether and to what extent they are more inclusive and democratic. Multiple authorship allows for the emergence of dissonant histories that challenge and compete with the official readings of the events, yet the individuals' ability to speak may be hampered by the actions of moderators, the mere design of the digital space or by the level of intervention it consents.

Finally, sustainability represents another crucial issue. If memory is grounded on notions of permanence, the instability and ephemerality of digital memorials prompts the development of new paradigms and ontological models for interpreting their power to shape our individual and collective memories. As argued by David Glassberg, public historians are in the ideal position to investigate how individual memories of the past are shaped and established through group communication, and how in turn they relate to the collective memory of a community.[49] Cybermemorials represent focal points that enable ordinary people to construct their understanding of the past through the sharing of their own multiple vernacular "collected memories."[50] Digital technologies thus provide new opportunities for the creation of a communal, participatory historical culture where historians and the public can engage in a dialogue with one another.[51]

Bibliography

Foot, Kirsten, Barbara Warnick, and Steven M. Schneider, "Web-Based Memorializing after September 11: toward a Conceptual Framework." *Journal of Computer-Mediated Communication* 11.1 (1 November, 2005): 72–96.

Haskins, Ekaterina. "Between Archive and Participation: Public Memory in a Digital Age." *Rhetoric Society Quarterly* 37.4 (2007): 401–422.

Hess, Aaron. "In Digital Remembrance: Vernacular Memory and the Rhetorical Construction of Web Memorials." *Media, Culture & Society* 29.5 (2007): 812–830.

---

[48] Stacey Hebert, "Digital memorialization: Collective memory, tragedy, and participatory spaces" (Master of Arts Thesis, University of Denver, Colorado, 2008), 73–74.

[49] David Glassberg, "Public History and the Study of Memory," *The Public Historian*, vol. 18, No. 2 (Spring 1996): 10.

[50] See James E. Young's definition of "collected memory" in James E. Young, *The Texture of Memory: Holocaust Memorials and Meanings* (New Haven: Yale University Press, 1993).

[51] Meg Foster, "Online and Plugged-in? Public History and Historians in the Digital Age," *Public History Review*, vol. 21 (2014): 12.

Moncur, Wendy, and David Kirk. "An Emergent Framework for Digital Memorials." In *Proceedings of the 2014 Conference on Designing Interactive Systems*. DIS '14. Vancouver, BC, Canada: Association for Computing Machinery (2014): 965–974

Veale, Kylie. "Online Memorialisation: The Web as a Collective Memorial Landscape for Remembering the Dead." *The Fibreculture Journal* 3 (2004), http://three.fibreculturejournal.org/fcj-014-online-memorialisation-the-web-as-a-collective-memorial-landscape-for-remembering-the-dead/, accessed May 12, 2020.

David Dean
Living History: Performing the Past

Abstract: This contribution explores a variety of ways in which history has been performed digitally in the hope of making the past come to life and imbuing it with significance for audiences. Bringing the perspectives of a public historian to an understanding of performing history digitally, it explores a range of living history practices from the earliest digital projections to contemporary uses of virtual and augmented reality.

Keywords: digital performance, immersion, interactivity, living history, public history, video games, virtual reality

When public historians think about living history, what immediately comes to mind are the ways in which the past is embodied through movement and space most often associated with interpretative programming in living history sites, heritage houses, and museums.[1] There are of course other forms of living history performances, including the formal re-enactment (restaging past events), the theatrical (re-presenting the past on stage or *in situ*; off-stage scripted or unscripted live performances), the cinematic (documentaries, feature films, television), and the virtual (immersive video games, virtual reality, augmented reality). Before surveying the varieties of performing living history digitally, it is necessary to give some precision to what we mean by performance in general and by digital performance in particular.

Folklorist and oral historian Richard Bauman describes performance as "a mode of communication, a way of speaking, the essence of which resides in the assumption of responsibility to an audience for a display of communicative skill" situated in a performance event.[2] Bauman's definition speaks to the primary concerns of public historians: the forms and mediums by which publics engage with and consume the past; the way historical meaning is shaped through performance by creative agents (actors, interpreters, designers etc.) and audiences; and the distance between a past event that gifts content and a present that experiences it anew. These concerns with historical

---
[1] Jay Anderson, *Time Machines: The World of Living History* (Nashville, Tennessee: The American Association for State and Local History, 1984); Jay Anderson, *A Living History Reader: Museums* (Lanham, Maryland: Rowman and Littlefield, 1991); Scott Magelssen, *Living History Museums: Undoing History through Performance* (Lanham, Maryland: Scarecrow Press, 2007); David B. Allison, *Living History: Effective Costumed Interpretation and Enactment at Museums and Historic Sites* (Lanham, Maryland: Rowman and Littlefield, 2016).
[2] Richard Bauman, *Story, Performance, Event* (Cambridge: Cambridge University Press, 1986), 3. See also Steve Benford and Gabriella Giannachi, *Performing Mixed Reality* (Cambridge, Massachusetts: The MIT Press, 2011).

production, historical representation, and historical distance have been affected deeply by digitization and we are only slowly coming to terms with what performing public history digitally means in our contemporary world and how it will affect and reshape the field of public history in the future.

Steve Dixon describes digital performance as including "all performance works where computer technologies play a key role rather than a subsidiary one in content, technique, aesthetics, or deliver forms".[3] Of course, what one considers to be "a key role" is open for discussion. It could be argued that uploading images or videos of non-digital performances onto digital platforms for wider public access is not really digital history but simply offering a new form of documentation. Alternatively, such relocating could be seen as being at one end of a spectrum of digital histories which culminates at the other end in performances that have been created digitally, such as augmented reality programs or performances using multi-sensory body suits. What these have in common is the use of computer technologies in representing the past to publics.

One of the earliest forms of performing living history digitally took the form of turning non-digital images, films, and sounds into digital form so that they could be projected. These could form backdrops to live stage performances, thus illuminating, illustrating, reinforcing, or sometimes contesting what audiences were witnessing. Such practices promoted a degree of intellectual audience interaction similar to that envisioned by earlier theatre practitioners such as Erwin Piscator, Bertholt Brecht, and Antonin Artaud. Indeed, in arguing that theatre created "la réalité virtuelle" for audiences, Artaud gave us the language by which we most frequently describe digital living history in English: virtual reality.[4]

One of the earliest proponents of digital technologies in theatrical performances (in productions such as *The Anderson Project* and *Jean-Sans-Nom*) was the Canadian theatre artist Robert Lepage and his multi-disciplinary production company Ex Machina.[5] In 2008, for the four hundredth anniversary of the founding of the city of Québec, they transformed eight one giant concrete grain silos in the city's old port into a single massive screen (600m x 30m). *Le Moulin á images/The Image Mill* focused on the daily life of everyday people, and the production was intended to be an entertaining, playful, and emotional tribute to the city (Fig. 1).[6]

---

3 Steve Dixon, *Digital Performance. A History of New Media in Theater, Dance, Performance Art, and Installation* (Cambridge, Massachusetts: The MIT Press, 2007), 3.
4 Antonin Artaud, *The Theater and Its Double* (New York: Grove, 1938).
5 Ludovic Fouquet, *The Visual Laboratory of Robert Lepage* (Vancouver, British Columbia: Talonbook, 2005), 162–80.
6 Thomas Bigelow, "Re-Imag(in)ing *The Image Mill*: Québec City's 400th and Remembering in the New Media," (MA in Public History Research Essay, Carleton University, 2010), 15–20.

Fig. 1: "Image Mill, Quebec City" by Colorado_Chris is licensed with CC BY-NC-ND 2.0. To view a copy of this license, visit https://creativecommons.org/licenses/by-nc-nd/2.0/.

In re-imaging the past by projecting it onto an actual industrial site, this public history event invited audiences to think through relationships between the real (the site itself), the remembered (personal, family, and community experiences living in the city), and the imaginary (the "what it must have been like" in the years before living memory). Lepage has continued to offer audiences innovative uses of computer technology in staged performances about the past, most recently in *887* where private memories and public histories of his growing up in mid-late twentieth century Québec intertwine through a variety of theatrical strategies and digital technologies.[7]

Le Moulin á images/The Image Mill built on earlier analogue multimedia and multi-disciplinary history-telling that took the form of *son et lumière* shows that were popular across the globe since the 1950s. Offering narratives of place projected onto heritage sites or sites of significance, particularly for tourists, such shows have become more sophisticated through digital technologies. While audiences traditionally sit or stand to watch these spectacles, the use of mobile devices is increasing, enabling participants to ambulate at their own pace, even selecting which narratives to listen to and which ones to skip.[8]

---

[7] Photographs and video clips of *Le Moulin á images/The Image Mill* can be found at http://lacaserne.net/index2.php/other_projects/the_image_mill/. The promotional videos for *887* illustrate the digital elements in Lepage's creative works; see, for example, those for the Barbican, London, England (https://www.youtube.com/watch?v=awnwBgfFfRo) and Rome, Italy (https://www.youtube.com/watch?v=kYswTsuzDFQ), all accessed February 20, 2018.

[8] There are many examples, the author's most recent experience being the Forum of Caesar in Rome, Italy, http://www.viaggioneifori.it/en/, accessed February 20, 2018. See also the many installations by Unicity, http://www.unicity.eu/index.php/en/hp-en.

This, albeit limited, degree of interactivity can be found in other forms of digitized local history performances such as those which turn public spaces into living history museums. In 2010 the Museum of Copenhagen opened The Copenhagen Museum Wall in the city center. It consists of a large multi-user interactive digital screen (actually four plasma touch screens) where visitors can select stories featuring thousands of images of Copenhagen past and present. Users can search and look according to their own interests and at their own pace, and they can also add their own images and stories, or comment on others, either at the site or online.[9] In 2015 the city of El Paso, Texas in the United States opened a similar 3D digital wall, Digie (Digital Information Gateway in El Paso), inside the El Paso Museum of History as well as a mobile version.[10] In both cases digitization allows publics not only to experience and interact with, but also participate in, the making and curating of a crowdsourced living history museum.

The technologies behind such installations have also transformed ways of seeing and generated immersive possibilities. Building on eighteenth and nineteenth century spatial illusions such as painted 360-degree panoramas or the *camera obscura*, German based artist and architect Yadegar Asisi created pictorial and digital reconstructions of heritage buildings in Berlin as well as panoramas imagining the redevelopment of four squares. From performing heritage Asisi moved on to create historical panoramas. *Dresden 1945* (2006), *The Wall* (2012), *Leipzig 1813* (2013), *Rome 312* (2014), *Rouen 1431*, and *Luther 1517* (2016) offer visitors the illusion of time travel to witness the destruction of Dresden by Allied bombing, a divided Berlin at the time of the Cold War, Leipzig in the aftermath of the Napoleonic Battle of the Nations, the triumphant entry of the Emperor Constantine, the medieval French market town at the time of Joan of Arc, and Wittenberg as the heart of the Reformation (Fig. 2).[11]

Typically, these panoramas are viewed from a platform accompanied by realistic sound effects and evocative original compositions. Asisi's installations create past moments in time and space through a meticulous re-presentation of what we might call historyscapes.

What all of these forms of digital living history performance share is that, on the whole, audiences remain consumers rather than producers of history. While allowing audiences a new way of seeing, and even a sense of really "being there", such activities also reinforce historical distance, because even if given some agency through a range of choices they have to make, publics are viewers and listeners of a reconstructed past rather than participants in an actualized past. However much as

---

9 The website of the company that built the installation offers links to a video and a conference presentation on the touch wall: http://www.gibson.co.nz/visitor-experiences/copenhagen-touch-wall. See also https://www.youtube.com/watch?v=GlxIa0OUcYc, both accessed February 20, 2018.
10 See http://digie.org/, accessed February 20, 2018.
11 Asisi offers a detailed description of his work at https://www.asisi.de/en/homepage/, accessed February 20, 2018.

Fig. 2: "asisi-Panometer-Leipzig-1813-Alt-Connewitz-16" by Hotel Alt-Connewitz is licensed with CC BY 2.0. To view a copy of this license, visit https://creativecommons.org/licenses/by/2.0/.

they are marketed as immersive experiences, this is achieved less because of the medium and more because audiences are able to suspend their own present and actively imagine what might have been though being stimulated by the sounds, images, and narratives provided. This is time travel experienced as a momentary illusion, much the same as what occurs at particular points during visits to living history museums, heritage houses, or sites that feature authentic or accurately recreated spaces and artifacts animated by costumed interpreters speaking in first or third person.

Remote access technologies have also enabled audiences to witness streaming of living history performances wherever they might be, or to access them later through platforms such as YouTube. More adventurous efforts have been the ways in which social media platforms have enabled publics to experience the past in real time. In 2006, Private Harry Lamin's letters home during the First World War were released daily on the platform Blogger exactly ninety years to the day they were sent between 1916 and 1920.[12] The Danish National Museum opened up new possibilities in digital living history by launching the Facebook page of a young Danish woman, Ida Charlotte Finnelstrup, where she chronicled her daily life in eighteenth century Copenhagen in real time. Over eight hundred and fifty followers, primarily

---

[12] See http://wwar1.blogspot.ca/2006/07/private-harry-lamin.html, accessed February 20, 2018.

women between eighteen and thirty years of age, engaged with Ida in real time over a six-month period in 2010 (Fig. 3).[13]

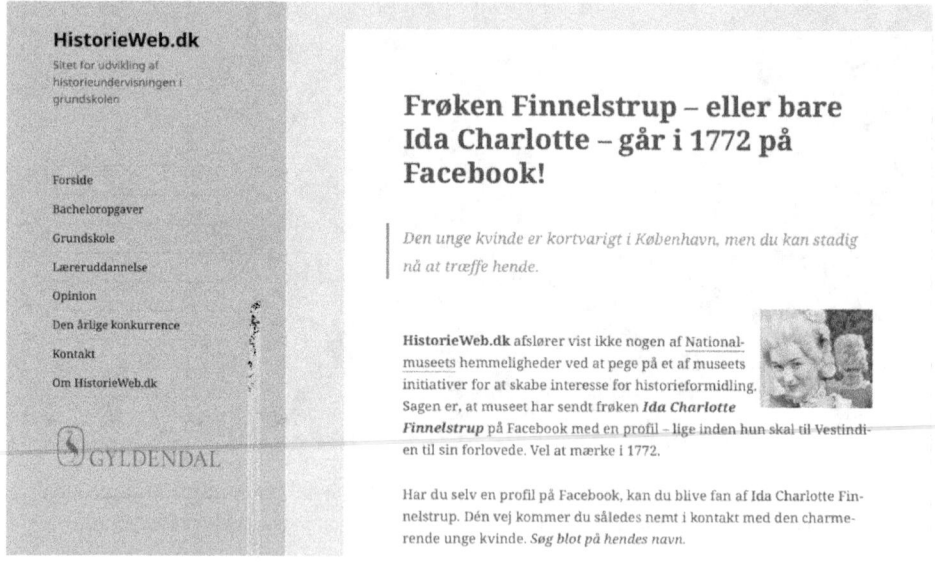

Fig. 3: Danish National Museum, Ida Charlotte Finnelstrup on Facebook, URL: http://historieweb. dk/2010/03/10/froeken-finnelstrup-eller-bare-ida-charlotte-gaar-i-1772-paa-facebook/, Screenshot taken by author 10 September 2021.

More recent examples include the project Detroit 1957 where real-time tweets were released as the riots in that city unfolded.[14] While also momentary, such digital performances enable a much more sustained involvement in the past over time – weeks, months, and even years – than is of course possible with visits to living history heritage sites.

Time travel has become more immersive through virtual reality (VR) and augmented reality (AR) technologies. Mobile VR and AR have enabled museums and heritage organizations to offer visitors more interactive experiences. An early example was Archeoguide (Augmented Reality-Based Cultural Heritage On-Site Guide) which sought to exploit "recent advances in mobile computing, augmented reality, 3D visualization, networking, and archiving to present users with on-site and online tours of

---

13 Mette Boritz et. al., "Digital levendegørelse – 1700-tals faktionsleg på Facebook," *Nordisk Museologi* 1 (2011): 60–80. Boritz and her colleagues were among the first to use the phrase "digital living history". See also https://idacharlotte1772.wordpress.com/, accessed February 20, 2018.
14 Jennifer Vannette, "In Real Time: Twitter as Public History," *[Re]Collection*. Accessed February 20, 2018, https://www.recollectionhistory.com/blog/2017/7/24/bqqe4kbce4zewham0thj6ejyspip5c.

the physical site according to their profile and behavior during the tour."[15] A more recent service declares that it revives history so effectively that "the future is in the past".[16]

Mixed reality – performing in environments that utilize both AR technologies and the real world, with virtual and augmented reality at one end of the scale and augmented virtuality at the other – promises much for the future of performing living history digitally. The Mixed Reality Laboratory's collaborations with artistic group Blast Theory provide two examples. *The Shape Living Exhibition* offered visitors four interfaces through which they could experience the history of Nottingham Castle: the "Augurscope" (3D renderings of the medieval castle displayed on a mobile screen unit that could be pushed around the open spaces where the castle once stood offering different perspectives); interactive flashlight technologies triggering images and audio clips in the caves underneath the castle; and two indoor installations (an immersive projection environment housed in a tent and a projection onto a sandpit). In *Ulrike and Eamon Compliant* participants in an ambulatory performance in Venice could choose to become, or engage with, the lives of Ulrike Meinhof, a member of the Red Army Faction in the 1970s, or Eamon Collins, a member of the Irish Republican Army in the 1970s and 1980s (Fig. 4).[17]

It is especially through digital video games that VR and AR technologies have enabled publics to experience the past as history.[18] Often involving the adoption of a persona or avatar to navigate through a series of physical – frequently combative – and intellectual challenges, programmers write code designed to take the player through a progressive series until they reach the ultimate end game, often accumulating useful materials, knowledge, and rewards along the way. The adoption of a persona or personal identification with a particular character mimics strategies considered to be especially effective in creating empathy and emotion in visitors to living history sites (so, for example, becoming a fugitive slave at Connor Prairie in the United States or taking on the identity of a victim or survivor at the

---

15 Vassilios Vlahakis et. al., "Archeoguide: An Augmented Reality Guide for Archaeological Sites," *IEEE Computer Graphics and Applications* 22, no. 5 (September/October 2001): 52–60. Accessed February 20, 2018. doi:10.1109/MCG.2002.1028726.
16 The promotional video carries the slogan: see https://lithodomosvr.com/, accessed February 20, 2018.
17 Steve Benford and Gabriella Giannachi, *Performing Mixed Reality* (Cambridge, Massachusetts: The MIT Press, 2011), 2–3, 147–52, 194–201. See https://www.blasttheory.co.uk/projects/ulrike-and-eamon-compliant/ and https://www.blasttheory.co.uk/projects/dial-ulrike-and-eamon-compliant/, both accessed February 20, 2018.
18 Kevin Kee, ed., *Pastplay: Teaching and Learning History with Technology* (Ann Arbour, Michigan: University of Michigan Press, 2011); Adam Chapman, *Digital Games as History: How Videogames Represent the Past and Offer Access to Historical Practice* (London and New York: Routledge, 2016); Jeremiah McCall, "Video Games as Participatory Public History," in *A Companion to Public History*, ed. David Dean (Hoboken, New Jersey and Chichester, West Sussex: Wiley Blackwell, 2018), 405–16.

Fig. 4: Ulrike and Eamon Compliant, Blast Theory, URL: https://www.blasttheory.co.uk/projects/ulrike-and-eamon-compliant/, Screenshot taken by author 10 September 2021.

United States Holocaust Museum).[19] AR offers participants nuanced opportunities to exercise a degree of agency in their experience because it combines virtual reality with additional computer-generated content. In "serious" historically themed video games, one can virtually step back into the past which becomes the player's present. Examples include Czechoslovakia 38–89[20] which uses testimonies to allow players to explore multiple perspectives;[21] others draw on documentary evidence, including oral histories and on-location scenarios, to help players "get to the truth

---

[19] On Connor Prairie, see http://www.connerprairie.org/things-to-do/events/follow-the-north-star, accessed February 20, 2018, and Thomas Cauvin, Joan Cummins, David Dean and Andreas Etges, "'Follow the North Star': A Participatory Museum Experience," *Journal of American History* 105, no. 3 (2018): 630–36. On the United States Holocaust Museum, see https://www.ushmm.org/remember/id-cards, accessed February 20, 2018.

[20] See http://cs3889.cz/;jsessionid=BAB9D4B374DC8626BA0890DE7CD19A1E, accessed February 20, 2018.

[21] Vit Šisler, "Contested Memories of War in Czecholovakia 38–89 Assassination: Designing a Serious Game on Contemporary History," *Game Studies* 16, no. 2 (December 2016), accessed February 20, 2018, http://gamestudies.org/1602.

(s) behind the presentation" and even encourage a degree of self-reflection.[22] Such games can encourage an exploration of alternative outcomes and counterfactuals;[23] often requiring collaboration during play, they can lead to further communication once the game has finished.[24]

Once their day out in the past is over, digitization will have enabled publics to showcase their experience or even to re-present it for public consumption using their digital cameras, smartphones, and portable devices by uploading them onto social media platforms such as Flickr, Pinterest, YouTube, Facebook, Twitter, and Instagram. Such postings can generate varying levels of interaction with others, from likes and retweets to comments and replies that sometimes generate lengthy conversations. Living histories thus re-imaged, re-configured, and re-presented stimulate further reflection and encourage conversations both local and global.

Bibliography

Chapman, A. *Digital Games as History: How Videogames Represent the Past and Offer Access to Historical Practice*. London and New York: Routledge, 2016.

Dixon, S. *Digital Performance. A History of New Media in Theater, Dance, Performance Art, and Installation*. Cambridge, Massachusetts: The MIT Press, 2007.

Kee, K., ed. *Pastplay: Teaching and Learning History with Technology*. Ann Arbour, Michigan: University of Michigan Press, 2011.

Magelssen, S. *Living History Museums: Undoing History through Performance*. Lanham, Maryland: Scarecrow Press, 2007.

McCall, J. "Video Games as Participatory Public History." In *A Companion to Public History*, edited by D. Dean, 405–16. Hoboken, New Jersey and Chichester, West Sussex: Wiley Blackwell, 2018.

---

[22] Aaron Oldenburg, "Abstracting Evidence: Documentary Process in the Service of Fictional Gameworlds" *Game Studies* 17, no. 1 (July 2017), accessed February 20, 2018, http://gamestudies.org/1701.

[23] Jan Simons, "Narrative, Games, and Theory," *Game Studies* 7, no. 1 (August 2007), accessed February 20, 2018. http://gamestudies.org/0701; Ryan Lizardi, "Bioshock: Complex and Alternate Histories," *Game Studies* 14, no. 1 (August 2014), accessed February 20, 2018. http://gamestudies.org/1401.

[24] Tony Manninen and Tomi Kujanpää, "The Hunt for Collaborative War Gaming – CASE: Battlefield 1942," *Game Studies* 5, no. 1 (October 2015), accessed February 20, 2018. http://www.gamestudies.org/0501/; Carrie Anderson, "'There Has to Be More to It': Diegetic Violence and the Uncertainty of President Kennedy's Death," *Game Studies* 15, no. 2 (December 2015), accessed February 20, 2018. http://gamestudies.org/1502.

Lara Kelland
Activist Digital Public History

Abstract: Digital Public History can provide social movement activists with tools for cultural activism, and collaborations between activists and academics have advanced social justice discourse within the field. Activists, archivists, and digital public historians have authored public-facing work that advances LGBTQ rights, racial justice work, and anti-colonial knowledge production.

Keywords: activism, social movements, LGBTQ history, black history, collaboration

With the development of Web 2.0 tools like Wordpress, Facebook, Instagram, and Omeka for archiving and interpreting the past, digital public history offers a possibility for a more robustly democratized practice of history-making. By putting these tools into the hands of anyone with a computer, such a shift in authorship means archival work and curatorial responsibilities could be assumed by cultural activists with relatively basic digital skills. Individuals and identity-based groups have long nurtured historical scholarship and authorship, and social movement activists have contributed to the public presentation of the past as a cultural intervention in support of their political goals. The promise of digital public history has certainly advanced such kinds of projects authored by grassroots activists. Yet the ideal envisioned for democratized cultural production, in which anyone could preserve and interpret any aspect of the collective past, has yet to be fully realized. Instead, partnerships between public history organizations, universities, and grassroots groups remains the most common network of digital public history work.

This article traces the ways in which social movement activists have made interventions in public understandings of the past through digital means. Many of the examples in this piece highlight the work done by US activists, academics, and library professionals, a framing that both highlights the proliferation of such work in the US as well as belying my research orientation. Still, I draw on global examples to gesture towards the significant work taking place in non-US and non-Western places. By engaging the question of institutional support and positionality here, the intersections between activist and academic reveal where digital public history brings such groups together, as well as revealing where such work diverges independently. As emerges from a comparative look at the examples engaged here, partnerships between academic and social movement-based digital historians have facilitated productive collaborations, but the centrality of academic or activist leadership can inform the shape of the final project. Generally, academic institutional goals tend toward the documentary and activist goals lean into visions for significant social change.

At the center of a survey on activist digital public history is a definitional problem: what constitutes activism? What are the bounds of social movements? In one much celebrated case of digital public history, 911digitalarchive.org has long been considered an exemplar of user-generated content, but the site lacks a unified goal of social or political change.[1] Engaging publics, then, I argue, is not enough to count; activist digital public history also seeks transformative change. Thus, I consider two significant strains of activist digital public history here: 1) LGBTQ archiving and interpretive initiatives and 2) born-digital archiving efforts sprung from on-the-ground social movements in the 2010s, including the Occupy Movement, Black Lives Matter archives from Baltimore and Ferguson, and documenting mass gun violence events. Each corpus has slightly different goals. LGBTQ projects seek primarily to rectify archival silences. By contrast, born-digital efforts emerge from a concern about abundance that is also unstable. Although it might seem that digital materials are safe from the challenges that characterize analog archives, such as deterioration of paper and accessibility of materials, preservation in the digital era has brought about a whole new array of issues related to preserving born-digital materials, for traditional and activist archivists.[2]

Activists and social movements leaders have used community history and memory practices as an organizing strategy, long before the emergence of the professional field of public history. From as early as the late nineteenth century, grassroots leaders who focused on social change related to race, gender, class, and sexuality have made interventions into the public remembrance of the past. Through the development of memorials, archives, museums, and community education efforts in the twentieth century, participants in the racial justice, labor, feminist, and queer movements researched, documented, and authored their collective pasts with a focus on narratives of resistance, survival, and social change. Although twentieth-century efforts tended to be separatist in origin as movement leaders deliberately turning away from mainstream institutions and towards autonomous organizations, movement historians both created independent institutions and made inroads into mainstream archives, museums, and universities. Twenty-first-century activists continued this work, and through the uses of digital tools have continued to reframe historical authority, while also

---

1 Stephen Brier, and Joshua Brown. "The September 11 Digital Archive," *Radical History Review* 111 (Fall 2011): 101–109.

2 See Kodjo Atiso and Chris Freeland, "Identifying the Social and Technical Barriers Affecting Engagement in Online Community Archives: A Preliminary Study of 'Documenting Ferguson' Archive," *Library Philosophy and Practice* 1377 (2016). https://digitalcommons.unl.edu/libphilprac/1377/; Laura Carroll, et al. "A Comprehensive Approach to Born-Digital Archives," *Archivaria* 72 (2011): 61–92, https://archivaria.ca/index.php/archivaria/article/view/13360; Roy Rosenzweig, "Scarcity Or Abundance? Preserving the Past in a Digital Era," *The American Historical Review* 108.3 (2003): 735–762.

continuing to blur the distinction between grassroots projects and academic public history.³

As a professional and academic field, public history's attention to power in the production of historical knowledge made it a natural partner for the cultural fronts of social movements. While academics in fields like history, anthropology, folklife studies, and women's studies began to explore what would become known as "shared authority," activists simultaneously began to critique the centering of historical authority in scholarship, demanding that lived experience be included in national and community narratives.⁴ From the 1950s through the 1970s, activists organizing for the Civil Rights, Black Power, Chicano Rights, Women's Liberation, Gay Liberation and other social movements worked outside of mainstream liberal organizations to articulate, preserve, and promulgate historical narratives. By the 1970s, such activism had moved into academic departments and scholar activists in the new fields of Black Studies, Women's Studies, and Gay Studies began to pressure universities to support such scholarship. In one of the earliest examples, activists within the Gay Liberation Movement formed the Gay Academic Union, an overlapping space of academic and independent scholars dedicated to documenting and interpreting same-sex loving practices across time and space.

The culture wars of the 1990s served as proof that activists had succeeded in demanding representation in mainstream cultural organizations.⁵ By the early 2000s, the lines between activist history and traditional historical scholarship had begun to erode, due in no small part to the theoretical and practice-based advances made by the field of public history. As public historians continued to institutionalize collaborative models, they also provided leadership in academic engagement with digital tools. This cultural and professional shift in academic history departments, by no means complete but significant nonetheless, paved way for the collaborative social movement history-making practices discussed here.

LGBTQ history is an instructive example of the trajectory from separatist, autonomous collective memory work towards collaborative, university-partnered projects that

---

3 For more on social movement activists' engagement with public history work, see Andrea A. Burns, *From Storefront to Monument: Tracing the Public History of the Black Museum Movement* (Amherst: University of Massachusetts Press, [1976] 2013); Lara Kelland, *Clio's Foot Soldiers: US 20th Century Social Movements and Collective Memory* (Amherst: University of Massachusetts Press, 2018).
4 For more on *shared authority*, see Katharine T. Corbett and Howard S. (Dick) Miller, "A Shared Inquiry into Shared Inquiry," *The Public Historian* 28.1 (2006): 15–38; Michael H. Frisch, *A Shared Authority: Essays on the Craft and Meaning of Oral and Public History* (Albany: State University of New York Press, 1990); Bill Adair, Benjamin Filene and Laura Koloski, *Letting Go?: Sharing Historical Authority in a User-Generated World*, edited by Bill Adair, Benjamin Filene, and Laura Koloski (Philadelphia: Left Coast Press, 2011).
5 For an excellent perspective on the late twentieth-century culture wars, see Andrew Hartman, *A War for the Soul of America: A History of the Culture Wars* (Chicago: University of Chicago Press, 2015).

retain the centering of activist voices.[6] The very emergence of LGBTQ history in the academy is a direct outcome of social movement activism, and as such the flow between activist and academic communities was especially fluid in the early years and even remains so today. In March 1973, a handful of academics and community intellectuals gathered in a New York City apartment formed the Gay Academic Union (GAU), a critical network during the early years of LGBTQ collective memory-building. Motivated by negative professional interactions and inhospitable academic experiences, queer scholars sought solace and community, but also quickly formed collaborative projects. The first author to publish an LBGTQ history book was Jonathan Ned Katz in 1979, and other community and academic historians undertook archival, public, and scholarly history projects in the late 1970s and early 1980s in Chicago, Boston, New York, Los Angeles, Central Indiana, San Francisco, Toronto, and numerous other cities.[7]

LGBTQ history still has a strong connection to community organizations such as archives and libraries. However, by the mid-1990s historical authorship had transitioned from primarily being located in grassroots community projects and individual labors of love towards a highly professionalized academic endeavor, while still often retaining some connections to grassroots organizations and the larger social movement. The emergence of digital history practices at this time paralleled the embrace of LGBTQ studies in academe. In 2003, when Jonathan Katz created www.outhistory.org, the site was initially envisioned as a project run entirely by grassroots activists. Katz built out the site with reproductions of sources from his *Gay American History* and *Gay/Lesbian Almanac*. Yet pressures to enhance the site and ensure its long-term sustainability led Katz to seek institutional support. In 2011 and 2013, John D'Emilio and Claire Potter joined Katz as co-directors, bringing in university partnerships that facilitated the growth of the crowdsourced site.[8]

Another example of queer digital public history work is the Digital Transgender Archive, a project which also reflects the fluidity of community-based activism and academic cultural production. The vision for the DTA emerged out of conversations at the 2008 Transsomatechnics: Theories and Practices of Transgender Embodiment conference, a space which sought "to extend and deepen a global network of scholars and activists."[9] Launched in 2016, the digital archive project brings together documents, objects, and knowledge from 50 organizational partners, serving as a portal to collections across the globe. While a model collaboration for large projects

---

[6] Although early historian-activists usually identified as either gay or lesbian, I use LGBTQ interchangeably to indicate all activists and historians concerned with same-sex loving practices and gender-non-normative experiences.

[7] For more on the emergence of LGBTQ history in activist and academic circles, see Jeffrey Escoffier, *American Homo: Community and Perversity* (New York: Verso, 2018), 104–118.

[8] Lauren Jae Gutterman, "Outhistory.org: An Experiment in LGBTQ Community History-Making," *The Public Historian* 32.4 (2010): 96–109.

[9] See www.sfu.ca/~wsweb/documents/TST_Prog_Layout_Finalnewapril29webrevised.pdf.

seeking to link disparate collections, the majority of organizational leadership are from universities or professional archival settings. However, a number of (primarily) activists serve on the advisory board, and the organizations represented include a number of organizations that are squarely focused on political movement goals, not cultural work. This balance ensures that the goals of the social movement frame the public history work rather than locating decision making power away from grassroots activists.

The core of digital public history activism has generally focused on archiving and documentation first, then interpretation and curation second.[10] For LGBTQ history, this mirrors the work of an earlier generation of cultural activists. LGBTQ history initiatives in the 1970s and 1980s often focused on creating repositories of primary sources. Early LGBTQ archivists initiated this work after frustrated researchers often found mainstream repositories disinterested in same-sex loving individuals and communities at best and actively "closeting" such past experiences at worst. Other movements with primarily born-digital artifacts and documents have contributed to this broad endeavor as well, and these projects reflect some of the most grassroots-driven work in the field. Movements in response to police brutality and gun violence have led the charge, although digital public historians have been forward thinking in archiving tweets, photos, and personal narratives from the Occupy and #metoo movements.[11] Again, in most cases, such initiatives have been linked to academic structures, either library archives or digital humanities centers; www.http://occupyarchive.org/, the primary site collecting Occupy's visual culture and personal narratives, was an initiative from the George Mason University's Center for History and New Media. Likewise, in 2018, The Schlesinger Library on the History of Women in America at Harvard's Radcliffe Institute for Advanced Study announced that it planned to "to comprehensively document the #metoo movement and the accompanying redefinitions of gender-based harassment and sex in the workplace," by no means a modest endeavor.[12] While some of the archivists or public historians involved in these projects undoubtedly see themselves as sympathetic observers if not participants in the social movements, it would be incorrect to locate these projects squarely within the social movements themselves.

In contrast, projects that emerged from the Black Lives Matter movement tend to be more centered in the movements themselves, albeit with university and community organization partnerships. As Web 2.0 tools proved invaluable to on the

---

[10] Krista McCracken argues that a commitment to documenting social movements are central to the profession's values and practices; see "Archives as Activism, April 20, 2017," http://activehistory.ca/2017/04/archives-as-activism/.
[11] For more on documenting the Occupy movement see John Erde, "Constructing Archives of the Occupy Movement," *Archives and Records* 35.2 (2014): 77–92.
[12] See www.radcliffe.harvard.edu/news/press-releases/schlesinger-library-awarded-grant-digital-archive-metoo.

ground organization strategies for the movement itself, archival strategies have also benefited from crowdsourcing. Three significant model projects have emerged, *Baltimore Uprising 2015, Documenting Ferguson*, and *A People's Archive of Police Violence in Cleveland*.[13] These projects also reflect activist-academic partnerships, but robustly foreground the interests and perspectives of on-the-ground activists. All three act as web-based item collecting interfaces, allowing anyone to contribute digital assets to the collection.

All three projects emerged at about the same time, but they vary in how directly connected they are to the goals of the political movement. Acting as an extension of BLM, the Cleveland project's founders directly tied the project to the role of healing from the traumas of Michael Brown's killing and other acts of state-sponsored violence; they identified the need "to find other people to be mad with, and move that anger into action."[14] This sentiment emerges throughout such efforts, underscoring that remembering and documenting the contemporary political moment is bound up with a hope for a different future as well as a commitment to ensuring self-representation in the archives for future research. Project directors also compared their work to archival activism in South Africa, continuing the long tradition of locating the US black freedom struggle in transnational contexts.[15]

Central to these projects, also, is the foregrounding of first-person accounts. The Baltimore project centers oral histories and offers a toolkit for anyone interested in conducting their own interviews. In contrast, the Ferguson project feels the most oriented towards collecting a significant moment in national history, seeing themselves "as an institution with a strong regional presence, feel[ing] an obligation to the people of the St. Louis, Missouri region and to future research and scholarship of cultural events in our area."[16] Although the faculty and staff who work on this project are certainly to be commended for collecting an event that once would have been abjectly ignored by archivists, the user experience of the Ferguson project receives a much less movement-goal oriented experience than the others. Cleveland's project, for example, offers up collections on police reports, protest posters created by families of police violence, and testimonies from juvenile detention abuse victims. Likewise, Baltimore project offers site visitors easy access to objects like personal videos made in response to Freddie Grey's death and visual items from the collections of 55 different content creators.

---

13 See www.baltimoreuprising2015.org, digital.wustl.edu/ferguson, and www.archivingpoliceviolence.org, respectively.
14 Jarrett Drake, 27 August, 2018. http://rhizome.org/editorial/2018/aug/27/building-a-community-archive-of-police-violence/.
15 Stacie M. Williams, and Jarrett M. Drake, "Power to the People: Documenting Police Violence in Cleveland," *Journal of Critical Library and Information Studies* 1.2 (2017), DOI: https://doi.org/10.24242/jclis.v1i2.33.
16 See digital.wustl.edu/ferguson/DFP-Plan.pdf.

Ferguson's site appears to be the most motivated by primarily documentation goals, as the interface is the least friendly of the three, offering a less consumer-oriented searching experience than the other two. Their project goals echo this, as they envision their task as "providing diverse perspectives on the events in Ferguson and the resulting social dialogue."[17] Indeed, this goal can be achieved primarily through collecting and preserving. This might well be explained by the leadership team for the project, all of whom are faculty or staff at Washington University and are also primarily not themselves Black.

A number of digital public history projects of note advance grassroots political causes outside of the US. The Macleki project features place-based storytelling in Kenya. The first iteration of the map features student essays on historic sites, the project intends to draw in more voices through crowdsourcing. The Movement History Timeline managed by Global Action Project imagines its scope to go beyond national borders, but thus far the published timeline projects are anchored in the US.[18]

Cultural geographers have partnered with other organizations on a number of ARCGIS projects. *The Genesis of Exodus* is a storymap that engages the history of migration in Central America in support of contemporary immigrant communities, purporting to "to deepen your understanding of the issue and help frame a response."[19] Similarly, indigenous groups have made powerful use of digital public history linked to contemporary movement goals. The Naonaiyaotit Traditional Knowledge Project Atlas serves as a robust place-based history project documenting the indigenous national knowledge of Kitikmeot Inuit of Nunavut. Likewise, although less far-reaching is the Lakota Language GIS storymap, a digital exhibit that blends place-based interpretation and language instruction. As the creators note, "geography, place, location, and culture" are embedded in the Lakota language, and thus digital maps are an ideal tool for the transmission of heritage.[20] All of these examples but one were created in partnerships between community organizations and universities, save for the Lakota example, which was developed in partnership with ESRI, the GIS software company.

Other forms of digital storytelling have emerged that appear to be further democratizing digital public history practice. For example, podcasting has emerged as an important forum, largely engaged by non-professionals, which offers a possible platform for activist digital public history. A number of social movement history podcasts exist, but few are strictly tied to activist groups. A number of journalists have taken to the form to popularize histories of mass resistance like Malcolm

---

17 See digital.wustl.edu/ferguson.
18 See www.movementhistory.org/#gallery.
19 See storymap.genesisofexodusfilm.com.
20 See community.esri.com/community/education/blog/2015/05/22/lakota-wicowoyake-canku-owapi-lakota-language-story-map.

Gladwell's *Revisionist History* or Eric Marcus' *Making Gay History*. A number of LGBTQ history podcasts have emerged in the past few years, mostly hosted by amateur historians but lacking a direct connection to social movement activism. They feature provocative titles like *Yesterqueer, History is Gay, The Mattachine Podcast*, and the explicitly international *Queer as Fact*. Creators of these podcasts generally identify that they lacked access to LGBTQ history and were inspired to rectify that, although given the rapid expansion of LGBTQ history initiatives, such moments may become fewer. Similarly, none of the authors could be called activists in a traditional sense, but they surely see their efforts facilitating more acceptance for LGBTQ people. Similarly, most black history podcasts remain under the purview of museums and journalistic organizations. The occasional exception, like the People's Black Panther Party and others who offer occasional history episodes but lack a robust engagement with change over time.

In many ways, the kind of partnerships seen in the examples engaged here reflect a culmination of the collaborative ethos that is central to the field of public history. Projects that bring together social movement goals and on-the-ground activism with university and cultural organizational partners reflect the longstanding mantra of shared (and sharing) authority. Partnership with university-based public historians can lend a stability to a project that might prove too onerous for a group of volunteer activists.[21] Certainly we should laud academic-based activists and social justice-minded cultural workers for cultivating such relationships and projects.

Digital history tools and Web 2.0 have been roundly celebrated for their perceived ease of access and democratizing potential, a vision which has yet to be realized. Certainly, identity-based social movements are well-poised to disrupt authority and normativity in digital history work. Conversations around the consolidation of the subfield of Black Digital Humanities is but one example of this.[22] Perhaps it is worth considering if the distinction between social movements and cultural makers still holds up in our present moment, but it is important that we consider the social relations, institutional confines, and professional goals involved in the production of social movement digital history. Certainly, digital public historians should continue to undertake such work and continue honing the field's reflective practices along these lines. But, too, we must be honest about the application of these tools and recognize that we have somewhat romanticized (or failed to achieve) the democratizing promises of digital public history.

---

[21] One example of a project that was unsustainable for social movement activists was the Gay History Wiki, a project documenting the life histories of gay Philadelphians lost to the AIDS crisis spearheaded by Christopher Bartlett. For more on the development of the project prior to its digital silence, see Gutterman, "Outhistory.org"; Christopher Wink, "TNT: Christopher Bartlett of the Gay History Wiki Project," 26 October, 2009, https://technical.ly/philly/2009/10/26/tnt-chris-bartlett-of-the-gay-history-wiki-project/.

[22] See dhdebates.gc.cuny.edu/debates/text/55.

While I am in no way critiquing any of the particulars of such projects here, it remains imperative that we continue to reflect on power dynamics as the dominant model for digital public history centers on university-initiated projects. As digital humanities tools and projects continue to originate in academic environments and are becoming increasingly specialized, we must continue to recognize how power informs the relationships in such collaborations and continue to be mindful in how we seek to share authority in the digital world.

Bibliography

Atiso, Kodjo, and Chris Freeland. "Identifying the Social and Technical Barriers Affecting Engagement in Online Community Archives: A Preliminary Study of 'Documenting Ferguson' Archive." *Library Philosophy and Practice* 1377 (2016). https://digitalcommons.unl.edu/libphilprac/1377/.

Brennan, Sheila. "Public, First," *Debates in the Digital Humanities 2016*. https://dhdebates.gc.cuny.edu/projects/debates-in-the-digital-humanities–2016.

Erde, John. "Constructing Archives of the Occupy Movement." *Archives and Records* 35.2 (2014): 77–92.

Gutterman, Lauren Jae. "Outhistory.org: An Experiment in LGBTQ Community History-Making." *The Public Historian* 32.4 (2010): 96–109.

Williams, Stacie M., and Jarrett M. Drake. "Power to the People: Documenting Police Violence in Cleveland." *Journal of Critical Library and Information Studies* 1.2 (2017), DOI: https://doi.org/10.24242/jclis.v1i2.33.

Jerome de Groot
Digital Public History: Family History and Genealogy

Abstract: This chapter looks at the use of digital resources in family history. Increasingly, family history is being supported by digital means, and participants are often leaders in terms of using online and digital tools in their historical investigations. The digital tools that family historians use are becoming more sophisticated, and the types of information that are being included are becoming more interoperable and shareable. Family history is a global, enormously popular public history activity. It is undertaken around the world and for the most part online, using digital tools and engaging users in networks and online communities. As its digital tools evolve and develop, the practice of family history will similarly evolve. More and more, the practice of family history is being undertaken on websites and using the software provided by major international information companies, and it is important to take into account the tension between individual usage and that supported in this commercialised way.

Keywords: family history, genealogy, family trees, DNA, genetic genealogy

Family history and genealogy have a very long tradition as public historical activities, going back centuries.[1] Investigating family history through looking at records and archives became increasingly codified through the twentieth century in Europe and the USA as national and local record offices began to open their official collections to the public. Family history and genealogy are complex ways for individuals to engage with historical techniques such as research in archives, palaeography, codicology, and the like. Digital family history refers to the hugely augmented possibilities for doing such research online.

Whilst a long-standing activity, the great expansion in family history was particularly driven in the post-war period by an interest in social history.[2] In the United States the boom in genealogy first developed among a set of predominantly white middle-class amateur historians in the 1960s and 1970s, but also was driven by the popularity of the television series *Roots* which aired for the first time on ABC-TV in 1977. Similarly, across Europe, the development of genealogy and family history

---

[1] See the articles at http://ncph.org/history-at-work/tag/jerome-de-groot-on-genealogy/ and also Francois Weil, *A History of Genealogy in America* (Harvard, MA: Harvard University Press, 2013). See also Jerome de Groot, *Consuming History: Historians and Heritage in Contemporary Popular Culture* (London and New York: Routledge, 2016), 73–87.
[2] See Alison Light, *Common People* (London: Penguin, 2014).

was driven by the opening up of archives and record offices to wider publics. Family history practice has developed in different places for different reasons. Different communities have used it for particular purposes, such as the Church of the Latter-Day Saints which encourages its members to create extensive family trees for retrospective baptism of the dead. The Church has developed an extensive set of digital resources, which is the best available on the web, largely as a consequence of this institutionalized practice.

The foundational practice of the family historian is the creation of a family tree based around a particular person and expanding sideways and backwards through time. Family history is a public history practice because this is a way that the "public" can "do" history. It began as a distinctly amateur mode of accessing the past, although those who undertake it have become increasingly skilled, including developing specialized practices and modes of representing family history. Indeed, there are many online university courses that are now available for those who want to make their work methodologically precise.[3] There are also many professional outlets, such as the Society of Genealogists, who will undertake family history research as a paid activity. Family history is a public history practice because the research and information generated is often shared, either with other users privately or online through public family tree software. Family trees are also evidence of historical practice, as they are a "published" creation with a linear narrative, as well as sources of evidence. Family trees also represent a rendering into a specialized format of the language or text of the physical bodies of those who had lived previously.

Family history and genealogy were transformed as practices by the advent of multiple digital resources, including databases, FTP, discussion forums, email, and noticeboards, and, in the 90s, by the expansion of the web.

Digital resources have led to exponential growth in users undertaking their own family histories. In the United Kingdom, for instance, the massively successful television series *Who Do You Think You Are?* was developed with the National Archives as a way of publicizing the online publication of census data in 2004.[4] The program, and its website, were wildly successful, far beyond what had been anticipated, with the television series now syndicated around the world. Perhaps more importantly, access to digital information allowing family history research has expanded hugely in the past fifteen to twenty years. As the number of digital records has grown, the ability to expand family trees far further has been enabled. The activity is now enormous, and worldwide. Public historians need to be aware of this practice and to understand how it works. The methodological challenge here is to

---

3 See, for instance, the courses at the University of Strathclyde, https://www.strath.ac.uk/studywithus/centreforlifelonglearning/genealogy/.
4 See Amy Holdsworth, *Television, Memory and Nostalgia* (Basingstoke: Palgrave Macmillan, 2011), 65–95.

understand the practices of family history, and also the effects (emotional and intellectual) that it has on those who undertake it.

Family historians have often been early adopters of new technologies, from microfilm to particular database software (GEDCOM, the foundational record system for most family history work, was an early open-source initiative although developed by the Church of Latter Day Saints).[5] Indeed, new groups and discussion forums were early modes for family historians in using the Internet, and it could be argued that their practice drove the development of particular models for presenting and accessing information. Certainly, the way that online records are kept, accessed, and shared owes much to the family history internet subcultures of the 1980s and 1990s.

During the first years of the twenty-first century, most genealogical record-keeping moved online. Presently, most family historians now access data and build their family tree online. They tend to use particular research and storage software provided by massive information companies such as Ancestry.com, Findmypast.com, and FamilySearch.org. These large companies provide umbrella access to the databases around the world and software interfaces that allow the user to mine the digital various archives. The user is given direct access to the database via their account. For a monthly fee the family historian will have instant access to libraries and archives around the world, to billions of records relating to employment, tax, property, the military, immigration, births, marriages, and deaths. They might be able to access library records, newspaper archives, and information about locale and maps. The web companies provide simple access to these databases; their websites also enable the building of family trees. Whilst the records are largely public, having been collected by governments and such agencies, the access to their digital elements is licensed.

Critically, users' family trees have emerged as a central element of the business model of most genealogical web services.

The companies also provide access to all the other family trees in their network, meaning that, as with most major web companies, the users are also producers (known as prosumers), creating content through their research and digital labour which contributes to the financial value of the company and the services it provides. Such prosumption is foundational to online family history, and the notion of the user as producer and collaborator is important. Most users recognize that they are creating content and sharing data to enable the database to grow and gain complexity, but are happy to do so in exchange for the wide access they are given to archives and users around the world. However, some more sophisticated family historians criticize the major companies or refuse to use their services.

---

5 See Jerome de Groot, "The Genealogy Boom: Inheritance, Family History, and the Popular Historical Imagination," in *The Impact of History? Histories at the Beginning of the 21st Century*, ed. Bertrand Taithe and Pedro Ramos Pinto (London and New York: Routledge, 2015), 21–34.

Additionally, the genealogical practice from the dusty archive to the web has transformed the production of family trees in other subtly important ways. For example, while many family historians continue to use physical records, books, and archives, they nonetheless tend to process and store their data using the various database technologies made available by the websites. More serious family historians may use bespoke software to build their family trees and keep their information. However, the majority will use the web and/or a combination of software networked to the web to maintain their data. The advantage of working within these online communities is that an individual family tree can be plugged into an entire global network of information, instantly crowdsourcing research and bringing a huge amount of work, context, and documentation to bear without the user having to move. As a result, the umbrella websites also function as social networks, as family historians communicate with one another (although they also use more obvious communication tools such as email, Twitter, and Facebook). They connect people around the world in a particular set of activities. Practical history-making becomes something that creates unlikely communities globally, connected through websites and social networks and united in a particular practice.

The digital tools that family historians use are becoming more sophisticated, and the type of information that is being included is becoming more interoperable and shareable. Genealogists will access government records, census data, graveyard information, maps, immigration information, and photographs. All of this is to be found online and can be linked to individuals within the family tree. Indeed, many of the larger family history groups, of which there are thousands, have created large archives of information on, for instance, particular local names, local locations, or single surnames. The users are, therefore, often also those who create the data. They sell this to the big web companies, ensuring that they are also part of the process of commodification of information. The development of digital tools for family history has also made the practice a very international, globalized one. Users will interact with records from around the world, and with users from many other countries. Again, whilst this was common before the development of the Internet, the development of database technology and online interfaces has meant that global access to this information has become more immediate and more easily available, expanding the ranks of these erstwhile historians.

The fact that family history is now curated and created online, engaged with and consumed through software and computers, underscores that it has become almost purely digital history. Of course, it often retains a clear connection and reference to "physical evidence". The interplay between the "real" thing and the digital version has become an increasingly complex negotiation. Users can look at images of the "real" record from thousands of miles away, simultaneously calling up a newspaper report, birth certificate, census account, and immigration record. They can also, at the same time, see how others have transcribed these records—correcting misspellings or correcting poorly written script in the Census records for instance.

Alternately, using notes and comments features, researchers can annotate their work for others to see. Research is conducted at all times of the day and night, on smartphones, tablets, laptops, as well as pen and paper. Historical information online is visualized, shared, revised, added to, and used by a huge number of researchers. Indeed the type of information produced by family historians is increasingly informing academic history, as historians use family records and data in their research.

Whilst the majority of users still tend to be in the developed world—North America, Europe, and Australia—the major Internet companies have expanded to include South Asia and South America, with use of their sites and interest in the activity growing. This might jar with local practice because obviously the undertaking of family history has cultural association and heritage in different locales. In many ways such practice could be seen as the imposition of a particular knowledge structure (the tree, the record, the database entry), imposed by largely Western companies such as Ancestry or MyHeritage onto non-Western contexts.

Family historians are increasingly being encouraged to use new, scientific techniques to augment their research. In particular, the use of DNA sequencing has been offered by Internet companies. A user submits a sample for consideration, and the company analyzes it for various markers. This includes looking at DNA markers suggesting male inheritance, or suggesting a common female ancestor many generations ago, or combining DNA analysis with population genetics to suggest shared historical ethnicity. More recent advances give researchers the option to share their DNA results with others, allowing them to see those with whom they share some DNA connection, whether it be a relationship of first or sixth cousins.

These types of investigation can produce excellent results and are increasingly well respected. In the public imagination DNA testing – for paternity, for family, and the like – is considered relatively infallible, and hence DNA tests are popular for their perceived authenticity. DNA testing opens up a new frontier for the sense of self and historical narrative that family history engages with, as Christine Kenneally argued: "DNA and our life experiences make our bodies palimpsests. As we learn how to interpret the body in the context of its genetic code, we begin to understand how the hand of fate, the choices of families, and the enormous journey of DNA through deep time affect our lives right now".[6] DNA evidence links the individual to the wider species, whilst encouraging a sense of the unique quality of the contemporary.

All of the DNA information that is provided is held online, and the self is rendered as digital data on the company websites. There are many ethical issues to resolve here, including those relating to the holding and storing of biodata. The relationship between the individual and the "big data" archive is complex and at present still evolving. Users sign privacy clauses that release the company to be

---

6 Christine Kenneally, *The Invisible History of the Human Race*, 2014, 264.

able to manipulate the DNA and also share the findings in various ways. Similarly, it is important for the company that the network grows, as individual results only acquire meaning when related to a wider whole. The interpretation of the data depends on the different company, with some offering a very low-resolution service and some a much more enhanced, detailed profile. However, this is still problematic for some mainstream family historians, as they are unable to access the raw information and need to have it interpreted for them. Elsewhere, the size of the archive is increasingly overwhelming to those without specialist software or ways of "reading" this "big" data.

Scientists have acknowledged that some of the practices involved in using DNA testing—such as using nineteenth century racial and ethnic designations—are deeply problematic.[7] Additionally, some scholars have expressed concerns that such practices reduce complex and socially-constructed categories of identity to a simply biological marker—essentially reifying ethnic and racial categories. Nonetheless, the possibilities of discovering hidden genetic connections—including potentially useful medical information—appear in company advertising. And, broadly, DNA testing has proven to be highly popular.

On the positive side of the ledger, DNA testing suggests a longer ancestry and can sometimes act as a link to family and relations that had been obscured by the archive. It also provides a service for those families and communities whose records might be incomplete, or have never existed. It has, for instance, been very high profile in the African American community, and Henry Louis Gates, Jr.'s series *African American Lives* (2006) provided a good example of the way that investigating family history could be augmented by DNA work. Louis Gates reminded readers that "searching for my ancestry was always a fraught process, always a mix of joy, frustration and outrage, as the reconstruction of their history – individually and collectively – must always be for any African American".[8] His public history – television series and popular book – was intended to address this ongoing issue. DNA science, he argued, allowed a further analysis: "when the paper trail would end, as it inevitably did, in the horrid darkness of slavery, we traced our African roots through our DNA".[9]

Louis Gates Jr.'s series showed how family history is never a neutral activity, and illustrated the importance of public historians engaging with the practice. As suggested, family history is public history as it engages a wider public with the practices and activities of "professionals". It allows the public to take up the tools of history themselves, assembling and reading evidence, presenting arguments, working in the archive. It is also distinctly political as a practice, outlining discussions about ethnicity,

---

[7] See Deborah A. Bolnick et al., "The Science and the Business of Genetic Ancestry Testing," *Science* 5849, no. 318 (2007): 399–400.
[8] *In Search of Our Roots: How 19 Extraordinary African Americans Reclaimed their Past* (New York: Random House, 2009), 5.
[9] *In Search of Our Roots*, p. 11.

the keeping of records and evidence, identity, and selfhood, all in relation to historical knowledge and investigation. Discussions of ancestry, roots, origins, and legitimacy are all fraught with political considerations, and these mean that the family historian must always be alert and careful about their practice, perhaps drawing lessons from public historians about how to deal with challenging or controversial pasts.

A good example of the "public" and political nature of the work is found in the Youtube advertisement that Ancestry.com posted on July 4, 2017. Whilst the Ancestry company was clear that the work was not politically pointed, it clearly had resonance. The film focuses on a set of people sitting down, whilst the words of the Declaration of Independence are read. Eventually the moving images resolve into a tableau imitation of John Turnbull's famous 1817 *Declaration of Independence* which is currently in the United States Capitol Building in Washington D.C. The tagline is simply: "Everyone we've assembled here is descended from a signer of the Declaration of Independence".[10] The trick of the advertising campaign was that the assembled descendants are a range of genders and ethnic backgrounds, with the message seeming to be that America is highly ethnically mixed and that this is the fundamental feature of the country, from its beginnings to now. The advertisement, which is shared entirely online, telescopes American history and makes a political point about the multicultural origins of the United States at a particularly tumultuous moment in Americans' ongoing culture wars. It is an important piece of contemporary digital public history whilst showing no historical moment, event, or personage.

Family history is an enormously popular, global, public history activity. It is undertaken around the world and for the most part online, using digital tools and engaging through networks and online communities. This has been inflected by the development of online tools and resources. As the digital tools evolve and develop the practice of family history will similarly evolve. Increasingly, the practice of family history is undertaken within the website and software of major international information companies, and the tension between this and individual usage is important to note. Public history practitioners and theorists need to be careful about how they understand and engage with family history organisations, and how they gather and read the data that is being produced by these users. Family historians produce and contribute to a discourse of historical sensibility, understanding themselves in relation to the past.

---

10 "Declaration Descendants," June 29, 2017, https://www.youtube.com/watch?v=R1PMt8bnz34.

Bibliography

Bishop, R. "In the Grand Scheme of Things: An Exploration of the Meaning of Genealogical Research." *Journal of Popular Culture* 41, no. 3 (2008): 393–412.

de Groot, J. "The Genealogy Boom: Inheritance, Family History, and the Popular Historical Imagination." In *The Impact of History? Histories at the Beginning of the 21st Century*, edited by B. Taithe and P. Ramos Pinto, 21–34. London and New York: Routledge, 2015.

Evans, T. "Secrets and Lies: The Radical Potential of Family History." *History Workshop Journal* 71 (2011): 50–73

Holdsworth, A. "*Who Do You Think You Are?*: Family History and Memory on British Television." In *Televising History*, edited by E. Bell and A. Gray, 234–47.

Rutherford, A. *A Brief History of Everyone Who Ever Lived*. London: Weidenfeld and Nicolson, 2017.

Valérie Schafer
Digital Personal Memories: The Archiving of the Self and Public History

Abstract: By providing a facilitated access to data storage, digital technologies seem to make expression and preservation of the self more straightforward. They reconfigure the means and forms of access to data, thus also affecting the relationships and participation of individuals in heritagization and history, and potentially impacting historians. This renews questions that scholars already know well, such as the place of memories in the making of history, and that of self-narratives.

Examining how "ordinary voices" can/could archive digital/digitized data and documents, this chapter aims at investigating this increased interest in preserving the self and memories, the heritagization of these data, and finally the role played by user-generated contributions in Digital Public History projects and in historical research in general.

Keywords: self, archiving, history, memory, personal data, heritage

Introduction

> Experience is neither completely lived nor entirely mediated, as the encounter between the two is a continuously evolving life-project to define the self in a larger cultural context. What makes mediated experience today differ from lived experience two hundred years ago is the fact that individuals need no longer share a common locale to pursue commonality [. . .].[1]

In the wake of ideas developed after World War II by Vannevar Bush, who imagined the multimedia based Memex (Memory Extender), the computer researcher Gordon Bell created MyLifebits. His project aimed to record and store all possible information about his life. In this "lifetime store of everything," he not only digitized his personal documents, home movies, voice recordings, and collections, but also stored his GPS data and the photos of his environment, taken by a wearable camera. In his book *Total Recall*,[2] he presented the developments he made in this domain with Jim Gemmel (and with the support of Microsoft Research from 1999 to 2007). This approach

---
1 José Van Dijck, *Mediated Memories in the Digital Age* (Stanford: Stanford University Press, 2007), 19.
2 Gordon Bell and Jim Gemmel, *Total Recall* (Paris, Flammarion: 2011).

Acknowledgments: The author wants to thank Joanna Lignot for her constructive and helpful proofreading.

https://doi.org/10.1515/9783110430295-033

makes him a forerunner of the "quantified self", as well as a pioneering experimenter of e-memories, attaining both organisational and patrimonial goals.

Other roots such as Boltanski's ambition to record all the moments of lives may be regarded as a recall of the Memex and an anticipation of lifelogging and self-tracking.[3]

These utopia and issues were taken up by commercial companies such as Evernote, which promises to "remember everything" via a software it describes as "a second brain." Other online services dedicated to "virtual eternity" belong to the second category, with online packages such as E-mylife enabling users to leave documents, photographs, or videos for close relatives after death, and send post-mortem messages on chosen dates to selected recipients.

Examining how "ordinary voices" can/could archive digital/digitized data and documents, this chapter aims at investigating this increased interest in preserving memories, the heritagization of these data, and finally the role played by user-generated contributions in Digital Public History projects and in historical research in general.

Multiple Voices, Multiple Tracks

The comparison of Gordon Bell's experiments and websites promoting "digital eternity" reveals different approaches to the digital preservation and organization of the self.

For instance, Gordon Bell describes his project as lifelogging, which he distinguishes from lifeblogging: in the first case the storage of individual data is private, and in the second it is public.

One can also distinguish between digitized heritage and born-digital heritage[4] without opposing them, as the two can often be entwined.

We can also underline the diverse range of spaces, devices, platforms, and media supporting the recording and storage of memory (from daily updates and blogs to podcasts and camcorder footage).

The creation of digital personal memories through user-generated content and crowdsourcing activities and the creation of a "mediated self" via the web and social media can also play different roles, from fulfilling a family goal to researching an artistic or historical project, or carrying out activism. There are several examples of the second category, such as the *Guantanamo Public Memory Project*, which seeks to build public awareness of the long history of the US naval station. The *Sep-*

---

[3] David Houston Jones, "*All the Moments of our Lives:* Self-archiving from Christian Boltanski to Lifelogging," *Archives and Records* 36 (2015): 29–41.

[4] Resources for which "there is no other format but the digital object," as defined by UNESCO in 2003, http://unesdoc.unesco.org/images/0013/001331/133171e.pdf#page=80.

tember 11 Digital Archive collects data and memories, inviting participants to fill in a form and answer the question, "how has your life changed because of what happened on September 11, 2001?"[5] The *Charlie Archive* at Harvard university seeks to collect, organize, and preserve a wide array of materials that represent diverse perspectives from different media on the events that took place in Paris in January 2015. It also invites people to share documents, underlining that, "The most exciting aspect of this project is that we don't know where it can lead us and how it will evolve".[6] *NC HB2: A Citizens' History*, launched by Tammy S. Gordon in 2016, establishes itself as "an archive of materials related to North Carolina's House Bill 2," inviting individuals to share experiences which "will help others get a fuller understanding of the significance of HB2 from multiple perspectives, including yours."[7]

These examples question the complex relationships between personal, private, and public memories. In fact, the borders between these types of memory are porous. In *Save as . . . Digital Memories*, the authors postulate that social network memory is a new hybrid form of public and private memory, where "the instantaneity and temporality of social network environments disguise their potential as mediatised ghosts to haunt participants far beyond the life-stage of their online social networking."[8]

In addition, the intentional storage and organization of traces through threads, timelines, and interfaces does not have the same meaning as those generated by digital platforms without the direct intervention of the user.

But it is also worth exploring the different facets of the self, which specialists paint in many shades. Fanny Georges distinguishes the declarative, active, and, finally, calculated identity, adding that: "By opening up the use of websites to a wider audience, web 2.0 sites have in return standardized forms of self-presentation, and valued certain information that was not even present in the first personal web pages, such as the number of visits, of posts, the name of friends. This presentation of the self is not neutral."[9] In addition, the mediated-self is also mediated by others on social media, through comments, likes, retweets, and interactions, therefore introducing several layers and identities.

---

[5] http://911digitalarchive.org/contribution. All websites mentioned in footnotes were accessed on March 3, 2019.
[6] http://cahl.io/#context.
[7] See Tammy S. Gordon's chapter in this Handbook "Individuals in the Crowd: Privacy, Online Participatory Curation, and the Public Historian as Private Citizen", pp. 317–325.
[8] Joanne Garde-Hansen et al., eds., *Save As . . . Digital Memories* (London: Palgrave Macmillan, 2009), 6.
[9] Fanny Georges, "De l'identité numérique aux éternités numériques" (paper presented at the Sixième Université d'automne des RAMM Les nouvelles technologies, Aix-les Bains, France, 2013), https://halshs.archives-ouvertes.fr/halshs-01576152/document.

This finally reveals nuances between digital platforms, which can be open or closed, commercial or free, produced by digital industry or by a community (sometimes academic).

Although the vast amount of personal data and testimonials on blogs and collective websites can be seen as "sources at hand" to feed public history, with these "distributed memories" converging within new forms of knowledge communities[10], the reality is of course much more complex and embeds several mediations, introduced by platforms and their design and/or curators, participants, or historians through digital public history.

"Self-archiving," Digital Heritagization, and Digital Public History

Several historical researches include the self in collective projects such as *Immigrant Nation* (IN), which started in 2014.[11] Aimed at sharing the immigration stories of US citizens, it has already gathered over a thousand stories online:

> Participants are invited to become co-creators in the website by creating and sharing their own stories with their own photo archives and voices. Anyone can get involved by creating a profile, searching others' stories and comparing those stories with the official immigration waves data sets. [. . .] Anyone can post comments in other people's stories and it is also possible to add tags in the stories, allowing users to search according to topics and countries.[12]

This project is aligned with Bodnar's analysis[13] on the special role played by immigration history in the history of the USA and its stated goal of defining national values. The IN team specifies this on their website: "The topic of immigration often divides communities across the country, but bringing these stories to the surface has the potential to create commonality between new arrivals and those whose families have lived in the U.S. for generations.[14]" This statement is also in line with Roy Rozensweig's and David Thelen's study,[15] in which they highlighted a certain

---

10 Henry Jenkins, *Convergence Culture: Where Old and New Media Collide* (New York: New York University Press, 2006).
11 https://www.immigrant-nation.com.
12 Carles Sora, "Expanding Temporal and Participative Digital Horizons Through Web Documentaries for Social Change," in *Temps et temporalités du Web*, ed. Valérie Schafer (Nanterre: Presses universitaires de Paris Nanterre, 2017), 257.
13 John Bodnar, "Symbols and Servants: Immigrant America and the Limits History," *The Journal of American History* 73 (1986): 137–151.
14 See http://inationmedia.com/interactive/.
15 Roy Rosenzweig and David Thelen, *The Presence of the Past. Popular Uses of History in American Life* (Columbia: Columbia University Press, 1998).

user distrust of history when written by "official or academic bodies" and a desire to remove intermediaries from the memory creation process (we will discuss this illusion in terms of technology later on).

This wish to be "face to face" with history[16] also explains the interest for the collection or creation of historical sources and resources for sensitive historical topics and events such as the September 11 attack, which struck the USA to its core. Another interesting phenomenon was the massive archiving of Twitter and of the web after the terrorist attacks against *Charlie Hebdo* by the institutional bodies (the French National Library and the National Audiovisual Institute) in charge of the legal deposit of the web in France[17], or the gathering of November 13, 2015 in Paris.

Of course, it is also appropriate to examine Web archiving institutions in order to understand how historians could use these sources. Indeed, the life but also the rapid death of digital blogs, platforms, and services (as illustrated by the case of Geocities) indicates the need to look closely at the institutionalized archiving, which aims to guarantee the authenticity and permanency of resources. Serge Noiret noted that digital public history brings "a great change in documentability".[18] Archival centers nevertheless remain a landmark for historians and a guarantee of the conservation and provision of primary sources.

In the field of born-digital heritage, we can underline both the success and limitations of preserving the self. Brewster Kahle, who was a pioneer in 1996 with the foundation of the Internet Archive, had a broad ambition. He did not distinguish between individual websites and more institutional websites: his *Wayback Machine*[19] thus contains multiple forms of self-expression. However, there is no guarantee of their regular preservation: despite the abundance of crawls and data, gaps and silence still exist in web archives.[20]

Several findings can be made about recovering the presence of the self in national Web archives.

First, it is clearly easier to archive some contents than others: for example Facebook, which features a closed system and many private contents, remains a challenge. The archiving of the self may therefore largely depend on media platforms and their terms of service, but also on their technical characteristics (e.g. the ephemeral flow of Periscope, which is a live streaming video mobile app).

---

[16] Serge Noiret, "La digital history: histoire et mémoire à la portée de tous," in *Read/Write Book 2: Une introduction aux humanités numériques*, ed. Pierre Mounier (Marseille: OpenEdition Press, 2012). http://books.openedition.org/oep/258.

[17] Web archiving initiatives related to the COVID crisis are also numerous and international. See for example the IIPC initiative: https://archive-it.org/collections/13529.

[18] S. Noiret, *Op. Cit.*

[19] https://archive.org/web/.

[20] Francesca Musiani et al., *Qu'est-ce qu'une archive du Web?* (Marseille: OpenEdition Press, 2019), https://books.openedition.org/oep/8713?lang=fr.

Second, not all archiving perimeters allow the archiving of these data: French Web archives include ordinary and vernacular traces of users, whereas Swiss Web archives have a more institutional and restricted archiving policy. In France, the frequency and depth of archiving still varies according to websites. Whilst the BnF (French National Library) archives press websites on a daily basis, it generally only archives other French websites once per year during the annual collection of seven million domains.[21]

The consequent risk of permanent data loss is of course not specific to Web archiving: there is a continuity of selection, loss, and oblivion that refers to a long history of preservation.

Historical Consequences

Although the projects referred to earlier are often established outside the sphere of historians, the latter can nevertheless provide them with support and curation. This is the case of the Guantanamo project, which benefits from the input of historical advisors.

The archives of the self are not yet a central primary source in historical research, although they are more and more becoming, on the web and through crowdsourcing activities, important archives of the self and of family memories. Their increasing use will depend, however, on several conditions being satisfied.

First, their use could be improved by optimising their portability, interoperability, and interaction with other sources through transmediality for example, which also depend on openness, searchability, and sustainability.

Second, historians will have to develop their ability to solve and manage gap/abundance, individual/collective, and micro/macro paradoxes. As noted by William Merrin: "Whereas broadcast media were concerned with communicating with, informing and uniting 'the social' – with the abstract social body formed by the population conceived of as 'the public' or 'the masses' – today's 'social networking' media derive their name from 'social life'."[22]

Furthermore, the data can never be considered to be "raw" (in this field too, "raw data is an oxymoron"[23]). Historians have to consider heritagization as a set of practices,

---

[21] Valérie Schafer, Francesca Musiani, and Marguerite Borelli, "Negotiating the Web of the Past," *French Journal for Media Research* 6 (2016), http://frenchjournalformediaresearch.com/index.php?id=952. See also Niels Brügger, *The Archived Web: Doing History in the Digital Age* (Cambridge, MA: The MIT Press, 2018).

[22] William Merrin, "Media Studies 2.0: Upgrading and Open-sourcing the Discipline," *Interactions: Studies in Communication and Culture* 1 (2009), https://clairemacme4.files.wordpress.com/2011/05/w-merrin-we-need-media-2-01.pdf.

[23] Lisa Gitelman, *"Raw Data" Is An Oxymoron* (Cambridge, MA: The MIT Press, 2013).

as recalled by Fanny Valois Nadeau,[24] who highlights the fact that heritage is not a passive process, but rather an active and creative link between the present and the past.

Another challenge for historians is that of contextualization and intelligibility, as the migration of contents over time does not safeguard from a potential loss of intelligibility.[25] Therefore, experts in documentation, digital archives, digital history, and media history are needed to fully contextualize and mediate data and digital content.

In addition to the visible and sudden disappearance of some social networks (e.g. Geocities and MobileMe), more discrete yet significant changes also occur in digital cultures (such as the changing meaning of hypertext links, gifs). The historian should therefore consider the conventions and frameworks of the media, and be aware of "the self-fashioning, the image-making, at work."[26] However, as Van Dijck states, it would be a mistake to underestimate the creativity of the users, as "it's a fallacy to think of memory as purely constraining or conformist."[27]

Finally, historians can certainly gain valuable insights into interdisciplinarity by working with experts in the sociology of innovation, in software studies, in information and communication studies, in memory studies, and in media studies.

If the interdisciplinary and transdisciplinary approach (which is already a basic concept in public history) is likely to modify the historians' view, the contents found in the archives of the self are also likely to modify not only the methodologies, but also the objects and subjects of their studies. The archives of the self raise the question of the relationship between history and memory, but also between the academic interests of historians and those of the general public, and consequently the relationship between these two entities. As Diane F. Britton, who specializes in Public History, aptly pointed out, the following issue is not new, but has yet to be fully understood: "How do we continue to confront the issue of 'who owns the past?' Who determines which stories or interpretations are legitimate, what should be remembered and saved?".[28]

---

[24] Fannie Valois-Nadeau, "Rethinking Heritagization Through the Digitization of Familial Archives," *RESET* 6 (2017), http://reset.revues.org/773.
[25] Bruno Bachimont, *Patrimoine et numérique. Technique et politique de la mémoire* (Bry-sur-Marne: Ina Editions, 2017), 195.
[26] Gunnthorunn Gudmundsdottir, "The Online Self: Memory and Forgetting in the Digital Age," *European Journal of Life Writing* (2014), http://ejlw.eu/article/view/100/254.
[27] José Van Dijck, *Op. Cit.*, 7.
[28] Diane F. Britton, "Public History and Public Memory," *The Public Historian* 19, no. 3 (1997): 11–23.

Conclusion

By providing a facilitated access to data storage and new ways to organize and display these data, digital technologies seem to make expression and preservation of the self more straightforward. These data are currently probably of more interest to commercial companies than historians. However, these initiatives will renew questions that historians already know well, such as the place of memories in the making of history, and that of self-narratives. Some projects reconfigure the means and forms of access to data, thus also affecting the relationship and participation of individuals in history, and potentially impacting historians.

Given the stakes involved in Digital Public History and archiving the self, the question "who owns the past?" also points to the need for an understanding of economic and ethical issues. Digital Public History projects sometimes show open distrust of a history written by professional historians, yet their contributors should perhaps be more concerned about the risk of memory privatization in locked platforms and closed services held by IT companies.

Although Gordon Bell considers digital storage to be "the perfect memory," the historian of ideas Abby Smith Rumsey warns that it will be extremely difficult to avoid collective amnesia[29] if data preservation and control is entrusted to private companies alone. I therefore underline the conclusion drawn by Louise Merzeau, who, when considering the illusion of total recall, highlighted "the imperative to collectively rethink oblivion in order to regulate and structure it so that it makes sense."[30]

Bibliography

Garde-Hansen, J., A. Hoskins, and A. Reading, eds. *Save As . . . Digital Memories*. London: Palgrave Macmillan, 2009.

Noiret, S. "La digital history: histoire et mémoire à la portée de tous." In *Read/Write Book 2: Une introduction aux humanitésnumériques*, edited by Pierre Mounier. Marseille: OpenEdition Press, 2012. Accessed March 3, 2019. http://books.openedition.org/oep/258.

Rosenzweig, R., and D. Thelen. *The Presence of the Past. Popular Uses of History in American Life*. Columbia: Columbia University Press, 1998.

Smith Rumsey, A. *When we are no more. How Digital Memory Is Shaping Our Future*. London: Bloomsbury Press, 2016.

Van Dijck, J. *Mediated Memories in the Digital Age*. Stanford: Stanford University Press, 2007.

---

29 Abby Smith Rumsey, *When we are no more. How Digital Memory Is Shaping Our Future* (London: Bloomsbury Press, 2016).
30 Louise Merzeau, "Il n'y a pas de mémoire sans une pensée de l'oubli," *Archimag*, September 13, 2016, http://www.archimag.com/archives-patrimoine/2016/09/13/louise-merzeau-memoire-pensee-oubli.

Pierluigi Feliciati
Planning with the Public: How to Co-develop Digital Public History Projects?

Abstract: Digital public history, when possible, should be planned with the public, not merely for the public. The involvement of an audience in projects has to be pursued considering the dimensions related to human-computer interaction and adopting the best techniques to guarantee the highest degree of satisfaction to all stakeholders: the conceivers and the developers, the programmers, and the final users. Such a participatory approach, to be effective, should be enacted during the whole project lifecycle. This contribution presents synthetically which competencies are requested, which methods could be adopted and when is it more appropriate to activate them, which results could we expect and how to evaluate the impact of projects on final users.

Keywords: project management, digital users, user studies, user engagement, user-centered design

Introduction

Digital public history demands broad goals related to engaging public audiences. They extend beyond merely granting publics online access to scientific papers written by historians or to digital/digitized primary sources. As well as for librarians and archivists, open access remains an important goal for publishers, but public historians should embrace digital tools in ways that expand the historical conversation. The broad community of public historians (including librarians or archivists, as well as a host of professionals in related fields) is meant to promote and engage the public understanding of the past. We all agree that acting on the Internet presents both challenges and opportunities. For example, it opens up a substantial risk of "replacement of knowledge and analysis by opinions" and that "digital public historians have to work at the creation of knowledge and scholarship, and not to the multiplication of pure opinions."[1]

The goals of public history should be planned with the public, not merely for the public. The involvement of an audience (target or general) in projects regarding historical questions, events, persons, places, and any possible matching of all this should be pursued proactively. We are aware that during the last several years, many good projects, supported by robust theories, opened up the highway of what

---

[1] Thomas Cauvin, *Public History: A Textbook of Practice* (New York/London: Routledge, 2016), 180.

https://doi.org/10.1515/9783110430295-034

we define as digital public history (DPH), discernable from the mere online publication of digitized collections. These projects were initiated by galleries, archives, libraries, and museums or were the result of digital humanities research outcomes.

The implementation of DPH projects has embraced experimentation with emerging – and even disruptive – technologies, tools, channels, languages, formats, such as crowdsourcing, annotations, wikis, tagging, feedback, comments, learning objects, semantic tagging, GIS, A.I., blockchain, etc.[2] Furthermore, some exemplary projects have provided activities of self-evaluation, typically carried out after the online publishing, and adopting the methods of log analysis and web questionnaires.

However, a broader approach that fosters digital users' involvement is possible. To tackle such goals, different technical dimensions must be considered, including those related to human-computer interaction. Also critical are techniques to guarantee the highest degree of satisfaction to all stakeholders: the conceivers and the developers, the programmers, and the final users. The best way to achieve such an ambitious target is to activate these endeavors since the very conception of the DPH project. Such a participatory approach – based on collaboration and sharing of authority – should also be enacted during the whole project lifecycle.

Complicating the effort to involve users is that the ongoing research about digital user studies (defined below) gives an impression of fragmentation. Various types of users of digital services exist in different contexts, missing a coherent and supportive methodological framework. Also, many studies carried out involving users' samples are based on very specific localized questions and indicators that do not address broader issues. The adoption of this localized view hinders any opportunity of standardization and benchmarking, so it is not possible to compare single studies or to rate projects objectively considering the point of view of their final addressees. Finally, and paradoxically, sometimes our present project-driven culture – with its focus on the end product – makes it challenging to dedicate the time and resources to consider user experience.

The main issues related to implementing a user-centered approach to DPH projects will be presented. The following issues will be considered briefly:
- which competencies are requested,
- which methods could be adopted,
- when is it more appropriate to activate different methods,
- which results could we expect,
- how to evaluate the impact of our projects on final (remote) users.

---

[2] See Meg Foster, "Online and Plugged In?: Public History and Historians in the Digital Age," *Public History Review* 21 (2014): 1–19.

User Studies Planning and Management

Since it is evident that no results are achievable without investing some resources (temporal, organizational, and human), the first issue to tackle when considering the sustainability of user involvement activities is typically to ask which competencies are needed to plan, organize and analyze DPH projects. Digital public historians must acquire some elemental professional skills to launch simple user studies. They need to consider a group of users representing a sample of the targeted public during the lifecycle of their DPH projects. As Sharon Leon argues, "the best digital public history work requires a blend of applied technical skills, targeted engagement strategies, disciplinary ways of knowing, and deep content knowledge."[3]

Several guidelines and best practices are available in order to develop adequate user interaction strategies. These can be tailored to a planned scenario and should draw a specific protocol to be applied. Typically, it is useful if the interaction with the sample users is controlled by someone who has a strong involvement in the DPH project and, in addition, by someone who has an in-depth competence in managing user studies to also be aware of the project itself.

The best results could be obtained by sharing the planning and development of a public history project with a significant number of representatives of the broadest target audience. It is helpful to go over the common myths about internet users, their competence, their interests, the context where they live and operate, their expectations in terms of technologies provided (performance) and the real usefulness of the offered resources and tools. For example, the digital literacy of young users, professionals' behavior and skills, or the necessity of being up-to-date with the last technical solutions are often taken for granted.

Digital user studies are an open field of research that aims to check the potential interests of designated communities or engage them.[4] This field covers a wide range of applications, starting with the digital version of the tradition of launching a public call asking for contributions to a collection, turned now into the harvesting of User Generated Content. Then, organizing user-centered assessment of prototypes and checking the efficacy of human-machine interaction. Finally, collecting and reusing users' feedback (even adopting big data analysis).

The participatory action, research and design are based upon the participant's involvement to provide solutions to eventual problems rather than solely documenting

---

[3] Leon, "User-Centered Digital History."
[4] A guide to these studies can be found in MINERVA EC Working Group Quality, Accessibility and Usability, eds, *Handbook on cultural web user interaction* (MINERVA publications, 2008): accessed May 22, 2020, https://www.minervaeurope.org/publications/Handbookwebuserinteraction.pdf.

them.[5] The core of this approach is to involve potential stakeholders (e.g. employees, partners, customers, citizens as end-users) in the design process, to develop solutions answering as closely as possible to their needs and behaviors. Initial stages of projects usually request involvement in activities of immersion, observing, and contextual framing to increase familiarity with the context. Consequent stages may be based on community brainstorming, modeling and prototyping, and implementation in community spaces.

The adoption of *Human-Centered* Design (HCD) – or *User-Centered* Design – methodologies may become the best solution. It is an approach to systems development based on interaction with the users and focused on the usability and usefulness of final products. The users stay at the core of this framework of methods, with their needs and requirements tackled by applying human factors/ergonomics, usability knowledge, and analysis techniques.[6] This approach, in addition to increasing ethical correctness,[7] has clearly shown how to enhance effectiveness and efficiency and improve human well-being, user satisfaction, accessibility, and sustainability.[8]

Projects' Lifecycle and User Involvement: When and Why?

What will be described in the following is a widely accepted schema proposal to orient choosing the best user study or involvement methods in the different stages of any DPH project.[9]

1 Conception Phase

In this crucial stage, when researchers focus on the main goals of the project and the selection of content, the involvement of the public is beneficial to identify

---

[5] See Jacob Trischler, Simon J. Pervan, Stephen J. Kelly, and Don R. Scott, "The Value of Codesign: The Effect of Customer Involvement in Service Design Teams" *Journal of Service Research* 21.1 (2018): 75–100.
[6] See Jansen and Marchionini, *Understanding User-Web Interactions via Web Analytics*.
[7] Zinaida Manžuch, "Ethical Issues In Digitization Of Cultural Heritage," *Journal of Contemporary Archival Studies*, 4 (2017), Article 4: accessed May 22, 2020, http://elischolar.library.yale.edu/jcas/vol4/iss2/4.
[8] Norman and Draper, *User-Centered System Design*; WWW Consortium, *Web Accessibility Initiative, Notes on User Centered Design Process (UCD)*, Version: 2004.04.01: accessed May 22, 2020, https://www.w3.org/WAI/EO/2003/ucd.
[9] Dobreva et al., *User Studies for Digital Library Development*, 248–249.

typical user groups, understand their needs and expectations,[10] and shape accessibility issues, or even collect and select content.[11]

During the planning phase and when conceiving the main functionalities and interfaces of the digital project, the staff could also call "fictional users," i.e. applying user types and roles, scenarios and personas.[12] In addition to these tools and to the valuable information gathered from the research literature on similar solutions, since the primary need of involving real users is to draw a clear picture of the target public, their particular needs, expectations, functional and non-functional requirements, the questions to be answered might be the following:

- Who are the target users of the DPH project?
- Who exactly needs it? Could different users be addressed in different ways? And how?
- In what context are they expected to access the DPH products?
- What accessibility issues need to be tackled (i.e. do I expect the adoption of/ need for specific user requirements and devices)?
- What are the foreseeable needs of the target user groups?
- What are the expectations of the target groups regarding the DPH project?
- Which users outside of these groups are most likely to benefit from involvement?
- What metrics could be used to measure user satisfaction in subsequent evaluations?
- Which functionalities are probably needed by this group?

---

10 The *Europeana Collections 14–18 project* (https://www.europeana.eu/portal/it/collections/world-war-I), in collaboration with the Clio-online Institute and the Department of History of the Humboldt-University of Berlin launched "a survey: experts from research institutes and universities, also from libraries, archives and museums developed a questionnaire to evaluate research interests, identify types of source materials that are of particular relevance to current and future research projects" in order to support "the selection process of the materials and sources, which will be digitized and published in the Europeana Collections 1914–1918 project." See Thomas Meyer, *Europeana 1914–1918: Remembering the First World War – a digital collection of outstanding sources from European national libraries. Deliverable D2.3 Report on the results of the survey of research interests* (2012), 4: accessed May 22, 2020, http://www.europeana-collections-1914-1918.eu/wp-content/uploads/2012/08/D2_3_Report_results_survey_research_interests_-_rev1_1.pdf.

11 The Italian portal *1418: documenti e immagini della Grande Guerra* (http://www.14-18.it/) was launched in 2007 to present digital collections of various materials concerning the First World War. As well as the 110 institutions who made their collections available, many citizens offered their family relics, asking the portal to digitize and publish them. Recently, the project staff organized a *Trascribathon*, in collaboration with *Europeana* 14–18 (https://transcribathon.com/en/), an open race for volunteer transcribers, to produce transcriptions of the unpublished documents and send the text back to the digital archive, to make their contents more accessible. Finally, they will study the impact of their huge collections on communities with different levels of specialization.

12 MINERVA EC WG Quality, Accessibility and Usability, eds, *Handbook on cultural web user interaction.* (September 2008): accessed May 22, 2020, http://www.minervaeurope.org/publications/handbookwebusers.htm: 86–91.

2 Formative Evaluation

The formative evaluation covers the development stage and focuses on the testing of a prototype (or the current version of the DPH service under re-development). It helps mostly to evaluate if something does not work and checking how users feel about the project outcomes. User studies could take the form of iterative circles of design and evaluation, adopting a user-centered design approach. Typically, the evaluation focus on usability, i.e. the ease of use of the service produced by the project,[13] but could also be used to identify critical issues as well as to receive pro-active feedbacks and suggestions. Usability testing is expected to be helpful for involving real users. Common questions during this stage of the evaluation could be:
- What is the general look and feel of the product/service?
- Are the intended functionalities working correctly, without errors and do they meet all user expectations?
- What do users prefer and dislike?
- What needs to be changed, and what is not essential?
- Are there functionalities and content we had not considered, and which were significant and attractive for the targeted public?
- Are they any suggestions that are worth considering before the public launch of the product/service?

3 Summative Evaluation

In this stage of the evaluation of the project, the focus is on its final outputs and how they achieve the expectations and requirements of the target communities/organizational structures/disciplinary domains. User involvement may support the valorization and dissemination of the project after it has already been launched. It has to be considered that users often tend to be more critical in evaluating a final product. Instead, during the development stages, they accept more readily that some features will not fully correspond to what they expect. The typical questions at this stage of the evaluation could be:
- Are the users satisfied with the project/ service?
- Can users efficiently perform their tasks? Furthermore, do they orientate themselves among the results?
- What should has to be scheduled to be changed in the next version?
- Are there any disadvantaged users? If yes, which developments can help to increase the accessibility of the project/ service: extension to other devices, interface refinements, addition of special features?

---

13 Usability is "the degree to which a software can be used by specified consumers to achieve quantified objectives with effectiveness, efficiency, and satisfaction in a quantified context of use" according to *ISO 9241–11. Ergonomic Requirements for Office Work with Visual Display Terminals: Part 11: Guidance on Usability*, 1998.

Channels/ Methods of Study, Involvement, Interaction, Co-Creation, Evaluation

"Probably one of the most confusing elements of user studies is that there is no clear allocation of types of studies for particular purposes, and the same methods can be used on different stages of the Digital Library development."[14] By extending this opinion to every type of project/service, let's give a look at the utility of some studies along with the stages summarized below.

1. In the *Conception* stage, a simple web questionnaire can be used to address a potentially large community of future users and collect feedback, which helps define scenarios and target users. Another solution could be the adoption of a persona method. To foresee the potential expectations and needs of target users in case an interested community is already reachable through a direct contact (in a department, library, archive, museum, city, etc.), it could very useful to organize focus groups and in-depth interviews, in order to gather qualitative data, ideas and inspirations, likes and dislikes. Finally, experts could be involved to face better the project goals and intended solutions, as well as accessibility and usability issues.

    The UK DiSC map project (Digitization of Special Collections: mapping, assessment, prioritization) may be considered a best practice of user-centered study organized in this phase. It was launched to study user needs before digitizing special collections,[15] and to be used in UK higher education institutions.[16]

2. In the *Formative* stage, to test the quality of the front-end, it is good to organize activities based on methods that ask for direct user involvement (like focus groups or even studies involving eye-tracking techniques). This prototype stage is quite valuable for assessing the product and testing it with the help of a sample of final

---

[14] Dobreva et al, *User Studies*, 249.
[15] The working group of the DiSCmap project discussed an acceptable definition of what a special collection is in Milena Dobreva et al, "The DiSCmap Project: Digitisation of Special Collections: Mapping, Assessment, Prioritisation" *New Library World* 112.1/2 (January 2011), doi: 10.1108/03074801111100436: 2–3.
[16] For more about the DiSCmap project, see Birrell, Duncan et al., "The DiSCmap Project: Overview and First Results," in *Research and Advanced Technology for Digital Libraries, Lecture Notes in Computer Science*, 5714 (Berlin/Heidelberg: Springer, 2009): 408–411. The project was commissioned by JISC in 2008 to the Center for Digital Library Research of the University of Strathclyde, Glasgow and was completed between September 2008 and May 2009. It turned the usual strategies upside-down that are led by supply rather than demand, adopting a series of inter-connected tasks to assess the current landscape of digitization from the point of view of researchers and teachers. The researchers used a combination of methods to gather data: web questionnaires, focus groups, interviews, and social networking.

users. Thus, it is recommended dedicate as much time as necessary to it, even if this phase is often skipped over to move more quickly to the public release.

A robust case to be inspired by could be the international user study of the 1.0 prototype of Europeana, the European Commission cultural portal, which provided useful suggestions and guided some future choices.[17] Among the results were the impact of the quantity and the language of resources on final users' perceptions of Europeana's utility, and some detailed recommendations on the homepage layout.

3. Finally, during the *project's ongoing* stage, when the product has been publicly released, user studies' real practice could be collected and included as part of the iterative process of measurement and improvement of service quality. As soon as the DPH project is released on the web, an initial check on how users have received the application is possible by collecting opinions, for example, during public presentations. These occasions should be carefully evaluated, bearing in mind the importance and meaning of "first impressions" in web usage. Then, comments and suggestions, collected through questionnaires, requests for assistance, forums, etc. must be taken under serious consideration in case of adjustments or improvements to be carried out. In this phase, the server log analysis represents a popular technique because of its useful results. It is a census data method (i.e. without defining a sample) which can be carried out in different ways (server, browser or network based), at different levels of complexity and based on commercial or open services. In any case, a server log analysis returns valuable results about the audience without involving anyone directly.[18]

Conclusions

The expectations and behaviors of target users in Digital Public History projects represent an unknown territory, too often distorted by considering popular myths as regards categories of digital users (millennials, professionals, digital newbies, Generation X, etc.). We wrongly presume that digital users like to have a lot of functionalities, the least disruptive technologies, and all possible content available. Conversely, most research shows that people, while accessing digital archives, adopt quite

---

[17] This articulated study was commissioned by the Europeana Foundation involving Strathclyde University (Glasgow), jointly with the University of Macerata, Italy, and the Emotion Lab of Glasgow Caledonian University. It was carried out between 2009 and 2010 in four EU countries, Bulgaria, Italy, Scotland and Netherlands. It adopted a unique and coherent protocol comprising several study methods (focus groups, interviews, eye-tracking) and involving different types of users (high-school students, university students, general public, experts).
[18] See Jansen, *Understanding User-Web Interactions*.

different behaviors according to different needs, scenarios and even at different stages of their lives.[19] For example, sometimes we might be searching for a piece of specific information (i.e. a date, a name) without being attentive to its provenance, while at other times we could be more interested in contexts than in specific data, more in relationships then in single information entities.

Research also demonstrates that the same person, engaged in different contexts, could apply extremely differentiated information literacy skills.[20] User needs should thus not just assumed but need to be studied and explored within specific project contexts.

If we agree with the statement that the quality of a digital cultural project reflects decisions that are taken at the earliest stages, DPH projects should invest part of their available resources in activities aimed at meeting the target users' needs, expectations and behaviors and, as much as possible, offering easy online facilities. Applications must be user-centered from their very first conception. As such they should adopt some of the methods and tools quoted above.

Bibliography

Milena Dobreva, Andy O'Dwyer, Pierluigi Feliciati, eds. *User Studies for Digital Library Development*. London: Facet Publishing, 2012.
Bernard J. Jansen, and Gary Marchionini. *Understanding User-Web Interactions via Web Analytics*. San Rafael: Morgan&Claypool, 2009.
Sharon M. Leon "User-Centered Digital History: Doing Public History on the Web." (2015): https://www.6floors.org/bracket/2015/03/03/user-centered-digital-history-doing-public-history-on-the-web/.
Donald S. Norman and Stephen W. Draper. *User-Centered System Design: New Perspectives on Human-Computer Interaction*. Boca Raton, Florida: CRC Press, 1986.

---

[19] See Pierluigi Feliciati and Alessandro Alfier, "Archives Online from Simple Access to Full Use: Towards the Development of a User-centered Quality Model?" *Archivi & Computer* 2 (2013): 104–105.
[20] Information literacy was defined by the Association of College & Research Libraries, "Framework for Information Literacy for Higher Education," 2016, http://www.ala.org/acrl/sites/ala.org.acrl/files/content/issues/infolit/framework1.pdf, as a "set of integrated abilities encompassing the reflective discovery of information, the understanding of how information is produced and valued and the use of information in creating new knowledge and participating ethically in communities of learning" (8).

Brett Oppegaard
As Seen through Smartphones: An Evolution of Historic Information Embedment

Abstract: People who want to learn about history also want to learn about it in the ways and through the media that they prefer. Sometimes it happens by reading a book, with the learner at home in a comfy chair in front of a fire. But sometimes – especially now, in the smartphone era – meaningful history-learning moments can occur just about anywhere. So, historians need to adapt. This chapter outlines how history-seeking audiences have always followed advances in communication technologies and how mobile technologies today simply offer opportunities for the next period of field expansion. The desirable affordances of smartphones can be traced conceptually back to the earliest people who read about historical events on papyrus scrolls (much more mobile than stone monuments), through volumes of bound papers cranked out on the printing press (prompting the need for mass literacy), and in complicated multimedia contexts (like with text and graphics overlaying video on television screens). As a confluence of the media that have come before it but also as a bridge to emerging forms of new media, mobile media are only now starting to be understood as viable media for history. This piece puts the intellectual foundations in place for such an exploration and also presents some reflections on work like this from a pioneer in the field, who has been designing locative historical experiences for more than a decade.

Keywords: locative, mobile, interactive, narrative, 5G, digital media, tourism

The practice of making and sharing historical discourse must adapt to society's emerging communication technologies, in an evolutionary sense, or risk irrelevance. Not vice versa. Based on professional experience forged through more than a decade studying the implementation of new media at historic sites, and as this handbook illustrates, people are now expressing digital forms of history narratives in all sorts of novel and exciting ways. The potential for such innovation in the field is clear and bright. But how exactly to realize that potential for public audiences still remains elusive.

Until sturdy and transferable blueprints get drawn, many institutionalized actors – from individuals to organizations – might be inclined to cling to traditions. Such a passive mindset, though, makes the unstable and unwise assumption that audiences patiently will stick around and that they will keep coming back to check on how cultural organizations and history professionals are sharing digital resources at their favorite historical site. In other words, if they don't find what they want, these audiences just might not come back for a second look.

https://doi.org/10.1515/9783110430295-035

Such flaws in assumptions ignore what research and experience tell us. Audiences expect media when, where, how they want it, for what they want to do with it, and without excuses; also, if they don't get it that way, they will turn to a bevy of readily available and easy-to-use alternatives. History does not possess a guaranteed value (or privileged position) in public discourse any more now than other recently challenged humanities pillars, such as English literature, philosophy, journalism, or even a liberal-arts education in general. Like it or not, how much these cultural cornerstones are worth will be determined by present and future audiences, who must in some respects find them to be accessible and useful.

As media convergence continues to obliterate physical boundaries, all types of information will be competing for the attention of future eyes and ears and also the hearts and souls of people as societal priorities shift and realign to changing media ecologies and cultures. Will they want to visit museums as physical places? Will they want to learn history? Will they be amenable to the interpretive positions of historians, especially those presented in antiquated idioms? More importantly, though, will they need history? Or will they consider purely ahistorical discourse as good enough to get by?

Social media illustrates how disruptive such a sudden emergence in the media ecosystem can be, especially when partnered with powerful and ubiquitous new communication tools, such as smartphones. Media makers on these channels are not waiting around for permission to comment upon the past or restricting their reminisces to curator jargon or even saving a spot on the panel for the experts. These prolifically circulating commentaries – inherently in hand and competing with all the other media options on a mobile device – come in irregular forms, personal, professional, political, etc., and in variable quality, often without established expertise. But the content that aligns best with the emerging technologies appears freshest and most fun, and it has been freed of the usual analog tethers, such as specific sizes, shapes, and locations of use.

In these smartphone-boosted social-media channels, such messages can be spotted and collected abstractly – from their topical clouds floating by – as thoughts within these systems get batted around like badminton birdies. Yet these discourses can also be grounded once again, and redeployed with a new sense of purpose, from a physical-space perspective but through the powers of new technologies. They can be brought back onto hallowed ground and embedded into a precise GPS position and anchored in place, through location metadata and responsive mobile devices.

Such locative media – as in digital media embedded in a physical place and experienced through technologies – reconstitutes shape to historical discourse in a sustainable and durable way, to be understood as created during distinct times, by authoritative sources, and within a particular "genius loci."[1] This connection of

---

[1] S. Eriksen, "Localizing Self on the Internet: Designing for 'Genius Loci' in a Global Context," in *Social Thinking-software Practice*, ed. Y. Dittrich, C. Floyd, and R. Klischewsk (Cambridge, MA: MIT

information to place, invariably encountered by people in that location, who are proximate to each other, can be considered an embedment experience. That term, *embedment*, has been chosen to indicate that digital media and physical sensory data are intertwined in a specific ephemeral yet grounded context. This mixture is dynamic in both predictable and unpredictable ways. The embedment sensation, in turn, creates a distinct type of mental-physical engagement for the senses. Likewise, historical discourse at its highest level, has multiple mapping qualities.

By that choice of phrasing, I mean the setting and context of the situation inherently matters, at least to people in that spot, as they cognitively map physical data accumulated by their senses in-situ with the historical layer of information delivered to them on their device and gathered together in an effort to make sense of what happened, how, and where.

In such concrete and territorial terms, locative dispatches become immaterial-yet-material expressions of historians as well as distinct artifacts of our smartphone medium.[2] As the interface through which we experience humanity today,[3] these pieces of media become worthy of attention and study as they appear, as communicative curio of our time but also as potential antecedents of where public history has room for development and growth in the realm of mobile media (and whatever comes next).

In the museum studies field, for example, Nina Simon has suggested as much when she argues that social media has created conversations that transforms historical artifacts into "social objects."[4] If informal and untethered messages made on social media, as an example, can benefit and engage audiences in place, mostly by happenstance, imagine what could be done with them by direction, with a creative designer, with the smartphone as the powerful communication channel directly linked to an in-place audience, and with the audience's location known and always in mind. Exigencies for providing novel types of historical context could become both bountiful and widespread, especially under the expanding infrastructures of 5G data, and especially if sufficient resources are devoted to such inquiries and experimentation. Freed from current constraints on data speed and storage, emerging capabilities could open mobile media in museums to radical new forms of interpretation, such as three-dimensional holograms, elaborate multisensory feedback systems, and immersive virtual-reality simulations.

Each industrial advance pushing forward the chaotic contemporary spread of information, including historical discourse, creates particular opportunities like

---

Press, 2002), 425–449. See also B. Oppegaard and M. Rabby, "Proximity: Revealing new mobile meanings of a traditional news concept," *Digital Journalism* 4.5 (2015): 621–638.
2 J. Frith, *Smartphones as locative media* (Cambridge: Polity Press, 2015).
3 J. Farman, *Mobile Interface Theory: Embodied Space and Locative Media* (New York, NY: Routledge, 2012).
4 N. Simon, *The Participatory Museum* (Santa Cruz, CA: Museum 2.0, 2010).

this. These specific locations can be related to the possible people-information-place interactions, affording certain agencies in those situations among audiences and designers while also constraining others.[5] Because of the quantities and complexities of changes in the global media ecosystem materializing today, at the dawn of the Internet's convergence with mobile technologies, this chapter does not aim – or even attempt – to encompass and explain the entirety of this complicated situation. Instead, the approach here is to parse off the location-awareness portion of the larger puzzle, to focus on embedment within that portion as an area of exigency, and to consider its relationships with smartphones, as a way to highlight what history-oriented producers and patrons might be overlooking or underappreciating when considering the nature of history related to place and place related to historical audiences.

When humans did not have many options for traveling or communicating across great distances – say for tens of thousands of years, pre-1850s – hyperlocal and place-oriented information was all that most people knew. While no one alive today directly experienced that sort of extremely immobile media ecosystem, its influences intertwine with evolutionary traits about how we value information, along the basic principles of Tobler's First Law of Geography,[6] which asserts that near things are more related than distant things.

Ascribing meaning to a place, including creating inscriptions about that place, is an ancient art, practiced widely across cultures and around the world.[7] Space,[8] as a term, can be distinguished from related labels – such as place,[9] and locale[10] – by the extent of the inscriptions and meanings made about the physical setting. In shorthand, then, the less inscribed and meaningful a location is, the more space-like. The more inscribed and meaningful, the more place-like and perceptually developed it becomes, toward a locale. The fine-tip description of *genius loci* even associates a specific incorporeal spirit.

For the first tens of thousands of years of humanity, information circulated primarily through oral methods. Writing didn't come into vogue in Ancient Greece, for

---

5 J.J. Gibson, *The ecological approach to visual perception* (Hillsdale, NJ: Lawrence Erlbaum Associates, Inc, 1979).
6 W. Tobler, "A Computer Movie Simulating Urban Growth in the Detroit Region," *Economic Geography* 46 (1970): 234–240.
7 B. Oppegaard, "From orality to newspaper wire services: Creating the concept of a medium," in *Communication and Technology*, ed. L. Cantoni and J.A. Danowski (Berlin: De Gruyter Mouton, 2015), 21–34.
8 Yi-Fu Tuan, *Space and Place: The Perspective of Experience* (Minneapolis, MN: University of Minnesota Press, 1977).
9 H. Sun, "Toward a Rhetoric of Locale: Localizing Mobile Messaging Technology into Everyday Life," *Journal of Technical Writing and Communication* 39.3 (2009): 245–261.
10 A. Giddens, *The Constitution of Society: Outline of the Theory of Structuration* (Cambridge, UK: Polity Press, 2007).

example, until around 400 BC, when it initially was scoffed at by Socrates but later adopted wholeheartedly by Plato,[11] and later generations of thinkers including Aristotle. Place-based inscriptions developed slowly from there, along with the literacy needed to decode the inscriptions, over hundreds of years, leading to a progression of information-sharing technologies about places, from the advent of docents to wall texts, from the development of object labels to brochures, from the multimedia extensions of texts into audio tours, websites, and mobile apps.

While analog audio tours of a place might seem sufficiently historic by today's standards, they were considered revolutionary communication technology not that long ago and only have been used in practice for a few decades. The first "Short-Wave Ambulatory Lectures" at the Stedelijk Museum in Amsterdam were offered in 1952, and the ground-breaking, taped "Treasures of Tutankhamun" exhibit toured the United States in the 1970s. The Louvre didn't have an audio guide until the early 1990s, and most major public places – from the Empire State Building to the Forbidden City – only added audio to their inscriptions in the 2000s, during the rapidly transitioning technological period involving cassette tapes, compact discs, and then fully digital media, migrating from Mp3 players to smartphones.[12] In similar ways, discourse forms we might marvel at today, such as interactive locative-media apps, are destined to become commonplace in the future, once infrastructure, expertise, and economics fully support them. So what can we learn about how those formed and are forming, in preparation for whatever comes next?

The mobile-media epoch in effect began on June 29, 2007, with the release of the initial iPhone, followed about a year later by the opening of the Apple App Store, which allowed third-party development of mobile media. Artists, scholars, and various other enterprising spirits have been trying to make sense of the smartphone's fertile academic and entrepreneurial potential since. With smartphones providing powerful, user-provided, and ubiquitous hardware, and with mobile-app software development options open to the general public – and less costly and more accessible than most previous digital-media platforms – place-based interpretation suddenly became intriguing again, especially to historians and people who enjoy learning about history at particular places, rather than abstractly.

Digital media meanwhile allows multiple voices operating on multiple layers to inscribe a place simultaneously and endlessly. Where a carefully curated physical sign might have once existed, limited to a few sentences, in a contested arena necessitating content compromises, smartphone hardware and ambitious developers make claims to the place now, too, allowing different channels, diverse perspectives, and new kinds of embodied-learning experiences.

---

11 Plato, *Phaedrus*, trans. R. Hackforth (Cambridge, MA: Cambridge University Press, 1972).
12 L. Tallon, *Digital technologies and the museum experience: Handheld guides and other media* (Landham, MD, Altamira Press, 2008).

Economics, in this case, has not effectively led these discussions. Even though the entry point for participation is extremely low, profits have been scarce. Audiences have yet to coalesce in large numbers around any number of novel forms of digital public history emerging through mobile technologies, and technopolists have yet to figure out how to spin gold out of the situation (i.e., the inertia on Google's Field Trip app). It's therefore a case in which ideas have been able to lead these inquiries for a lengthy period of time, rather than commercial products or bureaucratic systems. There has been no industrial-scale breakthrough for historical discourse apps, like the King Tut tour was for audio guides, or even what Pokémon GO has been for mobile gaming. Pokémon GO is an app in which people find informational digital treasures in everyday places, through physical gameplay, and some of that information includes historical snippets about particular places. Pokémon GO therefore could be a model for what digital public history can become but does not serve as a great example of what it is. In that regard, historians need to design mobile games with their perspectives and priorities in mind.

Historical sites, including museums, consider preservation, maintenance, and storage of their collections as prime directives.[13] Without the artifacts and protected places, this logic goes, there would be no reason to have site and object interpretation. Regardless of how great the interpretive experience might be, for example, no one gets to try on Lincoln's hat at the Smithsonian's National Museum of American History. Traditions of interpretive work, such as at history museums, in turn, are often presented as clinical in nature and founded on empirical evidence, authoritative perspectives, and apolitical rhetoric.[14] But the counter argument for this protectionist position could be just as provocative, in that, if few members of the public really engage with history, in modern contexts through contemporary technologies, then what public value does it really hold any longer?

After the advent of the World Wide Web, and the release of the iPhone, many early attempts at digitizing public history involved porting over ideas from the analog world and relatively minor extensions of traditional strategies. From a mobile perspective, that included the implementation of Quick Response (QR) codes. These codes allowed content creators to make websites of extensive depth, or at least deeper than analog equivalents could go, and connected those to users in place, through a scan of a code on a smartphone camera, which then hyperlinked the phone to the website.[15] QR codes can add some value to place-based historical

---

[13] M. Achiam and J. Sølberg, "Nine meta-functions for science museums and science centres," *Museum Management and Curatorship* 32.2 (2017): 123–143.
[14] M. Carnall, J. Ashby and C. Ross, "Natural history museums as provocateurs for dialogue and debate," *Museum Management and Curatorship* 28.1 (2013): 55–71.
[15] T.J. Soon, "QR code" *Synthesis Journal* (2008): 59–78.

discourse, but they also turned out to be not necessarily what audiences wanted, reflected in their light use, and primarily one-way broadcasts in nature.[16]

Many other physical-mobile mechanisms, with diverse iconography, appeared in the mid-2000s, such as Yellow Arrow stickers that served as similar physical triggers for digital hyperlinks.[17] Other projects, such as QRator, experimented with interactive experiences designed to turn a QR code into a thoughtful discussion prompt and data-collecting tool of public responses.[18] Low-cost but high-quality platforms, such as Curatescape, emerged a few years later, allowing systematic annotation of physical spaces and embedment of that information via mobile devices in dozens of cities, such as London, New Orleans, and Cleveland, where that project started.[19] And along came a flurry of ad hoc interactive mobile narratives, too, some related to history, intended to be integrated with physical space, including experimental forms that emanated from the Augmented Environments Lab at Georgia Tech University.[20]

Fort Vancouver Mobile (my research project in this realm) emerged during that formative era of interactive mobile narratives.[21] It was the basis of my dissertation and also many of my early research efforts. It could be called a locative "mobile app" focused on historical discourse, but it really was more of a generative idea about investigating mobile media as a medium that evolved into several mobile apps, academic presentations and papers, grant proposals, community events, field research sessions, public programming, and public exhibitions of its media artifacts. After a few years away from this project, I recently earned a community grant to refresh the programming on the Android and iOS versions of it, and to update its interface and basic interactions. During that 2018 rehabilitation process, which included a quick overview of recent academic literature published on this subject, I

---

16 Schultz, M. K., "A case study on the appropriateness of using quick response (QR) codes in libraries and museums," *Library & Information Science Research* 35.3 (2013): 207–215. See also, B.L. Smith, "QR Codes," in *Adult Education, Museums and Art Galleries*, eds D.E. Clover, K. Sanford, L. Bell, and K. Johnson (Rotterdam: SensePublishers, 2016), 243–255.
17 G. Goggin and A. Crawford, "Geomobile web: locative technologies and mobile media," *Australian Journal of Communication* 36.1 (2009): 97. Paper in special issue entitled "Placing Mobile Communications," edited by Clare Lloyd; Scott Rickard, and Gerard Goggin.
18 C.R. Ross et al, "Engaging the Museum Space: Mobilising Visitor Engagement with Digital Content Creation," *Digital Humanities* (2012): 348.
19 M. Souther, "From Exhibition to Conversation: The Elusive Art of Digital Storytelling," paper presented at *Network Detroit 2016*, Wayne State University, Detroit, MI, September 30, 2016. See also, M. Tebeau "Listening to the city: Oral history and place in the digital era," *The Oral History Review* 40.1 (2013): 25–35.
20 J.D. Bolter, M. Engberg and B. MacIntyre, "Media studies, mobile augmented reality, and interaction design," *Interactions* 20.1 (2013): 36–45.
21 B. Oppegaard, "Mobile media embedment: Lessons learned from making durable journalistic models at a national historic site," in *Civic Media Reader* eds, E. Gordon and P. Milhailidis. Cambridge: MIT Press, 2015. (Online only).

was reminded of how many fascinating ideas about embodied learning through mobile technologies have been circulating for a decade or more, as related gear has advanced tremendously, yet still without gaining major public traction. In an effort to give some of those ideas another nudge forward, here are a few of my reflections from the past decade, and projections about future prospects related to digital public history:

- Just since the iPhone was released, as a cultural and historical milestone of sorts, conceptualization of this core communication tool has evolved from being a cell phone (relating to the marvel of the cellular grid of towers, transmitting voices) to a mobile phone (focusing more on the mobilities the phone provides) to a mobile device (deemphasizing telephony altogether and emphasizing its all-purpose computational potential). More mobile devices are around the planet now than people, and young adults, ages 18–29, per the PEW Research Group,[22] are decidedly mobile-oriented. The next generation of people engaged by historical discourse is going to come from the pool of smartphone users today, so designers need to be thinking of them often, if not first. As I conducted field research at US National Park Service historic sites, such as Fort Vancouver, I often noticed people looking at their mobile devices and being engaged in smartphone activities that either were not history-related or not expert-vetted. They rarely were impressed by shovelware apps or nonresponsive websites. They often did use internet searches to seek place-based information, including facts about cultural artifacts and other curiosities around them. If only those searches (and answers) could be geolocated. But wait, they can be!
- I also saw people engaging in many other place-based smartphone activities with the potential for greater engagement. Going back to the Lincoln hat example: Not everyone can try on the original, but could a few replicas be made and those used as props for hashtagged selfies? Maybe with a prompt like, "What do you want to know about this hat? #lincolnhat." That type of activity could combine engagement in historical discourse and embodied learning with a bit of free marketing to boot. The questions could be fielded by historical experts, opening a discussion that then could lead into many other veins of related discourse, such as about nineteenth-century fashion, Lincoln's best speeches (he sometimes kept the scripts under his hat), and even into bigger topics, such as Lincoln's leadership role in the Civil War. In terms of embedment, having such interaction based in nearby Ford's Theatre, where Lincoln was assassinated, could add physical texture and grounding to the experience. Curating and then embedding those questions and answers into the locative media of the site could create another layer of connections for learners.

---

[22] PEW Research Group, Demographics of Mobile Device Ownership and Adoption in the United States, February 5, 2018, http://www.pewinternet.org/fact-sheet/mobile/.

- When I looked back at many of my favorite public history projects that used mobile devices, I was saddened to find mostly broken links. While Fort Vancouver Mobile lives on – in a semi-frozen state – most of its inspirations and peer projects have vanished from public view. Some writings about them still exist, including social media posts, press releases, and news coverage. But many of these were massive undertakings, with only a few of them still operational. Some of the novelty of mobile technologies might have worn off by now,[23] but mobile apps still are so new that they haven't even been properly defined and categorized yet, let alone included in any sort of archival organization. Their disappearance is a great loss to our communal knowledge about this field but it also appears to be causing a lot of wheel reinvention in this area of study, as people keep doing the same kinds of ad hoc projects over and over again, repeating discoveries (and mistakes) yet without enough scaffolding to gradually reach the next level of inquiry to move the ideas onward. Conceptualizing digital public history in genres of discourse might be helpful in coalescing thoughts about any number of promising approaches.
- When I first starting working on mobile media projects at Yellowstone National Park, interweaving scientific and historical discourse, I noticed signs hanging throughout the park that had an image of a mobile device inside an international prohibition symbol, the one with a red circle and a line through it. Therefore, before any mobile-app designs could be made and adopted, our research team first had to address the culture at the institution, which was significantly anti-mobile. We then had to convince them to take down the signs. In turn, many history-oriented mobile projects of the past decade have been focused on what new technologies can do, working within severe cultural constraints (i.e., no mobile use in Yellowstone), instead of locked into the ideas of what the audiences want and what can be done about that. This design-facing paradigm, whether motivated by organizational culture or technological curiosity, has generated a lot of fascinating ideas about what is possible, but it has also often left out of the discussion *the* key stakeholder, the person using the technology to engage in history. That should change, dramatically, and immediately. A great starting point is to determine exactly what the user wants, and where, and then reverse engineer the experience to ensure the desired outcome.

From that final point, I suggest a global reorientation to the wants and needs of the audience member of digital public history, especially when breaking new ground in mobile-media studies. An affordance of the smartphone as a medium is that many different voices can coexist within the same small device in the same place. In that

---

23 R. Ling, *Taken for Grantedness: The Embedding of Mobile Communication into Society* (Cambridge, MA: MIT Press, 2012).

way, digital history can be layered with navigational information, allowing audiences to seek their own paths, even when together with friends and family. Depending on the audience member's interests, and the rhetorical situation,[24] the experience could be tailored by age, ethnic culture, diverse topics of interest, and so on. For example, imagine the nuanced differences available through a set of digital data at a historical site, such as the USS Arizona at the World War II Valor National Monument, in Pearl Harbor, Hawaii, which could be designed specifically for a teenage local girl interested in mechanical engineering, or, in contrast, the same massive data set could be aimed at pleasing a visitor from Japan in his 80s, learning to play music of the war era on his ukulele. The rhetorical frames might overlap and interest both in some places but also diverge significantly in others.

Enough amazing history-making technology has emerged in the past decade to keep all of us engaged with this topic for the rest of our lives. To avoid unnecessary and inefficient loops, though, we can learn from much of our history of public-discourse developments to date and then make a radical shift toward what our audiences really want. And give that to them.

Bibliography

Farman, J. *Delayed Response: The Art of Waiting from the Ancient to the Instant World*. New Haven, CT: Yale University Press, 2018.

Frith, J. *A Billion Little Pieces: RFID and the Infrastructures of Identification*. Cambridge, MA: MIT Press, 2019.

Humphreys, L. *The Qualified Self: Social Media and the Accounting of Everyday Life*. Cambridge, MA: The MIT Press, 2018.

Wilken, R., Goggin, G., and H.A. Horst. *Location Technologies in International Context*. New York, NY: Routledge, 2019.

---

24 L.F. Bitzer, "The Rhetorical Situation," *Philosophy & Rhetoric* 25 (1968): 1–14.

Part 4: **Technology, Media, Data and Metadata**

Matteo Di Legge, Francesco Mantovani, and Iara Meloni
What does it Meme? Public History in the Internet Memes Era

Abstract: The aim of this chapter is to investigate the risks and the potentialities of internet memes (units of culture spreading online from user to user and mutating along the way) in terms of historical narration on digital platforms. After exploring their definition and evolution from the 1980s to recent years, it will be highlighted how history is represented through this online phenomenon. This chapter provides some examples taken mostly from Italian Facebook pages or groups that combine forms of popular culture with figures or topics of the past, in order to examine which challenges and ethical issues public historians may encounter when working with this digital tool.

Keywords: internet memes, historical narration, social media, communication, digital culture, humour

1 Introduction

1.1 Definition

In a world where the Web 2.0 has remarkably increased the number of "history creators," the contribution of digital public historians remains a topic of discussion:[1] also on the internet, non-academic audiences play an important role in the representation

---

[1] For the development of the links between public history and digital history, see Daniel J. Cohen et al., "Interchange: The Promise of Digital History," *Journal of American History* 95.2 (September 1, 2008): 452–491, https://doi.org/10.2307/25095630; Serge Noiret, "Storia pubblica digitale", *Zapruder. Storie in movimento* 36 (2015): 9–23; Thomas Cauvin, *Public History. A Textbook of Practice* (New York/London: Routledge, (2016) 2nd edition 2022), Chapter 8; Enrica Salvatori, "Storia digitale e pubblica: lo storico tra i 'nuovi creatori' di storia", in *Public history: discussioni e pratiche*, ed. Paolo Bertella Farnetti, Lorenzo Bertucelli, and Alfonso Botti (Milano: Mimesis, 2017), 189–197.

Notes: The title is an Italian wordplay on "me ne frego" (I don't care), one of the slogans used in early 1920s by Mussolini's troops; most of the following titles use wordplay too, based on some famous memes' series (True Story, Challenge Accepted, etc.). This chapter draws on the analysis of the panel *La Storia al tempo dei meme. Una sfida per la Public History tra potenzialità divulgative e rischi di semplificazione*, presented at the 2nd AIPH Annual Conference (Pisa, June 11–15, 2018). We thank Igor Pizzirusso and Gabriele Sorrentino, who participated in the organization and presentation of the panel.

https://doi.org/10.1515/9783110430295-036

of the past through different tools, including Internet memes, whose popularity should be taken seriously as objects of curation and collection.

This study aims to contribute to this growing area of research by exploring a category of Internet memes, namely those dealing with history. Spreading from one online community to another and gaining new meanings and functions, memes represent one of the most visible examples of cultural artefacts, whose diffusion and influence within and outside the web should encourage scholars and public historian to devote more attention to them.[2]

Fig. 1: Typical internet meme image format. Wikimedia Commons, the free media repository, url: https://commons.wikimedia.org/wiki/Category:Internet_memes#/media/File:Typical_internet_meme_image_format.svg.

The study of memes as a cultural parallel to genes began in 1979 with the publication of Dawkins' *The Selfish Gene*: according to the author, meme is a cultural unit that is spread from one person to another through copying and imitation.[3] Nevertheless, of all different types, Internet memes – the focus of this chapter – are relatively new, in the same way as the academic interest in them, mostly among communicators, linguists, political and social scientists. So far, creating a shared definition has seemed

---

[2] One of the first studies about how and why public historians should give memes their attention was Jim McGrath, "'This Is Fine.'" (accessed September 17, 2020). In the history of visual media and communication, memes can be considered the last online application of posters, satirical illustrations (e.g. Francois Cavanna's works in the 1970s) or political cartoons, which included several elements of today's meme, see Vasiliki Plevriti, "Satirical User-Generated Memes as an Effective Source of Political Criticism, Extending Debate and Enhancing Civic Engagement," Centre for Cultural Policy Studies, University of Warwick, 2014.

[3] See Richard Dawkins 1989, where the author acknowledges that a considerable part of human behavior comes not from genes (the basic units of genetics) but from culture. However, Dawkins' attempt to revolutionize cultural studies by adopting a Darwinist approach, in order to explain the success of specific behaviors or ideas, did not receive much approval from scholars over the last decades.

impossible:⁴ however, the term 'Internet meme' concerns a user generated content, i.e. a union of different semantic units (typically still images and text, or animated GIF, or a video), that spreads online and changes along the way. Beginning with the first "academically accredited" definition by Davison, according to whom "an Internet meme is a piece of culture, typically a joke, which gains influence through online transmission",⁵ scholars have distinguished "static" viral contents (only shared from user to user) from "remixed" memes, which are "replicated via evolution, adaptation or transformation of the original meme vehicle" (see sub Section 1.2).⁶

Besides their entertaining subject, the secret of memes' success in the late 1990s and early 2000s lies in their own increasing generativity,⁷ including five principal factors: the leverage for creating memes provided by graphics editing programs and the Internet; the adaptability to a wide range of uses, communicating jokes, emotions, advertisements; their ease of mastery, since most of them are made by using cut-copy-paste and text tool functions; the accessibility of memes, which depends on the accessibility of their habitat, the Internet; lastly, their transferability, relating to their most important quality, namely replicability in different cultures.⁸ Furthermore, the high generativity of remixed memes entails not only online sharing but also users' participation, stimulating people to usually anonymously modify and repost the joke.⁹

1.2 True (Hi)story

The history and development of Internet memes have, until recently, been largely ignored by scholars, but in recent years an increasing amount of literature has begun to focus on reconstructing the "genealogy" of today's memes (Fig. 2). Many researchers

---

4 See Michele Knobel and Colin Lankshear, "Memes and Affinities: Cultural Replication and Literacy Education" (Annual Meeting of the National Reading Conference, Miami, 30 November 2005), 1–22; Linda K. Börzsei, "Makes a Meme Instead. A Concise History of Memes," *New Media Studies Magazine, Utrecht University* 7 (2013), 1–28, 3.
5 Davison 122.
6 Knobel and Lankshear 13.
7 Generative systems are "a set of tools and practices that develop among large groups of people." See Jonathan Zittrain, *The Future of the Internet – And How to Stop It* (New Haven: Yale University Press & Penguin, 2008), https://dash.harvard.edu/handle/1/4455262, 74. Remixed internet memes are a generative system built on another one, the Internet.
8 Zittrain, 71; Börzsei, 10–12.
9 For Internet memes as individual and collective form of participation see, Ryan M. Milner, *The World Made Meme: Public Conversations and Participatory Media* (Cambridge, MA: MIT Press, 2016); Asaf Nissenbaum and Limor Shifman, "Meme Templates as Expressive Repertoires in a Globalizing World: A Cross-Linguistic Study," *Journal of Computer-Mediated Communication* 23, (2018): 294–310, https://doi.org/10.1093/jcmc/zmy016; for the role of memes as a form of electoral participation, especially in the 2016 US presidential election, see Benita Heiskanen, "Meme-Ing Electoral Participation," *European Journal of American Studies* 12 (2017), https://doi.org/10.4000/ejas.12158.

Fig. 2: A brief anthology of the most famous internet memes.
- a: All Your Base Are Belong to Us. Know Your Meme, url: https://knowyourmeme.com/memes/all-your-base-are-belong-to-us.
- b: Examples of LOLcats series. Linda K. Börzsei, "Makes a Meme Instead. A Concise History of Memes", New Media Studies Magazine, Utrecht University (F2013), 17, url: https://www.academia.edu/3649116/Makes_a_Meme_Instead_A_Concise_History_of_Internet_Memes.
- c: Photoshopped image of Bert and Osama bin Laden. Know Your Meme, url: https://knowyourmeme.com/photos/1516-bert-is-evil
- d: Some of Rage Comics characters. Know Your Meme, url: https://knowyourmeme.com/photos/183379-rage-comics/

have identified the "sideways smiley face" emoticon created on September 19, 1982 by Scott E. Fahlman as the earliest internet meme.[10] While emoticons share simplicity and universal application with memes, the images hosted on the website *Bert is Evil* (1997) can be considered examples of the first remixed meme.[11]

Just before the launch of the Web 2.0 in 2004, users began to contribute directly to the creation and spread of Internet phenomena, becoming both consumers and

---

10 Just like memes, emoticons' functions were to entertain and to communicate non-verbal information, sometimes even complex ideas or emotional states. See Davison 124; Börzsei 6; Lolli 44–45.
11 A significant difference between the *Bert is Evil* series and modern memes is, however, that in the first case the participation was not open, as his creator, the artist Dino Ignacio, was the only one remixing images.

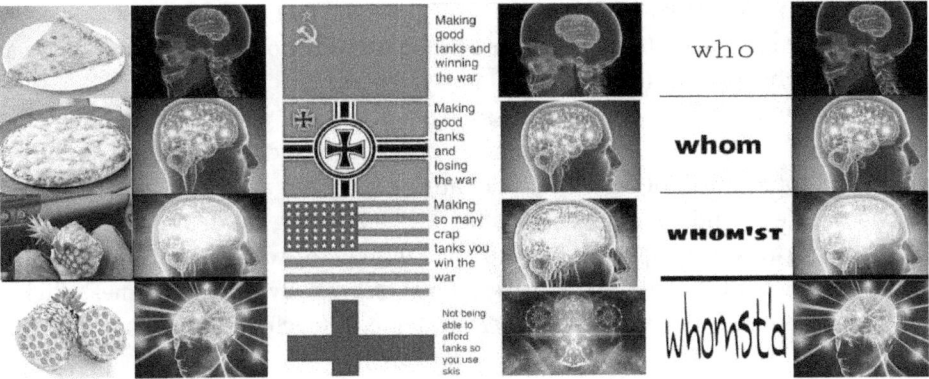

Fig. 3: Three adaptations of Expanding Brains meme.
  – Left: Know Your Meme, url: https://knowyourmeme.com/photos/1224659-galaxy-brain
  – Centre: Facebook, @420DankMemeBlazeIt.
  – Right: Know Your Meme, url: https://knowyourmeme.com/photos/1217719-whomst

producers (prosumers). All Your Base Are Belong to Us was one of the most significant examples among new remixed memes, "popular enough to reach out of the circles of Internet subculture into the mainstream."[12] By the mid-2000s, memes gained, so to speak, self-awareness, crystallizing into a predominant format: the image macros, pictures with a caption (generally in white letters with black borders, and in Impact font, Fig. 1) superimposed. Then, starting from the so-called "memetic frames" (the fixed part of the meme), by remixing images and captions entire series or "memetic families" have been developed across years (Fig. 3).[13]

Considering their diffusion throughout the Internet, memes have aroused interest of several disciplines, such as communication studies, sociology, and philosophy. Some contributions show how Internet memes' humour is changing our perception of the world and the way we communicate political satire;[14] others highlight their ambiguous language and the parallelisms with the propaganda styles of 'alt-right' and

---

[12] Börzsei 12. This meme originated from an awkward translation of "all of your bases are now under our control," which originally appeared in the opening dialogue of Zero Wing, a 16-bit 'shoot'em up' game released in 1989. See *KnowYourMeme*, All Your Base Are Belong to Us. https://knowyourmeme.com/memes/all-your-base-are-belong-to-us (accessed September 17, 2020).

[13] Lolli 58–59. Remarkable examples include *Advice Dog*, and *LOLcats*, both image macros with the caption written in "LOLspeak," a subset of internet slang. There are clearly many similarities between comics and some of these "memetic families," e.g. the *Rage Comics*, a phenomenon that appeared on 4chan in 2008.

[14] Börzsei 25; Limor Shifman, "Humor in the Age of Digital Reproduction: Continuity and Change in Internet-Based Comic Texts," *International Journal of Communication* 1 (2007): 187–209, 204; Anushka Kulkarni, "Internet Meme and Political Discourse: A Study on the Impact of Internet Meme as a Tool in Communicating Political Satire," *Journal of Content, Community & Communication* 6 (2017): 13–17.

'white supremacy';[15] furthermore, some scholars argue that "meming" (producing or remixing memes) is a fruitful practice for educators to focus on the new forms of social participation through the Internet.[16]

After having presented the main issues about memes, one could ask where the archives and the libraries are, in which it is possible to study, collect data, and fact-check this topic. Much of the current literature on memes pays particular attention to two different kinds of source: websites where they are created and spread, for instance, forums or blogs (4chan, Tumblr), aggregator websites (9GAG, Reddit), and social media (Facebook); databases, which essentially explain memes' origins and development, for example KnowYourMeme, Encyclopædia Dramatica, and Memebase.

Fig. 4: Medieval Macros, the Bayeux Tapestry Parodies. Know Your Meme, url: https://knowyourmeme.com/memes/medieval-macros-bayeux-tapestry-parodies/photos/sort/favorites.

1.3 Challenge Accepted: Digital Public History and Memes

Some memes can summarize – though in a simplified manner – even complex historical issues. Indeed, there are some points of contact with the 'public' approach to digital history: the users' active participation in reworking a meme, the language's simplicity, and entertainment. There are certainly several problems to be

---

15 See, Angela Nagle, *Kill All Normies: The Online Culture Wars from Tumblr and 4chan to the Alt-Right and Trump* (Winchester, UK; Washington, USA: Zero Books, 2017); Lolli, Chapter 4.
16 Knobel and Lankshear, "Memes and Affinities: Cultural Replication and Literacy Education," (Annual Meeting of the National Reading Conference, Miami, November 30, 2005), 17.

faced: by their very nature, memes have no author, because they are "frequently incorporated into systems and among practices that actively prevent and dismantle attribution";[17] of course, the risk of simplification and deliberate manipulation is not so unlikely; lastly, one can wonder if it is possible to laugh at everything, even at controversial or still raw public debate issues.

Given these premises, what are the possible risks and the advantages that memes have for the (not only) digital narration of history?

2 History through Memes

2.1 From Ancient Rome's Senate to Feudalism. Memes about Ancient and Medieval History

Is it possible to describe ancient and medieval history through memes?

Cultural studies researcher Kim Wilkins wrote about the bond between memes and medieval history, exploring how the meme series dedicated to the Bayeux Tapestry helped the real object to gain new relevance in popular culture.[18]

For the author, the web may be a fertile soil for a humor made of medieval memes; they are generally oversimplified, sometimes offensive, but they also represent an interesting opportunity to adapt ancient and middle age history images and concepts to modern times.

This peculiar "memetic family" found in the Italian Facebook community offered a quite good environment probably because ancient history is familiar in Italy and influenced the birth of some Facebook pages dedicated only to ancient history memes.

"Apostrofare Catilina in senato" is a Facebook page, created by a young Italian archaeologist who works as a tourist guide, and takes its name from a real event: the accusation of Catilina by Cicero in the Roman senate, in 63 BC, also known as the First Catiline Oration. Starting from the name that recalls a real historical fact, the page makes jokes about ancient Roman history using memes.

In Fig. 5 (a) the meme is created by merging two distinct structures: the traditional background is taken from a Pokemon video game and two historical figures that fit this specific situation: here, the meme adapts this mechanics, even grossly, to the vicissitudes of Augustus and his daughter Julia who, in fact, rebels against the *mos maiorum* imposed on her by her father. Figure 5 (b) uses a sentence that became viral on social media, used by vice-prime minister Luigi di Maio in the

---

17 Davison 132.
18 Kim Wilkins, "Valhallolz: Medievalist Humor on the Internet," *Postmedieval: A Journal of Medieval Cultural Studies* 5 (2014): 199–214, https://doi.org/10.1057/pmed.2014.14.

(a) *Augustus vs Julia.* (b) *A fake Caesar quote.*

Fig. 5: Two memes about ancient Rome. Facebook, @apostrofarecatilinainsenato.

aftermath of the diplomatic incident with France in Bardonecchia, when the French Gendarmerie crossed the Italian border without authorization to look for migrants. The phrase "the Foreign Ministry did well to convene the French ambassador. What happened to Bardonecchia must be fully clarified in all its aspects" was seen by social networks as an example of Italian weakness and stigmatized here with a cunning historical reference: Julius Caesar, always looking for a *casus belli* to invade Gaul congratulates himself because the senate has called the ambassador of the Gauls for clarification.

2.2 On the Battlefield. Memes and Military History

For their simplicity and communicative immediacy, memes fit particularly well together with the macro-theme of military history, maintaining, at the same time, their first purpose: joking about a specific theme through the juxtaposition of a text and the symbolic value of a specific image.

The biggest difference between common memes and this peculiar type is the preponderance of memes built with the specific task of not only remembering a war event, but also summarizing with few details almost the entire military tradition of a country or, in case of memes dedicated to civil wars or homologous factions, to outline some peculiar military features, derived from widespread beliefs about the military history of that specific country.

One of the most common types of memes that fits quite well with military history are those dedicated to specific characters, for example generals and famous leaders. A very rich trend born in the USA of such "military memes," built on notorious figures, presents Unionist and Confederate generals as protagonists; in Europe, this "meme family" ranges from Napoleon to Stalin, following a very similar structure that tends to highlight qualities, well-known victories or famous failures, e.g. Little Big Horn for Custer or Waterloo for Napoleon.

Memes concerning military history have evolved, "invading" the field of animation, using characters and situations taken from famous cartoons. The intent is always to simplify a more complex concept by adapting it to a repeatable frame, but in this case, the frame is more "mobile," more ductile and able to show details that a still image cannot transmit.[19]

Concerning military history, the classical meme is not meaningful enough: a more dynamic approach is therefore necessary. With the right quantity of dynamism, achieved thanks to the combination of basic concepts of memes and cartoons or to a deeper and articulated transformation that moves away from the actual meme while maintaining some traits, these structures can help communicate historical knowledge, in a simplified yet precise manner. They can also be excellent tools for synthesis, because they can get to the roots of a territorial or national rivalry by simply stylizing it, making it more understandable and therefore potentially useful.

2.3 There's Very Little to Joke About! Memes and Totalitarianism

The most controversial historical memes may be the ones on the totalitarianism of the 1900s – Nazism, Fascism and Stalinism – and their charismatic leaders.

It is difficult to joke about these periods and the tragedies associated with them, with their widespread violence, systematic violations of human rights and genocidal policies.

Moreover, totalitarianism's memes are a kind of case study that heavily depends on the cultural context: in every country each totalitarianism is perceived differently according to the respective national history. For example, in Italy Fascism represents the most controversial topic. Online pages that deal with this historical period are often deleted, because of complaint reports and the 'flame wars' that usually occur. In contrast, Italian prosumers are generally less sensitive about Stalinism, as it was less connected to their own national history. Nazism on the other hand is still a taboo topic and there is some reluctance to tell jokes about it. Pages where these memes appear are often very volatile and stay online for short time spans, as they are frequently closed for violating social networks' policies. This also happens because many website administrators are not actually being ironic but are apologists and these kind of pages are mainly followed by neo-Nazis and totalitarianisms' sympathizers. The highest risk here is oversimplification, as their creators often do not have a deep knowledge of the field. The features of truth and entertainment within memes are very entangled, and it is often difficult to separate one from

---

19 Examples of this way of illustrating military history through frames from famous cartoons or the language of rap battles are the YouTube channel "Cartoon History Memes" and "Epic Rap Battles of History."

the other. In addition to this, memes are characterized by a strong leaning towards references to current events, and for this reason, they are increasingly seen as a source of information. The union of all these aspects make these memes a powerful vehicle to spread hate, preconceived ideas, and fake news about history.[20]

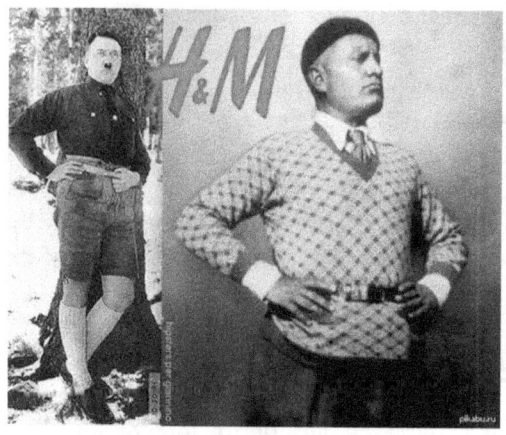 

(a) *Hitler & Mussolini. From @facciabucosocial* (b) *Mvsolini. From @mvsolini*

Fig. 6: Memes about totalitarian figures.

On the other hand, memes can also be a means of deconstructing Fascist and Nazi rhetoric about certain topics. On social networks, this is mainly performed by using an expedient: the sarcastic use of a regime's icons and slogans.

For instance, in some memes the irony comes from famous portraits of the dictators, that were at the center of the cult of personality and photographed in many different contexts. These memes are funny because they show dictators in commonplace settings such as sports, politics and fashion. One of the most known memes uses wordplay derived from H&M, the clothing-retail company, and the initials of Hitler and Mussolini who are depicted as hipster fashion icons (Fig. 6 a).

In other memes a pun is delivered using propaganda slogans in a caricatured style. In Fig. 6 (b) the comic effect is provided by the assonance between Mussolini's "Molti nemici, molto onore" (Many enemies, much honour) and the joke "Molti mici, molto onore" (Many kitties, much honour).

In conclusion, memes about totalitarianism are often subject to political and ideological use of history, no real attempts of storytelling using the characteristics of such a media.

---

20 See Leonardo Nolasco-Silva, Maria da Conceicao Silva Soares, and Vittorio Lo Bianco, "Memes and the Coup D'etat," *Periferia* 11 (2019): 111–130, https://doi.org/10.12957/periferia.2019.37034.

3 Conclusion: Is this Digital Public History?

Memes, as part of popular culture, are first and foremost an accurate mirror of society, as they reflect the changes in our perception of a world in which humor seems to be the "unique key for the understanding of social and cultural processes."[21] For this reason, digital public historians should start to think of how to use some memes both as a source and as a learning tool for historical content for the benefit of those who are digitally literate.

In public history, a critical outlook is a cardinal aspect of our understanding of the past, particularly if historians share their authority with the audience. Still, the cited cases suggest that memes can provide some pieces of information, although they cannot make the process of historical understanding and interpreting explicit per se. The "radical anonymity" and its spread on Internet forums through nicknames and avatars, enables a new type of freedom and creativity, but at the same time it sweeps away any trace of authoriality.[22] Moreover, anonymity facilitates oversimplifications or, as shown in sub Section 2.3, ill-concealed revanchisms.

While working with digital native audiences, memes are undeniably an easy tool to condense even complex historical matters into a single image or video. Conversely, being a union of different semantic units, it could be difficult to grasp the meaning of a meme without knowing its cross-references to popular culture and to historical debate: digital literacy means indeed understanding intertextuality and having the ability to evaluate information by examining different sources. Concerning memes, the faster the decoding process, the better the entertainment.

In conclusion, despite the evident limitations of using Internet memes in constructing a shared narration which is able to render the complexity of the historical process, it is important that public historians learn to understand these ever more popular units of culture "as records of public discourse, modes of coping with a terrible world, material objects that get more complex the more you unravel and contextualize them."[23] On the other hand, memes could prove to be useful both to stimulate students' creativity and to test their learning in contexts such as at the end of a lesson plan, a seminar, or a museum itinerary.[24]

---

21 Limor Shifman, "Humor in the Age of Digital Reproduction: Continuity and Change in Internet-Based Comic Texts," *International Journal of Communication* 1 (2007): 187–20, 187.
22 For the anonymity in online communities, see E. Gabriella Coleman, *Hacker, Hoaxer, Whistleblower, Spy: The Many Faces of Anonymous* (London; New York: Verso, 2014); Lolli, 87–90.
23 McGrath 14.
24 For examples about how a responsible use of the internet language may help to go beyond a pedagogy of transmission recognizing the importance of interactivity in the construction of the historical knowledge, see Diego Leonardo Santana Silva, "Os memes como suporte pedagógico no ensino de história", *Periferia* 11 (2019): 162–78, https://doi.org/10.12957/periferia.2019.36408; Luisa Quarti Lamarão, "O uso de memes nas aulas de história", *Periferia* 11 (2019): 179–92, https://doi.org/10.12957/periferia.2019.36442.

For digital public history, Internet memes represent an open challenge to be faced, if only as a valuable source for a future history of mass media and an indicator of public opinion. It might be pointless – as well as counterproductive – to attempt to stop this Internet phenomenon, by means of legislative procedures.[25] It could be more productive to investigate which role of mediation a "memer-historian" could play in this context, both online and offline.

Finally, some of these memes about history are simply brilliant: why should we turn them down?

Bibliography

Börzsei, Linda K. "Makes a Meme Instead. A Concise History of Memes". *New Media Studies Magazine* 7 (2013).

Davison, Patrick. "The Language of Internet Memes." In *The Social Media Reader*, edited by Michael Mandiberg, 120–134. New York: New York University Press, 2009.

dos Santos, Rosemary, and Felipe da Silva Ponte de Carvalho, eds. *Revista Periferia*. "Memes e Educação: práticas educativas em rede" 11 (January–April 2019).

Lolli, Alessandro. *La guerra dei meme. Fenomenologia di uno scherzo infinito*. Orbetello: effequ, 2017.

McGrath, Jim. "'This Is Fine': Reading, Making, and Archiving Memes after November 2016." *NCPH Twitter Mini-Con: (Re)Active Public History* (2018). https://twitter.com/i/events/1053259123100393472.

---

25 In 2016, articles 11 and 13 of the proposal for the EU's new copyright directive had fed fears that memes will effectively be banned, but the approved directive on April 2019 protects uploading memes and GIFs as quotations, caricatures, and parodies. Nevertheless, it will probably be problematic to distinguish between memes and other copyrighted contents.

Paolo Mogorovich and Enrica Salvatori
Historical GIS

Abstract: The historical GIS is, without any doubt, a powerful means of communication of historical phenomena for the public and also of collecting georeferenceable historical source through crowdsourcing activities, but the complexity of the data model underlying a GIS can also distance the public from understanding the complexity of the phenomena themselves. From this point of view the role of the Digital Public Historian is essential: not only will he/she have to be able to construct a GIS with a methodologically correct data model, but he/she will have to find the right ways of communicating it in order to make the GIS an effective tool of understanding and sharing the past.

Keywords: GIS, web GIS, cartography, historical maps

Introduction

Digital Public History (DPH) as a discipline involves a set of technologies for data acquisition, storage, processing and distribution used in order to interact effectively, consciously and transparently with the public on issues related to history. This includes the management of geographic information and in particular map creation. A map is a very effective and familiar medium to show special types of information. For example, on a map we can evaluate with immediacy and clarity both general and particular features, as well as the relationship among different types of objects. Since information technology began to deal with geographic information in the late 1960s, the communicative power of a map has been enriched by important components, mainly from the point of view of graphics and DataBases. The DataBase approach has enriched the potentialities of abstraction and analysis made by the geographer: what in the past was only drawn on a paper, now can be put in a DataBase and this has given rise to important considerations on the nature and the characteristics of the object itself. Since the 1990s, the incredible technical potential of telematics – that unifies IT and telecommunication methodologies trying to integrate remote information processing and transmission systems – and its social applications transformed the management and the use of geographical information as a powerful tool easily used by the public, as shown by GoogleMaps, OpenStreet Map and similar initiatives.

GIS for DPH: Opportunities and Problems

The union between traditional cartography and informatics has produced the Geographical Information System (GIS), that can be defined as a coordinated set of resources (data, skills, logistic, IT tools, network infrastructure) dedicated to the acquisition, integration, processing, distribution and presentation of geographical data.[1] Despite traditional cartography, the data processed by a GIS are grouped in classes or layers, each one containing the description of data of a unique type (e.g. only roads, only buildings). The GIS manages two main types of layers: vector or raster model. Vector model: in the layer defined entities are represented as well, geometrically described by a "feature," i.e. points, or lines or areas, with several attributes. For example, an area representing the shape of an administrative entity with the values of its population is a typical basic GIS representation of the administrative entity itself. Raster model: a geographic phenomenon is represented by a quantity, in general continuous, defined in a certain domain, sampled to a regular grid. For example, by regularly dividing a large area into small squares, the set of numbers that define the elevation of each square is a raster.

The presentation of a map is the most common feature of a GIS and involves different tools, such as the selection of one or more layers, both vector and raster, the flexible use of symbology, the possibility to zoom and pan to best frame the area of interest, the selection of background layers (Google Map, Open Street Map, etc.), the automatic selection of what to represent and how to show it according to the scale, in order to always have optimal management of the graphic space available (a PC display, a large paper, a smartphone).

GIS tools also allow the user to interact with the map, such as selecting a feature to obtain information about the attributes of the feature itself, other documents (text, photo or video) or from atlases. If in a GIS the data displayed are historical, either because they are taken directly from sources, or because they are re-elaborated in a more complex and mediated way, the interaction with the user is obviously based on layers dedicated to historical concepts and/or information: for example the extension of a country/political power over time in relation to the population and the Gross Domestic Product; the distribution of the fortifications in relation to the position of churches, villages, houses but also rivers, valleys, mountain passes and other geopolitical realities. However, as explained below, the possibilities of the research depend on how the GIS data model is conceived and built.

Unlike traditional cartography – where the different types of objects are drawn on the same support, – in a GIS each object type is managed separately in a dedicated layer.

---

[1] Burrough et al, *Principles of Geographical Information Systems*; Longley et al. *Geographic Information Systems and Science*.

Let's put emphasis on the word *managed* instead of *drawn*, because a GIS is devoted to process data, not necessarily to draw them, even if a map is almost always produced. Separate management of different layers gives the user the possibility to construct maps for different purposes and allows the exchange and re-use of data among different operators. In this way a historical GIS can allow different users to map certain phenomena according to the query.

GIS have a lot of advantages over traditional cartography, which include the possibility to manage an unlimited number of different layers and to describe entities with an unlimited number of attributes. For example in *Mapping Decline: St. Louis and American City* there are four interactive series of maps dedicated to white/black people residencies,[2] the relationship between race and property, the municipal zoning and the urban renewal: all this "layers" can be animated by a chronological slidebar and/or they can be put in relation with municipal borders, the presence of roads or highways or the disponibility of documents. The data considered in this project are numerous and of different kinds, but the geographic database that supports their visualization is able to receive other data too: this is because with the GIS we have the possibility of carrying out heavy processing operations and quantitative analysis and applying, where possible, evolutionary models. Another important feature is the strong expressive capacity in drawing a map, due to the possibility of selecting the most suitable object type (layer) and to use a quantity of graphic tools (color, symbols, lines, 3D models, etc.). Additionally, a GIS can access Internet resources so that it also be allowed access to data and processing resources; it is also suitable to involve people with different levels of expertise distributed globally and it encourages exchange experience and resource sharing, thanks to the User Interface that adopts the well known metaphor of the map. From this point of view, historical GIS is a powerful tool to illustrate effectively and to various audiences (students, communities, institutions) not immediately evident but historically significant relations between phenomena.

Nevertheless, the enormous potential of GIS applied in the historical field is not exempt from considerable problems, partly inherited from the past, or rather from the traditional relationship between geography and history, and on the other hand related to the peculiarities and the complexities of a geographical database.

Looking at traditional historical maps we will notice that they usually describe a situation as a picture: reality is frozen in a certain moment, while for the historical data the concept of evolution is critical. This impasse could be overcome in a GIS creating different layers or working on data attributes, but the operation is not easy and implies a profound reasoning on the quality of the data model (for example by establishing a predetermined chronological range). Indeed it is easier to find historical GIS

---

[2] "Mapping Decline St. Louis and the Fate of the American City," http://mappingdecline.lib.uiowa.edu/; GIS that accompanies the book Gordon, *Mapping Decline*.

projects with a reduced dynamic time component, processed from sources that "take a picture" of a situation in a given moment, rather than illustrate it over time.[3]

Both the vector model and the raster model are not perfectly suitable to handle elements with undefined boundaries:[4] for example, they describe very well administrative limits in the modern sense of the term, but not the uncertain and variable realities of the castreous districts in Europe in the twelfth century. This uncertainty can be visualized in a GIS using particular symbologies that express probability criteria, but this relies on blind trust from the user, because the critical reading would imply a profound knowledge of the methods used by the GIS authors.

In short, the processing of historical data in a GIS makes it possible to effectively represent the complexity of the unfolding of a historical phenomenon over time in an area; however, the operational choices that have to be made in order to create the data model and to obtain a good visualization of temporal passages and/or spatial uncertainties does not allow, or rather does not facilitate, the awareness of the complexity underlying the GIS itself. This makes the GIS a powerful tool for representing historical data, but a problematic tool for a conscious public participation.

DPH: The Actors

In DPH initiatives various roles are active: scholars, lecturers, researchers, disseminators, archivists, conservatives, etc. A possible classification is to consider, on the one hand, the professionals of history (those who work daily in sectors where history as a discipline is a prevalent issue), who can make use of infrastructures and technical skills of a certain importance and, on the other hand, the non-professionals, typically the common public, who generally operate only with their own device (smartphone, tablet or personal computer) and have very different needs. Between these two types of users the public historian could find its maneuvering space. In order to understand it well, we first examine the two most common work paths that can be found on the net: the top-down (from professionals to the public) and the bottom-up (from the public to professionals) flows.

---

[3] For example, the "Atlas électronique du Saguenay. Lac-Saint-Jean" shows individual maps for each significant moment of the past (http://uqac.ca/atlas/saguenay-lac-saint-jean).
[4] Cohn, "Representing Regions with Indeterminate Boundaries," 957–961.

The Top-Down Flow

The top-down flow can be considered the expression of scholars' commitment to research and to transferring their knowledge to others. From this point of view, the GIS applied to history has greatly expanded the potentiality of history in creating new research paths, in teaching or rather in editions of historical texts integrated with geographical data.

An example of a GIS elaborated on a literary work that has clear research purposes, but which obviously is also free access to everyone, is "Mapping Dante."[5] This website hosts the first interactive digital map with the places mentioned in Dante Alighieri's *Divine Comedy* and is a very good example of geo-criticism and literary mapping, developed by Price Lab for Digital Humanities at the University of Pennsylvania. Users are able to visualize and sort places according to a number of literary, cultural, and geographical categories, in order to explore the connections between Dante's text and geography.

With this GIS a teacher or a scholar can use the maps to pursue his/her own research but also clearly explain to students or the public the importance of Dante's vision of the world by selecting different layers or by making specific queries. There are many examples of this type of GIS.[6] Here we outline one of our DPH projects – TraMonti – carried out by a team from the University of Pisa and ISTI-CNR of Pisa in 2011.[7] TraMonti aimed to enhance and promote the historical-archaeological heritage and oral memory of Val di Vara (Ligury, Italy) through surveys and research and the construction of a website. The GIS includes an archaeological historical census to identify the remains of human activity from prehistoric to ancient times, the settlement revolution that took place during the Middle Ages, the relationship between the medieval network of the castles and the roads, the evolution of the settlement from the modern to contemporary ages, and the most recent structures and productive activities, in particular manufacturing, mills, crushers and quarries. The material surveyed was then enriched with photographic documentation and interviews to retrieve the memories of the oldest inhabitants of the valley.

A dynamic map can be created with three layers that can be displayed independently: elements from the archaeological census, elements derived from historical documentation, and some tourist routes. Points are used for the first two levels and lines for the third. Each item on the map is linked to a structured card that describes its content. The three thematic levels are superimposed on Google Land, but you can also use OpenStreetMap, Google Satellite or Google Map. The basic display functions

---

5 "Mapping Dante: A Study of Places in the Commedia," https://www.mappingdante.com/.
6 Knowles and Hillier, eds, *Placing History*.
7 Salvatori, "Un progetto di Public History nel cuore della Liguria," 12–32, http://tramonti.labcd.unipi.it/; GIS http://tramonti.labcd.unipi.it/val-di-vara/mappa-dei-beni-culturali/.

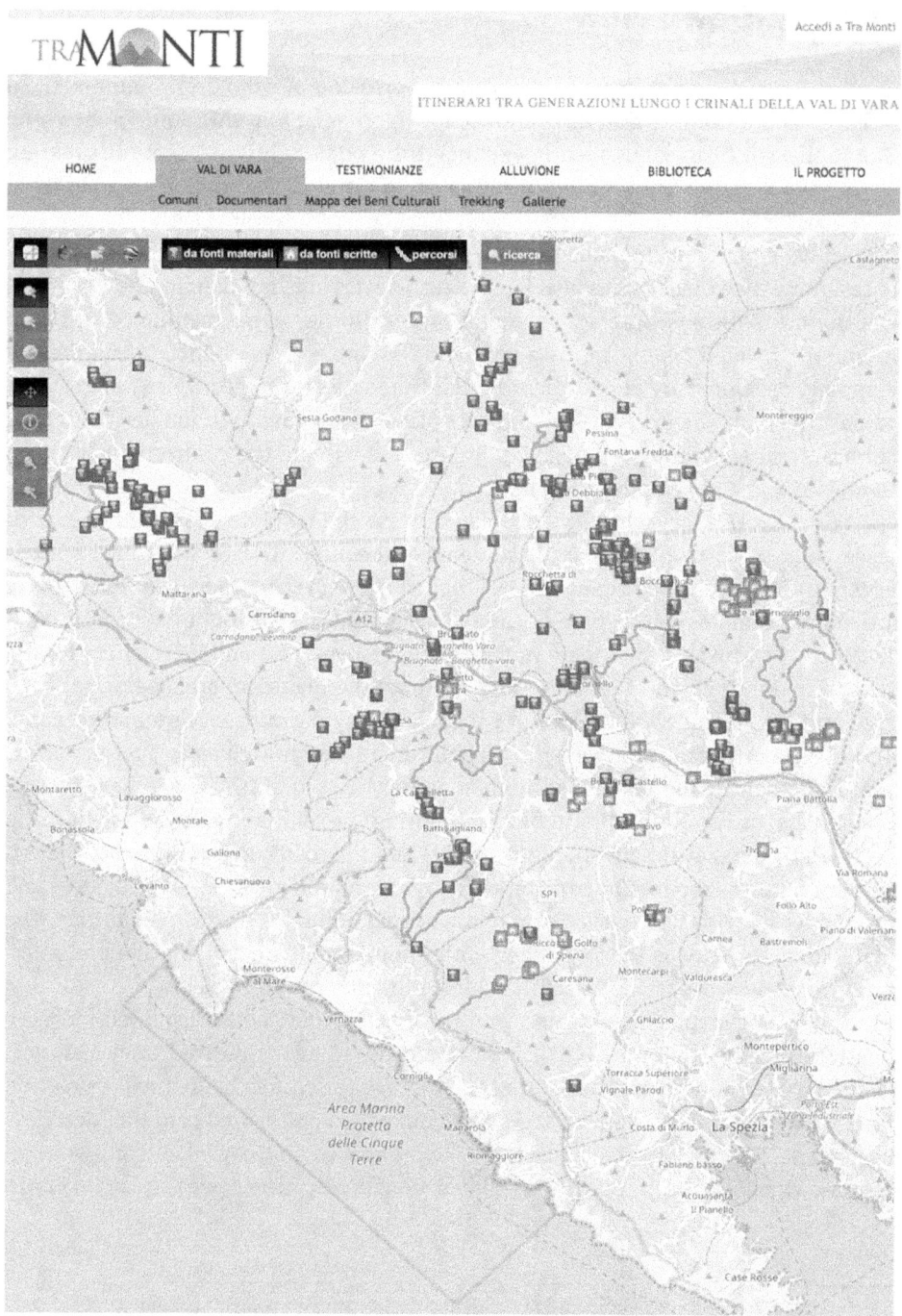

Fig. 1: "TraMonti" project Web GIS. Salvatori, "Un progetto di Public History nel cuore della Liguria".

are available and queries can be made on layers' attributes. Inside the project site the GIS allows an interaction with the public limited to the query of historical-archaeological emergencies in the valley and to the identification of preferential paths. It aims to be a service to particular categories of public: administrators for example or tourists; however, none of them can put their hands directly on the service in order to modify it or add data. However, all the tools are included in a website that collects and presents other materials from past and recent local history, some of them spontaneously collected among the population: the map of the cultural heritage of the territory does not exist as an autonomous object, separate from the context but as an element, among others, of a DPH project. In short, the GIS in the "Tramonti" project is only one element among others of a set of contents that allows and favors the sharing and discovery of one's own history by the inhabitants of a valley.

A Bottom-Ip Case

Of particularly interest is the bottom-up flow, where the public can produce historical georeferenced data. Potentially, the impact and the social importance of this new opportunity could be very high, because it gives voices to groups, minorities, realities that do not feel sufficiently represented in the official historiography, and it can facilitate cultural innovation policies at different levels of citizens' involvement.

In a DPH GIS project using on a bottom-up flow, we have a data flow created by people who use special applications on the web on their device, to build archives of information, typically stories, pictures, videos, oral records and geographical data, or even to add information to an already existing data set. A classic example of this kind of activity is the possibility given by Google Maps to add a missing place, or a shop or a label or also to create a "personal" map to share with others.

One example among many is the map of the US Civil War made in Google Maps by an anonymous author.[8]

Smartphones and other devices often have integrated tools for acquiring geographic information to associate with the database in a semi-automatic way. For example, photo cameras integrated in smartphones usually combine images and movies with the date and time of shooting and, thanks to the GPS system, they also show an accurate geographical position that could be put automatically in the DataBase. Often these devices also allow data transmission to storage and to publication sites. If the GIS is designed to provide services through the web (webGIS), it can create and deliver a map that displays positions, metadata and labels of all the items spontaneously

---

8 https://www.google.com/maps/d/u/0/viewer?hl=it&mid=11fCNn0u_5ZqXHjuS3DEpgxehc3c&ll=38.175729132316896%2C-95.8510205&z=3.

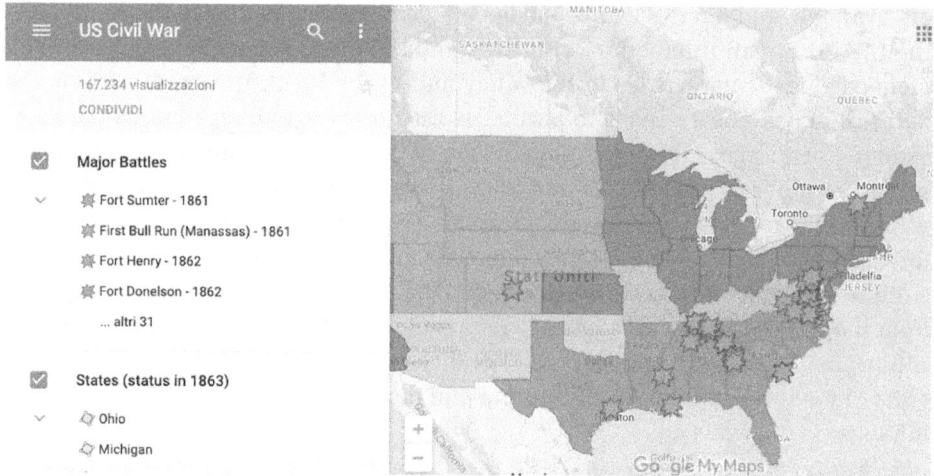

Fig. 2: US Civil War GIS on Google Maps, https://www.google.com/maps/d/u/0/viewer?hl= it&mid=11fCNnOu_5ZqXHjuS3DEpgxehc3c&ll=38.175729132316896%2C-95.8510205&z=3.

uploaded by people. In "Honoring our Veterans" by ESRI, for example, it is possible to insert the picture, name and hometown of a veteran, adding a description of his life and automatically the geographical position.[9]

In a DPH project, founded on crowdsourcing activity, it is therefore possible to "ask" the public to communicate data of historical interest to a webGIS and thus construct in a collective and shared way a coordinated repository of georeferenced historical information. An example is the mapping of city epigraphs, the places of a territory that have been visited and portrayed by a particular artist, or the places of memory of a particular phenomenon. Two examples among many. The British Library engages the public's help in geoferencing historical maps:[10] people can place historic maps over the latest maps and so compare the past with the present and the contribution helps the British Library make its maps fully searchable and viewable. The Tate Museum in the "Artmaps" project features georeferenced artworks that anyone can relocate or enrich with comments.[11]

---

9 https://storymaps.esri.com/stories/honoring-our-veterans/index.html.
10 Http://www.bl.uk/georeferencer/.
11 "Artmaps," http://www.tate.org.uk/about-us/projects/art-maps.

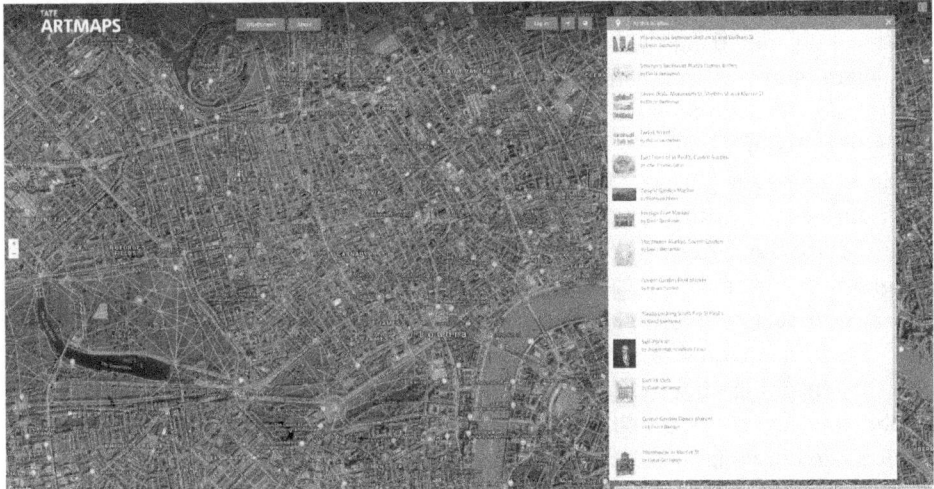

Fig. 3: "Artmaps" project Web GIS. Gabriella Giannachi, *Art Maps Project,* on the Tate site https://www.tate.org.uk/about-us/projects/art-maps.

The Time Dimension

In a map it is possible to frame the geographical space by choosing the area and the scale, so that we define the "part of the territory" visible on the screen; similarly, in a historical context, it is important to define the time interval which the map refers to. As mentioned before, the maps that we normally use derive from an ancient cartographic tradition that considers the map as a picture of a situation, taken at a certain time, deliberately ignoring the before and the after. This probably is due to the impossibility, in the past, of representing on a piece of paper the temporal evolution of entities.

However, the most important dimension of history is time and, just as it is possible to graphically represent the spatial dimension, it would be an essential outcome to graphically represent time together with space. This is often a difficult technical challenge.

In the modeling phase, managing the time and space variables could be a difficult task, due to the nature of historical data and in particular the lack of accuracy. In cases where historical data is accurate and clear, for both the dimension of space and time, using GIS is straightforward. For example, if we know the buildings (and their locations) where one or more people were affected by an epidemic, it is easy to map that data. Modelling this kind of data in a GIS is simple because we are sure of the geographic data (houses), numerical data (sick people) and temporal data (year). The simplicity and clarity of the original data obviously makes the interaction with the public more transparent, in the sense that it does not hide mediations or interpretations of the data themselves.

There is also the case where the data are accurate in space, but with uncertainty relative to time, such as we might encounter when mapping the different walls or parts of a wall of a castle. The challenge is how to compare restorations made in different periods, for example, those identifiable in a delta temporum (mid-thirteenth century) or other restorations or modifications occurring earlier or later (before the thirteenth century or after the eleventh century). In this case the geographic representation is simple, but the temporal data model should be able to describe uncertainty and give appropriate consistent answers to user queries. In this case it is essential to provide the public with greater transparency and clarity, and the reasoning underlying the data model; in the case of the participation of the public, it is also necessary to provide users with clear input forms in which the time choices are unambiguous and well explained.

There are also cases where data are accurate in time but uncertain in their positioning – e.g. in a year a number of settlements were attested in a place, but today those places do not exist anymore, either in whole or in part. They cannot be placed with accuracy on a map but are still positioned within an area. In this case, modelling time is easy, but we have to invent a suitable model for space, and obviously the map we create must emphasize the uncertainty. In this case the public can be useful in finding a correct geo-reference for a place, thanks to local memory, to the relevant knowledge of a territory that only a resident of a community can have. However, interaction with the user is not easy, as they may be asked to provide hypothetical geo-referencing that however should then be confirmed using strict methods and comparisons.

Often historical change is represented as a "map collection," even an ancient one: maps which refer to different dates may be displayed in a variety of ways, so as to convey the evolution of a historical phenomenon.[12] In a more sofisticated example GIS can use animation tools to show the evolution of a phenomenon; they are based on a time bar or a clock, in general reproduced on the map, that moves in the temporal dimension. Over time the entities on the map change position and shape, others appear, and others disappear, as in HGIS de las Indias.[13] The transition between the images can be gradual (fading, venetian blinds, etc.) in order to simulate the swiftness of evolution, depending on the kind of phenomena depicted. Interestingly, the solution used in the Firenze in Guerra's Collection project inside Historypin for the seventieth anniversary of the liberation of Florence, saw photos crowdsourced that were added on the google map of the city and put in the exact places where they

---

[12] "Euratlas," https://www.euratlas.com/; "Timemaps," https://www.timemaps.com/.
[13] "HGIS de las Indias," https://www.hgis-indias.net/index.php/webgis.

were taken in 1944; people had the possibility to fade the old picture and replace it with the google street view of today.¹⁴

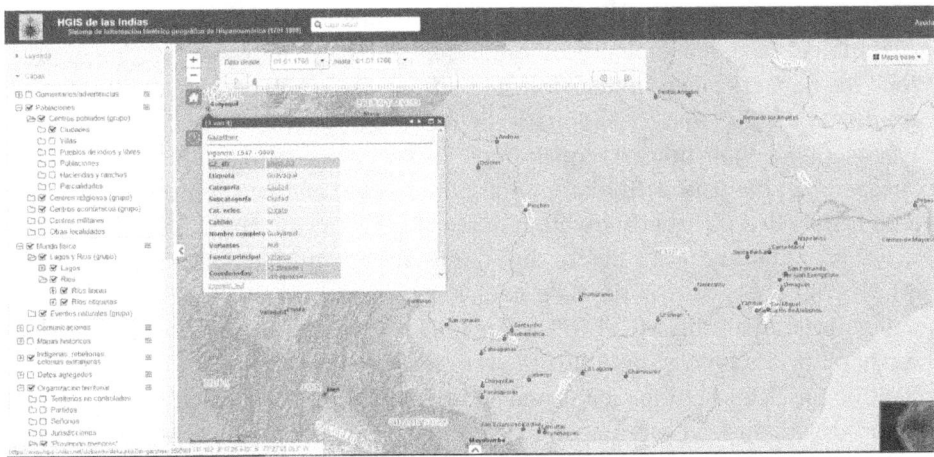

Fig. 4: "HGIS de las Indias", https://www.hgis-indias.net/index.php/webgis. Gil, T., and L. Barleta. "Digital Atlas of Portuguese America" presented at DHLU 2013, Proceedings of the Third Conference on Digital Humanities in Luxembourg with a Special Focus on Reading Historical Sources in the Digital Age, Luxembourg, December 5–6, 2013.

In another possible solution, GIS can build historical maps dynamically. Historical data are stored in a database and each entity has its geographic position, shape and attributes marked with a start time and end time concerning validity; given a certain date, the software selects and represent the entities with their characteristics at the date, so that the map you see does not exist as a real map, but is an actual map of an old stage.¹⁵ This is a product of the highest quality and of great technical complexity, useful for showing historical changes to the public, but hardly suited to encourage their participation.

Conclusions

Setting up a DPH applications when the historical GIS component is concerned involves a great deal of work for data preparation: in the retrieval of textual historical information and historical maps, in extracting data that have to be structured and

---

14 https://www.historypin.org/en/firenze-in-guerra-s-collection/geo/43.771594,11.254386,5/bounds/29.917453,-0.416528,55.028419,22.9253/paging/1.
15 Gil and Barleta, "Digital Atlas of Portuguese America."

formalized and in the management of historical maps with a current and homogeneous cartographic criteria.

To set up geographical databases with historical information, we have to begin by creating a data model, where the entities are unequivocally defined and, in the geographical case, are geometrically represented by a primitive point, line or area. When the data are taken from historical maps, we face problems of geometric accuracy due to the fact that the old maps are often highly symbolic and limited by the instruments of their time. Complications also arise from the evolution of certain concepts, e.g. the very definition of an entity's edge, and because the same entity could be labelled differently in different epochs (e.g. a city, could have been previously a hospital and even before that a military camp). This uncertainty clashes with the rigidity typical of the data model supported by a GIS. Such issues imply, for the authors of a historical GIS, a great clarity of method and an equally clear transparency of choices in publishing the result of their work. If we move from a scientific publication to the management of a GIS in a DPH project, such attention and accuracy must be even more accentuated. The historical GIS is, without any doubt, a powerful means of communication of historical phenomena for the public and also of collecting georeferenceable historical source through crowdsourcing activities. But the objective difficulties in understanding a data model underlying a GIS makes GIS itself a powerful filter that can, if not well managed, distance the public from understanding the complexity of the phenomena themselves. From this point of view the role of the Digital Public Historian is essential: not only will he/she have to be able to construct a GIS with a methodologically correct data model, but he/she will have to find the right ways of communicating it in order to make the GIS an effective tool of understanding and sharing the past.

Bibliography

Burrough, Peter A. *Principles of Geographical Information Systems for Land Resource Assessment.* Oxford: Clarendon Press, 1986.

Cohn, Antony G. "Representing Regions with Indeterminate Boundaries." In *Encyclopedia on GIS*, edited by Shashi Shekhar and Hui Xiong, 957–961. Springer, 2008.

Gil, T., and L. Barleta. "Digital Atlas of Portuguese America" presented at DHLU 2013, Proceedings of the Third Conference on Digital Humanities in Luxembourg with a Special Focus on Reading Historical Sources in the Digital Age, Luxembourg, December 5–6, 2013.

Gordon, Colin. *Mapping Decline: St. Louis and the Fate of the American City.* University of Pennsylvania Press, 2014.

Knowles, Anne Kelly, and Amy Hillier, eds. *Placing History: How Maps, Spatial Data, and GIS Are Changing Historical Scholarship.* ESRI, Inc., 2008.

Longley, Paul A. et al. *Geographic Information Systems and Science.* Chichester: Wiley, 2005.

Salvatori, Enrica. "Un progetto di Public History nel cuore della Liguria." In *Storia e territorio della Val di Vara*, edited by Enrica Salvatori, 12–32. Pisa: Felici Editore, 2012.

Gerben Zaagsma
Content Management

Abstract: The use of content management systems (CMSes) in public history is a relatively new phenomenon that has greatly enhanced the possibilities of presenting, curating and narrating history online. As CMSes have become increasingly powerful and easier to use, they obviate the need for comparatively costlier custom solutions, both in terms of time and financial investment. Archives, libraries, museums, institutions, scholars and educators are making use of CMSes to showcase collections, accompany exhibitions, tell histories online and to build online communities and networks. This chapter discusses how content management systems support these activities and projects while also delving into more technical aspects. In doing so the chapter focuses on open source systems which can be used by any scholar without incurring licensing fees, and are often supported by large user communities.[1]

Keywords: digital history, public history, content management systems, digital storytelling, web 2.0, internet

There is an intimate connection between public and digital history.[2] Given that many digital public history projects take place on the web, a central question is what technologies can assist us in that effort. Since the early days of the web, historians have built websites to tell stories, to collect materials, and to extend their audiences. It is no exaggeration to say that such efforts have been transformed decisively by the advent of (open source) CMSes, such as Wordpress, Drupal, and Omeka. From the late 1990s onwards, content management systems re-shaped the ways in which public historians, heritage institutions and organizations engaged and built audiences through the Internet. As CMSes continue to develop, the possibilities to engage and involve audiences also continue to evolve.

Telling history online in the early days of the web meant building a static website using the HyperText Markup Language (HTML) whose layout was controlled through Cascading Style Sheets (CSS). While this enabled historians to construct non-linear hypertextual narratives online, they still had to manually code the websites themselves, requiring a substantial investment of time, a willingness to learn the relevant technology or hiring programmers, designers, and technical experts. While HMTL and CSS are still the building blocks of any website, as far as the underlying code is

---

[1] I would like to thank my co-editors of this volume, Serge Noiret and Mark Tebeau, for their critical feedback and careful editing, and Sinem Adar for her comments on an earlier version of this chapter.
[2] See for example, Fien Danniau, "Public History in a Digital Context: Back to the Future or Back to Basics?" *BMGN – Low Countries Historical Review* 128.4 (2013): 118–144. http://www.bmgn-lchr.nl/index.php/bmgn/article/view/9355.

concerned, a modern CMS no longer requires individual users to manually build websites. This allows project teams to focus on content strategies, editing, and more advanced functionalities and designs.

What, exactly, is a CMS? According to Barker, "a content management system (CMS) is a software package that provides some level of automation for the tasks required to effectively manage content" and "a tool to assist in and enable the theoretical ideal of content management. How well any one CMS successfully brings that ideal to life is the subject of great debate and Internet flame wars."[3] On the most basic level, a CMS enables editors and/or users to easily manage and create content. For example, using a content management system, such as WordPress or Omeka, historians can easily create basic websites and digital narratives through the use of ready-made themes and/or templates. In addition, many CMSes allow users and/or developers to extend core functionalities by using add-on modules. Omeka, for example, allows users the option of deploying add-ons, such as Dublin core subject vocabularies, to enable the easy addition of key metadata for digital objects.

The challenges of developing projects without a ready-made CMS are well illustrated by one of the classic early examples of online history: the Valley of the Shadow project, a "digital archive of primary sources that document the lives of people in Augusta County, Virginia, and Franklin County, Pennsylvania, during the era of the American Civil War."[4] Another example is the website American History from Revolution to Reconstruction and Beyond which was created in November 1994 by a group of students from the Arts Faculty of the University of Groningen in the Netherlands under the supervision of George Welling.[5] These early hand-built projects required extensive work and resources. Some of them, such as the Cleveland Cultural Gardens Project, started out as hand-coded websites and were later migrated to a CMS.[6]

Well-known CMSes such as Drupal and Wordpress, launched in 2001 and 2003 respectively. Initially, these systems emphasized the features of Web 1.0 in which information was merely published, rendering audiences into passive consumers of content produced by others. Yet, as they developed, they adopted features that would fundamentally alter the relation between historians and their audiences. Wordpress, for example, first emerged as blogging software that invited comments from audiences. This was part of the transition to what is often called Web 2.0, which turned users (or 'the crowd') into active participants and co-producers of knowledge whose collective intelligence and wisdom has been, and is, harnessed broadly, including by historians.[7]

---

[3] Barker, *Web Content Management*, 5, 7.
[4] http://valley.lib.virginia.edu/.
[5] http://www.let.rug.nl/usa/.
[6] http://www.culturalgardens.org/.
[7] Tim O' Reilly, "What is Web 2.0: Design Patterns and Business Models for the Next Generation of Software," *Communications & Strategies*1 (2007): http://oreilly.com/web2/archive/what-is-web-20.html, 17–37.

That is not to say that historians have jumped on the CMS bandwagon easily. As late as 2006, four years after the publication of the first edition of Bob Boiko's classic *Content Management Bible*,[8] Cohen and Rosenzweig could still avoid talking about CMSes in their chapter on 'Designing for the History Web,' focusing instead on elaborate discussions of the principles of (HMTL-based) web design. Even when talking about collecting history online through blogs they suggested that the "most powerful and flexible way to receive collections is through an interactive website of your own design."[9] Despite this slow transition and uptake of CMS among historians, digital history projects also drove the development of dedicated CMSes such as, most notably, Omeka, a CMS developed from 2007 onwards by the Roy Rosenzweig Center for History and New Media (RRCHNM). Omeka was built to publish collections and narrative exhibits; it was partly based upon other systems and plugins which were used, for instance, to ran the Center's Hurricane Digital Memory Bank, a key example of an early online collecting project.[10]

CMSes obviate the need for custom built websites, thereby potentially reducing costs and time to deploy. Because of their relative ease of use, content editing also becomes much simpler. Moreover, the use of a CMS makes digital history projects more sustainable because it reduces the risk of building a website that can no longer be updated after its original developer has left. All of this, however, is relative; a CMS-built website can be anything from a single-user Wordpress-hosted site, which can be set up in minutes, to an institutional Wordpress or Drupal-based website which can take many months to develop, test and deploy against significant costs; a good example of the latter is the Digital Web Centre for the History of Science (DWC).[11] Nonetheless, by using software with large developer communities, the challenges of long-term maintenance are significantly reduced.

---

8 The 2nd edition was published in 2005. See Bob Boiko, *Content Management Bible* (Indianapolis, Ind.: Wiley, 2005).

9 Daniel J. Cohen, and Roy Rosenzweig, *Digital History: A Guide to Gathering, Preserving, and Presenting the Past on the Web* (Philadelphia: University of Pennsylvania Press, 2006). http://chnm.gmu.edu/digitalhistory/collecting/3.php.

10 See: http://hurricanearchive.org/, accessed 13 August 2020. For a very short history of the Omeka project: https://omeka.org/news/2018/02/20/omeka-now-public-10-years/. Digital memory banks are an interesting phenomenon in itself, once described as "an in-between digital space" and a Web 1.5 endeavor as, for one thing, it cannot "succeed in an entirely digital and editable mode." See Sheila Brennan, "What's Next for Digital Memory Banks?," Lot 49 (May 6, 2013), accessed December 22, 2017, https://www.lotfortynine.org/2013/05/whats-next-for-digital-memory-banks/; Sheila Brennan and Mills Kelly, "Why Collecting History Online is Web 1.5," *RRCHNM Essays on History and New Media*, accessed December 22, 2017, http://chnm.gmu.edu/essays-on-history-new-media/essays/?essayid=47.

11 The DWC is hosted by the Huygens Institute for the History of the Netherlands, one of the humanities institutes of the Dutch Academy of Sciences (KNAW). See http://www.dwc.knaw.nl/?lang=en.

The choice of which particular CMS to select depends, *inter alia*, upon the general aims of the website, an individual or organization's specific needs in terms of design, functionality, and editorial options, envisaged future extensions, already available (technical) expertise, and budgets. Of course, the relative importance given to these factors in the process of decision-making has serious implications regarding the accessibility of content, the project scope, and modes of presentation in the final product. Thus, choosing a CMS always entails trade-offs, although the significance and impact of these choices are not always well recognized by digital historians.[12]

Of equal important to the selection of a CMS is the implementation of that content management system. Indeed, implementation is key to any successful project; as argued by Boiko, the "most perfect CMS in the world can be rendered all but useless by a poor implementation."[13] This pertains especially to complex projects with various stakeholders and competing visions and/or interests. In order to realize the full potential and possibilities offered by CMSes several factors are of key importance. A CMS serves to satisfy informational needs and thinking through how users can find the information they are looking for is key.[14] Interface and user interaction design are therefore crucial as a badly designed website may inhibit discovery of content and can put off users altogether.[15] A clear content strategy and a well-thought out plan of what type of interaction with users is envisaged, is of equal importance, and a central aspect in any digital public history project.

Wordpress is probably the best-known free open-source CMS and currently (2022) powers over 40 percent of the world's websites.[16] It is mostly known as a highly versatile blogging platform with excellent editorial functionality. Yet it is also suitable for anything from simple to medium-complex websites. Wordpress offers hosted as well as self-hosted solutions. In the former case (and this applies to many blogging platforms), a user only has to sign-up and choose a domain name and the service takes care of creating the actual website. Users can also host their own CMS, whether a more complex tool such as Drupal or more easily deployed

---

[12] For a useful overview and advice on making the best choice, see Dean Rehberger, "Getting Oral History Online: Collections Management Applications," *Oral History Review* 40 (1) (2013): 83–94.

[13] Cf. Barker who defines implementation as "the process by which a CMS is installed, configured, templated, and extended to deliver the website you want." See Barker 2016.

[14] Boiko, *Content Management Bible*, 147–173; on the non-digital roots of information science in a humanities context, see Charles van den Heuvel, "Historical Roots of Information Sciences and the Making of E-Humanities," in *Historical Roots of Information Sciences and the Making of E-humanities*, ed. Rens Bod, Jaap Maat, and Thijs Weststeijn (Amsterdam: Amsterdam University Press, 2014), 465–478.

[15] Design should also take into account issues of accessibility. See George H. Williams, "Disability, Universal Design, and the Digital Humanities," in *Understanding Digital Humanities*, ed. David M Berry (Houndmills, Basingstoke, Hampshire: Palgrave Macmillan, 2012), 202–213.

[16] See: https://w3techs.com/technologies/details/cm-wordpress/all/all.

system like Wordpress. Self-hosting involves downloading and configuring the software oneself. Most hosting companies these days offer easy install procedures, automating and simplifying much of the work of configuring the underlying database.

Self-hosting allows for the greatest degree of flexibility in terms of customization (whether it's about design or enhancing functionality through plugins or self-coded custom solutions). More complex CMSes, such as Drupal or Joomla, offer more advanced ways to present content and add functionality and can be used to build highly complex websites. Drupal, in particular, is a well-known CMS in the digital humanities world and there's even a book *Drupal for Humanists* by Quinn Dombrowski.[17] The Mediawiki software that powers Wikipedia can also be regarded as a CMS. Dombrowski has made a useful distinction within the public history context between generic open source CMS and those developed specifically for academic or heritage purposes such as Omeka and Scalar.[18]

Omeka, as already mentioned, was released by the Roy Rosenzweig Center for History and New Media (RRCHNM) in 2008 and provides "open-source web publishing platforms for sharing digital collections and creating media-rich online exhibits."[19] It can be extended with Neatline which "allows scholars, students, and curators to tell stories with maps and timelines."[20] It is also used in conjunction with humanities data repositories as in, for example, the French NAKALA project.[21] Scalar is a "free, open source authoring and publishing platform that's designed to make it easy for authors to write long-form, born-digital scholarship online."[22] As it is clearly geared towards academic historical publishing, it is of less importance within our current discussion. Another tool worth mentioning is Scripto, an open-source transcription tool which enables community transcriptions of document and multimedia files and can be integrated with Omeka, Wordpress and Drupal.[23]

Because of their ease of use, flexibility and extensibility, open-source CMSes afford and enable a wide variety of uses. As such, they are deployed in myriad ways in digital public history projects. Archives, libraries, museums make use of CMSes to showcase collections and accompany exhibitions or use crowdsourcing to involve and solicit help of the public in transcription and other citizen science type projects. Historians use blogs to narrate histories online and many historians collaborate with heritage institutions on digital history projects whose results are showcased online. CMSes are also used to build online communities and networks.

---

[17] Quinn Dombrowski, *Drupal for Humanists* (College Station: Texas A&M University Press, 2016).
[18] Dombrowski, "Drupal and Other Content Management Systems."
[19] http://omeka.org.
[20] http://neatline.org.
[21] For more information on the resulting NAKALONA project, see: https://www.nakalona.fr.
[22] https://scalar.usc.edu.
[23] http://scripto.org.

A very interesting example of the latter is the Ottoman History Podcast (OHP) which was initiated in 2011 by two scholars from Georgetown University, Emrah Safa Gürkan and Chris Gratien, as an "experiment aimed at finding an alternative form of academic production that explores new and more accessible media and allows for a collaborative approach." The OHP "is dedicated to offering a multivocal and inclusive discussion of history in the Ottoman Empire and elsewhere that showcases the numerous perspectives on the past within our field of study."[24] Offering a diverse group of guests on the program, the OHP is non-affiliated and aspires to reach scholars and the public alike. The podcast runs on the blogging platform Blogger and illustrates how easy individual or small teams of scholars can engage in online storytelling and education, and build online communities with relatively little effort, by using a CMS.

With a CMS like Omeka it has also become relatively easy to create online exhibitions. A good example is the project Gent 1913 Virtueel, an initiative of the Institute for Public History at the University of Gent, which revolves around the 1913 World Exhibition that took place in the Belgian city of Gent.[25] The website, built with Omeka, has an image database, several online exhibitions, a timeline and a 3D model of the premises of the World Exhibition that allows users to navigate the exhibition site through a virtual spatial representation.

If these are all examples of comparatively small projects, CMSes are also deployed to build and showcase huge online collections by archives, libraries and museums. The Dutch website *Netwerk Oorlogsbronnen*, for example, operates a collections portal through which it provides access to millions of digital resources from hundreds of heritage institutions about World War Two and the Holocaust in the Netherlands. The portal, which continues to expand, is built with Drupal and has involved a massive multi-year effort to engage a wide variety of stakeholders, allowing for the ingestion of their digitised objects into the portal.[26]

Crowdsourcing constitutes another form of engaging and interacting with the public. The Smithsonian Institution's online Transcription Center, for instance, is built with Drupal and allows so-called digital volunteers to make historical documents and biodiversity data more accessible.[27] Another interesting example of a project in which professional historians and the public collaborate to collect and narrate history online is the Virtual Shtetl (VS), launched in 2009, and run by the POLIN Museum of the History of Polish Jews since 2012. The VS is a Drupal-built website that "aims at describing all the Jewish communities that have lived within

---

[24] http://www.ottomanhistorypodcast.com/p/mission-statement.html.
[25] http://gent1913virtueel.be.
[26] https://www.oorlogsbronnen.nl/.
[27] https://transcription.si.edu.

the ever-changing borders of the Polish Commonwealth."[28] Its content is in part contributed and created by its base of around 22.000 users.[29]

The projects mentioned here illustrate the myriad uses to which CMSes in digital public history settings are being put and the affordances of new digital technologies for new forms of non-linear digital storytelling and interaction with our audiences. Yet caution is also advised: CMSes are not magic out-of-the-box solutions that obviate the need for a careful assessment of a project's requirements and editorial strategies. Sharon Leon has suggested that "creating public history for the Web requires that we take advantage of the medium to deliver content that honors the complexity and contingency of history and that we communicate those characteristics to our audience."[30] It is beyond the scope of this chapter to discuss how CMSes could enable historians to do so, but safe to say: the basic interpretive work remains up to digital public historians themselves as they construct their projects.

Bibliography

Barker, Deane. *Web Content Management: Systems, Features, and Best Practices*. Sebastopol, CA: O'Reilly, 2016.

Dombrowski, Quinn. "Drupal and Other Content Management Systems." In *Doing Digital Humanities: Practice, Training, Research*, edited by Constance Crompton, Richard L Lane and Ray Siemens, 342–359. London: Routledge, 2016.

Leon, Sharon. "Complexity and Collaboration: Doing Public History in Digital Environments." In *The Oxford Handbook of Public History*, edited by James B Gardner and Paula Hamilton, 44–66. New York: Oxford University Press, 2017.

---

[28] See Pauline Sliwinski,"Museum as Memoryscape: The Virtual Shtetl Portal of the Museum of the History of Polish Jews," *Museums and the Web 2012* (April 11–14, 2012): https://www.museumsandtheweb.com/mw2012/papers/museum_as_memoryscape_the_virtual_shtetl_porta.html.

[29] https://sztetl.org.pl/en.

[30] Leon, "Complexity and Collaboration," 44–66, 49.

Carlo Meghini
Linked Open Data & Metadata

Abstract: This article considers linked data, starting with the four rules drawn up in 2006 by the inventor of the web, Tim Berners-Lee, to produce this kind of data: (1) to use a web standard, the Internationalized Resource Identifier (IRI), to name things within the data; and, in particular, (2) to use IRIs of the HTTP protocol, so that data associated with these IRIs can be retrieved and accessed in exactly the same way that web pages are retrieved and accessed; (3) to use a second web standard, the Resource Description Framework (RDF), to format the data, and a third web standard, the SPARQL Query Language, to query those data. Finally, (4) to use IRIs from other datasets within the data, so as to connect one's own data with those of other people.

This article comments on these rules and discusses their implications, highlighting in particular the fact that they lay the bases for the creation of the Semantic Web, that is, a new web, parallel to the web for humans as we have known it for the last two decades. The Semantic Web is made up of pages containing formal knowledge expressed as linked data. This knowledge is consumed by artificial agents carrying out trivial, time-consuming, and error-prone tasks (such as counting the occurrences of a certain syntactic construct in Dante's Comedia), freeing humans from such tasks and letting them use their time for more intellectual activities (such as figuring out the evolution of Dante's culture). The vision of the Semantic Web is presented along with two basic ingredients for its establishment: the Resource Description Framework (RDF), the language for expressing linked data, and ontologies – that is, vocabularies – that axiomatize the definitions of the terms used in linked data. For the realization of the Semantic Web, RDF is necessary but not sufficient, because RDF provides the mere structure of linked data, without indicating any particular way to represent a specific domain. This is the role of ontologies, without which any linked data dataset would remain confined within a (possibly very small) community, defeating the vision of a common, global data space. Finally, the article discusses the role of the Semantic Web for the scholarly domain. In fact, linked open data and ontologies play a very important role in the scientific and scholarly world by offering tools for the creation and sharing of data and vocabularies. The key concept here is interdisciplinarity. It has been long recognized that significant progress can be achieved in all branches of science in research projects that are able to combine tools, data, and knowledge from different domains. Research infrastructures such as D4Science are complex systems that allow users to realize interdisciplinarity in science by offering scientists virtual research environments where they can find the tools, data, and knowledge that they need for their work. They also provide them with the communication and collaboration facilities that are necessary to cooperate with their colleagues. D4Sceince is also supporting the humanities with virtual research environments like those of the PARTHENOS and ARIADNE infrastructural projects.

https://doi.org/10.1515/9783110430295-039

Keywords: linked data, ontologies, semantic web, resource description framework, ontology web language, data interoperability, research infrastructures

Linked Open Data are data that combine two independent features: as Linked Data, they are structured according to four rules proposed by the inventor of the web, Tim Berners Lee, in a note published in 2006.[1] As Open data, they are accessible and re-usable "without restrictions from copyright, patents or other mechanisms of control".[2] This article elaborates on the former feature; readers interested in the latter can find more information e.g in the footnote.[3]

Linked Data and the Semantic Web

Since their introduction in 2006, the four rules defining Linked Data have been increasingly followed by institutions and individuals willing to make their data accessible and interoperable, and are nowadays a *de facto* standard. Indeed, according to official statistics,[4] the Linked Open Data cloud, consisting of the datasets formatted as Linked Data, counted 295 datasets in 2011 and 1,014 datasets in 2014. At present, 9,960 datasets are identifiable on the web,[5] with the number expected to grow for the reasons explained below.

The four rules of Linked Data can be stated as follows:
1. To use a web standard, Internationalized Resource Identifiers (IRIs), to name things within the data, and in particular
2. to use IRIs of the HTTP protocol, so that data associated to these IRIs can be retrieved and accessed in exactly the same way web pages are retrieved and accessed.
3. To use a second web standard, the Resource Description Framework (RDF), to format the data, and a third web standard, the SPARQL Query Language, to query these data.
4. The fourth rule is in fact a re-statement of the first: to use IRIs from other datasets within the data, so as to connect one's own data to those of other people.

Despite their simplicity, these four rules have wide implications, as witnessed from the size and the volume of activity of the World Wide Web Consortium (W3C), the "international community that develops open standards to ensure the long-term

---

1 https://www.w3.org/DesignIssues/LinkedData.html.
2 https://en.wikipedia.org/wiki/Open_data.
3 https://en.wikipedia.org/wiki/Open_data.
4 linkeddata.org.
5 http://stats.lod2.eu/.

growth of the Web".[6] Overall, the rules aim at establishing for data a network structure similar to the web. Such network structure, generally called *Semantic Web*, is not expected to actually replace the web, but rather extend it. How? While web pages are human-to-human messages that convey information on a multitude of topics using natural languages (text, images, graphics, and the like), Linked Data are machine-readable messages, often called *metadata*, that convey information on a multitude of topics using an artificial language, RDF. So, the extension of the web to the Semantic Web is one that complements the informal knowledge carried by web pages, with the formal knowledge carried by Linked Data.

The rationale behind the pursuing of the Semantic Web is similar to that of the Web: to improve the quality of people's lives. However, the means are different. The web tries to achieve this goal by making knowledge available to people at the lowest possible cost. In contrast, the Semantic Web tries to achieve the same goal by increasing the level of automation. The expectation is that by making more information available to artificial agents such as Linked Data, it will be possible to multiply the number of such agents in carrying out trivial, time-consuming, and error-prone tasks, freeing humans from such tasks and letting them use their time for more intellectual activities. A case in point is the DanteSource project[7] which has built a Linked Data dataset of Dante's works and of references to primary sources of these works. The dataset is based on an ontology for representing the knowledge on literary works and on the primary sources embedded in the commentaries to these works. A web application allows users to explore the dataset in various ways and to visualize statistical information, such as the total amount of references to a certain work, or to an author, in each of the parts of the works of Dante. Such information is gathered from several heterogeneous sources and offered as a coherent whole via a single access point to the scholar, who may use it to reconstruct the evolution of Dante's cultural background, a task clearly beyond the capabilities of any artificial agent.

RDF and Ontologies

RDF is the language recommended by the W3C to be used for Linked Data. Its first specification was issued in 1999,[8] followed by a new specification in 2004.[9] The latest version of RDF, known as RDF 1.1, was released in 2014.[10]

---

[6] https://www.w3.org/.
[7] http://perunaenciclopediadantescadigitale.eu/dantesources/.
[8] https://www.w3.org/TR/1999/REC-rdf-syntax-19990222/.
[9] https://www.w3.org/TR/rdf-concepts/.
[10] N. Guarino, D. Oberle, and S. Staab, "What Is an Ontology?" In Handbook on Ontologies, Second Edition, ed. S. Staab and R. Studer (Springer-Verlag, 2009).

RDF uses a very simple format for expressing data: its basic unit of representation is a *triple*, consisting of a subject, a predicate, and an object. A triple represents a natural language statement in a formal way. The statement expresses that a binary relation, the triple's predicate, holds between two individuals, the triple's subject and object. For instance, a triple may express the statement that Edgar A. Poe is the author of the tale "The Black Cat" by using an IRI for Edgar A. Poe as subject, an IRI for "The Black Cat" as object, and an IRI for the authorship relation as predicate.

A Linked Data dataset is just a (possibly very large) set of RDF triples. Faithful to the Linked Data principles, RDF uses IRIs to identify each element of a triple. Standard values such as strings and dates that occur as objects in triples can be represented by *literals* drawn from the XML data space, another element of conformance to the web. Individuals not worth to be globally identified via IRIs are represented as unnamed individuals, termed *blank nodes* in RDF.

Compared with the rich structures of traditional data models, RDF appears dramatically poor, confining itself to binary relations and to a minimal syntax. However, this simplicity is RDF's strength: it reduces the cost of developing tools for managing RDF documents; it avoids by design all structural problems that arise when integrating data from different sources; it naturally offers itself as a natural basis on top of which sophisticated modelling languages can be developed. In fact, RDF lies at the basis of the architecture proposed by T. Berners Lee for the realization of the Semantic Web, depicted in the figure below:

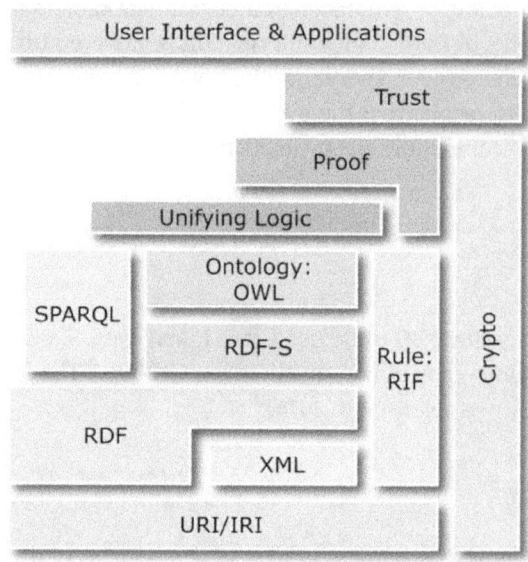

Fig. 1: The Semantic Web stack of languages (this picture is taken from Wikipedia at https://it.wikipedia.org/wiki/File:Semantic_Web_Stack.png).

For the realization of the Semantic Web, however, RDF is necessary but not sufficient, because RDF provides the mere structure of Linked Data without indicating any particular way on how to represent a specific domain. To make RDF useful for the realization of the Semantic Web vision, another fundamental ingredient is needed, namely, common vocabularies offering the *terms* to be used as subjects, predicates, and objects in triples that can be understood and used by people and programs other than those who have created them. Without such vocabularies, any Linked Data dataset would remain confined within a (possibly very small) community, defeating the vision of a common, global data space. This is what Europeana has done to build its very rich Linked Data dataset, which sits at the centre of the Digital Library. The Europeana dataset includes descriptions of dozens of thousands of objects in the Cultural Heritage domain obtained by first collecting the metadata from thousands of Cultural Heritage institutions all over Europe, and then by transforming these metadata according to a common ontology, the Europeana Data model.[11] The ontology is built on top of well-known vocabularies, notably the CIDOC CRM, giving the Europeana Linked Data dataset the maximum potential for interoperability, as explained below.

The terms of such global data space can be conveniently divided into IRIs for representing *particulars*, such as individuals, things, time periods, space regions, and the like, and IRIs for representing *universals*, that is the general categories of discourse. Universals, in turn, are usually divided in classes (e.g., people, object, time, space, and the like) and properties (to be a friend of, or the father of, or the author of, and so on). IRIs for particulars are typically provided by *terminologies*, while IRIs for universals are typically provided by *ontologies*. Sometimes the term *ontology* is used for both.

While the term ontology has a long history in philosophy, where it is used as a synonym of metaphysics, it is a relatively new acquisition of computer science, where it is understood as the formal specification of a conceptualization of a domain of discourse.[12] More specifically, ontologies are logical theories providing symbols for the universals of a certain domain of discourse, and axioms establishing the proper relationships amongst those symbols. For instance, an ontology of social relations might include classes such as persons, organizations, and mailboxes, and properties such as to-be-a-friend-of, or to-work-for. Typical axioms in such an ontology might establish that persons are either males or females, and that every organization has to have a certified mailbox.

---

11 M. Doerr, S. Gradmann, S. Hennicke, A. Isaac, C. Meghini, and H. van de Sompel. The Europeana Data Model (EDM). In World Library and Information Congress: 76th IFLA General Conference and Assembly, pages 10–15, Gothenburg, Sweden, August 2010.
12 N. Guarino, D. Oberle, and S. Staab, "What Is an Ontology?" In *Handbook on Ontologies*, Second Edition, ed. S. Staab and R. Studer (Springer-Verlag, 2009).

Three different kinds of ontologies are typically recognized:[13]
- *Top-level* ontologies describe very general concepts like space, time, matter, object, event, action, etc., which are independent of a particular problem or domain.
- *Domain* ontologies and *task* ontologies describe, respectively, the vocabulary related to a generic domain or a generic task or activity, by specializing the terms introduced in a top-level ontology. A well-known domain ontology in the domain of Cultural Heritage is the CIDOC CRM,[14] an ISO Standard since 2006, largely used to describe the assets and activities of libraries and *musea*.
- *Application* ontologies describe concepts depending both on a particular domain and task, which are often specializations of both the related ontologies. The ontology underlying the DanteSource dataset, mentioned above, is an example of an application ontology.

An ontology is a fundamental complement of a Linked Data dataset. The Linked Data dataset provides factual knowledge about a slice of a certain domain, while the ontology provides lexical knowledge about the same domain, offering definitions of the terms used in the triples of that dataset. The expectation is that the largest possible number of datasets share the same ontology, thereby being fragments of one global dataset and as such *semantically interoperable*. This idea is at the core of the Data for History project,[15] recently launched to connect history data expressed in the CIDOC CRM ontology into a global network.

In the Semantic Web picture given in Fig. 1, ontologies occupy a central position. The W3C has made several important recommendations for the expression of the ontologies. There is an RDF Vocabulary for expressing simple ontologies, named RDF Schema, offering IRIs for defining classes and properties, and for laying down some basic lexical knowledge about them, such as taxonomies. There is a whole family of languages for expressing more articulated ontologies, the Ontology Web Language (OWL) family. OWL directly derives from a family of mathematical logics, called Description Logics, devised in the field of Artificial Intelligence as expressive knowledge representation languages. As logics, these languages come equipped with a sound and complete inferential apparatus that can be effectively (but not always efficiently) implemented. The youngest representative of the OWL family is OWL 2, recommended in 2012.[16]

One might wonder why in Fig. 1 ontologies sit on top of RDF. The reason is that ontologies themselves can be considered as data; as such, they can be represented

---

[13] N. Guarino, D. Oberle, and S. Staab, "What Is an Ontology?" In *Handbook on Ontologies, Second Edition*, ed. S. Staab and R. Studer (Springer-Verlag, 2009).
[14] http://www.cidoc-crm.org/.
[15] http://dataforhistory.org/.
[16] https://www.w3.org/TR/owl2-overview/.

by the following four rules of Linked Data. These rules can be contextualized to ontologies as follows:
1. to use a web standard, Internationalized Resource Identifiers (IRIs), to name classes and properties, and in particular
2. to use IRIs of the HTTP protocol.
3. To use the Resource Description Framework (RDF) to format the data; and a third web standard, the SPARQL Query Language, to query these data.
4. To use IRIs from other datasets within the data, so as to connect one's own classes and properties to those of other people.

Needless to say, these rules have been strictly followed by the W3C in developing the languages for ontologies mentioned above. More precisely, both in RDF Schema and in OWL, classes and properties are identified by IRIs of the HTTP protocol (according to rules 1 and 2), and the axioms that encode the lexical knowledge on these classes and properties are expressed as RDF triples (according to rule 3). Finally, IRIs of classes and properties defined in other ontologies can be used within an ontology (rule 4), thereby realizing the required interconnections at the level of the vocabulary.

As a result, Semantic Web ontologies are Linked Data, so that they can be accessed on the Web like any Linked Data dataset. For example, the RDF expression of the CIDOC CRM ontology can be retrieved from the web at,[17] as any Linked Data dataset.

The Semantic Web and the Scholarly Domain

Linked Open Data and ontologies also play a very important role in the scientific and scholarly world, by offering tools for the creation and sharing of data and vocabularies, such as the CERIF (the Common European Research Information Format) Ontology.[18] The key concept here is interdisciplinarity. It has been long recognized that significant progress in any branch of science can be achieved through research projects that are able to combine tools, data, and knowledge coming from different domains. Research Infrastructures such as the D4Science[19] are complex systems that allow realizing interdisciplinarity in science, by offering scientists Virtual Research Environments where they can find the tools, data, and knowledge that they need for their work, along with the communication and collaboration facilities that are necessary to cooperate with their colleagues. D4Science also supports the Humanities through the Virtual Research

---
17 http://www.cidoc-crm.org/sites/default/files/cidoc_crm_v5.0.4_official_release.rdfs.
18 https://www.eurocris.org/cerif/main-features-cerif.
19 https://www.d4science.org/.

Environments allocated to the PARTHENOS[20] and the ARIADNE[21] infrastructural projects. These technologies are enablers of e-science, a new area where Information and Communication Technologies are employed to support the work of researchers to the end of accelerating scientific progress. This is also achieved through the creation of Open Access repositories for scientific literature and data such as OpenAire.[22]

However, sharing data across scientific communities requires that the data are semantic interoperable, and ontologies and Linked Data play a fundamental role in achieving semantic interoperability, as has been argued above. As a consequence, they are very relevant in the e-science scenario. In particular, Linked Data ontologies are the ideal *media* for the development and the exchange of vocabularies and terminologies specific to scientific domains, and for interconnecting them to top ontologies supporting the integration of the scientific domains. Linked Data datasets expressed in terms of those ontologies are the ideal *media* for the development and the exchange of data providing evidence on specific phenomena. The interconnections of domain ontologies through top ontologies allow the re-use of Linked Data datasets across scientific domains, thereby offering the basis for interdisciplinarity.

Bibliography

Guarino, N. "Formal Ontology and Information Systems." Amended version of a paper in *Formal Ontology in Information Systems. Proceedings of FOIS'98*, Trento, Italy, June 6–8, 1998, edited by N. Guarino, 3–15. Amsterdam: IOS Press, 1998.

Berners-Lee, T. *Linked Data*. https://www.w3.org/DesignIssues/LinkedData.html.

Antoniou, G., and F. van Harmelen. *A Semantic Web Primer*. Cambridge, Massachusetts, and London, England: MIT, 2004.

Manola, F., E. Miller, and B. McBride. "RDF 1.1 Primer. W3C Working Group Note." June 24, 2014. https://www.w3.org/TR/rdf11-primer/.

Hitzler, P., M. Krötzsch, B. Parsia, P. F. Patel-Schneider, and S Rudolph, eds. *OWL 2 Web Ontology Language: Primer (Second Edition). W3C* Recommendation. December 11, 2012. https://www.w3.org/TR/owl2-primer/.

---

[20] http://www.parthenos-project.eu/.
[21] https://ariadne-infrastructure.eu/.
[22] https://www.openaire.eu/.

Frédéric Clavert and Lars Wieneke
Big Data and Public History

Abstract: In this chapter, we define big data in history in three ways: (1) big data implies the use of an amount of data that the historian's personal computer cannot deal with; (2) the data historians are using must be either directly linked to primary sources (digitized primary sources) or must be a primary source itself (born-digital primary sources); (3) big data implies a redefinition of some aspects of historians' methodologies. We then try to identify the challenges and uses of big data in public history, which we consider as multifaceted ways to study, deepen and empower public connections to the past. For instance, the study of social networks online can help us better understand public uses of the past while the provision and application of large databases for historical primary and secondary sources can help us establish links with a wide non-academic audience. In particular, we discuss two opportunities offered by big data to public historians: the study of artefacts of collective memory as well as crowdsourcing, especially to collect primary sources that would not be accessible otherwise, or to improve them by collaboratively transcribing images of sources into texts.

Born-digital sources are now quite numerous online (newsgroups, web archives, social media), and we illustrate the potential that born-digital primary sources offer public historians through the #ww1 project, which is based on a large database of Tweets written during the centenary of World War I. Using distant reading techniques and by looking at the specific case of the French "dead for France" database and how it was tweeted, we show how we can study the way that people engage with their own national collective memory and national history. We argue that this kind of study does not necessarily require a strong digital infrastructure.

The chapter then focuses on en masse digitization projects, particularly when they involve crowdsourcing as part of the digitization effort. Going beyond very well-known examples (Google Books, Gallica, and Europeana newspapers, for example), we look at the case of "What's on the menu?" a project to digitize the New York Public Library's historical collections of the city's restaurants' menus. Looking at the crowdsourcing part of the project, we show that it solves the pitfalls of the most well-known large digitization projects, in particular poor OCR quality. It also invites citizens to participate in the development of their town's historical narrative, together with historians.

In conclusion, we draw the reader's attention to the limitations of big data. Focusing particularly on two of its pitfalls – inequality of access and what is outside big data – we emphasize that big data does not mean complete or representative data. Data, datasets, and big data remain socially constructed objects. Inequality of access is here understood in two ways: data itself is not always accessible, and not everybody can access online services. For instance, big data does not document life in rich Western urban areas the same way as it documents life in the same countries' poorer rural areas. To put it another way: inequalities in data accessibility undermine the possibilities of creating public history projects that are not mainstream or based on mainstream data. Furthermore, many aspects of our lives are not documented by big data. In other words, the large-scale digitization of sources casts shadows on and influences both our research and the way that citizens empower themselves to develop their own historical narratives. Nevertheless, the pitfalls of big data should not prevent us from making use of it in public history, but the historian's and citizen's critical thinking is key to its proper use.

Keywords: big data, digitization, born digital, distant reading, metadata, visualization, crowdsourcing, collective memory

What is Big Data?

Big data has been around as a marketing term for several years. Its initial definition dates back to 2001[1] and defines "3V" as core engineering challenges for big data applications: volume (dealing with large amounts of data), velocity (dealing with high frequency real-time data) and variety (dealing with diverse sources of data). Working with big data implies the setup of a workflow, based on data acquisition, data analysis, data curation, data storage, and data usage. Though the concept originated from the broader sphere of on-line corporations – Google, Amazon, social networks online and many others –, over time big data made its way into academia, including the Humanities and Social Sciences. Several history projects associate themselves with big data, such as the "Venice Time Machine"[2] project or Seshat: The Global History Databank,[3] while an ever-increasing number of history books or articles have big data at the center of their reasoning.[4]

Looking closely at these projects, the history-oriented definition of big data slightly differs from the engineering perspective. Historians are barely dealing with high frequency real-time data (velocity) that are more related to the present than to the past. On the contrary, the two other "Vs" (volume and variety) are at the core of historical big data: the historian's primary sources cover a large variety and are often "messy" – i.e. not structured, with few metadata, etc. –, and, with the many

---

1 Laney, "3D data management," 1–4.
2 https://vtm.epfl.ch/. See Alison Abbott, "The 'time machine' reconstructing ancient Venice's social networks," *Nature News* 546.7658 (2017): 341–344.
3 http://seshatdatabank.info/. See Pieter François, J.G. Manning, Harvey Whitehouse et al, "A Macroscope for Global History: Seshat Global History Databank, a methodological overview," *Digital Humanities Quarterly* 10.4 (2016).
4 See Manning, *Big Data in History*, or Jo Guldi and David Armitage, *The History Manifesto* (Cambridge, UK: Cambridge University Press, 2014).

mass-digitization projects that are going on, the volume of primary (and secondary) sources that we can include in our corpora as well as the cross-referencing and inter-connection of previously separated datasets is drastically increasing.

Thus a more suitable definition of historian's big data could be the following threefold one: (1) Big data implies the use of an amount of data that the historian's personal computer cannot deal with; (2) The data historians are using must be either directly linked to primary sources (i.e. digitized primary sources) or be primary sources itself (i.e. born-digital primary sources); (3) Big data implies a redefinition of some aspects of the historian's methodologies.

This practical definition should remind us that historians, like many other humanists and social scientists, are faced with new challenges when dealing with massive amount of inter-connected data and information from which we need to extract knowledge.

Those challenges also need to be taken into account by public historians. In this chapter, we will use a broad and simple definition of public history. Considered as the numerous ways to study, deepen and empower the public connections to the past, public history is concerned by big data in several ways: for instance, the study of social networks online can help us better understand public uses of the past while the provision and application of large databases for historical primary and secondary sources can help us establish links with a wide non-academic audience.

In this chapter, we will try to describe the characteristics of big data in public history through use-cases that are partially based on the authors' experience. Big data offers many opportunities to public historians, and two of them will be discussed in the following pages: to study artifacts of collective memory – in a broad sense, including every aspect of citizen's relationships to the past – as well as crowdsourcing, especially to collect primary sources that would not be accessible otherwise, or to improve them by collaboratively transcribing images of sources into texts.

Citizens' Relationship to the Past and Born-Digital Primary Sources

Besides fears of an imminent digital dark age,[5] the Internet and its applications, including the World Wide Web, today offer a wide range of primary sources: usenet groups, Web Archives (such as Internet archive, the Web archiving program at

---

[5] Pallab Ghosh, "Google's Vint Cerf warns of 'digital Dark Age,'" BBC News, February 1, 2015, http://www.bbc.com/news/science-environment-31450389, accessed January 24, 2017; Tremonti Anna Maria, Ian Milligan (guest), "Preserving digital history is imperative to save cultural history," The Current, CBCRadio, May 11, 2015, http://www.cbc.ca/radio/thecurrent/the-current-for-november-5-2015-1.3305130/preserving-digital-history-is-imperative-to-save-cultural-history-1.3305263.

Library and Archive Canada or the *dépôt légal du web* at the French National Library), online social networks such as Twitter, archived by the Library of Congress, or Facebook. Though access policies from one service to another differ significantly, finding ways to access historical data en masse can be easy,[6] not always expensive and does not systematically require a strong technical infrastructure.

To illustrate the potential that born-digital primary sources on-line offer to public historians, we will focus on one use-case, based on our research on the centenary of the Great War that helped us to better understand how citizens perceive the past.

In this research, we collect data from Twitter in order to try to understand how people (or, rather, Twitter accounts) are engaging with the many British or French ceremonies of commemoration around the centenary of the Great War, that started in 2013. We started to collect tweets, based on keywords, in April 2014 and plan to do so until the centenary of the Versailles treaty (June 2019).[7]

Working with more than seven million tweets that were acquired so far, requires applying a set of methods and tools called distant reading. Distant reading, an expression coined by Franco Moretti,[8] implies asking a computer program to read and analyze our primary sources for us. One of the more common approaches is to use text-mining techniques, software that will try to derive the meaning of the corpus content. In our case, text mining allowed us to understand that Twitter accounts writing in French were not tweeting in the same way on official commemoration days as during the rest of the year. In both cases, French speaking members of Twitter were paying homage to the French soldiers (or *Poilus*) who "died for France." While this homage focuses on particular individuals throughout the year, it becomes more general during official commemorations. We found the reason for this difference by analyzing the links that were tweeted: references to individual *Poilus* were directed to the database of the *"morts pour la France."* This is a database that assembles official acts declaring people (mainly, though not only soldiers) as *"morts pour la France."* In general, this database consists of scans of official documents (Fig. 1) and therefore – from the point of view of the computer – images. Nevertheless, the French Defense Ministry, publisher of the database, opened a module to allow people to transcribe those images into actual text that can be analyzed as text by computer. It will allow large scales studies about the French fallen soldiers (and some civilians, whether male or female).

As this example shows, thanks to the harvesting and analysis of tweets, we are able to see how people engage with their own national collective memory and national history. In our example, indexing a database not only involves technically transforming a database of scanned pages into genuine text, it in fact means truly creating a

---

[6] For instance, we use DMI-TCAT to collect data on Twitter. With some savoir-faire, setting up a server is rather easy, see https://github.com/digitalmethodsinitiative/dmi-tcat.
[7] Frédéric Clavert, "Les commémorations du centenaire de la Première Guerre mondiale sur Twitter," *Ricerche Storiche* 46.2 (2016): 147–166.
[8] Moretti, *Graphs, Maps, Trees*.

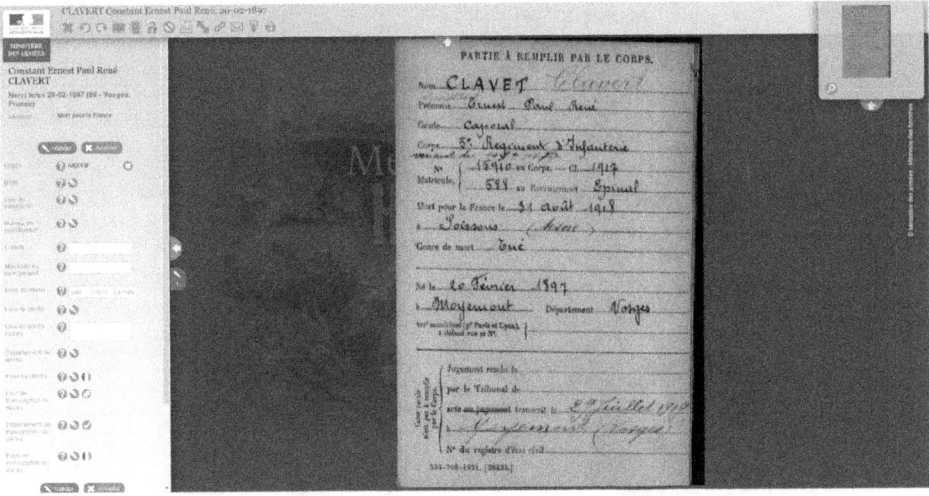

Fig. 1: One record of the *Morts pour la France* database, with the indexation module on the left. Source: "Base de données des Morts pour la France", *Mémoire des Hommes, Ministère des Armées*, https://www.memoiredeshommes.sga.defense.gouv.fr/fr/article.php?larub=24 (December 2020).

virtual *lieux de mémoire:*[9] through user generated content, French citizens become thereby actors in the never-ending construction of collective memory.

Though this kind of project does not necessarily need a strong digital infrastructure, collecting historical data requires planning and a sense of anticipation. It requires being able to learn distant reading techniques that have, technically and, more important, methodologically, a steep learning curve, or to set up interdisciplinary teams. It is also necessary to be able to circumscribe what the collected data is about and what should be excluded. For instance, in the example developed here, we will probably never be able to speak about artifacts of the French collective memory on the first battle of the Marne (September 1914),[10] as on this occasion French memorial institutions used keywords or hashtags that were either too precise or too loose to be caught up or to be collected without massive noise. It was different in 2016 with the centenary of the battle of the Somme due to the official use of a very explicit hashtag, #Somme100. The result is that we cannot consider our seven million tweet database to be a representative sample. Furthermore, lots of tweets may speak about the Great War without using keywords that a historian would think of as linked to this event, or that are answering a tweet that is in our database (Fig. 2).[11] It does not mean that this database is not usable for research, but that, as with all primary sources, our database has blind spots and gaps.

---

9 Nora Pierre, *Les lieux de mémoire, tome 1: La République* (Paris, Gallimard, 1984).
10 In our case, we could have brought the missing data to a branch of Twitter, Gnip, Inc. Asking commercial suppliers can unfortunately be very costly.
11 D'Heer et al, "What are we missing?".

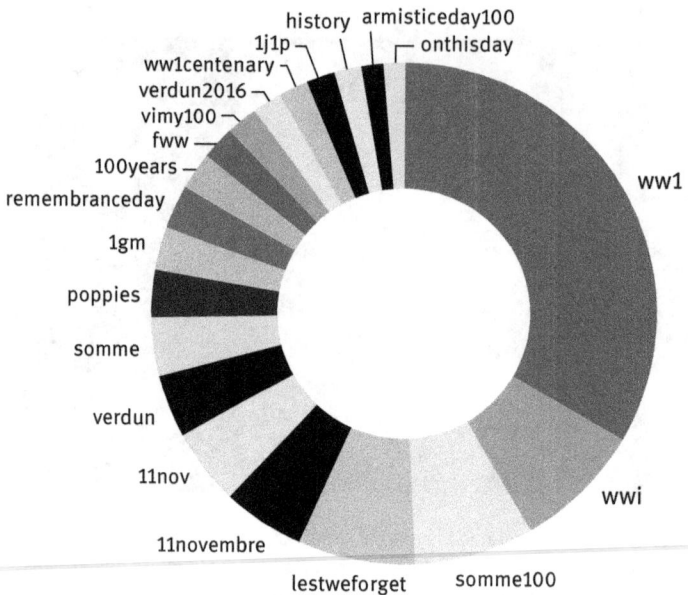

Fig. 2: The twenty most used hashtags in our database (proportion, based on a sample). Note the presence of "1j1p" for "1 jour – 1 poilu", the hashtag used by French citizens to discuss the indexation of the *morts pour la France* database. Source: author.

If born-digital primary sources are valuable to public history, notably to study citizen's relationships to their past, the case of en masse digitization of large corpora must also be looked at closely, particularly when it implies crowdsourcing part of this digitization effort.

From en Masse Digitization of Paper-Born Sources to Citizen Participation

Several programs of mass digitization of primary (and secondary) sources have been carried out since the late 1990s and 2000s, such as the French Library led Gallica,[12,13] or Europeana Newspapers.[14]

---

[12] http://gallica.bnf.fr/.
[13] http://books.google.com/.
[14] http://www.europeana-newspapers.eu/.

Google Books has become an unavoidable resource for many historians since its launch in 2004 despite the many legal troubles Google encountered.[15] Beyond digitization, Google "datafied" books by delivering the Google Books Ngram Viewer (Fig. 3).[16]

One of the most common uses of the Google Books Ngram Viewer is to display long-term (since 1800) trends. We will take here the example of the expression "public history." Surprisingly enough, this expression has been used more often (in relative frequencies) during the nineteenth century than at the end of the twentieth or the beginning of the twenty-first centuries. Looking further in Google Books, it appears that "public history" was opposed to private lives: the book *A history of the four Georges, kings of England* published in 1860 claims to contain at the same time their public history and the history of their private lives.[17]

One of the major reproaches made against en masse digitization is the poor quality of its text recognition and, more generally, of their digitization.[18] While scanning paper documents operates with relative ease and a significant workload, the transcription of such scans from images of texts to actual text poses severe challenges. Even though software and algorithms improve day by day, it is sometimes useful to apply other means than optical character recognition to improve the quality of transcription and to create texts that are searchable and can be automatically processed by a computer. One possible avenue for this process is through digital public history. Our case study here is the New York Public Library (NYPL)'s project *What's on the menu?* (fig. 4)

Want to know the average price of a beer in New York in the 1930s? Want to know the price differences of this beer from one neighborhood to another? In other words, want to do economic and social history thanks to a collection of menus?[19] The NYPL has a very large collection of menus, that have crucial information for (not only) economic and social historians with very diverse possible uses.

Nevertheless, trying to answer a question about the prices of beer in New York during the 1930s will be a long process if done based on the original paper archives or based on a digitized version of this archive without proper character and layout recognition (OCR). With very different fonts, layouts, etc., the transcription of menus

---

15 James Somers, "Torching the Modern-Day Library of Alexandria," *The Atlantic* (April 2017).
16 https://books.google.com/ngrams/graph?content=public+history&case_insensitive=on&year_start=1800&year_end=2000&corpus=15&smoothing=3&share=&direct_url=t4%3B%2Cpublic%20history%3B%2Cc0%3B%2Cs0%3B%3Bpublic%20history%3B%2Cc0%3B%3BPublic%20History%3B%2Cc0%3B%3Bpublic%20History%3B%2Cc0.
17 For instance: Smucker Samuel Mosheim, *A History of the Four Georges, Kings of England: Containing Personal Incidents of Their Lives, Public Events of Their Reigns, and Biographical Notices of Their Chief Ministers, Courtiers, and Favorites* (D. Appleton and Company, 1860), iii.
18 See, with an optimistic tone, Goldsmith Kenneth, "The Artful Accidents of Google Books," *The New Yorker*, (December 2013), https://www.newyorker.com/books/page-turner/the-artful-accidents-of-google-books, consulté le 13.02.2018.
19 See the "about" page of the project: http://menus.nypl.org/about and "Food Glorious Food: The New York Public Library's Menu Collection | Urban Agenda Magazine,",accessed February 13, 2018.

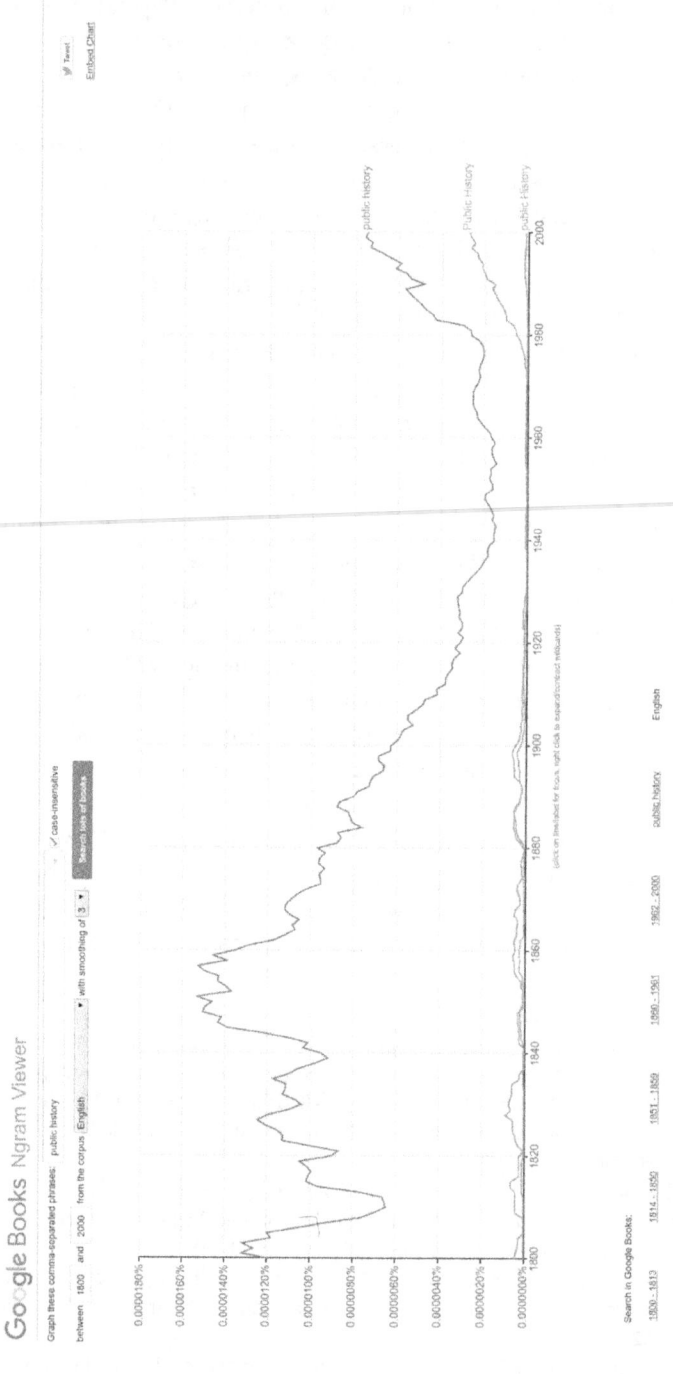

Fig. 3: Google Books Ngram for "public history". Source: "Ngram Viewer", *Google Books*, https://books.google.com/ngram (December 2020).

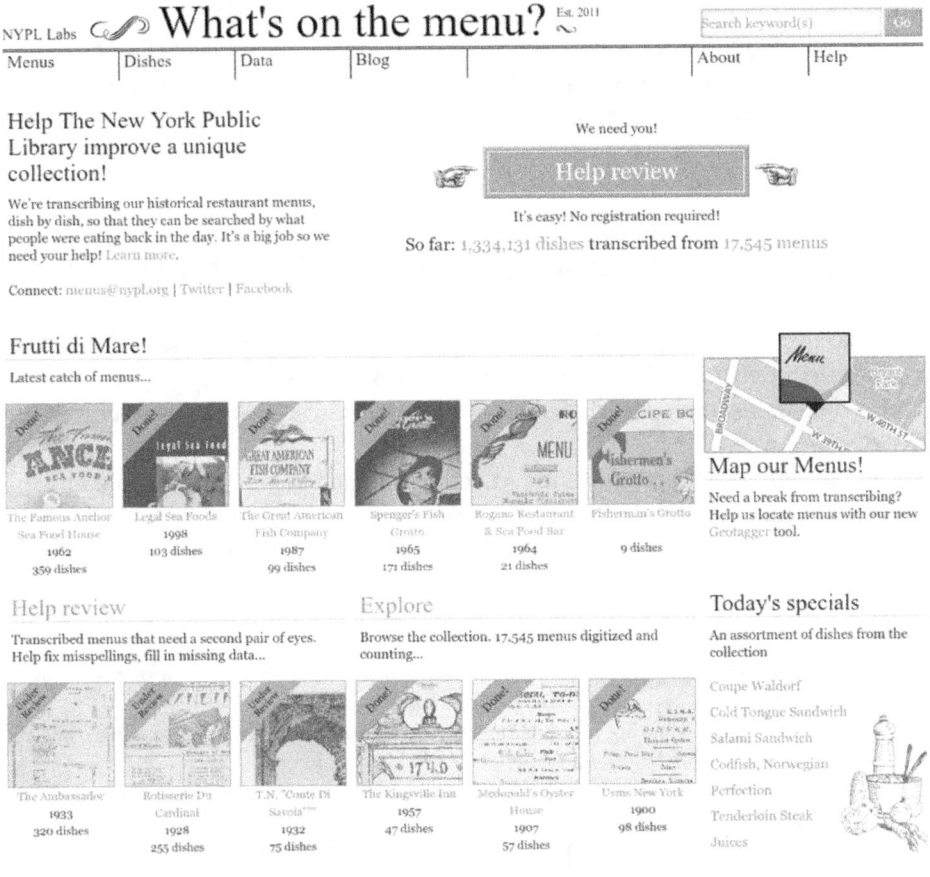

Fig. 4: Snapshot of *What's on the menu?* project homepage. Source: *What's on the Menu*, New York Public Library, http://menus.nypl.org/ (December 2020).

is not an easy task, if at all feasible by automated means. As a consequence, the NYPL appealed to a large audience: in other words, it crowdsourced text recognition to the wider public.

This initiative knew a large success from its beginning,[20] making the New York's menu collection a researchable one, available freely on the web. It is also, through several ways to export data, an archive for historians and citizens that can be processed and analyzed with computers.

Crowdsourcing the treatment of large amount of data, as the NYPL's *What's on the menu?* project example shows, opens up the participation of people to the elaboration of their town's historical narrative, and allows cooperation between citizens and

---

20 Rebecca Federman, "Happy Birthday to . . . Us! A Year of Menus," *The New York Public Library*, https://www.nypl.org/blog/2012/04/20/happy-birthday-to-us-menus.

academic and non-academic historians. With the availability of relatively easy to use open source platforms such as pybossa,[21] the necessary technology can be used for public history, while the main challenges of crowdsourcing remain: how to engage a large enough crowd of people that are willing to spend their time and effort on the task at hand? The answer to that question lay with each particular project.

Conclusions: Beyond the Big Data Mythology

The use cases we developed in this chapter both produced great results. We should nevertheless be careful in our use of big data. As mentioned earlier for our Great War centenary example, big data does not mean complete data or even representative data.

In his 2008 WIRED article, Chris Anderson claimed that big data would end theory. He imagined sciences where hypotheses would be born from data rather than a world where data would derive from theories.[22] The two sociologists danah boyd and Kate Crawford responded to this claim by developing a conceptual definition of big data:

> We define big data as a cultural, technological, and scholarly phenomenon that rests on the interplay of:
> (1) Technology: maximizing computation power and algorithmic accuracy to gather, analyze, link, and compare large data sets.
> (2) Analysis: drawing on large data sets to identify patterns in order to make economic, social, technical, and legal claims.
> (3) Mythology: the widespread belief that large data sets offer a higher form of intelligence and knowledge that can generate insights that were previously impossible, with the aura of truth, objectivity, and accuracy.[23]

One of the elements that boyd and Crawford emphasize here is quite well-known from the historian's point of view, as they are trained in building primary sources corpora: how data (and corpora) are created, how metadata are defined have strong implications. Data, metadata, and corpora are the results of social, economic and technical processes, that must be explicated even when using big data.

---

[21] Https://pybossa.com.
[22] Chris Anderson, "The End of Theory: The Data Deluge Makes the Scientific Method Obsolete," WIRED (2008). http://www.wired.com/science/discoveries/magazine/16-07/pb_theory.
[23] Danah Boyd and Kate Crawford, "CRITICAL QUESTIONS FOR BIG DATA: Provocations for a cultural, technological, and scholarly phenomenon," *Information, Communication & Society* 15.5 (2012): 662–679, 663, doi: 10.1080/1369118X.2012.678878.

A fitting example for the mythologization of big data was published in 2010 in *Science*, in an article that claimed to build the history of cultural phenomena thanks to a quantitative analysis of the Google Books corpus alone,[24] without the intervention of historians, and which was harshly criticized.[25]

The use-cases presented in this chapter should not prevent critical thinking about big data but rather stimulate it, in particular as there are several pitfalls to take into account when historians are working with large amounts of data. To deconstruct big data as a myth, we will try to analyze some of its features: inequality of access and what's outside big data.[26]

Thinking in terms of inequality of access is relatively difficult, as the potential inequalities of access are numerous. We will therefore emphasize two aspects: first, data itself is not always accessible, and second, not everybody can access online services. If we consider the example of born-digital sources, it is, for instance, easier to get data from Twitter than from Facebook or from a web-based forum: however, the user population of the former is not necessarily the same as for the latter. The population studied is hence not the same, and crowdsourcing the digitization of a corpus online means from that perspective to ask a precise part of the population with very specific interests and motivations to participate and collaborate in public history projects. Here again, this population is hard to define in sociological and demographic terms. In his book *Big Data in History*, Patrick Manning states that some areas of our world are "data-poor."[27] As a world historian, he was thinking mainly of African countries, but big data does not equally document life in Western (and rich) urban areas and life in Western (and usually poorer) rural areas in the same way. This element is all the more important to public history, that easily accessible data are not always the most useful to public historians: inequalities in data accessibility undermine the possibilities of creating public history projects that are not mainstream or that are not based on mainstream data.

That leads to another pitfall of big data: several aspects of the process are not documented at all in big data, independently of whether primary sources are born-

---

24 Michel J.-B., Shen Y. K., Aiden A. P. et al, "Quantitative Analysis of Culture Using Millions of Digitized Books," Science 331.6014 (2010): 176–182, doi: 10.1126/science.1199644.
25 For instance: Alexander Koplenig, " HYPERLINK "https://academic.oup.com/dsh/article-abstract/32/1/169/2957375/The-impact-of-lacking-metadata-for-the-measurement"\h. The impact of lacking metadata for the measurement of cultural and linguistic change using the Google Ngram data sets – Reconstructing the composition of the German corpus in times of WWII." *Digital Scholarship in the Humanities* 32.1 (2017): 169–188. doi:10.1093/llc/fqv037. ISSN 2055-7671.
26 We will not expand here on two other kinds of pitfalls, regarding ethics and laws. For the first ones, we strongly suggest reading Moravec Michelle, "What would you do? Historians' ethics and digitized archives," *Medium* (2016). For legal aspects, there are too many differences between countries, notably as for as personal data are concerned, to be developed here.
27 Patrick Manning, *Big Data in History*.

digital or not. This is what Ian Milligan[28] and Lara Putnam[29] argue in two separate articles. The large-scale digitization of sources casts shadows over and influences our research and, in the case of public history, influences the way citizens empower themselves to elaborate their own historical narratives.

Nevertheless, the potential pitfalls of big data should not prevent us from making use of big data, in particular combined with crowdsourcing approaches. (Digital) public history is all about writing (digital) history with citizens. For this reason, no public historian can ignore the potential of big data: thanks to massive amounts of data, we know more about the public connection to the past and can call for public participation when needed. More generally, it allows all of us, historians and citizens, to participate in the elaboration of the narratives of our own history and to participate in the making of primary sources, through crowdsourcing, and through participation in online platforms such as online social networks.

Bibliography

Laney, Doug. "3D data management: Controlling data volume, velocity and variety." *META Group Research Note* 6 (2001): 1–4.

Manning, Patrick. *Big Data in History*. New York, Palgrave Pivot, 2013.

Moretti, Franco. *Graphs, Maps, Trees: Abstract Models for Literary History*. Verso, 2007.

D'heer, Evelien. Baptist Vandersmissen, Wesley de Neve et al. "What are we missing? An empirical exploration in the structural biases of hashtag-based sampling on Twitter." *First Monday* 22.2 (2017), doi: 10.128.248.156.56.

Putnam, Lara. "The Transnational and the Text-Searchable: Digitized Sources and the Shadows They Cast." *The American Historical Review* 121 (2)402: 377–402, doi: 10.1093/ahr/121.2.377.

---

[28] Ian Milligan, "Illusionary Order: Online Databases, Optical Character Recognition, and Canadian History, 1997–2010," *Canadian Historical Review* 94.4 (2013): 540–569, doi: 10.3138/chr.694.

[29] Putnam, "The Transnational and the Text-Searchable," 377–402, doi: 10.1093/ahr/121.2.377.

Gioele Barabucci, Francesca Tomasi, and Fabio Vitali
Modeling Data Complexity in Public History and Cultural Heritage

Abstract: The publication by Galleries, Libraries, Archives and Museums of metadata about their collections is fundamental for the creation of our shared digital cultural heritage. Yet, we argue, these digital collections are, on one hand, of little use to scholars (because of the inconsistent quality of the published records), and, on the other hand, they fail to attract the interest of the general public (because of their dry content). These problems are exacerbated by the current move towards public history, where citizens are no longer just passive actors, but play an active role in contributing, maintaining and curating historical records, leading some to question the trustworthiness of collections in which non-scholars have the ability to contribute. The core issue behind all these problems is, we believe, a (doomed) search for objectivity, often caused by the fact that data models ignore the derivative and stratified nature of cultural objects, and allow only one point of view to be expressed. In turn this forces the publication of bowdlerized records and removes any venue for the expression of disagreement and different opinions. We propose an approach named "contexts" to solve these issues. The adoption of contexts makes it possible to support multiple points of view inside the same dataset, not only allowing multiple scholars to provide their own possibly contrasting points of view, but also making it possible to incorporate additions, corrections and more complex kinds of commentaries from citizens without compromising the trustworthiness of the whole dataset.

Keywords: trustworthiness, multiplicity, contexts, disagreement, cultural heritage metadata

Introduction

One of the core tenets of public history is that all levels of society must play an active role in the construction of its cultural identity, in particular by participating in the valorization of its culture and of the artefacts that its culture has produced through its history. It is thus the responsibility of cultural institutions to not just make cultural artefacts, or in the digital case, raw metadata about such cultural artefacts available, but also provide critiques and reflections on said artefacts. The ability to contribute reflections should, however, not be limited to renownedscholars, but extended to amateurs and the general population. Doing so, however, poses a series of issues, common to all crowdsourcing activities and exacerbated by the use of digital technologies: e.g., how can trustworthiness be maintained? In which way can rich and complex reflections be faithfully expressed? How can one attract new active contributors?

Let's take a step back. What do we use digital technologies for when dealing with cultural heritage? A quick overview in the field of public history as well as of GLAMs (Galleries, Libraries, Archives and Museums) identifies two principal aims: first, preservation of knowledge, i.e., the need to associate to our physical or cultural artefacts what is known about them, should they get destroyed or forgotten about; second, circulation of knowledge, i.e., the desire to allow larger audiences (scholars, students, general citizens) to improve themselves by gaining access to information about our cultural artefacts that otherwise (for fragility, physical distance, obscurity) would be hard or impossible to reach.

Yet, we notice, we are failing on all the abovementioned counts: on the one hand, we frequently find poor digital records, as an extremely limited quantity of information ends up being associated with our physical and cultural artefacts; on the other, we are more or less failing to interest a substantially larger audience to our digital collections.

In many ways, we believe, both failures stem out of a single cause: a (doomed) search for objectivity, often caused by the fact that models ignore the derivative and stratified nature of cultural objects, and allow only one point of view to be expressed, bringing forth unbalanced and incomplete descriptions of our artefacts. In turn, this forced objectivity eliminates conflict and disagreement, the very matters that have the best chance to create and maintain interest in lay audiences.

We suggest, on the contrary, that we should explicitly aim at representing competing points of view and opinions, and make sure that we fully document their existence and strengths, as well as the supporting ideas and providing backing, so that our audiences can finally perceive representations that are truer and more interesting than the sterilized and boring renditions forced by so-called objectivity.

From its inception, digital public history has been well aware of the challenges and potentialities of the use of digital tools to narrate multiple viewpoints, even if competing between them (Noiret 2018).[1] Whether these points of views represent the distance between two similarly accredited scholars with different opinions, or between a recognized expert and an Everyman submitting his/her own private records, the possibility for the data structure to allow, accept and represent faithfully the multiplicity of points of view over our past and our cultural heritage. So far, this complexity has been unavailable in our digital tools. It is our desire and plan to amend this limitation.

---

[1] Serge Noiret. *Digital Public History*. In: *A Companion to Public History*, David Dean (Ed). 2018. Wiley doi:10.1002/9781118508930.ch7.

Starting off with an example of the record of an image in Europeana (see figure # 1), we derive a classification of the issues and a methodological approach that we name "contexts" to express multiple points of view in data models. Our approach draws from a number of existing data models and modelling techniques, and can be implemented using current Semantic Web technologies, although with limitations due to the current state of the standards.

Scholarship, Truth, Disputes: An Example

In many disciplines of the humanities, truths are hard to come by and facts are rare. In most cases, we use words such as *facts* and *truths* just to mean "statements for which there is an acceptable trail of supporting sources," or "statements that are more or less accepted by the majority of the relevant scholars" or even "statements that so far haven't been disproven."

This is not a surprise, as precise knowledge in many cases is impossible or outside our reach. Yet scholars can easily deal with incomplete or conjectural knowledge, and even when they are personally convinced of the truthfulness of some information, they are aware and able to accept that different viewpoints, dissent and speculations may exist about them.

Unfortunately, the ability to contemplate and handle different or opposing interpretations over the same piece of information is not embodied in the software and in the digital data structures that we use to represent them: single points of view and unique data items are usually expected in our digital collections. The inevitable conflicts and disagreements cannot be expressed explicitly, and need to be simplified, resolved and eliminated before committing information to the digital realm.

Yet, unknowns, disputes and dissenting opinions are often what in the first place attracted, fascinated and still keeps fascinating scholars into their respective fields of expertise. Neutered, undisputable and unequivocal data as expressible in our digital world have the twin problems of a) being a poor representation of what we know and think and b) being fundamentally boring and unable to attract anyone, especially lay people and younger students.

Even the ever important dialogue between experts and collective memory must recognize that this dialogue does not always . . . in fact, almost never ends up converging into an agreed, shared, resolved piece of knowledge that is also, at the same time, engaging and fascinating to all. In public history, just like everywhere else, increasing the number of voices participating in the cultural debate about something tends to increase divergence and diatribe rather than solve it, and our software simply cannot keep up with this additional complexity.

Allow us to make an egregious example by considering figure #1, taken from a record in Europeana, and itself coming from the Bildarchiv Foto Marburg (cfr. Peroni,

Tomasi, Vitali 2012).² The image was present in 2012 in two separate and dissimilar records in Europeana (See Fig. 2), and is now (2020) present in only one, the second having been removed probably due to being a duplicate and because of the number of issues in its description.

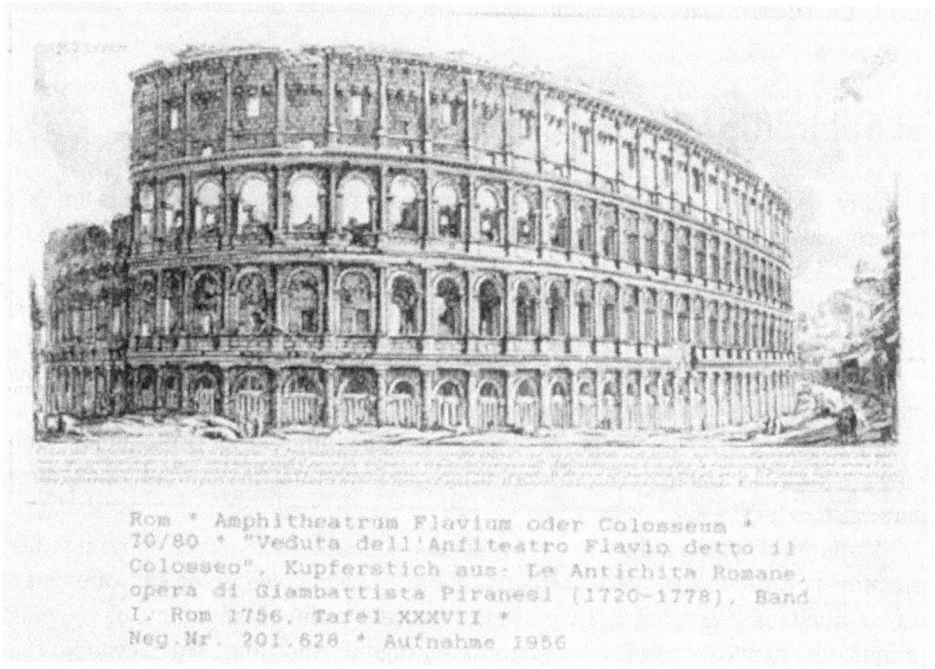

Fig. 1: An image taken from Europeana.

The existing record³ (Fig. 2a) is accompanied by metadata stating that the item being described is a 53.9 x 41.3 cm print by G.B. Piranesi, dated 1756 (and/or 1787), titled "Veduta dell'Anfiteatro Flavio detto il Colosseo," showing a table number and a signature, and describing as subjects James Caulfield and King Gustaf III of Sweden. The deleted record (Fig. 2b) described the (very same) item as "Amphitheatrum Flavium / Colosseum", a 70 to 80 A.D. building by Vespasianus, and, in a plain text description, represented via a 1960/70 photo by Konrad Helbig of a print by G.B. Piranesi.

Both records are clearly incomplete and wrong. They contain objective and factual information (e.g., 53.9 x 41.3 cm being the size of the item), some more or less

---

2 Silvio Peroni, Francesca Tomasi, Fabio Vitali. 2012. *Reflecting on the Europeana Data Model*. IRCDL 2012: 228–240.
3 https://www.europeana.eu/en/item/2064137/Museu_ProvidedCHO_Bildarchiv_Foto_Marburg_obj20089555_T_001_T_071.

acceptable interpretations (e.g. the nature of the work, the title, and the author) and some much less acceptable assertions, in fact errors (James Caulfield and King Gustav III are clearly NOT the subject of the image, this item is NOT a building and its creation date is NOT 70 to 80 A.D.).

At the same time, questions abound: what is the record about, a first century building, an eighteenth-century print or a twentieth-century photograph? Who is its author, Vespasianus, G.B. Piranesi or Konrad Helbig? Why two dates: 1756 and 1787? What was the role of James Caulfield and Gustav III?

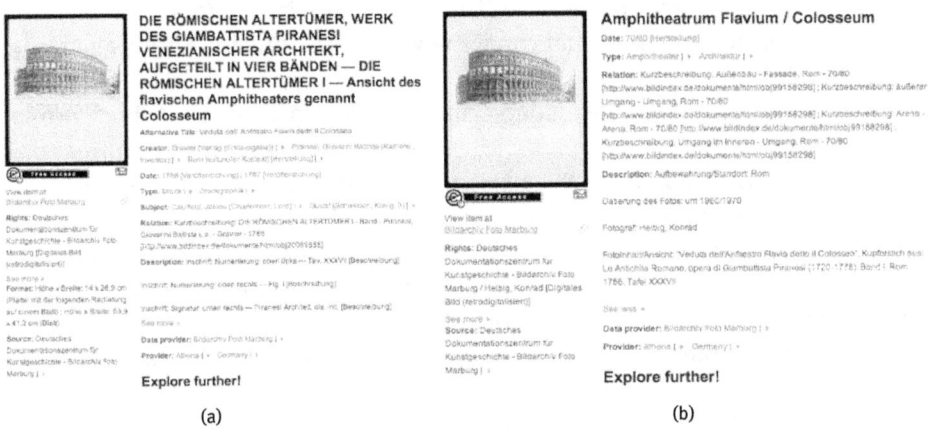

Fig. 2: Two records for the same image from Europeana in 2012.

As we see, the facts are few, and actually constitute the most boring and uninspiring part of the data we are given, while many additional details, although wrongly characterized, paint a much more complex and interesting story than the physical dimensions, once we take pains to understand and explain them. Most interestingly, the more incorrect of the two records (i.e., the one that ended up being deleted) is also the one that contains the most details that can help clarify the whole story.

The following could be a better story: in the 1990s, the Bildarchiv Foto Marburg organized a retrospective of the works of Konrad Helbig (1917–1986), a famous German photographer and art historian, known for his groundbreaking early photographs of Italian classical works of art, and of naked, tanned, underage Sicilian boys. Among the pictures selected, there was one (53.9 × 41.3 cm) of Piranesi's print of the Colosseum. The dimensions as posted are of the exhibition's cardboard, as demonstrated by the typewritten label and the fact that Piranesi's book has a completely different size.

"Antichità romane" by Giovan Battista Piranesi (1720–1778) is a four-volume book of high quality etchings of various scenery of Rome and its countryside, a famous bestseller of the eighteenth century, often brought back home by the young nobles and high society bourgeois of the age upon their return from the so-called "Grand Tour" in Italy. In particular, table thirty-seven of volume I is titled "Veduta dell'Anfiteatro Flavio detto il Colosseo."

The first edition of the book (1756) was dedicated to James Caulfeild, Lord Charlemont (1728–1799), a 28 year old Irish patron of the arts on his third year of a grand tour in Italy. At that time, in 1756, Gustav III (1746–1792) was only 10 years old, not a king yet, and likely uninterested in the arts. Yet, some years after Piranesi's death, his son Francesco had problems financing a new printing of the book, and found another patron in King Gustav III of Sweden, to whom he dedicated the new edition (1787). This explains both the two dates and the double dedication of the volume in the Europeana records.

This may be a better story, but can we now suggest fixing the Europeana record accordingly?

Well. First, ours is just one among many possible explanations: it should not be promoted as truth only because it is richer or more plausible than the current one. Second, and most importantly, this explanation deals with many different levels of abstraction of the artefact (the chain of reproductions, the physicality of these reproductions, the people associated with them, etc.), and the data model employed by Europeana (Doerr 2010)[4] does not possess the necessary concepts, nor does it allow for the expression of level-specific annotations. Unfortunately, Europeana's problems are not unique as these limitations are common to most data models used in the humanities.

In public digital history, the role of the final users in adding complexity and variety to the description of artefacts is a key requirement. What can the readers add to the interpretation of the observed reality? How can we allow and manage information coming from crowdsourced initiatives for data enrichment? Europeana, with the CrowdHeritage project,[5] is in fact moving toward this direction, but unfortunately still with the unexpressed expectation that only one reading of reality can be preserved, and dissimilar points of view must be reconciled and made to converge outside the data model and before committing them to the digital world.

Common Issues in Representing Metadata

The example in the previous section has shown various typical problems in representing metadata (digitally or otherwise) about our history and cultural heritage. We can classify these issues in a few broad categories:

---

[4] Martin Doerr et al. The Europeana Data Model (EDM). World Library and Information Congress: 76th IFLA general conference and assembly, 2010, 10. http://www.ifla.org/en/ifla76.
[5] https://pro.europeana.eu/post/crowdheritage-a-crowdsourcing-platform-for-enriching-europeana-metadata.

- *reticence*: information that was probably known at the time of the digitization was not recorded due to haste, lack of skill, or, more probably, lack of policies and software support for this kind of information. The role of Helbig, the retrospective held about his work, the relationship between table thirty-seven of volume I and the whole of Piranesi's four-volume work, etc. are missing.
- *flattening*: the fact that an artefact is derived from another artefact and that other artefact is derived from yet another artefact is never made explicit. A single set of metadata is used to describe the content of the image, the physical support, and the long chain of entities represented, leading to inconsistent and meaningless information.
- *coercion*: information that was felt to be important, but for which no appropriate field was found, was forced into inappropriate fields (e.g., the dedication of the book to James Caulfeild and Gustav III ending up as the subject of a single page of the book), leaving to the puzzled reader the task of making things straight, and forever baffling any automatic tool tasked with indexing and searching collections by subject.
- *dumping*: some important information, for which no appropriate field was found, was placed as plain text inside a descriptive field, easy for humans to read but forever lost to any automatic management of the data. In particular, the existence of Helbig, the date of the photograph and the placement of the image as an individual page within a four-volume book are narrated in the description field, rather than being formalized in any specific field.

And, a few remaining problems we should also consider:
- not all statements of the story we told have the same reliability;
- all statements are clearly authorial (we are expressing our own personal interpretation); and
- we ourselves have fairly diverse levels of confidence about the events described: while the position of the image within the 1787 edition of the work has been verified *de visu*, we know that the roles of Francesco Piranesi and Gustav III are plausible but unverified, and, worse still, that the 1990 retrospective about Helbig is an interesting but purely hypothetical invention.

In the following section we propose an approach called "contexts." Contexts cohesively address these issues and enable data models to express not only finer details about the artefacts, as they do now, but also a wide variety of opinions, points of views and conjectures that constitute the largest part of our knowledge about cultural heritage.

Contexts for Qualification of Metadata

We can find many data models to represent metadata, facts and information about our history and cultural heritage. These data models are able to encode many fine details about artefacts and historical events, but cannot handle situations like the one presented above and cannot describe the circumstances within which these details find their place, their role, their correctness, their plausibility. The approach we suggest, in order to achieve these goals, is that of *contexts*.

Contexts provide boundaries to opinions and make them comparable to facts. Identifying and expressing the context of all statements is fundamental for their correct interpretation and use. Without the proper context, it is easy to draw false conclusions from data.

In general, we define contexts as sets of statements meant to characterize the metadata about an entity, rather than the entity itself (the entity can be an artefact, an event, a person, a concept or, in general, anything worth describing). For instance, assigning a provenance attribution to the creation date of a print is not a statement about the print, but a statement about a statement about the print.

The following are a few contexts that we have identified:

- *Temporal relationships*: facts and assertions are rarely absolute, and more often constrained by a temporal interval. For instance, Gustav III was in fact the King of Sweden, but only between 1771 and 1792; although he was alive in 1756, he certainly was not the King of Sweden then, and hardly the addressee of a dedication from a Roman printer.
- *Spatial relationships* (or, better, *jurisdictional*): geopolitical entities are evolving concepts and statements that refer to them must be qualified. For example, was Caulfeild Irish? James Caulfeild, 1st Earl of Charlemont (1726–1799),[6] was a noble of the Kingdom of Ireland, then under the rule of the Crown of England, with little or no direct connection with the current Republic of Ireland. Describing him as Irish is therefore just a handy simplification for a much more nuanced characterization of his true affiliation.
- *Part – whole relationships*: the item being described in Helbig's photograph is only one page in a four-volume book, itself published in at least two editions. It is important to be able to distinguish between the statements regarding the individual page (the heading of the image, the subject, etc.) and those regarding the volume as a whole (the author, the publication date[s], the dedications, etc.)
- *Object-subject relationships*: Object-subject chains can be particularly deep, intricate and fascinating. In our example, what we are describing is, in fact, a JPEG image created in the 2000s, derived from a high-resolution TIFF scan dated

---

[6] The authors would like to express their gratitude to Daniel Kiss for his clarification about the name and title of James Caulfeild.

somewhere in the 1990, about a photograph by Konrad Helbig dated 1956, about an etching dated 1756 by Giovan Battista Piranesi, about a 70 to 80 AD building called the "Colosseum" in Rome. Each one of these entities deserves descriptive metadata about them, but they must be correctly associated with the entity actually being described.

– *Provenance*: All statements present in the metadata come from a source that should be identified: an individual, a text, a direct analysis of the artefact, etc. Provenance information is needed, not only to give backing and responsibility to the statement itself, but, most importantly, to allow multiple different and competing statements, possibly in contrast with each other, to coexist in the same metadata collection. Without provenance there is no complexity, there is no dissent, there is no public history.
– *Confidence*: the sources themselves expose varying degrees of confidence in expressing this or that fact. Recording a confidence level allows for conjectural, hypothetical and even whacky statements to correctly coexist with established and settled information.

The use of contexts brings back the objectivity and truthfulness that software needs and that computer scientists crave for, without giving up the richness of information favored by scholars in the humanities. Consider the statement "at the end of twentieth century the Marburg Foto Archiv organized a retrospective about Konrad Helbig." It is clearly speculative, non-objective and conjectural. Adding a few contexts, the previous statement becomes "Barabucci, Tomasi and Vitali (2020) speculate that it is possible that at the end of twentieth century the Marburg Foto Archiv organized a retrospective on Konrad Helbig." By flatly stating the conjectural nature of the hypothesis, we made the statement as a whole more objective and easily verifiable: the addition of the contexts around the statement made it stronger and usable in a scientific discourse.

In summary, contexts have the undeniable advantage of being able to accept a much larger quantity of information than simply the official and established data, allowing for multiple conflicting views over the same items, and, ultimately, allowing a much more interesting and nuanced representation of our cultural past.

Representing Contexts in the Semantic Web

Models adopted for the description of cultural objects are various and heterogeneous. Traditionally, metadata in cultural heritage are classified depending on their role (e.g. descriptive, administrative/technical and structural). Riley (2009–10)[7]

---

[7] Riley Seeing Standards: A Visualization of the Metadata Universe 2009–10, http://jennriley.com/metadatamap/.

identifies instead four macro-categories: community, purpose, function and domain. This classification allows us to deal, in an effective and explicit way, with the complications that arise when metadata descriptions are created by different communities (e.g. libraries, archives and museums), for different purposes (e.g. description, preservation, technical features, structure or rights), with different functions (e.g. structure standards, content standard, conceptual model, controlled vocabularies, markup languages, record format) and while dealing with different domains (e.g. cultural objects, moving images, datasets, geospatial data, music materials, scholarly texts, visual resources).

Originally, data models were basically content standards, created as the result of reflections about theories on data description elaborated within different scholarly communities. The AACR2 rules[8] for libraries, or ISAD[9] and ISAAR-CPF[10] for archives are examples of this type of content standards.

These early theoretical models, fairly distant from actual implementations, were later rethought as structural standards, especially after XML started providing an adequate syntax to formalize existing vocabularies (DTDs first, XSD Schemas later). Examples of such structural standards, designed to support the description of data through markup languages, are EAD[11] and EAC-CPF[12] for archives, TEI[13] for literary texts and MODS[14] for libraries.

We now live in a yet more sophisticated world where we talk about ontologies as a new form of formalization methodology for enriching the expressivity of Schemas. Ontologies such as OAD,[15] EAC-CPF,[16] CIDOC-CRM,[17] RDA,[18] Bibframe[19] are behind the conceptual modelling of the new Linked Open Data cloud.[20] Add to the mix controlled vocabularies for managing the value of the attribute for person, places, subjects, concepts and objects (e.g. VIAF, DDC, UDC, LCSH, Getty vocabularies,

---

8 Anglo-American Cataloguing Rules (AACR): http://www.aacr2.org/.
9 General International Standard Archival Description (ISAD(G)): https://www.ica.org/en/isadg-general-international-standard-archival-description-second-edition.
10 International Standard Archival Authority Record for Corporate Bodies, Persons and Families, 2nd Edition (ISAAR (CPF)): https://www.ica.org/en/isaar-cpf-international-standard-archival-authority-record-corporate-bodies-persons-and-families-2nd.
11 Encoded Archival Description (EAD): https://www.loc.gov/ead/.
12 Encoded Archival Context for Corporate Bodies, Persons, and Families (EAC-CPF): https://eac.staatsbibliothek-berlin.de/.
13 Text Encoding Initiative (TEI): https://tei-c.org/.
14 Metadata Object Description Schema (MODS): http://www.loc.gov/standards/mods/.
15 Ontology for Archival Description (OAD): http://culturalis.org/oad/.
16 Encoded Archival Context – Corporate bodies, Person and Families (EAC-CPF) Ontology: http://culturalis.org/eac-cpf/.
17 CIDOC CRM: http://www.cidoc-crm.org/.
18 Resource Description and Access (RDA): see the registry, https://www.rdaregistry.info/.
19 Bibframe: https://www.loc.gov/bibframe/.
20 The Linked Open Data Cloud: https://lod-cloud.net/.

Geonames, Dbpedia and Wikidata[21]) and you obtain a fairly complete and sophisticated set of domain models for the description of a large part of cultural heritage artefacts and historical sources and knowledge.

To summarize, metadata element sets, controlled vocabularies, schemas and ontologies – and in general any relevant standard such as those proposed by domain associations such as IFLA,[22] ICA[23] and ICOM[24] – clearly show us how rich and detailed the description of cultural objects can become (Isaac et al. 2011).[25] Yet, although each of these models in fact exposes a rather complex, multidimensional and interconnected landscape, none of them gets close to the very issues we are discussing here, because of the underlying and implicit assumption that data description should be neutral and objective.

Many past and current reflections of Digital Public History as a discipline bring forth the importance of allowing and handling crowdsourced contributions from all sectors of the society, not just scholars, thus reinforcing the need for multiplicity of points of view on data. These contributions must be documented in order to generate more expressive and complex descriptions.

Already the notion of the neutrality of data models is being challenged by proposals such as HICO[26] (Daquino and Tomasi 2015),[27] in order to deal explicitly with interpretation acts (hico:InterpretationAct as well as classes such as Criterion and Type) as fundamental tools for expressing provenance of semantic interpretations; similarly Mauth[28] (Daquino 2019)[29] is useful to express the authoritativeness of existing statements with explicit paternity, and to let final users become active parts of the description process.

---

21 See in particular from Isaac et al. 2011 the section devoted to "Value vocabularies": https://www.w3.org/2005/Incubator/lld/XGR-lld-vocabdataset-20111025/#Value_vocabularies.
22 International Federation of Library Associations (IFLA) standards: https://www.ifla.org/standards.
23 International Conuncil on Arcives (ICA) standards: https://www.ica.org/en/standards-and-tools.
24 International Council of Museums (ICOM): https://icom.museum/en/resources/standards-guidelines/standards/.
25 Isaac Antoine [et al.], Library Linked Data Incubator Group: Datasets, Value Vocabularies, and Metadata Element Sets, W3C Incubator Group Report. October 25 2011, <https://www.w3.org/2005/Incubator/lld/XGR-lld-vocabdataset-20111025/>. A complete overview of ontologies could be read in Linked Open Vocabularies: https://lov.linkeddata.es/dataset/lov/.
26 Historical Context Ontology (HiCO): http://hico.sourceforge.net/.
27 Marilena Daquino, Francesca Tomasi. 2015. *Historical Context Ontology (HiCO): a conceptual model for describing context information of cultural heritage objects*. MTSR 2015: 424–436.
28 mining Authorithativeness in Art History (Mauth), http://purl.org/emmedi/mauth.
29 Marilena Daquino, *Mining Authoritativeness in Art Historical Photo Archives: Semantic Web Applications for Connoisseurship*, IOS press 2019.

Other ontologies such as PROV-O[30] for describing the provenance, SPAR[31] for publishing data, FaBiO[32] (as an FRBR-aligned ontology), PRO[33] for managing roles, or CiTO,[34] for representing the citations are able to add other types of contexts to data description. Similarly, the CMV+P (Barabucci 2019)[35] document model is based on the fact that most cultural artefacts reference or embed other artefacts explicitly and integratably into other data models.

Finally, the recent RiC-O[36] model uses the similarly named notion of "contexts" to indicate a plurality of paratextual information used to translate the classical siloed approach to data descriptions into a graph of connections between vocabularies and ontologies.

Contexts can also be seen as a generalization of the Factoid model (Bradley and Short 2005)[37] used in prosopography, where it is common practice to treat information found in old records not as objective truths, but as utterances of partially trusted sources. This mistrust of sources, and the consequent need for contextualization, is reflected in the design of modern APIs for querying historical datasets (Vögeler 2019).[38]

Some recent projects (Daquino et al. 2017;[39] Daquino, Giovannetti and Tomasi 2019[40]) demonstrated the possibility of a semantic enrichment through a contexts-aware approach, especially in the Linked Open Data workflow. This is the reason why Semantic Web, and RDF/OWL, are our starting point for the following reasoning on contexts.

---

[30] Prov-O: https://www.w3.org/TR/prov-o/.
[31] Semantic Publishing and Referencing Ontologies (SPAR): http://www.sparontologies.net/.
[32] FRBR-aligned Bibliographic Ontology (FaBiO): http://purl.org/spar/fabio.
[33] Publishing roles Ontology (PRO): https://sparontologies.github.io/pro/current/pro.html.
[34] CiTO, the Citation Typing Ontology: http://purl.org/spar/cito.
[35] Gioele Barabucci: *The CMV+P document model, linear version*. In *Versioning cultural objects*. IDE, 2019. urn:nbn:de:hbz:38-106539.
[36] Records in Contexts Ontology (RiC-O): https://www.ica.org/standards/RiC/RiC-O_v0-1.html.
[37] J. Bradley, H. Short: *Texts into Databases: The Evolving Field of New-style Prosopography*. Literary and linguistic computing 20: 3–24. 2005.
[38] Georg Vogeler, Gunter Vasold, Matthias Schlögl. *Von IIIF zu IPIF? Ein Vorschlag für den Datenaustausch über Personen*. In: Patrick Sahle (Ed.): *DHd 2019 Digital Humanities: multimedial & multimodal*. Frankfurt / Mainz. DHd. 2019. DOI: 10.5281/zenodo.2600812.
[39] Zeri & LODe project: http://data.fondazionezeri.unibo.it/.
[40] Semantic Digital Edition of Bufalini Notebook: http://projects.dharc.unibo.it/bufalini-notebook/. Si veda anche Marilena Daquino, Francesca Giovannetti, Francesca Tomasi, *Linked Data per le edizioni scientifiche digitali. Il workflow di pubblicazione dell'edizione semantica del quaderno di appunti di Paolo Bufalini*. Umanistica Digitale 7, 2019. https://umanisticadigitale.unibo.it/article/view/9091.

Accommodating Contexts

The natural habitat for contexts as presented in the previous sections is in datasets expressed with Semantic Web standards, frequently used to represent metadata for cultural heritage artefacts. RDF[41] and OWL[42] are the two such technologies.

RDF is used to express statements about well-identified entities. In the RDF model each statement is expressed using a so-called triple, composed of a subject, a predicate and an object, the subject being the entity being described. For example: "Antichità Romane" (subject) has author (predicate) "G.B. Piranesi" (object).

Expressing metadata using RDF is easy, and most of the existing metadata models have an RDF representation. Modelling contexts means expressing statements whose subject (the entity being identified) is not the artefact being described, but another statement in RDF that expresses some quality about the artefact. For instance, in example #1, _s is a statement that expresses the fact that the book "Antichità Romane" was authored by G.B. Piranesi (numbers 1 and 2). The context _c added at the end (numbers 3, 4 and 5) affirms that statement _s was created by GBarabucci, FVitali and FTomasi by introducing a ctx:Context class that assigns a clear and unambiguous provenance to it.

```
:AntichitàRomane rdf:type ex:Book .                                ①
:_s rdf:type rdf:Statement;                                        ②
rdf:subject :AntichitàRomane;
rdf:predicate dc:author;
rdf:object :GBPiranesi .
    :_c rdf:type ctx:Context .                                     ③
    :_c ctx:forStatement :_s .                                     ④
    :_c ctx:assertedBy [:GBarabucci,:FVitali,:FTomasi] .           ⑤
```

Example #1: A contextualized statement.

We cannot, however, simply add a couple of RDF statements to existing RDF collections. For instance, although these statements are meant to represent the sentence "Barabucci, Vitali and Tomasi assert that G.B. Piranesi is the author of the book 'Antichità Romane,'" they would actually be understood by RDF processors (reasoners) as expressing two slightly different, independent sentences: "G.B. Piranesi is the author of the book 'Antichità Romane' and Barabucci, Vitali and Tomasi assert this." The authorship of the book is placed on the same level of truth as the provenance of the statement. This is unfortunate, because the provenance of context _c

---

41 Resource Description Format: http://www.w3.org/TR/rdf11-concepts/.
42 OWL 2 Web Ontology Language: http://www.w3.org/TR/owl2-overview/.

does not factor in, nor restrains, the statement of authorship, as we were hoping to obtain.

Extending current data models with the ability to assert statements as true only within and depending on the truth of a given context is problematic due to shortcomings of the underlying RDF meta-model. The same issues arise not only in the Semantic Web, where RDF and OWL are used, but also in traditional databases, where the ER model (Chen 1976)[43] is used.

We could, of course, overcome this limit by introducing ad-hoc interpretation rules in our own metadata processors, e.g., by having them ignore assertions outside of explicitly activated contexts. This approach would work in practice, but would be project-specific and would prevent the sharing of our data with the rest of the world, e.g. in the Linked Open Data: we cannot expect all participants in the LoD to use of our modified rules instead of standard RDF reasoners to process this and other RDF datasets.

Or, we could adopt the RDF extension called "nested named graphs" (Gandon and Corby 2010),[44] that introduces the concept of "local truth" and changes what RDF reasoners are allowed to infer from a dataset. Example #2 provides the same example using nested named graphs.

```
:AntichitàRomane rdf:type :Book .
:C {
  :S {
    :AntichitàRomane dc:author :GBPiranesei .
  } ctx:assertedBy [:GBarabucci, :FVitali, :FTomasi] .
}
```

Example #2: A nested named graph of the same contextualized statement.

In this reformulated example we are nesting the authorship attribution:*S* inside graph:*C*, and explicitly specify that the graph:*S* is asserted by "GBarabucci," "FVitali" and "FTomasi." In other words, the outermost graph guards the content of the subgraph and blocks reasoners from considering the inner content as true independently of the truth of the outer context.

This approach is correct, working and in line with the best practices of the W3C, the authority behind Semantic Web technologies. Nonetheless, as of 2020, nested named graphs are not yet fully standardized, nor supported by reasoners.

---

43 Peter Chen. *The Entity-Relationship Model: Toward a Unified View of Data*. ACM Transactions on Database Systems. 1(1): 9–36. doi:10.1145/320434.320440.
44 Fabien Gandon, Olivier Corby: *Name That Graph, or the need to provide a model and syntax extension to specify the provenance of RDF graphs*. 2010. https://www.w3.org/2009/12/rdf-ws/papers/ws06/.

Adopting them or not constitutes a foundational problem that must be addressed by scholars and data modelers before they are able to apply our approach, or any similar one that looks towards allowing multiple reciprocally inconsistent datasets to be associated to the same entities.

With this model it becomes easy to express not only different opinions by established scholars, but also statements that are the result of crowdsourced activities, while providing, at the same time, the consistency and the truthfulness needed to support the complexity of heterogeneous point of views.

Conclusions

The push towards a single and objective description of cultural artefacts in digital systems is causing an impoverishment of our data collections, to the point that they end up as neither useful to scholars nor captivating for lay audiences. We believe that this happens because current data models and their underlying meta-models lack the ability to express, first, conflicting interpretations and, second, the stratified relations that exists between artefacts (e.g., a JPEG image being derived from a photo, that in turn depicts a painting, that represents a building). These problems stem from a root issue: the lack of support for multiple points of views in data models. To address this issue, we propose an approach in which all assertions are contextualized by associating various facts about them such as tempo-spatial relations, object-subject relations, provenance, etc.

Nevertheless, as Digital Public History recognizes, the general public must be allowed to have a voice in enriching our cultural tradition. Context information is key to this much needed participation, because it allows the role of contributors to be recognized, while at the same time, preventing the dilution of trust that may arise in such crowdsourced activities.

The adoption of this approach makes it possible to support multiple points of view inside the same dataset, allowing not only multiple scholars to provide their own possibly contrasting points of view, but also addressing key issues related to the public crowdsourcing initiative, such as the fear of contamination of curated datasets with unreliable information. Most importantly, with this model it is possible to incorporate additions, corrections and more complex kinds of commentaries from citizens without compromising the trustworthiness of the whole dataset.

With respect to sharing metadata with other institutions, our notion of contexts is in line with the ethos and the direction towards which the Semantic Web, the Linked Open Data cloud and modern data models are moving, but its practical adoption is at the moment hindered by its reliance on technologies that are not yet standardized nor widely implemented.

Still, the core principles behind our approach (in particular, the ability to express conflicting opinions) are necessary steps for our future digital collections to truly become useful, trustworthy and engaging for scholars and citizens alike.

Bibliography

Barabucci, Gioele. "The CMV+P document model, linear version." *Versioning Cultural Objects: Digital Approaches*. Eds. Roman Bleier, and Sean M. Winslow. IDE, 2019. urn:nbn:de:hbz: 38–106539.

Daquino, Marilena, Francesca Mambelli, Silvio Peroni, Francesca Tomasi, and Fabio Vitali. "Enhancing Semantic Expressivity in the Cultural Heritage Domain: Exposing the Zeri Photo Archive as Linked Open Data." *ACM Journal of Computer Cultural Heritage* 10.4 (July 2017). http://dx.doi.org/10.1145/3051487.

Peroni, Silvio, Francesca Tomasi, Fabio Vitali. "Reflecting on the Europeana Data Model." *IRCDL* (2012): 228–240.

Vitali, Fabio. "Beyond Three Dimensions: Managing Space, Time and Subjectivity in your Data." *SUMAC '19: Proceedings of the 1st Workshop on Structuring and Understanding of Multimedia heritAge Contents*. October 2019. https://doi.org/10.1145/3347317.3352728. 3–4.

Yannick Rochat
History and Video Games

Abstract: The aim of this chapter is to highlight some of the constraints present in the development of games with historical settings, and to explain why historical fallacies are sometimes included in games, even though the authors most often know that these are mistakes. Such choices are strongly dependent on gameplay traditions (what we have learnt to play, and how) as well as technological restrictions carried by the gaming platforms (computers, consoles, mobiles) and the game engines (the tools used to create games).

Keywords: 3D modeling, game design, game engine, game studies, modding, narrative design, simulation, world building

Videogames and Historical Accuracy

Following their apparition around the 1960s in universities, digital games have been sparsely studied prior to the emergence at the turn of the millennium of the field of game studies,[1] which was interested in the art of creating video games, storytelling and aesthetics of such a nonlinear medium, and the act of play, among many other topics.[2]

Developing a video game is a complex and expensive task. Large projects need a team with many different skills.[3] In this context, history "has much to offer [to] video game developers, including ready-made settings that can activate players' prior mental schemas to provide a sensation of verisimilitude."[4]

Video games integrated historical events quite early on, not only as narrative backgrounds, but also for educational purposes. This is the case of *The Oregon Trail*,[5] released in 1971 for schools as the student project of a young teacher.[6] His goal was to help pupils realize how difficult it had been for American colonists to follow the nineteenth-century Oregon Trail.

---

[1] Frans Mäyrä, *An Introduction to Game Studies* (SAGE Publications, 2008).
[2] James Newman, *Videogames* (Routledge, 2013 [2004]).
[3] Katie Salen Tekinbaş, "Game Development," in *Debugging Game History: A Critical Lexicon*, ed. Henry Lowood and Raiford Guins (Cambridge, MA: The MIT Press, 2016), 185–198, 195.
[4] Metzger and Paxton 2.
[5] Minnesota Educational Computing Consortium, *The Oregon Trail* (Minnesota Educational Computing Consortium, 1971).
[6] "Classic Game Postmortem: Oregon Trail," Games Developer Conference 2017, accessed March 5, 2020, https://www.youtube.com/watch?v=vdGNFhKhoKY.

In recent years, studying how history is depicted in video games has been a recurring topic both in the fields of history and game studies.[7] Like any cultural object, a video game might influence a player's interest in history but also raises the question of historical accuracy.[8] "Similarly to film advisors, historians have to decide whether the distortions in video games change the overall understanding of the past they wish to convey."[9]

Should game developers fictionalize history, or should they stick to what we know of the past? To debate these questions, I focus here on two case studies highlighting this tension over historical accuracy. In *Assassin's Creed Origins*,[10] a historical past is virtually reconstructed in the narrative. In the case of *Sniper Elite 4*,[11] curators from the Royal Armouries Museum in Leeds were consulted. They documented their collaboration with Rebellion, the video game development studio, on the weapons represented in the game which had to be as accurate as possible.[12]

Two Case Studies

1 Assassin's Creed Origins

At the time of writing, the *Assassin's Creed* series franchise,[13] developed and published by Ubisoft between 2007 and 2020, is composed of 11 main episodes in different historical periods (Italian Renaissance, American Revolution, Paris during the French Revolution, nineteenth-century London, etc.), a few secondary episodes, downloadable contents, reissues, books, a live-action movie, etc. They take place in various historical eras. Substantial budgets allowed historical contexts to be recreated based on consequent archival fieldwork that were used as backgrounds for the conspiracy-inspired narratives of the games. Most of the episodes in the series tell fictional stories, yet they include historical facts in extra-diegetic vignettes that the

---

[7] Here are a few references in historical game studies. On this topic in general, see Kapell and Elliott, ed., *Playing with the Past*, Chapman, *Digital Games as History*, and Alexander von Lünen, Katherine J. Lewis, Benjamin Litherland, and Pat Cullum, ed., *Historia Ludens* (Routledge, 2019).

[8] Tara Jane Copplestone, "But that's not accurate: the differing perceptions of accuracy in cultural-heritage videogames between creators, consumers and critics," in *Rethinking History – The Journal of Theory and Practice* 21.3 (2017), https://doi.org/10.1080/13642529.2017.1256615.

[9] Thomas Cauvin. *Public History: A Textbook of Practice* (New York, NY: Routledge, 2016).

[10] Ubisoft, *Assassin's Creed Origins* (Ubisoft, 2017).

[11] Rebellion Developments, *Sniper Elite 4*, (Rebellion, 2017).

[12] See Lisa Traynor, and Jonathan Ferguson, "Shooting for Accuracy. Historicity and Video Gaming," in Historia Ludens, ed. Alexander von Lünen, et al (Routledge, 2019), 243–254.

[13] A *franchise* is a "general title or concept used for creating or marketing a series of products, typically films or television shows" according to Oxford Dictionary of English (2017).

player can activate optionally, making the *Assassin's Creed* franchise a recurring example in the debates on historical video games.[14] One year after the release of *Assassin's Creed Origins*, in 2017, a game situated in Ancient Egypt, Ubisoft separated fiction and history in the game by including an educational extension called the *Discovery Tour by Assassin's Creed: Ancient Egypt*.[15] This extension is standalone and not accessible from within the original game. The player can choose to either enter a fictional (and violent) universe or a pacified world, with historical guided tours about Ancient Egypt. Such a *Discovery Tour* is presented as an educational program, even if the player still incarnates a fictional character in a virtual environment and follows a trail like playing a game (Fig. 1), or a serious game,[16] a term used to describe games aimed at teaching or communicating narrative contents, often at the expense of gameplay.

Fig. 1: The player is invited to follow a trail in the "Discovery Tour" (screenshot).

---

14 See for example Adrienne Shaw, "The Tyranny of Realism: Historical accuracy and politics of representation in Assassin's Creed III," *Loading* 9.14 (2015): 4–24, http://journals.sfu.ca/loading/index.php/loading/article/view/157/185, Alexandre Joly-Lavoie, "Assassin's Creed: synthèse des écrits et implications pour l'enseignement de l'histoire," in *McGill Journal of Education / Revue des sciences de l'éducation de McGill* 52.2 (2017), 455–469, https://doi.org/10.7202/1044475a, Aris Politopoulos, Angus A. A. Mol, Krijn H. J. Boom, and Csilla E. Ariese, "'History Is Our Playground': Action and Authenticity in Assassin's Creed: Odyssey," *Advances in Archaeological Practice* 7.3 (2019): 317–323, https://doi.org/10.1017/aap.2019.30, and Lisa Gilbert, "'Assassin's Creed reminds us that history is human experience': Students' senses of empathy while playing a narrative video game," *Theory & Research in Social Education* 47.1 (2019): 108–137, https://doi.org/10.1080/00933104.2018.1560713.
15 Ubisoft, *Discovery Tour by Assassin's Creed: Ancient Egypt* (Ubisoft, 2018).
16 Minhua Ma, Andreas Oikonomou, and Lakhmi C. Jain, *Serious Games and Edutainment Applications* (Springer, 2011).

In both modes, players can move an avatar embodying a third-person point of view, in the 3D environment modelling Ptolemaic Egypt. In the story mode, history is used as an environmental and narrative background aiming at purely fictional adventures, in which the player needs to fulfil objectives, often by murdering fictional or historical characters. In the discovery mode instead, "players can freely explore the interactive 3D reconstruction of ancient Egypt [. . .] without violence, narrative plot and gameplay constraints."[17] It is intended as a means to learn/teach history (Fig. 2).

Fig. 2: Illustration and explanations in the "Discovery Tour" (screenshot).

The co-existence of these two modes highlights the existing layers of a video game: one mode favours gameplay over historical accuracy, while the other favors historical accuracy over gameplay. Is it possible to reunite both historical accuracy and gameplay?

Historians were consulted during the development of *Assassin's Creed Origins* in order to document the period and provide knowledge and expertise on language and hieroglyphs, but more generally to help simulate the daily life of Ptolemaic Egypt. During a talk at a games conference in 2018, Maxime Durand, a historian who has been working on the *Assassin's Creed* franchise for years (as a Ubisoft employee), described the role of historians in these video games and the involvement of game developers with history: "Every time, we try to work [. . .] with people experts in their field of research, and these are helping us to create credibility. We are

---

[17] Own translation of Ubisoft press release titled "Le Discovery Tour d'Assassin's Creed transforme l'Egypte antique en un véritable musée vivant," February 20, 2018, email.

not aiming at one hundred percent historical accuracy. [. . .] We are trying to get inspired by history to create a fun game."[18]

Being able to see the Giza pyramids from Alexandria lighthouse is a mistake, but it is fun at the same time. Developing a historical video game might be a more difficult task than it appears at first: games' creators have to develop both fictional and sound historical contexts, that can be rewritten at will by a player according to the main narrative, while vouching for historical accuracy at the same time, when possible.

2 Sniper Elite 4

Sniper Elite 4 is a video game set in Italy during World War Two,[19] in which the player receives missions and must kill different human targets with the help of firearms and explosives. Curators from the Royal Armouries Museum, in Leeds, were consulted for their expertise on historical weapons. They provided high quality pictures, organised workshops with the game developers, and suggested improvements based on previous video games in the series.

In this context, recreating reality would ruin the game. Video games are fantasized models. Here, in a war context, with an accent on long-range weapons, the one individual incarnated by the player must be able to wipe out a whole regiment in one or two hours (Fig. 3).

Video games with a focus on action carry these kinds of codes. This lack of realism will not surprise many players. However, the in-game contents, be it the environments, the clothes, or the weapons, are not judged in the same way. A game is built around its game design. An implicit contract is formed between the developer and the player, implying that the game must be entertaining. Players are thus tolerant of a lack of global realism in this case. However, all the graphical assets and narrative elements will contribute to their immersion in this other universe, and the tolerance threshold in this case might be lower.

The curators list how the collaboration proceeded, how they were useful, and what they could not influence. For example, historically some weapons had to be held at the hip in order to shoot, but shooter game mechanics require bringing the sight close to the eye in order to aim and shoot naturally (as a first-person viewer). Thus, in the game these weapons are manipulated like in any first-person shooter (abbreviated to "FPS") in which the player sees through the eyes of the protagonist. Since they had let the designers and programmers manipulate the original weapons

---

[18] Maxime Durand, David Lefrançois and Marc-André Éthier, "Keynote – Beyond Gaming: How Assassin's Creed Expanded for Learning," filmed June 28, 2018 at Games for Change, New York City, NY, 1min45–3min10, video, https://www.youtube.com/watch?v=OdROuGMNHXg.

[19] Lisa Traynor, and Jonathan Ferguson, "Shooting for Accuracy. Historicity and Video Gaming," in *Historia Ludens*, ed. Alexander von Lünen et al (Routledge, 2019), 243–254.

Fig. 3: The fictional city of "Bitanti" in Sniper Elite 4, inspired by Porto Venere, Italy (screenshot).

and had provided pictures and documents to model them inside the games, the mistakes introduced by the game creators could have appeared as a result of lack of rigor "with a risk of historical misrepresentation or misinterpretation."[20] Through the use of a curator's experience, we can learn about the process of developing video games, how choices are made, and why often they cannot be realistic.

In serious games, developers often push for the narrative to be a central element. Using or creating video games in the context of public history does not necessarily need to follow this logic. In many cases, the work done in collaboration with game developers can have a high potential for teaching/learning history or just talking about it. However, even if the historical background in a video game seems promising, the public historian should never forget first to check what works, then what does not work, before using it. One must be aware of the reasons behind the mistakes in order to comment on them.

Today, video games are popular objects well-known among younger players and many people know the language of video games. In "those digital games that make meaning out of the past,"[21] they will be able to mentally sort what is supposed to be wrong (e.g. game design that is often unrealistic) from what is supposed

---

[20] Traynor and Ferguson 247.
[21] Chapman 14.

to be accurate (environments, historical context): "Gamification requires that history, however useful as scenery, cannot be allowed to interfere with playability."[22]

Compared to a book or a film, a video game offers "the ability to recreate the lost worlds of the past."[23] Video games are continuous universes: at any given moment, a player can leave the storytelling and explore the environments. Moreover, this implies a need for game developers to fill the gaps in the game world with buildings, living beings and side stories. This is history that is probable: in the absence of sources, game developers and historians determine what is the best (hopefully the most probable) scenario according to their knowledge. In this respect, video games can be of powerful assistance in teaching history and cultivating the imagination,[24] and complement other forms of learning. Historians who co-curate video game content contribute to create the "learning environment" of a scholarly game. As with the game design process itself, to fully assess the possibilities a game must be put into development and iterative research must be used to explore the best practices in translating historical scholarship into gameplay that meets the standards of the discipline. A video game thus offers far greater potential for the creation and presentation of history than any other entertainment or interactive media.[25]

Platforms, Genres and Historical Themes

Based on the analysis of a corpus of 1,690 historical video games, a recent study shows that the proportion of historical video games to the number of video games released on all gaming platforms between 1981 and 2015 is relatively constant.[26] We can observe a constant interest in historical video games, from the educational video game *The Oregon Trail* to actual strategy and simulation video games like *Total War: Rome II*,[27] set in Antiquity, *Crusader Kings II*,[28] set in the medieval period, and *Rails across America*,[29] set in the nineteenth and twentieth centuries, or FPS' like *Medal of Honor*,[30] set during World War Two.

---

22 Metzger and Paxton 25.
23 Kathryn Meyers Emery and Andrew Reinhard, "Trading Shovels for Controllers: A Brief Exploration of the Portrayal of Archaeology," in *Video Games, Public Archaeology* 14. 2 (2015): 137–149.
24 James Paul Gee, *What Video Games Have to Teach Us about Learning and Literacy* (New York: Palgrave Macmillan, 2003).
25 See Spring, "Gaming history."
26 Yannick Rochat, "A Quantitative Study of Historical Videogames (1981–2015)," in *Historia Ludens*, ed. Alexander von Lünen et al (Routledge 2019).
27 The Creative Assembly, *Total War: Rome II* (Sega, 2013).
28 Paradox Development Studio, *Crusader Kings II* (Paradox Interactive, 2012).
29 Flying Lab Software, *Rails across America* (Strategy First, 2001).
30 Published by Electronic Arts (1999–2012).

By comparing the video game genres and the platforms on which historical video games were released, it appears that "strategy" and "simulation" genres are significantly more represented on personal computers than on consoles because of their interfaces (the need to use a keyboard and a mouse in order to select large groups of persons and pick orders in the menus). Examples of such video games are the *Total War*,[31] *Civilization*,[32] *Age of Empires*,[33] and *Hearts of Iron*[34] series, all of which are strategy games, or even wargames, and digital versions of the tabletop wargame tradition.[35] In the meantime, there were as many action historical video games released on computers as on home consoles, especially with platform, third-person shooter, and FPS games, a genre which gained popularity on consoles too.[36] Eventually, among the many historical settings that we can trace in video games, we can identify periods or events: World War Two is invoked in 30% of "historical video games" in the database. For a given topic, the availability of games is usually not related to the gaming platforms. However, global simulation games are better represented on computers.

Game Engines

This section is focused on game engines, which are tools frequently used to develop video games in projects aiming at recreating the past. Resorting to a game engine allows access to 3D modelling technologies.

Today, many of the bigger game studios use their own, private and regularly iterated game engines. Nevertheless, many game engines are open to game developers, artists, scholars and amateurs,[37] either as open source software (e.g. *id Tech 1* to *4* developed by game company id Software), with a unique license fee, or with progressive license fees.[38] It is not mandatory to create a new video game when it comes to displaying historical content. Certain games allow the practice of modifying their con-

---

31 Published by Electronic Arts, Activision, and Sega (2000–2018).
32 Published by MicroProse, Activision, Hasbro Interactive, Infogrames, and 2K Games (1991–2016).
33 Published by Microsoft Studios (1997–2018).
34 Published by Strategy First, and Paradox Interactive (2002–2016).
35 Jon Peterson, *Playing at the World: A History of Simulating Wars, People, and Fantastic Adventure from Chess to Role-Playing Games* (Unreason Press, 2012).
36 Michael Hitchens, "A Survey of First-Person Shooters and Their Avatars," *Game Studies* 11.3 (December 2011).
37 Kirk Woolford and Stuart Dunn, "Experimental Archeology and Serious Games: Challenges of Inhabiting Virtual Heritage," *Journal on Computing and Cultural Heritage* 6.4 (2013):1–15.
38 Epic Games, Inc. Accessed October 17, 2018 https://www.unrealengine.com/en-US/faq.

tent (i.e. "modding"), which gives birth on several occasions to vibrant communities exploring historical sources and scenarios together.[39]

> Through modding the game, players challenge its authority as a text that represents the official version of history. By producing a version of history that is a dialogue between the official history of the game, their own understanding of feasibility and verisimilitude, or their counterfactual imagination, players contribute to an understanding to the past as plural and contingent. In this sense, *Europa Universalis II* encourages players to mod the historian's code by challenging the authority of the hegemonic and linear official history.[40]

This practice is frequent in historical video games and allows for some levels of shared authority for the players, a concept that is central to digital public history methods. Video games might be also useful to teach/learn history, but they are more relevant as simulations of the past.[41]

Bibliography

Chapman, Adam. *Digital Games as History: How Videogames Represent the Past and Offer Access to Historical Practice*. New York, NY: Routledge, 2016.
Champion, Erik. *Playing with the Past*, London: Springer-Verlag, 2011.
Kapell, Matthew W., and Andrew B. R. Elliott, eds. *Playing with the Past: Digital Games and the Simulation of History*. Bloomsbury Publishing USA, 2013.
Lowood, Henry, and Raiford Guins, eds. *Debugging Game History*. Cambridge, MA: MIT Press, 2016.
Metzger, Scott Alan, and Richard J. Paxton. "Gaming History: A Framework for What Video Games Teach About the Past," *Theory & Research in Social Education* 44.4 (2016): 1–33.
Spring, Dawn. "Gaming History: Computer and Video Games as Historical Scholarship," *Rethinking History: The Journal of Theory and Practice* 19.2 (2015): 207–221.

---

[39] Gareth Crabtree, "Modding as Digital Reenactment: A Case Study of the Battlefield Series," in *Playing with the Past: Digital Games and the Simulation of History*, ed. Matthew Wilhelm Kapell and Andrew B.R. Elliott (Bloomsbury Academic, 2013), 199–212.

[40] Tom Apperley, "Modding the Historians' Code: Historical Verisimilitude and the Counterfactual Imagination," in *Playing with the Past: Digital Games and the Simulation of History*, ed. Matthew Wilhelm Kapell and Andrew B. R. Elliott (Bloomsbury Academic, 2013), 185–198, 195.

[41] The organisation in 2018 of a course aimed for a general audience, on that topic, with fellow researchers from the University of Lausanne (Dominique Dirlewanger, David Javet, Selim Krichane, Giuseppina Lenzo, Matthieu Pellet, and Sandrine Vuilleumier) helped me prepare this chapter. A film of the event can be found at https://www.youtube.com/watch?v=zXWFB6XniVk (accessed 3 March 2020).

Dominique Santana
Historians as Digital Storytellers: The Digital Shift in Narrative Practices for Public Historians

Abstract: Innovations in digital technology have profoundly affected all areas of a historian's professional practice, offering unprecedented opportunities to the (co-) creation and impactful dissemination of historical narratives. In practical terms, the digital shift has set the stage for non-linear, cross-media and participatory narrative practices. This chapter aims at assessing the distinct tendency towards novel forms of digital storytelling, along with its potentialities and risks for the field of digital public history and cultural heritage institutions such as museums, archives and libraries. By exploring a selection of inspiring examples from the new media industry, it seeks to identify the potential role of public historians in digital storytelling.

Keywords: digital storytelling, interactive narrative practices, transmedia storytelling, shared authority, co-creation, new media industry, cross-platform hybridity

Storytelling in the Digital Age: A Proliferation of Forms and Approaches

We can no longer deny that the unsettling paradigm shift from a culture of scarcity to a world of abundance through digitization, online dissemination and participatory digital technology has fundamentally shaken the hegemonic traditions of history as a profession.[2] The digital shift has mutated the role of the public from a passive consumer towards an (inter-) active user demanding not only valuable reasons to interact, but also a certain amount of agency to engage with our stories. As a result, academic historians are increasingly forced to adapt their historical narratives to recent digital advances and reconsider their engagement with their audiences.

Michael Frisch's ground-breaking notion of "shared authority" in oral and public history (1990) – notably coinciding with the rise of the world wide web (1989) – has

---

[1] Schank, Roger, *Tell Me a Story: Narrative and Intelligence* (Illinois: Northwestern University Press, 1995), 219.
[2] Rosenzweig, Roy, "Scarcity or Abundance? Preserving the Past", *The American Historical Review*, Vol 108, No. 3 (2003), 739–757.

Notes: "People think [and] understand the world in terms of stories."[1]

https://doi.org/10.1515/9783110430295-043

profoundly shaken the foundations of academic historical narrative practices, formalizing a shift from author-driven to community-driven storytelling. Digital public history is about "presenting history and creating digital narratives with and for the public."[3] Consequently, the loss of exclusive control over historical narratives has raised vivid discussions around who owns the narrative and, thus, the past.[4]

In the early 1990s, historians began to experiment with the blossoming World Wide Web, CD-ROM discs and multimedia authoring software such as HyperCard.[5] One of the best-known examples is still the *The Valley of the Shadow* (1993), which let users explore a digital archive of source documenting life in two communities during the American Civil War. Since then, digital advances have resulted in a range of new formats for interactive storytelling, for instance virtual or online exhibitions, serious games and interactive web documentaries, which build their interactive historical narratives by creatively combining archival footage with animated multimedia archival documents (for example, The Goggles' *Welcome to the Pinepoint* or Katerina Cizek's *A Short History of the Highrise*). With the growing interest for and wider accessibility of digitized or digital-born archives and ego-documents, archiving gains a new significance. Several institutional digital archive collections were created, such as *Europeana* or the *Digital Library of Congress*. Moreover, through crowdsourcing activities on dedicated online platforms, these collected digital/digitized archives are greatly brought to life to tell their stories on the web. In virtual and online exhibitions, they are contextualized and creatively curated by archivists, museum practitioners or historians in interactive design interfaces, such as *Éischte Weltkrich – World War I*, which offers different modes of navigation through its digital collection, an interactive geo-referenced map and a timeline. Seeking a more immersive storytelling experience, other projects resort to 360 degree videos, augmented, virtual, locative and mixed realities, for example *Bagan*, a 3D virtual tour of the UNESCO World Heritage Site Bagan in Myanmar, using photogrammetry, 3D modelling, 360 degree cameras and drones to reconstruct a heritage site particularly at risk by a recent earthquake. Innovative technology actually allows visitors to experience these sites in ways that the human eye cannot capture in real life.

The flowering era of the participatory Web 2.0 in 2004, has raised new approaches to storytelling, both in terms of form and content. In the digital story world, narrative forms are user-centred, shape-lifting, navigational across many temporalities and spaces, generally mosaic-structured moulding a polyphonic collage of multiple

---

[3] Serge Noiret, "Digital Public History," in *A Companion to Public History*, edited by David Dean (London: Wiley-Blackwell, 2018), 117–118.

[4] Bill Adair, Benjamin Filene, and Laura Koloski, eds., *Letting Go? Sharing Historical Authority in a User-Generated World* (Philadelphia: Pew Center for Arts & Heritage, 2011).

[5] Chris Hales, "Interactive Cinema in the Digital Age," in *Digital Narrative: History, Theory and Practice*, edited by Hartmut Koenitz et al. (New York-London: Routledge, Taylor & Francis Group, 2015), 43.

viewpoints.⁶ Subsequently, these new forms of narrative content are built on iterative and collaborative storytelling design to bring in previously marginalized voices, in line with the bottom-up approaches of microhistory. They offer empowering possibilities of active engagement in forms of instant feedback through liking and commenting, impactful participation or co-creation through crowdsourcing or sharing their own stories, massive sharing through retweeting and re-posting on social media platforms.⁷ Driven by the democratic potential of the interactive web, numerous visual artists and filmmakers have adopted community-based narrative approaches around complex topics to generate social change – an occurrence which has also been increasingly observed in the growing field of digital public history. What all digital storytelling projects have in common is that they need their creators to "integrate creative and functional design across interface, production, distribution, and experience, above and beyond the narrative at the core of their work."⁸ They carve out spaces for dialogue, allowing historical narratives to be structured to a collaborative and horizontal practice.⁹ How do these digital interactions with narratives of the past actually function on the web?

Media theorists distinguish between different levels of interaction.¹⁰ In the conversational mode, the author is a facilitator/initiator allowing user-generated content (UGC). In the hypertext mode, users cannot add to the story, excluding any form of co-creation. Still, "they depict a world that emerges afresh at each of the user's steps," an approach which Lachman calls "the magician's force."¹¹ The experiential mode generally places the users' interaction in a location-specific physical space resulting in an embodied interaction. Finally, the participatory mode empowers users to change "the original database/content, making this form potentially more transformative of the artefact itself than other forms."¹² New media artists and few digital public historians have been progressively experimenting shared authority and with transmedia

---

6 Patricia R. Zimmermann, and Helen de Michiel, *Open Space New Media Documentary: A Toolkit for Theory and Practice* (New York-London: Routledge, Taylor & Francis Group, 2018), 57.
7 David Dean, "Introduction," in *A Companion to Public History*, edited by David Dean (London: Wiley-Blackwell, 2018), 11.
8 Richard Lachman, "Emergent Principles for Digital Documentary," *VIEW Journal of European Television History and Culture* 5.10 (2016): 108.
9 Patricia R. Zimmermann, and Helen de Michiel, *Open Space New Media Documentary: A Toolkit for Theory and Practice* (New York-London: Routledge, Taylor & Francis Group, 2018), 99.
10 Henri Jenkins, *Confronting the Challenges of Participatory Culture: Media Education for the 21ˢᵗ Century* (Cambridge, Massachusetts: MIT Press, 2009); Sandra Gaudenzi, "The Living Documentary: from representing reality to co-creating reality in digital interactive documentary," PhD dissertation, University of London (2013), 178–179.
11 Richard Lachman, "Emergent Principles for Digital Documentary," *VIEW Journal of European Television History and Culture* 5.10 (2016): 104 and 105.
12 Sandra Gaudenzi, "The Living Documentary: from representing reality to co-creating reality in digital interactive documentary," PhD dissertation, University of London (2013), 244–252.

storytelling to develop cross-platform narrative practices. These new exploratory digital landscapes, functioning as hybrid spaces, generate open-ended, interactive and community-based digital stories which "migrate across archives, dialogues, essays, live media, performances, websites, and video."[13] Digital storytelling is most impactful when untethered, continually evolving across various digital platforms, physical installations or participatory events involving local and global, physical and digital communities. By embracing cross-platform hybridity and transmedia storytelling, digital public historians adopt a more inclusive approach to co-creation and transcend temporal, spatial, generational and digital barriers.

The Digital Shift: Challenges and Opportunities

The digital turn has led to a merging of the once distinct functions of historians, museum curators, archivists, web designers, filmmakers and audiences.[14] This blurred "messiness" is, in fact, an oasis of unprecedented opportunities. Breaking the scholarly wall creates an open space for truly transdisciplinary partnerships to creatively interweave new approaches and forms of digital storytelling. For disciplinary historians, this demands discomforting effort as "creativity [. . .] goes against every principle they have received during their training."[15] However, the ocean of opportunities comes along with risks and challenges. Serge Noiret alerts that "the Internet has eroded the distinction that once existed between academic research and Mr. Everyman's public handling of the past, by allowing anybody to upload memories and historical documentation on the Web."[16] If in theory anyone could become a digital narrator of the past, what is the added value of professionally trained historians as digital storytellers?

---

[13] Patricia R. Zimmermann, and Helen de Michiel, *Open Space New Media Documentary: A Toolkit for Theory and Practice* (New York-London: Routledge, Taylor & Francis Group, 2018), 1–18.
[14] Steven High, "Storytelling, Bertolt Brecht, and the Illusions of Disciplinary History", in *A Companion to Public History*, edited by David Dean (London: Wiley-Blackwell, 2018), 163–174.; Katerina Cizek, et al., *Collective Wisdom: Co-Creating Media within Communities, across Disciplines and with Algorithms* (Cambridge: MIT Press, 2019), https://wip.mitpress.mit.edu/collectivewisdom, accessed 19 September, 2020.
[15] Thomas Cauvin, *Public History. A Textbook of Practice* (New York-London: Routledge, Taylor & Francis Group, 2016), 110.
[16] Serge Noiret, "Digital Public History," in *A Companion to Public History*, edited by David Dean (London: Wiley-Blackwell, 2018), 114; Guido Koller, *Geschichte digital. Historische Welten neu vermessen* (Stuttgart: W. Kohlhammer GmbH, 2016), 77–79.

A Detour into the New Media Industry

The new media industry has been exploring the potential of digital technology and has released several hundred remarkable interactive, immersive and co-creative projects in the last ten years. This hybrid movement is being thoroughly researched by the Co-Creation Studio at MIT Open Documentary Lab.[17] Intending to bridge the copious participation gap between historians and new media storytellers, this section explores a selection of interactive digital storytelling projects from the new media industry, which, in light of their originality in dealing with historical narratives, might be considerably inspiring for digital public historians.

#uploading_holocaust revolves around remembrance work in the digital age by approaching the question of how teenagers handle the memory of the Holocaust today. This cross-media project produced by Gebrueder Beetz confronts YouTube videos entirely shot by Jewish students from Israel on their trip to Auschwitz with captured impressions of German and Austrian teenagers and combines this authentic video footage with a thought-provoking interactive questionnaire. Suited for individual users or entire classes, on each thematic block of this multimedia project, users are confronted with direct questions and their answers are put in relation to others with real-time visualization. Further, the project website provides freely downloadable educational material to be used in German schools.[18]

The interactive documentary *Jerusalem, We Are Here* consists of a color-coded interactive map and three virtual tours of the Katamon area of Jerusalem guided by Palestinians whose families were expelled from their homes in 1948. Together with a team of researchers and developers, filmmaker Dorit Naaman virtually remaps Jerusalem via Google Street View as a mosaic of stories built around houses and places with text, audio and video, like a virtual reclaim of a once Palestinian neighbourhood. The project also allows former residents to enrich the interactive map by submitting their stories and archives. Particularly interesting here is the intersection of scientific

---

17 The Co-Creation Studio at MIT Open Documentary Lab is an interdisciplinary centre founded in 2017 under the direction of Katerina Cizek and William Uricchio. Their research project *Collective Wisdom: Co-creating Media within Communities, across Disciplines and with Algorithms* assembles international experts from various backgrounds to map and identify the different types of co-creation in storytelling. Out of the nearly 300 projects mapped for their research, none was initiated by or led by academic historians. Committed to sharing knowledge, networks and tools, the research team has recently published an online version of their study results, *Collective Wisdom*, open for online reviews and discussions: https://wip.mitpress.mit.edu/collectivewisdom.

18 Gebrueder Beetz is also known for its previously produced cross-media project *Farewell, Comrades!* about everyday life in the former Eastern Bloc comprising an extensive interactive documentary, a book and an exhibition "Farewell Comrades the web project is not dry archives, it is living history!" (trailer extract). All the digitized items were put together in their respective context by a team of historians. Postcards gathered from all over the former block as memory fragments, lead to individual life stories of ordinary people with extraordinary lives.

research and new media storytelling as this project was directed by a filmmaker, yet funded by the Canadian federal research funding agency, the Social Sciences and Humanities Research Council.

David Dufrense's *Fort McMoney* is a hybrid documentary-game blending nonfiction content and gaming strategies, which problematizes the considerable impacts of Canada's oil sands industry on the town of Fort McMurray and its surroundings. The structure of the gameplay enables its players to participate in debates as part of a democratic and inclusive community to foster collective decision-making. This powerful participatory storytelling format has raised discussions around the boundaries between evidence-based representation and simulation of the past. When simulating the past in a historical game, the players' choices and inputs change the outcome of the gameplay and with it the historical narrative. McCall explains this process as one of shared authority between designers and players.[19]

Triangle Fire Open Archive was initiated in 2011 by the Remember the Triangle Fire Coalition in collaboration with Buscada, an interdisciplinary team of place-based urban designers. Activists, descendants, artists and – indeed – historians, together envisioned this digital living memorial a user-generated digital archive collecting multimedia archives and testimonies about an industrial fire at the Triangle Shirtwaist Factory in New York, killing 146 immigrant and Jewish female textile workers who were locked in their working room in 1911. This ever-growing open archive is designed in thematic categories to facilitate navigation and all the items are cross-tagged by the donors themselves. In addition, the Coalition has been organising public gatherings and raised money to build a physical memorial where the fire took place. This digital archive has even experienced occasional incarnations as a physical *Open Museum* in several host institutions across the city. A similar project is *Sandy Storyline*, an online crowdsourced archive collecting stories from witnesses of Hurricane Sandy on the American East Coast in 2012.

We find few equivalent examples of interactive digital storytelling directed by academic historians, such as *The Valley of the Shadow* (1993) about the American Civil War conceived by the University of Virginia or the *September 11 Digital Archive*, created by the Roy Rosenzweig Center for History and New Media in collaboration with the American Social History Center, an online platform collecting stories related to the attacks and preserving them in a collaborative digital archive.[20] Likewise,

---

19 Jeremiah McCall, "Games as Participatory Public History," in *A Companion to Public History*, edited by David Dean (London: Wiley-Blackwell, 2018), 409; William Uricchio, "Things to come: the possible futures of documentary . . . from a historical perspective," in *i-docs. The Evolving Practices of Interactive Documentary*, edited by J. Aston, S. Gaudenzi and M. Rose (New York: Columbia University Press, 2017), 191–205.
20 This living digital storytelling repository was designed with their in-house digital tool called Omeka, a content management system for online multimedia collections and interactive memory banks.

historians worldwide are currently creating community-generated online archives, such as *covidmemory.lu* or *coronarchiv.de*, to harvest stories about life in times of a global COVID-19 pandemic.

116 cameras – Holograms for Holocaust Memory uses co-creative oral history holograms and natural language processing to create new dimensions in testimonial representation. With 116 cameras capturing Holocaust survivors' testimonies in all directions, the production team captured the emotional experience of such a first-hand testimony in the most immersive way through artificial intelligence and natural language processing. Digital technology has undeniably shifted perceptions of time and space in the remembrance of the Holocaust.[21] Can artificial intelligence immortalize Holocaust survivors by recording and preserving every single aspect of their voices, emotions and deepest thoughts? This project enables future generations to interact with Holocaust survivors who will go on telling their stories even when they are no longer amongst us.

Merging Spaces: How Can the Digital Support the Analog?

As Cohen and Rosenzweig observed already in 2006, "The past was analog. The future is digital."[22] However, considering the present as a hybrid sphere merging analog and digital, how can digital and analog best support or enhance each other? Digital tools and techniques are increasingly explored in cultural heritage institutions to support their physical exhibitions and as a response to the changing demand of visitors who "want to do more than just "attend" cultural events and institutions."[23] In the digital age, exhibitions are no longer "attended" but immersive spaces to be truly "experienced" with all our senses. An illustrative example is the *Museum of Tomorrow* in Rio de Janeiro, which examines the past, considers current trends, and explores future scenarios in a hybrid space for innovation and experimentation in technology, science and arts. In collaboration with researchers, scientists and visual artists, the museum curates "exhibitions to interact, feel and think"[24] through digital

---

[21] Eva Kovács, "Testimonies in the Digital Age – New challenges in research, academia and archives", in *Interactions: Explorations of Good Practice in Educational Work with Video Testimonies of Victims of National Socialism*, edited by Werner Dreier et al. (Berlin: Erinnerung, Verantwortung und Zukunft [EVZ], 2018), 76–77.
[22] Daniel J. Cohen and Roy Rosenzweig, *Digital History: A Guide to Gathering, Preserving, and Presenting the Past on the Web* (Philadelphia: University of Pennsylvania Press, 2006), 80.
[23] Nina Simon, *The Participatory Museum* (Santa Cruz: Museum 2.0, 2010).
[24] Translated from Portuguese: "Exposições para interagir, sentir e pensar" is the museum's resolution which resonates in all corners of its physical and virtual spaces: https://museudoamanha.org.br/pt-br, accessed September 19, 2020.

technology. Their narratives move across multimedia experiential exhibits, immersive 360 degree video projections, large interactive touchscreens, as well as virtual and mixed realities.

Once limited to bulky audio guides, the supporting toolset for exhibitions now contains iPads, VR headsets, immersive video installations and "the new locus of self":[25] our smartphones. In 2019, for example, the *Lëtzebuerg City Museum* launched <LMC>, a smartphone application with multiple functionalities for its physical and digital museum visitors. This innovative and user-friendly interface offers a virtual 3D and VR reconstruction of their permanent exhibition, topic-specific audio tours and quizzes for adults and children, as well as an "open book" promoting dialogue and instant feedback. All the digitized items with their respective stories can be browsed online and are easily shareable in several social media platforms.

Conclusion

There is no outright recipe for digital storytelling and, as we have seen, many forms of digital storytelling in which the past plays a role exist today. Yet, one question remains unanswered: If technically "Mr. Everyman"[26] can become a digital storyteller, why do trained historians matter in digital public history projects? Although new media storytellers are sensitive to the authenticity of the narratives they craft, their projects often lack external and internal digital source criticism.[27] Historians can bring a "new historicism" into play, give historical meaning and importance to the collected stories or any other crowdsourced material in the digital story world, the practice of hermeneutics being "the combination of "textual" and "contextual" analysis."[28] In other words, it is our responsibility and even our duty as digital public history storytellers to not only facilitate dialogue and public participation, but also to weave the collected stories and fragments of the past in their historical contexts.

Finally, there is an urgent need to – in a similar fashion to our colleagues from the digital media industry at the MIT Open Documentary Lab – further historicize and study this kinetic transformation process of historians as digital storytellers in

---

25 Andrew Hoskins, "The Restless Past. An introduction to Digital Memory and Media," in *Digital Memory Studies – Media Pasts in Transition*, edited by Andrew Hoskins (New York-London: Routledge, Taylor & Francis Group, 2018), 21.
26 Serge Noiret, "Digital Public History," in *A Companion to Public History*, edited by David Dean (London: Wiley Blackwell, 2018), 114; Guido Koller, *Geschichte digital. Historische Welten neu vermessen* (Stuttgart: W. Kohlhammer GmbH, 2016), 77–79.
27 Serge Noiret, "Digital Public History," in *A Companion to Public History*, edited by David Dean (London: Wiley-Blackwell, 2018), 114.
28 Andreas Fickers, "Towards a New Digital Historicism? Doing History in the Age of Abundance," *VIEW Journal of European Television History and Culture* 1.1 (2012): 25.

the making. The internationalization of Public History (IFPH) fiercely accelerated by the Internet gives new opportunities for the mapping of all the digital storytelling projects mediated by public historians worldwide, as has been happening recently on social media platforms.[29] Such initiatives constitute an essential step towards historizing practical and theoretical advances of this emerging field on a global level.

Mentioned Digital Storytelling Projects

- #uploading_holocaust: http://www.uploading-holocaust.com/#screen/start
- <LMC>, Lëtzebuerg City Museum: https://citymuseum.lu
- 116 cameras: https://www.116cameras.com
- A Short History of the Highrise: http://www.nytimes.com/projects/2013/high-rise/
- Bagan: https://artsexperiments.withgoogle.com/bagan
- Collective Wisdom: Co-creating Media within Communities, across Disciplines and with Algorithms: https://wip.mitpress.mit.edu/collectivewisdom
- Coronarchiv.de:https://coronarchiv.geschichte.uni-hamburg.de
- Covidmemory.lu: https://covidmemory.lu/
- Cowbird: http://cowbird.com
- Digital Library of Congress: https://www.loc.gov/
- Éischte Weltkrich – World War I: https://ww1.lu/?lang=en
- Europeana: https://www.europeana.eu/en
- Farewell, Comrades!: http://www.farewellcomrades.com/en/
- Fort McMoney: http://www.fortmcmoney.com/#/fortmcmoney
- Highrise: http://highrise.nfb.ca
- Isungur: http://www.isungur.de
- Jerusalem, We Are Here: https://jerusalemwearehere.com
- Museum of Tomorrow, Rio de Janeiro: https://museudoamanha.org.br/en
- Sandy Storyline: https://www.sandystoryline.com/
- September 11 Digital Archive: https://911digitalarchive.org/
- The Valley of the Shadow: https://valley.lib.virginia.edu
- Triangle Fire Open Archive: http://open-archive.rememberthetrianglefire.org/
- Welcome to the Pinepoint: http://pinepoint.nfb.ca/#/pinepoint

---

29 You can follow such global mapping initiatives on the IFPH Facebook group: https://www.face book.com/groups/ifphgroup/, or consult Thomas Cauvin's recent collaborative Google Doc "Start: Mapping Public History Projects": https://docs.google.com/document/d/1iyOre6tkXhCxC6inV XOQVKCO_W8JYPfVBF3f9ddx-1o/edit?fbclid=IwAR0oEouPl4X8F9EtWx8It9UnChqIMn6AC cy5CTH7c2W-YPqw-5YEWTGYgZ4.

Bibliography

Cizek, Katerina, et al. *Collective Wisdom: Co-Creating Media within Communities, across Disciplines and with Algorithms*. Cambridge: MIT Press, 2019. DOI: 10.21428/ba67f642.f7c1b7e5, accessed 19 September, 2020.

Koenitz, Hartmut, et al. *Interactive Digital Narrative: History, Theory and Practice*. New York-London: Routledge, Taylor & Francis Group, 2015.

Lambert, Joe. "The Central Role of Practice in Digital Storytelling." In *Digital Storytelling. Form and Content*, edited by M. Dunford and T. Jenkins, 21–26. Hampshire: Palgrave Macmillan, 2017.

Nash, Kate, Craig Hight, and Catherine Summerhayes. *New Documentary Ecologies. Emerging Platforms, Practices and Discourses*. Hampshire: Palgrave Macmillan, 2014.

Zimmermann, Patricia R., and Helen de Michiel, *Open Space New Media Documentary: A Toolkit for Theory and Practice*. New York-London: Routledge, Taylor & Francis Group, 2018.

Enrica Salvatori
The Audiovisual Dimension & the Digital Turn in Public History Practices

Abstract: The historical tale has always been more effective and engaging with the use of sounds and images than with the fixity of the written word. In a certain way, the audio/visual dimension allowed by the digital turn brings the tale back to its original fluidity, returning it to its original identity. As a tale made by sounds and images, the "story" must have its own styles, special effects, pauses, and rhythms, which have a decisive and primary importance related to its contents. The current digital revolution has emphasized this ability of the storytelling to influence, invoke and evocate and captivate by multiplying the ways and the tools in order to produce and pubish audio-visual "stories" and increasing and modifying the impact force of the historical audiovisual narrative.

Keywords: audio, video, podcast, docufiction, storytelling

The historical tale has always been more effective and engaging with the use of sounds and images than with the fixity of the written word. In a certain way, the audio/visual dimension brings the tale back to its original fluidity, returning it to its original identity.[1] As a tale made by sounds and images, the "story" must have its own styles, special effects, pauses, and rhythms, which have a decisive and primary importance related to its contents. This is also true, of course, for the written text: just think of the different reactions that an essay, historical novel, or partially fictional text can incite in a reader. However, an audiovisual product has a greater ability to influence, invoke, evocate and captivate than the written word, even if it is an exciting novel. The current digital revolution has not changed this assumption; indeed, we can say that it has even emphasized it by sharing the production tools to a vast public. Subsequently, this has multiplied the ways of creation and publication, thus increasing and modifying the impact force of the historical audiovisual narrative.[2]

The most important innovations in the digital audio-video environment of the last twenty-five to thirty years can be identified, firstly, in the discovery of peculiar

---

[1] Walter J. Ong, *Orality and Literacy* (Routledge, 2013). I wish to thank Stefania Manni for the suggestions received for writing this essay.
[2] Andrew Tolson, "A new authenticity? Communicative practices on YouTube," in *Critical Discourse Studies* 7, no. 4 (2010), http://www.tandfonline.com/doi/full/10.1080/17405904.2010.511834; Ann Gray and Erin Bell, *History on Television* (Routledge, 2013); Michelle Caswell, "Seeing Yourself in History: Community Archives and the Fight Against Symbolic Annihilation," *The Public Historian* 36, no. 4 (2014): 26–37. https://doi.org/10.1525/tph.2014.36.4.26.

compression formats of audio-video files,[3] which produced, as an obvious consequence, a generalized growth of the simplicity in using the tools for recording, post-producing, and publishing audio and video.

For what concerns the recording, if ten years ago, in order to make a good audio, you had to equip yourself with a decent microphone and, on the other front, to shoot a video it was absolutely necessary to own a quality camera; today these tools are basically optional, as they are integrated into other devices (smartphones, tablets) and their use depends exclusively on the degree of quality and professionalism of the products you want to create. Now there are several high quality versions of software, free or for a fee, to produce audio-video files, such as Audacity or Garage Band for audio, and Movie Maker, Imovie, Final Cut Pro, Adobe Premiere or Lightworks for video (the complete list is long and constantly changing). Each software shows different degrees of difficulty, but all allow a basic production with only a minimal learning curve. The reduced file weight and easiness of the production process has made it possible and useful to create publishing platforms where the user can place, share, and distribute histories in audio-video files, for instance City of Memory,[4] My House of European History,[5] or Storicorps.[6] There are also initiatives that have created a particular "channel" on Youtube, such as the Italian Pinte di Storia.[7]

It is useless to examine these aspects individually, mainly because of the fast changing market that continuously enriches and modifies itself. It is far more important to consider this concept globally, focusing on the fact that the common user can now easily access the basic tools for creating, producing, and publishing audiovisual content, which has had and will continue to have far-reaching effects in the way stories are "told". The new "storytellers" not only have "pen and paper", but a set of tools to give voice and images back to their stories. Furthermore, the places where they can publish their own audio-video stories have multiplied and globalized: social networks (i.e. *Youtube*), thematic platforms (i.e. *Memoro*), personal blogs, and sites (i.e. *Historycast*).[8]

---

[3] Riccardo Finocchi, *Ipermedia e Locative Media: Cronologia, semiotica, estetica* (Edizioni Nuova Cultura, 2016); Marco Furini, *Comunicazioni multimediali: Fondamenti di informatica per la produzione e la gestione di flussi audio-video nella rete Internet* (FrancoAngeli, 2018).
[4] http://www.cityofmemory.org/map/index.php#, a repository for "all New York City's stories".
[5] https://my-european-history.ep.eu/myhouse/allStories, a collaborative project incorporating our testimonies on Europe.
[6] https://storycorps.org/, whose mission is "to preserve and share humanity's stories in order to build connections between people and create a more just and compassionate world".
[7] https://www.youtube.com/channel/UCDRxSxN2je0AyZNeVVymHgQ.
[8] *Youtube* is a very well known video sharing social network, available at https://www.youtube.com; *Memoro* is an international non-profit archive which everyone can contribute to by using audio and video to collect the life experiences of people born before 1950, available at http://www.memoro.org; *Historycast* is a podcast on history that I made in 2006, available at https://itunes.apple.com/it/podcast/historycast/id126956772?mt=2 and http://historycast.org/.

Audio or Video?

Regardless of the different "technical" skills that the two mediums require,[9] the choice between audio or video content depends essentially on what aims our story wants to reach. Here is a summary of the main advantages and disadvantages of the two options:

Audio:
- Audio requires a high quality output, since the human ear cannot stand a distorted sound;
- An audio file is easier to produce than the post-production of a video file;
- Audio files are generally much lighter than video files, which facilitates their publication, sharing, and storage;
- Theoretically, there are no limits to the duration of an audio file. The format of the product must obviously be appropriate for the context of the story and the user, but a good historical audio tale can have a very long duration, even more than an hour. This is because audio can complement other activities, such as travel, sport, or manual labor, while it is impossible to watch a video while completing these activities;
- Dramatization of the audio is essential since the listener cannot read the words with the proper punctuation, or see the gestures or the images to integrate what he/she is listening to: everything is played on the tone of the voice, the sound, and the pauses.

Video:
- Although it is advisable to produce videos with good image quality, the interest for a certain visual content can compensate for non-optimal recordings (this situation does not occur for audio);
- Processing a video file implies greater technical skills than working on audio files;
- Video files "weigh" a lot, even if produced in low definition, so the producer has to carefully consider how to publish and where to store the large file;
- Video imposes a more active visual attention while watching the story, which does not allow multitasking with more challenging activities. This consequently requires a very careful reasoning on the format (duration and structure) of the product;

---

9 Walter Fischer, *Digital Video and Audio Broadcasting Technology: A Practical Engineering Guide* (Springer Science & Business Media, 2010).

– Video obviously involves a particular attention to non-verbal language: gestures and expressions, distance between people, clothing, and set design. This can be very challenging if we want to reconstruct a scene from the past.

In summary, building a half-hour historical video-documentary takes advanced skills, not only technical-digital ones, but competences related to screenwriting, scene creation, and the ability to direct and edit. If you don't pay enough attention to the rhythms and format of the video, the public will be unreceptive to the product and therefore the video would be unable to convey the message. On the other hand, audio grants much more freedom of movement and makes directing, screenplaying, and editing activities of minor importance for acceptance of the tale.

To exemplify the concept, let's look at the "taught" history in an educational environment. A one-hour video lesson, recorded with a fixed camera on the teacher-speaker, is a product that does not reach a great audience, while the simple audio-lesson-conference is able to fulfil this task. In Italy, in 1997, a TV channel was launched on satellite television to broadcast university lectures in collaboration with the Ministry of Education, University and Research. The format of the video lesson was completely "traditional": fixed camera on a teacher with a chair and a blackboard, but without any visible audience and with standard educational content.[10] The service has been certainly useful, but the video products were unbearably boring for the general public. Nowadays, the UniNettuno formats are a little bit more varied and articulated; however, for a truly effective visual teaching product, you need a good staff, technologies, high competences, and funding. An example is the series of famous video lectures of the universities of MIT (i.e. *Physics I & II* by Walter Lewin[11]) and Harvard (i.e. *Justice* by Michael Sandel[12]), whose teachers have become celebrities of the educational sector. The credits of each video demonstrate how much the producers needed the generous contribution of sponsors.[13]

In my personal experience, as a small producer of audio-lessons and founder of a podcast dedicated to history (*Historycast*[14]), the first recorded by an iPhone in the classroom, the second with a simple dynamic microphone in my bedroom, I can say that the audio is easy to produce and modify, allows ample room for experimentations and solutions, and normally meets a good rating among listeners.[15]

---

10 UniNettuno: https://it.wikipedia.org/wiki/UniNettuno_University_TV and https://www.uninettuno.tv.
11 https://www.youtube.com/channel/UCiEHVhv0SBMpP75JbzJShqw.
12 http://justiceharvard.org/.
13 Nowadays the panorama of platforms offering online courses and in particular MOOCs (Massive Open Online Courses) is wide and varied: Coursera (https://www.coursera.org/), EDX (https://www.edx.org/), Future Learn https://www.futurelearn.com/), and Fun MOOC (https://www.fun-mooc.fr/).
14 See note 5. For the lessons see https://itunes.apple.com/it/artist/università-di-pisa/1280874168?mt=2.
15 Enrica Salvatori, "Hardcore History: Ovvero La Storia in Podcast," *Memoria e Ricerca* 17 (2009): 171–87.

But, despite the huge limitations of the video production, the digital world nowadays tends to foster more and more image-based stories and prefers the video to tell and spread tales. In this way we see a real hyper-production of videos that, given these premises, can only last a very short duration (five minutes on average) and have incisive content, conditions not always ideal for expressing the complexity of history.[16]

The Format

The audio or video historical products can have extremely different formats, depending on the context of publication, the intended audience, and distribution goals. Below there is a summary of the main formats that can be found on the web, related to the potential and the limitations of the historical communication they offer.

Original primary sources: original audio or video sources that can be collected and published in a platform, blog, ebook, or site in order to carry forward a project/historical message. They require a minimum post-production, but instead require an accurate description of their metadata.[17] This section also includes journalistic or research interviews (e.g. a collection of oral sources) that entail a greater attention to the construction of the plot and editing. If the original audio or video source is not available, primary or secondary sources can be transformed into audio or audio-video content through acting.[18]

Following the primary sources in historical practice we find their reading and interpretation (i.e. *lectures, conferences, documentaries*). These products have in common the educational content and the eminently popularizing purposes, but they can assume very different formats, from a really simple structure (*lesson*) to an extremely complex and sophisticated plot, with the insertion of music, original or recited sources, interviews, and so on. If the format tends to replicate the lesson, it is strongly recommended to choose audio over video as the medium. If this is not possible for various reasons (i.e. a lesson in History of Art) then it is necessary to edit by alternating appropriate images with the framing of the speaker. In both cases, audio or video, the diction, the balance between speech and pauses, and the "dramatization" of the discourse are not secondary elements to make the product effectively communicated and therefore functional.

---

16 Michael Strangelove, *Watching YouTube: Extraordinary Videos by Ordinary People*; Amit Agarwal, "What's the Optimum Length of an Online Video," in *Digital Inspiration* (February 17, 2011), https://www.labnol.org/internet/optimum-length-of-video/18696/.
17 See for example *The Black Media Archive*, a multimedia collection of speeches, interviews, movies and music about African-American History, http://www.dubyakaygee.com/BMA/theBMA.html.
18 See for example several speeches by Simon Bolivar, available on Youtube, such as *Discurso ante el Congreso de Angostura*, https://www.youtube.com/watch?v=6Kddt0RtqZg.

At the top of the possible hierarchy of audio-video products related to history is the *docufiction*: here the content is always educational, but the storytelling is characterized by various styles, from the lesson to the novel, mixed in a new original object, whose quality derives from the abilities and the resources of the author/director. The MIT or Harvard lessons mentioned above, or the more famous and fitting example of *Last Stand of the 300*, the History Channel documentary by David Padrusch, broadcast in 2007 in direct criticism of the movie *300* by Zack Snyder, are extremely expensive and complex products.

The Broadcast/Publication

Depending on the outputs and their aims there may be more ways of publishing audios and videos online. It is possible to archive them in a database/collection, or periodically publish the contents to subscribers using RSS Feed (by podcast/channel), or organize contents in a site by creating a multimedia path (*storytelling*).

Database/Collection

This typology includes all the initiatives that promote the collection of historical audio and video contents with a common theme or feature. Prime examples include the *RAI-Teche Archive* or the *United Nations Audiovisual Library*,[19] but also places where oral sources are collected, such as *Memoro – the Memory Bank* with video interviews of the elderly, *Mémoire orale* on the oral sources of Wallonia and Brussels,[20] the *Médiathèque en visualisation « fresque » – INA – Jalons* with hundreds of videos on a century of contemporary history for educational purposes,[21] or *British Pathé*,[22] the great collection of newsreels, documentaries, and footage produced from 1896 to 1976. The common characteristic of these collections, even in the extreme variety of realizations, is to become digital libraries of searchable audiovisual sources. Other uses through search engine/interface or thematic paths could be used to enrich explanatory texts and scientific essays. In this context, the attention of the public historian must be placed on two factors: the presence for each object of all metadata needed to contextualize the audio-video source (author, date, technique, context,

---

[19] Rai-Teche: www.teche.rai.it/; UN Multimedia: http://www.un.org/fr/multimedia/videolibrary.shtml.
[20] *Memoro*: http://www.memoro.org; Mémoire orale: http://www.memoire-orale.be/index.php.
[21] https://fresques.ina.fr/jalons/fresque.
[22] https://www.britishpathe.com/.

conservation, etc.) and the navigation interface that should, as much as possible, facilitate the research and the retrieval of data, as well as their possible analysis.

Podcast/Channel

This choice of publication is not suitable to directly broadcast primary or secondary sources, but is more useful for elaborate content: lectures, conferences, documentaries, and docufictions. The name *podcast* is a neologism born in 2004 from the fusion of two words: broadcast, the English term that indicates the broadcasting, and the commercial name iPod linked to the famous mp3 player of Apple.[23] At the base of the pure and simple podcast, as of the personalized "video channel", there is the same mechanism that allows the user to subscribe to the service, usually for free, and then be automatically notified when a new episode is available. The podcast/channel modality allows the user to create his / her personal palimpsest, which can be activated at the time and in the circumstances that one wishes. It is a powerful and extremely widespread communication tool, in theory one of the most agile and functional solutions to implement distance learning, even if not always fully exploited by educational institutions, at least in the European context.[24] The podcast/channel of cultural and historical content is also an extremely useful tool for museums, libraries, archives, and cultural institutions that intend to take care of the community of their visitors, since it favors the periodic transmission of content on the importance of their collections, cycles of readings, seminars, and meetings.[25] The panorama of the podcasts is clearly growing and promises to have greater stability than that of independent podcasts. This growth, which clearly does not concern only History but several other disciplines, indicates that there is a growing demand for good information and culture from the public. I report among the best to my knowledge the various podcasts of History Hit network,[26] BBC's Witness History,[27] and the Radio GDR Podcast.[28]

---

23 Lionel Felix and Damien Stolarz, *Hands-On Guide to Video Blogging and Podcasting: Emerging Media Tools for Business Communication* (Taylor & Francis, 2013).
24 Enrica Salvatori, "Can You Graduate from MIT by Using ITunesU?" in *Mobile Science Learning*, edited by Enrique Canessa and M. Zennaro (Trieste: ICTP, 2012), 59.
25 Enrica Salvatori, "Hardcore History: Ovvero La Storia in Podcast," *Memoria e Ricerca* 17 (2009): 171–87; Enrica Salvatori, "Listening to, Watching, Living and, Ultimately, Learning History. On and off the Web," in *L'histoire Contemporaine à l'ère Numériqe. Contemporary History in the Digital Age*, edited by Frédéric Clavert and Serge Noiret (Bruxelles, Bern, Berlin, Frankfurt am Main, New York, Oxford, Wien: Peter Lang, 2013), 331–346.
26 https://www.historyhit.com/podcasts/.
27 https://www.bbc.co.uk/programmes/p004t1hd.
28 https://radiogdr.com/category/podcast/.

Unfortunately, institutional and academic podcasts are often made by people who are inexperienced in communication tools and recording techniques.[29] This results in a product that highlights an obvious contrast between the validity of the content and the poor quality of the podcasts. The direct consequence of this is a certain level of difficulty in listening; and if there are no listeners, there is no communication. On the other hand, the opposite can happen: a flawless technical production made by very skilled people in editing software, but who do not know, or superficially know, the method of the historian and who therefore cannot communicate the complexity and problematic nature of the historical talk. The consequence in this case is – paradoxically – even more negative than the previous one: the listeners/users are reached and connected with, but the message conveyed could be erroneous.

The podcast can be published independently or on dedicated platforms. The most famous is undoubtedly Apple's iTunes, but there are several, one different from the other, some even addressed to research in the cultural field, such as the podcast section of H-Net.[30] The audiovisual platform – among the best known being YouTube and Vimeo – has the advantages of being specialized in publishing audiovisual content and being made of essentially well made social networks, both of which considerably increase the potential audience of the audiovisual tale.

Storytelling/Site

This category includes all the publications in which the audiovisual content is only one medium inside a complex and articulated historical narration that can also include text, images, three-dimensional reconstruction, timeline, and data. In this case, each of the four formats of contents listed above can easily find its place. Indeed, they all can find an optimal collocation, when and if the structure of the digital historical tale (*storytelling*) is well thought out. In the multimedia story of the *Viareggio massacre of 2009*, made by the newspaper *Il Tirreno* and the IIT-CNR center,[31] there are galleries of images, video interviews, journalistic reports, written sources, timelines, and three-dimensional reconstructions, all bound by a well written text. The storytelling, trivially the art of telling stories, is a term that appeared in the United States in the first half of the nineties in direct relation to the digital turn and refers to

---

[29] Such as UniNettuno channel mentioned above, but also the podcast of Luigi Gaudio about History, derived from his lectures to students (https://www.spreaker.com/show/storia-medievale), or other podcasts not supported by adequate funding.
[30] https://networks.h-net.org/h-podcast.
[31] Donatella Francesconi, "Viareggio: La Strage Che Viene Da Lontano," *Il Tirreno*, 2014. http://static.repubblica.it/iltirreno/viareggio-la-strage-che-viene-da-lontano/.

an activity that "uses very different types of narration, from the oral story done by the singers up to the digital storytelling, which practices the virtual immersion in multi-sensory universes based on screenplays".[32]

This technique is applied in different ways, from the simple to the extremely sophisticated one, in the most various sectors; it is based on the awareness that stories have the power to construct and reconstruct reality, and consists in the diffusion of intentionally targeted and expertly elaborated narratives. This is a real twist toward the narrative realm, to the writing of history that, coinciding with the explosion of the internet and with the progress of new information and communication technologies, has become widespread far beyond the boundaries of research, touching politics, education, psychology, and marketing.

Because of this peculiarity, the historian who uses (or analyzes) this communicative meta-medium must be profoundly and critically aware of all its implications, in order to guarantee that the verifiability of the sources and methodological rigor are always clearly perceived by the user.

Conclusion

With this quick review of the different ways in which digital video and audio can be used to tell histories, I hope to clearly demonstrate that the spectrum of possibilities for audio-video use in projects of Digital History or Digital Public History is extremely wide and we cannot suggest precise solutions that would be doomed to grow old in a rapidly changing world. Some overarching recommendations include: in projects that include the collection of spontaneously recorded stories from the public, it would be of use to pay close attention to the metadata and at the same time the navigation of the site, so as to facilitate the discovery, the study, and the sharing. If you prefer the dissemination of your own interpretation of history, that it is for educational or entertainment purposes or following other instances, it would be of use to pay close attention to the format, especially for videos, and, in any case, to choose the podcast solution with the release of RSS feeds to encourage the loyalty of the public.

However, whatever solution is adopted, it is very clear that in today's world, an inextricable mixture of material and digital, real and virtual, it is unthinkable to promote a Digital Public History project using only one or two mediums and excluding the audio and video dimension. A digital public historian must therefore not

---

32 The original in Italian: "fa uso di tipi di narrazione molto diversi, dal racconto orale come lo praticavano i cantastorie fino al digital storytelling, che pratica l'immersione virtuale in universi multisensoriali basati su sceneggiature" (Christian Salmon, *Storytelling. La fabbrica delle storie* (Fazi, 2008)).

necessarily become an expert in the management of these media, but rather know their limits, potentials, and formats to be able to use and to understand them in an appropriate manner that optimizes on their use.

Bibliography

Felix, L., and D. Stolarz. *Hands-On Guide to Video Blogging and Podcasting: Emerging Media Tools for Business Communication*. Abingdon: Taylor & Francis, 2013.

Fischer, W. *Digital Video and Audio Broadcasting Technology: A Practical Engineering Guide*. Kent: Springer Science & Business Media, 2010.

di Marco, F. *Comunicazioni multimediali: Fondamenti di informatica per la produzione e la gestione di flussi audio-video nella rete Internet*. FrancoAngeli, 2018.

Salvatori, E. "Listening to, Watching, Living and, Ultimately, Learning History. On and off the Web". In *L'histoire Contemporaine à l'ère Numériqe. Contemporary History in the Digital Age*, edited by F. Clavert and S. Noiret, 331–46. Bruxelles, Bern, Berlin, Frankfurt am Main, New York, Oxford, Wien: Peter Lang, 2013.

Strangelove, M. *Watching YouTube: Extraordinary Videos by Ordinary People*. Toronto: University of Toronto Press, 2010.

Tolson, A. "A New Authenticity? Communicative Practices on YouTube." *Critical Discourse Studies* 7, no. 4 (2010), http://www.tandfonline.com/doi/full/10.1080/17405904.2010.511834.

Raffaella Biscioni
Digital Public History and Photography

Abstract: This essay intends to analyze the current contribution of photography to Digital Public History (DPH) starting from the perspective of changing relationship between photography and memory in the new web context.

Keywords: digital public history, cultural memory, photography collections, digital humanities, audience engagement, crowdsourcing

In its original historical form, photography constitutes a direct and immediate link with the past; a form of permanent memory whose *noema* is expressed with the words "it has been."[1] The current "technical revolution" and dematerialization into a network environment and the possibilities of immediate and multiple sharing, have emphasized the changing and fluid nature of the image, constantly renegotiated on the basis of the new contexts it passes through.[2]

The new spaces offered by the Internet therefore represent a new environment where photography can take different and sometimes apparently conflicting roles. For example, photography gets very easily into the logic of "disintermediation" typical of the web and takes up important space within social networks through user generated content. At the same time, it is central to large operations of "cultural memory" directed from the top.[3] In the latter case, such operations are often centralized and have a strong cultural-political meaning, oriented by governmental institutions or by very important private subjects. These cultural institutions must deal both with the interactive and participatory nature of the web,[4] and with the new great private digital companies (like Google), which have made important strategic choices from the outset in the direction of cultural heritage, using their technological advancement to structure new networks and control of resources.

The historical photographic heritage is also traditionally disseminated, articulated and rooted in the territory, but at the same time the universality of the photographic language makes it particularly attractive for the new digital communication channels that lead to it being widespread in new global communities.

---

[1] The best-known statement about the documentary dimension of photography concerning the past is in Roland Barthes, *La Chambre claire. Note sur la photographie* (Paris, 1980).
[2] For example, André Gunthert theorized the diffusion of a "conversational" use of digital photography, completely oriented towards the present, see André Gunthert, *L'Image Partagée. La photographie numérique* (Paris: Textuel, 2015).
[3] Jan Assmann, *Cultural Memory and Early Civilization: Writing, Remembrance, and Political Imagination* (Cambridge: Cambridge University Press, 2011).
[4] Faye Sayer, *Public History: A Practical Guide* (London: Bloomsbury, (2015) 2nd edition 2019); *Participatory Archives*, ed. Edward Benoit and Alexandra Eveleigh (London: Facet Publishing, 2019).

All these aspects have stimulated practices of DPH, but since it's difficult to compare the vast universe of photos shared in the DPH projects which runs on social media,⁵ this chapter will focus mainly on the use of photography in some important national or international "cultural memory" projects on the web which share historical narratives with photographs. We will observe the interactions of these projects "from above," trying to understand their characteristics both in relation to participatory practices "from below" and to the examples of some public and private "mega-projects" that use historical digital photography in a quite different perspective from that of DPH, but very much linked to it.

Europeana

Europeana was born in 2008, about 15 years after "American Memory," a pioneering digital project on American cultural memory⁶ (Fig. 1) and represents an experience allied to an important effort to digitize the heritage but also with a clear political intent. In fact, on the whole, Europeana is a major undertaking to construct a shared "cultural memory" for the European Union, in the sense given to this term by Jan Assmann, that is, processing memories as a means of constructing a shared cultural identity.⁷

This operation found a privileged space online: according to Jill Cousin, Europeana "is Europe's most visible representation of our common European cultural heritage",⁸ and a situation that can engage users through new participatory practices and support the new telling of old stories.⁹

Through Europeana, therefore, the images of cultural institutions and private citizens, find a new dimension, strongly oriented in terms of common European identity, and for this reason the cultural themes on which it has invested most in recent

---

5 It is estimated that Facebook has 300 million new photos uploaded every day, Instagram 40 billion photos shared from 2010 to today and 95 million new images every day, while for Pinterest, the total number of pins is above 100 billion; see *Social Media Statistics 2020: Top Networks By the Numbers* https://dustinstout.com/social-media-statistics/.
6 Sally Stieglitz, *The American memory project*, in *Cases on electronic records and resource management implementation in diverse environments*, ed. Janice M. Krueger Hershey (Pennsylvania: Information Science Reference, 2014), 106–116.
7 Jan Assmann, 'Communicative and Cultural Memory' in *A Companion to Cultural Memory Studies*, ed. Astrid Erll, Ansgar Nünning, (New York: De Gruyter, 2010), 109–118.
8 Jill Cousins was Director of Europeana Foundation since its beginnings in 2005/2006 until 2018, see Jill Cousins, http://www.culturaitalia.it/opencms/en/contenuti/focus/Jill_Cousins_Europeana_s_success_receives_a_boost_from_CulturaItalia_and_other_national_aggregators_.html?language=en, [last accessd 10.02.2020]. See also Bjarki Valtysson, "EUROPEANA. The digital construction of Europe's collective memory", *Information, Communication & Society*, 15, (2012) 151–170.
9 Sharon Macdonald, *Memorylands: Heritage and Identity in Europe Today* (London: Routledge, 2013).

Fig. 1: Europeana homepage.

years are significant: the Great War, European migration, European society of the 1950s engaged in reconstruction after the Second World War.

We can consider Europeana an emblematic example of how web 2.0 and Digital Public History practices have progressively changed the role played by institutions in the policies of memory and access to European cultural heritage, which become more dynamic and innovative in digital form, while also hosting private heritage assets.

Europeana organizes digital collections from different countries and, over its 12 years of activity, has added more than 58 million digital artefacts: works of art, books, videos, photos, audio materials, organized into specific thematic collections. In terms of photography, more than five million items have been accrued. A very complex infrastructure collects digitized heritage from more than 3,500 European institutions thanks to the work, knowledge and skills of professionals in the Digital Humanities.

One of the collections that had the greatest amount of collaboration from private users is *Europeana 1914– 1918 – Untold stories and official histories of World War I*, (Fig. 2) which collected more than 370,000 digital artefacts (books, newspapers and magazines, maps, archive documents, videos, propaganda material, school books, posters, photos, memorabilia, etc.).[10]

In fact, not only does the portal bring together collections from the principal European institutions, but it also invites users to upload their own materials and share their family story, through "Adding your story to Europeana 1914–1918" page. Thanks to special online collection forms, the user is able to upload materials and relevant information, by specifying the type of document (a postcard, diary, photo, etc.)

---

10 https://www.europeana.eu/portal/en/collections/world-war-I.

and adding the story that they wish to share (for example, who the person in the photo is, how they came to have it, what is known about the artefact). Once added, the contribution is reviewed by an expert from the Europeana team and, ultimately, made available to everyone, and included in a participatory context.

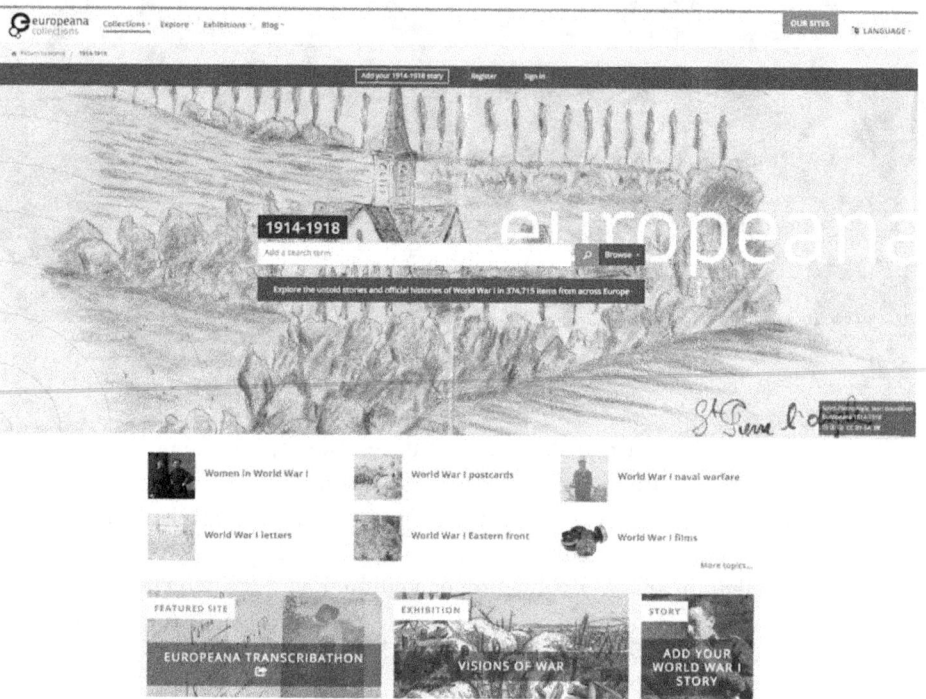

Fig. 2: Europeana 14–18 Collection Homepage.

One of the first tools that Europeana used to engage the public for the creation and implementation of online collections are the Collecting Days held in various European cities: during these events, anyone who owns letters, memorabilia and historically interesting photos was asked to participate. A team of experts helped to digitize the materials and record the oral history testimonies. All the materials were returned to the owners on the same day, while the digitized artefacts were reviewed and added to the Europeana collections. In this way, they became part of a shared heritage.[11] It is not only the remarkable number of photographic documents in these collections that is important: especially in a multilingual and multicultural context such as the European

---

11 Since 2011 to date, over 50,000 pieces of memorabilia have been digitized. See https://blog.europeana.eu/2014/04/documenting-the-great-war-behind-the-scenes-at-a-14-18-community-collection-day/, last accessed February 10, 2020.

Union, the universal language of photography becomes an important facilitator for sharing and comparing story and experiences.

In the summer of 2017, Europeana Transcribathon[12] came into existence as a competition between EU countries to digitize crowdsourced materials in Europeana 1914–1918. Participants were asked to transcribe maps, diaries, letters and postcards which were already digitized as best as possible, and as quickly as possible. The finale Transcribathon took place in the House of the European History in Brussels in November 2018.[13]

Europeana Photography is one of Europeana's thematic collections. Launched in 2012, it was dedicated to the digitization of photographs with a high level of historic, artistic and cultural value related to the first century of photography (1839–1939).

In 2014 virtual and multimedia exhibitions began:[14] these included *Untold Stories of the First World War*, curated by historian Peter Englund,[15] which was based on private and personal stories and images that people had uploaded to Europeana 1914–1918.

Blue Skies, Red Panic. A Photographic Perspective on the 1950s in Europe is the latest online exhibition, telling stories about society, culture and politics in European countries "between East and West, freedom and oppression, cliché and normality."[16] The exhibition is related to the Europeana project Fifities in Europe Kaleidoscope (2018–2020) (Fig. 3), dedicated to the 1950s in Europe.[17]

The case of Europeana, and its relationships with new digital channels and DPH practices from the top-down, is only a part of photographic digital content on offer. The first great experience of this type was American Memory, ended in the same years in which Europeana was born. Her legacy was substantially carried forward by the Library of Congress, thus taking its place within the large LoC digital catalog. At the same time (since 2009) a part of the LoC photographs has been made available through Flickr, the famous photosharing platform which was created in 2004.

As specified by the Library: "Offering historical photo collections through Flickr is a welcome opportunity to share some of our most popular images more widely."[18]

---

[12] https://transcribathon.com/en/. To date, this has yielded more than 38,472 documents, a number that is continuously increasing.
[13] https://pro.europeana.eu/event/centenary-tour-finale-europeana-1914-18-transcribathon.
[14] It is possible to consult the list of exhibitions at https://www.europeana.eu/portal/en/exhibitions/foyer.
[15] https://www.europeana.eu/portal/en/exhibitions/untold-stories-of-the-first-world-war.
[16] https://www.smb.museum/en/exhibitions/detail/blue-skies-red-panic.html.
[17] The final conference of the project was dedicated to "New strategies for user engagement and digitized photographic heritage," see https://www.photoconsortium.net/kaleidoscope-accomplishment/.
[18] https://www.flickr.com/people/library_of_congress/ The photos posted on Flickr, currently more than 36,000, do not have the accurate cataloguing and the philological-critical analysis that accompanies the LoC website: here the users tag the images and add their comments, sometimes

Fig. 3: Kaleidoscope Project postcard.

In this way, a clear distinction was made between the creation of a "digital library" as a professional and orderly tool according to advanced cataloguing and digitization criteria, and a dissemination area that offered a "pre-packaged" selection, although rather large, of very "popular" images.

While American Memory had established approximate criteria for the first digitization campaigns of photographic materials, leading to a large contribution of images from peripheral territories towards the centre, the use of Flickr allowed a simplified distribution oriented towards a "consumer" using a top-down logic.

Due to the open access policy of institutions like the LoC, which makes an immense photographic heritage freely available, photography appears as an instrument available to all, to scholars as well as the generic public, but without any predisposition for any specific disciplinary approach: in practice it is a valid tool for PH practices for scholars of different disciplines or those who are simply enthusiasts.

extemporaneously. For example, in the case of the famous "migrant mother" by Dorothea Lange, there are some posts by "pro" users that underline some key points for a philologically accurate reading on a historical level (in this specific case the "thumb after retouching": https://www.flickr.com/photos/library_of_congress/3551599565/in/photostream/) but overall the presentation of these photographs aims for a faster and more aesthetic "consumption" of images.

In this regard, we can recall the Public Library of America (DPLA),[19] launched in 2013. Also, in this case, it is a very large repository, which serves as an aggregator of over 4,000 American archives and institutions, with a total offer of more than 30 million items. Designed at the Berkman Klein Center for Internet & Society at Harvard University, supported by the Alfred P. Sloan Foundation, it was established after preparatory work that "brought together hundreds of public and research Librarians, innovators, digital humanists, and other volunteers." DPLA appears on the web without an explicit reference to DPH, but has some very interesting tools, like a section dedicated to searching for sources of family or community stories.[20] DPLA has a strong ethical imprint based on the principle of free and universal accessibility of information. Another aspect interesting for DPH is the attention to the educational uses of images and documents and for the connection with schools and teachers, as well as the fact that it endeavors to make the material available thematically through the "exhibitions," or specific topics.

Flickr Commons

Since 2009, Flickr Commons[21] (Fig. 4) supports public engagement between cultural institutions and individual users. Due to this collaboration, the Library of Congress, and other institutions, have taken advantage of the most popular channels to improve access to its collections thanks to an active and numerically very important online audience.[22] It has also harnessed the rich and structured interface where those who publish and view photos can leave comments, provide short metadata tags, organize their photos in a pool and share and disseminate the photos.[23]

---

[19] https://dp.la/.
[20] It can be used for four types of activities: Education, Family Research, Lifelong Learning, Scholarly Research.
[21] The Commons was created in 2009 through an agreement between the Library of Congress and Flickr https://www.flickr.com/commons. Approximately 115 institutions are now members of the project.
[22] As can be read on its homepage, today it hosts "tens of billions" of images and 2 million groups. In the case of LoC the dissemination was more limited: "During The Commons' first year, Flickr users tagged and commented on digitized heritage: more than 67,000 tags were added and more than 2,500 users got involved. More than 500 photos have been verified by the US Library of Congress and transferred to the library's permanent records. In a relatively short period of time, the Library has managed to get a group of amateur historians involved in the construction of a heritage asset." See Barbara Orbach Natanson "A Happy Anniversary: Four Years of Sharing on Flickr," *Library of Congress Blog*, January 16, 2012, https://blogs.loc.gov/picturethis/2012/01/a-happy-anniversary-four-years-of-sharing-on-flickr/.
[23] Historypin, a platform expressly dedicated to history, allows you to upload historic images and "pin them" to a map, creating mash-ups if the historical picture is overlaid in Google Street View.

Fig. 4: The Commons homepage on Flickr.

The presence of users' vernacular, family photography and private collectors is also very common on this sharing platforms (Fig. 5). Through the thematic groups, the images are organized in a pool, and generally they deal with the widest possible range of subjects, from history, arts landscapes, design, fashion, etc. In many cases, they become a veritable *wunderkammer* (cabinet of curiosities) for the contemporary era.[24]

There are numerous groups related to history, and one of the first crowdsourcing projects was conducted on Flickr, *The Great War archive*, promoted by the University of Oxford in 2008.[25] In these groups we find an important part of the DHP's bottom-up practices. The nature of private memories in this groups is not static and the same image is not anchored to a specific Group, but can be shared on different groups not necessarily related to the same topic: in some cases it may even be possible to have over 30 or 40 shares in different groups. Thus the traditional classifications give way to a strong component of unpredictability, which contemplates not only indexing, but also the formats and quality of the images.

To date, Historypin has attracted 100,454 members and 35,232 collections, and approximately 3,000 cultural institutions who use its technology.
24 Melissa Terras, "The digital wunderkammer: Flickr as a platform for amateur cultural and heritage content" *Library Trends*, 59.4 (2011): 686–706, 689.
25 The group collects around 17,000 images, https://www.flickr.com/groups/800965@N21/.

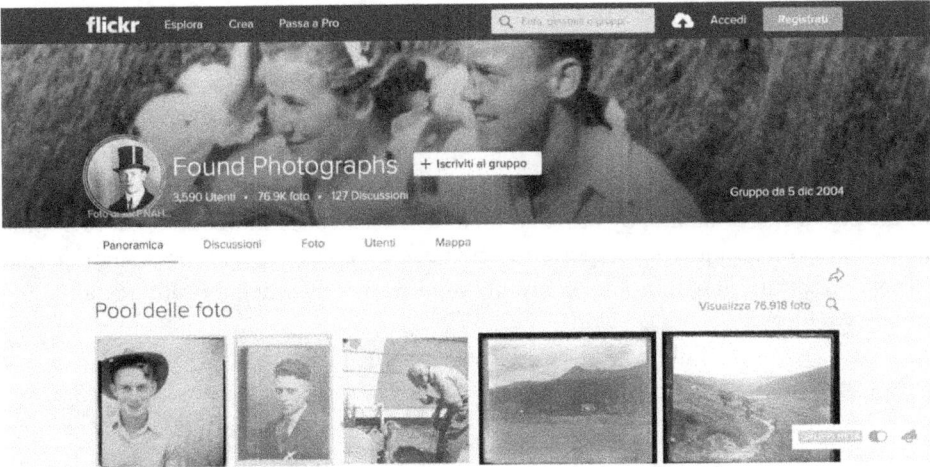

Fig. 5: Found Photographs group homepage on Flickr.

Although the presence of user generated content is central, it is easy to find groups where photographs of users and cultural institutions are mixed. These are not just images posted by The Commons collections, but also shared by other platforms, such as, for example, on Europeana, Google Arts and Project or institutional websites, which make it possible to share images on social media.[26]

Google Arts & Culture

Google Arts & Culture[27] hosts the most important museum collections in the world, including digital exhibitions that have been curated by private or public institutions or cultural professionals. The online exhibition service provides storytelling tools, which include a high-resolution zoom view for admiring photos in greater detail, the ability to search photos by place, person, event and date, the creation of videos with expert narration and the ability to display notes and maps. These possibilities have attracted an increasing number of institutions. When the online exhibition tool was launched in 2012, it hosted 42 virtual exhibitions, including those curated by the Imperial War Museum in London, The Anne Frank House and the Smithsonian Institution.

---

[26] This is a benefit of the new open access-oriented policy. This type of sharing is widespread in all the main social networks, including Pinterest and Instagram in particular, where massive parts of the photographic collections of the main world museums are shared.

[27] The portal hosts more than 9,000 online collections produced by more than 1,500 partner institutions in 70 countries and approximately six million images, see: https://artsandculture.google.com/, last accessed June 10, 2019.

They wanted to tell the story of major historical events and enhance images that were disseminated on the Internet for the first time ever: "Each exhibition features a narrative which links the archive material together to unlock the different perspectives, nuances and tales behind these events."[28] (Fig. 6).

In 2018 it launched a new app that also makes this heritage available on the smartphone, with the slogan "Play with art using only your phone," and every image in the portal can be shared by users on their own social account. From a photographic point of view it has its own importance, because it allows access from a single portal to very important photographic archives, even private ones such as Getty image or the Alinari Archive.

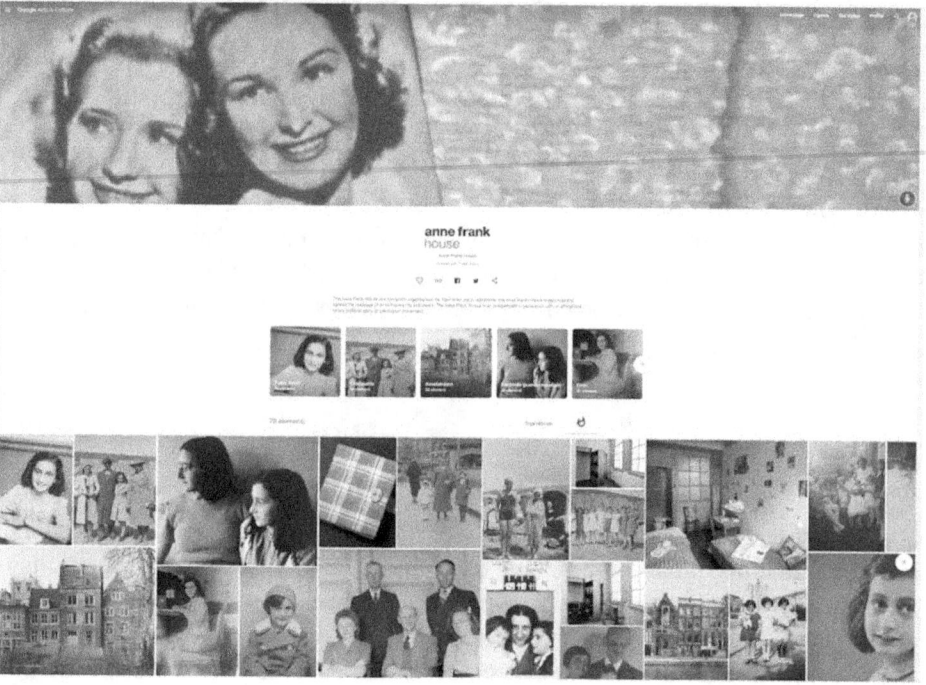

Fig. 6: Anne Frank House on Google Cultural Institute.

Naturally, we cannot forget the very strong role of the Google image search engine, which, even if it has elementary functions and a search system that produces very approximate results from a heuristic point of view it has, however, integrated a reverse search system and probably also plays an important practical role for many DPH searches.

---

28 Mark Yoshitake, "Bringing history to life," Google Official Blog, October 10, 2012, https://www.blog.google/outreach-initiatives/arts-culture/bringing-history-to-life/.

Conclusion

The picture we have drawn of the relationship between photography and DPH is very general, and moreover is concentrated geographically between the USA and Europe; while surely many very interesting uses of digital photography in a "public" dimension are located in several emerging countries, also for the purpose of consolidation or "invention" of a national identity.[29]

However, it can be seen that the drawing of the relationship between photography and DPH is in full swing, and that rapid technological changes have a very complex effect on the social uses of photography, difficult though they are to fully understand while they are happening. We hope that the picture we have drawn here may help increase understanding of how some recent development dynamics are moving along the axes of those different polarities that we indicated at the beginning (such as top-down, local-global or private-public) which are central to the field of DPH practices.

Bibliography

Assmann, Jan: *Cultural memory and early civilization: writing, remembrance, and political imagination*, Cambridge: Cambridge University Press, 2011.
Benoit, Edward and Alexandra Eveleigh, eds., *Participatory Archives*, London: Facet Publishing, 2019.
Caraffa, Costanza and Tiziana Serena, eds. *Photo Archives and the Idea of Nation*, Berlin: De Gruyter, 2015.
Gunthert, André, *L'Image Partagée. La photographie numérique*: Paris: Textuel, 2015.
Sayer, Faye, *Public History: A Practical Guide*, London: Bloomsbury, (2015) 2nd Edition 2019.

---

[29] Interesting case-studies in Costanza Caraffa and Tiziana Serena, ed. *Photo Archives and the Idea of Nation* (Berlin: De Gruyter, 2015).

Seth van Hooland and Mathias Coeckelbergs
Exploring Large-Scale Digital Archives – Opportunities and Limits to Use Unsupervised Machine Learning for the Extraction of Semantics

Abstract: The current excitement in regards to machine learning has spurred enthusiasm amongst collection holders and historians alike to rely on algorithms to reduce the amount of manual labor required for management and appraisal of large volumes of non-structured archival content. The Digital Humanities and commercial archival software promote out-of-the-box tools for auto-classification, but is the adoption of machine learning as straightforward as it is currently presented in both the popular press and the Digital Humanities literature? This chapter brings a sense of pragmatism to the debate by giving an overview of both possibilities and limits of machine learning to extract semantics from large collections of digitized textual archives. Two methods have gained substantial popularity: Topic Modeling (TM) and Word Embeddings (WE). This chapter introduces these non-supervised machine learning methods to the community of historians, based on an experimental case-study of digitized archival holdings of the European Commission (EC).

Keywords: machine learning, metadata, information extraction, big data, digital humanities, digital archives

Introduction

With the captivating slogan "Kill time, make history", the New York Public Library (NYPL) offers probably one of the best examples of how crowdsourcing initiatives have contributed to the creation of public history.[1] Through various projects, ranging from the transcription of nineteenth century menu cards ("What's on the menu") to the cross-referencing of U.S. Census data with old phone books ("Direct Me NYC: 1940"), the NYPL has demonstrated in recent years how end-users can participate in making digital collections available. Other individual institutions and large aggregators such as https://europeana.eu have set up similar crowdsourcing projects to leverage the visibility of large collections with little to no existing metadata. In parallel to contributing comments, correcting OCR errors or transcribing handwritten text,

---
[1] For an overview of their various projects, see https://www.nypl.org/collections/labs.

https://doi.org/10.1515/9783110430295-046

end-users often can also use these crowdsourcing platforms to create their own personal online collections, helping historians for example to gather and analyze primary source materials.

However, even if crowdsourcing holds significant value to make large-scale historical collections available, automated tools are needed to provide access paths to make sense of ever-increasing collections of digitized primary source materials. Libraries, archives, and museums have in this context been inspired by the seminal work "Graphs, maps and trees", in which Franco Moretti (Moretti 2007) demonstrates how computational methods can be used to analyze the totality of the literary production for a genre or an epoch. Moretti argues that the "close-reading" tradition from the Humanities, in which scholars read and interpret a small selection of canonized works, should be complemented with "distant viewing" methods, allowing the inidividual to process computationally all available works of a genre or time frame. The distant reading paradigm has resonated strongly with the Digital Humanities community. One good representative example is the "Mining the dispatch" project, which proposes a computational analysis of an archive of over 112 000 articles from the *Richmond* Daily Dispatch, covering the period 1860–1865.[2] Through the use of TM, for example, fugitive slave ads can be identified in an automated manner within the corpus. Once these results are obtained, historians can interpret sustained spikes in the number of fugitive slave ads by mapping them to the evolution of the Civil War. This example underlines how algorithms can assist historians – they can help to automatically create subsets of primary source material, which facilitates a particular research question. Without TM, gathering all relevant journal articles containing a fugitive slave ad would be close to impossible when merely using full-text indexing, due to the variation in phrasing and terms used.

The objective of this chapter is to provide a better understanding for historians on how machine learning tools operate. This raises the question what specific role historians are expected to play within these projects: passive consumers of the end-results produced by engineers who collaborate with archivists and librarians, or active users of these technologies within their own research practice. Depending on the context, both scenarios are possible. Large-scale research infrastructures such as Text Grid offer "off the shelf" methods which can be easily embedded by end-users within their day to day research practice.[3] In parallel, historians might want to export subsets of corpora to perform certain customized operations, which are not available in the standardized toolkit of a virtual research environment. Even if historians are considered to simply re-use the results of clustering and classification methods configured by librarians or archivists, they need a critical understanding of how these tools extract semantics from primary source materials.

---

2 For more information, see http://dsl.richmond.edu/dispatch/.
3 For more information, see https://textgrid.de.

If we believe media such as the *New York Times*, Artificial Intelligence (AI) and machine learning techniques have the potential to automate a wide range of societal challenges, ranging from the detection of cancer to self-driving cars.[4] Given enough content to analyze sufficient training sets for practice, algorithms can develop statistical models to replace decision-making ordinarily thought to require human intelligence or discernment. Digital Humanities scholars are currently applying statistics and machine learning to make sense of large volumes of non-structured text. In this context, historians and archivists can "function as a partner in the analytic process, providing information about data's location, and improving the visual analyst's understanding and trust of data through explaining their context of creation, the history of their structure and semantics and their chain of custody" (Lemieux 2014).

However, misunderstandings and false hope circulate among historians on how machine learning can be used. This chapter therefore provides a conceptual introduction to machine learning by focusing on two specific methods: Topic Modeling (TM) and Word Embedding (WE). Both approaches are extensively used within Digital Humanities projects for the analysis of large non-structured corpora.

Automating What and How?

Two different strands from computer science should be distinguished when automating the description and usage of large digital collections:
- **Rules**: This approach is based on an abstract model of the content and its application domain, on top of which decisions on content can be automated. For example, http://schema.org provides an ontology of how movies, music, or books can be described in a manner which is re-usable by computers.
- **Statistics**: This approach is based on statistics derived from the content itself, making use of either supervised or non-supervised machine learning techniques. For example, auto-classification tools categorize email as having business value or not. They make these decisions based on a training set prepared by an expert who has manually labeled which emails have business value and which don't.

Both approaches have their advantages and limitations. The rules-based approach is complex and expensive, as one needs to develop a complex model on top of which the rules can be built. The statistics-based approach requires less resources for the development of a model, but you often need training data, which are not always available.

---

[4] See articles such as https://www.nytimes.com/2016/10/17/technology/ibm-is-counting-on-its-bet-on-watson-and-paying-big-money-for-it.html.

Defining Rules: The Road from Artificial Intelligence to Rules Engines and Linked Data

Beginning in the 1960s, the artificial intelligence community developed methods to represent known facts and assertions, from which new knowledge can be inferred. Rules-based systems require the user to define rules, so that a software can infer what to do in a certain situation. In the 1980s, this strand of research culminated in the creation of the then-called expert systems. This type of software consisted of knowledge bases or ontologies containing a large amount of facts and statements that were connected through formal logic. The drawback of this approach was the lack of adaptability: the system can only function based on the information it has. This implies that these systems can only be operational within well-delimited specialized application domains, such as specific medical disciplines (epidemiology, virology, . . .) where expert systems could help to diagnose a disease based on a combination of symptoms. However, the cost of creating and maintaining the rules tended to be prohibitive.

The complexity of developing and applying ontologies on a large scale across application domains has been illustrated by the difficulties of implementing what Tim Berners-Lee promoted as the Semantic Web. The Semantic Web seeks to make information on the Web machine usable by formalizing the meaning of data published there. It does this by applying a conceptual data model – the Resource Description Framework (RDF), developed by the World Wide Web Consortium (W3C). Due to the complexity of implementing ontologies on a large scale, Berners-Lee reformulated in 2006 his vision for a more structured Web by rebranding the Semantic Web as Linked Data (van Hooland and Verborgh 2014).

As power users of libraries and archives, historians might have observed over recent years efforts by collections holders to make their collections and the metadata about them available in a more structured manner. The Library of Congress, for example, has invested considerable effort into the promotion of Bibframe, a format which should allow the conversion of Machine Readable Cataloging (MARC) files into Resource Description Framework (RDF) compatible metadata. Despite major efforts, there is still no international consensus within the library world on the feasibility of the endeavor, due to the complexity of maintaining data quality consistent across very large volumes of data represented in RDF. The difficulty of developing and applying ontologies is also reflected by the efforts made by the archival community to venture into the Linked Data territory. The International Council of Archives (ICA) has initiated the Records in Context (RiC) project, which aims at packaging into one global ontology the semantics of pre-existing ICA standards such as ISAD(G) and ISAAR(CDF). The W3C's initiative under the name Architypes offers another approach. The project tries to re-use existing mark-up from Schema. org and keep the development of new definitions limited to a strict minimum.

Relying on Statistics: Machine Learning

In parallel to these developments, we have seen a dramatic increase in the volume of data collected and therefore also unprecedented volumes of primary source material for historians to analyze. This shift in the landscape has made the rules-based methods that thrived in approaches to AI in the twentieth century outdated at best and often obsolete. In the context of the surge of big data, Guruswamy has designated rules-based approaches as "dinosaurs in the big data world".[5] Hence, a shift from knowledge-driven methods to data-driven methods has been seen, which means that traditional rules are in general left behind. This has opened new space for the use of statistical systems to try and find structure in the wealth of information available today. The tremendous advantage of statistical approaches of machine learning is that there is no need to develop an a priori model of an application domain, which is then used to apply the rules.

When introducing machine learning algorithms, an important distinction has to be made between so-called supervised and unsupervised methods. This analogy to child-rearing is misleading because it implies that you first develop methods for supervising children before children cope with the world using unsupervised methods. In machine learning, it is not the case that supervised methods would precede unsupervised methods. It is difficult to state where exactly machine learning practices first developed, but many attribute it to the theories of Hebb (Cooper 2005). In his book *Organization of Behavior*, originally published in 1949, Hebb explained the adaptation of neurons in the brain during a learning process as an unsupervised process, stating that "cells that fire together wire together." This directly puts emphasis on one of the main characteristics of unsupervised methods, namely their bottom-up generation of results, whereby it is a priori not known which form the results will take. For supervised methods, by contrast, we must first give correct examples as training input, thereby determining the structure of the output in the number of categories we assign the input data to. Thus, one of the most important tasks of supervised learning is to classify data into a priori designed categories. By contrast, unsupervised methods cluster data together without knowing in advance what these clusters might be or what they might represent. This makes unsupervised methods suitable to deal with large amounts of unknown data, allowing it to assist in tasks such as information retrieval or summarization. Topic modeling is one of the most prevalently used examples of unsupervised approaches to the use of algorithms for textual data. At the same time, since no "correct examples" are given to an unsupervised learning algorithm, the evaluation of the results can be quite difficult.

---

5 See http://bigdata.teradata.com/US/Articles-News/Data-Science–Machine-Learning-Vs–Rules-Based-Systems/.

Over the last few years, the library and archives communities have almost exclusively experimented with supervised machine learning methods. Big software vendors, such as OpenText, offer auto-classification tools allowing archivists to put documents into predesigned categories. The software offers easy-to-use interfaces allowing archivists to select a test corpus, perform the manual classification of documents into a limited number of categories, and then to check the quality of the auto-classification based on sampling. However, software developers typically provide neither benchmarking studies nor clear methods to assess the quality of their tools in an objective manner.

Given that the application of supervised machine learning is not as straightforward as many believe, and is so labor intensive, we must explore other methods, including those of unsupervised machine learning. These methods – in particular Topic Modeling (TM) and Word Embeddings (WE) – offer promising paths forward. TM clusters a determined number of keywords extracted from a document collection together into so-called topics. An example of a topic (topic 33 from our results) based on the archival holdings of the EC, which we will present in a moment, is the following cluster of ten terms:

---

gas fuel energy electricity coal power nuclear supply industry production

---

Upon reading the cluster of terms, we understand that the subset of documents from our corpus with this topic probably addressed how the EC dealt with the usage and supply of energetic resources.

This example points to both the power of and problematic aspects of TM – namely the interpretation of the topics. As Chang et al. (2009) have indicated, it is difficult to present objective standards to monitor which interpretations of the topic model are valid and which are not. The interpretational difficulty arises from the fact that it is psychologically attractive for humans to give a meaningful interpretation to a list of words they are presented. This results from an interpretational difficulty inherent in topic models – namely that we would like to find that they represent concepts hidden within the text. Although we know that the clusters of keywords are merely a representation of their occurrence within the document collection, we expect them to correspond to clear-cut concepts. This is due to the distributional hypothesis within the field of linguistic semantics, which states that the meaning of a word is determined by the company it keeps. Expressed differently, this hypothesis understands words which occur in the same documents to have a semantic relatedness. In practice, topics are often difficult to interpret as they cannot be mapped easily to one single concept, but rather are usually a combination of two or more concepts. In the example provided above, seven terms immediately refer to the concept of energy (gas, fuel, energy, electricity, coal, power, and nuclear) and three terms to the concept of industrial production (supply, industry, and production).

In contrast to the topic models, which allow us to understand how documents are related between one another based on identified topics, WE are used to understand how words are related to one another semantically. The term was made popular by the seminal paper of Mikolov et al. (2013) in which they describe Word2Vec, an online, freely available toolkit to either train WE on a corpus, or to use their pretrained word vectors based on the Google Press corpus. Through a statistical analysis of a massive corpus, one can determine for example that the terms London and England have the same relation to one another as for example Paris and France. The algorithm is agnostic of the semantics of the relationship, but allows an individual to monitor how these terms interact with one another in vector space, allowing them to extract semantic relations like the aforementioned "is capital of". Due to the vectorial representation of these words, we can answer questions such as "what is the capital of France?" by simply starting with the vector for "London," subtracting the vector for "England," and adding the vector for "France". The corresponding vector should lie closest to "Paris," hence answering our question correctly. Examples from an experimental case study will now demonstrate how an original method has been designed to apply WE to the results of TM.

Experimental Case-Study: Archives of the European Commission (EC)

The mass digitization of the EC's archives offers in this context new exciting possibilities to query and analyze an archival corpus in an automated manner. Currently, researchers can only perform full-text queries in order to make sense of this massive corpus, as illustrated in Fig. 1. In the context of a research collaboration, the authors received a local copy of the corpus from the EC archives, allowing us to process and apply various machine learning methods.[6]

Specifically, the case study used a combination of topic modeling and word embeddings to explore research questions related to policy development within the EC Archives: When and how did environmental considerations start to influence the agricultural policy development from the European Commission (EC)?; What are the key documents to analyze the debate on nuclear energy production from the

---

[6] The dataset has been created following the Council Regulation (EEC, Euratom) No. 354/83 of February 1, 1983 concerning the opening to the public of the historical archives of the European Economic Community and the European Atomic Energy Community. The legal text and all its amendments are available at http://eur-lex.europa.eu/legal-content/EN/TXT/?qid=1475395564392 \&uri=CELEX\:31983R0354. After the signature of a Non-Disclosure Agreement (NDA), the MaSTIC research group of the Université libre de Bruxelles obtained a 138.3-GB, 24,787-document corpus from the European Commission Archives.

1960s onwards? These are two examples of typical research questions historians might have in mind with regards to the archival holdings of the EC.

Fig. 1: Search interface of the COM files of the EC archives, available at http://ec.europa.eu/historical_archives/archisplus/.

The research team accessed a dataset spanning a period ranging from 1958 to 1982. The dataset is multilingual: it contains documents in French, Dutch, German, Italian, Danish, English, and Greek, as those were the then official languages of the now-called European Union. For this experimental case study, only the English corpus was taken into account, which represents a total number of 11 868 documents. In the context of the first exploratory study, Latent Dirichlet Allocation (LDA), which is the most popular TM algorithm, was applied on the corpus. As was already mentioned, the dataset presents close to no metadata: apart from an XML file corresponding to each PDF and containing basic information such as a unique identifier, a creation date, the number of a reference volume and the language and title of the document, little additional information is given. There is no insight as to what the documents encompass in terms of topics and themes, which makes the dataset difficult to use for historians. In the context of this first exploratory study, the authors manually interpreted the topics, in order to attach a descriptor from the EUROVOC thesaurus. Fig. 2 gives three examples from topics and the EUROVOC descriptors which were manually attached to the topics.

URI	label	tokens			
http://eurovoc.europa.eu/2965	agricultural aid	agricultural premium farms	areas directive production	aid number	measures eec
http://eurovoc.europa.eu/852	ECSC aid	coal industry measures	steel production community	ecsc iron	aid decision
http://eurovoc.europa.eu/1418	textile industry	fabrics crocheted products	textile fibres yarn	woven community	knitted agreement

Fig. 2: Manual labeling of TM results with Eurovoc.

It is important to underline that the authors within this first exploratory study were unable to attach a label to around thirty percent of the topics, due to either the very general nature of the terms (e.g. *agreement community parties negotiations*) or the fact that the authors were unable to find a semantic link between the terms (e.g. *lights bmw brazil eec coffee*). For some topics, OCR noise resulting in terms such as *cf, ii,* or *ir* was the main cause.

The manual labeling of topics with descriptors from the EUROVOC thesaurus was, of course, suboptimal. One of the key problems is the interpretation of the clusters of terms that form a topic. Throughout the examples, one can sense that in the majority of cases, topics do not point to one clear concept, but often are a combination of concepts. This aspect makes the manual labeling process inherently subjective and troublesome. Ideally, one would also want to perform an automated reconciliation process, as described in van Hooland et al. (2013). Unfortunately, the semantic heterogeneity of topics also constitutes a stumbling block for this process, as there is no way to indicate within the reconciliation process how the different concepts within a topic should be tackled separately.

The research team turned to WE, seeking a way to leverage the outcomes of the topic model. The state-of-the-art recommended that TM can be viewed as a method to learn more about the topics addressed in a large corpus of documents, whereas (pre-trained) WE can be seen as a general, vectorial representation of language itself, allowing one to understand the distance between words. In the context of his doctoral research, one of the authors designed an original methodology which brings together both sources of information.[7] As WE allow one to produce vectorial

---

[7] Mathias Coeckelbergs is currently preparing an in-depth paper to present the usage of WE to interpret the results of TM.

representations of language as a whole, this then allows the individual to estimate the semantic relatedness of terms found in the same topic. In other words, we sought to automate the identification of different concepts present in one topic.

The research team discovered that two situations are present when applying WE embeddings to the results of TM, which are dealt with in the following section. The results described below illustrate that some topics are used to mark a single concept and topics as concepts, whereas others – by far the largest amount of topics – were used to indicate a collocation of two or more concepts. As a result, the chapter will refer to these topics as collocations.

The results were intriguing. LDA was applied on the English-based subcorpus, as described above. The full results can be analyzed on Github.[8] Within the dataset, three different color codes are used, which help to understand the following different outcomes of WE on the TM results:

- Terms in orange indicate a topic which represents one single concept
- Blue and red are used to indicate the first and the second concept in a topic consisting of two different concepts
- Terms in light blue do not indicate a clear link with the terms from the topic which surround them

Examples of these results can be visualized on https://github.com/MathiasCoeckelbergs/Concepts-within-Topics. Using the vectorial representations of the terms within a topic, we discover that some topics indicate a general concept, represented by terms displayed in orange. A good example can be found in topic 17, indicating territorial authority. Since within our corpus the authority of several structures of living are discussed, we discover them as terms in our topic, showing semantic relatedness, namely "community," "territory," "national," "country," "state," and "states". On the other hand, the different ways in which their authority can be discussed are found in the words scoring highest in the semantic coherence hierarchy, namely "authority," "legal," "rights," "authority," "undertakings," "directive," "provisions," "rules," and "law". We remark in passing that the words "authorities" and "authority" are not ranked next to each other, which we would expect for words having the same lexeme. However, in this case it is clear that both words have a vastly different usage, given that "authority" indicates the power of judgment and acting a person or instance possesses, whereas "authorities" can refer to this power but also to the instances of authority themselves, such as the police department or the jurisprudential body.

---

8 https://github.com/MathiasCoeckelbergs/Concepts-within-Topics. More information and in-depth discussion can be found in: Coeckelbergs, M., van Hooland, S. "Concepts in Topics. Using Word Embeddings to Leverage the Outcomes of Topic Modeling for the Exploration of Digitized Archival Collections." Proceedings of the EAI International Conference on Data and Information in Online Environments, 2020, 41–52.

In some cases, we see that the semantic coherence of terms is attested, but it does not pinpoint a clear concept. For example, in topic 31, the WE cluster together all ten terms, which are "vocational," "labor," "education," "employment," "health," "social," "migrant," "worker," "work," and "working". One can assume that the topic relates to social security of migrant workers, but the documents clustered under this topic might also relate more to the impact of education on employment of migrant workers, for example.

This analysis brings us to the possibility where a topic is the collocation of two concepts, the first represented in blue and the second in red. This situation is far more common than topics representing only one concept, depicted in orange. These collocations indicate that an important relationship between those two concepts exists, since they are prevalent throughout the document collection. Some clear examples of these collocations are found in the data. For example, topic 30 brings together two concepts, namely those of industry and studies. Hence, documents which have a high score for this topic can be attributed a high probability of dealing with industry studies, assessing the progress of markets and work. Our methodology clusters together industry-related terms "project," "development," "market," "industry," "industrial," and "system", and secondly study-related terms "study," "survey," "data," and "statistic". The concept of industry can be found multiple times within the topics. For example, next to topic 30 which we have now explained, in topic 33, we find the terms "industry," "supply," and "production," constituting the industry concept, which is collocated with the resources concept, expressed through the words "gas," "fuel," "energy," "electricity," "coal," "power," and "nuclear".

However, WE do not always manage to group together terms from a topic into one concept. This is, for example, the case with topic 27. There are two distinct concepts, the first one consisting of "price," "market," and "product"; and the second one of "milk," "sugar," and "wine". Four terms are then displayed in light blue, indicating terms which do not have a clear link with the terms from the topic which surround them: "production," "quality," "variety," and "marketing".

Based on the examples analyzed, there are clearly cases where WE deliver significant added value to the interpretation of the outcomes from TM. By doing so, historians can have access to subsets of documents which relate to their specific research questions. If one is interested in the evolution of the agricultural policy of the EU for example, running the above described methods can significantly help to aggregate individual documents spread out across this enormous corpus.

Conclusions and Future Work

With the help of an experimental case study, this chapter has provided an introduction, in particular, to the extraction of semantics from large-scale digitized archival holdings and the usage of unsupervised machine learning techniques. With the exponential growth of digitized primary source materials, historians need additional tools when facing digitized text collections which have insufficient metadata. The current enthusiasm with regards to machine learning to automatically extract semantics is justified. Non-supervised methods, such as TM and WE, offer tantalizing alternatives in the absence of traditional manually created metadata to make sense of corpora through the identification of statistically relevant terms. A real-world case study based on digitized archival holdings of the EC suggests reasons for enthusiasm. However, this chapter also identifies challenges historians should be aware of. Regardless of whether technically savvy historians implement these technologies on their own specific corpora or whether they "passively" consume the results of algorithms implemented by collection holders, scholars and end-users should have a basic understanding of how machine learning operates and at which steps their input is needed.

As already outlined in the existing literature from the domain of computational linguistics, the interpretation of the results of TM is complex and requires a manual analysis of how the various terms reflect a topic present in a large corpus. In addition, the configuration of the k-parameter, the number of terms per topic, and the terms included as stop words all have a big impact on the results. The currently available scientific literature does not offer a clear examination of how these parameters affect the results, which underscores the "black box" character of the usage of these methods. However, there are also enough reasons for archivists to keep a close eye on machine learning methods. By using WE, the complexity of interpreting the outcome of TM can be simplified, as WE can help to automatically identify the different concepts hiding within one topic. This method holds the potential to facilitate at a later stage the automated labeling of topics with headings from a controlled vocabulary. Also, importantly, the method is language independent and can be applied across a wide variety of application domains.

All in all, this chapter underlines the semi-automated nature of applying machine learning techniques. At crucial stages of the process, historians with an already solid understanding of the context of the corpus must help to make strategic decisions when configuring the algorithms. We can therefore conclude that historians need to be actively involved in the usage and uptake of unsupervised machine learning methods.

Bibliography

Coeckelbergs, M., S. van Hooland. "Concepts in Topics. Using Word Embeddings to Leverage the Outcomes of Topic Modeling for the Exploration of Digitized Archival Collections." Proceedings of the EAI International Conference on Data and Information in Online Environments, 2020, 41–52.
Chang, J., S. Gerrish, C. Wang, J. L. Boyd-Graber, and D. M. Blei. "Reading Tea Leaves: How Humans Interpret Topic Models." *Advances in Neural Information Processing Systems*, edited by M. Jordan, Y. LeCun, and S. Solla, 288–296. Cambridge: MIT, 2009.

Cooper, S.J. "Donald O. Hebb's Synapse and Learning Rule: A History and Commentary." Neurosciene and Biobehavioral Reviews 28, no. 8 (2005), 851–874.
Lemieux, L., V. Brianna Gormly, and L. Rowledge. "Meeting Big Data Challenges with Visual Analytics: The Role of Records Management." *Records Management Journal* 24, no. 2 (2014): 122–141.
Mikolov, T., W. T. Yih, and G. Zweig. "Linguistic Regularities in Continuous Space Word Representations." *HLT-NAACL* 13 (2013): 746–751.
Moretti, F. Graphs, Maps, Trees. Abstract Models for Literary History. New York NY, Verso Books, 2007.
van Hooland, S., and R. Verborgh. *Linked Data for Libraries, Archives and Museums. How to Clean, Link and Publish your Metadata*. London: Facet, 2014.
van Hooland, S., R. Verborgh, M. De Wilde, and J. Hercher. "Evaluating the Success of Vocabulary Reconciliation for Cultural Heritage Collections." *Journal of the American Society for Information Science and Technology* 64, no. 3 (2013): 464–479.

Federica Signoriello
Infographics and Public History

Abstract: This chapter focuses on the role of infographics in public history. In the last few years, infographics have become increasingly popular both on- and offline. My aim is thus to identify best practices in order to bridge the gap between academic research and the wider public. The chapter is therefore divided into four main sections. It starts by asking what infographics are and how can we distinguish data visualisation from infographics. The next section discusses public history and infographics, identifying the main uses of infographics in the discipline. The chapter then focuses on which steps to take in order to compose an infographic for the purpose of communicating historical research to the public, including orientation, content, and software and online resources, before drawing some conclusions in the final section.

Keywords: infographics, public history, graphic design

Even though the term "infographic," the union of the words "information" and "graphic," first appeared in 1969,[1] it has only become common relatively recently. Several kinds of graphic design labelled "infographics" have found their way and are enjoying increasing popularity both on and offline, especially in newspapers and magazines, in various forms, ranging "from tasteless chart junk to interactive forms of civic engagement."[2] While the need to disseminate the outcomes and outputs of academic research via visually engaging and appealing means is pressing, infographics are only one of the latest trends in this sort of communication. Like other disciplines, public history is no exception. This is why now that more and more infographics are being used to bridge the gap between academic research and the wider public, it is worth shedding light on the best practices. This chapter will first define the concept of infographics against that of data visualization, moving then into the relevance of infographics in public history with a few examples of their use in this field. Finally, it will deal with the main practicalities of composing infographics, from their layout to some useful resources.

---

[1] "Definition of Infographics," *Merriam Webster*, 2019, https://www.merriam-webster.com/dictionary/infographics.
[2] Murray Dick, "Infographics and Data Visualization," in *The International Encyclopedia of Journalism Studies* (American Cancer Society, 2019), 1–7.

What Infographics Are

In a way, infographics have been part of human life for a very long time, as drawing symbolic pictures to represent reality has always been a way to communicate information. Hieroglyphs, frescoes and maps guided men through the millennia,[3] for the simple reason that vision overcomes all the other senses when it comes to learning.[4] The studies on learning styles have confirmed this tendency, that is especially true for those people identified as visual learners, who "like information to arrive in the form of graphs, charts, and flow diagrams," and "draw maps of their learning sequences or create patterns of information," working easily with symbols.[5]

It is only in 1982 that information design took a turn with the self-published book *Visual Design* (*The Visual Display of Quantitative Information* in its second edition),[6] which first set the standards for statistical graphics, charts and tables. The development of office-oriented software and, later, of data visualization tools, led to a greater employment of visual designs.[7] The word "infographic," however, is incorrectly used to encompass many representations that fall under other categories, mainly into data visualizations. Unlike those who argue that "there is no threshold at which something becomes an infographic,"[8] in this chapter we maintain that "a genre of visuals appears to be clearly recognised as infographics."[9] It is therefore appropriate to extrapolate an accurate definition of infographics against that of data visualization, which is explored in another section of this handbook.

On the one hand, data visualization is "the art and science" of communicating information through visual presentations that "may take the form of traditional charts and tables or may include new, interactive visualisations created by software."[10]

---

[3] Clive Thompson, "The Surprising History of the Infographic," *Smithsonian*, accessed 25 February 2019, https://www.smithsonianmag.com/history/surprising-history-infographic-180959563/.
[4] John Medina, *Brain Rules: 12 Principles for Surviving and Thriving at Work, Home, and School* (Seattle: Pear Press, 2010), 233.
[5] Neil Fleming, "I'm Different; Not Dumb. Modes of Presentation (VARK) in the Tertiary Classroom," in *Research and Development in Higher Education*, ed. A. Zelmer, vol. 18 (1995 Annual Conference of the Higher Education and Research Development Society of Australasia (HERDSA), HERDSA, 1995), 308–313.
[6] Edward R. Tufte, *The Visual Display of Quantitative Information*, 2nd edition (Cheshire, Conn: Graphics Press, 2001).
[7] Yuvaraj, "Infographics," 6–9.
[8] Lankow, Ritchie, and Crooks, *Infographics*, 20.
[9] Dunlap and Lowenthal, "Getting Graphic about Infographics," 42–59.
[10] Sue and Griffin, *Data Visualization & Presentation with Microsoft Office* (Thousand Oaks: SAGE Publications, Inc, 2016), http://methods.sagepub.com/book/data-visualization-and-presentation-with-microsoft-office.

A simple example of interactive data visualization is that of Fig. 1, *Life Chart* by the Digital Panopticon Project.[11]

As well as giving an overall idea of the stories of the lives of 1,526 convicts born in 1800 and tried at the Old Bailey courthouse, every line in this life chart in the Digital Panopticon project website is clickable and leads to the complete life story of the corresponding person and its sources. The chart itself, however, does not provide any context or any interpretation of the data, and these reflections are left to the reader.

On the other hand, an infographic may include elements of data visualization, but its purposes are different. As an object constructed to deliver abstract, complex and dense messages, an infographic "reveals the hidden, explains the complex and illuminates the obscure through illustrations, some short written explanations and data visualisation."[12] Hence, what makes infographics stand out is the presence of a narrative. According to Krum, "a good infographic is about storytelling by combining data visualisation design and graphic design."[13] Its layout should be divided into three main parts:
1. An introduction that presents the topic to the audience
2. A key message that contains something new, i.e. a previously unknown piece of information
3. A conclusion, which might even be a call-to-action.

The *National African American History Month* infographic Fig. 2 is a good example of this structure,[14] as it displays a brief explanation of the information presented below, a main body made of pictures, dates and names that exemplify the contribution of African Americans in the US Navy following a chronological order, and a conclusion reiterating how important their presence is for the Navy in the present day.

On the same website, that of the Naval History and Heritage Command, the *Pearl Harbor* infographic provides a good example of a call to action, as it invites the reader to learn more about the impact of the attack on Pearl Harbor by watching a linked YouTube video.[15]

---

[11] "The Digital Panopticon Search Builder; Results", *The Digital Panopticon Project*, 2018, https://www.digitalpanopticon.org/search?e0.type.t.t=root&e1.type.t.t=tried&e0.born.y.l=1800&e0.born.y.h=1800&e1.offence_category.to.x=&tf-scatter-color=offence&tf-scatter-major=major&targ=scatter.
[12] Yuvaraj, "Infographics."
[13] Krum, *Cool Infographics*, 27.
[14] "The National African American History Month Infographic," *Naval History and Heritage Command*, 2019, https://www.history.navy.mil/news-and-events/multimedia-gallery/infographics/history/african-american-naval-history-.html.
[15] "Pearl Harbor Infographic," *Naval History and Heritage Command*, accessed July 4, 2019, https://www.history.navy.mil/news-and-events/multimedia-gallery/infographics/history/pearl-harbor-infographic.html.

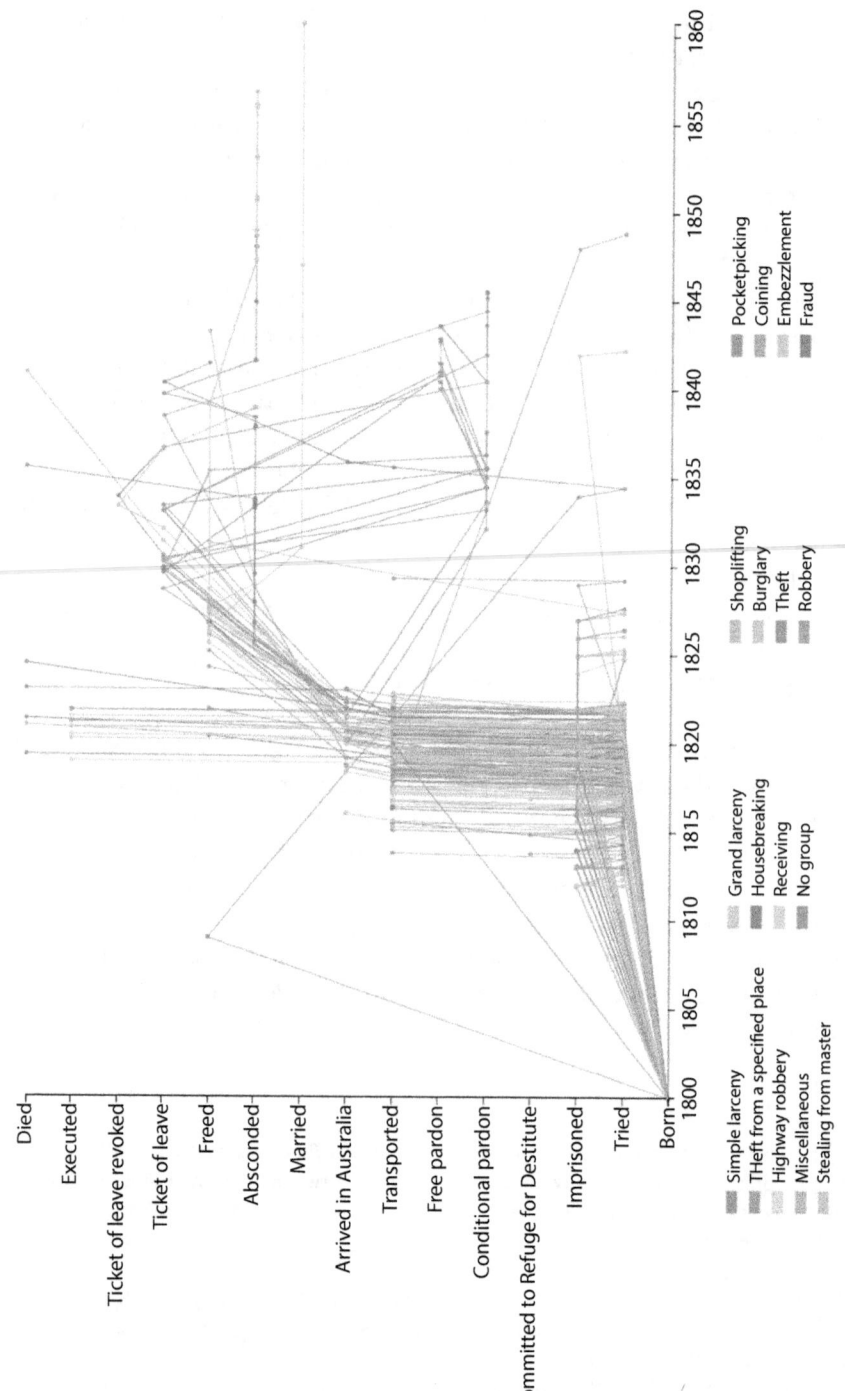

Fig. 1: The Digital Panopticon Search Builder (consulted 6th September 2021). Copyright owned by the Universities of Liverpool, Sheffield, Oxford and Sussex, reproduced with the kind permission of Prof. Robert Shoemaker.

Fig. 2: African Americans in Naval history. U.S. Navy, graphic by Annalisa Underwood. Creative Commons licence Attribution 4.0 International (CC BY 4.0).

Media formats of infographics are classified by Krum according to their level of complexity:[16] static infographics are the simplest and most common (JPG, PNG, GIF files), designed to be printed or viewed on a webpage; the other kinds of infographics build upon this simple design and provide, usually via a web browser, different levels of interaction: they can be zooming, clickable, animated (also called gifographics), video,[17] and interactive.[18] Krum classifies infographics also according to their content: informative, persuasive, visual explanations, infographic advertisements, press release infographics and infographic posters for sale.[19]

Public History and Infographics

The definition of public history comes with a recognition of the significance of the audience. Public historians, therefore, choose ways of communicating to suit their audiences,[20] and benefit from the development of digital technology, which offers a considerable variety of new tools for dissemination to non-academic audiences.[21] It has been noted how opening up to the public is a feature of digital history, of which history professionals should take advantage.[22] The potential of infographics – as defined in the paragraph above – is therefore particularly significant in digital public history. Their added value, i.e. the possibility to convey a narrative within their forming elements, definitely holds the power of "communicating, describing, interpreting and showing local historical experiences."[23]

As Cairo maintains, the goal of information architecture, of which infographics are part, is to make reality visible, so that information can be navigated effortlessly and used effectively.[24] This goal is achieved when large graphics are printed on panels, or when interactive timelines, enriched by videos and texts, are displayed in museums to help the visitor making connections between the objects displayed

---

16 Krum, *Cool Infographics*, 31–51.
17 See for example *The Infographic History of the World*, 2013, https://youtu.be/GZk0H9nHdlE.
18 See for example Curtis Harris, "Kennedy – A Data Biography of the 35th President of the United States," *Tableau Public*, June 24, 2016, https://public.tableau.com/en-us/s/gallery/kennedy-data-biography-35th-president-united-states.
19 Krum, *Cool Infographics*, 69–91.
20 David Dean, "Introduction," in *A Companion to Public History*, ed. David Dean (Chichester, UK: John Wiley & Sons, Ltd, 2018), 1–11, 3.
21 Serge Noiret, "Digital Public History," in *A Companion to Public History*, ed. David Dean (Chichester, UK: John Wiley & Sons, Ltd, 2018), 111–124, 120–121.
22 Tim Hitchcock and Robert Shoemaker, "Making History Online," *Transactions of the Royal Historical Society* 25 (December 2015): 75–93.
23 Noiret, "Digital Public History."
24 Cairo, *The Functional Art*, 19–20.

and a broader historical context. Infographics, nevertheless, have seeped deeper into public history.

A pointed example is provided by the large use of infographics by Colombian media, government and non-governmental organisations, academia and citizen groups to publicize the process and scope of the peace agreements with the Revolutionary Armed Forces of Colombia (FARC) in 2016. One of the aims of these designs was that of raising awareness of the country's recent history, the civil war and its complexities, despite the fact that population was not the target audience of the final peace agreement. This graphic content reached a wide public, eased the understanding of dense subjects and highlighted the potential of infographics and their educational value.[25]

The great adaptability of infographics is being used in the field of education. The experience told by McCracken, teaching Canadian history at the Shingwauk Residential Schools Centre, is revealing.[26] In the classroom, infographics may be projected in Microsoft PowerPoint presentations or may be printed, and their role is that of communicating the main facts and drawing connections between data and events, whilst the teacher provides context and nuances.[27] Asking students to create infographics also trains their ability to summarize content, it stimulates their creativity,[28] and, most importantly, their skills in visual literacy, i.e. "the ability to interpret and create visual messages for learning and performance."[29]

Finally, online channels such as blogs and social media have become popular means for research dissemination with varied kinds of public. Blogs such as Versus History publish informal blogposts, podcasts, quizzes, lists of curious facts and infographics as ways to explain the unfolding of historical events.[30] If a single social media is to be singled out, that would be Pinterest.com by virtue of its functionality. On Pinterest, users visually share and discover new interests by "pinning" images to their own or others' virtual boards and browsing what other users have pinned. This platform, therefore, hosts many thematic boards of infographics and history infographics, especially on military history. The advantage of browsing Pinterest is

---

[25] Marín Ochoa, "Treatment of Post-Conflict Colombia through Infographics and Data Visualisation," *Revista Latina de Comunicaciòn Social* 73 (April 6, 2018): 700–717.
[26] In her blogpost, Krista McCracken explains how, together with her colleagues, she used infographics to update handouts, brochures and educational material at the Shingwauk Residential Schools Centre (Canada), following other history teachers who employed infographics as educational tools in the same country.
[27] "Using Infographics to Teach about Canadian History," *Active History*, 18 March 2019, http://activehistory.ca/2019/03/using-infographics-to-teach-about-canadian-history/.
[28] Charee M. Thompson, "Creating 'Visual Legacies': Infographics as a Means of Interpreting and Sharing Research," *Communication Teacher* 29.2 (April 3, 2015): 91–101.
[29] Dunlap and Lowenthal, "Getting Graphic about Infographics," 42–59.
[30] "Versus History – Versus History Blog," *Versus History*, 2019, http://www.versushistory.com/versus-history-blog.

that the author or the original hosting website of an infographic can be easily traced, hence revealing more specific sources.

Composing Infographics

The public historians should carefully consider how to devise and organize the content of their infographics according to their audience, whether they create them by using a free online tool or whether they commission a professional graphic designer. We discuss below three main aspects of composing a history infographic: orientation, content and resources.

Orientation

The first choice to make when preparing an infographic is its orientation. Vertical designs are indicated to be uploaded on webpages, as they can easily be read from the top to the bottom by scrolling, as in Fig. 3, *World War I, 1914–1918*.[31] Horizontal layouts are suited for print or full screen presentations and develop their narrative from the left to the right, for example in the design by Alberto Cairo, *À Espera da Santidade*, published by the Brazilian newspaper *Época*,[32] but also available online.[33]

Content

The organization of content should follow a clear pattern. The following categories of content organization reflect the kind of information represented and may be combined together.[34] The most common component in a history infographic is the timeline. An infographic developing a timeline is suited for unfolding a sequence of events such as a chronology or a biography, and the layout can vary from a centred line with dates to its left and right, to dates aligned to the left and

---

[31] Potashova, Laykova, Mizinov, and Denis, Z. (2014). World War I, 1914–1918. https://www.behance.net/gallery/18865975/World-War-I.
[32] Cairo, *The Functional Art*, 158.
[33] Casadei, "Infografia Revista Época | Café Expresso," 2010, https://jcasadei.wordpress.com/tag/infografia-revista-epoca/.
[34] Thompson, "Creating 'Visual Legacies': Infographics as a Means of Interpreting and Sharing Research," *Communication Teacher* 29.2 (3 April 2015): 91–101.

longer descriptions to the right, or to a more challenging zig-zagged or curved line that looks like a roadmap (Fig. 2).[35]

Mixed charts/data visualisation are suitable when quantitative data are the main kind of information displayed. Different charts and graphs may be combined to convey a message. Qualitative data may be represented in easier and more effective ways than charts, for example by an image replicated in different colours – for instance the military casualties in Fig. 3.

Two attractive and telling designs are comparisons and maps. In a comparison design, the area is usually divided vertically and symmetrically to highlight the differences between two people, ideas or events. Maps are convenient to compare data across cities, regions and states.

When combining these elements with text and images, the different areas should be clearly marked, and empty space is essential to improve readability between the different sections and between charts, text and images. A blogpost by See Mei Chow illustrates some simple combinations of these components in vertical layouts.[36]

Fig. 3 exemplifies an infographic which, even if dense and compact, displays several sections marked by subtitles. In Fig. 4 we highlighted its layout, its sections and the underlying narrative becomes evident. The contrast between the maps at the top and at the bottom stresses the changes between states and boundaries before and after World War I. The timeline is divided into numbered subsections marking the role of the six main countries involved before and after the war, the events themselves and a clear break happening with the assassination of Franz Ferdinand. Moreover, the data visualisation and chart between the timeline and the final map are set up as comparisons between the loss and gains of the Triple Alliance and the Entente.

What to Use: Software and Online Resources

For those public historians capable of using software for graphic design it is worth paying for subscriptions, for instance, to the Adobe Creative Cloud in order make the most of Adobe Illustrator and Adobe InDesign. Most software packages which include presentation tools offer solutions for the less-skilled designer, especially when they can integrate charts made by data stored in spreadsheets. Open-source

---

[35] "Infographic Layout: How to Portray History Using Timelines," *Piktochart*, September 28, 2015, https://piktochart.com/blog/layout-5-portraying-history-with-timelines/.
[36] See Mei Chow, "Layout Cheat Sheet for Infographics: Visual Arrangement Tips," *Infographic Blog | Data Visualization Blog | Piktochart*, accessed July 11, 2019, https://piktochart.com/blog/layout-cheat-sheet-making-the-best-out-of-visual-arrangement/.

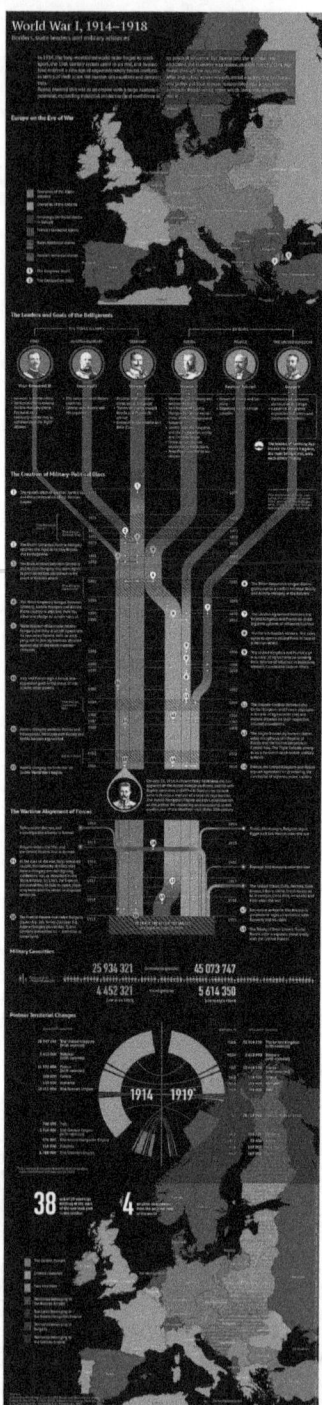

Fig. 3: World War I. Infographics for Russia Today. Editors: Masha Potashova, Yana Laykova. Design: Anton Mizinov, Denis Zaporozhan. Licensed by Creative Commons by attribution-NonCommercial 4.0 International (CC BY-NC 4.0).

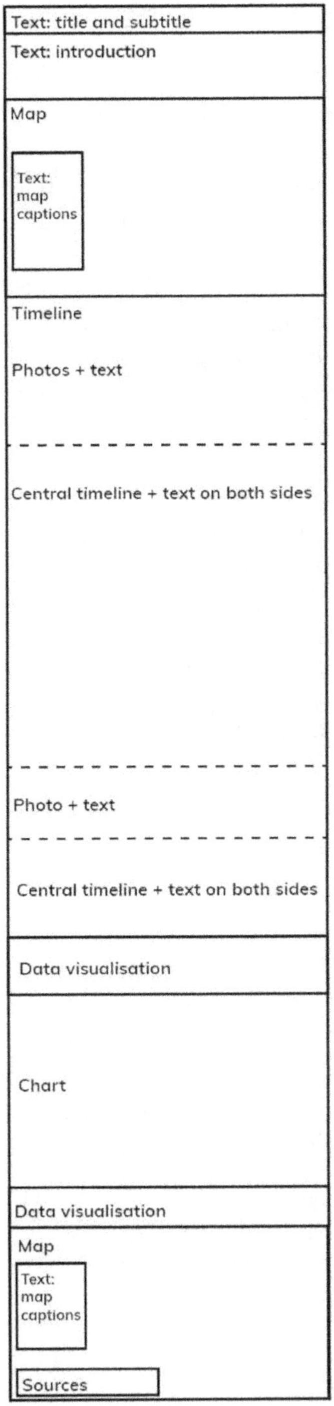

Fig. 4: Layout of the infographic World War I (figure 3), by Federica Signoriello. Creative Commons licence Attribution 4.0 International (CC BY 4.0).

software like Inkscape is also at hand to create ad hoc vector graphics for customised infographics.

One of the reasons why the use of infographics has increased is the presence of free or relatively inexpensive tools online allowing anyone to arrange content into virtual canvases. The lists provided here are destined to be outdated soon and therefore the general advice is to be proactive in periodically scouting the web for new resources. The most comprehensive list of tools is currently that by Krum on his website *Cool infographics*.[37]

Online infographics design tools such as Canva,[38] Infogram,[39] and Piktochart[40] offer, often with the option of keeping a free and basic account, infographics templates plus vector graphic elements and data visualization tools to populate them. Fig. 5, *Occupation of the Ruhr Valley*,[41] represents a good history infographic from the Versus History blog made with Canva. Simple video-infographics can be created with Animaker,[42] and Biteable.[43]

Free JavaScript charting libraries for interactive and clickable infographics, are found on Google Charts,[44] Timeline JS,[45] and Shanti Interactive.[46] Photo, image and illustration databases are numerous on the web. Incorporating these elements in an infographic means necessarily having the permission to do so, and often it is easier to find material shared directly with a Creative Commons Licence. Pixabay is one of the many databases holding royalty-free photos, illustrations and vector graphics,[47] while good websites to find icons – some require attribution, depending on the use of the images – are the Noun Project,[48] Pictofigo,[49] and the Orion Icon Library.[50]

---

37 Krum, *Cool Infographics*.
38 "Canva," accessed January 12, 2019, https://www.canva.com/.
39 "Infogram," 2019, https://infogram.com/.
40 "Piktochart," 2019, https://piktochart.com/.
41 "The French Occupation of the Ruhr Valley in 1923 (Simplified)," *VERSUS HISTORY*, 2019, http://www.versushistory.com/2/post/2019/04/new-infographic-the-french-occupation-of-the-ruhr-valley-in-1923-simplified.html.
42 "Animaker," *Animaker*, 2019, https://www.animaker.com/infographics.
43 "Biteable," *Biteable*, 2019, https://biteable.com/templates/category/infographic/.
44 "Charts," *Google Developers*, 2019, https://developers.google.com/chart/.
45 "Timeline JS," *Timeline JS*, 2019, https://timeline.knightlab.com/.
46 "SHANTI Interactive," 2019, http://www.viseyes.org/.
47 "Pixabay,", 2019, https://pixabay.com/.
48 "Noun Project," *Noun Project*, 2019, https://thenounproject.com.
49 "Pictofigo," 2019, https://www.pictofigo.com/.
50 "Orion Icon Library," 2019, https://orioniconlibrary.com/.

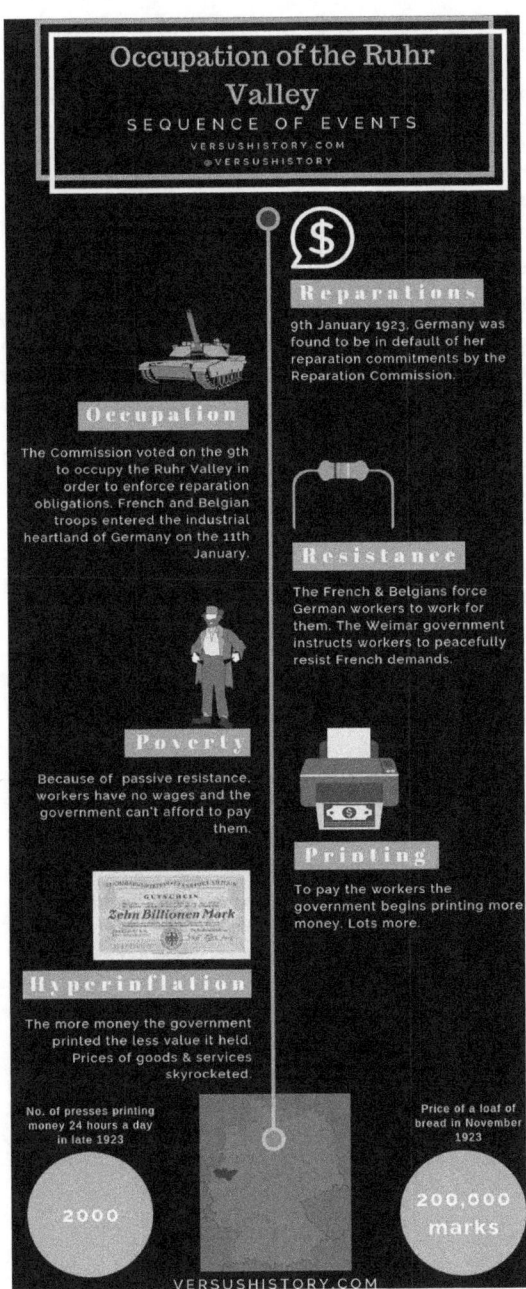

Fig. 5: Occupation of the Ruhr Valley, by Versus History Blog. Copyright owned by the blog editors Patrick O'Shaughnessy, Elliott L. Watson, and Conal Smith, reproduced with their kind permission.

Conclusions

The increasing number of software and online tools allowing anyone to create infographics offers an excellent chance to the public historian. Their communicative potential, not limited to their mere visual nature but enhanced by the power of narrative, is definitely a very exploitable asset for communicating, describing and interpreting history. Recent experiences demonstrate how infographics are effective in museums, in printed and online newspapers, in all levels of education and in the multi-faceted world of online blogging and social media.

The fast-paced evolution of the web will soon drive infographics towards more interactivity, as we can already witness in the development of the tools mentioned in the last paragraph above. All our clues suggest that infographics in the near future will be even more relevant to digital public history.

Bibliography

Cairo, Alberto. *The Functional Art: An Introduction to Information Graphics and Visualization*. New Riders, 2013.

Dunlap, Joanna C., and Patrick R. Lowenthal. "Getting Graphic about Infographics: Design Lessons Learned from Popular Infographics." *Journal of Visual Literacy* 35.1 (January 2, 2016): 42–59.

Krum, Randy. *Cool Infographics: Effective Communication with Data Visualization and Design*. John Wiley, 2014. https://coolinfographics.com.

Lankow, Jason, Josh Ritchie, and Ross Crooks. *Infographics: The Power of Visual Storytelling*. Hoboken: John Wiley & Sons, 2012.

Yuvaraj, Mayank. "Infographics: Tools for Designing, Visualizing Data and Storytelling in Libraries." *Library Hi Tech News* 34.5 (July 3, 2017): 6–9.

List of Contributors

Florentina Armaselu is a research scientist at the Centre for Contemporary and Digital History (C^2DH) of the University of Luxembourg. Her research focuses on digital history and historiography, text analysis and text encoding, and human-computer interaction.

Gioele Barabucci is Associate Professor of Computer Science at the Norwegian University of Science and Engineering (NTNU). He received his PhD in Computer Science from the University of Bologna. He has been Marie Skłodowska-Curie Experienced Researcher at the University of Cologne as well as Director of the Cologne Center for eHumanities. His main research topics are the design of knowledge (how to represent and store information) and the evolution of information (understanding and forecasting how data and its structure will change over time). His research focuses on comparison algorithms, versioning systems and document models, as well as ontologies, legal documents and multilingual systems. He is currently working on the formalization of the concept of 'document evolution': how documents change through time due to human edits, changes of format, or translation, https://gioele.io.

Raffaella Biscioni (PhD) is a researcher at the University of Bologna, in the field of Contemporary history and the history of photography. She has carried out studies regarding the use of photography as a mean of communication and a tool for propaganda, while also devoting significant attention to the method for preserving, managing and archiving photographic heritage with new digital technologies.

Dr. Chiara Bonacchi (PhD) is Senior Lecturer in Heritage at the University of Stirling, UK. She is an archaeologist, specialised in Public Archaeology and Heritage, with a focus on Digital Heritage. After a PhD in Public Archaeology from the UCL Institute of Archaeology and before joining Stirling, Dr Bonacchi worked as Post-Doctoral Research Associate and Co-Investigator Researcher at the University of Newcastle, Central Saint Martins and the UCL Institute of Archaeology. She has designed, participated in and coordinated a broad portfolio of collaborative research projects in the UK, Europe and the Middle East, focussing on the study of public perceptions and experience of the past, digital co-production and public engagement, data science and digital ethnographies in heritage studies, heritage values and the politics of the past. In Italy, she spearheaded the set-up of public archaeology as a field of study, in collaboration with colleagues from the University of Florence. Bonacchi has advised arts and culture organisations and funding bodies in the UK and Europe and her work has been reported in an array of popular outlets, including Nature News, the Guardian, the Times, the Telegraph, le Scienze, La Repubblica, Culture 24 and Discovery.

Sandra Camarda is Assistant Professor in Public History and Transmedia Storytelling at the C^2DH – Luxembourg Centre for Contemporary and Digital History. She holds a Masters in Museum Anthropology and a PhD in Anthropology from UCL (University College London), with a specialization in visual culture and in the history of photography. Her research interests focus on visual and material culture, transmedia storytelling, edutainment, the history and memorialization of World War One and the strategies of use and display of museum collections in both real and virtual environments. She teaches a course in Cultural Heritage at the University of Luxembourg and is involved in the development of digital public history projects and museum exhibitions. She is the curator and project coordinator of *Éischte Weltkrich*, a digital platform on the history of the Great War in Luxembourg.

Thomas Cauvin (PhD) is Associate Professor of Public History at the University of Luxembourg. President of the *International Federation for Public History*, he published *Public History: A Textbook of Practice* (Routledge) in 2016.

Priya Chhaya is a public historian and preservationist. She is the associate director of content at the National Trust for Historic Preservation where she directs digital content for Preservation Leadership Forum and SavingPlaces.org. For more information visit: www.priyachhaya.com.

Frédéric Clavert is associate professor in contemporary history at the C2DH, University of Luxembourg. Though trained as a political scientist and historian dealing with monetary history, his current research interests focus on the echoes of the Great War and its Centenary on digital social networks and on EEC and EU-related debates on online forums. He is co-head with Caroline Muller (University Rennes 2) of the "allure of the digital archive" project (http://www.goutnumerique.net). He is also managing editor of the Journal of Digital History.

Mathias Coeckelbergs is a teaching assistant and PhD researcher in information science at the Université libre de Bruxelles (Belgium). He is working on a joint PhD project in cooperation with the Quantitative Lexicology and Variational Linguistics (QLVL) department at KU Leuven (Belgium) on the use of text mining methods to detect and model intertextuality in ancient Hebrew. His broader research interests include the application of machine learning to ancient literature, archives and libraries. ORCID: 0000-0003-1827-3931

Kimberly Coulter leads a digital project at the Bavarian State Painting Collection in Munich, Germany, to enrich public engagement with the collections of the Alte Pinakothek. From 2009–2021 she led the Environment & Society Portal at the Rachel Carson Center in Munich. She has been a visiting researcher at the Deutsches Museum, a lecturer at the University of Munich, a DAAD research fellow at the University of Bonn, an architectural draftsperson, a cartographer, and a lecturer at University of Wisconsin–Madison, where she earned her Ph.D. in Geography. ORCID: 0000-0001-5856-6005

Jerome de Groot teaches at the University of Manchester. He is the author of Consuming History (2008/2016) and Remaking History (2015).

David Dean teaches British history and public history at Carleton University, Ottawa, Canada. Recent publications include A Companion to Public History (ed., 2018) and Migration and Stereotypes in Performance and Culture (co-ed., 2020). He is a member of the steering committee of the International Federation for Public History and co-editor of International Public History.

Michelangela Di Giacomo PhD, is a historian specialized in contemporary history. Since 2015 she has been designing the permanent exhibition of M9 where she still works in the Research, Development and Educational Department. She published, among others, "Servono ancora i musei di storia?" in P. Bertella Farnetti, L. Bertucelli, A. Botti (eds.), "Public History. Discussioni e pratiche", Mimesis, Milano, 2017.

Matteo Di Legge (MA in history and master's degree in public history from the University of Modena e Reggio Emilia) works as an archivist and digitalization technician for Archimedia s.r.l., specializing in 3D printing. As member of the PopHistory association, he is working on several projects related to public history and is helping to develop the association's website.

Emily Esten is the Arnold and Deanne Kaplan Collection of Early American Judaica Curator of Digital Humanities at the University of Pennsylvania Libraries. As a practitioner, Esten's work bridges digital humanities and public history to consider how technology facilitates community engagement in museums and cultural institutions.

Pierluigi Feliciati is Associate Professor in Records and Information Science at the University of Macerata, where he is the vice-president for University Archival services. Previously he has worked as an archivist at the Italian Ministry of Culture, where he coordinated the National Archives web information system. He is the coordinator of the archival science section of the international scientific journal JLIS.it and member of the scientific board of several scientific journals (Il Capitale Culturale, Archivi, Digitalia). In 2013, he was the director of the 2nd International Summer School in Policies and Practices in Access to Digital Archives, funded by CEI and OSF. In 2019, he was visiting professor at the School of the University of British Columbia (Vancouver, Canada) and teacher of Records and Information Governance for the Master in Archival Science. He is member of the Italian CRUI Commission on Open Science and of the Metadata Research group of the Italian Central Institute for Library Catalogue (ICCD).

Andreas Fickers studied history, philosophy and sociology and specialized in the field of history of technology. He earned his PhD from the University of RWTH Aachen / Germany. After positions in the field of media history at the Universities of Utrecht and Maastricht in The Netherlands, he joined the University of Luxembourg in 2014 as Professor of Contemporary and Digital History. Since 2017 he has directed the Luxembourg Centre for Contemporary and Digital History (C2DH) where he is also Head of the Doctoral Training Unit on Digital History and Hermeneutics (https://dhh.uni.lu).

Sophie Gebeil is an Associate Professor in contemporary history at Aix Marseille University in France. As a member of the TELEMMe laboratory (UMR 7303 AMU-CNRS), she leads the transversal workshop Visual Studies and Digital Humanities. Interested in born digital history, she is working on how the past is portrayed online in the French web archives. Her PhD thesis, entitled "The Digital Building of the North African Immigration Memories on the French Web" (1999–2014) was the first history thesis in France to be written on the basis of web archives. As a researcher associated with the National Audiovisual Institute (INA), her current research focuses on how social movements are remembered in the INA web archive.

Fred Gibbs is an associate professor of history at the University of New Mexico. His work explores the intersection of spatial humanities, digital heritage, critical cartography, and community mapping.

Tammy S. Gordon is Professor of History and Director of Public History at North Carolina State University.

Wilko Graf von Hardenberg leads the DFG-funded research project "The Sound of Nature" at Humboldt University in Berlin. Until recently he was senior research scholar at the Max Planck Institute for the History of Science in Berlin. Trained as a political historian and a geographer in Turin, Brussels, and Cambridge his research activities are positioned at the intersection of environmental history, the history of science and technology, and digital history. He co-edited The Nature State: Rethinking the History of Conservation (Routledge, 2017) and is the author of A Monastery for the Ibex: Conservation, State, and Conflict on the Gran Paradiso, 1919–1949 (University of Pittsburgh Press, 2021). ORCID: 0000-0002-8704-6997.

Martin Grandjean is a Junior Lecturer in digital contemporary history at the University of Lausanne and the EPFL (Switzerland), where he teaches the history of international organizations and historical data analysis. Specializing in network analysis and visualization, he studies large sets of complex archival data and asks how historical sources transform into quantitative data. His experiments also sometimes lead him into the field of social media analysis and data journalism. Spokesman of the French-speaking association of digital humanities for six years, he is now co-chair of the Admissions Committee of the Alliance of Digital Humanities Organizations (ADHO). Website: www.martingrandjean.ch

Jesse Johnston (PhD) is an archivist and scholar based in Ann Arbor, Michigan. He has served as a Senior Librarian for Digital Content at the Library of Congress, Senior Program Officer for preservation and access programs at the National Endowment for the Humanities, and as an archivist at the Smithsonian Center for Folklife and Cultural Heritage. He holds a PhD in musicology and a Masters in archives and records management. He has taught archives and digital curation courses at George Mason the University of Maryland School.

Finn Arne Jørgensen is Professor of Environmental History at University of Stavanger, Norway. His research includes studies of waste and recycling histories in Scandinavia and the US, the history of the Norwegian leisure cabins, material culture and consumption studies, and the connections between environmental humanities, media studies, and digital humanities. He is particularly interested in how technologies mediate and enable human relationships with nature. He is the author of Recycling (MIT Press, 2019), Making a Green Machine: The Infrastructure of Beverage Container Recycling (Rutgers University Press, 2011) and co-editor of Silver Linings: Clouds in Art and Science (Museumsforlaget, 2020) and New Natures: Joining Environmental History with Science and Technology Studies (University of Pittsburgh Press, 2013).

Livio Karrer (PhD), is curator for the M9 Museum in Mestre (Italy). He worked on cultural and political history of Twentieth Century Italian history focusing on the evolution of civil rituals. He wrote several essays on civil funerals of major political actors of postwar Italy and on the political relationship among Italian communist and socialist parties in the 80's. Since 2014 he has been working with Fondazione di Venezia for the development of the M9 Museum project.

Lara Kelland is the E. Desmond Lee Endowed Professor in Museum Studies and Community History at the University of Missouri – St. Louis, where she directs the Museums, Heritage, and Public History MA program. She earned her PhD in 2013 from the University of Illinois at Chicago in U.S. History. Her first book, Clio's Foot Soldiers: Twentieth-Century US Social Movements and the Uses of Collective Memory (University of Massachusetts Press, 2018) traces the use of history in 20th century social movements, including Civil Rights, Black Power, Women's Liberation, Gay Liberation, and American Indian Movements. Her second book, Collective Memory in Isla del Encanto: Island and Diaspora Heritage during the American Imperial Century, engages Puerto Rican collective memory and public history and is under contract with the University of Massachusetts Press.

Mills Kelly is the Executive Director of the Roy Rosenzweig Center for History and New Media and a professor of history in the Department of History and Art History at George Mason University (USA). From 2017 to 2020 he served on the presidential team of the International Society for the Scholarship of Teaching and Learning and is the 2020 recipient of the Gutenberg Teaching Award at from the University of Mainz in recognition of his work in advancing history teaching and learning.

Mary Larson is the Associate Dean for Special Collections at the Oklahoma State University Library and a former president of the Oral History Association (US). Having earned her MA and PhD in anthropology from Brown University, she has worked as an oral historian for over thirty years, starting with the programs at the University of Alaska Fairbanks and University of Nevada, Reno, before moving to Oklahoma in 2009. Much of her research has revolved around the intersection of oral history and digital technology, and in 2014 she co-edited a book on that topic with Doug Boyd (*Oral History and Digital Humanities: Voice, Access, and Engagement*, Palgrave Macmillan). Some of her other writing has focused on the under-representation of women and minority groups in the cultural and historical record, as well as on ethics and the implications that technology has for oral history practice.

Joshua MacFadyen is Associate Professor and Canada Research Chair in Geospatial Humanities at the University of Prince Edward Island in Canada. His research focuses on energy transitions and traditional energy carriers in Canada, and he teaches digital humanities and history in the Applied Communication, Leadership, and Culture program in UPEI's Faculty of Arts. He leads the GeoREACH lab at UPEI which supports Geospatial Research in Atlantic Canadian History (http://projects.upei.ca/geolab/). His most recent monograph is titled Flax Americana: A History of the Fibre and Oil that Covered a Continent. It was published in 2018 by McGill-Queens University Press as part of the Rural Wildland and Resource Studies series. He also published an edited collection in the same series titled Time and a Place: An Environmental History of Prince Edward Island (McGill-Queens 2016).

Francesco Mantovani (MA in historical sciences from the University of Bologna in partnership with the University of Bielefeld and master's degree in public history from the University of Modena e Reggio Emilia) works as a teacher in secondary schools and collaborates with the Istituto storico della Resistenza e della società contemporanea in Modena. He is working to develop public history projects in the Modena region in collaboration with the PopHistory association.

Carlo Meghini graduated in Computer Science from the University of Pisa in 1979 and has worked for the Institute of Computer Science and Technologies since 1984. He is Prime Researcher and the leader of the Digital Library Group of the Networked Multimedia Information Systems laboratory. He has published more than ninety papers in international journals and conferences and participated in more than twenty European projects in the area of Information and Communication Technologies, contributing to the development of Europeana, the European Digital Library. He is an associated editor of the ACM Journal of Computing and Cultural Heritage.

Iara Meloni is a PhD student at the University of Milan. She completed her MA in historical sciences at the University of Bologna and a master's degree in public history with a thesis entitled "Tra la via Emilia e il West: An Italian Way to Public History." Her work focuses on fascism and anti-fascism in northern Italy. Her recent publications include *Memorie Resistenti: Le donne raccontano la Resistenza nel Piacentino* (2015) and *Un'altra giustizia: La punizione dei crimini fascisti* (2019).

Paolo Mogorovich is a Researcher of the Italian National Research Council since 1972, retired in 2009; lecturer at Iuav University of Venice and at the Dept. of Informatics (Univ. of Pisa). Actually he is lecturer of GIS at the Univ.of Pisain the MA degree in Digityal Humanities and collaborates with the Digital Culture Laboratory of the same University (LabCD). He studies Geographical Information System and related technologies; in particular the analysis of GIS tools, usability and freindliness, standard, integration with Remote Sensing; GIS application in planning, environment and others, with special interest in humanities such as Tourism, Management of the Cultural Paolo Mogorovich is a Researcher of the Italian National Research Council since 1972, retired in 2009; lecturer at Iuav University of Venice and at the Dept. of Informatics (Univ. of Pisa). Actually he is lecturer of GIS at the Univ.of Pisa in the MA degree in Digityal Humanities and collaborates with the Digital Culture Laboratory of the same University (LabCD). He studies Geographical Information System and related technologies and GIS application in planning, environment and others, with special interest in humanities such as Tourism, Management of the Cultural Heritage, History.

Pierre Mounier is deputy director of OpenEdition, a comprehensive infrastructure based in France for open access publication and communication in the humanities and social sciences. He has published several books about the social and political impact of ICT, digital publishing and digital humanities. As deputy director of OpenEdition, Pierre Mounier's work mainly revolves around the development of an internationalization strategy for infrastructure, in particular by establishing partnerships with platforms and institutions in Europe and elsewhere. To further this objective, he regularly participates in international conferences and seminars to present OpenEdition's programs and discuss subjects relating to digital humanities and open access. He also coordinates the development of OPERAS, a European infrastructure dedicated to open scholarly communication in SSH, gathering 45 partners from 17 countries.

Reina Murray is the geospatial data curator and applications administrator at Johns Hopkins University and formerly the GIS project manager at the National Trust for Historic Preservation. Her background is in GIS, historic preservation and urban planning.

Serge Noiret, Orc ID: https://orcid.org/0000-0003-0217-1228 History Information Specialist (Ph.D.) at the European University Institute, Florence. His research activity focuses on the (History of) Public History, Digital (Public) History and Information Literacy. His publications are listed in his blog Digital & Public History (https://dph.hypotheses.org/). He is member of the editorial boards of the journals: Il Capitale Culturale. Studies on the value of cultural heritage, Chinese Journal of Public History, Humanités Numériques, Memoria e Ricerca, Magazén, International Journal for Digital and Public Humanities and Ricerche Storiche. Member of these scientific committees: Museum M9 in Mestre-Venice; Réseau national de la Fondation Maison des Sciences de l'Homme (RnMSH) and of the Campus Condorcet, Paris. Member of the board of directors of the Festival dei Popoli (International Documentary Film Festival). Co-founder and first President (2012–2017), of the International Federation for Public History (IFPH); co-founder and first President of the Associazione Italiana di Public History (AIPH) from 2017.

Dr. Nico Nolden (PhD) is a teaching and research assistant for Public History at the Leibniz University of Hannover in Germany since 2019. From 2014 to 2019 Nolden was responsible for the working field digital games and history at Public History of the University of Hamburg. He built up the GameLab there, and established a diverse collection of digital games with the Ludothek. He is a founding member of the "Arbeitskreis Geschichtswissenschaft und digitale Spiele", the german-speaking research community for historical sciences and digital games. His doctoral thesis analyzes historical staging and commemorative cultures in digital games.

Brett Oppegaard is an Associate Professor in the School of Communications at the University of Hawaii at Manoa. His research has been supported by the National Endowment for the Humanities, the US National Park Service, and Google.

Trevor Owens (Ph.D.) is a librarian, researcher, policy maker, and educator working on digital infrastructure for libraries. Owens serves as the first Head of Digital Content Management at the U.S. Library of Congress. He is also a Public Historian in Residence at American University, and a lecturer for the University of Maryland's College of Information, where he is also a Research Affiliate with the Digital Curation Innovation Center. Owens previously worked as a Senior Program Officer and as Associate Deputy Director for Libraries at the United States Institute of Museum and Library Services (IMLS). Prior to that, he worked on digital preservation strategy and as a historian of science at the Library of Congress. Before joining the Library of Congress, he led outreach and communications efforts for the Zotero project at the Center for History and New Media at George Mason University. Owens is the author of three books, the most recent of which, The Theory and Craft of Digital Preservation, was published by Johns Hopkins University Press in 2018 and has won outstanding publication awards from both the American Library Association and the Society of American Archivists.

Eugen Pfister (Dott. Ric. Dr. phil.) is historian and political scientist. He leads the SNF-Ambizione research project "Horror – Game – Politics" at the Hochschule der Künste Bern – HKB. Born 1980 in Vienna, Studies in History and Political Sciences at the University of Vienna and the Université Paris IV – Sorbonne. PhD in co-tutelle at the Universita degli studi di Trento and at the Johann-Wolfgang-Goethe-Universität Frankfurt am Main. Founding Member of the research group "Geschichtswissenschaft und Digitale Spiele" (gespielt.hypotheses.org).

Anaclet Pons is professor at the University of Valencia (Spain) and Head of The Department of Modern and Contemporary History. His research focuses on social history, historiography and digital history. He is author or co-author of several books in Spanish, and of numerous articles and book chapters. His publications include *La historia cultural. Autores, obras, lugares* (Akal, 2013), co-authored with Justo Serna, *El desorden digital Guía para historiadores y humanistas* (Siglo XXI, 2013), and *Microhistoria. Las narraciones de Carlo Ginzburg* (Comares, 2019). He is also, at present, continuing his research on digital history.

Marcello Ravveduto is Associate professor in contemporary history and teaches Digital Public History at Universities of Salerno and Modena and Reggio Emilia. He is a member of the national executive Board of the Italian Association of Public History. He is the scientific director of the the "Joe Petrosino" virtual Museum.

Rabea Rittgerodt works as acquisitions editor at the De Gruyter publishing house, which publishes the e-journal of the International Federation for Public History, hosts the blog journal Public History Weekly, and is also the publisher of the present handbook. Her focus is on books (monographs, edited volumes, yearbooks) and digital projects in global/social and cultural history of the 19th and 20th century, with a particular focus on interdisciplinary and transnational history of Europe/Africa/US, and topics ranging from migration/intellectual/digital/public/military/labor history to feminism and violence studies.

Yannick Rochat is a scientist at the College of Humanities of Swiss Federal Institute of Technology in Lausanne (EPFL), Switzerland. He holds a PhD in Applied Mathematics for Humanities and Social Sciences from University of Lausanne (UNIL), Switzerland. In 2016, he co-founded the UNIL Gamelab, dedicated to the study of (video) games (https://unil.ch/gamelab). He studies among other topics the history of video games (local histories, minor platforms). His personal website can be found at https://yro.ch/

Enrica Salvatori is Associate professor in Medieval History at the University of Pisa since 2006, where she teaches Medieval History and Digital Public History. Since 2015, she has been the Director of the Laboratorio di Cultura Digitale (LabCD, Digital Culture Laboratory) of the University of Pisa. She is on the board of: Società Storica Pisana, Associazione Italiana per l'Informatica Umanistica e la Cultura Digitale (AIUCD), OpenEdition Italia, Associazione Italiana di Public History (AIPH); and on the editorial board of Umanistica Digitale and Annales du Midi. She is also President of Società Storica Spezzina and P.I. of Codice Pelavicino Digital Edition project project (http://pelavicino.labcd.unipi.it/).

Dominique Santana is currently a PhD researcher at the Luxembourg Centre for Contemporary and Digital History (University of Luxembourg), in co-tutelle agreement with the University of São Paulo. She holds a bachelor's degree in History and History of Art from *Université Libre de Bruxelles*, and a master's degree from *Humboldt-Universität zu Berlin* in History. Experimenting innovative ways of digital interactive storytelling and transdisciplinary co-design in Digital Public History, Dominique translates her current PhD research on steel-framed transatlantic migration into a participatory transmedia project involving the making of an interactive web documentary: A Colônia Luxemburguesa (www.colonia.lu).

Valérie Schafer is a Professor in Contemporary European History at the Centre for Contemporary and Digital History (C^2DH) of the University of Luxembourg. She specializes in history of computing and telecommunications. Her current research deals with the Internet and Web history, with digital cultures and Web archiving. She is a co-founder of the journal *Internet Histories. Digital Technology, Culture and Society*.

Federica Signoriello is a research librarian (MLIS University of Sheffield) at the European University Institute in Florence, Italy. She completed a PhD in Italian Studies at University College London and she published articles and book chapters about comic poetry, cultural history and history of scholarship in the Renaissance. In the past few years she also worked at the Warburg Institute Library, at Cambridge University Library and at the British Library. https://orcid.org/0000-0003-1581-4720.

Mark Tebeau is an urban, public, and digital historian, He is an Associate Professor of History at Arizona State University, where he leads the public history program. Previously, he taught at Cleveland State University for more than a decade, founding the Center for Public History + Digital Humanities. Tebeau has directed more than two dozen digital humanities, oral history, and public history projects. Notable work includes *Curatescape*, an Omeka-based framework for mobile publishing; the Cleveland Regional Oral History Project, which has collected more than 1200 oral histories to date; and *A Journal of the Plague Year: An Archive of Covid-19*, an international rapid-response and crowdsourced digital archive documenting the pandemic. Tebeau has received grants from National Endowment for the Humanities, and the National Science Foundation, and has held fellowships at the Smithsonian Institution and Harvard University. His recent scholarship explores the history of public gardens, monuments, and public art. He received his B.A. from the University of Chicago and Ph.D. from Carnegie Mellon University.

William G. Thomas III is the John and Catherine Angle Chair in the Humanities and Professor of History at the University of Nebraska. He was co-founder and director of the Virginia Center for Digital History at the University of Virginia. He is the author of *A Question of Freedom: The Families Who Challenged Slavery from the Nation's Founding to the Civil War* (Yale University Press, 2020).

Francesca Tomasi is Associate Professor in Archival and Library Science at the University of Bologna. Her research is devoted to Digital Humanities, with a special attention to knowledge organization theories, models and technologies. She is a member of different scientific committees of both associations and journals. In particular, she is President of the Library of the School of Humanities in the University of Bologna (BDU – Biblioteca di Discipline Umanistiche), Coordinator of the international second cycle degree in Digital Humanities and Digital Knowledge (DHDK), President of the Italian Association of Digital Humanities (AIUCD) and co-head of the Digital Humanities Advanced Research Center (DH.ARC), where she is scientific leader of a number of scholarly projects.

Seth van Hooland is a program manager at the European Commission and also teaches information science at the Vrije Universiteit Brussel (VUB). As an academic and consultant, he has worked extensively on the topic of metadata quality within the cultural heritage sector and the role linked data can play to facilitate the access and reuse of documentation. His current research focusses on semantic interoperability within public administrations.

Marii Väljataga holds a PhD in History from the European University Institute in Florence. Her dissertation, entitled A small nation in monuments: A study of ruptures in Estonian memoryscape and discourse in the 20th century considers a network of three socio-political upheavals for an exploration of how memory places and the memories connected to them survived, responded to, and participated in the political changes. In her role as Chief Specialist for Innovation at the National Library of Estonia, she launched a project set to transform the Estonian library network by rendering physical book collections mobile and creating a shared, countrywide database of knowledge, within which users may seamlessly navigate the features of discovery and delivery.

Fabio Vitali is Full Professor in Computer Science at the Department of Computer Science and Engineering (DISI) of the University of Bologna. He holds a PhD in Computer and Law from the

University of Bologna and has been working for a long time on digital document formats, hypertext systems, web technologies and usability and user experience design. He has been part of the W3C Working Group on XML Schema and is currently co-chair of the OASIS TC on LegalDocML. He is the main author of Italian and international standards on legislative XML such as NormeInRete, CEN Metalex and Akoma Ntoso, which became an OASIS standard in 2018. He teaches Web Technologies as well as Usability and User Experience Design at the Computer Science School and at the graduate course on Digital Humanities and Digital Knowledge of the University of Bologna.

William S. Walker is Associate Professor of history at the Cooperstown Graduate Program in museum studies, State University of New York at Oneonta. He is the author of A Living Exhibition: The Smithsonian and the Transformation of the Universal Museum and an editor of The Inclusive Historian's Handbook (inclusivehistorian.com).

Lars Wieneke has a PhD in engineering and is head of the digital research infrastructure group at the C2DH (University of Luxembourg). He has worked in multiple international projects and networks and acted as a work package leader in the FP7 funded project CUbRIK where he coordinated the development of histoGraph, a tool for the indexation, visualization, exploration and analysis of multimedia archives that incorporates different levels of crowdsourcing. He was also a co-head of the Europeana taskforce on User-Generated content and is currently co-head of the working group on visualization and interactivity in DARIAH.

Rebecca S. Wingo is a scholar of the Indigenous and American West, and the Director of Public History and an Assistant Professor of History at the University of Cincinnati. She is the lead editor of an open access volume called *Digital Community Engagement: Partnering Communities with the Academy* (University of Cincinnati Press, 2020).

Gerben Zaagsma is Assistant Professor at the Centre for Contemporary and Digital History (C^2DH) at the University of Luxembourg. His main research and teaching interests are modern Jewish history, digital history, and music history. He currently works on a two related projects that investigate the politics of digitisation and the history of digital history, in addition to ongoing work in modern Jewish history. He holds a Ph.D. in modern history from the European University Institute in Florence and was a research fellow at the Department of Hebrew and Jewish Studies at University College London and the Lichtenberg Kolleg, The Göttingen Institute of Advanced Study at University of Göttingen. As a web developer and editor, he was also involved in the creation of several online resources, including the recently launched portal #DHJewish – Jewish Studies and Digital Humanities (dhjewish.org). His book Jewish volunteers, the International Brigades and the Spanish Civil War was published with Bloomsbury Academic in April 2017. For more information see: gerbenzaagsma.org.

www.ingramcontent.com/pod-product-compliance
Lightning Source LLC
Chambersburg PA
CBHW081943230426
43669CB00019B/2907